JOHN R. MICKEY

JOHN R. MICKEY

JOHN R. MICKEY

JOHN R. MICKEY

Personality in Culture

Personality in Culture

John J. Honigmann

THE UNIVERSITY OF NORTH CAROLINA CHAPEL HILL

Harper & Row, Publishers

NEW YORK
EVANSTON
LONDON

Contents

6
SOCIALIZATION FROM WITHOUT AND WITHIN 157

7
SOCIALIZATION AND CULTURAL CONTEXT 188

8
CHILDHOOD IN CULTURE 214

9
AS THE TWIG IS BENT 263

10
LATER LIFE IS IMPORTANT, TOO 298

11
CULTURAL PSYCHIATRY 320

12
IN DEFENSE AGAINST STRESS 351

Preface

While writing this book I worked with the professional commitment and interests of an anthropologist. As an anthropologist I have selected heavily from the richness of already published studies dealing with the world's ethnological cultures; that is, with people like the Samoans, Hopi Indians, and Hindu villagers. Nevertheless, specialists in several other disciplines, including political science, social psychology, and psychiatry, are currently doing much research bearing on a number of topics covered in this volume. I have therefore ventured beyond my discipline, grasping vital conceptual tools coined by psychoanalysts, other psychologists, and sociologists and utilizing the empirical findings and theories of any discipline when they throw light on how individuals come to embody and respond to what, in customary anthropological fashion, I define as culture.

Thus the central theme of my book is: to promote understanding of culture by showing how, figuratively speaking, it deeply and conclusively etches its mark on persons. Even a quick look through the following pages will indicate the selectivity with which I have followed my interest in how persons respond to culture. For example, I have devoted considerable space to mental illness as a socially patterned response to culture. Also, I have emphasized the emotional aspects of personality, having little to say about studies of cognitive processes. Constantly I have been aware of objections directed against certain conceptions and ill-advised methods held or followed (sometimes only by allegation) in culture and personality. While myself formulating additional criticisms, I have taken pains to defend the responsibility and methodological rigor that are inherent in cultural anthropology and compatible with the type of knowledge the discipline has traditionally sought to acquire. Current procedures can always be improved, but too often, I believe, critics have arbitrarily proposed to substitute their own methods, standards, and assumptions, regardless of whether they suit anthropology's special research objectives. Alas, I am saying nothing new. A. L. Kroeber in his own way repeatedly (and rather fruitlessly, it would seem) made much the same point when he distinguished between history and science.

Contrary to my experience in writing *Culture and Personality*,[1] I found that in the present work I had to reflect much more seriously on controversial questions like cultural relativity and the importance of concrete cultural context versus the goal of abstract universal generalization or universal laws of human behavior. Sympathetic as I am with generalization, I am nevertheless very much persuaded that the first approach has continued value and that the extent of contingency in human life renders many correlations and determinants spurious if too much is claimed for them. This first controversial issue closely relates to another difficult question, that of personal freedom. I accept the fact that my behavior is influenced by social facts but preserve the conviction that, like other men, I am free to choose. (Of course, human choice is always limited by experience and by current cultural and other resources.) I wish that anthropology could say with Sartre: "I have tried . . . to show that freedom alone can account for a person in his totality; to show this freedom at grips with destiny, crushed at first by its mischances, then turning upon them and digesting them little by little. . . ."[2] I would hate any social science to allow any human act to be justified in terms of anything but human will.[3]

This book was written for my own education as well as to teach others how personality is patterned in different societies and social classes. Furthermore, I have sought to provide teachers and persons interested in further study with references that will guide them in going more intensively into many topics, including some that I have barely touched on. This is a suitable place to say that several times I have cited the latest (even paperback) editions of social science works when they contain new material, even if only a new, up-dating preface.

My debts are extensive; first, to many teachers, most of whom I never had in class. Above all, I owe much to the stimulating ideas and remarkable ethnographic reports of Margaret Mead, whose influence will be inescapably felt in many pages. Comments

concerning *Culture and Personality* made by David G. Mandelbaum, William Bruce Cameron, David B. Stout, Lewis Binford, and others helped me to write this new work, the manuscript of which George D. Spindler and Raymond D. Fogelson read critically to my benefit. I acknowledge also advice and cooperation provided by Arthur J. Rubel, Rosa Z. Castro, Dorothea Leighton, Richard Simpson, Richard Robbins, Richard Preston III (the latter two acting as my research assistants), J. M. Ritchie, the many people who sent photographs at my request, and Irma Honigmann, who carefully read every page and provided considerable editorial assistance.

The University of Research in Social Science, as well as other resources of the University of North Carolina, facilitated my research and the typing of drafts of the manuscript. I have drawn on results of fieldwork and travel generously supported by the Department of Anthropology and Peabody Museum of Yale University (Kaska Indians) (and once again acknowledge, the intellectual inspiration that I received there from Cornelius Osgood); the Wenner-Gren Foundation for Anthropological Research (Great Whale River Eskimo and Austria); Committee on International Exchange of Persons (Pakistan); University of North Carolina Research Council (Austria); American Philosophical Society (Austria); and the Government of Canada's Northern Coordination and Research Centre (Frobisher Bay Eskimo).

JOHN J. HONIGMANN

Chapel Hill, February, 1967

1 Honigmann, 1954a.
2 Sartre, 1963: 584.
3 Jaspers, 1933: 185.

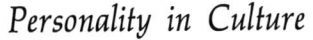

Personality in Culture

The Individual in Culture

1

Culture, as it is ordinarily constructed by the anthropologist, is a more or less mechanical sum of the more striking or picturesque generalized patterns of behavior which he has either abstracted for himself out of the sum total of his observations or has had abstracted for him by his informants in verbal communication. . . . The cultures so carefully described in our ethnological and sociological monographs are not, and cannot be, the truly objective entities they claim to be. No matter how accurate their individual itemization, their integrations into suggested structures are uniformly fallacious and unreal. . . . If we made the test of imputing the contents of an ethnological monograph to a known individual in the community which it describes, we would inevitably be led to discover that, while every single statement in it may, in the favorable case, be recognized as holding true in some sense, the complex of patterns as described cannot, without considerable absurdity, be interpreted as a significant configuration of experience . . . in the life of the person appealed to.[1]

EDWARD SAPIR

ONE WAY OF UNDERSTANDING

Anthropology aims to understand culture, our own along with others considerably more difficult to comprehend because they are removed in time, space, or simply familiarity. Cultural anthropologists aren't indissolubly wedded only to those cultural fragments of human society ambiguously called "primitive." They devote their efforts to ways of life found among all mankind.[2] Let's also recognize early that cultural understanding does more than mirror precisely what transpires in the acts, thoughts, and feelings of people who are collectively being studied. When he explores another culture, an anthropologist holds up no mirror to reflect reality. Instead, he arbitrarily selects, distorts, formulates, systematizes, exaggerates, and under his own signature stylizes the objective world. He incorporates its elements into his own being and transmutes them by whatever theory and concepts he employs, as well as by his logic, imagination, and good sense. Experience convinces me that an anthropologist confronting a way of life that he seeks to understand exists in a state of tension with his subject matter, tension that can wax strong and endure long and unrelentingly.[3] The understanding he finally reaches blessedly resolves the tension, but it no more copies

1

Edward Sapir

objective reality (which exists independently of the observer) than it merely portrays his subjective opinions, feelings, and fertile imagination. Imaginatively, like a synthesis, cultural understanding reconciles the observer's viewpoint with the challenging behavior he set out to comprehend. Whether his final interpretation is true or not is a question that depends on specific tests and criteria, some of which I will in due course examine. No truth, however, is ever fixed, immutable, or eternal. Truth basically consists of an unstable agreement between men who, armed with changing values, concepts, and other tools of research, confront a changing, objective reality.

Today's shrunken world gives cultural understanding special urgency, at home no less than abroad. Economic, political, and other ties creating far-flung social nets draw together people who possess extremely contrasting, even incompatible, expectations, ways of thought, and modes of expression. Laws propose to effect order across vast cultural and moral chasms. Nations unite social classes that act from nearly incommensurable motives and aspirations. As mankind becomes increasingly one family, its members more and more infiltrating and penetrating one another's thought,[4] cultural misunderstandings more and more often draw it close to a brink of disaster. Newer, deadlier weapons demand unequivocally that people with different lifeways exist together, not necessarily harmoniously but effectively, lest they perish.

Some anthropologists aren't primarily interested simply to learn more and more about particular cultures scattered over the globe, however practical such knowledge may be. What they cherish much more highly is to make broad scientific generalizations out of understandings they gain about specific cultures. They formulate comprehensive principles about how social behavior is normatively organized, how certain kinds of cultures affect personality and individual mental health, how personality gets formed in any society, and how culture in general changes or evolves. In addition, some anthropologists reach far less touted, more humanistic or philosophical generalizations. They strain to know better man's nature: man's fate as a culture-bearing creature, and the extent and vicissitudes of human freedom, particularly in view of the constraints that every society imposes on behavior. They ask whether some kinds of culture suit man's nature better than others. If they adopt that dynamic brand of modern philosophy, existentialism, they hold man free and human behavior indeterminate or highly contingent, assumptions that conflict radically with the search for laws about human behavior pursued by many social scientists.

The branch of anthropology called ethnology pursues cultural understanding by investigating, on the surface as it were, peoples' ways of life: the energy they put to work, the homes they build, the skills they master, the gods they worship, the magic by which they counter threats, and the social framework that prescribes who owes responsibility to, and takes precedence over, whom. Archeology painstakingly reconstructs prehistoric communities that flourished and disappeared long before writing, thereby augmenting our understanding of present culture in terms of the past.

Culture and personality, the subject of this book, is another approach to cultural understanding. Those of us who rely on this point of view, instead of devoting our attention to the vast array of traits that make up even a simple round of life, concentrate on the actors who keep a way of life going. Psychological anthropology, as this viewpoint has also come to be known, studies culture as it is embodied in its carriers' personalities. Other anthropological approaches, even archeology, occasionally direct attention to personality as they use psychological concepts to gauge the motivational sources of a style of sculpture, a complex ritual, fear of ghosts, or some other bit of behavior. In fact, everyone from time to time adopts a psychological vantage point as he probes in search of elucidating attitudes, values, thoughts, feelings, and motives or for the educative influences of early experiences. Nor—to anticipate what many of the following pages will amply demonstrate—is anthropology the only discipline that turns the personality spotlight on society and culture. Anthropologists by no means originated the practice of watching the interplay between culture and the individual or his psychodynamic states, and currently other disciplines

also find advantage in doing so, notably sociology and history.[5]

Actual accomplishments can best show what culture and personality is about. Therefore, I shall briefly report several investigations: research on Great Russian national character; trailbreaking work by Ruth Benedict and Margaret Mead; my own psychological understanding of the Canadian Kaska Indians; two psychiatrists' biographical study of a Navaho Indian diagnostician; 300 years of persistence and change in northeastern American Indians' personality; and, finally, a sociologist's interpretation of why Jews rarely become alcoholics.

OF NATIONAL CHARACTER

That members of each nation have a distinctive set of psychological qualities is far from a novel idea. The British philosopher David Hume made this point as long ago as 1748 in his essay "Of National Characters."[6] Men, he said, acquire similar manners through their relations with one another. From birth each man inevitably becomes caught up in networks of social interaction and so, nearly inevitably, comes to share others' sentiments. Similar sentiments "as it were, by contagion," come to permeate a group without erasing individual differences or preventing the members of "different professions" from also possessing distinctive characters, or, as we say today, status personalities. The priest's personality differs from the soldier's, and each arises through the roles that those specialists play. In Hume's words, "The uncertainty of their life makes soldiers lavish and generous, as well as brave."

In time as well as in concepts we travel a long way from Hume to Harvard University's Russian Research Center which, well financed by U. S. Air Force and other funds, collected anthropologists, sociolo-

Russians, like these Muscovites queuing for fresh fruit, possess strong interest in people and human affairs. They judge others leniently, perhaps because they believe that life for everybody is hard and subject to many deprivations and dangers.

gists, and psychologists to launch broad studies into Soviet society.[7] Through interviewing mainly young, well-educated, Russian émigrés, examining life histories they wrote, and studying results of psychological tests—like the TAT, or Thematic Apperception Test—the project collected abundant information bearing on the national character of European Russians. Interviews and psychological tests administered to a control group of Americans matched for age, sex, and occupation with Russian émigrés provided data that allowed an even more precise evaluation of distinctive Russian personality characteristics.

Comparison reveals that Russians possess strong interest in people and human affairs, their perception of others being rich, concrete, and lacking in stereotypes.[8] They infuse actors in fictious situations (like those created through pictures in TAT) with personal attributes, rather than viewing them schematically and abstractly as Americans tend to do. Compared to Americans, Russians less often evaluate a person in terms of his positive or negative attitudes toward the evaluator himself, but keep in mind characteristics that are the person's own. Russians do, however, evaluate freely and without overemphasizing positive at the expense of negative traits. Their perceptions of people, far from being impersonal and detached, probe for covert feelings and motivations more than they remain concerned with external achievements, overt behavior, and peripheral physical traits. Russians seem acutely aware that a person's words and actions don't always directly mirror his feelings and motives. Therefore, alternative explanations must be considered and tested if another's behavior is to be adequately understood. Americans, on the other hand, distinguish relatively slightly between the external act and the underlying attitude, assuming one to be isomorphic with the other. Russians may be more lenient in judging others because their view of people striving to meet their problems tends to be more pessimistic than Americans'. Russians not only concern themselves more with a person's social environment but are readier to perceive that environment in

Respect, loyalty, and sincerity from others are more important to a Russian than just being liked.

negative terms. Vital deprivations, losses, and dangers loom large in the responses which Russian subjects gave to TAT pictures. Americans take happier views. Russians have fairly easy access to their own feelings and don't give way to any enduring high degree of self-deception. Like Americans, they tend to regard themselves in terms congruent with the way they see others. Above all, the Russians tend to perceive each person as dynamically interrelated with other people, as actively participating in group life. Whereas Americans often expect a basic conflict between group-belongingness and personal integrity, in which the latter quality must give way to the former, Russians don't. They are also less worried than Americans over making a choice between conforming to social demands and risking isolation for nonconformity, between personal approval and personal achievement. More than caring

about just being liked—a conspicuous attribute of American national character—Russians care about receiving loyalty, respect, and sincerity from their group. They express fear, depression, and despair more frequently and openly than Americans and more greatly fear external authority. Puritanical about verbal discussion of sexual topics, Russians nevertheless exhibit little conflict about sex and appear less confused about their maleness or femaleness than Americans. Finally, Margaret Mead[9] has observed that whereas an American is guilty or afraid when he must rely on his greater strength or power over another person—we typically play down our strength lest we be charged with bullying—a Russian acts comfortably from a position of greater power, using the advantage that it gives him.

Few national character studies have been pursued with the thoroughness of the Har-

vard Russian Project or with better financ-
ing. Investigations of this kind became exceedingly popular in anthropology around
1940, growing out of the exigencies of
World War II and postwar problems, and
most of the extensive work was done on
Japanese, Germans, and Russians. Wartime
conditions obviously required anthropologists to give up their preferred way of working in face-to-face, clinical fashion with living informants in the informants' own
homes or villages and forced anthropologists to stand at a distance, drawing their
conclusions from émigrés and literary
sources without ever setting foot in the
communities whose members they sought
to understand. Their efforts at characterizing nations quickly became controversial.
Critics unbelievingly asked whether worthwhile generalizations could really be made
about large, highly differentiated nations
layered like a pousse-café into social classes
and broken into regions, each marked by
local customs and traditions.

Again and again in the following pages
you will confront this problem. It will challenge you in every statement that ascribes

widely pervasive personality characteristics
to a social system while obviously drawing
upon data obtained from only a small sample of people who, chances are, were selected too opportunistically to guarantee
that all the significant divisions would be
represented in the final study. Like any
statements, those describing national character have limited use; they make poor
guides for predicting behavior; but, as I
shall point out in Chapter 4, for scholars
who make and use them, they possess other
values and afford a special kind of understanding. Psychological characterizations of
nations sometimes ring like stereotypes;
that is, like oversimplified and uncritical
opinions which overlook a situation's full
scale of complexity. Anthropological accounts of complex social situations are indeed often deliberately simplified, just as
psychological or psychiatric characterizations are that overlook each individual's
many facets of behavior and discount the
way his behavior suits itself to different
situations.

Nobody can study everything. Every discipline abstracts and in doing so resigns it-

⟨ When National Characters Meet

*When a Russian talks to a Frenchman he feels irresistibly inhibited by the
Frenchman's individualism, reserve, urbanity and unconcernedness. The intellect
and the senses outstrip the heart. This is exemplified in the contemporary French
novel, in which there is little feeling and a great deal of intellectualité and
sensualité. On the other hand, the French know how to respect the personality
of their fellow men and do not encroach on their inner life. . . . They are more
unassuming than the Russians and do not feel themselves called to be the moral
judges of their fellow men. The Russians easily admit that they are miserable
sinners, and are ready to repent of their sins; but they expect others to do the same
and repudiate anyone who fails to acknowledge his sinfulness. The moral passion
of the Russians is duly reflected in their thought, in which ethical and metaphysical
interest preponderates over the concern for the truth of logical and epistemological
propositions. The latter is very characteristic of the Western mind, because it has
lost touch with ultimate realities and acquired a habit of hiding from them and
from those who remind it of them.[10]*

NICOLAS BERDYAEV

self to distorting the phenomena it grasps. Its practitioners draw from a complex, sometimes boundaryless whole whatever details they believe relevant. National character studies, while admitting the undeniable fact of complex variability among individuals, social classes, and geographic regions, abstract elements of behavior that are perceived to recur, albeit in shifting form, from one person to another, that glance off dozens of things people make and use, that appear in children's drawings and in adult codes, and that are echoed in movies and other commercial entertainments. Such abstractions are made far from uncritically, for severe criticism has taught researchers to accept them only after cautious inspection, and then carefully to formulate them to apply to as many of the available facts as possible. Anthropologists construct such generalizations tentatively, aware that future research may upset them all.

National character studies formulate generalizations about socially patterned attributes of personality with the assumption (which must be constantly reevaluated) that even though members of a nation speak different dialects or even several languages, the very fact that they remain parts of a viable whole means that they possess some, however few, shared psychological bases of understanding.[11] It is to those psychological bases, to those thin threads of uniformities abstracted from a sea of individual and other differences, that national character and similar research in culture and personality attends. The results of working only toward obtaining knowledge of this shared psychological substratum are much more meager than could be obtained by fully describing even only a single component social aggregate within the nation, like a particular class or region. In fact, each individual in a nation has more facets and can be more richly described than the paltry regularities that run through persons who comprise a social system.[12]

DESCRIBING CULTURAL CHARACTER

All cultures . . . exhibit patternings . . . a tendency to organize large areas of their content with reference to certain dominant attitudes or values.[13]

RALPH LINTON

"A culture, like an individual, is a more or less consistent pattern of thought and action," governed by its own characteristic purposes. "In obedience to these purposes, each people further and further consolidates its experience" so that the most ill-assorted traits accumulated by them during their history become characteristic of their cultural goals. Such is the configurational theory that Ruth Benedict develops in her celebrated book *Patterns of Culture*.[14] Historians like Wilhelm Dilthey and Oswald Spengler had already sought to understand historical cultures by regarding them as if they possessed the purposefulness of human beings. Dilthey[15] sought clues to driving attitudes and motives in the cultures' philosophies. Spengler[16] viewed the whole classical Western world as Apollonian, meaning that it saw life and the cosmos as ordered, and in harmony had discovered an integral virtue. In contrast, he branded modern culture as Faustian, endlessly engaged in combatting obstacles, making conflict the essence of experience and a challenge without which life becomes superficial and meaningless.

Ruth Benedict recognized the difficulty of summarizing large and complex civilizations segmented into many occupations, classes, and regions, but she refused to abandon the underlying idea of wholeness in culture, an assumption which she believed to be sound. To demonstrate her thesis that ways of life form consistent wholes, her book uses simple cultures which she and other anthropologists had originally studied for quite other purposes than to discover their over-all "character-

Ruth Benedict. A photograph taken early in her career. (Columbia University)

istic purposes." Her sensitive nature, creative talent, and imagination (she was a poet before she studied anthropology) provided her with valuable assets for her job.[17] Her early anthropological training took place at a time when anthropologists were heavily engaged in plotting the distribution of culture traits and making maps through which they hoped to unravel unwritten history. Such training wasn't wasted on the young poetess, for it impressed her with a respect for empirical data which she then proceeded to interpret in original, revealing fashion.[18] Her book's title uses the word "pattern" to mean a configuration, Gestalt, or integrated whole. Anthropologists in the 1920s often spoke of patterning to designate the way alien traits—like a folklore theme, a trait of social organization such as the mother-in-law taboo, or a material element like the horse—drawn into a culture

thereupon become harmoniously integrated into the scheme of life, receiving at least a newly assigned meaning if not a more compatible form.[19] Benedict applied this view. Through time a culture's distinctive configuration comes to pattern the existence and to condition the thoughts and emotions of individuals born to it, or who come to participate in its activities. She speaks of a culture's wholeness and its distinctive purposes emerging from "emotional and intellectual mainsprings," but she contented herself with inquiring into such psychodynamic mainsprings only by studying the culture itself. *Patterns of Culture* wasn't written only after she looked at specific individuals clinically, as Harvard's Russian Research Project did. From cultural facts, often reported by others who had recorded them firsthand, she proceeded to infer the psychological characteristics of the culture's actors, so that her approach to personality is anological and culturally deductive.* To avoid confusion, we can describe Benedict as dealing with cultural character rather than with personality.[20]

Benedict illustrates her thesis that cultures are wholes that encompass the personalities of individuals who participate in them by contrasting the Pueblo, or village, Indians living in the southwestern United States with other North American Indians, particularly with those who formerly flourished on the Great Plains west of the Mississippi River. Succinctly she expresses the difference between cultural characters in those two regions by contrasting two diametrically opposed routes for achieving worthwhile experience. Pueblo Indians, like the Zuni, distrust excess and outlaw extreme psychological states from their experience. They extol moderation; hence she

---

* This method no longer predominates in Ruth Benedict's *The Chrysanthemum and the Sword*, published in 1946, in which she describes Japanese national character.

calls their cultural character Apollonian.* Plains Indians, on the other hand, willingly annihilate ordinary limits of being. Those people, who live as if walking a knife-edge, she labels Dionysian. Unlike her students and later workers in psychological anthropology, Ruth Benedict in this book isn't concerned with socialization, or with how differences in cultural character came to be learned anew in every generation. (Later, she became very much interested in questions of personality development.) Many situations document the Pueblo's restrained Apollonian, in contrast to the Plains' exuberant Dionysian, cultural character. Where Plains Indians fast to force themselves into experiencing a vision, the Pueblo fast to clean themselves ceremonially. Plains Indians value highly the self-reliant, venturesome man who heroically demonstrates initiative and unflinchingly bears self-torture. Pueblo villagers prefer the mild-mannered, moderate man who never pushes himself forward. The Pueblo have resisted incorporating mind-changers, like peyote or alcohol, firmly into their culture, but Plains Indians have built a new religion around peyote. So, Plains people drive themselves to the frontiers of existence, pursuing extremes to the point of frenzy and even death as they reach for experiences that the southwestern Indians firmly refuse to meddle with.

Even more dramatic cultural characters are described when Benedict turns to the Dobu islanders living off eastern New Guinea in Melanesia and the Kwakiutl Indians of Vancouver Island and adjacent British Columbia. Jealousy, fear, suspicion, and a fierce sense of ownership are motives that run through the Dobuans' cultural character, judging from Reo Fortune's account of their culture.[21] They view almost every success as being won at the expense of a defeated rival. In fact, the good man is he who manages to gain something at the expense of another. His stronger magic not only induces his own crops to grow well but also alienates plants from another's garden. Should his own plants be similarly stolen, he unleashes sorcery to vent his resentment, performing it treacherously under the mask of obsequious friendship to bring about his rival's illness and death. The use of disease charms to protect one's property loads life with fear, and adds to the oppressive, constant sense of tension and danger. When they are grossly humiliated or frustrated, these laughterless, dour people attempt suicide in a desperate attempt to save face and win belated support from kinsmen.

From the sea, beaches, and forests of the North American Pacific Coast, the Dionysian Kwakiutl studied by Ruth Benedict's teacher, Franz Boas, manage to obtain ample comforts without excessive labor. Their material possessions as well as their privately owned immaterial wealth—songs, dances, myths, and names of house posts and of dogs—serve them as counters in deadly serious contests. In such contests, called potlatches, a man aims to outstrip and shame his rivals by loading them with more than they will be able to pay back in return. Individuals vie with one another according to their means, some going so far as to destroy their own property to vanquish others. "We fight with property," they say. When he has been victorious in contesting with wealth, a man shows his triumph in such uninhibited self-glorification that, judged by our cultural standards, it amounts to unabashed megalomania. Defeat and ridicule sting the Kwakiutl shamefully, and if humiliation can't be wiped out by distributing or destroying enough wealth to flatten the pretenses of another, it leads to sulking and suicide. Kwakiutl cultural

---

* Bear in mind that the present tense is conventionally used in ethnological descriptions of culture or personality. Many anthropologists prefer it to designate the so-called "ethnographic present," the situation prevailing at the time in which they are interested.

❲ Two Styles of Self-Expression Among American Indians

During the Sun Dance, Cheyenne Indian volunteers hang from a pole, supported by skewers driven through their skin. The photo (taken in 1903) shows the medicine man who inserted the skewers sitting next to a young man waiting to undergo the ordeal. Whereas the Plains Indians specialize self-torture into a technique for obtaining self-oblivion and power-conferring visions, the Pueblo Indians reject it outright. Nor do the Apollonian, village Indians of the Southwest try to bring on ecstasy through dancing. Ruth Benedict describes their dances as monotonous reiterations to compel natural forces. There is nothing wildly Dionysian in the blend of treading, drumming, and unified singing through which the masked Hopi dancers in Walpi pueblo, shown in the other photo (taken about 1891), bring together the mist in the sky and heap it into piled rain clouds, forcing the rain upon the earth.

character revolves around shame. Even accidents and death are fitted into the predominating view of life, being viewed as either due to overwhelming shame or as affronts that had to be retaliated. The Indians' emotions swing a gamut between feelings of superiority, in which the ego feels safe, and feelings of defeat, by which the individual knows he has fallen short of his culture's ideals. Perhaps because they are sufficiently close to our own culture, we find Kwakiutl attitudes to be more intelligible and less irrational than the paranoid suspiciousness of Dobu.

Patterns of Culture remains a unique work; its method has rarely been emulated. In the first place, few anthropologists have ever quite understood the principles that guided Benedict's approach and which she herself left inexplicit.[22] Would-be followers were even more dismayed by critics who pointed to faults in her interpretation of the Pueblo and Kwakiutl cultural characters. Li An-Che[23] claimed that she interpreted Zuni Pueblo culture too much in terms of her own values. Other researchers returned from the Southwest fully convinced that Pueblo life harbored far more tension, suspicion, drunkenness, and ambition than Ruth Benedict acknowledges in her Apollonian pattern. Also, a fieldworker came back from the Kwakiutl to report that those Indians possessed an amiable side to their character that Benedict had quite ignored.[24] A persistent and never adequately resolved problem has been how to account for behavior that is in opposition to a culture's dominant emphases, major purposes, or motivational mainsprings. Some such aberrant behavior serves the master elements in the configuration by providing opportunities for the release of tension.[25] Another view regards it as perfectly permissible to ignore contrary cultural trends, provided that the observer, after giving them careful attention, concludes that their incidence doesn't constitute grounds for giving them the weight or significance assigned to other, *dominant* cultural features.[26] At any rate, perplexity and controversy between Ruth Benedict's interpretations and other anthropologists' views indicate very plainly that cultural reporting and psychological characterization are far from wholly objective tasks. Cultural character isn't entirely external but emerges as a synthesis that an imaginatively sensitive human being, who also draws on his own values, forms to account for his experience with a culture.[27] It is one way of understanding culture.

THE STAR PUPIL GOES TO THE SOUTH SEAS

Margaret Mead, Ruth Benedict's star pupil, was only 23 years old in 1925 when she went to Ta'u, an island in the Manu'a group of the U.S.-owned Samoan islands. For nine months she lived there observing how adolescence affected Polynesian girls.[28] The problem she had chosen stemmed from her own total cultural setting rather than from academic psychology and anthropology alone. She grew up in a world where parents and teachers who had ceased to take childhood or adolescence for granted saw unrest and inner turmoil to be the inevitable concomitant of growing up.[29] This view held stress to constitute the mental accompaniment of the physiological changes attending arrival of puberty. It could no more be omitted from development than the young girl's budding breasts or the boy's deepening voice and downy cheeks. An anthropologist pondering this theory saw good reason to doubt it. The very attitudes by which adolescents overtly expressed their inner turmoil—rebelling against authority, stewing in philosophical and religious doubt, worrying about choosing the right career—formed too intimate a part of American culture and therefore

couldn't be inevitable concomitants of physiological puberty. Margaret Mead suspected
that adolescent stress was culturally conditioned rather than biologically rooted.

. To test her hunch that adolescent unrest
didn't stem from biology but rather marked
the growing person's attempt to deal with
difficult problems originating in a given way
of life, Mead went to Samoa, to a culture
radically different from her own.[30] Here
she found a good-natured, simple people
who had long impressed travelers with their
lack of sensuality, voluptuousness, and any
sense of indecency.[31] On Ta'u island she
studied a community blessed with an economy of plenty in which innovations borrowed from Western culture made life more
comfortable and where most individuals
regardless of rank found it possible to live
desirable lives. The Polynesians she came to
know lived much as they had in the past:
from coconut, bananas, and breadfruit
trees; yam and taro plants; poultry, pigs,
and fish. Islanders earned cash by selling
copra and in return bought cloth, soap,
metal goods, kerosene, sewing machines,
and writing utensils with which to write the
Samoan language in an orthography taught
them by Samoan Christian missionaries.
Families lived in villages headed by councils
formed of all family heads. Beehive-shaped,
unwalled houses with high thatched roofs
and coral pebble floors furnished little privacy to a family, except in bad weather
when blinds were lowered. Mead found the
islanders living in a world saturated with
rank. The population was stratified into two
broad classes, titled nobility—who among
themselves recognized many fine distinctions of rank and title—and untitled commoners. Religion, however, held little
importance for these Polynesians, and missionaries had not succeeded in giving their
morality a puritan tinge. Christianity interfered not at all with adolescent premarital
flirtations that often led to sexual experiments.

In her work Mead didn't abstract information about personality by examining
Samoan culture alone. She worked clinically, which in anthropology means that
she systematically gained knowledge about
individual Samoan girls aided by an inexplicit body of psychological theory that she
didn't feel any need to spell out because it
didn't rigidly confine her as she went about
collecting and analyzing her data. She
found that the adolescent Samoan girl
differs from her prepubescent sister in one
chief respect: bodily changes have occurred
in the older girl that remain invisible in the
younger. No other great differences, and no
evidence of inner turmoil, set adolescents
apart. Then what accounts for the storm
and stress American children experience as
they enter adolescence? Or, turning the
question around, how can the absence of
adolescent unrest in Samoa be accounted
for?

Toward the end of her book, *Coming of
Age in Samoa*, Mead cites two characteristics of Samoan culture that influence the
Samoan girl's comparatively easy transition
to adulthood. At this point in her report she
begins to generalize knowledge she gained
through studying Samoans. Adding to it
knowledge she possesses of her own culture,
in which she herself grew up, she sets down
principles about how certain kinds of communities are culturally constituted and how
they thereby affect the well-being of their
members. Such generalizations, I have said,
are a major goal motivating anthropological
research. First, Mead hypothesizes, the general casualness of Samoan life, which is so
strikingly absent from contemporary America, contributes to Samoan girls' easy adolescence. Second, Samoa shares with the
world's other small-scale communities a
homogeneity that favors young people's
harmonious development.

The general casualness that accompanies
growing up in Samoa is quite absent from
American life. Nobody dies for causes in

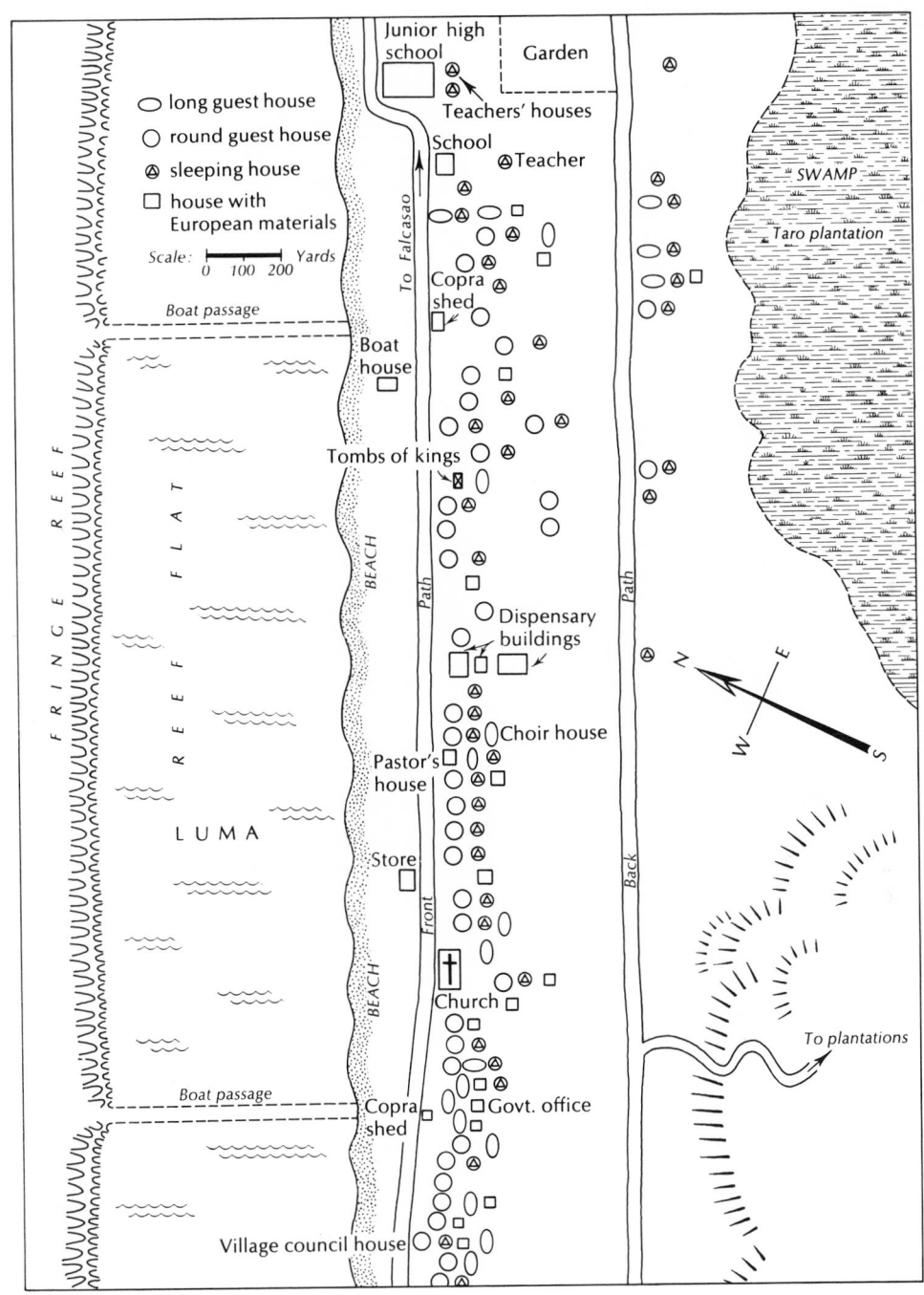

Lowell D. Holmes spent nine months in 1954 restudying
the island and one of the villages where Margaret Mead
worked. This map shows a section of Ta'u village as he
found it.[32]

Children in Western Samoa, a country that in
1962 became independent of New Zealand.
(Paul Popper Ltd.)

Samoa or fights to the death. Disagreements between parent and child are easily settled. Neither poverty nor disaster holds any great threat. No child is hurried along or punished for being too slow. No one person is overwhelmingly important in a child's life. Unlike American life, which generates strong feeling toward parents, duty, sex, religion, competition, success, and conformity, growing up in Ta'u is devoid of intensity. Where nearly everyone feels strongly, the adolescent girl is apt to be tortured by poignant situations that demand she choose, and by conflicting or mutually exclusive practices among which she is challenged to select. On the other hand, a way of life which teaches everyone the lesson of not caring, while it may generate no great art, encourages painless development from childhood to womanhood.

Prodigious and rapid change in Western civilization cuts generations and even peers asunder, but a small-scale social system like Samoa is marked by slow, even cultural change, so that it possesses considerable cultural homogeneity. People worship one set of gods and follow one accepted religion. Parents and children agree on one standard of morality, which men as well as women share. No radically divergent groups pursue special goals and compete with each other for the individual's allegiance. Margaret Mead therefore concludes that cultural heterogeneity and rapid change, such as until recently remained absent from most of the world's small-scale exotic communities, is partly responsible for adolescent unrest in the United States and elsewhere in Western civilization.[33]

The two conditions that vex our adolescents—the compelling necessity for them to choose and the bewildering variety from which they must select in a heterogeneous social setting—can't be pruned from our way of life. They form the flesh and blood of our culture. To dream of reforming our culture in the image of Samoa is an impractical, romantic fantasy. Instead, Mead recommends that we provide more wholesome conditions for development while preserving the intensity and heterogeneity characteristic of a large-scale, world-involved social system. A culture that confronts its young people with many dazzling choices and allows peddling many diverse ideas, she points out, must train its children to cope resourcefully with conditions they will encounter as they grow. Family and school must become more concerned than they have ever been with teaching young people *how* to think and choose, and less with *what* to think and choose. Adolescents need to learn tolerance for old and new ideas. They must understand that there are many ways, no one of which can objectively be proven better than another. Margaret Mead's thinking, as it moves from the problem of what produces adolescent unrest to recommended action, resembles the way economists and other scientists use their knowledge to intervene in culture. Whether such recommendations are correct and will be effective can only be found out by applying them, if only on a pilot scale, and observing what happens. Few anthropologists have been as bold as she has consistently been in bringing anthropological knowledge to bear on practical ends.[34]

SOCIALIZATION AND PERSONALITY IN NORTHERN CANADA

In 1944 and 1945 I lived among Kaska Indians whose territory in northwestern Canada overlaps the Yukon Territory–British Columbia border. The 200 men, women, and children constituting the tribe trap furs for their living while still obtaining some of their food by hunting and fishing, as they did in olden times.[35] As winter comes they quit the trading-post settlement of Lower Post and disperse themselves in small, winter, bush settlements located along river pathways that will soon freeze over. Each such settlement accommodates two or three related families, sometimes a couple, their unmarried sons and daughters, and their married daughters with their husbands and children. The men travel with dog team and snowshoes, covering a radius of some 50 miles, to set iron traps for mink, marten, lynx, and fox, and to hunt. Their work is cold, for the temperature sometimes dips to 60 or more degrees below zero Fahrenheit. The trappers keep a vigilant lookout for game, like spruce hens, grouse, moose, or bush caribou, food Indians relish far more than the flour, beans, and bacon they carried with them into the winter settlements. In late spring they desert their riverbank forest homes and travel by boat back to Lower Post, site of a church and of the stores that will buy their fur. They pass the summer living restfully in tents, subsisting on fish and more heavily on "store food" bought with the proceeds of their fur catch. Summer is a time of partying, and a good party requires an ample supply of home-made rice and apple wine or, if bootleggers can be located, whisky (when this study was made Canadian Indians were legally forbidden to drink alcoholic beverages). Frequent summer-evening dances lasting past dawn provide young people with op-portunities for flirting and sex. Old-style gambling games accompanied by pounding drums supply another popular form of rec-reation.

Like many studies in culture and person-ality, mine paid close attention to the way children are reared. I wanted to find out how Kaska adults socialize youngsters for roles in an atomistic system in which gov-ernment as we define it is unknown and where small family groups spend much of the year isolated in the bush. How are chil-dren prepared to carry on a culture in which individual resourcefulness is often the sole guarantee against the extreme danger posed by cold, accidents, and even starva-tion?

Kaska children are born with only an ex-perienced older woman attending the mother. She washes the newborn baby in warm water before laying it straight, hands at sides, to be swaddled in blankets. A week or so later the swaddled infant is laced firmly into a velvet or mooseskin pack easily carried on its mother's shoulders. On its first day of life, the child receives no food, but thereafter he both nurses from the mother's breast and drinks powdered or canned milk mixed in a bottle. Suckling is most casual. Neither my wife nor I ever observed any fondling of a nursing infant. The infant lies passively in its mother's lap or else simply reclines on a bed sucking from the bottle of warmed milk propped against a pillow. Whenever and wherever the infant cries, its mother offers milk. A few months after birth, if the weather is warm, the baby's arms come out of the

swaddling cloths. By 6 months, a mother discontinues the baby pack in favor of a shawl or blanket under which he sits astride his carrier's back. Thick diapers backed with soft moss continue to be used until walking commences, whereupon a child begins to wear trousers split open in the crotch to allow him to urinate and defecate freely. Small children remain almost solely in their mothers' care—they are not, as in many parts of the world, relegated to juve-nile nursemaids. They are never left alone in the house and they receive considerable loving attention from parents, aunts, and siblings. Relatives bounce a youngster on their knees, praise him with kinship terms, and cuddle his face with their lips and mouths. Adults don't push a child to hasten his maturation. Rarely did we see a toddler held upright to walk, and finger sucking is neither discouraged nor common. Weaning from the breast usually comes before two years and is accomplished gradually, rather than abruptly, by offering solid foods in-creasingly frequently. More and more the bottle takes the place of the breast. Wean-ing from the bottle comes even more gently. Soon after the child is about 2, by which time he has been weaned from the bottle, a sibling is likely to be born. At the same age social demands on the youngster increase; for example, he receives strong verbal en-couragement to defecate outside the house. But again the process is gradual rather than abrupt, for no one seriously expects sphinc-ter training to take firm hold until a child is about 3 or 4 years old. By that time scold-ing for wetting has sharpened ("You dirty boy!"). Fretting for attention soon disap-pears as a youngster learns to discontinue his appeals when they bring him no gratifi-cation or reassurance. A troubled 4-year-old simply goes off by himself to suck his fingers until the crisis passes. His father, who has never been demonstrative or atten-tive, retains some of his moderate warmth, and children of both sexes show closer at-

The little Kaska girl imitates grown-woman baby-packing. When families are isolated for the winter everybody must be resourceful, even burying the deceased should death occur. The young woman is helping to cover the coffin of her husband's mother. Summer life in Lower Post is relaxed and comfortable, and the owner of the unfinished log building is in no hurry to complete the job he began several years before.

Carried in a shawl, a Kaska baby rides astride its mother's back.

tachments to fathers than to mothers during this period.

Children are explicitly guided away from shouting, unruly behavior, and, especially, aggression. Disobedience merits scolding and physical chastisement, although the Indians disapprove of hitting a child. Education in cooking and the other skills is most unformalized. Children learn by emulating an older person, nobody explaining how and why a task is done. Youngsters draw

on experience to complete an assignment, like making a fire or cooking tea, doing the best they can. Next time it comes easier. Modesty training for both sexes, however, is inculcated quite forcefully and in early years includes suppression of anything smacking of sex. At adolescence, sex nevertheless bursts forth and parents realistically accept the inevitability of some premarital sexual experience. They object strongly only if a girl shows signs of becoming

*In the winter of 1945–1946 my family and I lived
in this house, located in an isolated bush
settlement of five families.*

promiscuous, and even then their power
isn't great. For Kaska parents don't force
themselves on children, their interference
especially declining with the child's increasing self-mastery. Hence they leave a youngster considerable room for his independence
and resourcefulness to blossom.

Out of this unhurried childhood (my
summary omits many details) emerges an
individual endowed with considerable self-
confidence and ability to cope with customary problems of living. Maturity doesn't require him to unlearn patterns of dependence. Long ago, before he was 4 years old,
he learned to do without intense emotional
dependence on others. He learned to cope
individualistically while imitating adult activities. Nothing in this unspecialized and
relatively homogeneous culture is specifically concealed from children, with the result that they enter adulthood knowing
quite a lot about the adult roles they will
play. The cultural milieu nurtures a person
endowed with a strong sense of responsibility for his own acts and for his own success
and failure, a person unaccustomed and

unwilling to grant anyone authority to
command his behavior or enlist his loyalty.

Despite always having been without indigenous police or authoritative leaders,
Kaska Indians' normal behavior to one another reveals strong and consistent controls
that guard against open flaring of hostility.
Aggression, which if unharnessed could
easily be suicidal in so atomistic a social
setting, usually remains tightly leashed.
Underneath the veneer of deference, however, there exists a fund of inhibited hostility that appears in dreams as well as in
drunken behavior. The blind force of suddenly unleashed, uncontrollable hostility
sometimes overwhelms an intoxicated man
or woman, who wildly directs it even
against himself. Emotional aloofness is another outstanding characteristic of Kaska
Indian personality. This is the same quality
that the Kaska mother turns on when she
discontinues her former warmth and attention to her 3-year-old child. Emotionally insulated, the Indian reveals only a limited
ability to tolerate affection or to express it

in interpersonal relations. He remains impervious to all intense emotional stimuli. This trait is well suited to reinforce his sense of independent responsibility for his own success and failure and, like deference, is also highly congruent with an atomistic social system. Instead of extolling togetherness, the Kaska community consists of a core of adults each of whom prefers to stand alone. People are kept apart not by mutual antagonism, as in some societies, but by a preference for independence and limited tolerance for strong interpersonal feelings. Finally, the Kaska Indian remains flexible rather than rigid. He lacks meticulous orderliness and compulsion about time or duty. His flexibility allows him to slip easily into passivity and to procrastinate when the going gets tough. I came to know well his tendency to procrastinate during the weeks when I searched vainly for someone to guide me and my family from the winter settlement back to Lower Post. My food supply, which I had brought along in the fall, was running low and with two young children I didn't want to risk surviving on the meat and fish that I or my hosts occasionally brought in. Others living in the settlement were themselves running short of store food. Yet, other things, like setting traps, had to be done before it would be profitable to make the 50-mile sled journey to the trading post. How exasperating it was, then, to see the men, despite favorable weather, delay day after day leaving for the trap line.

GREGORIO, HAND-TREMBLER

My next example of culture-and-personality research deals with only one individual, examining him at length in the context of the culture to which he is adapted. Instead of working through a number of subjects to discover the typical Navaho Indian personality (as I did among the Kaska), two psy-

chiatrists highly informed in anthropology, Alexander H. Leighton and his wife, Dorothea, studied the development of one Navaho man.[36] The result is one of the richest in a rich series of anthropological life histories.[37] They concentrated on a 38-year-old diviner named Gregorio, a man who uses his acquired gift of hand-trembling to provide clients with information about the cause and cure of disease.[38] A hand-trembler prays and sings while at the same time extending his hand, which begins to shake. He thinks of various diseases or causes of disease until something happens that tells him he is thinking of whatever is afflicting the patient. Then he begins to think of various curing rites until he hits on the correct one, and then of various medicine men to perform the rite that will finally cure the patient.

When he has secured all the information he needs, the shaking stops; divination is finished. What experiences led Gregorio to choose this career? How does Gregorio's role suit other facets of his personality? Answers to such questions should not only illuminate Navaho culture but also teach us about how any social system recruits people to carry out tasks that need doing.

At the going rate in Navaholand for anthropological information, 25 cents an hour, Gregorio told his story, at first willingly and then with growing reluctance, especially when it came to hand-trembling. He had grown up in an environment saturated with hand-trembling, and as a child saw much use made of the skill, particularly among his mother's Apache Indian relatives. His mother died when he was 7 and from then on aunts and his mother's mother reared him. His father, a recluse, ignored him. Around 14 he passed through an experience familiar to many adolescents. He began to doubt the effectiveness of many Navaho religious ceremonies that he witnessed and that had even been performed in his behalf. Around the same age came an involuntary attack of hand-trembling. Were both experiences related? Did he, from the depths of his being, unconsciously try to overcome his doubts by manifesting symptoms that stamped him as possessing an unusual gift? We know only that he never rebelled openly against the Navaho way or became a confirmed iconoclast. Far from exercising his ability as a diviner, Gregorio during the next eight years slipped from the orbit of Navaho life and worked with Mexicans as a herder. One incident he recalls vividly from this period is the time he tried to break a wild horse and slipped, hurting himself severely as the animal dragged him a long way while he lay unconscious. From this accident, despite a four-day and four-night curing ceremony promptly performed for him, he sustained a back injury that troubled him for the rest of his life. The next year, when he was 23, he returned somewhat as a stranger to live with the Navaho again. A marriage arranged for him by relatives turned out poorly. He quarreled with his wife, who once told him to stay with the Mexicans and never come back. He complained that she wouldn't stay in their hogan but had a tendency to "run around," a euphemism meaning that she led a promiscuous life. About then Gregorio unwisely volunteered to ride a wild horse, which he failed to control. "I couldn't do anything with it. It wouldn't mind the bridle or anything. . . . I sure got scared." He was living at a low ebb and drinking heavily when, following the strange experience that had occurred some years before, he began to practice

⟮ Gregorio in His Country

The psychiatrists provide this description of their informant:

We first saw Gregorio in the late winter of 1940, when we were living with a Navaho called Carlos and his family at the edge of a pinyon forest. . . . Gregorio would stroll across the sun-warmed clearing, under his large black hat, trailing big-wheeled spurs, and would often sit most of the day with his back against the wall or would shoot marbles with one of the children. Sooner or later he would come into the adobe house where we lived and sit for an hour or two, saying little and smiling much. After dark he would disappear in the woods, walking home under the moon, his pockets full of the cigarettes we had given at his suggestion.

We were told that he lived with his wife and two children about 3 miles away, was hard working, poor, but an expert in the practice of Hand-trembling.

• • •

We found that he lived in a little clearing in the pinyon woods near open grassy valleys. Firewood was everywhere plentiful, but water had to be hauled for miles in a rickety old wagon. The buildings consisted of a small Indian hut of the kind called "hogan," built with horizontal logs and chinked with mud, and a small square log cabin after the Mexican style.

The hogan's floor was the solid earth, sunk about 6 inches below the level of the outside. In the center lay the fire, covered by a stove made out of a bottomless can. . . . The utensils consisted of knives, forks, spoons, a frying pan, a home-made wire grill, various pots, a three-legged cast-iron Dutch oven, and some dishes. . . . A loom with a partly finished and poorly made blanket stood west of the fire, and before this sat his wife, the placid Nazba, smiling and friendly.[39]

ALEXANDER AND DOROTHEA LEIGHTON

A Navaho Indian hand-trembler in action.
(Navajo Tribal Museum, Window Rock,
Arizona)

hand-trembling professionally. Here is his account of what happened:

I wasn't feeling very good. You know some days you act like you are going to sleep, want to lie down. I felt that way. I was lying down . . . and I went to sleep for a little while. When I woke up my legs and feet and whole body felt all large, just like when you sit down and your legs go to sleep. I felt like that all over my body. And I could feel something through my arms there, as if it was running through my hands and out the end of my fingers. After that my hands started shaking. This happened right in the middle of the afternoon. My hands trembled all afternoon till toward sundown, then I stopped for a little while and started again after dark. . . . It was dark night, but I thought the sun was shining on me. I felt like the sunshine was coming in the door. The sun was shining bright like today in a little spot where I was sitting.[40]

His practice grew when clients who came to consult him benefited from his advice, so that he became one of the most successful diagnosticians in the community. He describes his gift by saying that it feels "like lightning or sunbeams coming from Heaven," striking down in the center of the house. "Everything is white and bright. Nobody could see that but you. You don't see that yourself, but you are having thoughts like that. The light doesn't stay long, then your hand starts shaking." But his success didn't improve his marriage, and his wife finally deserted him, taking along their only son. In 1932 he married again, a woman who had been prostituted by her mother, and this time the relationship turned out well.

What kind of man was Gregorio in 1940 when the Leightons questioned him? His settling down after his second marriage to follow a successful professional career didn't make him prosperous or enterprising. He still lived a hand-to-mouth existence, farming a little for himself, and hiring out his labor to Indians, whites, and Mexicans. Telling his story to anthropologists was, like hand-trembling, a way of earning a little money. Without economic reserves he was one of the poorest people in a community where everybody lived at a low level. Shy, he has nevertheless always been persistent and resourceful enough to get by, as well as perceptive and able to learn. Consistently he has tried to win social approval through obedience and conformity, traits that probably served him well when, as a partial orphan, he was reared by kinsmen. Constitutionally he seems unfitted for rebellion. Recall how quietly he resolved his doubts about religion. The Leightons measured his intellectual ability and found it average, or even on the dull side of average. Hand-trembling didn't exceed his intellectual capacities to the degree that some other Navaho religious role would have. Clearly he was no charlatan duping others, for he honestly believed that he possessed a gift to use his mind to discover hidden facts.

Gregorio's life history reveals how closely one's social role may be bound up with personal experience and personality characteristics. He chose to do professional hand-trembling after renewing his contact with Navaho life and religion following his absence among Mexicans. He returned to the Navaho as an outsider and a somewhat ridiculous man to boot. Hand-trembling effectively counterbalanced his marginal status by giving him a respected position that brought him considerable respect and prestige. Note how he chose a role which in childhood he had seen his mother's relatives perform many times. Undoubtedly Gregorio doesn't realize how he drew on the past to further his adaptation. As a role, hand-trembling suits his shy, passive, even timorous nature without straining his limited intellectual capacity. True, it doesn't meet all his needs, but where is the social system in which a person finds everything he needs in the roles open to him?

PERSONALITY IN HISTORY

Gregorio's life history accounts for how one man in part of his lifetime adapted in his culture by utilizing his biological and psychological resources and experience that augmented his other talents. As a biography it tells us rather more about the man than the culture, though it does give an inside view of what a Navaho Indian strives for and the meaning he attaches to some of his culture's goals. Biography is history writ small, covering only an individual's life span. Tribes, nations, and regions run longer histories that test their members' collective resourcefulness much as a person's lifetime tests his. Western Europe's shift to capitalism from feudalism was such a test, one that Erich Fromm[41] says radically transformed personality by putting every individual soundly on his own feet. Individualism had in fact begun earlier in the Reformation, which left man to face God alone, but capitalism added economic success to responsibilities for which a person had to rely primarily on his own efforts. Confronting the challenge to succeed, European man came to believe himself motivated largely by self-interest, but at the psychological cost of considerable insecurity and loneliness.

Every social history is a record of psychological changes in thought and feeling accompanying cultural changes—like the trough accompanying the cap of a wave, personality and culture are but different facets of the same events. To take another example, a French historian, Lucien Febvre, claims that the sixteenth-century Frenchman relied heavily on olfactory, tactile, and auditory information that he received about the world. As a result he saw the world in a vivid, emotionally highly toned fashion.[42] Today a Frenchman relies much more on vision. Reason confines his perception far more than during the French Renaissance, and other changes in French culture have made him considerably more independent of nonworldly forces and thrown him on his own abilities and the mundane environment. These are examples from fairly short-term social history. During the millennia occupied by human evolution man acquired new psychological abilities along with upright posture, bipedal locomation, and a larger brain.[43] In company with ever more specialized, powerful tools and new bases of social organization he learned to reflect on himself and on his condition in nature. He became capable of postponing gratification of his impulses. He set up ideals of good and bad, right and wrong, and on grounds of conscience came to insist on dutifully obeying those abstract notions. His psychological development as a fully human being taught him the experience of conflict between his hopes and his abilities as well as over what is possible but disallowed and what is attractive but

evil. His psychological evolution confronted him with anxiety and a concern for questions far beyond the ken of beasts pertaining to identity and autonomy: Who am I? What am I? How can I become someone better?

Between studying the microhistory of an individual and reconstructing the macrohistory of his genus we have the histories of particular communities and ways of life. Turbulence breaks out whenever communities with substantially different cultures come into contact or try to dominate and transform one another. Anthropologists immerse themselves in such turbulence (to which they refer more stiffly, using the word "acculturation") to learn as much as they can about change, including its psychological dimensions. One of the first investigators to approach acculturation psychologically, A. Irving Hallowell, rather surprisingly discovered that personality characteristics among Algonkian-speaking Indians in northeastern North America remained relatively unchanged, despite the people's 300 years of contact with French, British, American, and Canadian explorers, missionaries, fur traders, and government officials.[44] Ingeniously, Hallowell searched seventeenth- and eighteenth-century letters and other documents written by explorers and missionaries, to obtain a base-line picture of the aborigines' personality as it had been before any serious degree of cultural interference began. From those sources he learned that the Indian had possessed primarily a practical rather than an abstract type of intelligence and that he strongly preferred independence and individualism. "They hold it as a maxim," LeClercq, a seventeenth-century missionary, wrote, "that each one is free: that one can do whatever he wishes: and that it is not sensible to put constraint upon men." Parents used equally little constraint to rear their children. The Indians' renowned stoicism

The locations of some northeastern Indians.

under suffering testified to their rigidly suppressed emotionality, and other information indicates that they muted any show of joyful as well as painful feelings. In the face of provocation they tried to remain amiable and mild, inhibiting direct aggression to the extent of not even outrightly refusing a favor or contradicting somebody, though they may never have intended to comply with the request.

Interpreting those facts, Hallowell concluded that the Indians had aboriginally possessed a personality suffused with anxiety. They remained ever watchful lest their control break down and allow hostility or other strong emotions to escape. Were the

Indians at all hostile? Reports of occasional quarrels, sorcery, and homicidal behavior when they became intoxicated prove that they were. But, Hallowell reasons, because they deeply valued remaining in control of their emotions they cultivated indifference to anything likely to arouse them. As Le-Clercq wrote, "they rely upon liking nothing, and upon not becoming attached to the goods of the earth, in order not to be grieved when they lose them."

Some 300 years later, Hallowell in northern Manitoba and his coworkers in northern Wisconsin found essentially the same personality characteristics being refracted through the Rorschach inkblots and the

❲ Accustomed To Retain Emotional Control Even Under the Most Trying Circumstances, Traditionally Inclined Menomini Indians Greet a Returning Friend Without Any Pronounced Signs of Pleasure or Welcome

Whatever misfortune may befall them, they never allow themselves to lose their calm composure of mind. . . .

JOSEPH JOUVENCY (IN 1710)

No one was in sight at the houses close to the main highway where it cut through the dense forest, so we turned up one of the dirt roads leading back to the clusters of quonset style, board and roofing paper houses, bark wigwams, and log cabins in which the people lived. As we approached one of these clusters near the Zoar community hall . . . we saw a group standing and sitting about. Some of the men were playing poker on a blanket spread on the ground. Others were kibitzing. We parked our car, got out, and tried to walk casually, not run, into the circle of what we perceived as old friends who would greet us with the enthusiasm of long-lost members of the family. But we had forgotten what the native-oriented Menomini were like! Expressionless faces greeted us. Some even turned away, as though preoccupied with other matters more interesting. Only the children stared, but quietly. I walked over to the group of people clustered around the poker game and joined the kibitzers. Ranks opened so I had a place to stand and a clear view of the game, but otherwise no special notice was taken of my arrival. I stood across from a man about my age with whom I had, I felt, formed an especially close friendship, and who had been enormously helpful to me in my research in the past. He continued with his game, taking no notice of me whatsoever. I began to feel acutely uncomfortable. Perhaps there had been a long winter of gossip about the white strangers who had invaded their privacy for too long. Perhaps we were suspect of witchcraft, or at least of bringing bad luck. Finally, after several minutes of paranoid fantasy on my part, my friend Nepenahkwat glanced up, smiled quietly, and said calmly, "Hello George, I see you made it." And then continued with his game.

We stayed for several hours that afternoon. During the first hours we gradually became aware of the fact that the people were glad to see us, that they had thought about us during our absence, and that they had looked forward to our return. . . . We realized again that these were different people, with a different psychology, and a different set of norms for proper behavior. Overt emotionality is not displayed. The loud, overstated greeting normal for the situation in our own society would not only have been in very bad taste according to Menomini standards, but it would have been virtually impossible for a native-oriented Menomini adult, properly educated and formed in the traditional framework, to act that way even if he had, conceivably, wanted to.[45]

GEORGE SPINDLER

A. *Irving Hallowell*
(University of Pennsylvania—Jules Schick)

Ernestine Friedl

Thematic Apperception Test. Anthropologists found the Indians investing little energy in their environment. They tended to steer clear of people as much as possible, while at the same time controlling their thoughts and behavior so as not to get into trouble through dangerous impulses.[46] Among the Canadian Ojibwa Indians, Hallowell found those dwelling inland along the Berens River, who remained unchristianized and spoke little English, to be particularly introverted and on guard against upsetting emotional experiences. But these relative pagans didn't differ radically from the Christianized people who lived downriver on the shores of Lake Winnipeg, 20 percent of whom possessed mixed Indian and Caucasoid ancestry. The Lakeside peo-

ple gave Rorschach responses a bit faster, more like the tempo of Euroamericans, and showed a bit more extraversion (again in the direction of the Rorschach norms established by white subjects) but, as I said, manifested the same personality configuration revealed by their more isolated neighbors. In northern Wisconsin the Lac du Flambeau Chippewa Indians, 80 percent of whom possessed mixed Indian and Euroamerican ancestry and practically all of whom spoke English, again showed the same centuries-old basic psychological structure. Oddly enough, the Wisconsin Indians revealed even less emotional responsiveness to the outer world than the Inland Indians of Manitoba. Yet, the persistent, old personality didn't suit the Lakeside and

Lac du Flambeau people as well as it suited the Inland Ojibwa, whose way of life, after all, most closely resembled the culture that had been extant when the seventeenth-century missionaries and explorers arrived in Canada. On the relatively accessible shores of Lake Winnipeg and Lac du Flambeau new demands were being made on that personality which it wasn't equipped to meet. As a result, 36 percent of the Lakeside Rorschach records and 56 percent of the Lac du Flambeau ones bore signs indicating psychological maladjustment, compared to only 27 percent of the Inland Berens River Indians.

No one has yet found a very convincing explanation for the long-term persistence of these personality characteristics among the northeastern and other American Indians—for example, the Kaska. Hallowell offered two related reasons for such psychological resistance to change. First, the people still find it possible to get along with the old-time personality structure which, second,

gets firmly and unconsciously set very early in life. Ernestine Friedl[47] explained a single trait of Chippewa personality—namely, its detailed, practical, and noncreative intellectual approach to problems (akin to what the early travelers had also noted)—by the constantly changing conditions of Chippewa life during the ensuing two or three centuries. Almost every situation the Indians faced turned out to be unique, leaving them unable to depend much on abstract or general previous learning. In other words, a detailed, practical, and noncreative personality has remained congruent, even adaptive, in the Indians' restlessly changing circumstances. But through what mechanisms does it persist? Stephen T. Boggs[48] proceeded through a cleverly designed experiment to find out if he could account for a relatively unchanged personality by demonstrating unchanged patterns of childrearing. He proposed to examine childrearing and child behavior in families unequally assimilated to modern, Euroamerican cul-

⟮ Personality Traits Have Persisted Long in Northern North America

1691—LeClercq writes about the Micmac Indians of the Gaspé Peninsula:
In a word, they hold it as a maxim that each one is free: that one can do whatever he wishes: and that it is not sensible to put constraint upon men. It is necessary, they say, to live without annoyance and disquiet, to be content with that which one has, and to endure with constancy the misfortunes of nature, because the sun, or he who has made and governs all, orders it thus.[49]
1944, 1945—Honigmann observes the Kaska Indians of northern British Columbia and the southern Yukon Territory:
External sanctions are . . . resented because they imperil independence. Here is the root of the Indian's negativistic attitudes to the white man's law and the regulative functions of government. . . .

In his ingroup relations the Indian is also self-centered and nonauthoritarian. He does not seek authority in interpersonal relations, and others can scarcely tell him what to do—initiation of activity must come from within. Egocentricity thus leaves little room for patterns of leadership. . . . Within the Indian community, there is a consistent reluctance to give direction or, except in cases of manifest danger, as in adapting to the winter environment, even venture direct suggestion. "We do it this way," the Indian says when approached for help or advice, the implication being that the pupil may or may not follow the traditional pattern.[50]

ture—that is, in unequally acculturated families. If childrearing was really the medium that perpetuated the traditional personality, then it would remain similar regardless of differences in degree of acculturation. Boggs looked closely at childrearing practices and at parent-child interaction to see if certain specific characteristics, which Hallowell had cited as aboriginally typical of the Ojibwa, would alter with degree of acculturation. Such characteristics included not constraining others, not interfering with another person in face-to-face relations, and complying readily with requests, presumably in order to avoid giving offense. He found that childrearing did differ from one level of acculturation to another, as did the quality of interaction between parents and children, just as he predicted. Hence he concludes that the persistence of Ojibwa personality cannot be explained by claiming unaltered patterns of childrearing.

Bernard James[51] believes that the place to look for an explanation of Indians' personality is not in unchanging patterns of childrearing but in modern reservation conditions that, at least among the Lac Court Oreilles Ojibwa Indians in Wisconsin, have kept alive traits resembling the personality characteristics listed by Hallowell. The Indians' cultural deprivation, conflict between traditional and modern Euroamerican ideals of masculinity, and an unfavorable image of themselves bestowed by disparaging white neighbors create anxiety, necessitate emotional control, encourage indirection, and nurture other traits. This explanation, however, must be questioned, since far-northern Canadian Indians, being more isolated and self-sufficient, don't face as strong cultural deprivation and disparagement and don't live under reservation conditions. Nevertheless, they share the tight emotional control, indirection, and the other personality characteristics to which James calls attention.

CULTURE AND RESISTANCE TO ALCOHOLISM

Nobody doubts that culture influences both the frequency and style of mental illness or that it plays a large part in governing the success of psychotherapy. Just how culture exerts its power over mental health isn't at all well known; we don't really know how some cultures come to exercise a prophylactic effect on personal well-being, protecting a significant proportion of their members against the assaults of mental illness. Charles R. Snyder, a sociologist, demonstrates better than anybody ever has how Jewish culture protects Jews from succumbing to the temptation to drink regularly to excess.[52] Oddly, although Jews rarely become alcoholics they, unlike members of some abstemious Protestant denominations, use alcohol regularly as part of their religious ceremonies.

Snyder's investigation of Jewish drinking leads him to conclude that the Jew's socially patterned, religiously founded feeling of exclusiveness protects him from alcoholism despite his frequent exposure to alcohol. According to the Orthodox religious view, Jews are a group bound by a special covenant they have made with God. A chosen people, they must zealously avoid profaning contacts with cultural and religious outsiders, or goyim. Distinctive rituals, kosher food, and rigid endogamy are the principal devices by which Orthodox Jews cut themselves off from the surrounding profane world. It is especially noteworthy that Orthodox Jews also express their special status through the attitudes they reserve for drunkenness and sobriety. Many religions extoll sobriety but Judaism goes further and makes sobriety a specific and cardinal Jewish virtue, an indicator of the Jew's worth. Given this attitude, it is understandable that Jews are in no position to define drinking as something that gets one delightfully high and releases other

Jews drink regularly as part of their rituals.
(Sovfoto)

desirable effects, as rural Austrians do.[53] Jewish children learn early to stereotype gentiles as excessive drinkers. That this stereotype is unwarranted is quite immaterial. The point is that by means of the stereotype, Orthodox Jews sharply set themselves off from non-Jews and identify insobriety with non-Jewishness or with falling away from Jewishness. In other words, socialization into Orthodox Jewish culture uses alcohol to cultivate a sense of prideful exclusiveness as well as strong negative attitudes toward drunkenness and heavy drinking. As a result, Jews, who must drink as a part of their sacred rituals, resist carrying the taste for alcohol to a point where it ruins their lives or creates an inordinate dependence on alcohol's psychological effects.

Evidence supports the theory that a feeling of cultural exclusiveness helps the Jew to maintain sobriety and protects him from alcoholism. When Orthodoxy loosens its hold and Jews become more secular—that is, less careful about participating in daily and weekly rituals—the frequency of drunkenness among them also increases. True, Irish Catholics who are religious also stay

more sober than those who neglect their religious obligations, but the relationship between religious observance and sobriety is less pronounced in the Irish than in Orthodox Jews. Evidently something in Orthodox Jewish culture enables Jews to maintain their sobriety and, in the long run, protects them from alcoholism and its consequences. Theory says that the prophylactic mental-health factor is the Jew's sense of exclusiveness, the zeal with which he guards his special status. He dreads the consequences of being tagged a *goy*, or non-Jew, with which heavy drinking and drunkenness threaten him.

That this may not be the whole explanation is hinted by the fact that Jews are also remarkably well guarded from other forms of psychiatric disorder. For example, a study conducted in Manhattan shows Jews to have a markedly low rate of psychiatric impairment.[54] It explains little to say that "an impairment-limiting mechanism" must operate prophylactically in the Jewish family. What is that mechanism that reaches into personality and, despite the discrimination and prejudice from which many Jews suffer, protects them from the ravages of personality disorder?

PUTTING MAN BACK INTO CULTURE

That a pronounced concern with personality looked at in its cultural setting should emerge in American cultural anthropology during the 1930s was quite in keeping with the way that discipline had developed.[55] Few American anthropologists had ever been content to study culture as an abstraction, one entirely divorced from the people who create and internalize it. When anthropologists traced the diffusion of tools, domesticated plants or animals, folk tales, ceremonies, and other traits from any way of life to another, they recognized that psychologically motivated, individual choice

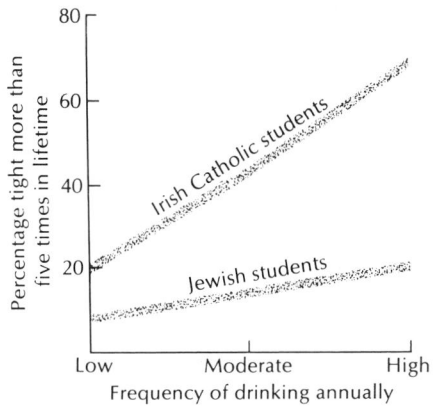

Religiously active Jewish students, drinking as frequently as religiously active Irish Catholic students, are less likely than the Irish to become intoxicated.[56]

governed borrowing, rejection, or reinterpretation.[57] Yet anthropologists' sights were fixed more on the trait than on the individual. The culture-and-personality movement, on the contrary, vigorously emphasized man in culture, at the same time singling out personality as suitable for cross-cultural comparison.[58] Culture and personality constituted a revolt against the tendency of the social sciences to be impersonal, to lose sight of the fact that people are the reality behind such abstractions as religion, democracy, war, and even culture.[59]

When I introduced national character studies, I indicated that the entry of psychological anthropology was hotly contested. Some anthropologists became so alarmed that, prophet-like, they cried out warnings that the study of culture was being neglected, as though paying heed to persons and how they embody culture isn't understanding culture itself.[60] Today many (but not all) social scientists acknowledge that certain social behaviors—especially problems like delinquency and certain psychiatric disorders that rest on cultural antecedents—cannot be adequately comprehended without using personality concepts.

Culture and personality answers two main types of questions: What are people like from one community, or from one part of a community, to another? How do people become as they are? The two questions are related. Psychological characteristics that people acquire or the culture they internalize depend on the experiences to which they are exposed. To isolate or segregate some people in a community means that they will learn different standards, learn in different ways, and embody relatively different cultures.[61] This is the case with U.S. social classes, where even forms of mental illness tend to vary from grossly disadvantaged persons of extreme lower-class status to those holding more favored

⟨ Anthropology Equipped for Understanding

With our holistic approach toward groups as well as individuals, our worldwide breadth and historical as well as prehistorical depth, our use of natural rather than contrived laboratories, our control of case counting as well as statistical methods and our appreciation of the need to account for every exception to our empirically based generalization, our emphasis on the group rather than the individual but without neglect of the individual's role in the group, our first-hand knowledge of all the cultural areas of the world, our control of languages, and our skills at face-to-face observation and interviewing, we are in a favorable position to contribute not only to the general description of contemporary world cultures but also to their understanding. . . .[62]

LAURA THOMPSON

social positions. Although psychological anthropology approaches cultural understanding through persons, it only rarely seeks answers to its problems using the methodological standpoint of existential phenomenology, that point of view which tries to grasp as directly as possible the nature of a person's experience of the world and of himself. Like much of psychology, the practitioner of culture and personality is too fond of psychological concepts and too habituated to separating subject and object, observer and observed, to try merging himself in the experience of the people he studies. To be sure, anthropologists value getting to know how other people think and feel, but they usually express their knowledge far more in terms provided by a theory, like psychoanalysis, than in relatively direct, existentially valid terms.[63]

FURTHER READING

Francis L. K. Hsu gives his conception of culture and personality in "Psychological Anthropology in the Behavioral Sciences" (1961b); so do Douglas Haring at the outset of the third edition of *Personal Character and Cultural Milieu* (1956), Margaret Mead in "Culture and Personality" (1963a), and Edward M. Bruner in "The Psychological Approach in Anthropology" (1964). For short histories, see G. Bateson, "Cultural Determinants of Personality" (1944), M. Mead, "Psychiatry and Ethnology" (1961c), and Milton Singer, "A Survey of Culture and Personality Theory and Research" (1961). Hallowell has also written on the history of relations between "Psychology and Anthropology" (1954) as well as on their then-current status, while "Interactions of Psychiatric and Social Theory Prior to 1940," by Thomas D. Eliot (1955), briefly reviews the psychological approaches of such sociologists and anthropologists as W. I. Thomas, E. R. Groves,

and John Dollard. In "Theoretical Setting —1954," M. Mead (1955b) sets out aims of childhood research in anthropology. I also recommend Abram Kardiner and Edward Preble's appraisal of "The Influence of Psychodynamics on the Study of Culture," an unnumbered chapter in their book *They Studied Man* (1961). Arvid Brodersen does lucidly what he promises in "National Character: An Old Problem Reexamined" (1957), and Weston La Barre reviews "The Influence of Freud on Anthropology" (1958). "The Influence of Psychiatry on Anthropology in America During the Past One Hundred Years," by Clyde Kluckhohn (1944) describes psychological anthropology's growth as a special field. For Edward Sapir's role in anthropology and the culture-and-personality movement, see Richard J. Preston, III, "Inherent and Imposed Structures and Writings of Edward Sapir" (1963). On the psychological concomitants of culture change, see A. Irving Hallowell, "Sociopsychological Aspects of Acculturation" (1945b); A. H. Maslow, "Resistance to Acculturation" (1951b); M. Mead, ed., *Cultural Patterns and Technical Change* (1953a: chaps. 5–6), and George D. and Louise S. Spindler, "Psychology in Anthropology: Applications to Culture Change" (1963).

REFERENCES

1 Sapir, 1934a: 411.
2 Kroeber, 1948: 4, 847; Dozier, 1955; Hsu, 1964.
3 Medley, 1964.
4 Teilhard de Chardin, 1959: 240.
5 Inkeles, 1963; D. J. Levinson, 1964; Homans, 1964: 967–971; Barbu, 1960; N. O. Brown, 1959.
6 Hume, 1898.
7 Nearly simultaneously, Columbia University and the American Museum of Natural History launched a large-scale

investigation of the values and assumptions that underlie the behavior of Great Russians, as most of the people of European Russia are called. See Gorer and Rickman, 1962: xvi–xvii, xix–xxx, 93–236; also M. Mead and Métraux, 1953. The Massachusetts Institute of Technology undertook similar research in the 1950s. See M. Mead, 1952a.

8 The following account takes much from Hanfmann, 1957; see also Inkeles, Hanfmann, and Beier, 1958, as well as the summary by C. Kluckhohn, 1955.

9 M. Mead, 1964b: 23–24.

10 Berdyaev, 1951: 278. By permission of The Macmillan Company.

11 Schneider, 1950. A. F. C. Wallace (1961: 26–28) favors a contrary view, stressing what he calls "the organization of diversity" over against "the replication of uniformity."

12 M. Mead, 1964b: 20–21.

13 Linton, 1938: 426.

14 R. Benedict, 1934b.

15 Dilthey, 1961.

16 Spengler, 1926–1928.

17 Barnouw, 1949; M. Mead, 1959a.

18 A. L. Kroeber, in a book review of *Patterns of Culture* in the *American Anthropologist* (1935, 37:689), aptly describes her approach as subjectively empirical. For a biographical memoir of Ruth Benedict by her brilliant pupil, see M. Mead, 1959a.

19 Goldenweiser, 1933: 85; *cf.* Morris Opler, 1948.

20 Singer, 1961: 47–49; A. F. C. Wallace, 1961b: 87. For other studies of cultural character, see Brickner, 1943; La Barre, 1945; Wolfenstein and Leites, 1950, and Lantis, 1953–1954.

21 Fortune, 1932.

22 A. G. Smith, 1964.

23 Li An-Che, 1937.

24 Codere, 1956; *cf.* Barnouw, 1957; Parker, 1964. See also the critique by Linton, 1956: 17–20.

25 E. Beaglehole, 1938: 123.

26 J. J. Honigmann and Honigmann, 1965a: 230.

27 Bennett, 1946.

28 M. Mead, 1928a; Sargeant, 1961.

29 *Cf.* G. S. Hall, 1904, *II*:71, 72, 73, 93.

30 M. Mead, 1949b: 405–412.

31 Samuels, 1964: chap. 1. Rorschach records from Samoa were collected by Cook (1941–1942 and 1942), who holds that the unchallenging Samoan culture has encouraged the development of a rather simple personality.

32 From Holmes, 1958. M. Mead reviewed Holmes' book in the *American Anthropologist*, 1961, 63:428–430.

33 Absence of adolescent stress or unrest has also been reported from Manus (M. Mead, 1930b: 189), the African Ngoni (Read, 1959: 170), Hawaiian Chinese (Hsu, Watrous, and Lord, 1961: 42), and the Hutterites (Eaton, 1964). Semin (1961) reports that Turkish adolescents in Istanbul have difficulty adjusting to adult norms and roles, as do town-dwelling Frobisher Bay Eskimo youth (J. J. Honigmann and Honigmann, 1965a: 179–180). For difficulties of Ethiopian teen-agers, see Bricklin and Zeleznik, 1963–1964. Havighurst *et al.* (1965) compare Buenos Aires and Chicago adolescents.

34 *Cf.* M. Mead, 1930a.

35 J. J. Honigmann, 1949; for the former culture, see J. J. Honigmann, 1954b.

36 A. H. Leighton and Leighton, 1949.

37 *Cf.* Dollard, 1935; C. Kluckhohn, 1945.

38 For more about Navaho divination, see Morgan, 1931, and Wyman, 1936.

39 A. H. Leighton and Leighton, 1949: 7–8.

40 *Ibid.*, p. 20.

41 Fromm, 1941.

42 Barbu, 1960: chap. 2.

43 Evolution of personality is discussed in E. Becker, 1962a; Hallowell, 1950, 1960, and 1963; Freedman and Roe, 1958; Spiro, 1954, and White, 1960.

44 My account follows Hallowell, 1946, 1951b, and 1952. *Cf.* Landes 1937 and 1938b. Barnouw (1963: chap. 9) and Holzinger (1961) summarize Hallowell's material, and Fogelson and Spiro (1965) discuss Hallowell's contribution to anthropology.

45 From G. D. Spindler, 1963: 357–358. By permission of Holt, Rinehart and Winston, Inc. Father Jouvency's observations, originally written in Latin between 1610 and 1613, were published in 1710. For his account, see Thwaites, 1896–1901, I:275–277.

46 A. F. C. Wallace, 1952b: 101.

47 Friedl, 1956.

48 Boggs, 1956 and 1958.

49 LeClercq, 1910: 243.

50 J. J. Honigmann, 1949: 253–254.

51 James, 1954 and 1961.

52 Snyder, 1958.

53 J. J. Honigmann, 1963b.

54 Srole *et al.*, 1962: 307–320.

55 Culture and personality owes little or nothing to nineteenth-century European attempts to develop systems of ethnic psychology, which belong to the era before Freud made his debut with psychoanalysis, and which concern mostly cognitive and sensory processes (*cf.* Piéron, 1909). Until recently, psychological anthropology has been heavily weighted in favor of studying emotional or expressive behavior. Darwin's contemporary, A. R. Wallace, cofounder of evolutionary theory, in his book *Malay Archipelago* (1894: 449–450) essayed into quite modern personality characterizations when he contrasted Malay and Papuan people in terms of relative undemonstrativeness and impulsiveness, respectively. Many years later Charles G. Seligman (1929) followed up this distinction and applied Jung's extrovert-introvert dichotomy to the same people. The famous Cambridge Anthropological Expedition to the Torres Straits in 1898 belongs to the older era of psychological anthropology (Haddon, 1901). Yet, one result of this expedition is quite in keeping with modern thinking about human behavior. The expedition's tests of certain psychological processes among Melanesian "savages" showed no disparity between those people and Europeans, thereby upholding belief in the psychic unity of mankind. Though contrary assertions are recurrently heard (see, for example, Garrett, 1960), the evidence isn't compelling enough to warrant acceptance.

56 Snyder, 1958: 107.

57 Goldenweiser, 1933: 59–88.

58 Kardiner and Preble, 1961: 223.

59 Sapir, 1932 and 1934a.

60 Meggers, 1946; *cf.* Morris Opler, 1946 and 1952.

61 Sutherland, 1942.

62 L. Thompson, in Wolfe, 1963: 7–8.

63 Laing, 1960: chap. 1. I distinguish between existential philosophy (for an excellent introduction to which, see R. G. Olson, 1962) and the existential phenomenological viewpoint that serves psychological understanding.

Diverse Approaches

2

It is . . . a natural desire of the human mind to perceive the whole spirit of an era in one well-rounded concept.[1]

ROBERT A. KANN

By way of introducing culture and personality I have presented several examples of what the field has accomplished, each illustrating attention centered on persons—Great Russians, Samoans, Indians, Jews—who embody distinctive cultures. Through their experience in different cultures they incorporated distinctive personality characteristics. In one case I refer to the personality of a particular Navaho Indian individual while in the others I speak of personality associated with cross sections of individuals, like Samoan girls, Ojibwa Indians, and Orthodox Jews. Several of the accounts inquire into socialization and trace personality characteristics back to the circumstances wherein they were acquired, sometimes back to childhood. I selected some of those studies largely for their historical interest and not because they are representative of the field. In this chapter I propose to range further through culture-and-personality literature to sample more approaches as well as trends and methods, though once more I have chosen brevity at the cost of omitting much, especially the careful reasoning with which the several authors whom I cite have supported and logically justified their conclusions.

MORE LIGHT ON THE PAST

Prehistory through the methods of archeology and history with help from written records study human behavior as it was. Compared to history, prehistory is able to deal with only limited aspects of bygone cultures because, being restricted to eras and societies that lacked writing, it has relatively poor and incomplete evidence to work with. Only rarely do the fragmentary cultural remains prehistory recovers from the earth—house walls, pottery, burials, and personal ornaments—betray to any significant extent the feelings or other personality characteristics of bygone populations. When the fog does momentarily clear so that, aided by fruitful theory or method, we glimpse a former world view, then immediately another handicap confronts us. When I work with a living culture, I can check the insight I gain in one situation, say a ceremony, against independent data from other situations, such as family life, children's play. Such additional information will provide grounds for keeping, rejecting, or revising my original insight. The prehistoric record rarely offers material rich enough to interpret psychologically, so how can it furnish enough data for cross-checking? As a result we perpetually wonder about Late Paleolithic man's attitudes toward the carvings, polychrome paintings, and incised drawings he left in Lascaux and other caves of southwestern Europe. Can we say that those people had adequately satisfied their lower needs—hunger, fatigue, and protection from cold—thereby allowing evolutionarily higher needs to appear? Such nonphysiological higher needs motivate people to express or actualize themselves. In persons who have adequately satisfied their physiological tensions and overcome their immediate survival problems, the higher needs come into play and instigate a search for beauty, creativity, or simply excitement.[2] Perhaps the Late Paleolithic

artists had shifted their attention from well-nigh exclusive preoccupation with sheer survival and came to perceive the world with augmented meanings. Their cave art, then, is a product of higher needs and of an altered view of the world. But did it really go so? Did the hunter indeed place high value on these paintings and drawings? May they not rather be analogous to grafiti we see casually smeared on the walls and pillars of public structures? The sparse prehistoric record gives little opportunity to check.[3]

Direct, written testimony posthumously bequeathed to psychologists, anthropologists, and professional historians by literate members of bygone civilizations greatly facilitates the interpretation of bygone personality systems. For example, the philosophies of an era can reveal unifying principles that point to patterns of thought and feeling; memoirs, diaries, and letters tell how particular men felt, and other literary genres (including drama) give clues to experiences that agitated human emotions. The nearer we come to the present, where history and ethnology overlap, the richer

⟨ Paintings and Other Art Reveal Ancient Mayan Psychological Characteristics That Historical Records and Modern Testing Partly Confirm[4]

If you grant that everything man-made expresses or, to use a modern psychological term, projects its maker's personality, then painting, sculpture, and other forms of an extinct society's art may contain valuable clues to the psychological characteristics of a long past people. If the art products are strongly stylized, their style remaining consistent from one piece to another rather than idiosyncratic and highly spontaneous, grounds exist for going so far as to infer the whole community's psychological characteristics from a few artists' products.

Mayan art tends to avoid sharp corners and to emphasize rounded corners, which demonstrates (according to one theory) that ancient Mayan men were introversive, creative, restrained, and preoccupied with self. Paintings show a preference for keeping human arms close to the body, which again reveals introversion, albeit of a mild type. The lack of background brings out a related psychological trait: The ancient Maya felt little inclined to relate themselves to objects in their environment. Conspicuously ornate headgear means that the men donned elaborate social façades, presenting themselves to the world in a self-preoccupied, restrained, and almost constricted way, severely repressing their aggressive impulses, as the avoidance of sharp points indicates. Short, thick necks and thick waists in many human figures reveal only slight development of conscience, a deduction that further upholds the view of the· Mayan as little interested in social relationships but endowed with creative ability, for witness the complexity of design in the paintings.

Some of these interpretations are supported by Spanish chroniclers who wrote about the Maya; others have been obtained by psychologists analyzing Rorschach-test protocols belonging to modern Mayan Indian males.

What feelings or motives impelled Late Paleolithic hunters to carve this figure, and what did the figure mean in the community where it was originally at home? (Musée de l'Homme, Paris)

the heritage for reconstruction. Judith Shklar[5] postulates three successive periods in European thought, starting with the Enlightenment, when people still possessed faith in progress and through reason confidently expected to regulate conduct and create a better world. The succeeding Romantic period saw faith in the power of reason collapse. The "Romantic mind" revolted against intellectualism and preferred to endorse art and emotion as paths to truth. People also shed the former optimism about the future. Today we live in an era when the Romantic sense of life as tragic has sharpened into feelings of defeat. Art has failed to subdue the world, and the blessings of science are more than balanced by its evils. In the language of some existentialist philosophers, man is homeless; he has been alienated from his existence.

Hampered though they have been by lack

of firsthand, clinical knowledge about people in the past, anthropologists have nevertheless paid considerable attention to psychological concomitants of cultural change. Often they concluded that change has been traumatic for personality, providing new threats to psychological security and self-esteem, undermining previous modes of adjustment, and triggering mental illness. One account describes how the entry of the "white brother," in the form of Mennonite missionaries, set up far-going, traumatic repercussions in Hopi life and personality.[6] The Mennonites wrecked the Hopi ceremonial system, in which men had played important roles that counterbalanced the disadvantages their sex invited in a matrilineal and matrilocal community. As the male role weakened and women's role strengthened, disturbing effects on male personality became apparent.[7] The spontaneity of Hopi boys has tended to decrease and constriction to increase, destroying the formerly balanced personality structure, particularly in those villages dominated by Mennonites. But the absence of historic documents, which could do for the Hopi what travelers' and explorers' accounts did in providing a psychological base-line for the northeastern Indians, leaves us without firm knowledge of how Hopi men in those villages formerly adjusted.

The near unanimity with which anthropologists have found cultural change to be traumatic suggests strongly that, following a prevailing bias to emphasize psychopathology above normal or healthy personality functioning, they may have lavished their attention too exclusively on unfavorable concomitants of change. This likelihood increases when we learn about substantial, heavy, and quick cultural transformations unaccompanied by serious personal maladjustment. In 1953 Margaret Mead revisited the Manus, on Great Admiralty island off the coast of New Guinea, after 25 years' absence.[8] She found those people—who had

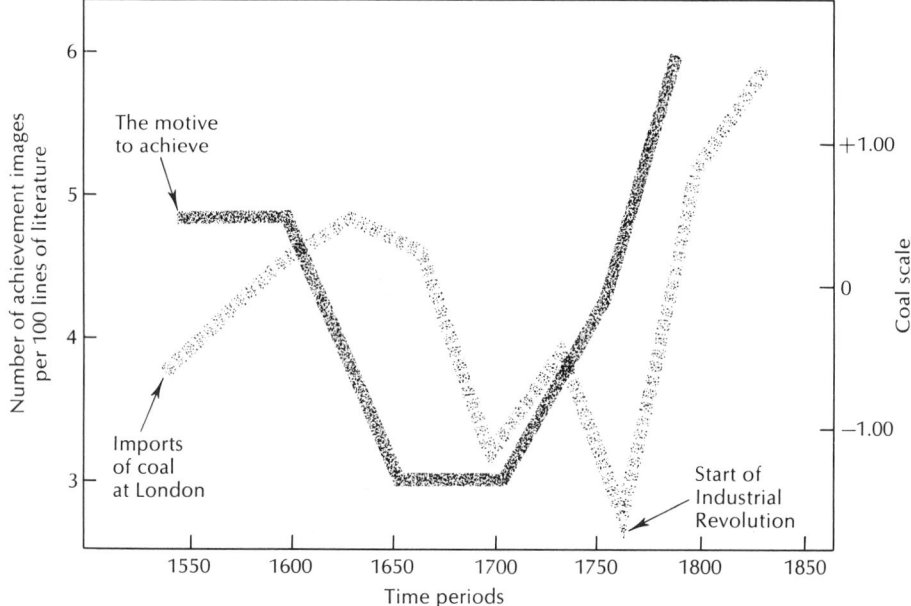

❪ Images of Achievement Keep Step with England's Industrial Growth[9]

It is reasonable to assume that as people become motivated to do well, excel, and achieve they will translate their drive into behavior. If opportunity exists, as it did in England from the seventeenth to nineteenth centuries, they will enter entreprenurial behavior, seeking to make their fortunes in business and industry. Then economic growth will reflect a rising achievement drive.

To measure achievement drive during six time-periods, from 1501 to 1830, researchers scanned 6,000 lines of plays, accounts of sea voyages, and street ballads, written by 295 authors. They counted each statement or phrase that set value on achieving excellence. For example, a statement urging adults to educate their children in order to bring about a more comfortable society, or extolling statesmen of the past for their per-severance was scored as containing an image favorable to achievement. The number of such images per 100 lines yielded a convenient achievement score. Scores ranged from a low of about 3 (in the period 1626–1676 and again in 1676–1725) to a high of 6 (1776–1830).

An independent measure of economic growth, derived from the number of tons of coal imported at the port of London, yielded a coal scale, an index reflecting British industrial expansion.

The graph shows both indices. Note that about 50 years after a rise in achievement drive, coal imports also begin to increase. As the motive to achieve starts to weaken, economic growth also goes into decline, again about a half-century later. Changes in motivation have apparently had far-reaching repercussions in England's industrial life.

been favorably inclined to change, who knew that a way of life could be altered, and who eagerly wanted something more satisfying than their traditional culture— participating in the modern world. The children Mead had known in 1928 in growing to adulthood had succeeded in transforming their unlovable culture through heavy borrowing from British, American, and other examples, and they had done so without psychological deformation.

Economic development and personality

In the 1960s one can't talk of culture change without including the idea of economic or technical development, that worldwide process of modernization which uses science to increase agricultural and other output and raise living standards. Chemical fertilizers, new plows and seeds, public health, and hitherto unexploited sources of energy are ingredients that spur modernization but they can't instigate the process unless favorable personality factors back their use. What those supportive psychological factors may be has engaged social scientists at least since Max Weber published *The Protestant Ethic and the Spirit of Capitalism* in 1905.[10] Weber, without analyzing people's motives clinically, grounded zealous profit making, careful planning, rational use of labor, and other earmarks of capitalism in ascetic Protestantism, especially in its central stress on religious grace. Ascetic Protestants, ideally motivated to earn God's grace through personal piety and individual good deeds, were considerably advantaged to make a success of capitalism. Their religion demanded a righteous way of life that avoided, as the deadliest of sins, wasting time. It also extolled work, citing St. Paul: "He who will not work shall not eat." Even recreation must serve some useful or rational purpose, not leading man

away from his work or calling. Such religious attitudes directly served emerging capitalism. Protestantism further recognized the legitimacy of pursuing wealth, claiming that wealth properly acquired evidenced divine grace. Let the capitalist not feel guilty if his pursuit of wealth promoted the unequal distribution of worldly goods. Why some Christians have more than others is God's secret, locked away from man. Did those attitudes to which Weber points actually exist as motivating forces in sixteenth-century, Protestant personality? Perhaps. At any rate, independent evidence suggests that some sixteenth- and early-seventeenth-century Englishmen increasingly showed attitudes favorable to economic development. Two investigators counted literary lines written in England between 1400 and 1626 that betray concern for achievement, and found that images bearing on the theme of achievement grew continuously from 4.60 per 100 lines in 1400–1500 to 4.79 in 1501–1575 and to 4.81 in 1576– 1625. By the Industrial Revolution (around 1830) they detected as many as 6 achievement images in every 100 lines of drama, of travel, and especially in street ballads.[11]

Recent inquiries into personality characteristics that favor economic development have frequently employed indicators of achievement drive, or n-achievement (i.e., need-achievement) as it is also called.[12] Indirect evidence of n-achievement in a population has been sought in literature (as noted in the previous paragraph); in children's readers; in the number of patents granted, games, and even certain pottery designs. Clinical evidence of the need consists of personality-test results that reveal achievement motivation in the subject, including results from the Thematic Apperception Test with its ambiguous pictures around which the subject builds a story that embodies his own feelings and needs. A person or group highly motivated to achieve derives pleasure through overcoming obstacles. Such people readily put out effort and take risks, financial and other, to win success. Communities and categories of people within communities vary in strength of n-achievement, just as individuals do. In a German city, for example, Protestant boys demonstrated more n-achievement than Catholic boys, other factors being kept equal.[13] Judging from achievement themes counted in folklore, communities that gain food through agriculture have a stronger achievement drive than those practicing techniques of gathering roots or fruit.[14]

PERSONALITY—DEPENDENT AND INDEPENDENT VARIABLES

Although the variety of approaches used in studying personality in its cultural context defies any simple method of classification, two main paths frequently utilized can be sketched to serve as at least a rough guide to such research.

Along the first path meander those studies that trace the consequences of a given culture on personality. Margaret Mead[15] follows it when she shows how the general casualness and homogeneity of Samoan culture leave the adolescent girl's personality free of conflict and unrest. Here culture becomes the independent variable and personality the dependent one. Personality varies in response to cultural differences. In *Sex and Temperament*, another book belonging to the early era of the anthropological study of personality, Mead[16] shows how each of three New Guinea communities bends the individual born within it to one type or emphasis of behavior, regardless of age, sex, and individual dispositions. In Arapesh, emphasis is put on passive growth, whether of plants, children, or brides. In Mundugumor, it is put on mistrust and hostility, which the Mundugumor believe occur naturally between individuals of the same or opposite sex. Tchambuli emphasize artistic

creativity and hold it to be especially important for men. These cultural emphases take hold starting early in a person's childhood and continue to pattern his behavior as he matures and assimilates increasing social responsibilities. The same general approach is taken by those who point out the influence that culture exerts on mental health and illness or, like Ruth Benedict,[17] assert that personality disorder occurs when the cultural demands are at variance with an individual's "native responses" as well as when cultural demands exceed his resources.

The second path is followed in studies that ask the opposite question: How do personality characteristics influence culture? Ruth Benedict[18] insists that human cultures aren't built simply from clues and resources cast up by geographic environments, nor do they simply arise out of physical drives like hunger, sex, and pugnacity. Environment and physical organism provide the merest hints, which become enormously elaborated in some communities and well-nigh ignored in others. Human pugnacity may be so small a hint that it almost escapes expression or, under the impetus of other motives, becomes tremendously exaggerated, as it was among the Sioux and other Indian tribes living on the U. S. Great Plains. People fashion their cultures largely unconsciously, as their motives, emotions, and values dictate, according to their canons of choice. (Their motives and values, of course, are far from wholly inborn but themselves arise as culture bends individuals to its own type of emphasis. The relationship between personality and culture is, therefore, partly reciprocal. What matters is where one breaks in, from what vantage point one begins to trace the process.) A number of anthropologists reject Benedict's relativistic idea that people shape cultures according to canons of choice. They view cultural development as largely beyond human control or intervention and as governed by impersonal laws. Even leaders count for little, being more products than makers of history.[19] Those who hold this position naturally see no point in investigating the cultural impact of the deviant or abnormal, as Benedict does looking at eighteenth-century, New England Puritan divines. These often psychiatrically disturbed people, she says, possessed tremendous social power. "They were the voice of God. . . . it is they, not the confused and tormented women they put to death as witches, who were the psychoneurotics. . . . A sense of guilt as extreme as they portrayed and demanded both in their own conversion experiences and in those of their converts is found in a slightly saner civilization only in institutions for mental diseases."[20]

The two paths meet. Through time a community unconsciously selects certain temperamental traits and dispositions as desirable, selecting them from possibilities inherent in human nature. Everyone must learn the socially desirable traits and dispositions regardless of his own, personal proclivities.[21] The approved temperament, socially incorporated in personality, in turn shapes the community's way of life, including elements of culture taken over from neighbors. How communities came initially to make their choice of temperament, like the Arapesh selecting passivity or like the Mundugumor choosing mistrust, from the many possibilities with which human nature confronted them, is a historical question. A detailed answer to it can't be found in a nonliterate community lacking historical records. Even among ourselves, the process that alters emphases in human behavior remains unnoticed. Suddenly we realize, for instance, that the personality demanded and most rewarded in university graduate-study and academic life is no longer unhurried, contemplative, and inner-directed but energetically endowed for rapid, constant productivity and respon-

Laura Thompson (*Moulin Studios*)

sive to social cues. Applicants endowed with such natures are best suited for graduate study. If others slip in, they must conform to the pressure or leave without obtaining a degree. The problem of tolerance becomes acute whenever some temperamental traits are held to be so desirable that they must be learned by everyone hoping to fill a given position, regardless of whether they conflict with his nature. Insistence on conformity to one narrow ideal creates unhappy people, people disadvantaged and perhaps doomed to rebel against the demands to which they are confined.[22]

HOLISM AND ITS PROBLEMS

Research on personality in culture need not be preoccupied with either the effect of culture on personality or vice versa. Some

The Hopi Indians, confronted by many hazards and pressures caused by their desert environment—including attacks by other Indian groups—evolved their own social system. As anthropologist Laura Thompson points out, this system seemed to be remarkably well suited to their needs: it both permitted and fostered the development of their latent capabilities.

Men and women had their special and essential roles in village life. Each person was expected to carry out his obligations to the tribe with very few external sanctions imposed by tribal leadership or by physical force. Social controls operating on the Hopi tended to originate with a socially patterned individual conscience that embodied the community's standards. But controls also reached outward to involve the Hopi natural and supernatural world in its many dimensions.

Some observers believe that the pressures confronting these pueblo Indians exacted a high toll in anxiety and frustration. On the other hand, a careful study which investigated Hopi personality and culture holistically suggested that the social system in its harmony with its environmental setting was reflected in a harmoniously balanced and healthy personality system. This complex personality was mature in social, emotional, and artistic ways (at least within many areas where artistic endeavor was socially encouraged) and was marked by a well-established internal control system and by an astute and analytical type of intelligence and an abstract kind of mental approach equipped with a readiness to cognize and deal with wholes.

Hopi babies are usually smiling and relaxed, and discipline of children is permissive. Nevertheless, the tribe's ways of initiating the child into the group life are rather more formalized and ritualized than those of other Indian tribes—the Papago, Sioux, and Navaho—with which they have been compared. Also, the Hopi are likely to use somewhat harsher methods when a child within a certain age group commits what are conceived to be social or moral transgressions. The result is often a child spurred on to premature development that is combined with emotional harmony and adult behavior.

Hopi Indian social personality possesses the character traits and the emotional and mental energy that are required to fulfill man's role in the universe as the Hopi conceive it to be. They believe the universe to be dangerous, but not unpredictable or devious. Instead of man being at the mercy of unpredictable forces, he is able to play a powerful, independent role in a universe that is complex, interrelated, and controlled by natural law. Man's role in this complex system is far from vague or inconsistent.

In these terms Laura Thompson analyzes in holistic fashion the manner in which Hopi culture and personality directly reflect the severity of environmental pressure, as well as other tensions under which the tribe lives. Ritual, art, mythology, language structure, social organization, child-training routines, and personality all interlock and fit into their geographic and historic context to constitute a congruous unity.

The result resembles the organic integration that ecologists discover in the way plant and animal groups relate themselves, in nature, to their overall environment. The Hopi example illustrates how isolated human communities also come gradually to integrate themselves logically, esthetically, and symbolically with their total setting.

anthropologists reject thinking in terms of cause and effect because human events are too complexly interdependent and too enmeshed with nonhuman factors, like geography, to allow one element to be pointed to as causing another. They would rather speak of congruence between certain elements of culture and personality. They assign priority neither to culture nor to personality. Each reflects the other. Personality is one feature related to, or integrated with, many other features of the universe they study. A holistic view holds personality to be integrated with all other features making up a whole community and its setting, even with the environment and the somatic constitution of the people who sustain it. Such a whole has been called a supersystem.[24]

Social scientists have for many years idealized holism, yet much of their actual research consists of teasing from the supersystem's many-stranded web isolated personality characteristics, separate dimensions of behavior, and particular variables. These they proceed to compare and correlate. They still lack precise enough concepts to grasp the working of wholes as wholes. They feel more capable when they work with discrete units of behavior or of culture, regardless of the lip service they periodically pay to the idea that culture, personality, and society each make up a system, and together combine into a total system. Available techniques and concepts allow them to work with a satisfactory sense of rigor and with painstaking, empirical exactitude only when they break up a system into its components.

DESCRIPTIVE ANALYSIS

Sometimes an author prefers to tell straightforwardly what persons are like in a certain cultural context, without specifying how they come to acquire their personality or the way in which personality is implicated in, say, social conflicts, a religious system, or readiness to change and adapt to altering historical circumstances. Take, for example, Kant's description of fellow Germans:[25] "The German . . . is home-loving; solid but not brilliant; industrious, thrifty, cleanly, without much flash of genius; phlegmatic, tough in endurance, persistent in reasoning; intelligent, capable, but lacking in wit or taste; modest, without confidence in his own originality, therefore imitative; overmethodical, pedantic; without impulse toward equality, but addicted to a painstaking hierarchical grading of society that sets title and rank above natural talent; docile under government, accepting despotism rather than resisting or altering the established order of authority." Such a description is compounded out of attributes that should be directly verifiable when we confront the subjects. I would contrast so attributional a description with a psychodynamic description in which all component elements are not immediately identifiable. Some are deeply hidden and can only be identified by somebody who has the theoretical key to unlock the meaning of what the subjects overtly do and say. Thus, attributes like docility, pedantry, and methodicalness are sometimes held to conceal a covert trait, anxiety. Weston La-Barre[26] describes Japanese personality psychodynamically when he characterizes the people as pervasively compulsive. That covert trait underlies their perfectionism, neatness, perseveration, persistence, and conscientiousness. He also sees Japanese to be endowed with a highly tyrannical conscience, by virtue of which they overtly present themselves as most self-righteous. Forbidden impulses not congenial to that conscience they strive to project onto others. Occasionally, aggression, which Japanese try energetically to control, escapes into masochistic impulses and hypochondriasis, which makes the people ready to respond to the most extravagant advertisements promising to remedy disorders or strengthen bodily functions.

Description always implies analysis which points to features, elements, or processes in the flow of events. Concepts to aid analysis can come from the realm of everyday common sense (as in the illustration from Kant), or they may be specially coined and rigidly defined to fit a theory like psychoanalysis, a theory which proved a great boon for culture and personality.

GENETIC ANALYSIS

Psychoanalytic concepts have especially been used genetically to analyze personality development in childhood. A genetic approach (which, needless to say, has nothing to do with genes!) concerns itself with how individuals acquire personality or learn their culture through socialization. Some genetic studies of socialization are primarily descriptive and little concerned with *how* the process occurs. A book like *Growing Up in an Egyptian Village* by Hamed Ammar[27] primarily describes in fine analytical detail and in straightforward, common-sense terms the sequence of growing up for children in the Muslim village of Silwa. We learn how a small child receives little deliberate teaching of how to walk and how casual are his sleeping habits. Ammar doesn't follow out the likely consequences of such early casualness for personality development; he interprets only at rare intervals. Similarly, he doesn't speculate about the subtler influences on personality of, say, adults' belief that they must actively force children to conform to social standards and must enforce obedience, subservience, politeness, and even fear, so that in later years children won't bring shame on the family or challenge elders' authority. In

distinction, Erik Erikson[28] illustrates a far more dynamic approach to genetic analysis. He employs psychoanalytic theory to trace in a child the repercussions of many incidents in his early socialization. Not that theory didn't also guide Ammar in what he looked for in the Egyptian village, but Ammar's theory is closer to common sense than Erikson's and less concerned with hidden repercussions or dynamics.

Genetic analysis doesn't have to be concerned with causes. It may simply attend to the sequence of development. "To give a genetic analysis much less information suffices than would be required to show that each link is sufficient for the occurrence of the next."[29] In practice, however, and this is particularly true of psychoanalysis, genetic analyses of personality often do trace cause and effect, sometimes rigidifying personality to the point where childhood has almost overwhelming power compared to later life.

We ought to avoid the mistake sometimes made by critics who misunderstand genetic analysis. Tracing adult personality characteristics back to childhood doesn't contribute a word regarding their historical origin. Genetic analysis inquires into how each new generation receives and comes to embody its cultural heritage, or the way in which each generation transmits its cultural heritage.[30] The historical development of that heritage is a problem that must be handled by historical methods. One variant mode of genetic analysis asserts that what happens in childhood repeats the history of the species. Psychoanalysts who claim that ontogeny repeats phylogeny (needless to say, without offering historic justification in the form of empirical evidence), derive culture from basic human impulses, problems, and situations that continue to recur in each generation in the same way they occurred in prehistoric times when they first called forth culture.[31] For example, myths

Sigmund Freud   (Dr. Ernst L. Freud)

in many parts of the world, even though they differ from one culture to another, are explained as originating in the universally present Oedipus complex: the situation that directs a child toward his parent of opposite sex, with consequent hate and jealousy for the like-sexed parent. The myths originally provided a devious channel wherein prohibited Oedipus strivings could be gratified and they still fulfill that function. When anthropologists denied the universality of the Oedipus complex, one psychoanalyst replied that their very refusal to acknowledge its role in culture arose from their own unresolved Oedipal tensions.[32] Freud[33] also explains the origin of culture phylogenetically when he claims that "Civilization is . . . built entirely on renunciation of instincts." Ontogenetically, "every individual on his journey from childhood to maturity has in his own person to recapitulate this development of humanity to a state of judicious resignation." Man has only a

limited quantity of psychic energy at his disposal, Freud reasons. What he uses up to gratify his impulses he takes away from culture building.[34] Historically, culture has been built up at the cost of sexual and aggressive instincts, which man has been forced to inhibit or repress. Yet, the very thwarting of these instincts generates frustration and fresh aggression, with the result that a vicious, self-regenerative cycle is instituted. Civilization costs man his happiness. He finds life hard, full of pain, full of suffering; he feels keenly his lack of liberty, and labors under an onerous burden of constant renunciation.[35]

PSYCHOLOGY AND CULTURE

Whatever its remote phylogenetic roots, culture is anchored in ever-present psychological processes. Exploring these in particular cultures is one of the tasks of psychological anthropology. Or else, elements commonly found in culture—clowning, money, male genital mutilations, and whatnot—are traced back to universal psychological tendencies that allegedly form part of human nature. Clowning, for example, may be explained as offering a chance to regress into infantile forms of sexual and aggressive behavior,[36] or as periodically providing license that helps people to cope with the tensions aroused by confining social values.[37] One shortcoming of psychodynamic explanations that purport in a single breath to account for patterns of culture no matter where they occur is their failure to take account of incompatible, or at least unexpected, personality characteristics present in some but not all communities where the cultural item is found. Often the universal explanations furnished are based on very little creditable evidence. Hence they have captivated few anthropologists.

The forms taken in particular cultures

by universal psychological processes them-selves—dreaming, defense, perception, and others—can be more satisfactorily investi-gated as products of social patterning. Dorothy Eggan[38] has over many years col-lected and analyzed Hopi Indians' dreams, assuming that the manifest content of dreams reflects specific cultural features as well as personal factors characteristic of in-dividual dreamers. Not even mechanisms of psychological defense, like repression, ra-tionalization, reaction formation, and oth-ers, are the same from one society to an-other. For one thing, the elaborateness of defense varies between cultures. Baffin Is-land Eskimo, with their lack of creative lying and posturing, possess a personality endowed with very simple defense maneu-vers.[39] Doubtlessly this leaves the Eskimo quite vulnerable to blows to their self-esteem and security, but it spares them from intrapersonal conflicts generated by many defense mechanisms themselves.

Cognition is a psychological process to whose social patterning anthropologists and other social scientists have paid much atten-tion. Alexis de Tocqueville[40] thought that a democracy like the United States, which leads every man to investigate truth for himself, "must" insensibly beget a tendency to form general ideas in the human mind. "When I repudiate the traditions of rank,

❰ Navaho Myths, Religion, Marriage Customs, and Kinship Behavior Reveal Prohibited Oedipal Strivings

In general, Navaho myths are concerned (a) *with the hero having done something he was warned not to do,* (b) *the death or dismemberment or transformation of the hero, and* (c) *the aid given by the gods including the ritual derived from the myth and the hero's ultimate restoration and apotheosis. More specifically, the hero's misdemeanor frequently is either mating with the wife of a god or eating food offered him by a zoomorphic god and subsequent identification with that supernatural being. The two themes may also be combined.*

Now what is the core of the Oedipus complex? The boy wishes sexual intercourse with the mother and wishes to be identical with the father. This phantasied identification takes place in the form of introjection, i.e., a phantasied incorporation or eating. If we discount the obvious camouflage of a goal being represented as a danger then we can see that the entire Navaho mythology and religion are based (a) *on the Oedipus complex, and* (b) *on magic or ritual in which Oedipal guilt feelings are allayed.*

· · ·

In this case I don't think anybody can say that I am just carrying over concepts that apply to Western Culture only and have nothing to do with the Navaho.

There are two institutions which show the Oedipal background as clearly as possible. One of the obviously Oedipal institutions is the polygamous marriage in which a man marries a woman and her own daughter by a previous marriage.

· · ·

While this father-daughter marriage reveals the incest aspect of the Oedipus complex, the teasing relationship with grandfathers certainly shows the father-son struggle.[41]

GÉZA RÓHEIM

professions, and birth, when I escape from the authority of example to seek out, by the single effort of my reason, the path to be followed, I am inclined to derive . . . my opinions from human nature itself, and this leads me necessarily and almost unconsciously, to adopt a great number of very general notions." Englishmen, he believed, display much less aptitude and taste for general ideas than Americans and less than their neighbors on the Continent, the French, but more than their forefathers did. To cognize is to classify by imposing categories of thought on reality, thereby imposing meaning. People don't merely see, smell, or feel, but also *know* what they perceive by their senses. A man stands before a painting: "It's modern . . . it's cubist . . . it's a still life by Picasso. . . .": He breaks down the painting into categories of knowledge—period, style, subject, and artist—by the same process he uses to discriminate between right and left or cabbages and kings. This ability to discriminate and classify different aspects of reality is part of cognition. Each culture has its own relatively distinct modes of cognition by which persons learn to order the world in which they live.[42] To a physicist the color spectrum is a continuous scale of light waves of different lengths, but the Philippine Hanunóo recognize only four general color categories—blackness, whiteness, redness, and greenness[43]—and speakers of Bassa in Liberia do with only two, one corresponding more or less to purple, blue, and green and the other approximating our yellow, orange, and red. Similarly, people categorize disease by the symptoms shown and order plant and animal life in their environment by its distinguishing features. According to one venerable notion, language orders how we classify. Since classification offers a way of thinking about reality, language to some extent governs thought. The tenses a verb utilizes—past, present, and future—guide our

conception of time. We conceive of things as either having been, being, or as they will be, but Hopi time falls into different categories because the Indians' tenses discriminate a period that extends up to and includes the present; a future, and a generalized timelessness governing things that have always been true.[44] If we really think of time differently than the Hopi, we can nevertheless with little trouble grasp their system. Owing to the fact that language names things it has another function. Cognitive features that make reality meaningful must be communicable to serve as guides to action. They are communicated by being reduced to symbolic formulations, of which language is one type.

Returning to the man standing before a painting, what would happen if in addition to recognizing correctly a Picasso, his admiration for the artist's work encountered contrary opinions expressed by a friend? Each would then be cognizing the same experience in opposed ways. Cognitive dissonance is a term for contradictions and attendant emotional conflicts that arise through opposed systems of knowing.[45] This common form of conflict must occur frequently among people who hopefully employ magic to obtain a good food supply, only to learn subsequently that their optimistic expectations remain unfulfilled: Their crop does badly.[46] Like the admirer of Picasso who confronts a contrary opinion, the farmer who relies on magic is confused and distressed by his crop's failure. People can select from several ways of reducing cognitive dissonance. They can abandon the practice that has run into opposition, drop admiration for Picasso (or cease to practice magic), thereby conforming to the new information. Or they can emphasize their habitual way of believing. By insisting vigorously on Picasso's excellence (or the value of magic), they minimize the contrary knowledge that has unwelcomely intruded on their consciousness. It is by no means extraordinary to find people who have made a heavy emotional commitment to a religious system rigidly preserving their faith despite regular disconfirmation.[47]

STRUCTURAL ANALYSIS

Spurred by sociologists, much interest has recently been taken in connecting personality and social structure, the enduring framework or skeleton of society. By way of example, note how Kaska Indians' amiability and their suppression of aggression aboriginally suited a stripped-down social structure, one lacking police, government, or any formal body empowered to maintain order and cooperation. Small hunting groups among the Kaska survived through voluntary cooperation. By interfering with mutual assistance, aggression in such small social entities would have imperiled survival. Such interpretations are easy for an anthropologist to reach, but they probably didn't occur to a Kaska Indian. Hence they don't represent a conscious purpose behind Kaska attitudes to aggression. In other words, the functions which an objective observer finds in behavior need not correspond to purposes held by the people being observed.[48] Another structurally oriented personality study by Dinko Tomasic[49] relates the thoroughgoing individualism of nineteenth-century pastoralists in what is now Yugoslavia to lack of centralized political authority. Absence of any effective superordinate government demanded that every man be ready to rely on physical force to maintain his rights. What we know about the Kaska Indians, who also live in an atomistic social structure lacking superordinate controls, indicates that we cannot generalize from the East European pastoralists to say that atomistic communities create

violent personalities. The Kaska suppress aggression and earnestly extol deference in interpersonal relations. According to one view, matrilocal communities (these are the type where husbands after marriage join their wives' families) will be most apt to suppress open expression of hostility, though aggression may be allowed release in such relatively nondisruptive forms as warfare against external enemies.[50] When, as among the East European pastoralists, patrilocal residence aggregates male kinsmen, aggressive behavior will be permitted to flourish.

PROLONGED CULTURAL IMMERSION

Great is the variety of techniques that have been invented or adapted for studying living personalities and their formation in cultural settings. I hardly propose to draft a technical manual for prospective investigators, and I don't claim personal competence in all the strategies that research-minded anthropologists, sociologists, psychologists, and psychiatrists utilize. Mainly, my aims are to set out some types of procedures and to show how resourceful and ingenious researchers have been in finding suitable ways of discovering the imprint that societies leave on their members.

The basic technique in culture and personality is fieldwork, the classic anthropological means of studying culture that requires prolonged and almost total immersion in another way of life. Undoubtedly there exist as many ways of doing fieldwork as there are anthropologists who go to the field, the basic technique being flexible enough to vary with each individual, the situations he encounters, and the specific problems he elects to study. As a result, would-be anthropologists spend little time practicing skills for collecting data. They are far less taught to follow rules than they are urged to be imaginative, flexible, and maximally creative under culturally strange circumstances where their customary modes of behavior provide poor guides to effective behavior. As a result of the intensely personal element that operates in traditional fieldwork, no ethnographic report can ever be strictly comparable to another; it won't be so even when, as occasionally happens, two ethnologists describe the same culture. Fieldwork makes culture and personality a clinical discipline in which, unlike under carefully contrived laboratory conditions, behavior is observed directly in its full, complex, frequently bewildering, natural setting.[51] Clinical disciplines are the most fecund when it comes to producing hunches and hypotheses, but they are also the most handicapped for testing their plethora of hunches.[52]

Using his whole being as a sensitive recording instrument, but protectively reinforcing his memory with written notes, a census, and maps, the fieldworking anthropologist regards his personal response to the culture wherein he lives as his major source of data. Learning a culture isn't so much a matter of digging out the facts of people's preferences, conflicts, modes of childrearing, or style of artistic expression—assumed to exist full-blown "out there" and to be had for the effort of asking—as it is utilizing countless bits of apparently unrelated information, obtained in remotely connected situations and consisting of spoken and unspoken behavior. That the Kaska Indians are emotional suppressers I learned from their feeble, denying humor; their muted response to death; their uncertain optimism when facing hunger; a widower's complaint that he needed a cook; an adulteress' preference for her paramour because he provided for her better than her husband; and the way people withdrew from the aged.[53] Juggling clues like these, an ethnologist constructs what he hopes will be

a reasonable model, which he then treats as though it were wholly external to him rather than in his head.[54] Even in a simple culture, a solitary fieldworker must cover an enormous ground in order to gorge himself with information and cover the variety of situations that add up to a total way of life. If his people enjoy night life, he learns to rest when they do. If they are mobile, he must strike his tent and move with them. He perceives not only what people do, say, and make but also how they do so; he remains alert for nuances of gesture, tone, and style that are very hard to conceptualize and of which his subjects may be oblivious.[55] Tuned in on personality, he is constantly preoccupied with such questions as "What does this mean?" "What does he mean?" For all the ground he covers, he has at his disposal only limited time, which he tries to use with maximal efficiency by heeding every likely event that comes to his ken. Simultaneously, however, he must do his housework, replenish supplies, treat illness, and find opportunity for relaxation—though that he prefers to do by joining his people in their own recreation, whereby he literally combines work and play. A fieldworker meets many people, but his time-consuming method allows him to work closely with only a few, each of whom becomes a representative example of some social experience, class, sex category, or age level.[56] When he recognizes that economic, social-class, regional, or religious differences stratify a community, he appraises each subject in terms of where he fits and tries to reach informants belonging to each significant social division. His rigor is analogous to the historian's critical evaluation of documents, except that the ethnologist's major sources are people rather than letters, journals, and newspapers. Many workers in disciplines biased in favor of interviewing many systematically sampled respondents, each of whom is asked to answer the same questions, are mystified that the anthropologist should confine himself to but a few informants, some of whom select *him*. Nevertheless, I hope to show that each approach has unique advantages.

PROJECTIVE AND OTHER TESTS

Frequently, anthropologists in pursuit of information about personality seek assistance from projective instruments, like the Rorschach and Thematic Apperception tests, and from other standardized aids. They test both in order to augment their psychological penetration of people and to secure strictly comparable, even measurable, information from a number of subjects. In simple terms, any test achieves its results by confronting a subject with a relatively standardized situation, one that remains in definite ways the same from individual to individual—objectively, at any rate, and that's what counts. Like a schoolroom examination, a test stimulates a subject to respond meaningfully while confining his responses to a narrowly designed channel. To be employable from one culture to another any such fieldwork aid must be largely culture-free. That is, everyone, regardless of his schooling, language, previous experience, and ability to read and write, should be equally capable of taking the test without facing handicaps imposed by a background that differs from the tester's. Probably no available test is 100 percent culture-free. Deliberate questioning is a new experience for some people. The Western skirts, suits, pale skins, and other features depicted on cards of the Thematic Apperception Test appear strange to South Sea islanders and to people of India who perceive them with special, culture-bound meanings. In order to offset this handicap, the TAT has been redrawn for use under exotic cultural conditions, human figures

and natural backgrounds, being more familiarly rendered. One insuperable limitation to testing occurs when subjects prove to be too inhibited to make up sufficiently rich stories to TAT drawings, or culturally disinclined to answer the examiner's questions, even when invited to do so in their own language. To be sure, those reactions in themselves reveal something about their psychological makeup, but they don't provide the kind of data on which tests and their interpretation depend.

Offsetting the disadvantages faced in cross-cultural use of projective tests is the big advantage they provide in the form of controlled stimuli to present to members of the same social system. Responses given to the Rorschach or TAT test are objective; they can be quantified, and they can be compared from one person or category to another. A researcher can use the responses to gauge the extent to which people differ psychologically who play different roles in the social system, and he can compare age categories to observe how personality changes from one period of life to another.

The Indian Education Research Project, which in 1943 began to study child development in six North American Indian tribes, is notable for the extent to which it relied on standardized procedures, many of them nonprojective, to acquire comparable information about young personalities from one tribe to another.[57] The instruments proved quite effective—though not without encountering a few difficulties—for getting easily comparable data on youthful emotional attitudes, relationships, values, aversions, and moral attitudes. Within a tribe, children as individuals differed widely from one another, yet group trends could easily be seen. Indian children showed up in especially sharp, contrasting fashion when their test-findings were compared to those of the non-Indian, midwestern U.S. youngsters who served as a control group. The Emotional Response Test, for example, asks whether you have ever been very happy, then invites you to tell about it. Similar questions are put about sadness, fear, anger, and shame, and the examiner also inquires what the best and worst things are that could happen to the subject. Southwest Indian children often ascribed sadness to the "badness of others" whereas Midwest children more frequently saw it as due to disappointment in others. "It is as though the Midwest children were more self-centered and felt a personal sadness when not given their own way in such matters as going to a movie or getting new clothes, while the Indian children were more group-centered, feeling sad when people were aggressive or bad, even though the aggression may not have been directed against them personally."[58] Let's see what else this test brought out. As good things, Navaho and Zia Indian children frequently reported receiving gifts and having property, such as sheep and cowboy hats. Generally, compared to Midwest youngsters the Indians cited securing property, food, clothing, and other possessions as sources of pleasant emotion. Loss, damage, or lack of those

things produced quite the opposite emotional state. Such facts don't speak much further for themselves. To extract more meaning from them, they must be interpreted in the light of other things we know about the people and their cultures. For instance, the facts made the researchers wonder whether, relatively speaking, modern, white society is quite as strongly attached to property as it is often ascribed as being. Perhaps Midwest children can afford to be more unconcerned about getting and losing possessions because their families are economically so much more secure, whereas the Indians are materially poorer. The Project also tested with questions originally set by the psychologist Jean Piaget to Swiss children concerning rules of games: "Can boys and girls like you make new rules for this game?" "Can the rules be changed?" "Is it right to play the game another way?" Such questions get at two sources of morality, one based on constraint, the other resting on social agreement among peers. The former comes early in a child's life as he accepts rules that come to him from outside authority and regards them to be absolute and unchangeable. Later, he reaches the second stage. As a result of the give-and-

❮ *Navaho Indian Children Reserve a Tight, Constraining Moral View for Native Games But Employ a Morality of Agreement for the White Man's Games, Which Aren't Sacred and May Be Altered*[59]

		6 to 11 years		12 to 18 years	
		Navaho games	White games	Navaho games	White games
Can rules be changed?	Yes	0	7	1	10
	No	14	3	24	3

Navaho Indian children nearly unanimously agreed that rules of Navaho games *cannot* be changed. They cited legends crediting the "Ancient Ones" and "Holy People" with the games and their rules. However, toward games belonging to white culture—that is, learned from teachers or older children—they extended a morality of agreement. As the figures show, Navaho children more frequently stated that the rules of white games could be changed and adapted to local conditions.

take of play in peer groups, he discovers rules to be man-made and learns that they can be changed. He joins others in making rules by common agreement. Comparison of the several Indian groups by their order of moral constraint shows Zuni Indian children to be consistently high—quite reluctant to change the rules—followed by Papago, Sioux, Zia, Hopi, and, finally, the Navaho youngsters. (Midwest children were not given Piaget's questions about rules of games.)

Skillfully drawn hypothetical situations to which the subject is invited to supply an outcome can test deeply implicit values that people rarely think about consciously. One investigation of this type sought to learn whether people living under varying cultures differed with respect to attitudes toward activity. Did they prefer people to do whatever spontaneously expressed their being? Or was it better to accomplish ends that could be measured by standards external to the individual and not necessarily expressive of his inner nature? Few Zuni and Navaho Indians or Texan homesteaders, to whom this research was directed, would understand such questions. Instead, the Indians and other testees heard a story about two men who lived differently. One kept his crops growing all right but didn't work them more than he had to, because he wanted to have time to visit friends and enjoy life. (The subject isn't told so, but this man, so far as his preferred mode of activity is concerned, emphasized *being*.) The other man liked to work in his fields and always put in extra time to keep them clean. As a result, he didn't have much time to visit friends or enjoy himself in other ways. (He emphasized *doing*.) Then the subject is asked, "What kind of a man do you believe it is better to be?" First and second choices are solicited.[60]

Projective tests consisting of stories or inkblots have enjoyed enormous appeal in anthropology, much of it stemming from their undeniable capacity to catalyze and bring into the open personality characteristics that it would take much longer and rare skill to discover in more natural situations or even through interviewing.[61] The person who takes the test isn't usually aware of how much he reveals when he obliges the examiner by saying what the inkblots might be or when he makes up stories for the TAT. The instruments are called "projective," because the vague, ambiguous stimuli of which they consist allow a subject to respond thoughtfully, emotionally, and verbally with a minimum of conscious deliberation, yet in ways that correspond to the way he normally behaves.[62] The TAT and Rorschach actually tap somewhat different aspects of personality: the former draws out a subject's manifest role behavior, interpersonal and self attitudes, and similar relatively conscious personality characteristics; the latter probes more deeply and exposes less obvious, usually more general, as well as completely hidden responses. Protocols containing a subject's responses are later scored and interpreted, after which the results are often expressed in an argot quite unintelligible to uninitiated outsiders. Take these sentences, for example, which refer to an analysis of Menomini Indian protocols: "The personality tends to be subject to unsystematized anxiety (presence of K) and apparently there is a tendency to attempt resolution of it by introspection (presence of FK). There is a relative looseness of control exerted over emotional responses (with CF dominating FC). . . ."[63]

Undoubtedly, you want to know whether any validity can be claimed for an interpretation of personality drawn from identifications of Rorschach inkblots or from stories made up to TAT drawings, especially when it applies to a subject following an exotic way of life. Let's consider a specific, simple interpretation. Assume that a U.S. person's

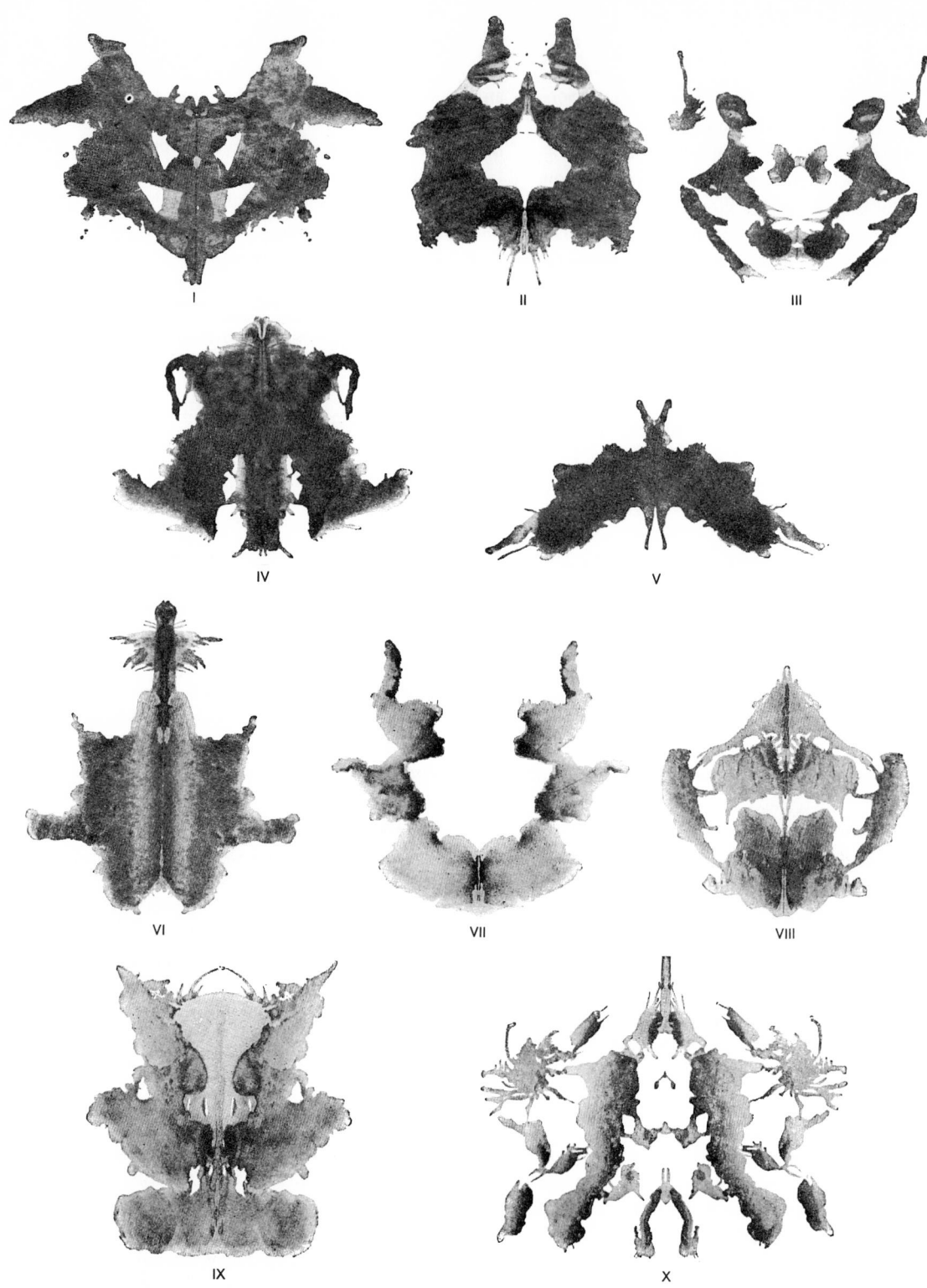

Ten inkblots—most in black, white, or shades of black, but a few in color—comprise the Rorschach test's stimuli.   (Hans Huber Publishers)

answers when he takes the Rorschach test slow down with the color cards because— here comes the interpretation—he is emotionally inhibited or for another reason blocks when the situation requires him to manage relatively strong emotional stimuli. Does slowing down on color cards mean the same thing when someone does it who has been reared in another culture? Let's face it, the Rorschach and other projective tests have not been very successfully validated objectively, even for American subjects. (Objective validation requires successfully predicting from one test, in this case the Rorschach, to another independent test or situation.) It is primarily a personal tool, in use much akin to the personal way an anthropologist does fieldwork as he combines thousands of remotely connected facts to construct models of culture and personality that he believes to be true. The Rorschach's validity depends largely on the consistency with which an experienced person uses it, together with many other clues to hidden personality states, in order to construct a model of the subject's whole personality. The consistency of this model at many points and its good fit with overt behavior attest to another kind of validity. Used in this way, even in foreign societies, the Rorschach as well as the TAT have won a high level of creditability. Quite a few tour-de-force attempts have been made to see if a psychologist or psychiatrist can blindly interpret projective-test protocols collected in another culture, the analyst being provided with the minimum of information about either culture or people.[64] Agreement between the blind analysis and what the fieldworker reports testifies to the test's validity. Blind interpretation of Rorschach protocols in particular may produce results of such vague generality that they could apply to almost anybody. Projective tests were not originally designed for such stringent use. They best provide auxiliary sources of in-

formation for a clinical psychologist or anthropologist to utilize along with an abundance of other knowledge that time allows him to gain about the people he is studying. Used in this way in the Indian Education Research Project with American Indian children, the Rorschach and a modified Thematic Apperception test distinguished personalities belonging to the different tribes as it brought out the children's orientation to the physical world; the nature and extent of adult pressures on them; the nature of parental authority; goals worth striving for; roles allocated to one sex or the other, as well as the emotional atmosphere enveloping those roles; the extent to which individual spontaneity is restrained or encouraged; the degree to which children accept and integrate influences from Euroamerican culture; and how their impulselife varies at different ages in response to changing cultural demands.[65]

Not every psychologically oriented anthropologist is equally committed to employing projective tests. The heavy, timeconsuming work of scoring and interpreting dozens of protocols deters some. Investigators also say that they don't want an instrument to create a barrier between them and their subjects; they prefer to approach their people directly, and to rely on their own sensitive insight in gauging psychodynamic states.

QUESTIONING AND RATING

Compared to an anthropologist acting as a living witness by immersing himself prolongedly in the culture he studies, much social science research sends out interviewers equipped with carefully prepared, pretested directives (schedules or questionnaires). They never get very familiar with the people whose culture and personality they are querying. The interviewers, rarely the same people who originally drew up the research, carry out instructions and inquire into a respondent's personal history; his current habits, feelings, attitudes and anxieties; and his future plans or wishes. Sometimes they rate what they learn, like a parent's degree of permissiveness or the level of a family's socioeconomic standing. Anthropologists can learn much from the well-planned strategies which sociologists and psychologists build to answer researchable questions, though to be adapted for fieldwork in other cultures those procedures may have to be modified. Before considering them more closely, I must warn you that the diversity of those techniques is too great to allow me to provide any easy, full, systematic account of each one.

Questioning. Formal interviews and rating procedures forcefully impose the investigator, together with his already shaped theory, hypotheses, and concepts derived from another culture, on the world he studies. Anthropologists, much more than sociologists and psychologists, prefer to remain receptively alert to that world's own concepts—in effect, allowing the culture to write its own program. As I have already suggested, they much more often come away from research building theories and hypotheses than they are likely to have tested any. The schedule of questions or of points to observe used by behavioral scientists selectively pinpoints the data that the investigator has reason to feel exist and that he needs to test his propositions. Why shouldn't he know what to expect? Most likely he is carrying out research on his own culture, which he knows from long, personal experience. He may have based his study on results that others previously obtained, a method that not only guarantees cumulative knowledge but allows him to forecast how people will act and, broadly, how they will respond to certain questions. Leo Srole[66] knew that some U.S. citizens are disenchanted with their political leaders and perceive the world in which they live as essentially fickle, unpredictable, and orderless. Hence they will strongly espouse few of society's norms and values. With this knowledge he constructed an instrument to measure the degree of alienation manifested by people in different social positions. When information is derived through interviews formally structured by schedules, the questioner doesn't stay around long enough to see if a person actually does become aggressive frequently, how a mother actually rears her children, or the extent to which a father participates in family life. He simply asks about those and many other things, often in ways that can gauge their quality and frequency. Deep and implicit values and attitudes can be tapped through well-put, thoughtfully phrased questions or, even better, through skilfully drawn hypothetical situations to which the subject supplies an outcome. Many times the interviewee must confine his responses to certain standardized alternatives provided by the interviewer. He can only say whether he does, believes, or feels something "often, rarely, or never." He can't answer at length, thereby producing unexpected information in his own words. At times interviewers run into problems similar to those anthropologists encounter when they test unresponsive people. For example, lower-class respondents may be unable adequately to express the way they feel. When asked "What do you like about school?" they may intend to say a great deal but answer "Nothing," whereas interviewees with more skill at communication offer detailed, critical evaluations of administrators, teachers, and the curriculum. When many people neglect to return a questionnaire or to admit an interviewer to their homes, the researchers run a risk of getting information from a skewed sample, assuming that those who do answer possess selected social characteristics likely to influence the information they give. To insure that every respondent, regardless of his educational level, interprets questions in the same way, they are worded as precisely as possible and are pretested to gauge their meaningfulness and effectiveness. However, even taking so much care at standardization, meaning varies with different subjects' experience, the answers possessing different underlying significance which the researchers shouldn't ignore. Middle-class and lower-class young men will both say that masturbation is wrong, but the Kinsey report indicates that masturbation is considerably more aberrant in lower-class culture than among middle-class youths, who find it invaluable in postponing full-scale sexual gratification which their cultural norms brand as much worse than masturbation.[67] Difficulties notwithstanding, interviewing allows so much information to be collected expeditiously in a relatively short time, about so many individuals, and pertaining to such a wide variety of situations that the method is continually being put to hard use. Answers can be gotten that lend themselves to precise scoring, which, in turn, allows very exact comparison of one person's previous experience or current performance to another's.

Rating. The focal problem in studying personality in culture is to assess personality characteristics, either in qualitiative or quantitative fashion. Some instruments that serve this purpose allow a person to rate himself as he answers questions; he checks attributes regarding his feelings, attitudes, likes, and dislikes, or makes up projective stories to pictures.[68] Other techniques are observational, as in the traditional, anthropological fieldwork method; here, the observer takes an active role in rating, perhaps under carefully planned, rigorously controlled conditions. Diaries, letters, and case histories built up through interviewing provide other sources for qualitative or even quantitative assessments. The basic feature of most devices for rating personality characteristics consists of a defined continuum along which some trait—say,

self-sufficiency—can be assigned a position. The number of steps or intervals on the continuum depends on the conditions of rating and the rater's training. Each position carries a numerical value so that scores can be computed for each subject. A well-known rating instrument, the Minnesota Multiphasic Personality Inventory, contains 550 items arranged under 26 headings, including general health, habits, sexual attitudes, religious attitudes, phobias, and morale. It yields scores on hypochondriasis, depression, hysteria, social deviance, masculine or feminine interests, paranoia, schizophrenia, and others. Despite all the practice and effort expended in rating personality, not all social scientists agree that human nature can be measured, and disagree even more among themselves about the feasibility and logic of particular rating instruments.

While I am on the subject of measuring of personality I will say just a word about procedures that psychological anthropologists have devised for rating aspects of personality and culture from one society to another, using literature that ethnographically describes those cultures.[69] Taking their clues about how personality relates to culture from theoretical writings, sometimes from works by psychoanalysts, these anthropologists proceed to rate the strength, severity, or indulgence attached to cultural routines affecting children, and then the strength of adult attributes of behavior presumed to have grown out of those childhood conditions. In due course I shall refer to a number of such studies and identify the variables that were rated as well as the bases on which the measurements were made. Anthropologists following this procedure sample the societies of the world in much the way social scientists sample individuals. But they identify and measure antecedent cultural variables and consequent personality factors much more rigorously than most fieldworking anthropologists who trace the consequences of child-rearing on adult personality.

Rather than accounting for all the approaches technically possible for studying personality in culture—what a job that would be!—I have spoken briefly about classic anthropological fieldwork, psychological testing, standardized interviewing, and rating procedures. Other methodological resources I have for the most part ignored, such as the life-history method, dream analysis, drawing, nonclinical procedures of content analysis applied to folktales and to other cultural materials, and photography. Some of these are referred to elsewhere in this book; for example, I have already spoken about life histories in presenting the account of Gregorio, the Navaho hand-trembler, and about content analysis in connection with achievement drive. Anyway, there isn't any finite list of techniques. Research demands imagination and creativity more than it calls for slavishly copying earlier models.

FURTHER READING

The newcomer looking for surveys of the field will obtain some help from review articles like A. I. Hallowell, "Culture, Personality, and Society" (1953); the chapters headed "Psychocultural Studies" or "Culture and Personality" in the *Biennial Review of Anthropology* for the years 1959, 1961, and 1963, edited by Bernard J. Siegel. John J. Honigmann and Richard J. Preston also survey "Recent Developments in Culture and Personality" (1964). Both *Psychological Abstracts* and *Sociological Abstracts* need to be scanned regularly by anyone who wants to keep up with writing on personality in culture. Psychological anthropology overlaps with modern social psychology, the scope of which may be gauged from J. E. Hulett, Jr., and Ross Stagner, *Problems in Social Psychology*

(1952) and the two-volume *Handbook of Social Psychology*, edited by Gardner Lindzey (1954). In their Introduction to *Child Training and Personality*, J. W. M. Whiting and I. L. Child (1953: chap. 1) relate their own to other approaches. S. Kirson Weinberg describes some major theoretical lines used in *Culture and Personality* (1958), and, at the end of my preceding chapter, I have already recommended Milton Singer, "A Survey of Culture and Personality Theory and Research" (1961). Everett E. Hagen, *On the Theory of Social Change* (1962), investigates the role of psychological factors in economic growth. In "The Anthropological Roots of Psychoanalysis," George Devereux (1958) explains how anthropology demonstrates the validity of psychoanalytic principles. A special publication by the *American Anthropologist* titled *Transcultural Studies in Cognition* (1964), edited by A. Kimball Romney and Roy Goodwin D'Andrade, explores psychological and other developments with respect to cognition, as does David French in his essay on "The Relationship of Anthropology to Studies in Perception and Cognition" (1963).

Coming now to techniques, John Bennett summarizes "The Study of Cultures" (1948), while Leon Festinger and Daniel Katz, editors of *Research Methods in the Behavioral Sciences* (1953), and Marie Jahoda and others, in *Research Methods in Social Relations* (1951), review much more fully manifold procedures, many of which are routine in sociology. "Interview Techniques and Field Relationships" (1953), by Benjamin Paul remains a singular analysis of the problems involved in establishing productive fieldwork roles. Bertha Stavrianos examines "Research Methods in Cultural Anthropology in Relation to Scientific Criteria" (1950), and Margaret Mead describes how an anthropologist works in *Male and Female* (1949b: chap. 2). Two more general discussions of anthropologists' purposes and methods are Grace de La-guna, "The *Lebenswelt* and the Cultural World" (1960), and Robert Redfield, *The Little Community* (1955), especially chapter 10. How we gain understanding of other people is discussed by Gordon Allport in *Pattern and Growth in Personality* (1961: chaps. 20–21). See too his essay, "Personality: A Problem for Science or for Art," published in *Personality and Social Encounter* (1960b). Irving Janis, "The Psychoanalytic Interview as an Observational Method" (1958), describes the dilemma of the researcher trained in a tradition of objectivity who wants to use psychoanalytic interviewing. G. M. Carstairs deals with the same method in "Cross-Cultural Psychiatric Interviewing" (1961). Dell Hymes, "Linguistic Aspects of Cross-Cultural Personality Study" (1961), points out the contribution linguistics can make and T. R. Williams acknowledges "The Personal-Cultural Equation in Social Work and Anthropology" (1959). "Obtaining the Facts," David C. McClelland calls chapter 2 of his book *Personality* (1951), in which he deals with psychologists' methods. *Motives in Fantasy, Action, and Society*, edited by John W. Atkinson (1958), treats methods for studying motivation via projective and other devices. Tests, scales, content analysis, questionnaires, statistical techniques, and projective methods are reviewed in Fred N. Kerlinger's readable *Foundations of Behavioral Research* (1964), while John E. Horrocks, *Assessment of Behavior* (1964), exhaustively discusses principles and techniques for measuring intelligence, development, aptitudes, and other personality features. Wise words about tests and interviews designed for personality measurement are offered in Julian Rotter, *Social Learning and Clinical Psychology* (1954: chap. 8). Recently Charles E. Osgood's semantic differential technique has been successfully used cross-culturally to compare attitudes of adolescents; see R. J.

Havighurst *et al.*, *A Cross-National Study of Buenos Aires and Chicago Adolescents* (1965: chap. 4). Semantic measurement itself is described by Charles E. Osgood and his associates in *The Measurement of Meaning* (1957). L. L. Langness reevaluates "Life-history Methods in Biography" (1964), and Oscar Lewis, "Seventh Day Adventism in a Mexican Village" (1964), shows how biography can be applied to culture change and acculturation. In "Folktales, Social Structure, and Environment in Two Polynesian Outliers" (1958), as well as in his review paper, "The Sociopsychological Analysis of Folktales" (1963), John L. Fischer describes the use and value of folktales in culture-and-personality research. Jane Belo, "Balinese Children's Drawings" (1955), Martha Wolfenstein, "French Children's Paintings" (1955a), and Rhoda Métraux, "Children's Drawings: Satellites and Space" (1961), illustrate how pictorial representations give insight into youngsters' conception of their world and furnish knowledge of their interests.

REFERENCES

1 Kann, 1960: 2.
2 Maslow, 1948 and 1951a.
3 Laming *et al.* (1953) are mainly concerned with interpreting prehistoric cognitive, rather than emotional states.
4 From A. F. C. Wallace, 1950. The drawings, from Morley (1946), are not the same as those used by Wallace. For problems of interpreting archeological remains, see also Hawkes, 1954.
5 Shklar, 1957; Kann, 1960; *cf.* H. S. Hughes, 1958.
6 L. Thompson, 1950: 119–120, 140.
7 Just as they are alleged to occur frequently in lower-class U.S. Negro men reared in mother-dominated households. See Rovere, 1965.

8 M. Mead, 1930b and 1956c. *Cf.* M. Mead's (1932a) account of the disrupted Omaha Indians.

9 Bradburn and Berlew, 1961. The chart is published by permission of The University of Chicago Press.

10 Weber, 1930. For a particularly good critique, see Means, 1965. For Weber applied in modern Detroit, see Lenski, 1963.

11 McClelland, 1961: 135.

12 Atkinson, 1958; McClelland, 1961.

13 McClelland, 1961: 54.

14 *Ibid.*, p. 69. See also Child, Storm, and Veroff, 1958.

15 M. Mead, 1928a.

16 M. Mead, 1935: chap. 17.

17 R. Benedict, 1934b: chap. 8.

18 *Ibid.*, chaps. 2–3.

19 L. A. White, 1949: 281 and chaps. 13–14.

20 R. Benedict, 1934b: 276.

21 M. Mead, 1935: chap. 17–18.

22 *Ibid.*, chaps. 8, 13, and 18.

23 L. Thompson, 1950: 176.

24 L. Thompson, 1961: chap. 5; *cf.* Lynd, 1958: 74, 75, 81; Edgerton, 1965: 445.

25 Paraphrased by Kroeber, 1948: 586.

26 LaBarre, 1945.

27 Ammar, 1954.

28 Erikson, 1963: chap. 4.

29 Beckner, 1959: 84.

30 M. Mead, 1951b and 1954b.

31 Róheim, 1943b.

32 Róheim, 1950: 362. Margaret Mead (1954c: 405) once used the same, logically fallacious type of argument to rebut critics who accused her of exaggerating the importance of childhood. The critics, she said, are unconsciously threatened by the sexual and excretory topics that belong with a discussion of childhood. " . . . the words *sex* and *infancy* can both be regarded as surrogates for those aspects of experience which cannot be recalled without special

operations and against which most persons have well-organized defenses."

33 Freud, 1961b: 207.

34 *Cf.* Unwin, 1934.

35 Freud, 1957: 91.

36 Levine, 1961.

37 J. J. Honigmann, 1942; *cf.* Gluckman, 1955: chap. 5.

38 Eggan, 1949, 1952, and 1961.

39 J. J. Honigmann and Honigmann, 1965a.

40 de Tocqueville, 1945, II, bk. 1: chaps. 3–4.

41 Róheim, 1950: 339, 340. By permission of International Universities Press, Inc.

42 *Cf.* Hallowell, 1951a; A. F. C. Wallace, 1962.

43 Conklin, 1955.

44 Whorf, 1956: 103.

45 Festinger, 1957; *cf.* Chapanis and Chapanis, 1964.

46 Rosenthal and Siegel, 1959.

47 Festinger *et al.*, 1956.

48 Emmet, 1958.

49 Tomasic, 1948.

50 R. F. Murphy, 1957.

51 Mayo, 1945: 18–19; M. Mead, 1952b: 401–403 and 1954a: 471–472; T. M. French, 1944.

52 Chapin (1947) shows how clinical disciplines allow for experimental testing of hypotheses.

53 J. J. Honigmann, 1949: 288–289.

54 C. Osgood, 1951.

55 M. Mead, 1933.

56 M. Mead, 1943: 137; 1952a: 9–15, and 1953b: 646–650, 652–655; *cf.* Mandelbaum, 1953.

57 Havighurst and Neugarten, 1955; L. Thompson, 1951.

58 Havighurst and Neugarten, 1955: 43.

59 *Ibid.*, pp. 139–141.

60 F. Kluckhohn and Strodtbeck, 1961; C. Kluckhohn, 1951b. For a critique of values theory, see Kunkel, 1965.

61 The following sources closely examine projective tests, especially the Rorschach

and TAT, and their place in cross-cultural research: W. E. Henry, 1960 and 1961; Lindzey, 1961; Abt and Bellak, 1950; Hallowell, 1954–1956; B. Kaplan, 1961a.

62 Lindzey, 1961: chap. 2.

63 G. D. Spindler, 1955: 144.

64 For some such experiments, see Oberholzer in Du Bois, 1944; Lessa and Spiegelman, 1954; B. Kaplan, 1954; James Ritchie, 1956.

65 L. Thompson, 1951; W. E. Henry, 1951.

66 Srole, 1956.

67 Kinsey, Pomeroy, and Martin, 1948: 375–378.

68 Here I draw from Horrocks, 1964; see also Lindzey, 1958; Beller, 1962.

69 Murdock and Whiting, 1951; J. W. M. Whiting, 1954 and 1961; Y. A. Cohen, 1964: chap. 9. For a brief account of errors likely in such cross-cultural studies, see Barnouw, 1963: chap. 20; M. Mead, 1963b.

Personality in Culture

3

A code of conduct; a kind of human being: two things. But the code or system of values dominates the culture and so controls the type of behavior of the people, makes the type of human being, and corresponds to character in the individual. In some sense the two ideas are one, or, if they are two, it is easy for the mind to pass from one to the other.[1]

ROBERT REDFIELD

To the anthropologist . . . the individual appears important only as a member of a racial or a social group.[2]

FRANZ BOAS

PERSONALITY AND, OR PERSONALITY IN, CULTURE?

Which is more useful: to conceive of personality as sundered from culture—connected with culture by the conjunction "and"—or to imagine personality as largely contained in culture?[3] Each view pictures the two realms as mutually related, so from that standpoint it makes little difference which you choose. But your further thinking about their relationship will very likely be influenced by whichever model you adopt. Conceiving of personality and culture as separate systems will tempt you to follow causal thinking: Culture acts on personality or vice versa. On the other hand, to conceive of personality as mostly part of culture encourages holistic thinking. Events in the realm of personality reflect the larger whole and change in tandem with changes in culture.

Even when his children are still young, an Austrian farmer in a village I know begins to assess their capacities and interests, as he plans to bequeath his farm to the one who most enjoys farming and promises to maintain the estate.[4] The decision he faces can't be lightly taken; it demands careful thinking. Now, the first model pictures the farmer's concern, a matter of personality, to be instigated by culture. Austrian rural

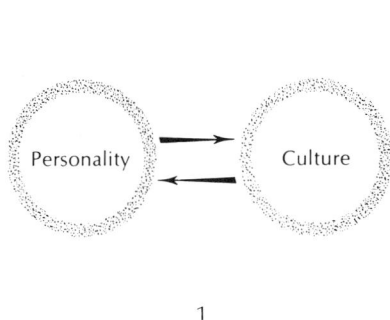

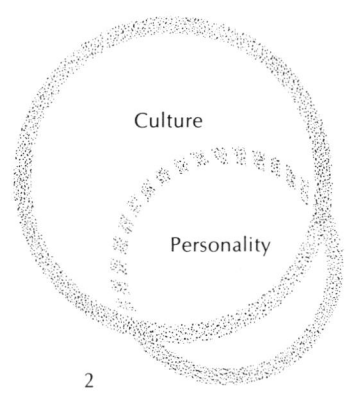

1

2

The first figure illustrates personality and culture as two distinct realms mutually related to one another. The second figure shows personality as partially in culture.

culture includes traits, like norms of inheritance, that guide a man in transmitting property to a successor. If the decision gives him concern, the concern derives from his culture. Were he a middle-class, urban American, he would be concerned about other matters, such as putting his children through college. In both lands, culture through socialization shapes individuals' hopes, fears, and concerns. An arrow running from the realm of culture to that of personality indicates diagrammatically how culture acts on people. The second model depicts culture and personality as inseparable. Without a farmer concerned with bequeathing and eventually transmitting his property there could be no cultural practice of estate inheritance in rural Austria. Culture is mainly what people do, think, and feel. Culture is partly the concerned forethought an Austrian farmer devotes to inheritance. True, each Austrian farmer experiences his concern differently. Only by ignoring individual differences, compressing a series of farmers into a generalization, does an anthropologist manage to describe a culture. But it is absurd to confuse such generalizations with something that acts on people, creating or influencing their personalities, unless we intend to speak figura-

tively only. The second model pictures a person immersed in culture from birth. The cultural world colors all his being.[5] Throughout life he actively adopts the hopes, fears, and concerns of others in his community. Not that anyone becomes a microcosm of his culture. No one participates in all of his community's culture, only in those portions which he is inclined and permitted to learn.[6]

Conceiving of personality as being *in* culture, making culture the larger realm and personality the smaller, corresponds to the way I defined the field of culture and personality in Chapter 1. The concept culture and personality calls for understanding culture by focusing attention on how persons in a given community embody their way of life in their psychological make-up. I want to approach culture from the vantage point of personality, to see how the smaller realm reflects the larger. To be sure, certain tangible elements of culture (like the plow, houses, tools) can't be considered part of personality except in the way people make, use, and think about them. As artifacts they are excluded from the realm of personality. In turn, a given personality contains idiosyncratic elements—like individual, temperamental proclivities present from birth—

A diligent girl in rural Austria who shows aptitude and love for farming can inherit her father's estate.

that can't be part of culture by the definition I shall shortly offer. Conceiving of personality as being part of culture has another virtue: Just as I can't sensibly speak of a chair being *in* a table, so I couldn't use the image of personality as being within culture if personality and culture were both substantive entities (things). To speak of personality *and* culture invites reifying each realm, whereas describing personality as being *in* culture repeatedly reminds us that we are dealing with abstractions—two imaginative, theoretical creations—neither of which is real in the way substantive entities are real. The usage I recommend has a practical significance too, for it implies that to change culture significantly one must simultaneously alter individuals' behavior. A plow introduced as a tool into a community where people hitherto farmed only with hoes demands new habits, attitudes, and knowledge if the new tool is to be seriously adopted. To use a plow, farmers must modify their personality by switching to new perceptions, perhaps adding a lust for profit which they previously lacked. I reject the idea that any firm boundary cuts envi-

ronment off from the person. The public world out there—other people with their expectations and habits—interpenetrates my private world of meanings. No firm line sunders my personality from the external world. One flows into the other. As I incorporate the world, so I act toward it and thereby recreate and perpetuate it. As I change my conception from the conception shared with others I begin to change my culture, more or less radically. I am neither wholly dependent on my environment nor does it wholly depend on my behavior, but we constantly influence each other creatively and dynamically.[7]

The remainder of this chapter will define at length the two concepts *culture* and *personality*. Mostly I shall take up personality. In going into its architecture and dynamics, its structure and operation, I follow the theory currently in widest use, psychoanalysis. It is, however, a modified version of Freud's original psychoanalytic theory, a version that is sometimes called neo-Freudian.

SOCIALLY PATTERNED THINGS AND BEHAVIOR

Let me introduce what I mean by culture with an imaginary book undramatically titled *Culture of the Mafa*. Like many ethnographic monographs, some parts appeal to the general reader more than others. When it describes the short-handled hoes Mafa use and how they wield them, it deals with facts that could fascinate only a specialist. But the anthropologist's astute explanation of why Mafa stick to short-handled hoes, though foreign missionaries have for years been pushing a long-handled kind, is much more interesting. His reasoning holds that distinctive motor habits have formed around the handles and that Mafa adults find it very difficult to change those habits.[8] The book also delineates Mafa social structure, showing how families combine into lineage, the lineage groups fitting into still larger descent groups, called sibs. Respected leaders in those groups possess authority to make decisions. Here the ethnographer again conspicuously steps forward to interject his professionally informed opinions about the process whereby leaders get recruited, chiefly on the bases of age and experience. The Mafa themselves aren't fully aware of that process; at least, they can't analyze it as clearly or fully. Several pages then reveal the tremendous powers possessed by Mafa gods and describe the tribesmen's worship. Once more the writer intrudes himself, pointing out that loved gods embody Mafa ideals, like loyalty, while feared deities indulge abandonedly in the most detested sins. The book accomplishes two tasks. First, it reports on artifacts, acts, thoughts, and feelings characteristic of an organized human collectivity, the Mafa, faithfully describing what those elements mean to the people. Second, the ethnographer lays bare interrelationships and functions of elements in Mafa life, and points up their meanings in terms of anthropological theory—a very different thing from the meaning they phenomenologically possess for the people themselves. The descrption of artifacts, acts, thoughts, values, feelings, adds up to Mafa culture itself. In his enlightening asides, the author comments *about* the culture. Except for photographs of representative hoes, shrines, and ceremonies, the description hardly goes into specific, individual artifacts or particular acts of hoeing performed by actual individuals. A description of culture consists, as a rule, of types and patterns, not of distinct instances; it reports the type of hoe and doesn't talk about individual hoes; the recurring pattern of hoeing, not specific acts witnessed by the ethnographer; not one occasion of worship, but the way Mafa regularly worship on stated occasions; not particular conflicts, but patterns of opposition.

To be in a position to generalize types and patterns, an ethnographer must either observe many instances of socially patterned hoes, hoeing, worship, and other acts; or he must have help from a native informant who is able and willing to provide generalizations about his own culture.

Several characteristics of culture should be incorporated into even a brief definition. First, its systematic nature: System implies that the constituent elements making up a way of life hang together in organized fashion. Anthropologists are much occupied with discovering precisely how, say, religion varies with social structure or social structure with technology. Second, culture is an open system, meaning it constantly transacts business with its geographic environment. Men take resources for building a culture—wood, food for energy, stimuli for science or poetry—from the world that surrounds them. Third, culture intimately involves man's biological organism in its operation. If we didn't get around bipedally, with the consequence that our hands are left free to manipulate paint brushes, machines, and weapons; if we didn't constantly demand air, wherefore we are land-based; if we lacked our large, complex human brain, which endows us for conceptual thought and valuation; if babies didn't get suckled, making their mouth the first organ to relate them with the outer world; if self-sufficiency came earlier than it does, thereby eliminating the prolonged helplessness that gives adults their strong advantage in commanding children's learning—then human culture as we know it would be very, very different.

Social patterning has touched all cultural elements, with the result that a hoe, prayer, or belief in any culture bears a social imprint. That is why distinctly individual proclivities—if any true idiosyncrasies exist—are by definition excluded from the realm of culture. By definition, they bear no social stamp. However, the overwhelming number of our acts, thoughts, and feelings are socially standardized, whether they have been taught us by others or have been cultivated simply through our awareness of other people or of the appliances that surround us. Culture, then, embraces only socially patterned things and behavior. When I say patterned, I mean more than learned. I find "learned" an inadequate characterization of cultural phenomena because the word carries too narrow a connotation, suggesting only formal, deliberate learning. We learn much, informally and unconsciously, through our relations with, and awareness of, others and through constantly dealing with artifacts that others have created. Some anthropologists claim that culture includes only behavior and things shared by two or more persons. To say that and nothing more is obviously false. At a given time nobody but the king shares the highly specialized behavior and regalia of kingship; yet, who would reject kingship from the realm of culture? Some anthropologists won't allow that a copywriter's just-coined slogan or a prophet's newly revealed religion forms part of culture; they claim that admission to culture comes only after others know of, or adopt, it. To my way of thinking, an innovation is cultural because, far from being wholly original, social factors have influenced its conception. Everything in culture, though it must by definition be socially patterned, need not be universal or shared by everyone in a community. Some cultural things are specialties, limited to one or a very few individuals; others are more or less approved alternatives, preferred by some people or representing versions of culture current in one social class and rejected by another.* A rich culture, like ours, abounds in alterna-

* Ways of life distinctive of social classes are sometimes called subcultures; I prefer to see them as made up of specialties and alternatives existing within a single culture.

tives among which to choose wisely can be most perplexing.[9] Like an iceberg, culture rides both in and out of sight. The overt side we readily know from observing people working, talking, wearing costumes, making artifacts. The equally patterned covert portion—norms, standards, and feelings—we infer or imagine. In their fieldwork, anthropologists employ special techniques to get at covert behavior, though, because the process of accurately learning about covert behavior is risky, some social scientists won't deal with it at all. They rally around "behaviorist" manifestos, whose blazoned key word, "behavior," designates only what can be directly sensed (like acts and words).[10] Beyond the iceberg's waterline, they claim, science cannot penetrate.

SOCIAL SYSTEM, SOCIAL CATEGORY, AND CULTURE

Culture flows from one inhabited region to another (and archeologists even find cultural remains in no longer inhabited areas), but customarily anthropologists study it in two kinds of demarcated, human collectivities: organized social systems (which I also call communities) and social categories. Very small social systems have been investigated for culture, like a street-corner gang or a unit of three Navaho Indian households; and also mammoth ones, like the United States. Social systems frequently contain subsystems (groups), each possessing specialized cultural elements; think, for example, of a tribe, with its council, fixed market, and military organization. Like boxes within boxes, subsystems embody yet smaller subsystems, and so on. Distinct from organized social systems are unorganized social categories, like Mead's adolescent Samoan girls or middle-class folk in the United States. For people to form a category merely requires that they share one or more characteristics, such as sex, age, income level, or a combination of behavioral traits. One can't understand the culture of sybsystems and categories belonging to a social system without having considerable knowledge about the larger culture to which they belong.* However, contrary to what some social scientists vehemently affirm, generalizing about the larger culture by no means necessitates sampling or screening all subsystems and categories.[11] Anthropologists, though, can fairly be accused of having mostly overlooked socially patterned variation within social systems. The result is a unimodal presentation of behavior falsely implying that everybody in the community is cast from the same mold and behaves in a uniform way. Other social scientists, notably sociologists and psychologists, lean the other way: they keep a close eye on diversity, that is, on the alternative ways of behavior people follow. Unquestionably, people are different. Consequently, the families and other groups they form come to acquire distinctive cultural forms. Generalizations may choose to overlook those differences, and for certain purposes it is right that they do. If we pursued variation too intently we would end up with a most uninteresting list of individuals and families and with no knowledge about why they are all different. We could scarcely speak of anything, for everything is always in flux. Even the individual whom the clinician tests and characterizes as being a certain kind of person varies from one situation to another. Nevertheless, it is worth bearing in mind that we may gain important knowledge from asking about the circumstances (income, poverty, education, isolation, etc.)

* Social categories also span several social systems. As a result, anthropologists engaged in cross-cultural research look for distinctive traits possessed by shamans, peasants, or other status categories, regardless of the community they occupy, and economists compare European and American top executives.

under which behavior varies and diverse alternatives come to be patterned.

FUNCTIONS OF CULTURE

At borders where cultures flow into one another each is open to its neighbors, so that cultural elements transfer more or less readily, but always selectively. Potential donor communities may guard their heritage (as the United States secretes military information) and prospective hosts may decline elements whose value they can't appreciate or whose consequences they rightly or wrongly dread. Successful cultural diffusion agitates a culture, for having entered one area of life, change impels compensatory and facilitating changes in others. Innovations that originate at home also stimulate compensatory secondary changes as they become more widely adopted in their own setting. One reason why people change their culture is because every way of life serves many vital and cherished ends for its carriers. When people encounter hitherto unknown behaviors and artifacts that promise to serve them better, they often veer to the new.

What ends do people achieve via culture —admittedly more or less satisfactorily— and hopefully pursue through change? Survival, for one. Culture guarantees survival through providing means of adaptation, like getting and preparing food, clothing and shelter, forms of regulating conflict, and ways of healing the sick. However, not every cultural element serves directly as an instrument of adaptation. Bureaucratic organization, grammar, reciprocal gift exchange, religious ritual, and the study of culture and personality don't protect survival; at least, not in the same degree as an oil stove in a modern Eskimo cabin or heart surgery. They serve other ends, providing means whereby people can effectively relate to one another, fortify morale, acquire knowledge, exchange ideas, and so on. Finally, culture furnishes its carriers with opportunity simply to express themselves in play, fantasy, worship, and art.

Now let's take a look at the darker side and face the fact that cultures also induce stress in their carriers.[12] Some of the stress serves positive or adaptive ends, as when threats keep men at peace or restrict illegal behavior. Other stress, like the confusing choices encountered by our adolescents, is less clearly helpful and people may wish strongly to minimize it. Stress, as it results from cultural arrangements or arises when a person for various reasons fails to cope appropriately, resourcefully, and flexibly with ordinary problems of living, has become a much pursued topic in psychological research and I shall have much more to say about it.

While talking of culture as instrumentally allowing individuals, groups, and social systems to adapt, I must also point out that a number of psychoanalytically minded social scientists, who have been strongly influenced by Freud, regard it as a front-line defense against the irrational, blatant, raw, striving impulses inherent in human nature that press for gratification regardless of personal or social consequences. Culture also operates, very like a neurotic symptom, these observers point out, to keep down anxiety generated by socially illicit impulses that approach too close to consciousness.[13]

I have been describing culture doing things, like serving ends and inducing stress. Such a figurative way of speaking mustn't be allowed to endow an abstraction with ability, purpose, and direction that it can't logically possess. Never forget, ultimately culture means people achieving their own goals through their own behavior with help from artifacts. People alone create more or less effective modes of organization, provide richer or poorer opportunities for expression, and stress themselves through the fears and confusion they admit

into their lives and the poverty they can't or won't alleviate.

Central to any culture is a stock of basic meanings and values which man's power of reflection has distilled from thousands of experiences. Such central world views motivate individuals and societies to recognize what in their lives is most significant; in terms of core meanings and value orientations people and groups choose, act, coalesce, and separate. Common world views enable people to communicate, support sustained social relationships, and protect social and cultural survival. Basic meanings and value orientations define tastes, being responsible for the delight men take in some things and their indignant rejection of others. Individuals also approach the world with private meanings, but their private worlds must complement one another harmoniously if social life is to continue.

His pattern of behavior

If a culture is a way of life followed by a human collectively, personality is the style of life grounded in a person—either an actual individual, like Gregorio, the Navaho hand-trembler, or a cross section of persons, like Samoan adolescent girls or Kaska Indians. To describe personality is to describe the pattern of behavior—of the acts, thoughts, and feelings—with which persons relate to peers and authorities, conceive of gods or nature, regard their own resources and failings, and manage artifacts. There are a number of reasons why it is difficult to describe personality and to study it analytically, but the major one is the variability people manifest in their behavior from one situation to another. So much variability, yet the object of personality study is to find consistency and pattern. The psychologist looks for signs of consistency in personal make-up while simultaneously recognizing that a person is complex and resourceful enough to permit a number of inconsistencies and unharmonized trends to exist in his behavior without producing wearing signs of strain. Personality suggests that something in a person's behavior endures for a relatively long time. Yet we must allow that an individual, despite himself retaining a sense of enduringness, constantly changes from birth to death. A bold, imaginative observer constructs personality much as an anthropologist constructs culture or a historian writes history; that is, by slighting particulars, overlooking some of the flux of constant change and variability, for the sake of more general and relatively immutable considerations.

Just as biological nature gives recurrent form to culture (culture wouldn't be recognizable, I said, if our biological make-up were substantially different), so personality utilizes resources inherent in human nature. Hope, anxiety, love, and the strength of our attachments to God and nation arise ultimately from the potentialities with which we are endowed. Personality as we know it would truly not be possible without the large, complexly organized human brain with its prodigious capacity for reflection and its extraordinary ability to store and manipulate symbols. Man, more than any other animal, survives by mulling over his experiences, in the process creatively adapting past experience to current reality. His experience is in large measure mediated symbolically, for we learn much that we don't actually see. In every generation personalities develop through utilizing previous generations' experiences that have been symbolically stored in memory or in those marvelous extensions of memory, like writing, pictures, and computer programs, all of which depend on the human brain. All this, important as it is to recognize, gives rather too much priority to the top of the brain, the cerebral cortex, the part that is first revealed when the skull is opened. Recent work in biochemistry and pharmacology calls our attention to the further role which deeper, subcortical levels of the brain play in personality. There, much normal behavior as well as personality disorder seem to be grounded in chemical states.[14] Although it has proven very difficult to correlate specific mental states with the release of specific chemicals in the brain, experiments do demonstrate that brain-functioning profoundly alters when certain drugs enter the body; presumably the drugs act on subcortical brain centers.[15] Yet, if biology provides the essential fundament of personality, it can't by itself account for everything we learn as we develop into adulthood. Personality is heavily influenced by the social relationships we enter, through which influence human nature acquires its distinctive cast from one community to another and from one individual to another.

PERSONALITY STRUCTURE

If we imagine personality to be built like a layered ball, then meanings, values, thoughts, and feelings belong below the surface. The surface itself reveals the primary, overt data of observation: what a person says and does, as well as the way he says and does it. Deep in the ball lies the personality's nuclear region, comprising broad, organizing value orientations, enduring dispositions, and policy-setting premises that guide an individual in a variety of situations.[16] This nuclear region I call *character structure*—the word "character," contrary to another use it has, implying nothing about morality. To speak about a personality core allows an observer to generalize about the whole man, though it may also mislead by suggesting a search for indwelling essences that rob man of his capacity to grow and change. Man is what he makes of himself. His character structure, too, belongs to what he makes of himself through the way he acts.

At some indeterminable distance beyond the nucleus begins the personality's peripheral region, comprising overt habits as well as *specific* covert attitudes and meanings. Some peripheral characteristics vary from situation to situation; they are lightly donned and easily shed. Others spring directly from the policy-making core, and are therefore much more consistent. One should guard against expecting isomorphy between core and periphery.[17] The character structure and peripheral region need not correspond in one-to-one fashion. A person who exudes confidence in his deeds and repeatedly affirms his happiness could thereby conceal quite a different character structure. The British field marshal, Viscount Alanbrooke, lost some of his unmatched repute once he allowed large parts of his wartime diary to be published, shaking many of his admirers by his self-exposure. "It was a shock to find that a man so outwardly calm was often inwardly seething; that a man who appeared just was privately apt to condemn those whose views differed from his own; that a man who had such an air of confidence was so often filled with gloomy forebodings in times of crisis and on the eve of great ventures."[18] Because the core area greatly interests many investigators of personality, much effort and ingenuity have been devoted to gauging it correctly. Correctly appraising the core area demands a sound knowledge of people; that is, it requires considerable data from a wide variety of situations. Acquiring those data necessarily takes time and a willingness to get beyond superficial acquaintanceships. In addition to close knowledge, one must also have a good stock of concepts, such as psychoanalysis furnishes, with which to think and talk about nuclear personality structure. Whereas psychoanalysis in the early 1920s conceived of anal, oral, and genital characters, the anal being best formulated,[19] neo-Freudians, like Alfred Adler, Karen Horney, and Erich Fromm,

subsequently greatly altered and vastly expanded concepts for grasping character structure.[20] They also broke with seeing its genesis directly in children's early bodily pleasure and came much more to view it as a response adapted to many life situations, especially to social relationships.[21] Others employ the term "character" differently. Sometimes it becomes synonymous with style of life or "response style."[22] Margaret Mead equates character (as in "national character") with a much broader range of socially acquired personality aspects than I do.[23] Her usage is illustrated in her contrast of two South Seas peoples, the Balinese and Iatmul.[24] The Balinese possess an extremely unresponsive character and, except when playing with small children, find no satisfaction in arousing responses from one another. In lieu of engaging themselves socially, they take delight in playing with small animals or puppets and in manipulating parts of their own bodies. The New Guinea Iatmul, however, rely strongly on emotional interpersonal relations, enlist themselves intensely in group activities, and grow very attached to leaders. That is their character.

Now I have another image to supplement the layered ball in describing personality structure. Imagine a relatively small building with a disproportionately cavernous cellar. Descending, we go from the glare of consciousness to the dark, or unconscious, level, on the way passing through an intervening twilight, or preconscious, basement.[25] Full consciousness implies that a person is aware of what he does. He deliberately chooses his course of action in a world of familiar forms and meanings. I am conscious now of describing the architecture of personality in the context of my major interest, cultural anthropology. But why have I chosen to write a book about culture and personality? What else does cultural anthropology mean to me? I don't fully know the ground from which my conscious behavior emanates. The unconscious affects, desires, identifications, and defenses which nudge my lifelong plans and influence my momentary decisions are hard to perceive. Only special techniques can plumb personality's cellar depths.

Yet, it is too much to say that everything beyond consciousness remains wholly beyond awareness. We glimpse our unconscious when it manifests itself in slips of the tongue that betray our true feelings; in impulses that must sometimes be subjected to tight reining, or not allowed any expression at all;[26] in fantasies that beguile us and draw us out of the frustrations and disappointments of reality, and, of course, in dreams. Dream interpretation is the single most valuable technique for gaining insight into the unconscious, the royal road to learning about hidden motivational states.[27] One way of unlocking the meaning of dream images is to use a theoretical key that presumes to interpret their unconscious significance to the dreamer. Then, for example, ferocious and frightening animals are identifiable as hostility harbored by the dreamer in his impulse life. Expeditious as this method seems, without help from the dreamer himself it remains highly equivocal, for it says nothing about the interpretation's plausibility. A better way of dream interpretation enlists a dreamer's cooperation. It calls on him freely to associate aloud to the dream and assumes that what he says will continue the line of unconscious thinking and feeling represented in the dream, thereby providing keys with which to unlock its true meaning. "Is that a good dream or a bad dream?" I asked my Kaska Indian informant to get him to begin associating by baring to me the feeling tone connected with the dream. "Where did you ever see a chain like that?" I asked on another occasion, picking out a prominent dream element, and thereby learned that the dream's latent meaning pointed to the male dreamer's son-in-law.[28] The tech-

nique of dream interpretation shows the wonderland of the unconscious to be dominated by a total disregard of ordinary logic, reality, and convention. In unconscious thought familiar things take on a most surprising cast. The most contradictory ideas flourish side by side, and in dreams they sometimes fuse into a single image that is almost unrecognizable under its weight of illogically related meanings. Are dreams really unconsciously motivated, as theory says and as the technique of dream interpretation assumes? A theory is supported by the productive leads it provides and the helpful questions it sets, but it can never be finally proven. Psychological experience thoroughly warrants the assumption that dreams contain meaning beyond the dreamer's conscious ken.[29]

Back of the question whether dreams convey unconscious meaning is an even more important one: Do we need an unconscious at all to understand personality in culture? Doesn't the concept pose more questions than it answers, at the same time complicating the search for clear, unambiguous knowledge? Opposed to it are those who would account for behavior primarily in terms of situation whose cues we obey without imagining hidden springs and tendencies that mitigate our responsibility as human beings and threaten to sap our freedom.[30] Personally, I am unready to chuck the unconscious, but I shall try to use it cautiously.

TEMPERAMENT

Individuality is very much a fact of life, whether a particular culture chooses to recognize it or not.[31] Everyone combines into a unique constellation physical features, temperamental qualities, level of metabolism, allergies, hopes, fears, and experiences. Here I propose to skim off one aspect of individuality, temperament, a subject about which—despite its long and active use—psychologists have little to say. Not even the boundaries of temperament are clear-cut, so that we aren't sure what marks it off from other aspects of personality. As I understand it, to describe somebody's temperament is to cover such qualities abstracted from his behavior as dullness or alertness, torpor or vigor, gentleness or brusqueness, passivity or assertiveness, apathy or readiness to flare into anger and into other emotions, emotional stability or restlessness, and so on. Temperament is also used to denote the strength, vividness, and other qualities attached to the senses and to basic drives, like hunger and sex.[32] Children with low sensory sensitivity, low autonomic reactivity, and low drive have moderate encounters with their environment compared to children with high sensitivity, quick autonomic reactivity, and high drive who make active, vivid, quick contacts with environmental opportunities, use a wider range of coping behavior, show a higher level of gratification—and also get into more trouble.[33] Speaking broadly, temperament points to activity level and to emotional reactivity, with the implication that those things are partly inborn. Not that a child inherits temperament as a single entity, the way he acquires brown hair or blue eyes. He inherits a constitution, including a range of metabolic and endocrine functions, sensory sensitivity, and drive strength, in which his temperamental qualities are implanted. Prenatal and postnatal experiences inextricably infuse the inherited, and probably largely biochemical, bases of temperament, so that even in early life temperament partakes of both heredity and environment and is by no means totally fixed or arrested.

Because men live in society, temperament inevitably comes up against social expectations. The confrontation need bring no clash but often one occurs, as when an infant who is temperamentally a restless sleeper is expected to sleep quietly; or an inactive and unassertive boy is asked to demonstrate the contrary qualities that adults expect boys, in contrast to girls, to exhibit. From the example of a few social systems that are flexible and culturally skillful enough to accommodate a range of temperaments, we learn that cultures can be built to allow varieties of individual temperament. They need not all insist on equally narrow conformity to one set of qualities. But in fact every group, despite comprising individuals who embody a broad range of temperaments, does select certain temperamental ideals. Inevitably the ideals fit some people's endowment more comfortably than they suit others, who find them uncongenial. It is reasonable to expect that those who are at home with such cultural emphases willingly assume and so perpetuate them, while temperamental misfits welcome change in cultural emphases that they find onerous,[34] and even manage to escape social demands. As an example, take delinquents who, temperamentally more impulsive than nondelinquents, have learned to channel their impulsiveness along delinquent lines.[35]

Much of what I have already said comes from Margaret Mead's book reporting field-work in New Guinea, *Sex and Temperament in Three Primitive Societies*.[36] She holds temperament to be one of the basic human materials out of which any social system derives its ideal personality type. She prefers not to say that temperamental qualities, such as passivity, pridefulness, brusqueness, or dominance, are inborn; only a potentiality for such traits may be inherited. Regardless of their source, some temperamental qualities appear more strongly in certain individuals than in others. Over many years a social system, confronted by a variety of temperamental traits, selects a few and makes them desirable qualities which everyone should manifest. Or, perhaps, they are only demanded of everyone who occupies a certain social position, like all men, all women, all leaders, or all graduate students. Such selection automatically rules out other traits as undesirable. Then, from infancy, children are treated in ways designed to bring out the desirable qualities while suppressing others. The word "selection" is used figuratively since the process occurs beyond awareness and as a rule rarely leaves any historical evidence of what happened. Selection isn't utterly perfect. A social system never eradicates all undesirable temperamental traits or manages to install a dead level of uniformity. Mostly the mountain Arapesh are temperamentally passive, gentle, warm, trusting, and unaccustomed to violence. Yet aggressive individuals do appear among them, despite the long and consistent encouragement that children receive to develop opposite qualities. Even an aggressive Arapesh, however, is affected by the passivity and gentleness that his culture emphasizes. As a result, the most active Arapesh child is far less aggressive than a normally active American youngster. But the Arapesh, unable to compare, can't appreciate the relative mildness of their aggressive youngster. By their own limited standards they see a big gap between him and his normal fellows. Still, they don't regard the deviant as a failure, as someone in whom educational aims failed to take proper hold, for they are too unselfconscious and unpurposeful in the way they shape temperament to become aware of having educational aims at all.[37]

Personality as a Whole

Covert and overt behavior normally occur in some orderly relationship to one another and to the physical organism whence they arise. In other words, personality forms a system that unites body and mind, in which covert and overt reflect each other, and wherein conscious ends are guided by un-conscious aims. It is a system that selectively stores past events to define present choices, strives toward future goals, and organizes both muscular and mental elements, so that physical illness has its counterpart in how the patient perceives his world and the emotions find their expression in bodily states. One of the system's most significant characteristics, as I have already pointed out, is its enduring temporal quality. Despite the fact that he grows and changes in every part, the individual remains the same person. His past experiences become consolidated into the whole, expressing themselves in present-moment decisions.[38] Youth lives into adulthood.

Strange that the self's continuum should outlast
The Virgin, Aphrodite, and the Mourning Mother.[39]

Personality also remains a system between situations. A worker's on-the-job behavior mirrors pleasures and crises he encounters at home and in his neighborhood involvements, and the old-time Sioux warrior, who bore the imprint of his childhood, carried over his military role to his family life. Insisting that personality forms a system hardly explains how, intellectually, the system is to be grasped as a whole. Without satisfactory concepts for grasping man configurationally, as a totality, social scientists have no recourse but to break down the whole into elements, levels, and processes, and then, in order to study their integration, laboriously to recombine the parts, constructing a model that represents their total functioning.

Engaging the World

Studying personality starts out by taking the existence of a system for granted. Armed with appropriate techniques, the investigator goes about collecting those facts of socially patterned overt and covert behavior which he requires, facts richly revealing the person's (or cross section of persons') mode of emotion, cognition, or perception—whatever the investigator happens to be most interested in. In collecting requisite data I note, for example, how my subject puritanically reins or hedonistically releases sexual and other appetites; clings to or shies away from power; identifies with or avoids female characters in the Thematic Apperception Test; prefers to deal with details far more than wholes while taking the Rorschach test; quickly gives up or perseveres when a challenge becomes very difficult; dreams often of violence; desperately risks all he owns in gambling; enjoys dancing; comes late, leaves ends of jobs uncompleted. All is grist—whether his response be instrumental (calculated, like persevering, to win a specific goal) or consummatory (the dance, after all, is an end in itself); whether his strategy for reaching the goal be inept or informed; whether his response be socially normal or deviant—for I want as reasonably full an account of his personality as possible. An account of personality is a record of how an individual or group engages the world—now to achieve valued ends, now to resist threat.[40] On one level an individual (or, as we say, a body) strives to fight off a virulent invasion of disease;[41] on another, individuals complexly organized and heavily equipped move in to repair damage caused by war or storm. The latter, being a deliberate maneuver that utilizes the distinctive human power of conscious reflection, exemplifies the kind of behavior social scientists are most prone to heed. Don't identify striving wholly with tension reduction. The fact is, a strong, healthy person *wants* to experience manageable tension; he regards it as a positive experience.[42] As an example, take the way a professor who overcommits himself to promised articles for professional journals is reaching out for challenges and growth.

People build opportunities for manageable tension into culture in such forms as mystery stories and competitive sports.

Obviously, the specific ends which men value or reject vary greatly from one social system to another. A Hopi Indian strives to bring rain so he can raise a harvest sufficient to carry him and his household over the winter. A Kaska Indian looks for fur, game, and fish and tries to preserve for himself a considerable measure of personal inviolability. Similarly, each individual pursues diverse goals which he has learned to value partly because of his unique constitutional endowment and partly on account of the unique set of experiences he has encountered. Yet, despite considerable variability between individuals and social systems, we can detect a number of ends pursued by every person.[43] We see man strive to grow, to actualize his potentials, and to realize himself in whatever degree his personal and social resources permit. Self-actualization is a goal realized in work as well as in play, in instrumental as well as consummatory behavior.

Another general human tendency, only partially different from self-actualization, aims to protect personal integration or to maintain a sense of coherent wholeness. Ambiguity so distresses human beings that sometimes they organize devastating revolutions to get rid of contradictions and inconsistencies embedded in their way of life.[44] Defense mechanisms, like denial, repression, and projection of unacceptable impulses on others, constitute attempts to cope with states that upset internal coherence. Personality uses means akin to the automatic way in which the body fights disease to maintain a sense of personal integration. Unconsciously we perceive in ways that maintain or enhance our sense of inner order. The apparent size of a coin isn't identical for everyone, but varies with the subject's financial status. A careful reading of more than 400 documents containing publicly available statements made by John

Foster Dulles between 1953 and 1959 concerning the Soviet Union reveals that the Secretary of State interpreted information reaching him in a manner consistent with his belief system, and so preserved his original image of Soviet bad faith. For example, when the Soviet Union began to behave less hostilely, Dulles perceived no change in intent but merely the necessity of adversity.[45] One's endeavor to retain personal autonomy reflects a very similar process. A person tries to regulate his life according to his own ends and percepts, in spite of the fact that social life forces him to accept restraint and direction. How much external direction a person can tolerate varies from one individual and social system to another and depends on whether direction promises to maximize or curtail personally desirable goals. Autonomy resembles the idea of authentic being, a goal that becomes difficult if conformism grows so demanding that it alienates us from our true self by obfuscating self-awareness and washing out all sense of uniqueness.[46] Despite seeking autonomy, we need nevertheless to relate ourselves to the world, for, as everyone knows, isolation constitutes the most unbearable punishment and loneliness can be excruciatingly painful.[47]

Enumerating fundamental human goals invites disagreement. Freud saw human striving to contain only two trends: one to build up, preserve, and unify; the other to return to an inorganic state at the expense of life itself.[48] In the former—the life instinct—sexual gratification plays a major role. In the other—the death instinct—there is no life trend. Erich Fromm builds up moral and philosophical anthropology around only a single, fundamental end of life, holding that, basically, man seeks new and higher forms of unity with nature, his fellow men, and himself.[49] Man literally creates the world he sees around him as he pursues this end. All the variable values encountered from one social system to another are rooted in this push, as well as all

emotion and anxiety. Man strives always to relate himself, thereby deciding his destiny and realizing his sense of identity.[50] Fromm would evaluate cultures by the degree to which they enable people to achieve an adequate sense of self. Kurt Goldstein also holds to a single basic trend in personality, self-actualization.[51] All such postulations of fundamental human strivings implicitly or explicitly take a position about which anthropology has been deeply ambivalent, namely, they assert that cultures can be evaluated. Basic trends like self-actualization, personal integration, and autonomy require properly nurturant environmental conditions; otherwise, people will become troubled and unrestful. Everyone agrees that physical health deserves high priority and that for its sake suitable environments must be created. But we aren't accustomed similarly to appraise environments in favor of mental health, largely because the latter remains more poorly defined. Everyone knows what it is to be free of gross personal disorder, but what does it take to actualize oneself or to be personally integrated? What is a proper measure of autonomy or of social relatedness? I feel more confident talking of concrete, specific goals or, like Alexander Leighton, of vital strivings for basic ends: physical security, sexual satisfaction, expression of hostility, expression of love, securing of love, securing of recognition, expression of spontaneity, and a sense of belonging to a definite human group and moral order.

SEARCH FOR MOTIVES

Most anthropologists instead of assuming fundamental, pan-human goals would rather learn how specific social systems develop special ends, or present distinctive conditions that pattern their people's striving. Taking for granted the basic unity of mankind, anthropologists prefer to look for differences between cultures in the specific goals held out to be worthwhile, as well as in any conditions—emotional, cognitive, or conative—that motivate behavior. Not that all behavior is aroused only when some inner need is awakened. Some playful or expressive behavior occurs precisely because all the vital needs have been met, and nothing unsatisfied presses to activity.[53] Observe the breadth with which I defined my interest in motivation. I mean it to be broad enough to include "any condition," including, for example, incongruities, dissonances, and frustrations that an individual encounters and that challenge him directly, as hunger impels someone to act.

People clearly differ from one culture to another in the goals they pursue, which, from the standpoint of personality, means that they have been endowed with different motives. Psychologists customarily distinguish between universal primary motives that are rooted in biological processes, like hunger, thirst, sex, fatigue, and pain, and learned, secondary motives that diverge sharply from one culture to another. Cultural appetite for rotten fish among the Eskimo or a stylish preference for very dry martinis among New York businessmen illustrate motives acquired through learning.[54] However, even primary motives, for all their intimate biological involvement, are susceptible to cultural influences. For example, the extent to which such drives regularly come up against conditions that frustrate them varies from one social system to another. Freud and his fellow psychoanalysts traced some of their patients' most severe conflicts and anxieties to sex frustration, most likely because they saw their patients in a puritanical culture whose moral prohibitions regularly blocked sexual gratification at many points in an individual's life. Among the Siriono, semitropical aborigines living under economically perilous conditions in northern and eastern Bolivia, hunger is the primary drive most greatly threatened and most laden with anx-

iety.[55] Westerners often use food as a substitute for sex (man has a remarkable capacity to substitute gratifiers), whereas the Siriono use sex to compensate for hunger. The Siriono practice food magic but have no sex magic, probably because their sex drive is rarely threatened to any great extent, so that they don't need to rely on magic to fulfill sexual desire. Why put so much weight on motivation? Because of how useful this dynamic concept has proven for explaining behavior ranging in magnitude from dreaming to social revolutions. Much in culture can be satisfactorily understood by exposing the, at times unexpected, sources underlying it. Such explanations become even more helpful when they include an account of how the motives were acquired and predict in general the situations that will arouse or curtail them. To be sure, anthropology and other disciplines studying human behavior have perennially been embroiled in debating the wisdom of explaining social facts by dipping into psychological states.[56] Admittedly some sciences have nothing to gain by it. A structural linguist views language as comprised of phonemes, morphemes, and implicit rules followed in organizing morphemes into meaningful statements. He doesn't care a hang what his speakers want.[57] An anthropologist occupied with cultural evolution can chart the successive energy levels reached by culture while never acknowledging conscious or unconscious motives brought into play while people were achieving greater control over nature. Other anthropologists, however, prefer to view religion as a means of coping; social control as based largely on willingness to conform; change as a matter of creativity or as something problematic for personal adjustment; and cultural evolution as resting on people's conceptions of nature, man, and time. Motivation and other explanatory concepts belonging to dynamic psychology bring valuable insights into such topics and become indispensable tools for dealing with other problems that directly front on psychology; for example, how culture is acquired in childhood and afterwards, or how mental illness is stimulated by stress originating in culture.

Note what happens when a person is blocked in his pursuit of vital goals.[58] Such blockage most dramatically arises when other people—rivals, authorities, or enemies—impede us. But it also originates with the individual himself, out of his personal limitations. He may lack resources—health, energy, intelligence, emotional stability, sexual potency—adequate to achieve certain ends. It also happens when he fastens his eye on unrealizable ends; perhaps on goals culturally prohibited to him. Then too, goals may be so vaguely defined that a person can't know how to pursue them effectively, or the choice of one forestalls access to another equally important, so that the striver is plunged into frustration or conflict. A person who is blocked when trying to reach important ends tends to respond with unpleasant emotion, the degree of unpleasantness depending on several conditions, including his ability to tolerate frustration. He may be vexed, mildly disappointed, saddened, heavily depressed, afraid, anxious, angry, or badly threatened. Such feelings flash the presence of danger; they testify that urgent motives, conscious or unconscious, are imperiled. To rid themselves of unpleasant emotion people resort to defense mechanisms, like reaction formation; they may resourcefully find substitute goals, or else they may intensify their efforts to reach the original target. Psychiatrists know that all such maneuvers often fail, so that stress remains unrelieved and even mounts in intensity. The necessity of coping with unrelieved or mounting stress wears down a person, strains him, and distorts his behavior. Other members of the community take note once the signs of strain or personality distortion assume forms like hypochondriasis, compulsiveness, or, more seriously, paranoia. Psychiatric symptoms differ a little from one culture to another, but that stress promotes strain holds universally. Note the sequence: I started with vital ends a person seeks—his motives. When those are blocked through cultural arrangements or for whatever other reason, he experiences stress under whose load his normal behavior may seriously disintegrate.

The study of motivation, then, is useful to account psychologically for both the abnormal and normal behavior that society patterns and so makes cultural. But like the equally useful concept of unconscious behavior (to which motivation, of course, is closely related), the study of motives carries dangers to be guarded against. The intensity with which we search for inner goals can conflict with recognizing the manifest ways in which people strive. The observer too obsessed with motives figuratively hides his eyes from the goals an individual visibly pursues. He neglects what a person is actually making of himself in favor of what the person once became and, presumably, is doomed to remain. Much can be learned about personality by observing the subject's overt being and doing, his contact with the world through which—whether as child or adult—he creates and develops himself to the extent that possibilities of action in his environment allow.[59] Of course, underlying meanings, by defining the situations he encounters, also guide his action. Traditional meanings not only motivate but limit our responses. My point is that a search for understanding should be directed to more than that which is within a person. An observer should also perceive the significance of situations in which a person is currently acting.

VALUES

Values—conceptions of the desirable and undesirable—also motivate, though, as we all recognize, people can be tightly insulated from the most lauded ideals to which they feel no sense of commitment, and can shunt aside ideals in situations that arouse the prepotency of other motives. All Kaska Indians value deference, but some of them readily release blind hostility when severely intoxicated.[60] Euroamericans endorse achievement highly and appraise one another in terms of abilities and standards of performance, while in rural Pakistan people who emphasize ascription more than achievement judge one another primarily in terms of fixed qualities.[61] We are accustomed to apply general standards that hold for nearly everyone, valuing a universal outlook that doesn't allow for too many personal exceptions; but in a small-scale social system, members treat one another in terms of specific, personal relationships. They emphasize particularism. People differ in the degree to which they value affectivity or neutrality in social relations and in the extent to which they tolerate inequalities; for example, holding that occupants of high positions deserve special respect and deference. Englishmen relate to one another diffusely, valuing and responding to many aspects of the other person, while in the United States we respond to specific dimensions of the other.

Some values are discrete, such as our endorsement of patriotism or doing well in life, and our condemnation of adultery and cheating. Other values are broad-gauge propositions concerning what people feel positively about; they influence both the means and ends of striving.[62] Let's call such broad-gauge propositions value orientations rather than values. In all societies, men confront the same basic questions, answers to which represent their value orientations. *What is the character of innate human nature?* Whether evil, good, mixed, or neutral, the answer preferred by a social system becomes a basis for dealing with other people, including children. *What relationship connects man to nature?* A view

that sees nature powerfully subjugating man will expect little from science and engineering, skills more apt to thrive where value orientations postulate man's mastery over nature. Some American Indians, like the Hopi, take a middle position. They affirm man's harmonious place in nature and thereby allow for mutual, ritual interdependence between a social group and the cosmos. *What time dimension is most significant: past, present, or future?* Whoever looks mainly backward or lives largely for the present will perforce restrict planning, more so than those oriented toward the future. *What is the significant end of human activity?* A social system that predominantly values being, will approve spontaneous expression of individuality. One that extolls doing, will deem it proper to appraise a person's accomplishments by external standards which he should achieve. An orientation to being-in-becoming, however, gives more weight to how potentialities develop than to self-expression or to external achievement. Finally, *How are men related to one another?* If lineally, then the hierarchical precedence of one person over another (an older over a younger brother, for instance) must be guarded; if collaterally, then mutual ties with peers count high; if individually, then individual goals deserve to be supported first. On any of those five basic questions we are very likely to order possible value orientations by rank. That is, I am not anchored only to the past, or the present, or the future, but I set greater value on one of those dimensions than on another, to which in turn I give higher priority than I assign to the third remaining one. Since situations cue behavior, the way I rank value orientations varies from one set of circumstances to another. Different groups and strata in a social system under similar circumstances will also vary in how they choose between directions. In the same person, value orientations can exist in tension; his commitment

¶[*Four Value Orientations Diverge Among Five Southwestern Peoples*[63]

	Zuni Indians	Navaho Indians	Spanish Americans	Texan Homesteaders	Mormons
1	Regard harmony with nature as preferable to a view of man as subject to nature, which in turn is preferred to the view that man can exert mastery over nature.	Regard harmony with nature as preferable to a view that man can exert mastery over nature, which in turn is preferred to a view of man as subject to nature.	Prefer a view that regards man as subject to nature over a view of man exerting mastery over nature, which in turn is preferred to a view that man should strive to live in harmony with nature.	Man can exert mastery over nature, which view is preferred to living in harmony with nature, which in turn is preferred to seeing man as subject to nature.	The view that man can exert mastery over nature is slightly preferred to living in harmony with nature, which in turn is preferred to seeing man as subject to nature.
2	Present orientation is preferred to a view which regards the past as the most important time dimension, which, however, is preferred to a future orientation.	Present orientation is preferred to a view which regards the past as the most important time dimension. A past orientation, however, is preferred to a future orientation (as among Zuni).	Present orientation is preferred to a past orientation, which in turn is preferred to a future orientation (just as among Zuni and Navaho).	Future orientation is preferred to a present one, which in turn is preferred to a view holding the past as the important time dimension.	Future orientation is preferred to a present one, which in turn is preferred to a view holding the past as the important time dimension (as among Texan Homesteaders).
3	Doing is preferred to an orientation that values spontaneous expressive activity (being).	Doing is preferred to being (as among Zuni).	Being is preferred to doing.	Doing is preferred to being (as among Zuni and Navaho).	Doing is preferred to being (as among Zuni, Navaho, and Texan Homesteaders).
4	Prefer a collateral orientation (that holds the individual to be not fully human unless he is part of a social order) over a lineal one (stressing continuity in time), which is preferred to an individualistic orientation.	Prefer a collateral orientation over a lineal one, which is preferred to an individualistic orientation (as among Zuni).	An individualistic orientation is preferred to a lineal view of social relations, which in turn is preferred to a collateral orientation.	Prefer an individualistic orientation to a collateral one, which in turn is preferred to a lineal view of social relations.	Prefer an individualistic orientation to a collateral one, which in turn is preferred to a lineal view of social relations (as among Texan Homesteaders).

to the past keeps troubled company with his concern for the future, so that from time to time as issues arise he must decide with anguish which of the incompatible dimensions shall dominate.

THE KNOWING EGO

Now I direct your attention to the way the ego, that buffer zone between inner and outer world, organizes motivated behavior. Although ego sounds like a thing and is even described as a "region" in personality, we come out much better if we hold to thinking about it as a process, partly conscious and partly unconscious. The ego confronts two dimensions of experience: first, internal impulses pressing for gratification regardless of consequences and, second, external reality, including social expectations and the gains and losses likely to be incurred through following a given line of behavior. Actually, the division between inner and outer reality isn't sharp because I can know reality only as I perceive it affected by my unconscious goals, state of health, feeling of safety or danger, and recollected prior experience. Between inner and outer realms, the ego mediates like a broker, now and again blundering, but often skillfully achieving gratification while heeding the physical and social worlds' demands. Another image pictures the ego as the control tower of the personality that directs the traffic of striving while consulting its memory for relevant past experiences capable of safely guiding behavior. Knowledgeably it integrates a thousand bits of information. Even in sleep, the ego remains active, dreams thoughtfully sizing up the dreamer's life situation and solving problems.[64] Normally, the ego operates with a sense of strength and freedom, which the individual subjectively feels as responsibility for his own acts. He experiences an autonomous sense of power over his impulses

and the external world's demands.[65] But at times the sense of control dissipates, leaving a person overwhelmed by inner and outer forces that outweigh him. Erich Fromm[66] says that when a person feels cut off from others, alienated, his ego jettisons its autonomy through intensified endorsement of conformism and heightened identification with leaders. He submerges himself in society to relieve his sense of aloneness. Industrialization has aggravated man's isolation and powerlessness. Although cheap, efficient media constantly broadcast information, modern men feel detached and unrelated to the people and events that make news and can rouse no responsibility for what occurs.[67] The way even vital events are reported strips them of significance. A broadcast tells me that a well-known man has been operated on for lung cancer. The message is hardly finished before the commercial comes on—"Kent satisfies best!" As playwright Arthur Miller puts it, "We smile, even laugh; we must, lest we scream. And in the laughter, in the smile, we dissolve by that much. Is it possible to say convincingly that this destruction of an ethic also destroys my will to oppose violence in the streets? We do not have many wills, but only one; it cannot be continuously compromised without atrophy setting in altogether."[68]

THREATS TO THE EGO

Periodically, I said, the ego is shaken by unpleasant feelings of stress that originate within and without. The external world threatens mortal danger; forbidden impulses seductively invite fulfillment through forbidden pleasures, and the superego inflicts its biting criticism, imposing a miserable feeling of shame or an awful sense of guilt because the ego has unwisely allowed the person to go beyond the limits socially set on behavior.[69] Some psychoanalysts reason that shame arises out of the ego ideal, the superego's stock of ideals, from which the ego has departed, thereby impairing the person's public image, while guilt stems from social prohibitions that the superego incorporates. Another way of seeing the distinction between shame and guilt is to picture guilt as warning the ego when it has transgressed rules that the superego has made its own; shame, however, is primarily other-directed and signals that the person has done something of which others disapprove. Guilt tags offenses against moral standards that have been incorporated into the personality and shame tags acts which call for social opprobrium, which the ego ideal dreads. Both sentiments may occur together, imposing a doubly crushing burden on the ego.

Shame and guilt do more than punish. A guilty person may be led to atone, as if to undo his wrong, or he may try bribery, as if to lure others into the same unhappy state in which his superego has landed him.[70]

The burden imposed by the superego may literally put a person out of commission, as it did an Eskimo woman we knew in northern Quebec. When her affair with a married man was discovered, she took to her tent, where she remained hidden all summer, most of the time in bed.[71] Some people think that early man relied so heavily on public opinion that he suffered only from shame and never from guilt. Obviously that's hard to prove, especially since it is even difficult to establish whether some living small-scale, exotic social systems are governed more by shame than by guilt. It has also been suggested that U. S. Americans are giving up guilt as the primary sanction of the superego and are coming mainly to rely on shame, the transition coinciding with our increasing other-directedness and growing insistence on conformity.[72]

The concept of shame touches closely on the currently popular idea of identity, which social scientists find useful in under-

⟨ The Gentle Superego of American Indian Children[73]

	Indicating guilt (%)	Indicating shame (%)	Questionable (%)	Total number of responses
Hopi Indians	26	59	15	192
Zuni Indians	12	81	7	171
Navaho Indians (of Navaho Mt.)	3	96	1	102
Sioux Indians	30	63	7	146
Midwest white children	46	42	12	443

When American Indian children in four tribes and Midwest white children were asked "Have you ever been ashamed?" they understood the question in two ways. Sometimes they reported instances when they had felt guilty, when their conscience had hurt them. At other times they recalled former experiences of embarrassment, times when they had made a poor showing in front of others. As the table shows, compared to Midwest white children, the Indian children reported experiencing embarrassment more often than guilt. As a matter of fact, the Navaho, Zuni, and, perhaps, Hopi languages lack even a word for guilt, a fact which supports the conclusion that these Southwest Indian children have much less conscience, or a far milder superego, than Midwest white children.

standing a person's career in society. The ego allows me to represent myself and, by drawing on others' norms and ideals that I have incorporated in my ego, to evaluate my reflected self. If I succeed in making myself measure up to what others expect of my age and sex, then others will be pleased and my ego will be satisfied. In a society like ours that values intelligence, honesty, physical health, attractiveness, and popularity, possession of those attributes goes far to confer a satisfactory sense of identity. With them I shall be convinced that I possess admirable traits and so maintain self-confidence. Objects, attributes, income, renown, and rank, also bolster self-esteem. Such props, however, should not become inseparably linked to a favorable self-image lest their loss prove utterly devastating. Philosophers express it somewhat differently when they say that a man only invites bruises from society if he attends too closely to his social self and ignores the real self that differentiates him from all other men and that is incommensurable with the superficialities demanded by conventional social life.

But most of us see ourselves very much as we appear to others, reading our image in their judgment.[74] As a result, when others denigrate me for what I have become in their estimation, I become dissatisfied, resentful, and ashamed, like the New York son of an Italian immigrant, who complained, "When an Italian boy sees that none of his people have the good jobs, why should he think he is as good as the Irish or the Yankees? It makes him feel inferior."[75] Bruised by the invidiousness that exacerbates inequalities of our class-ridden social system, lower-class people feel humiliated because they have parents who do "scummy" jobs or because they live in neighborhoods where, in the undisguised opinions of higher ranking teachers, policemen, and judges, people are shiftless and no good. In their egos, lower-class folk in-

corporate community-wide values exemplified by more successful and prestigious fellow Americans to which they themselves fail to measure up. Their dissatisfied self-image can't be easily repaired because their personal resources open few routes leading to higher prestige. Of course, many such people are partially resourceful in discovering workable defenses whereby their ego preserves a modicum of self-esteem and manages stress. For their plight they blame luck, God, or the racket one can't beat. They also resignedly lower their sights and slip into "dreaming in second gear."

Identity can be changed.[76] Psychoanalysis, religious conversion, and revolutionary reeducation as in communist China[77] transform the ego's image of itself, as do promotions in rank, demotions, banishment, and other drastic upheavals that gain their effect by altering our social relationships. Such transitions are ceremonially marked and publicized, removing any danger that others may neglect to treat us as befits our new social being. To minimize identity change, people have only to stabilize their social relationships, though sometimes they carry this too far, freezing their whole social environment and paralyzing their social effectiveness. No matter how much we change, a kernel of our identity persists through the overlapping transformations. Subjectively we remain ourselves, year after year, from childhood to old age.

A bodyguard of more or less self-deceiving, unconsciously motivated defense mechanisms stands at the ego's service to overcome threats from both without and within, and to maintain a relatively steady state of personal equilibrium.[78] Repression, best known of these, serves the ego by sweeping prohibited impulses under the carpet of consciousness; denial doggedly insists that no threat exists; reaction formation glosses over disallowed impulses by affirming only the noblest of aims to be at work; *substitution* and *compromise formation* cleverly find unexpected paths to gratification, the hope being that the superego won't detect their true character; *displacement* invests emotion in safe, nondangerous, or even hallowed objects; *renouncing control* finds more or less elaborate rationalizations for evading responsibility and escaping self-blame; *rationalization* whitewashes what has already occurred, appealing to the superego as well as to other people to be understanding; *withdrawal* and *detachment* try to encapsulate the ego, restricting it to as tiny a social space as necessary in an effort to preserve safety. Not to overlook *projection*, which throws temptation or disparagement on others—*they* are bad, not me. Although the list reads like a cast of live characters manipulating a person, you must look below the figurative language and visualize each defense mechanism as a purposefully and largely unconscious maneuver adopted by a harried but resourceful individual.

Projection is a heavily overworked word in personality psychology whose classic meaning St. Thomas à Kempis long ago summed up when he said, "What a man is inwardly that he will see outwardly."[79] Freud converted the concept into a defense mechanism, observing that the ego deals with impulses too powerful to master by externalizing them, casting them on somebody else. When we speak of projective tests, like the Rorschach, we employ the original broad meaning, assuming that what a subject perceives in ambiguous stimuli will be congruent with qualities in his personal make-up. Anthropologists have still further widened the concept's meaning by holding that people also project into real and imagined elements of the universe, notably supernatural entities. Abram Kardiner,[80] a psychoanalyst who with anthropologist Ralph Linton pioneered in psychological anthropology, delineates a subprocess of the ego that he calls the projective system. Made up of unconscious, emotional needs born of traumatic events in early life, it governs a person's projective behavior. A similar constellation of emotional needs constitutes a group's projective system, provided all the group's members have experienced relatively similar childhood conditions. The fewer the anxieties aroused in early growth that need to be compensated for, the simpler the adult projective system. The action of the projective system, Kardiner hypothesizes, registers most clearly in a culture's folktales and religion. Comanche Indian children grew up encountering few threats.[81] Permissive disciplines, abundant praise, and consistent rewards created a characterological groundwork for adult daring, freedom from inhibition, and high self-esteem. Hence, Comanche adults reveal not helplessness but resourcefulness in their relationships with the supernatural.

According to a somewhat similar view, emotionally significant human experiences like death, sex differences, and the Oedipal relationship of a child to the parent of opposite sex create tensions which people resolve symbolically.[82] They project the emotionally compelling experiences into the constituent symbols and themes of complex initiation rituals, drama, and other forms of art, which mostly they find and don't create in their culture. Some cultures are particularly rich in problematic interpersonal relationships, especially during childhood. They have much "plot." The more plot in culture, the more likely that people will be preoccupied with elaborating the problematic material into artistic forms of expression.

Wear and tear of stress

As this chapter must already have suggested, stress is undoubtedly one of contemporary social science's most popular and

Hans Selye   (André Larose)

useful concepts. Part of its popularity can be accounted for by its ability to connect vitally significant human behavior and cultural milieu. Culture stresses an individual, who then reacts defensively, with alarm, or with unpleasant feelings. But that doesn't wholly explain why social scientists dwell so devotedly on what instigates defense and suffering rather than, say, on stimuli that press for happier behavioral reactions. Oscar Lewis[83] holds that concern with what people suffer from is pragmatically more justified than investigating enjoyment because it produces more insight into the human condition and provides a lever for constructive change. In other words, to study stress will enable us to promote mankind's greater happiness. When applied to personality in culture, the concept of stress and its counterpart, strain, are of course used analogically to the meaning they possess in engineering. There, stress refers to a force exerted by one body on another. Materials, like wood, steel, concrete, and so on, are well known to vary in their ability to withstand stress and the engineer's task is to suit available substances to the load they must bear. Strain in engineering means deformation or change occasioned in the material's dimensions by stress. From engineering, stress spilled over into medicine, where it owes a good measure of its popularity to an 18-year-old medical student, Hans Selye.[84] It all started when Selye became more impressed with signs common to sickness than with the signs of individual diseases. Strongly discouraged by his teachers, who wanted to save him what they thought would be fruitless research, he nevertheless persevered with his interest and discovered a general symptom of disease which he called the general-adaptation-syndrome. Illness he viewed as a way organism has of adapting to noxious agents. The general syndrome of adaptation runs through three phases, beginning with an alarm reaction that initiates chemical changes in the body. The overt signs of this phase speak of a generalized call to arms in defense of the organism's integrity. However, no living organism can continuously maintain itself in a state of alarm. If life continues, a stage of resistance must set in to repel or control the virus, splinter, infection, or whatever threatens the organism. Arming to defend or repel threat, like the alarm reaction, also takes effort, so that the general-adaptation-syndrome's third phase consists of exhaustion—eloquent evidence of wear and tear. The struggle to adapt has literally worn down the body. Selye subsequently called the noxious agent producing the stress a "stressor" and reserved the name "stress" for the signs of wearing toil produced by combatting the stressor. Instead of stressor I shall generally speak of stress, while the evidence of combat and exhaustion I shall call strain. Social scientists have perceived poverty, cultural confusion, frustration, failure, cognitive dissonance, a sense of inadequacy, and many other internally and externally rooted experiences as stress or stressors. A person's behavioral responses to such stresses, like his feeling of pressure, tension, anxiety, or depression; his fantasies or obsessive-compulsiveness, or his more spectacular attempts to adapt through striking out at people and paranoiacally blaming his environment, constitute indubitable evidence of strain.

Unlike strain, stress is no extraordinary occurrence but rather a normal, fairly constant accompaniment of living.[85] Virtually every situation a person encounters and every role he plays between childhood and old age require a marshaling of adaptive resources in response to threats. It isn't only that stress is ubiquitous; there is also the contributory fact that human beings are imperfect, fallible, interdependent, and therefore inherently predisposed to suffer and to break when loads become too heavy.[86] To protect ourselves, we seek to regulate the invasion of our systems and to repair ambiguities that destroy our sense of cognitive and emotional coherence. Now, people differ in their ability to protect their integrity and to steer a comfortable course through life, just as they differ in their ability to digest food and to withstand the tubercle bacillus. They occasionally need help in their ability to safeguard themselves or to restore their well-being, wherefore social systems contain such professional specialists as shamans, curers, psychiatrists, surgeons, social workers. Obviously, stress theory in social science isn't as much interested in normal vicissitudes as in relatively great crises and in cumulative stress that piles up through perduring or successive threats—especially when those threats emanate from the patterned arrangements of a social system. Such stress involves very minute amounts of energy compared to many mechanical forces[87] and is also far less objective than mechanical stress, so that it can sometimes be safely defined by simply knowing what it is that a particular actor perceives.[88] Furthermore, whereas material bodies react to stress passively, a person actively "selects" meaningful stresses, to which he then responds actively with whatever psychological resources he possesses. What is stressful and the degree to which it threatens will vary among people, as well as at different points in the same person's life.[89] Common sense suggests that poverty, the death of close kin, and violence are nearly always threatening. Even though they may not be equal threats for everyone, their presence in a community is likely to affect a significant number of people. Thinking along those lines comforts social scientists, who prefer to define stress objectively and then look to see if certain predicted reactions to it, like the genesis of new religions, adjustments of belief, or personality disorder and other forms of deviance occur. Postulating basic needs, or vital human strivings for physical security, sexual satisfaction, love, recognition, support, encouragement, sustained membership in a definite human group, and others,[90] also enables an anthropologist objectively to locate stressors that, however dissimilar their form from one culture to another, act similarly to block the same basic needs or goals. Speaking even more generally, one can categorize two eternally likely sources of stress: internal psychological conflict, in which two opposed motivating forces clash; and the destruction of any familiar system of reality which a person has learned to manipulate and to live comfortably in.[91] For Freud,[92] expressing his unconsolable discontent with civilization, it was enough that man had culture. That very fact doomed him to stress because, being built out of mental energy of which man had only a limited amount at his disposal, culture could only be brought about and maintained by withdrawing energy from other aims pressing for gratification, sex and aggression. The more imposing a civilization, the stronger must be the sexual morality of those who built it and still wish to maintain

it; the firmer must be the men's renunciation of women, and the more resolute everyone's suppression of aggression. Freud's
view of personality told him that to block
gratification of sex and aggression engenders frustration, which in turn generates
fresh hostility that provokes still more aggression. Since the aggression isn't permitted to be released outward, it has only one
place to go—inward, against the self. Kept
from gratifying discharge by the demands
of society, part of the energy attached to
aggressive impulses becomes converted into
pangs of conscience that strengthen an indispensable adjunct of culture, the superego.
Aggression instigated by a frustrating social
order, by being turned against man himself
makes him more tractable; it is put to work
to serve the social order's demands, but at
the cost of stress. The price of cultural
progress is paid in forfeiting happiness
through heightening the sense of guilt. As a
result, men find social life hard, full of
pain, saddled with difficulties, and depriving
of liberty. Who can be wholly content
under such circumstances? Yet, illusorily
we deny that culture mainly causes pain,
claiming that its mechanisms and social arrangements actually enhance our power,
maximize and enlarge our satisfactions, and
secure justice. Such judgments are born out
of an unquenchable desire for happiness;
they don't really fool us, for we know, as
well as we know that we are alive, that every
advantage conferred by culture can be
matched by a liability. I can phone my
child, who is far away—that seems to be an
advantage brought about by culture—but
only my highly developed culture made it
possible for him to go far off, to my distress.

Not only do communities differ in socially patterned types of stress (somebody
called ethnographies compendia of stress).
Cultures also vary in the amount of stress
they engender. Thus, we have "tough" and
"easy" cultures.[93] Socially patterned arrangements in the former sustain tension
and block its reduction while the latter facilitate tension-reduction. In disintegrated
social environments, stress is high because
culture is ineffective, deprivations numerous, physical danger manifest, and morale
low as well as self-defeating. Raoul
Naroll[94] has tried actually to measure social
stress between social systems. He finds such
communities as the Toda and Copper Eskimo relatively low compared to Indians
like the Navaho, Northern Paiute, and
Tupinamba of eastern Brazil. All attempts
to deal with stress objectively, to delineate
its types or to measure it, demand finding
suitable signs by which the condition can be
clearly identified. Naroll, for example, recognizes social stress by four indicators:
voluntary suicide committed in such a way
as to come to public notice; deliberate
homicide committed so as to reach public
notice despite disapproval; the regular occurrence of physical assault among members of a community while they are intoxicated; and attribution of many deaths to
witchcraft. To distinguish stressful from
nonstressful neighborhoods in Canada and
the United States, such signs have been
used as a high frequency of broken homes,
few and weak associations, few and weak
leaders, scarce patterns of recreation, a high
frequency of hostility, a high frequency of
crime and delinquency, and weak, fragmented networks of communication.[95] Not
that those conditions all equally inflict
stress; rather, they identify an environment
in which goals assumed to be essential for
personal adjustment are likely to be chronically and cumulatively blocked. Another
study conducted in Manhattan's Midtown
identified such specific stressful experiences
as parents' poor physical and mental health;
economic deprivation in childhood; poor
physical health in childhood; broken homes
in childhood; worry about work and socioeconomic status, poor interpersonal affilia-

tions, and marital worries.[96] Robert K. Merton[97] has acquired considerable renown with his theory that the hiatus between available means and desired ends instigates strain that shows up in deviance.

Signs of stress vary and so does evidence of strain. Raoul Naroll doesn't really measure stress but, rather, symptoms of strain. The most familiar indicators of strain in current use are crime, delinquency, and personality disorder (mental illness). Another favorite sign of strain is alienation, or social isolation, which in lower-class Americans grows out of severely blocked economic opportunities and rejection from community life.

Anthropologists have perhaps been too ready to perceive stress in culture negatively and dismally. Some believe that culture change, especially total and rapid change, nearly always induces severe personal threat, though recent empirical evidence indicates quite the opposite.[98] Rarely do writers acknowledge that stress need not be inevitably noxious or detrimental to personality but that it can actually enrich life by promoting creativity and growth. "The only time the organism stops and thinks," says Ernest Becker, "doubles back on itself for a scanning of possible behavior, is when it meets a frustration in ongoing action."[99] (To be sure, frustration may also be too severe for constructive growth to occur.) A book like *Flight and Resettlement*, by H. B. M. Murphy,[100] hardly hints that growth-promoting opportunities might confront displaced persons. Psychiatrists come close to forgetting that stress disturbs even the lives of healthy people, not only those with disordered personalities; or that it not only calls up disturbing symptoms but also helps to remove them, as it cured the peptic ulcers of Dutch merchants in German concentration camps.[101] Wouldn't it be more judicious to recognize the variety of adaptations to which stress gives rise, noting that

it sometimes leads to creative redesigns of the social environment and higher levels of personal organization than had previously been achieved?[102]

From stress to revitalization

The way stress stimulates personalities to recreate their environment is dramatically seen in the creation of new religions. That religion, unless it consists merely in unthinkingly following rituals and in conformist church-going, can transform a person has long been clear. Durkheim noted: "The believer who has communicated with his god is not merely a man who sees new truths of which the unbeliever is ignorant; he is a man who is stronger. He feels within him more force, either to endure the trials of existence or to conquer them. It is as though he were raised above the miseries of the world. . . ."[103]

Using historical records illuminated by psychological theory, Anthony F. C. Wallace has documented one episode in which a new religion emerged to rescue some thousand New York State Seneca Indians from their low point of misfortune.[104] During the American Revolution they had joined forces with the losing side, in retaliation for which the American forces had devastated their village, scorched their cornfields, and hacked down their orchards. Untrustworthy Indian leaders, succumbing to rum and other inducements, and acting quite without legal right, had sold almost all the Seneca domain except for a tight little reservation. The people had less than enough to eat, needed new homes, and smarted under their white neighbors' contempt and pity. Alcohol, with the nearly unshakable grip it had on many, led to drunken brawls, that index of profound social stress that simultaneously aggravates community disorder. People suspected each

Anthony F. C. Wallace

other of witchcraft and there was other evidence of widespread disequilibrium—a disintegrated community if ever there was one. As though in response to the challenge of eradicating such pervasive malaise, several Indian prophets arose, citing authority derived from visions as they exhorted people to reform their lives. Mostly their preaching gained no appreciable attention until, in June, 1779, Handsome Lake swooned under the shock of the first of his visions, experiences which led him to transform Seneca life. Former warrior and veteran, Handsome Lake was 54 years old, sick, abandoned, bereaved, depressed, worried, and a confirmed drunkard, when one day he heard three angels from heaven explain to him not only his own plight but the sorry lot of other Seneca. Let him describe his first vision in the words that Halliday Jackson used to record the prophet's testimony:

. . . I saw three men standing by the house who appeared Like angels I then

fainted and fell Gently to the Ground without being any Sick. . . .

They told me there was four of them but one was not yet come whom I thought was the Great Spirrit whom the said was much displeased with the Indians getting Drunk and committing other Gross evils which many of them were guilty of . . . the great Spirrit knew not only what people was always doing but even their very thoughts, and the said there was some very bad people among us who would pison others. . . .[105]

Quitting his bed, Handsome Lake began to preach the advice his visions brought him: morality would pay off; someday a holocaust would destroy this world and the wicked would go to hell but heaven awaited those who lived upright lives; witchcraft, immorality, dancing, malicious gossip, and wife-beating had to be given up along with stinginess and greed. He extolled the wisdom of building sound frame houses, erecting fences, raising cattle, and breeding horses. He even prescribed that men should do the farm labor—not, as in former times, women—and that children should be sent to school. All those pragmatically sound activities formed part of the divinely sanctioned way of life which the Great Spirit sanctified. The Longhouse Religion, as Handsome Lake's Code and accompanying rites came to be called, spread not only among the Seneca but to other Iroquois Indian tribes as well, among whom, in much attenuated form, it still survives, offering more traditional Indians in New York State and southern Ontario a refuge from a society they can't fully accept.

Anthropologists have found other instances in which men, acting in situations of pervasive stress and cultural disintegration, and convinced they were carrying out divine will, successfully revitalized their followers' personality and culture. Such episodes include the origin of Christianity de-

An Iroquois longhouse in 1942. (*Mary Rowell*)

scribed by the Apostles; the Cargo Cults, by which twentieth-century Melanesians impatiently hasten a new day; and messianic movements in which Central Africans try to overcome the unevenness of an old way that doesn't jibe with a new one. Wallace has looked closely at several purposeful revitalization movements, as he calls them, and charted the course they take.[106] That revitalization in stress is at all possible must be credited to man's ability to reflect on himself and on his way of life. The complex image people develop of their own life and of their place in it, Wallace calls the "mazeway." Revitalization, such as Christ and Handsome Lake accomplished, restores coherence to a mazeway which has been fragmented and disjointed through drastic culture change or as the result of some other cataclysm. It can be traced back to the time when a social system begins to founder in a whirlpool of constantly mounting, cumulative stress created through culture's losing its efficacy to satisfy. Subjectively, people perceive that their mazeway

no longer suffices to cope with the reality they confront, and the realization that they are literally lost threatens them sharply. Rigid persons prefer to tolerate even such chronic stress rather than contemplate changing their way of life. Other people try vainly to restore personal equilibrium in piecemeal fashion; they take flight into alcoholism and drugs, or become inordinately dependent on strong and powerful leaders. Like war, rebellion, constitutional changes, and similar political attempts, such solutions mostly fail to come to grips with the underlying dislocation; often they only succeed in aggravating confusion and distress. At such times interest groups and selfish individuals begin to look out first for their own private interests and black-marketing, political favoritism, hoarding, as well as other forms of self-seeking, multiply. Revitalization begins the moment an inspired individual—not necessarily a religious prophet—or group conceives of an internally consistent, new, often utopian vision of what life can be. The reformulated mazeway recommended as a guide to action is, of course, never wholly new, but has grown out of a reshuffling, recombining, and reinterpreting of elements already in the culture. Some of them may even have been borrowed from a foreign culture; thus, Handsome Lake derived his new mazeway partly from Quaker doctrines and Muhammad's revelations embody Christian, Judaic, as well as contemporary Arab ideas and observances.

In any case, the leader—who is himself usually a very deeply stressed person, truly a victim of his times—can draw only on his own personal experience and segment of culture. He can recommend no more than his own previous life has taught him. Yet frequently he reports his code as having come to him annunciated full-blown in a dream of supernormal, ecstatic revelation; in vivid circumstances that Wallace sees partly to result from a chemical reorganization taking place in the prophet's deeply troubled organism. To be effective, the leader must communicate his discovery and at the same time persuade other people, who become his followers, to integrate his message into their personal mazeways. Heeding criticism, he also scales down his message to more acceptable proportions or puts it into more culturally suitable terms. He promises compelling rewards for those who accept and act on his advice, like spiritual salvation, social esteem, economic well-being, security. But his followers experience their chief reward directly: By obeying his terms and putting his teachings to work—thereby recasting their culture into a new mold—they obtain relief from stress and attain a sense of a clear, meaningful purpose in life. As the prophet's word spreads, signs of revitalization become apparent, especially among his adherents, who sometimes stand out in the population like bright new coins in a handful of change. However, as stress lifts in the social system and signs of strain dissolve, the very conditions that cre-

ated the need for revitalization disappear. As a result, fervor and enthusiasm decline, leaving the movement, which began so exhilaratingly, to become routine. What started as a new religion ends as an established church intent on preserving unaltered the founder's teachings, even though the conditions that originally warranted them no longer exist. So once again malaise piles up, engendering new stress and strain, making conditions ripe for another revitalizing episode.

FURTHER READING

Siegfried F. Nadel critically examimes the two concepts, culture and personality, in *The Foundations of Social Anthropology* (1951: 402–408), and Francis L. K. Hsu rebuts him in "Psychological Anthropology in the Behavioral Sciences" (1961b). In *Theoretical Anthropology*, David Bidney (1953: chap. 11) also comments on the intimate relationship of culture to personality, which is likewise the subject of Ralph Linton's little book *The Cultural Background of Personality* (1945). Clyde Kluckhohn's review of "The Study of Culture" (1951a) is well suited to the viewpoint discussed in the present chapter. See also Gisela J. Hinkle's "Sociology and Psychoanalysis" (1957). Leslie White's views on *The Science of Culture* (1949: chaps. 6, 7, 12, and 13) are especially challenging and, if endorsed, would quite cut the ground from under psychological anthropology. Personality is well introduced by Henry A. Murray and Clyde Kluckhohn in their "Outline of a Conception of Personality" (1953), and also in Edward Sapir, "Personality" (1934b); Hubert Bonner, *Psychology of Personality* (1961); Gerald S. Blum, *Psychoanalytic Theories of Personality* (1953); John W. Bennett and Melvin M. Tumin, *Social Life* (1948: chaps. 17–20); David C. McClelland, *Personality* (1951);

Donald W. MacKinnon, "The Structure of Personality" (1944), and J. L. McCary, ed., *Psychology of Personality* (1956). R. S. Peters reviews types of motivation theory in *The Concept of Motivation* (1958), a topic also covered in *Motivation and Personality*, by A. H. Maslow (1954). Henry A. Murray and others anticipate problems likely to be encountered in personality study in chapter 1 of *Explorations in Personality* (1938). For a brief review of major psychoanalysts' theories, see Benjamin J. Wolman, *Contemporary Theories and Systems in Psychology* (1960: chaps. 6–9). In chapters 5 and 6 of *The Revolution in Psychiatry* (1964), Ernest Becker stimulatingly describes post-Freudian and "post-scientific" personality concepts. "Motivation Reconsidered: The Concept of Competence," by R. W. White (1959), critically examines views of motivation that unduly limit it to the end of reducing tension. William I. Thompson looks at "Anthropology and the Study of Values" (1962–1963), but in not quite the broad historical and theoretical context that Wolfgang Rudolph adopts in *Die amerikanische "Cultural Anthropology" und das Wertproblem* (1959). For the dynamic role of the ego, see Talcott Parsons, "Social Structure and the Development of Personality" (1961), and Clara Thompson, *Psychoanalysis Evolution and Development* (1950: chap. 3), who evaluates culture as it has become increasingly relevant for understanding personality. Among further writings that take up the cross-cultural patterning of shame and guilt, mention must be made of Margaret Mead, *Cooperation and Competition Among Primitive Peoples* (1961a: 493–505), first published in 1937, and Richard B. Brandt, *Hopi Ethics* (1954: 55–72). In "The Superego and the Theory of Social Systems," Talcott Parsons (1952), adopts the restricted usage of culture preferred by many sociologists, holding that culture essentially comprises a system of symbols whose meanings members of a social system internalize; as they internalize moral standards they develop their superego. Coming now to stress, the "Effects of Social and Cultural Systems in Reaction to Stress" are explored by William Caudill (1958). Leo Simmons and H. G. Wolff examine "Links Between Stress and Disease" in chapter 5 of *Social Science in Medicine* (1954), a linkage that Wolff again follows up in "Stressors as a Cause of Disease in Man" (1960). H. C. Bredemeier and R. M. Stephenson, in *The Analysis of Social Systems* (1962: 128–135), delineate stress as it gives rise to deviance. *Students Under Stress* (1962: chap. 10), by David Mechanic, scans considerable stress research on the social, cultural, psychological, and physiological levels. One of the earliest ventures by social scientists into the social consequences of stress is *Frustration and Aggression* by John Dollard and others (1939). Alvin L. Bertrand utilizes much empirical data in "The Stress-Strain Element of Social Systems: A Micro Theory of Conflict and Change" (1963–1964).

REFERENCES

1 Redfield, 1955: 68–69.

2 Boas, 1932: 12.

3 A. F. C. Wallace (1961b: 8–15) and Caudill (1962: 178) endorse seeing the two as independent; C. Kluckhohn (1949: chap. 8) prefers, somewhat ambivalently, to see personality in culture. Spiro (1951) calls separation of the two concepts a false dichotomy, a view consistent with what Cooley (1902) also said.

4 J. J. Honigmann, 1963a.

5 G. Allport, 1960a and 1960b: 22–23.

6 Goldenweiser, 1933: 26.

7 *Cf.* L. Thompson, 1961: chap. 5; 1965.

8 Boas, 1932: 146.

9 M. Mead, 1928a: chap. 13.

10 *Cf.* Harris, 1964.

11 M. Mead, 1953b: 647 and 1956a: 207–208.

12 B. G. Anderson, 1964: 190–193.

13 Róheim, 1943b; G. Devereux, 1952; La-Barre, 1954: 240–248.

14 McGeer, 1962.

15 C. G. Barber, 1959.

16 C. Kluckhohn, 1949: 208; Lewin, 1948: 20–24; G. Allport, 1960b: 13; Angyal, 1941: 264, 268–269, 322–323.

17 C. Kluckhohn, 1954: 957; S. Parker, 153–154.

18 Liddell Hart, 1964: 337.

19 Abraham, 1949a, 1949b, and 1949c.

20 Adler, 1927; Horney, 1945; Fromm, 1941: appendix.

21 C. Thompson, 1950: chap. 3.

22 Stagner, 1961: 144.

23 M. Mead, 1956a: 215.

24 M. Mead, 1940.

25 Freud, 1949b and 1961a: chap. 1. Various concepts of the unconscious are reviewed in Mowrer, 1959.

26 *Cf.* Sartre, 1956: 570–573.

27 The classic work Freud's *The Interpretation of Dreams* (1933) first appeared in 1900. See also Fromm, 1951 and 1957; Gutheil, 1939; Lowy, 1942; Munro, 1955: chap. 2; Stekel, 1943; W. Wolff, 1952: pt. 4.

28 J. J. Honigmann, 1949: 329. See Róheim, 1947 and 1949 for dream analysis in anthropological fieldwork.

28 For a discussion of the biochemical sources of dreams, see Trillin, 1965.

30 E. Becker, 1964: 147.

31 Turnell, 1950: 16–18.

32 M. Mead, 1956a: 210–213; F. H. Allport, 1924: 107–108.

33 L. B. Murphy, 1962: 340.

34 M. Mead, 1951d: 79 and 1959b: 328.

35 Kelly and Veldman, 1964.

36 M. Mead, 1935.

37 *Ibid.*, p. 143.

38 Angyal, 1941: 10.

39 Raine, 1956: 83.

40 The concept of striving which I use owes much to A. H. Leighton (1959: chap. 5).

41 Dubos, 1959.

42 Goldstein, 1940: 140–142; Maslow, 1943; Murray and Kluckhohn, 1953: 36–37; E. Becker, 1964: 25, 38, 42.

43 With these basic goals I follow M. Jahoda, 1958. She provides more specific references.

44 A. F. C. Wallace, 1961b: 138–141.

45 Holsti, 1962.

46 May, 1958.

47 Solomon *et al.*, 1957.

48 Freud, 1924a.

49 Fromm, 1955; *cf.* Scharr, 1961.

50 *Cf.* Teilhard de Chardin, 1959: 239–244.

51 Piotrowski, 1959.

52 A. H. Leighton, 1959: 148.

53 J. McV. Hunt, 1960.

54 For the distinction between primary and secondary motives (drives) approached anthropologically, see N. E. Miller and Dollard, 1941: 54–68; Murdock, 1945; Malinowski, 1938–1939.

55 Holmberg, 1950: 92–99.

56 See, for example, Durkheim, 1938: li; Homans and Schneider, 1955; Needham, 1962; Coult, 1962.

57 C. Kluckhohn, 1961: 907.

58 A. H. Leighton, 1959: chap. 5.

59 E. Becker, 1964: 145.

60 The question whether the study of values in recent anthropology and sociology is primarily psychological or not is literally an academic one. Some prefer, as I do, to deal with values in personality, including Murray and Kluckhohn, 1953: 21–22; Vogt, 1951; McArthur, 1955; Lantis, 1959. Others overlook the personal basis of values, including Gillin, 1955–1956; Northrop, 1946; Kroeber, 1963: 16. Kunkel (1965) would do without the concept at all.

61 The classification of values that follows is from T. Parson, 1951b: 58–67 and 1960. See also Lipset, 1963.

62 Coriat, 1940. The classification of value orientations that follows is from F. Kluckhohn and Strodtbeck, 1961. For the idea of values existing in a state of tension, see Dasgupta, 1964.

63 F. Kluckhohn and Strodtbeck, 1961: 351.

64 T. M. French, 1954: chaps. 2, 4.

65 Lewy, 1961.

66 Fromm, 1941: 28–31.

67 *Cf.* N. O. Brown, 1959.

68 A. Miller, 1965.

69 Piers and Singer, 1953.

70 Rogow and Lasswell, 1963: 115–116.

71 J. J. Honigmann, 1962: 35.

72 Riesman, 1950; Kroeber, 1948: 612.

73 Havighurst and Neugarten, 1955: 74–80.

74 Strauss, 1959.

75 Langner and Michael, 1963: 454–459, 464.

76 Strauss, 1959.

77 J. J. Honigmann, 1963c: 362–368.

78 Maslow and Mittelmann, 1951: chap. 8.

79 Murstein and Pryer, 1959.

80 Kardiner, 1945b: 38–46.

81 *Ibid.*, pp. 85–97.

82 Róheim, 1934a; M. Mead, 1935–1936; 1939–1940; 1947a; and 1949b: 134; Y. A. Cohen, 1964.

83 O. Lewis, 1960–1961. See also the cautions expressed in J. J. Honigmann, 1965a.

84 Selye, 1956.

85 Angyal, 1941: 334.

86 B. Kaplan and Plaut, 1956: 102.

87 L. E. Hinkle, 1961: 291.

88 *Cf.* Basowitz *et al.*, 1955: 289; Simmons and Wolf, 1954: 113–115.

89 *Cf.* B. G. Anderson, 1964; Hill, in Tanner, 1960: 22.

90 A. H. Leighton, 1959: 148; Lindemann, in Tanner, 1960: 18.

91 A. F. C. Wallace, 1955.

92 Freud, 1957.

93 Arsenian and Arsenian, 1948.

94 Naroll, 1959.

95 A. H. Leighton, 1959: 318–319.

96 Langner and Michael, 1963: 104–105.

97 Merton, 1957.

98 See, for example, James E. Ritchie, 1956: chap. 7; M. Mead, 1956c; J. J. Honigmann and Honigmann, 1965a. Reasons for such skewing are examined in Langness and Rabkin, 1964.

99 E. Becker, 1964: 103.

100 H. B. M. Murphy, 1955.

101 *Cf.* Renaud and Estess, 1961; Langner and Michael, 1963: 384–394. The example is from Lindemann, in Tanner, 1960: 25.

102 K. Menninger, 1963: 81–86; J. Cumming and Cumming, 1962: chap. 3.

103 Durkheim, 1915: 416.

104 A. F. C. Wallace, 1961a; for other sources, see Deardorff, 1951; A. C. Parker, 1913; A. F. C. Wallace, 1952a.

105 A. F. C. Wallace, 1952a: 343.

106 A. F. C. Wallace, 1956a; 1956b; 1957; and 1961b: 16 and chap. 4. For a classification of cult movements, see A. F. C. Wallace *et al.*, 1959.

Social Personality and National Character

4

The important thing to know is not the way in which a certain thinker individually conceives a certain institution but the group's conception of it; this conception alone is socially significant.[1]
ÉMILE DURKHEIM

All our human thought and activity is either individual or social, according to how you look at it, the two being no more than phases of the same thing. . . .[2]
CHARLES HORTON COOLEY

SOCIAL PERSONALITY

In distinction to those psychiatrists and psychologists who devote their major efforts to understanding or treating personality in individuals, psychological anthropology definitely prefers to deal with personality characteristics attached to a plurality of individuals. The characteristics may in varying degree be shared by the great majority or all of the subjects or, in Boas' words, a characterization may be "merely a conceptualization of those traits that are found in a large number of individuals and are, for this reason, impressive" whereas "in another population other traits impress themselves upon the mind and are conceptualized."[3] The collection of traits itemized and systematically grouped will be called "the personality of the 'so-and-so,'" even though no individual member of the "so-and-so" perfectly portrays them all, just as no individual in the group perfectly represents the whole culture which men, women, children, royalty, and commoners jointly share and maintain. By the term "social personality"*

* In an earlier book[4] I used "modal personality" to express the same idea. I have now decided to restrict that term ("modal personality") and apply it solely to conceptions of social personality arrived at statistically by using the concept of the mode, something I shall explain very soon.

I intend to convey the idea that any culturally distinctive aggregate of individuals, if suitably studied with the help of psychological concepts and techniques, can be made to reveal a fairly general system of overt and covert behavior—a personality—which, however, no particular member of the aggregate need reveal in its entirety. Men have attempted such characterizations since the Periclean Greeks.[5] Hippocrates (c. 460–377 B.C.) and Galen (c. 130–200 A.D.) made them, using a notion of temperament, and the Arab social scientist Ibn-Khaldun (1332–1406) discerned common patterns of feeling in races, even though they were divided among several nations and cultures as well as in culturally defined peoples.[6] In 1748, as I have already said, David Hume[7] wrote an essay to clarify the idea of national character and to disprove the theory that environment caused it. Nineteenth-century German historians sought to capture in words a folk's unified spirit, soul, or mentality, clues which Wilhelm von Humboldt (1767–1835) sought in language.[8] Émile Durkheim,[9] Gustav le Bon, and other French sociologists stressed the socially derived collective consciousness that Durkheim regarded as "the highest form of psychic life," yet declared couldn't be studied by the tools of psychology, at least not those available in his time.[10] More recent terms, like group psychological trends, basic personality, ethnic personality, and collective world view, each possessing its own specifically designated shade of meaning, all denote what I call social personality; namely, personality characteristics found in social aggregates.

George Devereux,[11] who prefers to use the term "ethnic personality," visualizes it as starting on the basement level with an ethnic unconscious, which in small-scale social systems remains remarkably laxly repressed. As a result, its amoral contents escape readily, and in only slightly disguised form. (Devereux, a psychiatrist by profession, is largely alone among anthropologists in still clinging to the evolutionary doctrine that primitive people are uncivilized because they lack the psychic characteristics that only appeared with cultural advances.) Apart from blind, instinctual drives that press for gratification regardless of logic and morality, a community's ethnic unconscious contains shared emotions, residues of former bodily states, and shallowly buried fantasies. Shamans, Devereux believes, in practically every culture occupy a privileged niche that allows them freely to translate into action the most bizarre material from the ethnic unconscious, whose expression other members of the community readily comprehend, for their conscious egos perceive it as no distant stranger. Devereux cites men among the North American Plains Indians who, by donning the clothes and playing the roles of women, openly dramatized their homosexual fantasies without meriting social disapproval. Like Devereux, Bronislaw Malinowski[12] also suggested that defense mechanisms, especially repression, vary with culture, an observation that also serves to explain certain differences in the behavior of U.S. middle-class and lower-class youngsters.[13]

There are nearly as many ways of ordering a social personality as there have been investigators willing to attempt to do so, or as there are theories that enable one to grasp personality. Strongly influenced by psychoanalytic theory, many who ventured to study personality in culture have heavily concerned themselves with unconscious motivating states and other, equally "deep" psychological processes. Although to work on this level often provides an easy way of systematically reconciling a large number of discrete, often contradictory, attributes that people display in everyday life, it is not the only possible approach to studying social personality. If I picture an Eskimo community as being comprised of openly friendly, spontaneous, confident, and opti-

George Devereux

mistic people, who are somewhat narcis-sistically preoccupied with their public image, sensitive and easily hurt, and highly flexible rather than compulsive about calls of duty and order—that is descriptive of social personality, though it penetrates the system to only a very shallow depth.[14] Clues for such a description I take directly from the way Eskimos smile when we en-counter one another on the trail leading down to the river; I need no theory other than common sense born of experience to interpret the hidden meaning of the smile. I also draw on the ease with which a house-hold cooperates and on the way both sexes and all ages mix when the community plays ball in the summer evening. I note the way girls take pride in fresh, clean clothes, and the way a small boy sulks after a passing troop of Indians has mildly bullied him, and I use those facts as additional primary clinical data. What some writers have called

ethos[15] is often a psychological manner of describing a culture's style,[16] with empha-sis put on *how* people act, think, and feel, and make things, rather than on what they do, think, or make. One may be satisfied to stop with such an assessment of a people's expressive style of behavior, or go further and identify covert psychodynamic proc-esses that underlie the emotional over-tones, which are then regarded as efferes-cences mirroring the course of internal, motivational events.[17]

NATIONAL CHARACTER

Margaret Mead has unquestionably done most to refurbish the ancient idea of social personality, primarily with the aim of ap-plying it, under the name "national charac-ter," to contemporary practical problems.[18] Though methods, yet to be fully devised, appropriate for studying national character must be exceedingly complex since the sub-ject is so large, the concept itself is clear: A nation's culture—nationwide institutions, like the two-party system, education, and money—is embodied in the intrapsychic structure of its individual members, varying with their social position and degree of na-tional participation. Except that Mead spe-cifically mentions nations, this is the basic idea with which, following Edward Sapir, I introduced this book, when I defined culture and personality as an approach to cultural understanding that views culture as it is embodied in individuals. Mead proposes to study the way people learn their historically derived national character, starting in child-hood, and the way they daily live and ex-press it. "National character" isn't identical with my use of the term "character struc-ture" in the previous chapter. Instead of restricting her concept to nuclear motivat-ing states of personality, Mead saddles it with such relatively peripheral characteris-tics as attitudes to heat and cold; the conceptions of children's capacity to learn; attitudes to music or history; perception of the two-party system or the emperor; and so on. She explicitly dissociates herself from research that polls and tabulates the attitudes different countries hold toward war, peace, premarital sexuality, belief in God, and other subjects. Polling, she points out, demands precise sampling in order to measure variation between social classes and other categories comprising a national community, a matter of much less concern in national character research.[19] Also, she feels that putting too many questions to people so fragments their responses that it becomes virtually impossible to assemble systematically their answers so as to formulate the contours of their national character. She wants to deal with whole people, not with their discrete attitudes or their habits in this and that situation. In her conception, national character research avoids listing isolated attributes of national behavior; for example, after the fashion of Salvador de Madariaga,[20] who saw action dominant in Englishmen, thought in Frenchmen, and passion or feeling in Spaniards. (This approach is followed in many articles in the French quarterly *Revue de Psychologie des Peuples.*) Nor is the national-character approach, in her sense of the term, concerned with national self-images and studies of how others see us, worthwhile as such information may be.

The theoretical basis of the approach Mead recommends for studying national character—which is, I believe, also the approach followed by anthropologists investigating social personality in small communities—rests on four assumptions:

First, it regards each way of life and, within it, each system of personality, as a whole—a system. Consequently, how people behave in one area of culture—around the kitchen table, say—is significantly related to their behavior in other situations. Personality traits that children learn at

home can also be witnessed by them, and exercised, in other social situations extending into adulthood. Culture is a whole partly because the same people, who have learned the same basic ways of responding, participate in many different cultural situations. It is only logical that they should link those situations by infusing them with common ways of acting, thinking, and feeling. Largely on account of the holistic approach she adopts, Mead believes that national character doesn't lend itself to very precise measurement. Holism in anthropology demands skill in recognizing common patterns of behavior, picking them out as they run through diverse situations and appear in such highly varied materials as motion pictures, novels, Rorschach protocols, and comic books.

Second, anthropologists assume that, regardless of cultural differences, people everywhere possess the same basic human nature. A normal child born in China is endowed precisely like a Russian child (except for individual differences), and both are equally capable of learning any culture. Consequently, differences in the way they learn and in what they become must be accounted for in terms of socially patterned experience. It follows that human beings owe their social personality not to race or national origin but to other persons who mediated it—communicated it, verbally as well as nonverbally—in ways that I shall take up in later chapters. Anthropologists and other travelers who participate fully and for a long time in a culturally different community have the opportunity to learn a second personality, just as they can learn their hosts' language. Immigrants, of course, even more thoroughly recast their social personality as they learn a new culture. The assumption of psychic unity permits an investigator to apply the same principles of psychology to every people and to use his experience in his own culture (or with other cultures he has studied) as controls when he tries to grasp significant features in another.

Far more striking than these two rather commonplace postulates, is the third: the assumption of representativeness that confidently asserts that every member of a nation (or of any other social system that maintains a culture) is systematically representative of its culture: meaning that each member embodies it in an appropriate way, depending on age, sex, and other status characteristics. Rather than claiming that everyone is the same, as critics who have misread Mead accuse her of saying, she maintains that every person—ruler and subject, employer and employee, middle-class and lower-class—embodies the same culture differently, depending on his social position. When people of different statuses interact, however, each responds to a recognizable stimulus in the other. Throughout life, by participating in social interaction, we reinforce our national character; we confirm the version we originally learned as children or, should change occur, we alter it.

This leads to the fourth, primarily methodological, assumption: Even in a social system as large as a modern nation, any member of the system can provide some information about the national character. Hence, it isn't necessary to collect identical facts from all the informants. An anthropologist, as he describes the total pattern of learned behavior characteristic of the group, systematically assembles and combines data from a series of individuals.[21] He must, of course, screen out his informants' idiosyncratic personality traits, which contribute nothing to a knowledge of either national character or social personality. He must with equal vigilance evaluate each informant's place in the nation's social system, especially the degree to which each participates in it. An immigrant of ten years' standing will represent his new culture less fully than a 30-year-old, native-born citizen; an executive or lower-class person will each embody different regularities than a worker or someone of the middle class. Do not assume homogeneity when talking about national character no matter how holistically you may be oriented. Keep your eyes wide open to the manifold cultural distinctions that mark groups, classes, and other social categories in a modern national community; the job is to find out how every social subdivision in its own way embodies cultural patterns, and then to find common patterns. Careful study—a good deal more careful, no doubt, than any yet done—requires that occupants of all significant classes, ethnic groups, occupations, and geographic regions be included in one's roll of informants. So big an order demands costly, time-consuming research and teamwork of a new kind, for to remain holistic the teammates working with different samples of the population must be regularly brought together to share one another's information and to integrate their growing understandings, thereby replicating as far as possible the single fieldworker who controls all the known materials on a culture and integrates them in a single mind.[22] Any category of people who exert powerful political or other decisive social influence in the nation must certainly be studied. The Communist elite, engaged in deliberately forging a new Soviet character structure, could hardly be overlooked by anyone studying Soviet national character; and in Pakistan, West Pakistanis (especially émigrés from Uttar Pradesh in India) can't be skipped because they spearhead considerable planning for the new nation. Such powerful groups are particularly important from a practical point of view—something that Margaret Mead always bears in mind —for it is with their members that foreign governments deal through diplomatic channels.

In national settings of prodigous complexity and heterogeneity, where political parties or rival interest groups vie for power and diametrically opposed movements and policies compete for support, is it reasonable to expect to find any regularities of national character? Mead argues cogently that nations, however diversified they may be, also possess nationwide institutions to which everyone is in some degree and in his own characteristic way exposed; therefore it is quite reasonable to look for traces of such exposure in everyone. She could also claim that modern nations don't remain viable without diffusing among their members general principles; values; conceptions of past, present, and future; a national identifying image; perhaps a sense of threat, and quite likely feelings of patriotism. Modern means of mass communication are well equipped to disseminate such basic understandings. As new nations come into being, we can look for new national characters to take form, as a Soviet Russian national character and a Pakistani one have already emerged. On the other hand, as I have previously warned, the utility of statements of national character is restricted by the way in which they have mostly been obtained; for example, deduced from nonrepresentative samples of unknown size made up of persons, novels, movies, or other expressive social products. Such statements are imaginatively insightful, but, however critically they may have been composed, they provide only the roughest sort of map, one too general for a wayfarer to trust himself to who wants to find his way along foreign byways and in and out of unfamiliar social corners.

Up until the present at least, most reports of national character have resembled a public-opinion survey less than they have been like a historian's account of the temper of an age, or like Hogarth's pictorial representations of eighteenth-century London types. Perhaps you see no use for psychological interpretations of that sort, regardless of how tentatively they may be

Margaret Mead (Black Star—Bob Levin)

couched. Then you have company. Today, many scholars emphatically divorce themselves not only from national character and social personality research but also from other features of anthropology that perpetuate the discipline's humanistic heritage. Such scholars, who are trying out more precise ways of gauging socially patterned systems of thinking and feeling, will regard the comparison I just drew between a certain type of research and painting as most unfelicitous. It will call up such modes of knowing as intuition, which, however fully documented the conclusions may be, they reject out of hand as unworthy of cultivation. (I myself believe that to reject any path to knowledge is to choose to be that much poorer—but we'd better not get into *that!*) On the other hand, the destinations toward which alternative ways of knowing lead should not be confused with one another. National-character studies interpret and explain national styles of activity, thought, and feeling in a summarizing fashion that some people find helpful and revealing. They report the labor of fertile and creative minds which have grappled creatively with a multiplicity of exotic cultural cues. Should they not be judged by criteria appropriate to what they are about, rather than by standards more appropriate to some other mode of knowledge?

Experience has taught anyone who would make generalizations concerning national character to be prepared for the consequences, including hostility vented by subjects who believe they have been misrepresented or misunderstood. To reduce such risk and to curtail other unwelcome side effects—which nowadays threaten practically every anthropologist, for we mostly work with people who are learning to read—the investigator must observe continuous, watchful responsibility, anticipating how unqualified words or phrases might be perceived by people possessing a different self-view and world view. Despite the risk, open and even popular publication of national-character studies is extremely important, both in order to invite correction of errors and to prevent information from becoming a manipulative or destructive tool in the hands of a special-interest group.

Mirage of uniformity

Examine your own personality and you will find, along with features that you share with others in your social system, behavior that is distinctively you. With others you believe, albeit it your own way, that everyone deserves an equal break and that material possessions in fair measure are good because they enhance comfort, health, or similar desirable ends. You share with them patterns of doing hair, lips, or fingernails, of greeting friends, making dates, and drinking Cokes. But you have also your own way of expressing yourself, your private fantasies, your personal gait. Clearly, your social personality, no matter how meager or broad it is, doesn't negate your individuality, nor does it mean that you have been completely homogenized or absorbed into your group. Complete conformity is inconceivable.[23] At the same time, the reach of social patterning is nearly complete; traits you share with others may be individually styled to suit the pattern of your own personality, but even your most personal characteristics aren't wholly idiosyncratic; they bear the stamp of the culture by which you live. True, I lecture in a distinctive manner, but in that manner American—not British or Pakistani—national character stands revealed.

How about deviants? Aren't there people in every society who escape the reach of others' expectations, who strut aggressively where most men are obediently meek, or who prefer passivity where the ideal calls for forceful self-assertion? Among the mild, gentle Arapesh of New Guinea, deviants are the violent and aggressive men and women; nearby, among the Mundugumor, where men are supposed to be harsh and violent, it is the mild-mannered man who though he causes no trouble finds life congenial only in fantasy.[24] But deviance is more than failing to show the expected quality in behavior or going to the opposite extreme. A deviant may overplay the ideal, as a Mundugumor does who is *too* violent, who exceeds the approved style of behavior so grossly that he is put to death. Deviants are an undeniable fact in every social system, but even they have been reached by social patterning and so embody traces of the very expectations they violate. Recognizing the importance many Americans at-

(National Character Is Deduced from Many Different Cultural Clues

A few years ago we took three bodies of material—statistical work done on the
American soldier, the songs American soldiers sang, and the newspaper
published in the European theater by American soldiers—and put them
together. We found the same regularities running through all of them.[25]

MARGARET MEAD

I shall take a very small sample of data and use it to demonstrate how an anthropologist utilizes many different clues in formulating even a single dimension of national character:

Clue one: A French teacher criticizes her American pupils, saying, "American children enjoy too much liberty and independence."[26]

Second set of clues: Rorschachs taken from French adults reveal that subjects show
a tendency to dehumanize; see figures as mythological beings or toys rather than as
humans. The subjects also distantiate figures, making them remote in time and space,
rather than contemporary. Finally, they often immobilize animals and the few human
figures that they do project into the cards, so that the figures lack movement and appear stiff or static.[27]

Third set of clues: Paintings by French children, 11 to 16 years old, that deal with
the liberation of Paris from the Nazis show French civilians standing in the streets
simply looking at a parade of tanks and soldiers. In other pictures, child artists also
tend to suppress forceful action; for example, keeping the perpetrators of violence
offstage.[28]

A configurational-minded anthropologist suspects that these three kinds of data contain regularities that make them overlap in a variety of ways because they form part
of a single culture and have been executed by people who embody the same culture.
So he asks himself: What regularities do they reveal? What aspects of national character do they reflect? He keeps in mind that characteristics of national character are
learned, and so expects to get clues to whatever runs through the three sets of data by
taking into account what he knows about French children's socialization. He knows
the prevailing attitude behind education in the French family and school to be one
directed to making the child a proper person. The French believe that to attain this
goal requires a long apprenticeship and firm discipline; they liken an individual to a
fruit tree that must be carefully cultivated, grafted, pruned, and trained. Great emphasis is put on control of impulses, for only through such control can an adult be
produced who is capable of enjoying happiness, maximizing *bonheur* and minimizing
malheur. Lack of control resulting from insufficient training opens the way for all
kinds of dreadful possibilities; a person may become too self-denying or too indulgent,
both bad extremes. He becomes like an animal.[29] Knowing this emphasis in French
socialization makes it logical to deduce, merely as a hypothesis, that French national
character strongly approves of maintaining intellectual and emotional control. (Note:
I avoid claiming that childrearing alone causes the French to value emotional control.
I also don't say that every Frenchman actually supervises his thoughts, feelings, and
actions; I simply deduce that he greatly approves of doing so.) This deduction—that
French value control—is consistent with the three sets of data referred to. See how the

deduction fits the clues or, from another point of view, how the clues reveal that the French emphasize intellectual and, especially, emotional control:

Clue one: The teacher is objecting to American education which, from the standpoint of her own educational ideal and national character, she sees as imposing too little discipline and inculcating too little control.

Second set of clues: By dehumanizing, distantiating, and immobilizing Rorschach figures, subjects strive to maintain inner control. They are freezing their creations or removing them to a safe distance so that their dangerousness will be reduced. This is a mode of defending against impulses, especially aggressive ones.

Third set of clues: Let Martha Wolfenstein explain the lack of forceful human movement in French children's paintings: It "is indicative of the strong restraint imposed on energetic outward drives . . . a strong contrast between French and American children's art. . . ."[30]

One could go further, specifying the nature of the control that the French try to maintain. It does not lead to rigidity like that found among some northern Canadian Indians, including the Kaska. It fails to create binding inhibitions in French character. Rather, as de Madariaga said, Frenchmen are inclined to supervise their feelings in the name of intellect, but not utterly to suppress them.

The anthropologist will continue to work with other data from French culture, watchfully observing whether anything contradictory to the concept of control comes forward to demand modification of his hypothesis. In the same way that he formulated this regularity of French national character, he looks for additional regularities in the same as well as in other data, gradually building up a full, if tentative, model.[31]

tach to conformity, the Beats openly scorned it but their very rejection, like sacrilege that profanes the Host, symbolized its "reversed" presence in the rebels' social personality. Even the choice of whatever pattern of deviance a person selects may be made from a cultural stock of alternatives with which he is familiar and that suits the pattern of his social personality. A Manus might grow up in his Admiralty Island lagoon village to be a rapist, but he is unlikely to become a kind and considerate lover because his culture gives him no opportunity to attach those qualities to the sexual role.[32] Conversely, a sane Arapesh would find rape nearly incomprehensible, but not passive homosexuality. Among the Arapesh, the most active child having been raised in passivity will be less aggressive than a normal American child, though of course still conspicuously aberrant in the context of Arapesh life.[33] In any event, deviant no less than nondeviant behavior is socially patterned.[34] (Of course, nobody is deviant in everything, but only in some features of his behavior; he therefore embodies many of the same patterns of culture that others do.)

Now we can redefine social personality, noting that it designates any aspects of personality which an individual develops as a consequence of living in a particular society, at the same time that he develops his idiosyncratic personality. Clearly—and I have already cited Margaret Mead, who makes the same point most emphatically— it is incongruous to conceive of social personality or national character as a set of close uniformities which everybody embodies in precisely the same way.[35] Social personality is a general pattern of activity, thought, and feeling abstracted from a cross

(U. S. Department of Labor)

⊂ Corner-Boys Embody the American Social Personality's Goal of
Achievement But Don't Always Act It Out

*. . . the goals upon which the college-boy places such great value, such as
intellectual and occupational achievement, and the college-boy virtues of
ambitiousness and pride in self-sufficiency are not as such disparaged by the
corner-boy culture. The meritoriousness of standing by one's friends and the desire
to have a good time here and now do not by definition preclude the desire
to help oneself and to provide for the future. It is no doubt the rule, rather
than the exception, that most children, college-boy and corner-boy alike,
would like to enjoy the best of both worlds. In practice, however, the substance
that is consumed in the pursuit of one set of values is not available for the
pursuit of the other. The sharpness of the dilemma and the degree of the
residual discontent depend upon a number of things, notably, the
intensity with which both sets of norms have been internalized, the extent to which
the life-situations which one encounters compel a choice between them, and the
abundance and appropriateness of the skills and resources at one's disposal.*[36]

A. K. COHEN

section of individuals, none of whom manifests the total pattern perfectly. Mead[37] would say that social personality refers to a set of broad regularities running through behaviors manifested by an organized aggregate of people in a wide range of situations, as well as being reflected in the things they make and use. People living together in communities, especially in modern nations, differ too much from one another to allow thinking of them as uniform in any but the broadest sense.

SOCIAL CHARACTER

An author prefers his own terms to designate what others have already labeled in *their* favorite ways, and so it is with Erich Fromm, who uses "social character" for the way people sharing the same way of life feel and perceive.[38] Social character, the nuclear, regnant center of personality that combines ego and motivation in its operation, has a job to do. It channels people's energy in such a way that, without too much reflection and indecision, they will actually want to do the central tasks they have to do, because around those tasks their social system is pivotally organized. Some social systems are so set up, culturally speaking, that they encourage friendly, outgoing, receptive people, whereas others to get their jobs done demand exploitative social characters revealed in people who unhesitatingly manipulate each other for the sake of their own ends. Still other communities rear self-centered, hoarding personalities.

Fromm, a psychiatrist by profession, has consistently preferred to study his own society in both its historical and contemporary aspects. Many of his books examine today's industrial civilization with its demands that people be on time, produce and consume prodigiously, and get along easily with one another, especially on the job. He

sees our civilization meeting those and other demands by producing men endowed with a character structure that enables them to cooperate smoothly and unrebelliously and to cramp themselves into the impersonal slots of industrial and bureaucratic enterprises without feeling imposed upon. Bitterly, Fromm describes Western man's sense of individual powerlessness, which allows him readily to bow to authority; his hunger for social approval, which makes him fit into groups conformingly; his largely spurious sense of freedom, which enables him to be commanded by anonymous authority while yet illusorily believing in his own autonomy; and his readiness to appraise his worth and security by the number and amount of goods he possesses, which perfectly suits a capitalist economy that must produce or be doomed.

Fromm's view of social personality is probably the most selective of any similar concepts that you will encounter in this chapter, for it recognizes primarily those few governing motivations that gear people to the main goals toward which a social system is headed. His premise—that every system shapes human nature to conform to its needs—is quite in keeping with the dominant assumption of modern social science, which emphasizes society's primacy over the individual and even defines human nature in terms of learned behavior. Yet, unlike the more extreme social determinists, Fromm explicitly recognizes imperative physiological and psychological human needs that require fulfillment and that help to shape social conditions. Society cannot frustrate those needs beyond a certain threshold, or its members will try to change the social order to make it more compatible with their nature. Should they fail in that attempt, the society will probably collapse. When Fromm goes on to say that the mode of production plays an especially strong part in molding social character, industrial capitalism shaping modern man's along the

Erich Fromm (Bender, New York)

lines just summarized, he recalls what Karl Marx wrote in 1859: "The mode of production of material life conditions the social, political and intellectual life process in general . . . [for] It is not the consciousness of men that determines their being, but, on the contrary, their social being that determines their consciousness."[39] I don't fortuitously draw a parallel between Fromm and Marx, for the psychiatrist has been a long and devoted student of Marxian humanism. Like Marx, Fromm speaks with a strongly redemptorist tone, hoping to rescue men from economic and political conditions which block them from developing a healthy social character by alienating them from wholesome relations with fellow men, encouraging false values, and sapping independence.[40] He recognizes, of course, that no system of production can create social character except through social relations, and that it is parents and teachers who mediate the social system's needs. Through translating those needs into expectations,

rules, and rewards appropriate to nursery, home, and school, the cultural surrogates[41] bring a social character into being.

BASIC PERSONALITY

Abram Kardiner, another psychiatrist whom I mentioned when I spoke about the psychological process of projection, uses the term "basic personality" to identify his concept of social personality.[42] He dwells on the role of deeply unconscious motives whose play facilitates or hampers survival and other adaptive tasks in charge of the ego. Like Fromm, he is much concerned with elements in personality that control the individual's social relationships, especially those affecting his ability to establish satisfactory relations with others. Such interests, of course, belong to the major concerns of psychoanalysis, the theory which both men closely follow (though in somewhat different versions).

A basic personality arises out of relatively common experiences—"primary institutions" Kardiner calls them—that children in a social system meet in the way they are fed; are weaned; receive affection; become toilet-trained, and learn to handle sex, dependence, and hostility. The earliest such experiences center in the family; therefore any change in that group's tasks and organization can substantially affect basic personality formation. When Kardiner explains precisely how the primary institutions impinge on young individuals, he pays particular heed to traumatic experiences that children encounter in the primary institutions. The impact of such traumas exercises a powerful, formative influence, to the extent that subsequent, positive experiences do not outweigh or counter them. Early traumatic events leave lasting, unconscious traces in feelings that become consolidated, strangulate the ego, impoverish self-esteem, and set up a strong need for compensatory

Abram Kardiner

activities, thereby coming to play strong motivational roles that interfere with the ego's capacity to adapt and adjust. What determines a community's parental attitudes, family organization, and all-important childrearing practices? The society's larger organizaton, Kardiner answers, including the way people produce their subsistence. The primary institutions in any community depend closely on parents' economic roles, for a mother cannot be fully nurturant if her duties require her to spend entire days working away from home and child. Once basic personality is set—and that, remember, occurs early in life—it is no longer easily altered. The past lives on, consolidated in the constellation of feelings, and adults draw on it when, in a potentially endless chain, they treat their children as their parents treated them. People may even adopt new elements in their culture without changing their basic personality; they do so whenever they borrow a new religion or folktale which they projectively endow with

familiar meaning, or when they unconsciously refashion a borrowed element to make it congruent with their own, rather than the exporting group's, emotional needs. A decisive change in basic personality demands cultural changes far-reaching enough to alter primary institutions.

In addition to the motivating constellation of feelings implanted by early traumatic experiences, Kardiner reserves a place in basic personality for empirical knowledge and skills that provide a realistic basis for coping with environment. However, he underplays rational strategies in striving, even though in some communities (like the aboriginal Comanche Indians) they, rather than projective coping patterns, dominate basic personality. A basic personality dominated by its reality system, Kardiner acknowledges, adapts considerably more effectively than one in which emotional needs sit in control and press for compensation. Projection appears only slightly in the way people work with tools and use weapons in pursuit of food and for protection compared to the way it crowds into their religion, art, folktales, and other "secondary institutions," as well as in people's day-to-day concerns regarding scarcity or illness. Emotional needs can also be detected operating in social relationships; for example, in financial partners' mutual fear of being humiliated or in men's one-sided, exaggerated dependence on women. Secondary institutions and similar expressive behavior allow people to maintain relative equilibrium by periodically discharging accumulated tension emanating from those perduring traces of unhappy early experiences.

"THEY ARE NOT AWARE OF THEIR WRETCHEDNESS"

Kardiner achieved one of his best-documented interpretations of personality in culture when he delineated the basic personality of Papuan pagans living in Atimelang, a malarious village in the mountains of a small, obscure, Indonesian jungle island, Alor.[43] Let's start, as he does, by analyzing the primary institutions. These are themselves governed by the fact that during the wet season, women's economic role allows them to spare only about 10 to 14 days to devote themselves fully to a newborn child. Thereupon they resume their work in their vegetable gardens, leaving an older sibling or grandmother to care for the baby. Caretakers more or less conscientiously feed the infant premasticated roasted bananas and vegetable food, which it frequently spits back even though it remains hungry much of the time until the mother returns in the late afternoon to offer her breast. All during infancy, maternal care remains inconsistent and undependable, birth launching children on a long, largely unaided struggle with hunger and other tensions. Only sporadically are those tensions relieved by practices like sleeping on the mother's mat at night or masturbation, something a young caretaker may do when he cannot pacify an infant's hunger. A father lavishes attention on his child to the extent that he is not engrossed in financial and ceremonial occupations on which his prestige depends. A young child encounters no one in his environment with whom he can associate with dependable relief and gratification, nor does later childhood decisively change his predicament. In fact, his situation then worsens, because he is no longer carried and is even less provided with food

⟪ Basic Personality in Action[44]

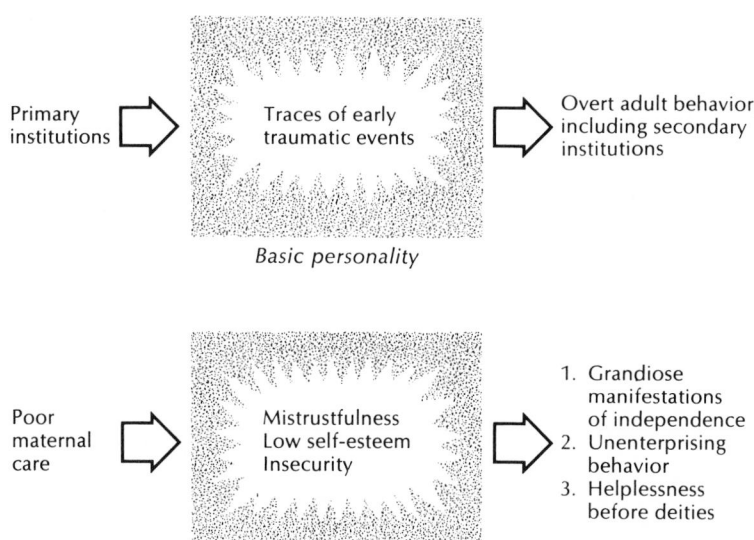

Basic personality

At the top, an abstract model shows basic personality mediating between primary institutions of childhood and adult behavior. Below it, data have been fed into the model to illustrate how poor maternal care in childhood creates painful feelings which generate certain overt, expressive adult behaviors. Mistrustful people with low self-esteem may overtly proclaim grandiose independence or, more isomorphically, may act unenterprisingly and openly admit their helplessness, in rituals directed toward powerful deities.

during the day than he was in infancy. Children suffer from a combination of hunger, desertion, and miscellaneous discomfort, including itching sores and augmented distress caused when the wounds are roughly medicated. During weaning, they are deliberately provoked to jealousy by the mother's teasingly putting another child to her breast.[45] Speech, walking, and other levels of independence they attain with a minimum of assistance or encouragement. Little wonder that youngsters show their frustration, protest, and rebellion in temper tantrums, but such attempts at vigorous self-assertion go as ignored as the children themselves, or else are violently suppressed. The child's chief resource is to take forcefully and by stealth that which he is denied, especially food. Foraging, widespread among freeroving bands of children and resented only when it becomes too constant or when food is scarce, as well as outright thieving from the gardens, provide the developing ego with opportunity to assert itself, to take vengeance on parents, and to test its growing independence. Boys can roam more freely than girls, for they aren't counted on to render any useful service until they are 13 or 14, but girls early join their mothers working in the gardens and help with cooking. This has the advantage of allowing them to eat more regularly than boys. Both sexes remain helplessly subject to adults' humiliation, teasing, ridicule, deception, and, where their personal possessions are concerned, contemptuous high-handedness. Any irritated adult freely administers corporal punishment for infractions that the youngster did not manage to conceal. With growing maturity, sex play as well as aggression come to be frowned upon, but sex merely goes underground, and children still vent aggression by taking revenge on younger children through spite and ridicule. Seldom if ever have anthropologists in their fieldwork discovered a harsher early milieu.

Now to the Alorese basic personality, which, theory predicts, should contain many feelings traceable to childhood's many unrelieved traumas. Early life indeed creates more tensions than it provides avenues of discharge for; as a result it loads the ego with many restrictive, defensive inhibitions and incapacitating confusions whose net effect is low self-esteem. People find it impossible to sustain great effort. In the face of danger and difficulty, they quickly collapse or surrender. As an aftermath of the childhood temper tantrums that adults sometimes violently suppressed, the individual cringes in considerable fear of using aggression. A general mistrust governs human relations but along with it, like a counterpoint, runs an incessant, unconscious search for some tension-relieving substitute of the kind, loving parent. The Atimelanger's weak superego reflects his lack of any inspiring parental model. Shame and fear rather than guilt form his major, internalized bases of social control. Women, however, possess a more comfortable, less traumatized internal situation than men, which reflects girls' more favorable early development, including their youthful productive roles at home and in the gardens that offered them opportunities to cultivate greater security and higher self-esteem. But the difference between the sexes is small. Kardiner concludes his interpretation of Alorese psychodynamics by stating that basic personality in Atimelang, which got off to a bad start, remains "anxious, suspicious, mistrustful, lacking in confidence, with no interest in the outer world." It is also "devoid of enterprise . . . filled with repressed hatred and free floating aggression over which constant vigilance must be exercised. . . . devoid of high aspirations and has no basis for the internalization of discipline." In a social system occupied by such people, "Cooperation must be at a low level and a tenuous social cohesion can be achieved only by dominance-submission at-

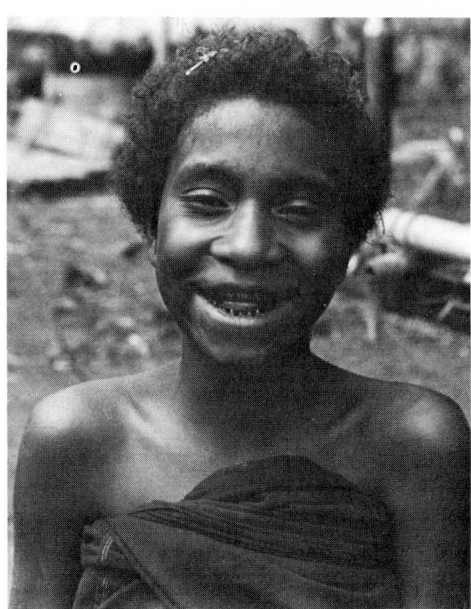

Fuimai is making string by rolling fibers on her thigh.
Padafan begs food from a baby lying in its mother's carrying shawl.
This Alorese girl's front teeth have just been blackened and filed.
Laying down tally sticks in reckoning a divorce settlement. (all Cora Du Bois)

WHAT HAPPENS IN ALORESE EARLY CHILDHOOD[46]

```
                                        ┌─ Desertion
  Poor maternal care  ◄────────────────── Hunger
                                        └─ Misrepresentation and lying

                                        ┌ Maternal image confused;
                                        │ neither inflated nor idealized
                                           ┌ Hatred ⎫
                                           │         ⎬ Ambivalence
                                           └ Love   ⎭

         Ego                              ─ Striving with outer world unaided;
                                            no interest in mastery
                                              └── Inhibited

                                          ─ Tendency to displace dependence
                                            on parent-surrogates

  Disciplines provide no early           ─ Ego-ideal, that portion deriving from mother,
  sense of responsibility, insist          possesses low achievement capacities
  little on obedience, impose
  no early economic                      ─ Superego operates chiefly by sanction of shame
  responsibilities, and permit
  sexual gratification for a time        └─ Low self-esteem and fear of outer world
```

Anxiety

Repressed hostility

Overvaluation of food and sex

Lack of self-confidence

titudes, not by affection and mutual trust." Predatory and exploitative trends take the place of tender and cooperative relations with others.

Now let's see how compensatory strivings in Alorese basic personality reveal themselves in a variety of Alorese behaviors, including secondary institutions. We discover lingering traces of a confused and ambivalent attitude toward the mother in men's distrustful relations with women. Men evaluate sexual potency highly because to them it symbolizes a means of finally winning the mother and bracing their self-esteem. But women resent giving themselves sexually to men and also dislike bearing and caring for children. Why? Because their own child-

hood stimulated too little desire to emulate their mother's role. Men require much compensation and show it through frequent demands for presents addressed to the ethnographer, great touchiness, and exaggerated concern with dress and regalia. Both sexes hugely appreciate sexual relations, for they offer an avenue to discharge some of the perduring tensions begun in early life. Keen competition between men engaged in financial transactions give evidence of the way Atimelangers overvalue wealth. The financial transactions serve them as means of bolstering their inadequate self-esteem, compensate for their pervasive lack of self-confidence, and help them symbolically to overcome the despotic father, whose latent image they carry. A strong fear of waste points to a high level of general insecurity, for actually these people rarely face real danger of shortage. Their consistent control over aggression isn't due to a strong, vigilant superego. Rather, the general absence of striking, killing, and even sorcery reveals their dread of aggression and is a consequence of their faulty ego development, which has blocked their whole system of self-assertion. Only in the financial system, with its competitive accumulation, does the basic personality project its enormous fund of hostility. Atimelangers can't plan well or systematize; they lack mechanical ability, and, stunted in their fantasy life, they rank far down on the scale of aesthetic development. These are all traits that can be traced back to early maternal neglect which strangulated the ego, arresting it in its ability to deal with the outer world. People manifest primarily negative attitudes to the supernatural, to their ancestral spirits whose powers for doing good they leave unexaggerated. They practice their religion in a highly formalized, rather than personal or meaningful, way. No trace exists of a bountiful god, and nobody tries to insure lasting supernatural good will by exemplary behavior. All of which goes to show that as children Atimelangers never found it worth while to try to influence their parents so that the latter would do good to them. As adults they find it similarly pointless to deal with supernaturals as though they could provide any benefits. For Kardiner, as for Freud, religion is built projectively out of the memories of childhood, and the people of Alor have only bitter memories to devote to that end.[47]

Boldly, Kardiner evaluates the Atimelang culture in terms of the people's psychological well-being:

The first thing that can be said about Alor is that it survives, and gives evidence of being an old culture. This is already saying a good deal; for to survive, a culture must have a sufficient number of staying qualities and compatibles to keep it going. However, in the case of Alor the continuance of the society must hang on a very thin thread, chiefly because of the low level of cooperative possibilities and because of its tenuous grip on the external environment. This culture has no place to go, not that progress is an essential factor, as we seem to believe in Western society, but because it must remain completely immobilized. Its survival can be accounted for largely on the basis of the absence of external enemies.

Yet there must be a sufficient number of gratifications for the individual[s] . . . they have plenty of good times and there is a good deal of socializing.[48]

Are the Atimelangers happy? Kardiner finds the question hard to answer, but concludes that at least "they are not aware of their wretchedness."[49]

Today, as I reread Kardiner's interpretation of the Alorese, which I originally read in 1945, I still admire the skill with which he puts his powerful, psychoanalytic theory revealingly to work. But more and more I have come to wonder if such theories don't overpower facts the way a bulldozer flattens a landscape. I know that an observer never mirrors reality, but I believe there is value in knowing how and to what extent distortion occurs. Many of the unconscious ideas and feelings attributed to the Atimelangers, I am quite sure, are really the analyst's own conscious theories, and the impossibility of disentangling those from what the Alorese phenomenologically experience dismays me.[50] Kardiner's nearly unrelieved, negative view of Alorese life, his preoccupation with unfavorable and pathological qualities in their personality, disturbs me now far more than it did in 1945. Since his theory equips him to listen for victimization with

both ears,[51] should he be surprised when
he finds the Atimelangers' wretched lives
hanging on a very thin thread? Without
denying all that he finds, I should still like
to know something about their happy experiences—for note, Kardiner can't bring
himself to say that they are totally unhappy.

ACROSS TRIBAL AND NATIONAL BOUNDARIES

In contrast to anthropologists accustomed
to working with culturally, linguistically, or
politically well-defined systems of varying
scope—like Atimelang village, the Kaska Indian tribe, or Great Russians—an occasional psychiatrist or philosopher has let his
glance escape the conventional boundaries
imposed by language, nationality, or culture
and talked about a Western personality,
Oriental culture, or the "mind of East
Asia."[52] "Area personality," a term more
embracive than social personality, has been
coined to refer to regularities of behavior
abstracted from several culturally different
peoples occupying a geographically intact
territory. Such an idea assumes an originally common tradition that historically
worked itself out in the region, or implies
that common myths, a common religion, a
heavy flow of communication and other
traffic, or conquest possesses the power to
pattern adjacent people's actions, thoughts,
and feelings.[53] The culture of the North
American Great Plains prior to civilization's westward expansion, where Black-
foot, Cheyenne, Comanche, and other
mounted Indian buffalo hunters ranged,
was probably accompanied by a coextensive
area personality which, figuratively speaking, packed the distilled essence of the
component tribal social personalities.[54] In
northeastern North America, including the
Canadian lands of the Cree, Ojibwa, and
Montagnais Indians, sage seventeenth-

century missionaries and explorers, as I
have already mentioned, clearly identified
transcultural personality characteristics.[55]

Cautionary signals greeted the area-per-
sonality concept almost as soon as it was
released. Examining closely two Indian
tribes, the Comanche and Cheyenne, who
both lived in the high Plains, Thomas
Gladwin[56] found their social personalities
to be quite dissimilar with respect to control
exercised over impulses, especially aggression. A Comanche child, who enjoyed remarkable freedom to express himself sexually and aggressively, stood a world removed from the mandatory restraint and
moderation saddling a Cheyenne youngster.
Adults likewise diverged in personality.
Compared to the Cheyenne, whose chiefs in
particular possessed fantastic ego-ideals of
pacifism, the more unrestrained Comanche
displayed aggression within the group almost as readily as outside it. The Cheyenne,
by contrast, hedged out-group aggression by
rules that made it more meritorious for a
warrior in battle to merely touch an enemy
than to kill him.

Carl Jung, who early parted from Sigmund Freud and subsequently withdrew
ever further from the mainstream of psychoanalysis, goes beyond the confines of a
geographical area and ascribes to all mankind a shared personality content that he
calls the "collective unconscious."[57] Innate, a precipitate of history containing
racial memories and traces of a lengthy,
phylogenetic past, the collective unconscious is something quite apart from the
socially patterned phenomena I have so far
mainly been talking about. I include it here
because it too extends beyond tribal and
national boundaries to include personality
characteristics that Jung claims can be perceived in every culture. Among the most
notable tenants of the collective unconscious are primordial images, called archetypes, around which social systems fashion
their cultural symbols, myths, and dreams.

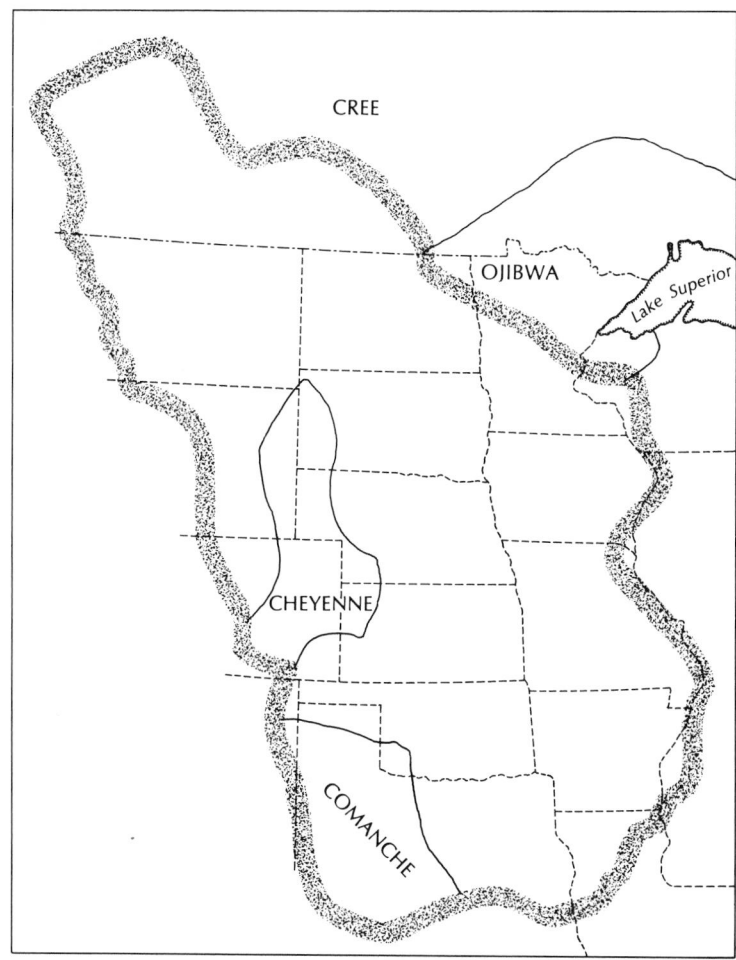

Map showing Great Plains culture area with the location of the Comanche and Cheyenne Indians and other Indian groups.[58]

The equivalence of the cow and mother, and the conception of the father as like a bull recur in many cultures and at many times in history, for they emanate germinally from the same old collective archetypes. Jungians explain phylogenetic memory by postulating it as built into brain itself. We don't inherit ideas but only as yet unidentified structures in the brain that enable archetypes to express themselves recurrently from place to place. Like other phylogenetic hypotheses, of which psychoanalysts seem to be fond,[59] Jung's provocative ideas have also been cold-shouldered by most anthropologists, though he has attracted many followers in other circles.

END OF THE HEYDAY

Some pages back I spoke of being ready in national-character research to face possible consequences, including the resentment and anger of people who are convinced that they have been misrepresented or maligned by what has been written about them. Now

I take up another kind of objection that anthropologists working with social personality and similar ideas have had to face, this one coming from their academic colleagues.[60] Under sharp, questioning criticism concerning the adequacy of the theory and methods being followed in studies of social personality, people who might have found culture and personality an exciting subdiscipline recoiled from it with dismay so great that work in the field began to slow down. Beginning in the late 1940s, when the heyday was over, a number of anthropologists attracted to psychological problems who sought more objective methods for studying social personality characteristics sought them in the Rorschach test and similar poorly defended projective techniques. Although such instruments partly relieved them of having to rely on their own imaginative and creative insights (words that have come to have almost a pejorative connotation in work of this kind), without other behavioral clues gathered through long, diligent fieldwork they are incapable of dealing fully with culture as refracted in individuals.[61] Not surprisingly, the critics' most strident and disheartening objection reiterated something that anthropologists might have readily acknowledged instead of being ashamed of it; namely, the difficulty any second person is likely to encounter who seeks independently fully to reproduce a view of social personality originally formulated by someone else. The process whereby thousands of unsystematically related facts are originally perceived, interpreted, and become integrated defies being set out operationally, like instructions for baking a cake. As with discovery in general, culture-and-personality research depends heavily on the personal qualities of a particular researcher and the conditions under which he works.[62] How one formulates patterns of culture or regularities of social personality is difficult to teach, being learned largely through apprenticeship and

by emulating published work that one admires. What I say will damn psychological anthropology for readers who have been urged to pursue objectivity in social and psychological research to the point where human beings can work with machinelike precision (or at least where different interviewers stationed in various places are getting comparable information). I don't mean to impugn the goal of objectivity, or the techniques that have been devised in sociology and other disciplines for attaining it. Fine work has come through this method, but in choosing it one must pay the cost of bypassing another method that experience proves can also be useful. "What is objectionable is not that some techniques are pushed to the utmost, but that others, in consequence, are denied the name of science."[63] Anyone irresistibly attracted only to objectivity that guarantees precise replication will be unsatisfied in culture and personality. On the other hand, someone who enjoys discovery saddled with few rules—other than the demands of logic and clarity—will prefer disciplines like criticism, history, psychoanalysis, or culture and personality. I exaggerate if I delay adding that those fields certainly allow interpretations to be confirmed, although—and this lends them added zest—on some questions a final verdict is harder to reach.[64] There are those who maintain that the traditional problems set by Sigmund Freud, Ruth Benedict, Margaret Mead, Abram Kardiner, Erich Fromm, and others, together with the methods they used to trace the impact of culture on personality, are on longer valid because social science today investigates different problems with an armamentarium of more rigorous methods.[65]

Accusing social personality and national-character studies of giving an oversimplified impression that psychological uniformity prevails in even culturally complex social systems is an objection that I have already anticipated. The impression may be quite

(*National Museum of India*)

❴ *The Mother Archetype Takes Many Manifestations*[66]

Everywhere the mother archetype manifests itself in various concrete forms, often appearing in things or localities that symbolize fertility and fruitfulness, that possess qualities akin to material solicitude and sympathy, or that exalt the female's spirituality.

Erich Fromm offers a different explanation for such recurrences. He says that to explain the universal character of certain symbols we need not postulate any kind of inheritance. Because every human being shares the same essential bodily and mental equipment—the same human nature—with the rest of mankind, he is capable of producing the understanding symbols based upon common biological attributes. Symbols in different cultures are strikingly similar because they derive from basic sensory and emotional experiences shared by all mankind.

unintended. Margaret Mead, who undauntedly persisted in national-character research, took the problem of internal variation into account, solving it not by sampling or looking for subtypes of national character but by reasoning that the same national institutions are differently embodied in people belonging to various social classes, regions, and occupational groups. Other anthropologists, notably Anthony F. C. Wallace, George Spindler, and Louise Spindler, met the question of heterogeneity by statistical means or by other complex methods which I will examine in the two sections that immediately follow this one. In effect, they acknowledge the suggestion that instead of looking for only one personality type, several should be sought, corresponding to significant groups and categories making up the community. Plausible as this suggestion sounds, it is logically little better justified than the older procedure of generalizing a national-character holding for the majority of nationals; that is, for anyone who has undergone certain common experiences and incorporated them in his personality. True, on this highest possible level of abstraction we fail to recognize subtypes corresponding to social variations by age, sex, class, or region, but by delineating several subtypes of personality attached to such categories won't we in turn be ignoring further variations discoverable by penetrating more deeply into each subtype? Ultimately we will be driven to saying that each individual is different from every other, which is certainly the truth; or to following the "flowing philosopher" Heraclitus, and recognizing that even an individual consists only of change, for his behavior varies from one time and place to another. Generalization is always possible, provided we are willing to abstract, to select logically necessary facts, and to sacrifice the richness of detail that closer focus provides. How far we go in making generalizations depends partly on the kind of knowledge we seek and is partly governed by shifting conventions that prescribe the level of knowledge it is meaningful to reach for.

In what amounts to a criticism of the psychological theories that anthropologists have favored in studying personality in culture, critics chide them for having been too utterly preoccupied with covert behavior, acting as though personality consists only of deeply rooted, difficult-to-verify motives that demand gratification or compensation and project themselves into cultural things. With such set concern for what is nuclear and unconscious, students of social personality neglected, or treated as secondary and "peripheral," more accessible thoughts and feelings as well as overt activity. (Kardiner,[67] taking a diametrically opposite view, accuses culture and personality of being too behavioristic and ignoring motivational phenomena!)

In assenting to the stricture that we anthropologists have been much too attracted to depth psychology, I would add that we have also tended too often to view social personality as not merely enduring but practically inflexible. The theoretical glass through which we peer exaggerates the stability of behavior, if only by putting blinders around our attention and directing it too exclusively to deep-seated, putatively fixed characterological traits. Consequently, the investigator has no equipment with which to observe the way changing conditions redirect, suppress, or release behavior. It is as though he expected Eskimo living under modern conditions in town to remain psychologically the same people they were when they turned out of their small coastal camps to hunt seal. Studies of men at war or surviving under brutalizing conditions in concentration camps indicate that such extreme situations affect human beings as severely as captivity transforms the behavior of nonhuman primates, for example, by increasing animals' aggressiveness. With respect to national character in particular, the tendency to rule out people's situation-bound attitudes from research (how people feel about current threats and other problematic issues, for instance) has been somewhat unfortunate. It has rigidified national character by barring close observation of day-to-day events that influence it.[68]

Anthropologists are also indicted for confusing fact and interpretation, a nearly inevitable result of heavily using psychoanalytic theory in cultural research. It is hard, the critics claim, to recognize what are facts of culture and what is an interpretation put on them. In a sense, this is a weak objection, a naively Baconian view which longs for facts that speak for themselves without needing to be given meaning through concepts supplied by theory. The critics, of course, realize full well that facts in themselves are mute. What they really demand is that the facts first be screened by common-sense theory or concepts, which will present them in familiar form. Then the Alorese men's troubled relationships with women, or the value those men place on sexual potency will be just that, and not vain, repetitive, symbolic attempts to find in women a kind and satisfying mother and in orgasm a substitute for maternal love. Let more abstruse theory be applied to facts only when their matter-of-fact nature has been made clear. I can see why the critics are troubled, but I doubt that they would feel as strongly if they had faith in the power of psychoanalytic theory meaningfully to resolve the symbolic properties of phenomena. After all, psychoanalysts don't trust common-sense concepts but charge them to be products of rationalization and other forms of defensive self-deception! So what is truth?

That Western observers studying exotic personality are inherently biased in their perception, another weakness cited in psychological anthropology, is all too true. But so would a description be biased that portrayed an exotic social personality or national character entirely from within, one insightfully written by a member of the community itself. Far be it from me to disagree with anyone about our need for better concepts with which to understand personality across cultural frontiers. We are far too likely to comprehend guilt, shame, parent-child relationships, stress, and other psychological phenomena primarily in terms of what they mean in our own familiar culture-bound experience, in Western psychiatric practice, and in the limited framework of Euroamerican children's development. Someday, perhaps, our concepts will be expanded and redefined, so that when with technical precision we speak of guilt it will connote more than the Judeo-Christian concept of moral blameworthiness and will incorporate significant nuances of meaning experienced by people who follow other historical traditions. To some extent we already do this with concepts like the family and parental roles, provided that we use them very thoughtfully, stretching our minds to encompass important features we have learned that families and parents possess in, say, India, China, Alor, or among Kaska Indians. We know that tears arise out of strong emotions other than grief, and that shaking signifies courage as well as fear. But much more effort will be required to overcome the ethnocentrism so readily taken for granted in our most common conceptual tools.

Projective tests so often employed in cross-cultural personality research have also been questioned. Are they at all capable of providing the kind of information that investigators confidently draw from them? I have already considered and replied to this objection in Chapter 2, pointing out that wise fieldworkers use the tests circumspectly and as adjuncts, checking what they reveal against other cultural data and, if necessary, modifying an interpretation to make it suit the cultural milieu. A test like the Rorschach provides them with a good opportunity to observe human behavior, but its validity can't be taken for granted.

MODAL PERSONALITY

By implication at least, if not by actual count, social personality or national character refers to psychological characteristics frequent among persons constituting a social system. How frequently? Anthony F. C. Wallace asked. How do we know they occur frequently? He proceeded to answer his questions by arithmetically calculating the types of response most often given to Rorschach test cards by adults in a small American Indian community, and then calculating the number of people who actually came close to sharing those features of behavior. Other anthropologists before him had used the Rorschach test quantitatively; for example, counting the number of times a panel of subjects taking the test used color in formulating their responses and the number of times they perceived humanlike movement in the blots. After dividing such sums by the number of subjects, the investigator took the resulting means as scores computed for an average Rorschach protocol representing a fictional, sexless person. Rather than calculating arithmetic means, Wallace made the mode his basic measure, using it to compare members of a carefully selected sample of Tuscarora Indian adults.[69]

The Tuscarora are an Iroquoian-speaking tribe whose ancestors in the eighteenth century migrated northward from piedmont and coastal North Carolina to join their linguistic congeries. When Wallace visited them in 1949, the Tuscarora were making little effort to maintain an Indian style of life on their thousand square miles of reservation overlooking the Niagara River. Yet their interpersonal relations definitely recall what Hallowell and perceptive early travel-

ers and missionaries had reported about Indians in northeastern North America. In their relations with one another, the Tuscarora impressed Wallace as notably unintense; they acted as though they didn't expect much satisfaction from each other. Social life, even in the family, revealed only shallow affect. They blandly disregarded many individual differences, showing instead a tendency to put people in sharply stereotyped categories, as friend, helper, enemy. Wallace, however, only incidentally heeded personality revealed in such unsystematic fashion. In search of more precise, quantifiable, objective facts, which could to some extent show up independently of his ability to perceive or interpret them, he relied on the Rorschach test, administering it to 70 carefully chosen people between 16 and 71 years old. He selected his sample to represent each adult age category in approximate proportion to its strength in the total population of 350 adults. After obtaining 70 Rorschach protocols from those subjects, he scored the records and for statistical use picked 21 of the scored items. The indicators he chose included the total number of responses given to the 10 cards, the number of humanlike movement responses, the number of color responses, and the proportion of responses which made use of the inkblot's form rather than some other determinant, like shading, color, or texture. From the scores obtained by his 70 subjects on each of the 21 items, he prepared a frequency distribution, asking in effect how many people gave no color responses, one color response, and so on for each of the selected items. Subject number one, for example, a 17-year old youth, gave a total of 10 responses, two of which reported humanlike movement and none of which utilized color; subject number 70, a woman 55 years old, provided a total of 23 responses, none of which recognized human movement in the blots but one of which employed color.

Next, Wallace used the formula for getting the mode and calculated the most frequent score obtained by his sample on each of the 21 items. For the total number of responses, the mode turned out to be 12.5; one single response turned out to be modal for human movement, more people falling in that interval than any other; for use of color, zero was the mode, and for the proportion of form to all other determinants, the mode was 42.5 percent. Using another formula, Wallace calculated a modal class for each of the 21 items, a range on each side of the mode within which, he reasoned, any variation is on mathematical grounds justified as being statistically insignificant. That is, any variation of total responses between 0 and 38 can be regarded as without statistical significance, and this broad range represents the modal class for that item. For human movement, the modal class includes any number of responses from 0 to 4, and for form-determined responses the modal class extends from 24.5 to 60.5 percent. Wallace doesn't assume that a person giving zero movement responses is psychologically identical with someone who offers 4 such responses; his argument is mathematical rather than psychological.

In his next step, Wallace counted the number of Indians who fall within the modal range, or modal class, on *all* 21 Rorschach items, and discovered that 26 do so, or 37 percent of his sample. That is, somewhat more than one third of the Tuscarora adults whom he tested belong to the statistically constructed modal personality type. Needless to say, he doesn't for a moment assume them to be all psychologically identical. An additional 16 individuals come so close to the mode in all 21 items that Wallace feels they could fairly be described in the same psychological terms as the modal group; in fact, for some items they actually fall within the modal range. This leaves him with 28 statistical deviants, individuals who fall within or close to the modal class on only a few items. So far, Wallace has found a statistically based modal personality type defined objectively by scores received for 21 kinds of behavior provoked by the Rorschach inkblots. Twenty-six Tuscarora Indians possess the modal personality, which is to say that they fall within the modal range on all 21 behavioral indicators. What are those men and women like, judging from the behavior they displayed when confronted by the projective test? Wallace hasn't yet told us. Prior to finding out, he took the records of the 26 individuals in the modal class and calculated arithmetic means for each of the 21 Rorschach scores: the mean number of total responses, the mean number of human movement responses, and so on. The central tendencies he derived by this procedure he treated as though they represented results obtained by scoring a single individual's protocol. We are back to the method used by other investigators, delineating the personality manifested by an aggregate of persons by constructing a typical picture which fully represents nobody. Wallace, however, has the advantage of doing so only for individuals who demonstrably share certain modes of response.

Here are some features of this typical Tuscarora Indian's protocol: He took 55.7 seconds to give each response; he gave a total of 12.8 scorable responses, including 8.5 in which he grasped the inkblot as a whole and 1.7 reporting human movement. In 37.6 percent he relied purely on the form of the card when he had the choice of attending to shading, texture, or color as well. To these scores Wallace is ready to apply standard interpretative techniques to the fictional protocol in order to express in psychological terms the personality of the typical statistically modal Indian. I won't detail his interpretation, but only report some features of it which, I remind you, Wallace believes apply also to the submodal category of protocols—hence, to 42 persons in

《 *Two American Indian Modal Personalities: Similarities and Differences Between the Ojibwa and Tuscarora*[70]

Quantification and statistical analysis sharpen cross-cultural comparison. Below are two composite Rorschach profiles (such as Rorschach analysts frequently make for individuals whose records they study) that represent the New York State Tuscarora Indian and the Canadian Ojibwa Indian modal classes. A. Irving Hallowell collected 102 Ojibwa records at Lake Winnipeg, and A. F. C. Wallace, his student, computed modes and means from them.

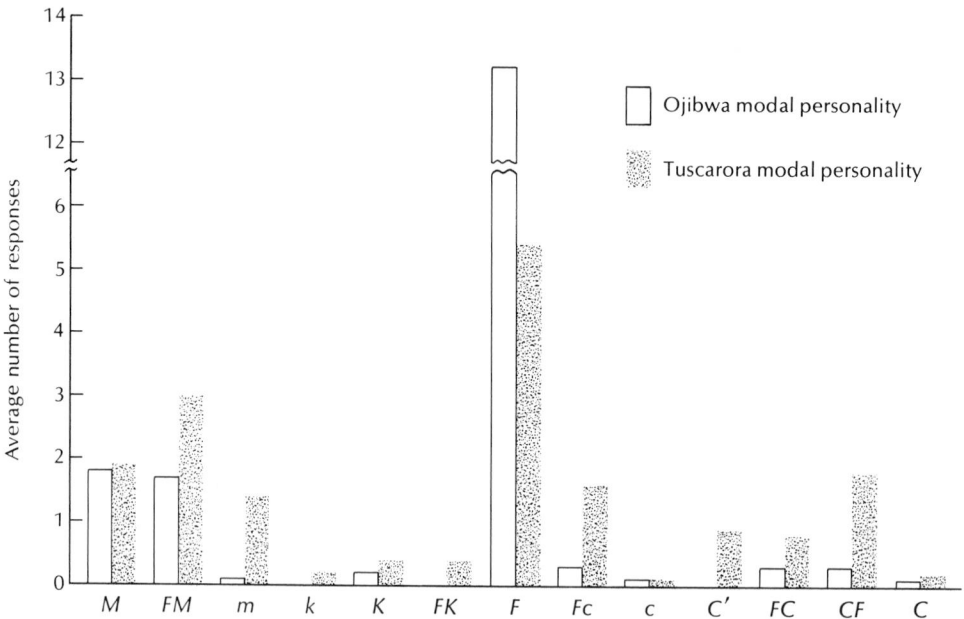

Here is a short key to the symbols used in scoring Rorschach records: *M*, human-like movement; *FM*, animal-like movement; *m*, inanimate movement or an impersonal force, like wind, acting on a figure; *k*, shading, as in an X ray or a topographical map; *K*, diffused shading ("smoke," "clouds," "steam"); *FK*, shading, as in vista and scenery; *F*, pure form, not enlivened; *Fc*, surface texture ("a furry cat"); *c*, texture without any object ("furry"); *C'*, achromatic color—black, white, or gray; *FC*, definite form with bright color ("man with red hat"); *CF*, indefinite form with bright color ("splash of red ink"); *C*, color only, not involving form or shape ("fire").[71]

Some marked resemblances show up, including an introversive tendency in both (*M* greater than the sum of *FC*, *CF*, and *C*), evidence of only slight degree of immediate anxiety (little *m*, *k*, *K*, and *FK*), the crude nature of emotional responsiveness (*CF* greater than *FC*), and a certain difficulty in handling dependence and anxiety. Although the Tuscarora and Ojibwa both shy away from emotionally charged social relationships, the Ojibwa are much more strongly inclined to do so. This is evident from the much slighter sum of *FC*, *CF*, and *C* and in the minimum *Fc*. But the real divergence comes out in the *F* scores. Compared to the modal Tuscarora, the modal Ojibwa exerts tremendous ego control over both fantasies and activities, ceaselessly guarding his impulses and watching over stimuli that reach him. He circumscribes his behavior within very narrow limits. Now we can understand the low *FM* (indicative of libidinal urges) and near-absence of anxiety indicators (m, k, K, and FK). The modal Ojibwa individual guards against such feelings. The towering F column means that he responds to the cards in terms of form, rather than by heeding movement, shading, or texture. By such meticulous, careful, rigid behavior he controls against upsetting stimuli.

all. The Tuscarora Indian sees life and all its problems in terms of broad, loose generalities. He thinks with stereotypes and preconceptions, rather than attending to the concrete details of each new situation, placing much reliance on rule-of-thumb thinking. This is not to be understood as the stereotyped thinking of unresourceful, unintelligent people. The Tuscarora adult's Rorschach protocol reveals that he is capable of a more original approach to life, though culturally he has no use for it. His stereotyped mode of approach helps him to avoid trouble, for, as you might expect, his ego strength endows him with only a limited capacity to meet crises adaptively and efficiently. The Indian also believes his social abilities to be inadequate for the situations in which he finds himself; hence, he relies on the rules of thumb that are everyone's common property. He also utilizes his stereotyped mode of approach as a means of coping with strong libidinous impulses, including aggression and dependence, which he can't fully deal with in more discriminating fashion. The Tuscarora is neither extrovert nor introvert but spends approximately equal energy responding to outside stimuli and to stimuli originating within. However, he prefers an introversive mode of adjustment, which leaves him more secure because the inner world threatens him less. Anxiety, although not of pathological significance, is present in the modal personality. Wallace also speaks of psychosexual immaturity as characteristic of the Tuscarora adult, being chiefly indicated by animal-like movement exceeding human movement in frequency. Strong aggressive impulses are active below the sur-

face, and strong dependency currents are still more deeply buried, probably never penetrating consciousness except through fantasy or in crises.

Little sets apart the 26 persons who fall within the modal range from other Indians on the reservation. The class contains two high-school students; four mature men, heads of families, who work regularly (two on high steel); nine unmarried men without regular employment; one semi-invalid, 66 years old; six married women who do housework, and four unmarried women. Wallace gives equally close attention to the social characteristics of the individuals from whom he obtained deviant Rorschach records. Generally speaking, they are deviant because they are more rigidly self-controlled than the already strongly controlled modal and submodal classes. A few are deviant because they are even more introversive than the other two categories. Observe how both the highly rigid and the extremely introversive people are deviant because they exaggerate characteristics normally present in the modal group. Rare are deviants who exert too little self-control or who manifest extreme extroversion; perhaps Tuscarora life with its pronounced emphasis on control and its preference for introversion suppresses all but the temperamentally most aberrant individuals with respect to contrary personality characteristics. In the same way that little sets the modal class apart from other people, deviants belong to no clear-cut social category, except that the highly rigid ones seemed to Wallace to have something in common. This highly rigid category, containing eight men and seven women, includes both herbal doctors in his sample, as well as one hospitalized paranoid schizophrenic; an aged hermit whom other people regard as peculiar; a man who when drunk came to the anthropologist asking to be given a Rorschach test; a young reputed mechanical genius, and two shy men more inclined to mechanical tasks than most Tuscarora. What does Wallace see linking those disparate people? He suggests that they not only avoid too close and continuous relationships with other people, but also try to relate themselves instead to nonhuman objects, like plants and machinery.

MENOMINI MODES OF ADAPTATION

Whether to examine culture as embodied in only a single mode of personality or to look for it incorporated in several personality types that coexist within the same social system depends partly on the extent to which its members are culturally variable.[72] True, Hallowell found some Berens River Ojibwa Indians to be more caught up in modernity than others, but, except for more signs of psychological maladjustment in the group that participated most heavily in modern life, he detected no other variations in the Ojibwa social personality. George and Louise Spindler also noted much uneven change among Algonkian-speaking Menomini Indians, a northern Wisconsin tribe experienced for over 300 years with European and American cultural pressures. By probing more closely than Hallowell, they also found that personality varied with where an individual stood on a gradient of increasing acculturation. They did not discover the most modernized Menomini Indian to exhibit many signs of maladjustment which could be ascribed to his psychological adaptation lagging too far behind his social opportunities.[73]

The Spindlers chose 68 men and 61 women to study, and classified them in one

or another of five steps, each succeeding one representing closer identification with Euroamerican, rather than native Menomini, culture. Primarily, they placed a person by the religion he professed and the religious group to which he belonged. However, the five categories also differ in amount and source of earned income and in the degree of prestige which occupants enjoy on the reservation; hence, they can be arranged not only horizontally, in terms of how close they come to native or Euroamerican culture, but also vertically, in terms of their relative socioeconomic standing. Lowest ranking is the *Native-oriented* group of least acculturated Indians living on the reservation. Most strongly committed to following the native way of life, they subsist by combining intermittent wagework with hunting, fishing, and gathering. Elders perpetuate a number of traditional ceremonies designed to prolong life, to protect them against sorcery, and to renew their supernatural power. The men keep in constant personal touch with the supernatural plane.

Mothers on this traditional level rear their children nonpunitively, warmly, and tolerantly, doing much "talking to" them in the form of giving advice and warnings. The two anthropologists found it very pleasant to spend most of their time with native-oriented Indians, whom they realistically saw not as fossil relics perpetuating an unaltered aboriginal past, but as a bridge spanning old and new Menomini ways of life. In the second category are members of the *Peyote Cult*, most of whom work for wages. Their prominent religious feature is the peyote ritual, in which they eat the mind-changing button of a cactus with the aim of tapping divine power. Occasionally such power, which they solicit to bring about physiological and psychological cures, manifests its arrival through visions.[74] Some peyotist parents practice the same lenient childrearing methods that na-

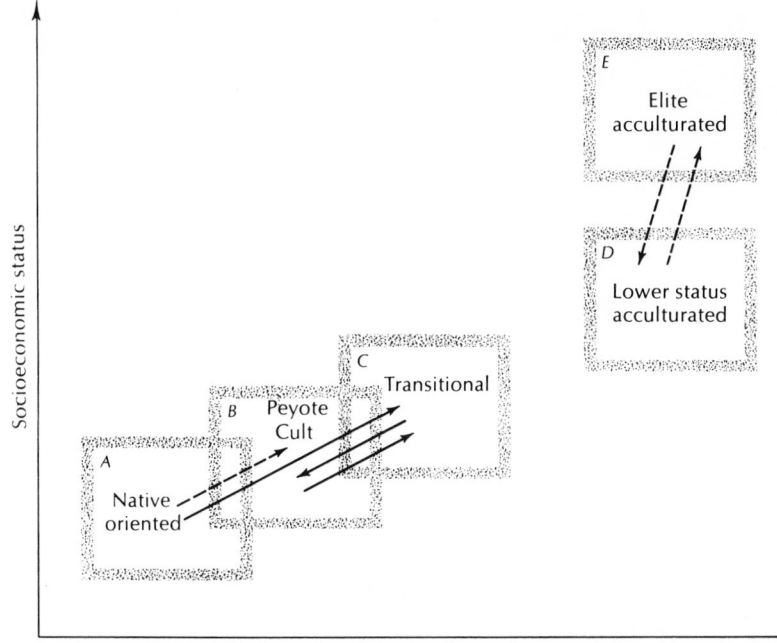

Menomini Indians fall into five socioeconomic categories, each oriented in a different degree toward native or Euroamerican culture. Arrows denote women's lines of upward or downward movement; dotted lines symbolize their infrequent mobility.[75]

tive-oriented Indians do, but others enforce their demands harshly, using brute force. A small number of Indians are *Transitionals* who still speak some Menomini and have had direct contact with the traditional, native-oriented ceremonies. But members of this third level don't identify with native-oriented people; instead, they have shifted to Catholicism, though some have occasional contacts with peyotists. Hence, this group lacks any clear-cut religious focus and, partly for that reason, can be called culturally dislocated. Generally they live poorly in overcrowded and unkept homes, and carry on skilled or unskilled jobs connected with the reservation sawmill and logging. They treat their children indulgently but inconsistently, occasionally when they are intoxicated beating them as well as their wives. Members of the *Lower-status acculturated* category were born Catholic and still maintain that religious identity but hold lower socioeconomic rank than the top-flight Catholic families on the fifth level. Lower-status acculturated people live in houses of fair-to-good condition, fill a variety of jobs which in some cases require special skills, and stay away from native-oriented religious rites. Yet they too speak some Menomini and are familiar with Menomini supernatural beliefs. The women spend much time socializing, using every available opportunity to attract the higher-ranking elite group's recognition. In the last, uppermost socioeconomic category, called *Elite acculturated*, the Spindlers place Roman Catholic families living in homes of excellent condition. Many of the men occupy supervisory jobs and, in recognition of their "superior Catholicism," be-

George D. Spindler

long to the Holy Name Society. Yet even they know some details of Menonimi magic and religion, and a few were even raised under typical native-oriented conditions. The wives of these men belong to the Catholic Holy Mothers' Group, whose leader is a Euroamerican woman; they work in church bazaars and busy themselves with other fundraising activities, including bingo parties.

Following Hallowell, Wallace, and other anthropologists, George and Louise Spindler studied their 128 Menomini subjects with the help of the Rorschach inkblot test. They believed that the test would bring out measurable variations in motives, interests, emotional balance, and other personality characteristics from one socioeconomic level to another. They too employed 21 indicators of Rorschach performance: like the average time needed for each card, the ratio of the sum of all humanlike movement responses to the sum of responses in-

volving color, and so on. After comparing the five levels to ascertain differences in the distribution of those 21 signs, they proceeded to interpret the differences according to the psychological meaning they were supposed to possess. Naturally, the Spindlers understood the uncertainty of applying to people of another culture a psychological technique whose validity remained very imperfectly established even in the culture where it was invented. Not only was it a question whether the 21 indices really meant what they were supposed to mean, but would such interpretations, if valid, likewise hold for persons reared in other ways of life? Tentatively, the Spindlers assumed that, with a few small restrictions, they could apply the test across cultural boundaries, though they admit that some day good evidence may prove they were badly mistaken. In that experimental spirit we should accept their results.[76] Despite the richness with which Louise Spindler portrays the women's varying modes of psychological adaptation, I shall from this point restrict myself to the Indian men, also omitting any consideration of the non-Indian control group which George Spindler utilized in order to sharpen his perception.

The native-oriented category became a psychological as well as temporal base-line against which to measure the other four levels—a temporal base-line which approximates Menomini social personality as it probably was before European contact. With this assumption, divergences from it on the other four levels can be regarded as alternative responses made by various categories of people to the impact of a dominant, foreign civilization. Tabulation of the 21 Rorschach indicators reveals 8 in which the 17 native-oriented men differ from the opposite extreme; that is, from 13 elite-acculturated male subjects. The probability that they do so by chance is less than 5 in 100, indicating that "these extremes are psychologically as well as socioculturally different—that the persons in the native-oriented and elite-acculturated groups have made different psychological adapations to their respective sociocultural environments." Equally significantly do native-oriented men diverge from peyotists in 13 Rorschach signs, from the transitionals in 5, and from the lower-status acculturated in 8. Psychologically, the native-oriented men are a homogeneous lot, greatly resembling Hallowell's description of the Ojibwa or the earlier travelers' generalized portraits of northeastern Indians. Highly introverted— that is, stimulated more by their inner fantasy life than by environment (especially other people)—they nevertheless remain quite sensitive to their surroundings, though emotionally they are too controlled to let their feelings ride them. The individual on this level is intellectually uncomplicated and considerably more responsive to biologically rooted drives (such as hunger and sex) than to imaginatively created ones. He accepts fate, retains his equanimity under duress, and omits the usual forms of anxiety, tension, and internal conflict. George Spindler believes that the native-oriented man's dependence on supernatural power, with which he strives always to live in harmony, preserves him from considerable anxiety of tension, but it is reasonable to add that other aspects as well of his carefully preserved, native-oriented mode of existence help to protect his narrow-based security. Psychologically adequate to demands made of him by his special mode of reservation life, he is clearly unsuited to roles played in a competitive and achieving society. You will see what happens to transitionals who have given in to Western cultural demands and who try to cope with them using primarily the native-oriented mode of psychological adaptation. Spindler is no better able than any other anthropologist to explain how the traditional person-

Louise Spindler administering a projective test to Canadian Blood Indians.

ality has managed to survive in northeastern North America as long as it has. For the Menomini, he believes, part of the answer lies in the native-oriented category's social isolation and in its ceremonies, even though the latter have undergone considerable change and attenuation. The ceremonies give people a strong sense of social identity, a sense of being culturally and psychologically Indian regardless of the clothing they wear or the occupations they follow.

One sees how far "out," how psychologically deviant, the peyotists are in the total Menomini population by noting that they differ from native-oriented men in more Rorschach indicators than separate the latter from the elite acculturated or even transitionals. The peyotists are more emotionally open than the native-oriented men, and less stoical, their affect being comparatively loosely controlled. They are also imaginatively inclined to creative fantasy and conversely more constrained in expressing their biologically oriented drives. Consciously they experience more anxiety, tension, self-doubt, and inner conflict. Yet on the whole they live introvertedly, which, Spindler suggests, means that their personality as a whole has failed to undergo a harmonious reorganization. Which came first, the far-out cult or the uniformly tortured psychological make-up of its members? Spindler believes that the peyotists, caught between two worlds and in search of stability, coherence, and relief from self-doubt, found help in the Peyote religion. Although the cult doesn't provide him with true self-confidence, it at least furnishes him with a route along which he can repeatedly find reassurance and salvation. After disturbed and stressed people have joined the cult it begins to shape their personalities, pushing them into greater self-involvement, ruminative introspection, pervasive anxiety, and fantasy accompanied by loosened emotional control.

The next category contains Menomini transitionals. Here we find men who are culturally as well as psychologically marginal. They resemble the peyotists in having experienced conflict between the old style and Euroamerican cultures and even show some of the same stressful psychological characteristics, notably tension and inability to control hostile feelings. However, they are less introspective about themselves than are the peyotists; rather, they recall Hallowell's highly acculturated but maladjusted Manitoba Ojibwa, Lac du Flambeau (Wisconsin) Chippewa, and other people caught between two worlds. The transitionals follow a broader range of intellectual interests than their native-oriented neighbors and are somewhat less governed by biologically anchored drives, though without compensatorially increasing their imaginative activity. A significant number of them are shift-ing toward a more Euroamerican way of life, emulating the emotional openness found in lower-status and elite-acculturated men, but without adding the same degree of control over feelings that the elite acculturated have acquired. Consequently, their personality reflects their disjointed social position, their loss of a meaningful place in society, and their lack of firm norms.

One might confidently expect lower-status acculturated men living with many trappings of Euroamerican culture to be psychologically sharply different from those cultural men-in-the-middle, the reservation's conflicted transitionals. Their Rorschach records, however, bear out nothing of the kind; judging from those, little distinguishes the more acculturated from the category standing immediately behind and a little below them. More sets them apart from the native-oriented base-line: lower-status acculturated men react more swiftly to problem situations, deemphasize their biological urgings, harbor a broader range of intellectual interests, and live in an emotionally more open fashion, though like the transitionals they often fail to retain adequate control over their affects. The typical lower-status acculturated man feels torn between his centuries-old capacity for introspection and the situational demand that he adopt an extraverted mode of adaptation. He finds it hard to pull loose from the introversive tow that tightly reins him back, though in fact he is actually in process of shifting over.

Finally, we come to the reservation's emotionally most relaxed group, the elite-acculturated men. They have both shifted to extraverted trends and learned to exert disciplined control over their feelings. Quick to react in problem solving, imaginatively creative rather than mainly heedful of biological drives, many-faceted in their interests, they have bent far from the native-oriented base-line. In a psychologically integrated fashion that matches their successful cultural adaptation, these prestiged Menomini leaders have carved out for themselves an original cultural identity, one very different from that guarded by the native-oriented men, whose equally well-ordered personalities are founded on a clear-cut Indian sense of identity. Hallowell and his coworkers among the Ojibwa and Chippewa report no personality characteristics comparable to those that Menomini elite-accultured men possess. Perhaps that is because those other Indians lacked the Menomini's favorable economic situation as well as the latter's abundant opportunities to identify with Euroamericans and to internalize Euroamerican values.[77]

FURTHER READING

In *La Psychologie des peuples* (1958: chap. 1) Abel Miroglio takes a *coup d'oeil* at the history of the social personality concept. Also in a historical vein, Kurt Lokasczyk follows events leading "Vom Volksgeist zur Modalpersönlichkeit" (1958). A. F. C. Wallace, in chapter 3 of his book *Culture and Personality* (1961b), evaluates a variety of approaches falling under the subject of his title, including his own form of modal personality description. Andre Siegfried, in *Nations Have Souls* (1952), deals with Latin realism, French ingenuity, German discipline, and so on in that vein. Martin Birnbach takes up differences among Fromm, Kardiner, and Horney over the relationship of culture to personality, in *Neo-Freudian Social Philosophy* (1961: chap. 4, pp. 149 ff.). In *Oasis and Casbah: Algerian Culture and Personality in Change*, Horace M. Miner and George De Vos (1960) see whether cultural alternatives that people will adopt can be predicted from a knowledge of their personality characteristics. In speaking of national charac-

ter, I omitted that usage of the term that refers to myths a nation holds about itself. Under the lengthy title "Ce que l'incident diplomatique de l'U-2 nous enseigne de la mythologie nationale, du caractère national et de la politique nationale des États-Unis," William E. Blanchard (1961) has written a stimulating treatment of a national self-view. Two useful summaries of national character research are Margaret Mead, "National Character and the Science of Anthropology" (1961b), and Ralph Linton, "The Concept of National Character" (1951). Regarding area personality, available evidence for speaking about "American Indian Personality Types and Their Sociocultural Roots" is summed up by George D. and Louise S. Spindler (1957). Robert Redfield, *The Little Community* (1955: chap. 5), examines problems associated with characterizations of social personality and ethos. Regarding the latter concept, *Naven*, by Gregory Bateson (1936), is a classic work; see also Kurt H. Wolff's detailed "Critique of Bateson's *Naven*" (1944). Daniel Katz reviews "Current and Needed Psychological Research in International Relations" (1961), offering suggestions which renewed interest in national character might heed. Bert Kaplan advises psychological anthropologists to match methods of "Personality Study and Culture" (1961c), something that experienced anthropologists probably do more often than even they realize. Nathan Leites' "Psycho-Cultural Hypotheses About Political Acts" (1948) must be kept firmly in mind in appraising the aims and logic of national-character research.

REFERENCES

1 Durkheim, 1938: xlvi.
2 Cooley, 1902: 342.
3 Boas, 1932: 44.

4 J. J. Honigmann, 1954a: 30–31.

5 *Cf.* Burnouf, 1960.

6 Hertz, 1925; Roginskiy, 1961: 45.

7 Hume, 1898.

8 Holzner, n.d.; Hurwicz, 1920: chap. 1; Kluback, 1956: 24 ff., 66 ff., 72, 78; H. E. Barnes and Becker, 1952: 879–886.

9 Durkheim, 1915: 444.

10 Goody, 1962: 10.

11 G. Devereux, 1956b. His is only one instance of parallel development, a subject discussed in Kardiner and Mead, 1959.

12 Malinowski, 1927: 92.

13 C. Kluckhohn, 1949: 211; Langner and Michael, 1963: 459–460, 468, 472.

14 J. J. Honigmann and Honigmann, 1959; for a description of another Eskimo social personality, see J. J. Honigmann and Honigmann, 1965a: chap. 6.

15 A word around which a jungle of variant meanings has grown up; see J. J. Honigmann, 1949: 9–14, 357–359.

16 Kroeber, 1957b: 73.

17 Asch, 1952: 110–111.

18 What follows is more fully stated in M. Mead, 1951c, 1951f, 1953b (her fullest discussion of the subject), 1954c, 1961b, and 1964b; also M. Mead and Métraux, 1953.

19 Compare Ruth Benedict's anthropologically executed study of national character, *The Chrysanthemum and the Sword* (1946), with Jean Stoetzel, *Without the Chrysanthemum and the Sword* (1955), which is based on public-opinion survey methods. However, see Métraux, 1943.

20 S. de Madariaga, 1928.

21 M. Mead, 1951f: 73.

22 M. Mead and Métraux, 1953: 85–101.

23 Collier, 1962.

24 M. Mead, 1935: chap. 13.

25 M. Mead, 1964b: 27.

26 Métraux and Mead, 1954: 31.

27 Abel, Belo, and Wolfenstein, 1954.

28 Wolfenstein, 1955a.

29 Métraux and Mead, 1954.

30 Wolfenstein, 1955a: 302.

31 For more about French national character, see Dolto, 1955; D. Lerner, 1961; Wolfenstein, 1955b; Wolfenstein and Leites, 1954; McClelland, 1964. Compare those authors' approach with that of Brownell, 1888; Miroglio, 1963.

32 M. Mead, 1949b: 147.

33 M. Mead, 1935: 143–145.

34 M. Mead, 1942. Richard Hauser suggests that this holds for male homosexuality in England, Scandinavia, and the United States. See his broadcast remarks in *The Listener*, 1965, 73: 141.

35 *Cf.* A. F. C. Wallace, 1961b: 24–30.

36 A. K. Cohen, 1955: 127. By permission of The Free Press of Glencoe.

37 For example, see M. Mead, 1954b: 737.

38 See Fromm, 1941 and 1955; Scharr, 1961; Birnbach, 1961: 76–89, 149; Weinberg, 1958: 24–26.

39 Marx and Engels, 1958, I:363.

40 Fromm, 1961 and 1962.

41 *Cf.* M. Mead, 1940–1941.

42 See Kardiner, 1939, 1945a, 1945b, and 1949; Kardiner and Ovesey, 1951; Kardiner, Karush, and Ovesey, 1959a, 1959b, and 1959c; Birnbach, 1961: 70–76; Dufrenne, 1953: 127–195; Weinberg, 1958: 22–24. Also see Du Bois, 1944: chaps. 1 and 9, the latter chapter being by Kardiner. When Kardiner and Ovesey (1951) extended the basic-personality concept to U.S. Negroes, they changed the term's original meaning, extending it to cover two distinct types of social aggregates: first, an organized social system like the Comanche Indians or the United States and, second, a relatively unorganized social category, U.S. Negroes. In the next chapter I present the term "status personality" to cover psychological characterizations of social categories or of people who occupy a common social status.

43 The following account is based on Du

Bois, 1944; Kardiner, 1945b: chaps. 5–9.

44 Kardiner in Du Bois, 1944: 12.

45 This also happens in Indonesian Bali; see Bateson and Mead, 1942.

46 Kardiner, 1945b: 169, 170. For a more complete diagram of what happens in Alorese early childhood, see Kardiner in Du Bois, 1944: 181.

47 Cf. Freud, 1953.

48 Kardiner, 1945b: 253. Published by Columbia University Press.

49 They became even more wretched during the invasion of Alor in World War II, when the Japanese beheaded five of Du Bois' Atimelang friends who had predicted victory for the "Hamerika" she had told them about. "There is no end to the intricate chain of responsibility and guilt that the pursuit of even the most arcane social research involves," writes Du Bois (1960: xiv–xv) in retrospect.

50 Cf. May, 1958: 5.

51 M. Mead, 1952b: 435; cf. Spiro, 1965: xii.

52 Fromm, 1941; Kardiner, 1945b: 339, 361, 412, 430 ff.; Northrop, 1946: chap. 9; Abegg, 1952.

53 Hsu, 1961a: 17; cf. K. W. Deutsch, 1953: chap. 4; Edgerton, 1965.

54 G. Devereux, 1951: 25–41.

55 Hallowell, 1946.

56 Gladwin, 1957; he secured his Comanche Indian data from Ralph Linton (1936) and also from Kardiner (1945b: chap. 3); his Cheyenne information came from Grinnell, 1923; Llewellyn and Hoebel, 1941.

57 Jung, 1953: chap. 5, 7; see also Fordham, 1953. The ideas of Lévi-Strauss (1963) seem somewhat related.

58 From Murdock, Ford et al., 1961: 128.

59 The most notable is Freud's (1918) reconstruction of the primal patricide, out of which we have inherited the superego.

60 I summarize mainly Lindesmith and Strauss, 1950; Inkeles, 1953; Inkeles and Levinson, 1954.

61 J. Henry et al., 1955.

62 Polanyi, 1962.

63 A. Kaplan, 1964: 29.

64 Kroeber, 1946, 1953, 1954, and 1957a: 191–204.

65 Cf. T. E. Graves' book review in the American Anthropologist, 1964, 66: 483–484.

66 Jung, 1959: 287, 289, 332, 333; Fromm, 1951: 18.

67 Kardiner and Ovesey, 1951: xiii.

68 Nett, 1957–1958.

69 What follows is based on A. F. C. Wallace, 1952b; see also A. F. C. Wallace, 1961b: 109–111. Quantitative Rorschach procedures are reviewed in Lindzey, 1961: chap. 7.

70 From A. F. C. Wallace, 1952b: 68, 100, 102–107.

71 Ibid., p. 49.

72 Cultural homogeneity and heterogeneity are explained in M. Mead, 1947d and 1949a. G. Wilson and Wilson (1945: 132 ff.) discuss uneven change and its consequences.

73 My account mostly follows G. D. Spindler, 1955. See also G. D. Spindler [1957]; L. S. Spindler [1957] and 1962; Slotkin, 1953, as well as L. S. Spindler and Spindler, 1958 and 1961. In the latter reference they apply Wallace's modal-personality technique to the Menomini Indians.

74 G. D. Spindler [1957].

75 From L. S. Spindler, 1962: 28.

76 Louise S. Spindler [1957] also procured a number of expressive interviews from which she inferred women's values and attitudes. I have not used them for my summary account.

77 In 1961 the 3000 Menomini shed their federal wardship status and became a separate county. See Ames and Fisher, 1959.

Personality and Social Structure

5

To the extent that a society insists upon different kinds of personality so that one age-group or class or sex-group may follow purposes disallowed or neglected in another, each individual participant in that society is the richer.

. . .

If we are to achieve a richer culture, rich in contrasting values, we must recognize the whole gamut of human potentialities, and so weave a less arbitrary social fabric, one in which each diverse human gift will find a fitting place.[1]

MARGARET MEAD

We are not lumps of clay, and what is important is not what people make of us but what we ourselves make of what they have made of us.[2]

JEAN-PAUL SARTRE

INTERPERSONAL RELATIONS HAVE FORM

In any social system or group, people's relations to each other and to persons outside possess form, order, or structure so that, as a result, they know what they owe to, and can expect from, one another. The relatively permanent arrangement of social actors to each other is their social structure.* In the past, a tyrant in a small band of Eskimo hunters might keep other members fearfully dependent on his will. Their subordination and his power gave the small band a form or structure, just as the relationships of husband, wife (or wives), and children gave an Eskimo family its form. Larger, modern Arctic communities inhabited by Eskimo have acquired a vastly different and more complex social structure. Their social arrangements would look very complicated if drawn on charts, like the organizational charts that define channels of command and responsibility in the army or in a business firm. In Frobisher Bay, a Baffin Island town of 1600 people, the rela-

* Because the form which interpersonal relations take in a given social system—their structure—is socially patterned, social structure must by one definition be considered part of culture. Nevertheless, I follow current fashion to the extent of treating the concepts separately.[3]

tionships of Eskimo to their Eurocanadian employers, foremen, and teachers, and to Government administrator, welfare officer, and projects officer illustrate important new structural arrangements.[4] Other bonds which Eskimo have created with one another by forming housing and fishing co-ops also bestow a form on their interpersonal relations that was aboriginally lacking.

I think I can best further explain social structure, a concept shared by both anthropology and sociology, by showing what one attends to when delineating it. Social scientists use half a dozen or so vantage points for spotting the form of the social system they are studying. Which perspective they take depends on the nature of their problem; on their preferences, theory, and methods, and even on the community they are observing, for just as a Geiger counter works only where radioactive substances occur in the earth, so some of these perspectives won't register a thing if the community lacks something to show up.

Status and Role. An anthropologist analyzes a social system in terms of its structure when he views it as a network of positions, or statuses, each with its in-built, expected role. A social system's business is divided up among such statuses as father, husband, plumber, and fisherman—a single individual usually acting versatilely in several such capacities, though at different times. An occupant of a status is counted on to play his role faithfully; he shouldn't be slow in claiming his rights or in executing his duties, and he ought diligently to perform the expected behaviors in ways that correspond to the controlling norms which he will very likely have internalized. In the case of an important status, if a person fails to live up to social expectations he can surely expect guilt, criticism, and even more severe external punishment, such as being removed from his position. Through such negative sanctions the social system, if

successful, prevents deviance from continuing and recurring.

A role, being a pattern of behavior regularly utilized by individuals who occupy a social status, is part of personality. It, overtly includes not only characteristic forms of speech, dress, and other actions but also an inner sense of identity, feelings of security, as well as more or less strongly felt responsibilities and expectations. On the other hand, failure to be sufficiently detached or casual about role obligations imposes a crushing sense of shorn autonomy.[5] A person often spends considerable effort mastering or polishing social roles appropriate to his age, to his shifting interests or growing experience, and to the changing world, for in a rapidly changing culture, failure to don suitable new roles can prove close to fatal. Witness the plight of the unemployed in the United States in the midst of an acute shortage of skilled workers and professionals. Many of the jobless will remain unemployable unless they can be retrained to master new roles which are in demand. The ability to change roles represents a valuable psychological resource, with which not all people are equally endowed. The Eskimo's sudden transformation after they moved off the land and into the town of Frobisher Bay can be explained by their readiness rapidly and surely to learn new roles: driving trucks, operating machines, handling telephones and other new apparatus, and meeting goals set for them by Eurocanadian administrators and foremen. Persons in a community who play more or less the same role—whether they be leaders, foremen, teen-agers, women, or men—possess a common status personality, a concept about which I will have more to say.

Component Groups and Categories. To analyze social structure for the purpose of identifying culturally variable conditions that influence human behavior requires locating people in social space. In a large

community like Frobisher Bay, people may from time to time be located in informal groups (like a teen-age gang) or in large, complex organizations, as well as permanently in ethnic and other categories. Within and between such structural groups, organizations, categories, and other social arrangements (like networks of interpersonal relations[6]), the social system gets its work done and provides its members with opportunities to find recreation and renew morale. From a psychological standpoint, to be located in such units is important because it calls for role-playing and helps carve out distinctive status personalities. For example, to belong to the teen-age Frobisher Bay Eskimo boys' gang, The Thirteens, calls for inking the number on the wrist as an insignia; cultivating a care-

fully managed, almost ritual hostility toward a rival gang, The Sevens; and being prepared lest the rivals "start something" when the two groups meet. Somewhat harder role-playing is demanded of men and women in Frobisher Bay's organization for rehabilitants. Here people are admitted to learn new, income-producing skills after serious illness has left them unable to continue with traditional, land-based careers as hunters or as the wives and children of hunters. Groups and organizations create tasks and rules designed to help them accomplish the ends for which they are organized. Thus, we get organizational needs that command fulfillment and must be incorporated in the personalities of the group's members. The organization's goals may actually only be those toward which a small

Relationships between Eskimo apprentice and Eurocanadian foreman (left) or between men organized into a fishing co-op and between the co-op and Government projects officer (right) illustrate new structural arrangements that affect the lives of Baffin Island Eskimo and impinge on their personalities. In the second photo, the projects officer addresses co-op members while his assistant interprets.

ruling elite is strongly motivated. But the elite pursues those ends with and through lower-ranking members, who cooperate for the sake of more immediate rewards and inducements. Groups and organizations also embody difficult-to-formulate atmospheres, or climates,[7] which, however, although they influence behavior in measurable ways,[8] many social scientists back off from trying to gauge and describe because they are too elusive.

In Frobisher Bay town a person's general status as an Eskimo, meaning his membership in an ethnic category, demands distinctive role-playing. When we talk about an ethnic category or refer to age and sex, we describe automatically ascribed statuses as contrasted with status that is achieved and earned by the individual. Ascribed status

can't be deliberately changed. I recall a Eurocanadian married to an Eskimo woman. He spoke Eskimo quite fluently and lived in a populous neighborhood of Frobisher Bay where all his neighbors were Eskimo. Yet his ascribed Eurocanadian status in Eskimo's eyes remained plain; in fact, he himself often enough called attention to it.

Social Stratification. Until now I have written as if statuses all exist on the same plane of power and social worth. People, however, are very prone to differentiate themselves and others, and even those of us who most piously affirm man's basic equality cling tenaciously to privilege and rank. Instead of classing everyone on the same level, many communities are structured like the Menomini Indians described in the last chapter: Their members are ranged as if on a series of ranked shelves between which there are no easy paths of access. (Not that many want to drop down; the problem mobile people face is to climb up!) Statuses in higher strata control more power, demand and receive greater respect, and members bask in higher esteem than those lower down, whose disadvantageous position the uppers try to ignore as long as they can and then try to repair with as little risk as possible to their own relatively good fortune. Groups and organizations also rank unequally, though I won't say anything further about that.

Just why inequality in social life should be more the rule than the exception has troubled many observers. India's caste system is grounded in Hinduism, though in Pakistan other bases are fully sufficient to maintain it. Karl Marx saw societies to be divided into real, sharply defined interest groups differently related to the means of production, and opposed to one another in actual or potential conflict for power. A more mitigated view, currently popular in American sociology, perceives classes to be much less real and far more poorly defined

❨ Group Atmospheres Influence Behavior[9]

1. Restrictions Imposed by Autocratic Leadership in an Authoritarian Atmosphere Generate Tension, Irritability, and Aggression*

Excerpts from Records

Immediately after coming in, the boys discover some slight damage done to their work by the "Monday gang." Sam is loudest in voicing his resentment: "Look around and see if they got anything we could bust up. We'll get them for that this time."

M. (the autocratic leader) heads off an attack on the "Monday gang's" property by very firmly outlining the day's work.

M. asks who left the scissors on the floor. Lyman says he gave them to Leonard. Leonard denies it: "No, you didn't." Lyman flushes with anger but says nothing except "I did, too." Observer writes, "I've never seen an outfit any busier in pointing out each other's faults."

Fred is definitely sullen, and responds to M. by muttering under his breath. He kicks the stool under the sign. Everybody is yelling at once and getting rather cross.

Interpretive Comments

Although most of the restrictions come from their autocratic leader, most of the boys' aggression and competitive self-assertion is directed against "scapegoats" like the "Monday gang," the other club which meets on the same day.

Continued restrictions make the boys tense and irritable.

Direct rebellious aggression against the autocrat is partly suppressed, and the footstool becomes an inanimate scapegoat.

2. Group Decision-Making in a Democratic Atmosphere Encourages Friendliness and Cooperation

Excerpts from Records

Van and Finn come in together. Van finds a bar of soap and says, "Look, here's the soap for the soap carving we decided on."

Bill and Eddie come in, and Bill says enthusiastically, "That's a good kind of soap!"

Bill holds up his piece with a laugh, "Look, Mr. W., I might make a bed out of this." Finn admires it, "Well, nice going, Bill." . . . Bill later returns the compliment, "Oh, that's good, Finn. . . .

Eddie, Bill, and Finn are busy on their projects, but Van is still casting around for the kind of boat he wants to carve; he is looking at pictures in the book. W. looks with him. W. exclaims, "Oh, boy, look at this model of a racing shell!" Van says doubtfully, "I was thinging of a canoe." W. agrees. . . . "Can you see there how almost straight it is for a long distance in the middle?"

Interpretive Comments

"We" decided—not "I" and not "our leader."

Interest in work is keen, even before the leader enters.

Pleasure found in a successful work project promotes friendliness: friendliness results in mutual praise; and praise, in turn, promotes pleasure in work.

The leader tries to follow up the boys' own ideas, and by giving necessary information, helps to make those ideas more effective.

* Aggression is in fact low in experimental groups where leaders exert their control to suppress such behavior.

than Marx thought, their inequalities being made very evident by diverse styles of life followed on the different levels. The levels themselves are sharply delineated by social scientists, who use various indicators. Some prefer income to define classes; others, years of schooling; and some combine a number of social characteristics, including place of residence and type of job. Depending on what indicators are used, the lines separating levels will fall at different places, though not too widely apart. Tough-minded social scientists implicitly betray their values when they appraise social stratification in a complex social system that requires vastly different skills, experience, and training[10] as both useful and inevitable. They assume that people will not make the heavy effort it takes to acquire socially useful skills unless they are promised unequal benefits in the form of money, prestige, and power, features that maintain a class-structured community. Opponents of this view admit other values when they point out that the way benefits get distributed often has little to do with a job's social usefulness. Aren't the garbage collector and the poet as socially useful as the physician and the movie star? Furthermore, the meager way benefits get distributed even deprives many people from learning more socially remunerative skills. Still bolder voices go further and point out that differentiation of skills is one thing and stratification another. Differentiation can exist without conspicuous, fixed inequalities in prestige and power.[11] Yet few American social scientists expect social classes marked by unequal power and prestige to vanish, though East Europeans, guided by Marxian principles, believe fully that they will.[12]

In a village in India people are self-consciously aware of the precise number of castes they represent, but in the United States some social scientists delineate three ranked strata, others five, and some six. We need not worry about how many classes

there really are; the number depends on how someone inquires, which, in turn, stems from the theory he uses or the problem on which he is engaged.[13] You may prefer to adopt a phenomenological perspective and ascertain social-class position only by asking people where they belong, in which case you would find the overwhelming proportion of your respondents claiming working class or middle class.[14] From an objective point of view, for many purposes it suffices to use a three-way breakdown, referring to a high-ranking, prestigeful upper class; a middle social level, and a low-ranking working class. The latter, however, is extremely complex for it comprises a heterogeneous assortment: regularly employed, low-skill, but stable poor families; unskilled, low-wage workers likely to exhibit wild, disturbing, and unstable patterns of behavior; families and individuals who have a rough time economically, but manage to keep themselves relatively intact (many Negroes belong in this category), and highly strained people and multiproblem families who enjoy neither economic nor personal security because they are chronically unemployed, or come from the residual bin of the aged, physically handicapped, and mentally disturbed.[15] A perceptive reader may charge me with applying the term social class when I should, more properly, say income bracket, socioeconomic status, educational class, or occupational level. To divide a community on those terms—by income, education, or type of occupation—is to use precise criteria that probably also demarcate ranked prestige levels out of which people rarely venture for friends, marriage, or social intercourse. Since social exclusiveness is an essential feature of social class it helps give rise to varying styles of life.[16]

Obviously, the arrangements that segregate people into castes, social classes, and other ranked strata bestow form on a community. From our point of view, what counts most in social stratification is, first, that social strata represent cultural variations that come to be embodied in personality and, second, that persons' unequal social locations in a community expose them to different types and levels of satisfaction, conflict, and stress, with varying implications for behavior.[17] In the United States, each social class possesses its own distinctive cultural alternatives and specialties[18] that persons in an adjacent class may find as offensive, and condemn as severely, as ethnocentric people in one community condemn unlike customs in another. Our social classes imply distinct ways of life, even though many behavior patterns are equally at home in all classes. Each class also patterns its own status personality, implanting it in the national character. Among the most important psychological characteristics that vary between social classes are those which help to maintain class structure in the community. I mean not only the invidiousness with which people compare and evaluate themselves, but the perception they have of cultural resources as well as

their own values and the goals they hold to be worth striving for. Compared to middle-class Americans, for example, working-class folk put a damper on ambition and realistically discount the American dream of unlimited upward mobility. They do so because they have learned through experience that ambition alone, unsupported by other qualifications which they lack, won't carry them to the top. They also value independence over having to take orders. Hence they have lowered their sights to give success no overriding place in the scheme of things.[19] The conflict they experience between the American dream of unlimited success, which they embody as part of their national character, and their more realistic, adaptive beliefs generates alienation, expressed when a person bitterly observes that "it isn't so much *what* you know as *who* you know." Although working-class people want their children to be successful, in reality it is unlikely that the youngsters will extend themselves to reach high if they have learned their parents' shortened view of success. Successfully up-

❨ How Many Social Classes Are There?

A varied number of U.S. social strata, differently designated by numbers, descriptive names, and letters, and delineated with the aid of somewhat different indicators, are the subjects of two recent studies in cultural psychiatry. The following chart tries to show equivalences:

The New Haven study[20] *(Refers to 5 classes)*		*Midtown (Manhattan) study*[21] *(Refers to 6 socioeconomic status levels)*	
I	Upper class	A	} High
		B	
II III	} Middle class	C	} Middle
		D	
IV V	} Lower class	E F	} Lower

ward mobile people possess personality characteristics which were better suited to promote them to higher rungs on the social-class ladder. They are strongly motivated to achieve success; capable of deferring gratification, including heterosexual gratification (for example, postponing marriage until after they become established), and skillful in forming relationships in social environments different from the one in which they grew up. They adopt higher ranking models and standards, even if this deviant choice renders them nonconformists in the eyes of their families and friends.[22]

Social Disintegration. The essence of community lies in the integrative ties that bind people. Some are obvious, like the dependence of a merchant on his customers, and vice versa. Others show up less clearly; for example, the sentiments that produce a settlement or a nation. However, analyzing social structure calls also for appraising possible community disintegration, a condition which, as A. F. C. Wallace's account of the Seneca Indians showed, carries considerable weight for personality.[23] Disintegration means that certain ties grow thin or snap, so that parts of the social system are virtually cut off, uncontrolled, and hold little or nothing in common with other parts of the community. Within the tissue of a disintegrated social system, individuals, groups, neighborhoods, and even organizations (like a mental hospital, for example) exist practically cut off from one another, either because they are determined to protect themselves from unwelcome interference, because they lack resources (personal and economic) for participating in common activities, or because they are ignored and shunned by others. As a result of such isolation, which naturally varies in degree, the individuals and groups in question internalize few common goals, values, and rules. Anomie prevails.[24] The cut-off segments may indeed covet community-wide goals

but lack the means and reject social rules for reaching them, instead anomically choosing their own rules as they go. As a result, physical aggression, crime, and delinquency, including white-collar crimes like tax-dodging and graft, flourish in the cut-off fragments—hence social scientists' assumption that here is where the trouble lies.* Component groups in a disintegrated system likewise don't cohere internally; families break up, businesses fail, schools grow into blackboard jungles, and hostility breeds apprehension. Churches lack power to foster common beliefs and to vivify sentiments of wider identification. A messiah or future-oriented social movement could relieve the high level of anomie by restoring a unifying basis of consensus, but until such a renascence dawns, the system remains disintegrated.[26] Culture in a disintegrated system may be grossly inadequate even to accomplish such basic ends as providing everyone with food, shelter, recreation, and protection of life and property. No wonder people stream away. Unwholesome conditions and insufficient physical resources drive them off, and their very exodus exacerbates further desocialization.[27]

However, disintegration also results from people being injected into a community

---

* By assuming that the trouble lies mainly in the parts, these social scientists spare themselves the need of explaining how—if at all—the disaffected parts can be effectively treated without changing the whole social system. (That they assume the possibility of partial treatment is clear from any textbook in social work.) Yet, the same social scientists, without perceiving any inconsistency, subscribe to the idea of a social *system*, i.e., of an organized whole. Evidence suggests strongly that piecemeal attempts to rectify disintegration through individual counseling, educational experiments, community houses, and slum clearance—all of which leave the larger, more powerful sectors of the community unaltered—are likely to fail, except as they help upward mobile persons who are predisposed to move out of the disintegrative situation.[25]

faster than they can be integrated, so that they take up their new lives in proximity to one another without establishing any sense of community. The very word "structure" implies permanence or chronicity, so if social disintegration is a *structural* characteristic it must be distinguishable from merely acute dislocations created by natural disasters, such as floods, air raids, and earthquakes, which prove to be much less devastating to personality.[28] In disaster, the community retains its coherence; the catastrophe itself marshals people's resources and morale, so that they organize themselves to relieve their predicament and thereby hasten the system's return to equilibrium. Social disintegration should also be distinguished from social atomism in northern Canadian forest communities, like the Kaska Indians, in which individualism is pronounced, relatively few traditional bonds and obligations link people, and members insist on psychological privacy. However, when such an atomistic community came to be conjoined with modern Canadian society, disintegrative characteristics tended to appear.[29]

Disintegration, like social integration, is, I repeat, a matter of degree, every social system revealing some points where the social cement is brittle. In Frobisher Bay a relatively thin seam joins Eurocanadians and Eskimo in a common community. Employment, service, and administration channel most of their interaction, and families form no close friendships, rarely visiting each other's home or enjoying common recreation together. Differences in language, incompatible interests, and impenetrable personalities help maintain the two groups' separateness and so, too, does the frank, invidious discrimination which originates mostly from some Eurocanadians. I won't dwell any longer on this degree of separateness because, compared to other instances of desocialization known to social scientists, Frobisher Bay scarcely deserves much at-

tention.[30] However, the situation undeniably slows down Eskimo and Eurocanadians establishing common values and meanings, and therefore may with time lead to graver problems.

Social disintegration becomes relevant for questions raised by psychological anthropology through the way it enters personality and influences individuals' enduring patterns of behavior, especially if it isn't somehow neutralized or masked by more benign relationships or social roles. Freud hypothesizes that the "power" which holds groups solidly together comes from the sexual instincts, Eros. We let others influence us because we want to remain in harmony with them; which is to say, for nonsexual or sublimated love of them.[31] Group identification endows us with enormous strength and morale and supports personality integration. Lack of social involvement, as I have said and shall illustrate abundantly, encourages people to achieve satisfaction deviantly by flouting social norms. Since people in cut-off segments of a social system suffer disparagement at the hands of more powerful persons occupying other social locations, social disintegration also poses threats to their identity and self-worth. Disparaged people feel demeaned, rejected, inferior, and relatively worthless. Social scientists go further. In addition, to seeing lower-class people stinging under the small respect shown them by people who stand higher in the social-class hierarchy, they look upon cultural conditions in lower-class life as imposing special psychological hazards. Broken families, for example, limit security, block boys' opportunities to identify with suitable male models, and place sheer physical survival in jeopardy. In the mother-dominated, lower-class households frequent in some U.S. cities, boys are at special risk of maladaptive consequences.[32] There is little question that poverty, a common symptom of social disintegration, deprives people of that buttressing of self-esteem which, in a society that values income and possessions, comes through owning socially valued goods. In brief, people in disintegrated communities strain under a manifold load of stress, for which, however, a wide assortment of cultural arrangements and people in all social classes hold joint responsibility.[33]

Stress and Strain. Stress, together with its behavior indicator, strain, crops up in some degree in every social system and has become a concept much used for analyzing social structure. I have just said that cultural arrangements in some communities or social strata result in more stress than others. Living in a "tough culture" naturally demands a high price in the form of strain.[34] Stress inheres not solely in social disintegration but also arises from class war, status rivalries, authoritarianism, prejudice and discrimination, strikes, and change wherein one segment of society outruns another, creating a chasm of misunderstanding between them. Mental disorder (some, by no means all), I have already said, constitutes one way of dealing with the unpleasant feelings that stress imposes on social actors and with which they must cope, effectively or ineffectively. Withdrawal, another mode of showing strain, appears in those few Eskimo families of Frobisher Bay who, distressed by certain features of town life, including their neighbor's somewhat overenthusiastic response to licensed alcoholic beverages, fled from town and for a few months resumed living on the land in modified traditional fashion.[35] Somewhat surprisingly, as I pointed out in an earlier chapter, social scientists interested in stress have largely failed to note evidence that people can cope with stress constructively, devising new ways of procuring food, more efficient systems of social control, and better modes of social coordination, while simultaneously discarding patterns of behavior with which they have become heartily dissatisfied. Stress in early life, while undoubtedly painful, may encourage greater resourcefulness, venturesomeness, and a higher threshold of fear, thereby actually increasing the person's capacity for adaptation.[36]

Structural Principles. Recurrently in many contexts—family, work, play, religion—social relationships are sometimes run through by clear-cut governing principles that bestow structural form on the social system as a whole and influence personality. Descent illustrates such a principle at work. Structural principles are highly stable, but they aren't usually enforced like laws and are also much harder to spot. When a person's rights and duties at almost every point in his life reflect his community's organization into groups that claim descent from some line of male or female ancestors, then we have a strong lineage principle at work. If emphasis is put on how high or low one is in a hierarchy of mounting power, responsibility, and respect, then a hierarchic principle patterns personality and bestows structural form. So, too, with principles like social atomism,[37] cooperation and competition,[38] or terror pervading a revolutionary period. In the plural community of Frobisher Bay the relatively great degree of power and autonomy possessed by Eurocanadians vis-à-vis Eskimo dominates social relations. Their powerful social role aids Eurocanadians to act as socializers who guide the Eskimo as the latter become full-fledged town dwellers.[39]

STATUS PERSONALITY

People who occupy a similar social status; who belong to the same group, ethnic category, caste, or class, and experience the impact of the same stressors possess a common status personality. Social structure is like a play in which status personalities amount to the social roles we play. As each actor comes on stage to take up his status role—as the executive opens his attaché case on arriving at the office or the husband drops off his commuter train to kiss his wife —he swings into an appropriate system of overt and covert behavior: He dons his status personality. At one extreme, when a status personality is very narrow and limited to short durations, it includes little more than wearing a uniform or greeting the customer with a drilled-in salutation. Such a thinly furnished system of behavior leaves character structure unaffected. At the opposite extreme, people like American

Negroes[40] or East European Jews,[41] because of their long and intensive socialization in an ethnic category, have been deeply affected in very many aspects of their outer and inner lives. They reveal rich, highly distinctive status personalities, in effect embodying alternative versions of the national character, just as their culture ("subculture" some anthropologists call it) constitutes a clear-cut version of the larger one.[42] Whether a status personality is as narrow as a part-time occupational role superficially carried out, or, at the other extreme, cuts

❨ *Personality Maneuvers in Response to Strain Reveal the Negro's Marginal Status in American Life*[43]

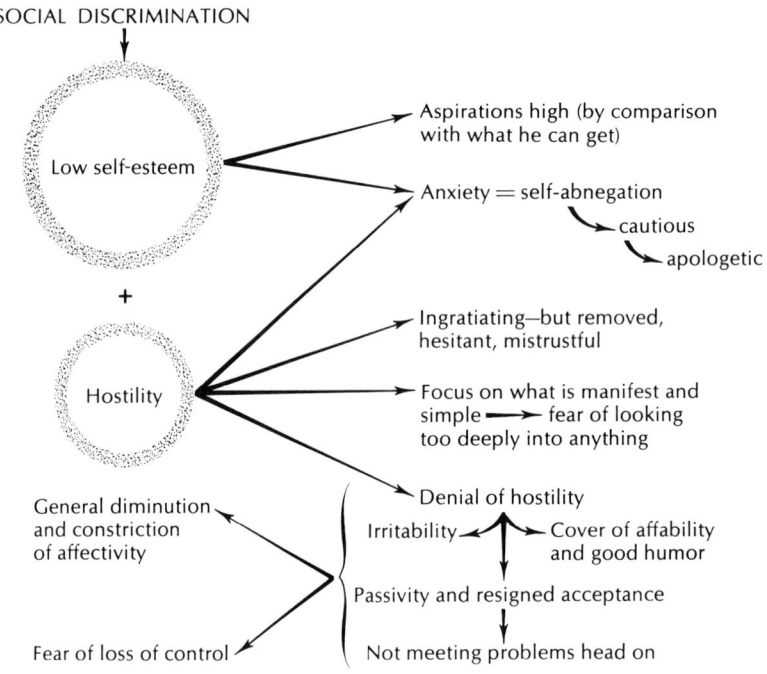

American Negroes must adapt both to social discrimination and to the strain promoted in their personality by the impact of that discrimination. The Negro's self-esteem suffers because others constantly feed him an unpleasant image of himself. To maintain his internal equilibrium and protect himself from being overwhelmed by stress, he automatically and unconsciously initiates adjustive maneuvers, some of which the diagram lists (at the points of the arrows). Note the central motivating roles which low self-esteem and consequent hostility play in his character structure; also how they suffuse his behavior as he copes with the resultant strain.

deeply into a major portion of total personality, the concept views social structure
psychologically from the standpoint of role-
playing actors. Usually, descriptions of
status personality are limited to a particular
social system, like the *American* executive
or *Samoan* adolescent girl. Sometimes, to
look for salient, transcultural features of
overt and covert role behavior promises to
be worth while. What do American and
Russian executives hold in common, despite
their dissimilar national characters?[44]
What personality goes with poverty wherever it is found, and why do peasants in
many parts of the world share the view that
all good things of life—even love, friendship, and honor—are severely limited?[45]
We hope for answers that are not too thin
or wholly obvious and superficial.

Status personality—those features of
behavior characteristic of individuals who
occupy the same social space and thereby experience similar rewards, stresses, and dominant principles—is always superimposed
on social personality,[46] and, of course, in
no way blots out the reality of accompanying individual differences. Status personality, social personality, and individual personality, all possess permeable membranes,
with the result that each level influences the
others and is penetrated by them as well.
Certain roles suffuse the whole personality,
with the result that the individual hardly
ever stops playing them, doing so even
when he is asleep. Hence, we witness an
executive personality, recognizable at the
conference table, at home, or on the golf
course.[47] A sex role—being masculine or
feminine—invariably colors the total personality, just as playing it daily vis-à-vis the
other sex confirms it. Simone de Beauvoir[48] describes how woman's situation
affects her social character. Inhabiting a
world fashioned, ruled, and dominated by
men, she can't consider herself responsible
for what happens in it and sees no need to
criticize, investigate, or judge for herself.

"Shut up in her flesh, her home, she sees
herself as passive before these gods with
human faces who set goals and establish
values." She experiences time in a characteristic way, as a matter of routine and rep-
etition that lacks much novelty and creative
flow. Her fate is bound up with perishable
things, and in losing them she loses all.
"Only a free subject, asserting himself as
above and beyond the duration of things,
can check all decay; this supreme recourse
has been denied to woman."

Although this is not yet the place to
launch into full discussion of socialization,
a few observations along that line will bring
out other things about status personality.
Acquisition of every status personality
doesn't arouse equal social concern. How
physicians learn their role in most countries
is a matter of major public interest; the
community not only passes on the educational process' effectiveness but continues to
review the physician's professional behavior. Many roles are learned and played
much more unconcernedly. The lifelong
process of role-learning, which brings status
personalities into being, relies heavily on
identification and imitation. The model may
be a parent, beloved teacher, or a respected
predecessor who held the same office and
now leaves his stamp on his successor. Or
the model may be a group, class, or other
category—a so-called reference group—to
whose norms the actor finds it advantageous to conform. He begins to further the
reference group's interests, adopts its symbols, and echoes the principles which summarize its views of reality. Largely it is
through interpersonal relations that our
status personalities become patterned. Our
faltering initial responses bring out corrective behavior in others, which in turn stimulates and maintains new responses.[49] In
one culture the father's assertiveness may
be of a sort that complementarily encourages submission in his son; in another, in
symmetrical fashion, the parent's assertion

stimulates the child's further assertion up to some limit.[50] Here I am talking about the expressive aspect of role-playing, the dimension in which roles otherwise similar from one social system to another will most sharply diverge. Applying standards of the culture itself readily shows me that people master their roles unequally well. Inherent individual differences, previous experience, and the very circumstances of learning make a difference, and also guarantee that no two individuals will possess precisely the same status personality. Consequently, status personality, like social personality, is an abstraction, a type that an observer constructs from any number of individuals acting in the same status and to which no one particular individual need perfectly correspond.

GRATIFICATION AND STRESSES IN ROLE-PLAYING

Almost every role carries its immediate rewards as well as its quota of fear and anxiety. If an actor understands his rights and duties and manages to execute them expertly, if his task isn't physically dangerous and doesn't arouse forbidden impulses, then he feels safe in his role, experiences the glow of success, and basks in his contemporaries' esteem. On the other hand, if his role exposes him to mortal danger, if his rights and duties are so cloudily defined that he doesn't know precisely what to do or to expect, if he is inept, and if he has much of his self-esteem or property staked on an uncertain outcome, then fear and anxiety ride high. Intelligent players of unpleasant roles easily learn to reduce their risks and to defend themselves against the full force of unpleasant emotions. Hence, they ingeniously devise new forms of adaptation which, should they deviate too far from what the community expects, sometimes land the inventor in new trouble. Men who

hold strong power are only too likely to insulate themsleves from unpleasant information. As someone put it, the power of criticism atrophies with success. But when an executive protectively restricts the flow of unpleasant news he also excises feedback that might help him correct costly errors and avoid serious later difficulties.[51] Role-players frequently encounter stress from contradictory expectations inherent in a status. A blue-collar worker must choose between loyally serving management or adhering to the norms of his small work group; an adolescent is torn between peer-group demands and contrary parental values. The "actor" who confronts such dilemmas has to choose which demand to satisfy, or how to reconcile them, while also coping with the stress imposed by the conflict. The Oedipus complex popularized by psychoanalysis represents a difficult early situation in which a young role-player faces what, phenomenologically speaking, constitutes mortal danger. Insistent on maximizing the gratification which he has been accustomed to receive unstintingly from his mother, a child encounters the rival claims of his father, whose power and strength he fears and resents. Psychoanalysts hold that how a boy or girl manages and resolves this crisis, fundamentally and lastingly affects his personality.

The Marginal Man. A special role-conflict affects the marginal man (who may well also be a woman).[52] He is the person of one race, of recent immigrant status, or of conspicuous religious affiliation who finds himself straddling two racial or cultural worlds that conflict in sentiments of mutual exclusiveness. Here stands the Jew who seeks acceptance in a gentile community but finds himself marginal to both Orthodox Jews and gentiles, and the American Indian who despite schooling that taught him skills and enabled him to speak English can't pass into the non-Indian world, though he can't any better identify with "those Indians." The very ambiguity of the marginal man's status motivates his behavior. Partially he can solve his dilemma through apathy and withdrawal, by overly identifying with one of the two sides even though it rebuffs him, or by allying himself with a third party made up of people like himself occupying a similar social no man's land.

BASES OF COMPLIANCE

Despite occasional contrary evidence, in every social system most people play their roles adequately, even well: cooking what the family enjoys, organizing entertainment the community flocks to see, killing when ordered to, haying industriously while weather permits, delivering goods as needed, and learning what parents and teachers impart. So wholeheartedly do some of us endorse our roles that we forget how to be spontaneous. When Arthur Koestler realized how complying with reason and routine had strait-jacketed his life, he resolved to find himself.

In order to do that I had to "get off the track." This metaphorical track I visualized very precisely as an endless stretch of steel rails on rotting sleepers. You were born onto a certain track, as a train is put on its run according to the timetable; and once on the track, you no longer had free will. Your life was determined . . . by outside forces; the rail of steel, stations, shunting points. If you accepted that condition, running on rails became a habit which you could no longer break. The point was to jump off the track before the habit was formed, before you became encased in a rattling prison.[53]

In a book about culture and personality, I can omit attention to how people press sanctions on one another to maintain role-

playing that remains faithful to the demands of a status.[54] True, any sanction, whether negative and painful like a diet of bread and water or positive and inspiring like a good grade, ultimately exerts its force psychologically. It influences personality, and my purpose is psychologically to explore conformity to social norms. But if I can explain why people without constraint faithfully play their parts, then I shall be dealing even more directly with the psychological basis of social control.

Social responsibilities are met, tasks appropriately accomplished, and courtesies observed because role-takers personally anticipate demands. Those portions of personality standing closest to the external world, the ego and superego, incorporate others' expectations, realize the significance of their threats, anticipatorily savor the tangible or intangible rewards that proper fulfillment will bring, and understand the importance to others of playing the part well. The actor imagines himself as he appears to others, and behaves so to maintain a likeable public image of himself. Fortified by his anticipation and understanding, he directs his energies along lines laid down by the status he occupies. As he does so, signals feed constantly back to him which indicate how well or poorly he is performing. Such signals help him to correct inappropriate behavior; in response to them he exerts a little more dominance, somewhat less submission, more care, or greater foresight. The signals also arouse shame and guilt, the superego exercises quick, sharp jabs of pressure when his behavior deviates too far, and those feelings, too, serve to correct role-playing. What we do with a role depends on how meaningful it appears in the light of our values and emotional needs and on the personal significance we attach to its probable outcome in particular situations. A young man knows he is duty-bound to put in military service, but he also respects the ideals of Christ as reinterpreted for an atomic age by Pope John XXIII[55] or A. J. Muste. After carefully weighing these conflicting convictions, he chooses to play the unpopular role of a conscientious objector, regardless of what others may say or do to him. More motivates my role as a professor of anthropology than the norms which others, including my university and profession, prescribe for my status. The personal opportunities I perceive in the role govern the way I teach and write and how I encourage my students to do research. Norms and sanctions continue to operate along with personal meanings and values, but in them-

⟨ Despite Considerable Strain, People Obediently Carry Out Orders to Inflict Severe, Nondangerous Pain on Voluntary "Victims"

A study at Yale University to assess the extent of . . . blind obedience found that an unexpectedly large proportion of a test population would follow orders, even if they could see that they were inflicting severe [but, they had been told, nondangerous] pain.

It has also shown, however, that such people do not enjoy being cruel. In fact, some of the subjects became distraught. The report of the experiment describes the reactions of one subject, a "mature and initially poised businessman."

He entered the laboratory "smiling and confident," the report said. "Within 20 minutes he was reduced to a twitching, stuttering wreck, who was rapidly approaching a point of nervous collapse."

At one point . . . "He pushed his fist into his forehead and muttered: 'Oh, God, let's stop it.' And yet he continued to respond to every word of the experimenter, and obeyed to the end."

The 40 subjects were men of various callings and ages recruited from the New Haven area. They were paid a nominal sum of $4.50 for their assistance. . . .

. . . they were seated at a console lined with 30 switches. According to labels on these switches, each of them, in succession, administered a more severe shock to what appeared to be a volunteer learner sitting in an "electric chair" in an adjoining room.

The first bank of switches was marked "slight shock" and succeeding banks were labeled for shocks of increasing severity to "Danger: Severe Shock," and finally two switches bearing the mark: "X X X."

[Within minutes, allowing no time for reflection] each subject was told he was the "teacher" and that he was to give the "learner" a memory test. Every time the "learner" made a mistake the "teacher" was told to flip a switch, increasing the dose each time.

Actually the "learner" was an accomplice of the experimenters and received no shocks at all. However, when the 300-volt switch was flipped, in the "intense shock" category, he began to cry out as though in pain. . . .

At this point there remained 10 switches, each of which seemed to inflict more pain. Only 14 of the 40 subjects defied orders and stopped before completing the sequence.

Among the 40 subjects, 14 displayed such nervous manifestations as unnatural smiles and "bizarre" laughter, particularly as they administered the most severe "shocks."[56]

selves the most cajoling and even painful external sanctions fail to guarantee some kinds of behavior. Without compatible personal values and insights, men won't act; or if they do, they can't be counted on to continue acting once pressure on them has been discontinued.

A social system or any component group within it (like a factory, school, hospital, or deliberative assembly) pursues goals: it produces flour, teaches children, treats the sick, worships gods, presents entertainment, and advances itself toward a desirable future. Those goals, we know, reside in members who have learned the goals and have incorporated them in their roles. Destroy a person's zeal or ability to play any role and you imperil the system's goals, as wartime propagandists well understand when they spread rumors to erode the enemy's morale. At the same time that people serve the factory or other organizations, and thereby move the total system toward its goals, they synergically benefit themselves. Tangible and intangible satisfactions accrue to them through role-playing; they augment their self-image and they attain good repute in the eyes of others. Reduce or wholly remove such personal satisfactions and the motivational fire to pursue goals valued by the community will die down, perhaps go out. Even motherhood will be shirked by the woman who derives no satisfaction from childbearing or childrearing and who sees children interfering with her career or impairing her identity.

In San Luis Jilotepeque, a Guatemalan town of thirty-five hundred, John P. Gillin shows that to play the role of Indian or Ladino is not only a matter of race or ancestry but follows from the type of world view the person endorses.[57] Indians are fundamentally ordered toward effecting a peaceful adjustment of men to the universe, whereas Ladinos seek to put man in control, to dominate the universe. In the Indian's collective scheme of things, individ-

John P. Gillin

uals count much less than the group, contrasting with the higher value Ladinos put on the individual. Indian and Ladino live in worlds of unequal breadth and depth. The Indian's is spatially limited and narrow in scale. The Ladino's is spatially and temporally larger. With respect to role-playing, Indian and Ladino approach things differently. The Indian tills land and cuts wood with his hands, aided by simple tools, and accepts weariness as one of the facts of life, not to be resented or regarded as punishment. Ladinos, preferring to work through other men whom they control, hold toil to be unbearably burdensome as well as disgraceful. Indians in their narrow world of kin and neighbors brand any show of envy and competitiveness as criminal, but the Ladino under his mask of ceremonial politeness constantly relies on competition and conflict to climb to greater power and prestige. I cite this example to reinforce the point that compliance, instead of being governed only by norms and sanctions also springs from other, less immediately related, motivating aspects of personality whose acquisition is often quite remote from particular roles we play. Such motivating sentiments can't always be gauged by the role itself. Dag Hammarskjöld's prominent position as a powerful international mediator, his autobiographical *Markings* reveals, grounded itself on considerable insecurity and doubtful soul-searching. Some scientists use their discipline as a battleground to act out tensions or to deny dependence.[58] Anxiety reinforced through strong discipline and aroused in an impoverished environment—not only warm fellow-feeling and security—motivates Hopi and other Pueblo Indians' tight cooperation and interdependence.[59]

A young Hopi monitor confessed that carrying her baby sister made her back ache.

Once I left her and ran off to play with others for a while. I intended to go right back, but I didn't go so soon, I guess. Someone found her. I got punished for this. My mother's brother said: "You should not have a sister to help you when you get older. What can a woman do without her sisters? You are not one of us to leave your sister alone to die. If harm had come to her you would never have a clan, no relatives at all. No one would ever help you out or take care of you. Now you have another chance. You owe her more from now on."[60]

From those warnings the little girl learned the Hopi meaning of interdependence. Each man, group, or social category invests roles with changing meanings developed out of experience and history. I play the role of professor with a share of the academic world's definition of it, but year by year to the distress of some of my colleagues I reinterpret it to conform to my personal value

system. Actors don't all endorse their parts with equal wholeheartedness, but even their halfheartedness or ambivalence, corresponding to the unsatisfying state of psychological ambiguity, helps motivate their behavior.

The degree to which a person identifies, consciously or unconsciously, with other individuals, with a group, or with a social category patterns compliance and explains noncompliance. The teen-age gang that enhances a lower-class boy's self-esteem becomes his reference group in the same way that the category of professional historians becomes the star by which a graduate student fixes his behavior. On the Menomini Indian reservation some years ago, Indians complained to an anthropologist that they saw little of a small number of Indian men who associated much with Eurocanadians, whom they also emulated.[61] A mobile person learns new roles as he identifies with models holding higher prestige, imitates them, and anticipates their expectations.

Character structure, said Fromm,[62] leads a normal person to act as he *has* to act in a given society and to feel satisfied with his activity. Americans' other-directed national character, with its built-in, highly sensitive radarscope responsive to others' demands and expectations, admirably suits a culture in which roles change rapidly.[63] It encourages flexibility that enables actors quickly to receive corrective signals by which to readapt their behavior. On the other hand, a tradition-directed social character is well suited for learning by drill; being more responsive to shame than guilt, it fits a culture that possesses great behavioral stability. Today's world favors a personality that alertly takes its cues from each social situation in which the individual is placed, and readily permits him to modify his behavior as the situation demands. This demonstrates how new cultural conditions may render a social character obsolescent, though it might continue to be ideally suited for role-playing in another social system. In Pakistan and India, a social personality endowed with highly particularistic loyalties to caste, kin, and even region and language, has proven ill adapted for learning new roles that embody strong identification with the new nations. Many Indians can't accept the constitutional value that all men, regardless of caste, deserve basically equal consideration. The South Asian's strong loyalty and sense of obligation to kin encourage nepotism, a trait at variance with rational management which holds that a job belongs to whoever is best suited for it, not to a relative or fellow casteman to whom one owes loyalty.

So much emphasis on congruence between personal inclination and social mandate oversimplifies. Individuals who will, are quite able to act in situations incongruent with their prepotent needs. Self-sacrifice, heroism, and courage are words by which we praise such dedicated role-playing. An instance of discrepancies between social demands and personal propensities is reported from Bang Chan, a rice village in Thailand.[64] Here a person enjoys being surrounded physically by others, though he does not necessarily look for emotional interchange with them, has no great need for others' concern, and feels that others have no strong need for strong concern from him.* Yet Bang Chan is not a village where everyone can comfortably cultivate his own garden. Demands by family and kindred must be met; deference is paid to seniors, and superiors with authority are heeded, at least as long as benefits follow in those relationships. Individuals adhere to those social demands voluntarily, despite being free to break off the role-relationships and go elsewhere. In other words, despite conflict between social demands and personal propensities, they master and play the roles. The effects of the stress consequently engendered they repress, project in fantasy, or deal with through other defense mechanisms.

Some social scientists believe that social norms operate *on* the individual rather than within him.[66] All we need posit to understand compliance, they say, is a willingness to conform to social norms. But why are people now willing and then unwilling to conform? Why do we want to do what society holds to be right, decent, and fitting in one context, but chafe when compliance is exacted in another? Why are the same roles differently enacted? The answer is that highly generalized dispositions—like other- or inner-direction—and broad basic values—like loyalty and warm fellow feeling—as well as less edifying impulses, also govern the parts we play in society. Situations that arouse those motivating states prompt a quicker response than equally important circumstances that conflict with them.

"PEOPLE ARE NO DAMN GOOD!"

Disillusioned, some Americans believe that it is useless to strive after long-range goals or for social betterment; really, nobody can be counted on, and nearly everybody is out for what he can get.[67] An idealistic, ambitious, middle-class, community-spirited citizen deplores such passive, self-defeating attitudes, the more so when he finds them endorsed by people living in forsaken slums in the grip of poverty, who use them to justify doing nothing to improve their condition.[68] Yet, one can look at alienation in another way than the one sociologists have mostly favored, and which practically outlaws alienation as a legitimate means of social adaptation. The pessimism that alienated people express in their attitudes resembles principles concerning the meaning of life that Schopenhauer, Voltaire, Goethe,

---

* Bang Chaners' psychological make-up contrasts definitely with Great Russians' strong need for affiliation. In its isolative features Bang Chan social personality resembles that of Balinese.[65]

and a number of other philosophers offer as the best part of wisdom.[69] What does it matter if a large proportion of alienated people saps the vitality of a community or group, rendering the group powerless to confer a sense of belonging or personal security or to serve as a yardstick for gauging one's success or failure, provided those alienated people have correctly faced up to the ultimate meaningless of life, their own included? Their unhappiness is warranted by the fact that they have not been trapped into investing undeserved faith in political action or in a vision of a better future. Of course, unlike the philosopher, the alienated slum-dweller didn't choose his position rationally after serious philosophical reflecting. But how it grew has nothing to do with its truth or falsity. Being wholly unprepared to evaluate the philosophical implications of alienation, social scientists are far more prone to regard that psychological state as expressing social powerlessness; for look how in the United States it increases as social-class level falls.[70] The sociologist believes that alienation results when structural arrangements cut off some individuals from utilizing socially approved means—

like schooling—to achieve good jobs, things money can buy, and other tangible proofs of success. Social scientists also view alienation as a precipitate of social stress, a sign of strain, and a dangerous one if an alienated person reaches the point where he withdraws his respect from authority, doubts the legality of sanctions, and disregards social values. Alienation so intense prepares him to commit serious offenses with impunity. However, not everyone reaches that degree. In fact, all alienated people are not of a kind, and therefore can't all be detected by the same objective interview scale.[71] For example, some lack conscience, and neither fear nor respect the power of society. Other individuals are autonomously inclined and conscientiously inner-directed by personal morals which happen to be at variance with society's looser standards. Still others are truly lost and confused. Karl Marx, followed closely by Erich Fromm, sees man to be alienated from himself and other men through the fact that society makes his labor and the products of his labor objective commodities in which he must deal solely in order to live.

ℂ Modern Man Plays Roles and Pursues Goals Supposed to Be His Own, But He Is Afraid to Delve Into His Own Aims

> . . . modern man lives under the illusion that he knows what he wants, while he actually wants what he is supposed to want. In order to accept this it is necessary to realize that to know what one really wants is not comparatively easy, as most people think, but one of the most difficult problems any human being has to solve. It is a task we frantically try to avoid by accepting readymade goals as though they were our own. Modern man is ready to take great risks when he tries to achieve the aims which are supposed to be "his"; but he is deeply afraid of taking the risk and the responsibility of giving himself his own aims. Intense activity is often mistaken for evidence of self-determined action, although we know that it may well be no more spontaneous than the behavior of an actor or a person hypnotized. When the general plot of the play is handed out, each actor can act vigorously the role he is assigned and even make up his lines and certain details of the action by himself. Yet he is only playing a role that has been handed to him.[72]

ERICH FROMM

Alienation is never complete but rather evolves situationally. "People are no damn good!" a person explodes in a momentary lack of social sympathy. Student leaders of the Berkeley Free Speech Movement felt alienated from some of the larger society's values, but they scarcely ignored problems confronting the campus or such traditional American goals as free speech and equal rights. As activists, they denied the virtues of caution and moderation, tactics that an established authority understandably preferred. "We have to justify everything in terms of the act itself," they asserted, in anything but an alienated mood. Instead of belittling the importance of alienation for a psychological understanding of culture, I am appealing for a less global, less pejorative, and less ethnocentric use of the term. Alienation derives its significance not only from the social context wherein it occurs,

but also from the examiner's frame of reference as well. Hence, social scientists using the concept ought to examine their philosophical assumptions and the cultural values from which the term derives a large part of its meaning.

Deviant role-playing

Wherever men find themselves out of joint with their social environment the fact will be reflected in some peculiarity of self-feeling.[73]

CHARLES HORTON COOLEY

In the preceding chapter I dealt with deviance as bearing the imprint of a culture. Now I shall examine deviance from the vantage point of social structure and point out its significance for both society and

❮ Srole's 5-Item Scale Measures One Type of Alienation[74]

Scores to Srole's Anomia Scale range from a possible low of o to a possible high of 10. Respondents tell if they strongly agree, agree, are undecided about, disagree, or strongly disagree with each of the propositions, their response being scored as shown:

1. In spite of what some people say, the lot of the average man is getting worse.
   - 2 *Strongly agree and Agree*
   - o *Undecided, Disagree, and Strongly disagree*
2. It's hardly fair to bring children into the world with the way things look for the future.
   - 2 *Strongly agree and Agree*
   - o *Undecided, Disagree, and Strongly disagree*
3. Nowadays a person has to live pretty much for today and let tomorrow take care of itself.
   - 2 *Strongly agree, Agree, and Undecided*
   - 1 *Disagree*
   - o *Strongly disagree*
4. These days a person doesn't really know whom he can count on.
   - 2 *Strongly agree and Agree*
   - o *Undecided, Disagree, and Strongly disagree*
5. There's little use writing to public officials because often they aren't really interested in the problems of the average man.
   - 2 *Strongly agree and Agree*
   - 1 *Undecided and Disagree*
   - o *Strongly disagree*

the individual. I follow prevailing usage: for convenience excluding deviance of which the community approves, like the hero's brave deed or the saint's magnanimity. I prefer to call such people cynosures.

From a structural viewpoint, deviance occurs when someone breaks rules or sets his behavior contrary to norms which govern role-playing. It may be the good boy who, holding back, runs afoul of norms sanctioning street conduct among peers in a high delinquency neighborhood; or boys from that neighborhood may be charged with breaking the larger community's laws. In a milder way, deviance means that instead of complying with social expectations we shirk from playing the role as fully as others expect, or we exaggerate it by going further than is welcome. In any event, deviance always results from a value judgment rendered by certain people in the community—peers, teachers, neighbors, police, or courts—who have power to make their opinion felt. Always it is possible that the deviant will refuse for one reason or another to concur in their judgment. But even if he disagrees with it, no question arises as to which party is the socially deviant one; right or wrong has little to do with the issue, for power alone suffices to render the judgment. Shifts in social power or changes in governing norms can overnight convert socially approved acts into serious deviance or make deviant acts perfectly right and proper. Now, it is a fact—at least in large-scale social systems—that people are always trying to change some rules and expectations governing the roles they play; perhaps they seek to evade responsibility, perhaps to increase responsibilities in order to acquire more power or other rewards, or perhaps to maximize their rights. Hence, what it is right or wrong to do—the definition and character of deviance—constantly shifts, making stability a very intermittent state, and ambiguity a practically chronic social condition. Such bending and twisting of roles is one way of bringing about change.

"In reading the lives of great discoverers," Angyal says, "one often wonders whether they excelled their contemporaries in intellectual endowment, or whether they were merely less socialized and more detached from scientific and other conventions."[75] Although personality disorder constitutes one source of deviance, all deviants are not mentally ill. Nor are they necessarily unhappy. Despite strenuous disapproval they incur, they may enjoy setting themselves against and baiting power inherent in the social system. Falling into deviance is easier in some statuses than in others where the norms, being tighter, allow little or no latitude or personal scope in role-playing. Among the mild and passive Arapesh, a violent and aggressive woman suffers more than a man, who has the possibility of winning public approval as a "big man," at least until people discover that he isn't acting and therefore can't be a genuine one.[76] It follows that some social structures are better equipped than others to prevent people from becoming nuisances to themselves or to others. The tighter the limits set around role-playing—that is, the more narrowly people insist on conformity—the more likely the community will be to show a high rate of crime, delinquency, and personal suffering.[77]

The theory of social stress applied to deviance explains it as a more or less successful response to a difficult situation that the individual has encountered.[78] He copes with it by reinterpreting his role in a manner compatible with his resources, temperamental proclivities, or previous experience, and executes his private phrasing in a way that runs afoul of others' expectations. Everybody bestows a private phrasing on all his roles, but the deviant, like the mental patient, goes too far. Another way the deviant meets his difficult situation is by selecting an alternative behavior pattern contained in his culture, one that he has had opportunity and talent to learn, but of which his community disapproves.[79] People not only learn existing, or innovate additional, illegitimate ways of coping; they also acquire styles of behavior that increase the likelihood of deviance.[80] For example, in a social system where role-playing ideally calls for postponing gratification, some people nevertheless learn to value immediate impulse-release and are frequently tempted to find it. On the other hand, individuals enjoy unequal opportunities to learn illegitimate patterns of behavior or to acquire the personality characteristics favorable to their use.[81] Hence, people in the same status differ in the likelihood that they will play their role deviantly. To see how this theory works, let's look at a situation highly likely to be met deviantly.

In the United States many people set the highest value on pecuniary success. Although success beckons Americans in all social strata, not everyone finds that goal equally attainable or the proper means for doing so equally readily at hand. Lower-class people, for example, though economically most deprived and therefore in greatest need of greater pecuniary success, find socially approved means for doing so furthest from their reach. They don't have what it takes to get ahead in modern society. The combination of pressure on them to succeed and lack of the right means for doing so puts them in a situation extremely favorable for deviance, one that tempts them to pursue the goal illegitimately with whatever means they can muster.[82] The insistent lure of the goal without adequate resources for winning it also generates frustration that instigates hostility, which in turn becomes capable of motivating sheerly malicious and negative conduct.[83] Delinquent boys of lower-class background, for example, sometimes steal not to acquire symbols of success but just for the hell of it. They show their strain by turning upside down the norms of the society that balks them.[84]

Few individuals in any community innovate original forms of deviance. In the same ways that socially approved modes of behavior are learned when a child or adult imitates others, identifies with esteemed role models, or internalizes the expectations of those whom he respects, so deviants acquire many of their means of striving from others. Not only is pressure to choose certain illegitimate means higher in economically disadvantaged than in more favorably placed United States social strata, but also models from whom we learn delinquent and criminal behavior are more abundant and conspicuous there, especially in cities. Hence, the incidence of certain forms of deviance is higher in lower-class neighborhoods, where deviants tutor deviants.[85] Similarly, among the Arapesh the violent and aggressive man or woman distorts for a growing child the picture of Arapesh life. Particularly the children of such deviants are likely to take over and adopt such clues.[86] I hasten to add that American middle-class culture facilitates its own patterns of deviance, including cheating on exams, fudging pupils' school grades, reckless driving, premarital sex relations, and drunkenness.[87] The sense of independence successfully nurtured in adolescent boys of middle-class background, together with the peer groups in which they center their strongest orientation and loyalty, also set the stage whereon middle-class delinquents act out their roles. Like lower-class youth, they strive illegitimately for socially esteemed prerequisites; but in their case it is those on which successful participation in normal middle-class, teen-age culture depends: dating, alcohol, pocket money—and, if possible, a car. Youth of this class don't readily learn violence and robbery; this is simply because the peer groups with whom they identify endow those avenues of masculine expression with not the slightest glimmer of prestige. Hence, middle-class teen-age delinquency is, at least to middle-class eyes, a pallid version of the delinquency known in lower social strata.[88] Nor are the lower-class people alone in being prone to act illicitly when confronted by a discrepancy between the importance attached to a goal and the availability of means to attain it. Wherever anomie prevails, almost anything goes; meaning not that the community approves of any and all means of coping but that many of its members—regardless of class—try whatever means they can readily master. As a result, infractions of law and ethics multiply.[89] Project Camelot, in which the United States defense establishment stationed social scientists in Chile to identify conditions leading to internal revolt, with the aim of learning how to prevent social revolution, showed that even highly respectable social scientists from prestige universities and government officials will overlook questionable means for the sake of achieving strongly valued ends.[90]

Deviance flourishes in a plural community marked by discordant norms. In culture-conflict one party poorly understands the other's rules, or doesn't sympathize with the other's expectations and hence frequently offends through acts of deviance.[91] After legal beer and spirits reached Frobisher Bay, Eskimo proceeded enthusiastically to drink, but without full awareness of consequences and without any tested pattern that would have regulated the speed and amount of alcohol consumed at any one time. As might be expected, heavy public drunkenness followed and arrests (made by local Eurocanadian police) more than tripled. Simultaneously, however, Eskimo and non-Eskimo leaders cooperated to establish common norms and new rules, and public drunkenness quickly declined.[92]

POWER OF NUMBERS

Psychological anthropology inquires into enduring modifications that persons adopt in response to social experience. By definition this rules out the temporary impact of mobs and crowds on personality. Yet, we should recognize that participation in such loosely organized social aggregates can so transform individuals that they will do things which they are morally and aesthetically incapable of doing alone. Normal superego controls seem to dissolve in some crowds, allowing sex and destruction to pour forth without moral censorship. No wonder established authorities fear the spontaneous organization of mobs, for such crowds are capable of nullifying their power and the power of conventional social norms. However, crowds also evoke good and healing deeds, and we can be impelled by zeal and courage through a crowd animated by noble sentiments. The very fact that disaster is shared appears to protect its victims from overwhelming anxiety and demoralization.[93] What probably helped Japanese, British, and German civilians to cope effectively with the stress of air war was the power of numbers, the awareness that no one was in it alone.

ADVANTAGES AND SHORTCOMINGS

Social structure has captured considerable popularity in anthropology and become one of the highly used, serviceable concepts of social science. Attending to personality in relation to social structure allows one to make statements of great specificity. Instead of talking about social personality as it characterizes a whole social system, especially a large one like a modern nation, a structural analysis traces specific variations in personal make-up associated with the statuses that comprise an intricate web of life. As a result, we see personality at work. We observe how it contributes to the social system's goals. We detect ambiguities, conflicting demands, blocked goals, and consequent strain in particular statuses.

It would be strange indeed if a serviceable concept like social structure didn't also possess inherent shortcomings. One resides in its very specificity, by which the whole person comes to be split into parts, roles, that nobody troubles to reassemble.[94] In structural theory, behavior very much depends on situation, a dangerous notion if it conveys the idea that anybody can be brought to do anything. An exclusively structural approach also slights both the individual and general cultural backgrounds of behavior. Executives, professors, and politicians don't execute demands inherent in their statuses like automatons. They perceive meaning in their positions, meaning that derives partly from previous experience and partly from the fact that they have been reared as Russians, Americans, or Chinese, and hence embody distinct national characters.

FURTHER READING

Admirable summaries of major issues in a structural approach to personality include Bert Kaplan, "Personality and Social Structure" (1957); Melford E. Spiro, "Social Systems, Personality, and Functional Analysis" (1961b); the same author's (1961a) "An Overview and a Suggested Reorientation" of culture and personality research; Bert Kaplan's "Editor's Epilogue: A Final Word" (1961b); and Talcott Parsons, "Personality and Social Structure" (1951a). Bronislaw Malinowski, in *Sex and Repression* (1927), was one of the first anthropologists to see personality and its formation in structural terms. Sarbin's comprehensive account of "Role Theory" (1954) and David McClelland's discussion of the same topic in his book *Personality* (1951: chap. 9), will be very useful. The concepts of status and role owe much to Ralph Linton, who developed the ideas in *The Study of Man* (1936: chap. 8). "Social Structure and the Development of Personality," by Talcott Parsons (1961), consid-

ers how personality factors become responsible for meeting demands imposed on statuses. Freud views the relationship of individual and group in *Group Psychology and the Analysis of the Ego* (1949). In "Jewish Personality Traits" (1946), Harold Orlansky describes difficulties in finding concepts to elucidate the Jew's status personality. On the other hand, W. Lloyd Warner and his associates have little trouble characterizing American executives psychologically in *Big Business Leaders in America* (1955) and *The American Federal Executive* (1963). Several hundred studies of Negro personality are reviewed by Thomas F. Pettigrew in *A Profile of the Negro American* (1964); he also helped edit a special issue of *The Journal of Social Issues* (1964, vol. 20, no. 2) devoted to the same topic. Anne Roe has made the scientist her special province. For a summary of her findings, see her paper "The Psychology of the Scientist" (1961) and also her book *A Psychological Study of Eminent Psychologists and Anthropologists* (1953). "Sons and Lovers," by George K. Park (1962), examines role-strain in European peasants. Justus M. Van der Kroef examines the fit between social structure and an acquisitive motive in "The Acquisitive Urge: A Problem in Cultural Change" (1961). Else Frenkel-Brunswik looks at the "Interaction of Psychological and Sociological Factors in Political Behavior" (1952), a perspective also frequently adopted by Harold D. Lasswell—for example, in *Psychopathology and Politics* (1934). Harold M. Hodges very readably reviews how *Social Stratification* (1964) has been approached in social science, literature, and philosophy. Charles J. Stokes, in "A Theory of Slums" (1963), offers fruitful ideas concerning the culture of poverty and its associated personalities, while Herbert Gans, to collect material for *The Urban Villagers* (1962), lived in a Boston neighborhood of moderate poverty; he presents it very well, partly in psychological terms. Charles McArthur applies Florence Kluckhohn's values schema and the TAT in order to delineate "Personality Differences Between Middle and Upper Classes" (1955). Social disintegration among Omaha Indians is the subject of Margaret Mead's *The Changing Culture of an Indian Tribe* (1932a). Using Ruth Benedict's concept, Alvin Gouldner and Richard Peterson, in *Notes on Technology and the Moral Order* (1962), speak of Apollonian impulse control as a structural characteristic associated with technological change. Dennis Wrong, in "The Over-Socialized Conception of Man in Modern Sociology" (1962), warns against failing to note that men often resist social demands. *Man Alone*, edited by Eric and Mary Josephson (1962), makes one appreciate the variety of ways in which "alienation" has been used. For its significance in capitalist society, see Erich Fromm, *The Sane Society* (1955), and Arthur G. Neal and Salomon Rettig, "Dimensions of Alienation Among Manual and Non-Manual Workers" (1963). Lorna H. Mui, "Social Structure and Anomia" (1961), shows how a test for alienation unintentionally favors relatively high-ranking U.S. respondents. Leslie T. Wilkins reviews several theories of *Social Deviance* (1965), as, in more severely critical terms, do Sidney Axelrad, in "Juvenile Delinquency: A Study of the Relationship between Psychoanalysis and Sociology" (1965), and David Matza, in *Delinquency and Drift* (1964). Two comprehensive examinations of Émile Durkheim's concept of anomie which Robert Merton so fruitfully applied are: Marshall B. Clinard, "The Theoretical Implications of Anomie and Deviant Behavior" (1964), and Ephraim Harold Mizruchi, *Success and Opportunity* (1964). The socially patterned nature of deviance and how it varies from one cultural setting to another are demonstrated by Margaret Mead, "Educative Effects of Social Environment as Disclosed by Studies of Primitive Societies" (1942), and Irving Spergel, *Racketville, Slumtown, Haulburg* (1964). Melvin Tumin, in "The Hero and the Scapegoat in a Peasant Community" (1950), regards certain deviants as social symbols; depending on what they symbolize and for whom, their deviance will be accepted or condemned. Mirra Komarovsky presents the predicament facing the individual who encounters "Cultural Contradictions and Sex Roles" (1946), and Erving Goffman, in *Stigma* (1963), examines the situation of the person whose social identity is spoiled through bodily abominations, character blemishes, or other socially devaluated signs.

REFERENCES

1 M. Mead, 1935: 316, 322.
2 Sartre, 1963: 49.
3 Kroeber and Parsons, 1958.
4 J. J. Honigmann and Honigmann, 1965a.
5 *Cf.* Ruitenbeek, 1964.
6 For social network, see J. A. Barnes, 1954; Bott, 1957; Epstein, 1961; Jay, 1964.
7 Selznick, 1957: 38–55.
8 Lewin, 1947; Lippitt, 1940; Lippitt and White, 1943; M. A. Deutsch, 1949a and 1949b.
9 From Lippitt and White, 1943: 493–494. 496. See also H. H. Anderson and G. L. Anderson, 1961.
10 K. Davis and Moore, 1945.
11 Bredemeier and Stephenson, 1962: 325; Wesolowski, 1962.
12 Kuusinen, 1961: 809–813.
13 L. S. Lewis, 1963–1964.
14 Centers, 1949.
15 S. M. Miller and Mishler, 1964.
16 For the theory of social class see Warner, Meeker, and Eells, 1949.
17 The point that social strata represent unequal opportunity locations is made in a forthcoming book by R. Jessor.

18 Linton, 1936: 272–273.

19 Chinoy, 1955: chaps. 5–6; *cf.* Mizruchi, 1964.

20 Hollingshead and Redlich, 1958.

21 Srole *et al.*, 1962: 213, 216; Langner and Michael, 1963: 436.

22 Lipset and Bendix, 1959: chap. 9.

23 A. H. Leighton, 1959: chap. 6; A. H. Leighton *et al.*, 1963: chap. 9; A. F. C. Wallace, 1956a.

24 Merton, 1957: chaps. 4–5.

25 For more on the subject of overcoming disintegration, see Gans, 1962: 270–271; D. C. Leighton *et al.*, 1963: 350; Meyer, Borgatta, and Jones, 1965; Rice, 1965.

26 A. F. C. Wallace, 1961b: chap. 4.

27 Homans, 1950: chap. 13.

28 Janis, 1951.

29 For social atomism, see Balikci, 1963: 133–137, 155; Barnouw, 1961; Helm, De Vos, and Carterette, 1960: 96; Helm, 1961: 12, 140; J. J. Honigmann, 1946: 94, 148; J. J. Honigmann, 1949: 146, 149, 153, 155, 253–254, 287; Slotkin, 1953; James, 1954.

30 *Cf.* Clairmont, 1963.

31 Freud, 1949a: 31.

32 Rovere, 1965.

33 C. C. Hughes *et al.*, 1960: chaps. 5 and 7; Langner and Michael, 1963: chap. 16.

34 Arsenian and Arsenian, 1948; Bertrand, 1963–1964.

35 J. J. Honigmann and Honigmann, 1965a: 11–18.

36 J. McV. Hunt, 1965: 91–92.

37 Rubel, in press.

38 M. Mead, 1937: 467.

39 J. J. Honigmann and Honigmann, 1965a: chap. 5.

40 *Cf.* A. Davis and Dollard, 1940; Rohrer and Edmonson, 1960; Kardiner and Ovesey, 1951; Dai, 1953.

41 Joffe, 1949; Zborowski and Herzog, 1952.

42 M. Mead, 1964a: 36.

43 Adapted from Kardiner and Ovesey, 1951: 303. See also Karon, 1958: chap. 9; Grossack, 1956.

44 Granick, 1960; see also Granick, 1962; Haire, Ghiselli, and Porter, 1963.

45 O. Lewis, 1961: xxv, xxx; G. M. Foster, 1965.

46 Linton, 1945: 130.

47 Gerth and Mills, 1953: 179. Dalton's (1948) study of the rate buster shows how a factory worker's role bears traces of his wider experience.

48 S. de Beauvoir, 1953: chap. 21.

49 Bateson, 1936: chap. 13 and 1946.

50 M. Mead, 1949b: 64–65 and 1947b.

51 Nokes, 1961.

52 Stonequist, 1937.

53 Koestler, 1952: 128. By permission of The Macmillan Company.

54 For means of social control, see J. J. Honigmann, 1963c: chap. 12.

55 In the encyclical *Pacem in Terris*, sec. 3, no. 127.

56 *The New York Times*, Oct. 26, 1963; bracketed material from Milgram, 1963.

57 Gillin, 1951 and 1952; see also Tumin, 1952.

58 Eiduson, 1962.

59 L. Thompson, 1950: 93; Siegel, 1955.

60 Eggan, 1956: 356–357.

61 G. D. Spindler, 1955: 96–103.

62 Fromm, 1941: 283.

63 Riesman, 1950; *cf.* Fromm, 1949: 5.

64 Phillips, 1963.

65 Bateson and Mead, 1942; M. Mead, 1937: 12; 1939–1940: 26, and 1940.

66 B. Kaplan, 1957: 104 and 1961b: 666–667.

67 Srole, 1956.

68 Srole *et al.*, 1962: 199.

69 M. Cooper, 1965: 331.

70 Mizruchi, 1964: chap. 5.

71 Lane, 1953: 390–391; *cf.* Simpson and Miller, 1963.

72 Fromm, 1941: 252–253. By permission of Holt, Rinehart and Winston, Inc.

73 Cooley, 1902: 227.

74 Meier and Bell, 1959: 190.

75 Angyal, 1941: 332.

76 M. Mead, 1935: 145.

77 M. Mead, 1945a: 480; G. Wilson and Wilson (1945: 89–90) call such insistence on conformity, magic.

78 A. K. Cohen, 1959.

79 M. Mead, 1930a: 186–187; A. K. Cohen, 1955.

80 Merton, 1957: 141.

81 R. Jessor, in press; Cloward, 1959.

82 Merton, 1957: chap. 4. For an enlargement of Merton's theory, see Hagen, 1962: 195–199, and Short, 1965.

83 A. K. Cohen, 1955: 336; Merton, 1957: 177–178; Sherif and Sherif, 1964.

84 Evidence shows, however, that many adolescent boys don't feel frustrated in their economically deprived position. See Reiss and Rhodes, 1963; Spergel, 1964.

85 Cloward, 1959.

86 M. Mead, 1935: 157.

87 J. W. Scott and Vaz, 1963.

88 Matza, 1964: 64.

89 Durkheim, 1951.

90 Silvert, 1965.

91 R. M. Williams, 1947; M. Mead, 1953a: 286–291; Keesing, 1958: 404–406.

92 J. J. Honigmann and Honigmann, 1965b.

93 Janis, 1951.

94 G. W. Allport, 1957: 10, 12–13.

Socialization from Without and Within

6

The traditional scheme [of education] is, in essence, one of imposition from above and from outside. It imposes adult standards, subject-matter, and methods upon those who are only growing slowly toward maturity. The gap is so great that the required subject-matter, the methods of learning and of behaving are foreign to the existing capacities of the young. They are beyond the reach of the experience the young learners already possess. Consequently, they must be imposed; even though good teachers will use devices of art to cover up the imposition so as to relieve it of obviously brutal features.

. . . Moreover, that which is taught is thought of as essentially static. It is taught as a finished product, with little regard either to the ways in which it was originally built up or to changes that will surely occur in the future.[1]

JOHN DEWEY

Moral choice is free, and therefore unforeseeable. The child does not contain the man he will become. Yet, it is always on the basis of what he has been that a man decides upon what he wants to be. He draws the motivations of his moral attitude from within the character which he has given himself and from within the universe which is its correlative. Now,

the child set up this character and this universe little by little, without foreseeing its development.[2]

SIMONE DE BEAUVOIR

AN INCLUSIVE PROCESS

From birth, or even as far back as conception, until his death, a person is being socialized, modifying his behavior constantly in response to circumstances that are themselves socially patterned. Common sense shows that some of those modifications endure, for a time at least remaining part of his personality. As the title I have given this chapter intimates, a person enlarges his repertory of behavior to meet his own hopes, fears, and values as well as others' expectations and prohibitions. The result more often than not turns out to be a compromise between inner and outer wishes, and inevitably it represents an individual's personal reinterpretation of whatever he takes over from society.

If patterning is a general term to denote the fact that with time objects, behaviorial traits, or total personality systems take on features congruent with the culture in which they exist, then socialization constitutes one means of patterning. It embraces all those processes in a specific community or group whereby human nature, by virtue of its profound plasticity, through significant experiences that individuals in their lifetime encounter, acquires socially patterned characteristics. For example, pre-Communist Siberian Chuckchee found that their imperfect system of reindeer domestication and their exploitative interpersonal relations prevented them from learning any high degree of confidence and social trust.[3] Instead, they favored each generation developing such adaptive personality characteristics as deep-rooted suspiciousness, an eagerness to exploit others accompanied by understandable fear of being likewise exploited, and brutal readiness to insure security at others' expense. I don't presume to know how suspiciousness, fear, and self-seeking originally appeared in Chuckchee history and social personality; I am only explaining that the cultural setting fostered such traits. Socialization is not, of course, unguided or left wholly to chance and personal inclination. Personal and impersonal agents, like parents, peers, teachers, and books, aid people to acquire definite social and status personality characteristics, including in certain instances deviant ones. More is involved in the process than conservation of current habits, traditional values, and tested skills from one generation to the next, for in every generation craftsmen, teachers, and prophets may conceive a need for new skills or fresh values and create educative conditions designed to engender them. A leading group in a nation, like the Bolsheviks in Russia, may set out determined to revamp the national character in order to induce strong new springs of motivation.[4] Often, however, socialization proceeds informally and wholly inexplicitly, so that its changing emphases in response to altering cultural and environmental conditions go quite unnoticed. Schools are merely one, culturally limited educational agency, their place in some cultures being marginal compared to the crucial impor-

tance with which certain Western countries endow them.

As I conceive it, the lifelong task of becoming socialized confronts us with a considerably wider task than learning to play required roles in organized social life. It extends along a broad front, in a rich, complex culture introducing one individual or another to thousands of cultural items from diet to space travel; wood-cutting, fishing, and philosophy; approved and conforming patterns as well as disapproved and deviant forms of behavior. A newborn infant begins almost at once to receive signals transmitted by its caretakers that call out learning, and such signals grow in volume and insistence as he grows and matures, until, with the disengagement that accompanies aging, they begin to decline, though without ever fully ceasing. A highly inclusive *Field Guide for a Study of Socialization*[5] alerts anthropologists bound for childrearing research to observe how various sectors of behavior are treated, beginning with succoring, which mostly characterizes infancy. Soon thereafter, even young children will in varying degree be oriented toward achievement, taught the importance or unimportance of self-reliance, variably trained for obedience, encouraged to some extent in nurturance, and directed toward a measure of responsibility. In great depth socialization systematically patterns every socially normal as well as deviant detail of an individual's posture, gesture, tempo, speech, dreaming, modes of defense, way of thinking, content of thinking, capacity to feel, and the forms that his feeling takes.[6] It enters the way he becomes mentally ill, and governs the chances that he will or won't break down psychiatrically. Socialization connotes finality and completeness; the grandson of European peasants socialized as a child in a Maine village becomes practically indistinguishable from a grandson of Old Americans. He can never go back to the land of his ancestors to become what he would have become had he been reared there among them by parents who had never migrated.[7] In this sense, socialization once under way limits what a person can become, an idea that some people hate to accept.[8]

What happens in socialization at any time becomes added to what occurred earlier, so that each new experience either affirms, counterbalances, compensates for, or overcomes modifications that a person previously admitted into his personality. A boy's strong, early identification with his mother or with women dominating a household sharpens his later struggle to achieve identification in a male role. In such circumstances dramatic initiation rites or the cult of toughness he joins in the city streets helps marshal his resources to counterbalance his early cross-sexual identification, and helps push him to adopt more appropriate role models. Not that consistency threads like a repeated musical motif through life, linking each bit of learning with every other. If that were true, then parents would have no cause to censor what a child sees on the TV or movie screen lest it counteract values they themselves teach; nor would they need to criticize what he reports his teacher to have said, dissuade him from playing with undesirable peers, confiscate forbidden literature in his possession, or move into a better neighborhood to control his friends.[9]

Even in small-scale, homogeneous social systems, contrasting temperamental bents from one parent to another confront a child with contrasting influences.[10] Although a social system that permits considerable early sexuality or aggression will very likely maintain the same indulgent note in those two areas of behavior (conversely, where early sex or aggression is severely dealt with, severity will probably continue to be the rule, a similar consistency doesn't hold for oral, anal (excretory), and especially not for dependence behavior from one

point in childhood to a later one. Also, no consistent quality links any one of those five areas with another. Knowing how adults respond to a child's sexual or toilet habits, whether indulgently or severely, allows no safe prediction about the character of the discipline they exert with respect to feeding, aggression, or dependence.[11] Inconsistency hardly means unrelatedness. I always proceed on the assumption that what happens at any one age or in any particular circumstance is systematically connected with what happens elsewhere in the life cycle.

My challenge, then, is to discover systematic connections between such events in a particular culture: to discover how a baby's earliest experiences anticipate his subsequent sudden weaning, buttressing him against the traumas that his mother knows must come, or how punishment is counterbalanced by almost immediate indulgence, as though the socializer sought to restore himself in the pupil's good favor, thereby enhancing his own power to guide. This view allows me to see that any slowly changing, homogeneous culture, despite its inconsistencies, systematically bridges childhood and adulthood by allowing children to witness daily the future roles they will play. (Psychological consequences of such prefiguring, however, vary; Manus children hardly enjoyed entering the adult roles they saw.[12]) Past experience also becomes relevant for future learning when it aids a person to assimilate later experience for which it provided analogous preparation. American children who grow up measuring their worth conventionally, first by gold stars and then by letter grades and grade-point averages, are fully capable of comprehending the precise significance of another gold bar, a second telephone on the desk, or a carpet on the office floor.

Enculturation. I have never been persuaded by M. J. Herskovits' distinction between socialization and enculturation, in

Socialization in childhood comes through many
varied experiences, as these scenes from the
Enns Valley in rural Austria show.

defense of which he points out that many animals live in society, whereas man alone possesses culture.[13] Through "socialization" all social beings, human and non-human, learn to live with fellow members in groups and come to play appropriate sex- and age-linked roles. Through enculturation, however, only human beings in each generation learn new and traditional skills and ideas; they come to embody culture, becoming persons accomplished in whatever ways a particular social system values.

Margaret Mead perceives the two concepts differently from Herskovits and, I fear, scarcely more helpfully.[14] She defines socialization as a universal process possessing varying forms and occurring through unidentical influences in different cultures, whereas enculturation means the particular pattern that learning follows in each unique culture or at some point in its history. The distinction is analogous to the universal act of eating as distinguished from what a particular community cooks and serves in a culturally distinctive way—its cuisine. In studying socialization, a social scientist makes generalizations concerning a worldwide process that varies from one time and place to another; but in studying enculturation, he strives to see learning as it is patterned in a single culture, yet proceeds differently from one individual to another.

Resources for Socialization

Throughout life a person strives to master new experience, and as he does so he perpetuates his culture. How does this vital process, which not only equips individuals to survive but simultaneously guarantees the perpetuity of culture and survival of society, come to occur? Whatever resources man has for being socialized, and they are considerable, he lacks any instinctual readi-

ness for goal-oriented behavior. Instead, he is plastic, plasticity providing his most valuable resource for becoming socialized. Plasticity isn't infinite. Some of its limits are clear: We can't be taught to fly, breathe under water, or memorize too vast a stock of detailed experience. We have restricted tolerance for ambiguity and other forms of stress, against which, if they become too strong, we will probably take protective measures. However, I prefer to exercise great caution in specifying limits to human learning lest I fallaciously project my own personal and cultural standards on mankind as a whole, as zealous reformers in another day sanctified their culture-bound ideals, calling them "God's will."

Socialization occurs for another reason. Childhood inescapably puts each growing being into a situation highly favorable for learning. His exclusive dependence on adults for survival, bodily comfort, and emotional security demands that they respond; and they do, mostly in accordance with ways they themselves have learned. In doing so, they subtly inform the child of their expectations, provide him with a traditional code for communication through which he will assimilate much future learning, and teach him his first lessons in the pleasures of sociability. That anything at all happens in socialization is very much due to the fact that individuals come into life moved to interact and integrate themselves with the world, a point to which I shall return.

Socialization thrives not merely on the extended period of human helplessness that follows birth but also on the way some cultures, our own being most notable, artificially prolong the period of dependence. This gives adults sustained power over the young, and enables the teachers to press forward a truly huge volume of cultural material that they believe must be learned. It was John Dewey who once defined edu-

Man-made things are important for transforming human nature. Through diffusion of artifacts, behavior associated with them spreads, an instance being seen in this photo of a Baffin Island Eskimo youngster and his father's outboard engine.

cation as having become "the art of taking advantage of the helplessness of the young." Our children sense their prolonged helplessness, especially when it blocks the awakening demands of their adolescent bodies, and sometimes they rebel outrightly against it. Rebellion may earn them a few concessions, individually or collectively. Or it may be put down with utter callousness, just as political struggles have periodically been suppressed when the stagers of revolt held too little power to alter the system.

The distinctive human ability to reflect on experience, leading to power to modify behavior in terms of such reflection, also underlies socialization. It isn't so much what a person experiences that determines his response as the construction that he puts on it. Socialization utilizes the whole human organism. Personalities are not only

formed through the resources of large, complex human brains; our sensory organs and highly sensitive mucous mouth tissue, our physical strength and our adept, limber bodily structure—particularly the flexible hands and fingers—also teach us about the world, and in terms of such information we shape our behavior.

Every normal individual has resources that allow some degree of socialization to take place, and his community likewise is prepared and equipped to transmit to him selected elements of its culture. However inexperienced parents of a first-born child may be, their culture includes a time-tried body of customs for rearing him. No people, in Lucian's words, "think it . . . sufficient that nature alone should supply what is wanting to the good qualities of both soul and body, but we join to them instruction and sciences, by which natural endowments are improved and defects are bettered."[15] Within a social system, any subgroup that periodically recruits new members is similarly ready to add "instruction and science" to natural endowments and so adapt the new members to the system they will help perpetuate. Practices to supply "what is wanting" can become very extensive indeed—witness basic training and other education in the armed forces. Every community or organization holds special attitudes toward the child or other untrained newcomer, assigning him certain rights and surrounding him with definite limitations, for his experience can land both him and others in jeopardy. The value placed on the newcomer is apt to be especially high in a small group, like the middle-class family, where his individuality and identity are relatively important. Deliberate berating and disparagement of a tenderfoot may also be the rule, the new arrival being hazed or subjected to ritual abasement that asserts and makes clear the power of the group.

SOCIALIZATION FROM WITHIN

Socialization is often used in a way suggesting that agents of society put facts, values, attitudes, and skills into a learner, as though he were a receptacle. The word then doesn't convey much about the pupil's active role, except that he may resist the socializers' efforts. Words like "influence," "mold," "inculcate," "impart," "train," and even "teach" all imply that the pupil, whether he be child or adult, remains largely passive and that socialization works primarily on him. Which calls to mind John Locke's seventeenth-century, empiricist notion that the individual comes into the world with his mind a blank slate, upon which society writes a program, in terms of which he thenceforth behaves:

Follow a child from its birth, and observe the alterations that time makes, and you shall find, as the mind by the senses comes more and more to be furnished with ideas, it comes to be more and more awake; thinks more, the more it has matter to think on. After some time it begins to know the objects which, being most familiar with it, have made lasting impressions. Thus it comes by degrees to know the persons it daily converses with, and distinguishes them from strangers; which are instances and effects of its coming to retain and distinguish the ideas the senses convey to it. And so we may observe how the mind, *by degrees*, improves. . . .[16]

Locke's ideas have dominated Anglo-American psychology and, for a long time almost without challenge, shaped the point of view commonly held in psychology, sociology, anthropology, and social engineering that emphasizes the primacy of society over persons. When Émile Durkheim and George Herbert Mead came along, they regarded minds and selves as essentially social products, creations of social experience. So imbued were social scientists with the view that society determines human nature that few could tolerate Freud when he visualized man as bringing instincts into the world with him, to be jointly utilized by him and society in personality formation. Though Charles H. Cooley[17] said that face-to-face groups enable man to develop a human nature that is neither in society nor inborn in him, social psychologists generally pay slight heed to how personality develops from the dynamic interaction of biologically founded potentials and the attention which society pays to them.

John Dewey[18] taught that behavior emerges from universal impulses interacting with environment or situation, but, unlike Freud, despaired of tying particular acts to specific mainsprings that propelled them. Dewey flatly denied that the child entered society as a blank slate; he comes with impulses that start him to assimilate information. Long before Dewey, Gottfried Leibnitz questioned Locke's views and pictured the intellect as perpetually active in its own right, manipulating and not passively receiving sense data.[19] To express his proactive conception of mind, Leibnitz invented the analogy of a block of veined marble that calls to the sculptor to chisel one kind of figure rather than another. Where Locke is the fountainhead of Anglo-American psychology, Leibnitz has been a source of Continental thought down to Gestalt psychology, Kurt Goldstein, Andras Angyal, and the modern existentialists, a brand of thought which until recently left sociology and anthropology practically untouched.

More is needed to comprehend the individual's active role in socialization than postulating instincts or other inherent talents of human nature. Keep in mind that what experience signifies to a person influences his behavior more than the experience an outsider sees. "If men define situations as real, they are real in their consequences."[20] Whatever meaning we attach to events isn't wholly dependent on others. Literally, we create the meaning of the world through our encounter with it, and we interpret each new event by drawing on the store of meanings already created in us.[21] The results may be highly creative and adaptive or calamitous, as when "the small group of people who make the vital decisions in foreign policy . . . fall victim to the stupefying effects of their own propaganda."[22]

Learning represents trying on and reaching out—eagerly when experience promises especially deep gratification and at other times reluctantly, but always actively. As we act, we change, and those changes that endure mark our personality. In Great Whale River, Quebec, I observed Eskimo children learn through executing the value that Eskimo set on sharing, as they went to beg tea from a neighbor, carried meat and fish to a relative, were urged by parents to offer others some of the candy they had brought home, or heard their parents express resentment against niggardly neighbors. I also saw the child below 7 cling to possessions and even fight for things he wanted: Here was no passive molding of behavior. Only with time do the children master their feelings and make the Eskimo pattern of sharing part of their personality.[23]

Needs determine the sentiments we learn. A child forms his first attitudes toward political authorities through projecting his nonrational needs on them, especially his dependence and sense of powerlessness, in the light of which the President and other figures of authority appear benign and protective.[24] The steps through which we add lasting meanings and dispositions to our personalities can occur intentionally—that is, with full awareness—or unintentionally. When the choice to become or to resist is made quite deliberately, it springs from knowing what isn't and visualizing what

can be.[25] But often we act far less intentionally, which may bring very troublesome consequences in the form of guilt and divided feelings. A transactional view of socialization is illustrated by Piaget's account of how through the very act of playing children learn that the rules of games are not immutably sacred but represent manmade outcomes of free decisions.[26] The child's discovery of this sets off a series of unanticipated consequences as he learns that he possesses autonomy in a world on which he hitherto felt overwhelmingly dependent.[27]

As socialization proceeds, a person creates the world, and in response to his creation he acts. Meanings alter as maturity increases or experience grows; in other words, he incessantly reshapes his personality anew. Consequently or unconsciously, people select what is relevant to them and choose how to learn it. To counteract such autonomous choice, agents of society resort to ample reward and drastic threat or punishment; they coerce and cajole, not to speak of subtler pressures they design to make nonconformists unhappy. But a determinedly resistant person will nevertheless refuse to accept the full, expected sequence of behavior. Sometimes, as Bob Dylan explains from his own life, pressure itself puts the pupil on guard.[28] As a child, Dylan knew that his parents acted as they did because "they were up tight" and concerned with their children—because they wanted their children to please them and to make them proud, not to embarrass them. Parents often want children to be what *they* want them to be, and as Dylan sensed the threat lurking in that kind of pressure he began to run.

When a person accepts and embodies a culture pattern into his own system of behavior, he invariably modifies it, leaving his own stamp on the cultural heritage according to how he interprets and evaluates it. As a result, culture is different for each individual.[29] His idiosyncratic version of the culture in turn becomes a model for others to emulate, and in doing so they too modify it.[30] Consequently, it can't be true that some cultures never change or "that education in societies of elementary culture tends towards uniformity and mediocrity."[31] Whatever uniformity we find between one person and another is a matter of degree or, more correctly, an abstraction created by an observer who looks for similarities while ignoring many points of difference. A person's autonomy in socialization makes culture not uniform but highly unstable. Consequently, socialization is much less predictable and controllable than people commonly believe.[32] Really, we can't dependably teach anything; the best we can hope for is to devise more and more effective conditions of learning, up to a point where they do not too greatly interfere with individual freedom of choice.[33]

The view that behavior creates meanings, and that meanings constantly shift, does more than recognize the considerable latitude that personality possesses; it warns us against rashly declaring that any period of life, no matter how critical it may be for certain kinds of learning, indelibly fixes any personality characteristics on whoever passes through it. Utter rigidity of behavior from childhood to adulthood, or from one situation to another, doesn't accord with facts. Therefore any statement about social personality or national character—the Kaska Indian's emotional isolation, for example, or the Great Russian's fear of external authority—must be understood as implying "sometimes," or "in certain situations but not in all," and hardly as saying that those characteristics won't change.[34]

PART OF DEVELOPMENT

Socialization occurs within a larger process: development, the sequence whereby a newly fertilized egg grows into a fully mature, highly involved organism that eventually disengages itself increasingly from the world and finally dies.[35] In this succession, a continuous chain of transformations leads from one stage of growth to another, each prior phase contributing well-nigh irreversibly to the form and substance of later ones. Only very partially can development be reverse; for example, through regression, in which behavior instead of progressing toward greater specificity becomes more primitive, perhaps only as the individual temporarily consolidates his growth. In greater part, development is final, the organism being forever prevented from returning to earlier forms and functions. Progression on all fronts isn't inevitable, however, for a fixated individual may tarry at some comfortable stage in growth at the cost of broadening his adaptive repertory. Within the developmental program much remains unfixed, including the length of life itself.

To take human development in particular, it is as though life develops along a broad plain surrounded by unscalable mountains that set effective limits. On the plain, considerable mutability marks the course of growth, which depends on hereditary predispositions, nutrition, climate, accidents, drugs ingested, viruses or other foreign bodies that invade the organism, and of course the social relationships it enters. So much leeway insures that each individual will develop uniquely; it also allows personality to be differently patterned from one culture to another.

Sequences in Maturation. Many years devoted to observing hundreds of children showed Arnold L. Gesell and his colleagues at the Yale Clinic of Child Development the order and fixity by which children gradually increase their capacities.[36] Although lapses and regressions occur, in general maturation continues predictably, repeating from one child to the next the

Observers take notes as they watch through a one-way screen while Arnold Gesell's colleague, Frances Ilg, gives tests to a child. (Yale Clinic of Child Development, New Haven, Connecticut)

same sequences of transformations. Four weeks after birth, babies stare at lights, windows, and nearby faces. By 16 weeks, they spend increased time in physical activity, can grasp objects, and put out more demands for sociability. Toward the end of the day especially, they demand attention, perhaps because at that time (in the United States) the family is together. At 28 weeks, babies bring a variety of objects to their mouths and bite on them with relish. They vocalize happily to themselves: gurgling, growling, and making squealing sounds. No question about whether they enjoy people at that age. Babies take to people for themselves as well as for what people can do and begin to respond to more than one person at a time. The 12-month-old baby likes to

creep, place things on his head, throw things from his playpen, and is quite capable of fine motor coordination, both in eating and playing. In this heyday of sociability youngsters hugely delight in social give-and-take. A 15-month-old child shows restiveness if kept too long in one place; he wants to shift. From this stage emerges the 18-month-old, who gets into everything, especially since he now begins to know where things are kept, and takes much interest in household activities, like sweeping and dusting, which he likes to mimick. Twenty-four months brings considerable understanding of others' property rights and also a lessened tendency to get into things. A child now enjoys helping around the house, running errands, and passing objects to people.

Half-a-year later, he shows himself to be a bit compulsive, insisting that everything be where it belongs even though his own belongings are often in a chaotic state. Others find his ways hard to accept. By three, he has fewer definite ideas about how the household should be run but remains helpful to his mother. Four sees him a truly social being who wants to be with playmates regularly. Play life now occupies him too heavily to allow him to carry on with his former domestic interests.

Developmental gradients, like the one I have just summarized, aren't so tightly fixed that they wholly exclude the influence of culture. A baby's imitation or sociability appear only with environmental stimulation, though neither is wholly determined by culture. Instead of asking what determines what, it is better to see such behavioral unfolding as reflecting a maturing organism's increasing potentialities while being simultaneously dependent on what a specific social system gives and expects. Maturation isn't precisely the same from one child to another; the ages at which particular capacities emerge vary, but the order of stages holds. Do the stages also hold in a community culturally different from New Haven (where Gesell's studies took place)? The answer seems to be Yes, at least for motor activity, but it is only right to say that we have little such data.[37] Gesell's neurological bias led him to take little interest in culture as a factor influencing development. He didn't even seek children from among New Haven's variety of socioeconomic backgrounds, but relied on the middle-class Yale faculty to fill his laboratory.

We know very well that cultures like individual parents hold contrasting attitudes toward development. Some people won't try to rush or push the stages. They tolerantly say that a child will walk when he is ready, and so wait until he reaches the level of development when he will be ready, even

eager, to acquire the new habit. Less permissive cultures often invite trouble, for parents and children alike, by gearing learning to a calendar. "A baby should feed itself at 15 months," people say, without asking if *the* baby is at all ready to feed itself at that age. The age at which a community poses some bit of learning may be critical for further unintended learning if at that age the task to be learned is particularly difficult. A Balinese child learns to walk early, but he frequently loses his balance, and adults discourage him strongly from getting around by crawling. Loss of balance preoccupies Balinese throughout their lives. Not that they only learn their preoccupation in early life; undoubtedly they learn the importance of balance several times. Each time, the significance of such learning is informed by the problem the child originally encountered in maintaining balance when his balance was so precarious.[38]

Social scientists noting Gesell's popularity in America have observed that mothers who read about his work tend to be patient with their children's development. They tend to allow biological rhythms of growth to emerge at their own pace and are disinclined to become irritable; they realize that growth patterns can't easily be changed or speeded up. Some psychoanalysts criticize Gesell for never exploring child behavior dynamically and for ignoring motivational springs of action. Yet, the psychoanalytic and developmental viewpoints can also be used together. A 5½- or 6-year-old who lets his tensions explode may be understood developmentally as showing evidence of a struggle to achieve greater independence in doing things, an endeavor in which he frequently feels frustrated. Psychodynamically, his behavior may be explained in terms of the way he is pitted against his father, frustrated in gaining a monopoly of maternal love and therefore deeply troubled. In America, children 5½ or 6 years old face still more difficulty through being started in school precisely at an age when, because they have temporarily lost some of the equilibrium they possessed in an earlier developmental state, they depend heavily on parents.[39]

Developmental Tasks. Less sharply marked than the maturational stages defined by Gesell, are the developmental tasks individuals encounter at given periods of life.[40] In infancy and early life, an individual's successful accomplishment of breathing, feeding, elimination, day-to-day dealing with environmental stimulation (including pain), and managing two-way gratifying exchanges with his environment are tasks of crucial adaptive importance fraught with long-range consequences. Developmental tasks like those and others arise out of both physiological maturation and social expectations. An individual's personal aspirations further define the significance of his accomplishments, on some of which society brings to bear a great deal of formal, explicit teaching. Certain tasks (like achieving independence in middle childhood—after age 6) recur practically invariably from one culture to another. Other, culturally highly specific ones (like learning to read) grow principally out of social expectations. Some crop up again and again, in one period of life after another, so that we are never through grappling with them. For example, getting along with peers is a problem that recurs as the individual develops from middle childhood to adolescence, then to adulthood, and finally to old age.

Early Development in Handling Ideas. No one has more assiduously sought orderly progression in the development of cognition than the Swiss psychologist Jean Piaget in his work with young, French-speaking Swiss subjects.[41] His method demands close, skillful, clinical observation and informal questioning of relatively small numbers of children, but makes practically no use of quantification. I have already described his discovery that in playing games

children first cling to the rules, which they regard as sacred and inviolable. Five-year-olds insist that the rules must have always been the same, and reject the suggestion that they can be altered. At this age, Piaget claims, a child has as yet established no genuinely mutual relationship either with adults or other children. In the main, he simply submits to constraints that adults impose on him. Age 8 in girls and 10 in boys ushers in a new attitude toward the rules, which no longer appear externally fixed and wholly unalterable. Rules now come to be seen as the outcome of free decisions and worthy of respect to the degree that mutual consent was enlisted in their construction. The new attitude correlates with truly cooperative relations that children now establish with adults and age-mates, supplanting earlier relations of adult constraint.

Another Piaget experiment tackled children's tendency to regard duty and the value attaching to it as self-subsistent; that is, as independent of the person and as imposing their urgency regardless of an individual's circumstances.[42] Such "moral realism" correlates with the constraint that adults exercise over powerless young children who learn to see parental injunctions as categorical, all-or-nothing obligations. As the child moves increasingly into cooperative relations with adults, he learns to judge acts in terms of the intentions behind them. Piaget sees room for culture to influence early moral realism, though he believes that some is inevitable even if adults' constraint should be reduced to a minimum. But, he says, it "will be more or less marked according to the nature of the home and . . . the combined characters of parents and child." Anthropologists know best Piaget's exploration into immanent justice, the animistic belief that punishment emanates automatically from things themselves:[43] The bridge cracks under a thief because he stole some apples; a rotten plank gives way under a disobedient boy because he touched the teacher's forbidden scissors. As the Swiss child's age increases, he gradually reduces his conviction that things themselves have the ability spontaneously to punish, and instead allows a greater role for chance, a development that also accompanies declining constraint in his relations with adults. Piaget reasons that belief in immanent justice originates when a child transfers to *things* (like an ax or a bridge) feelings he has acquired under the influence of adult constraint. Experience with more usual forms of causality can't budge him from his magical conception of justice. Rather, emotional experiences stemming from more cooperative relations with adults play the greatest role in weaning him from animistic thinking.

Piaget's postulate that development carries children gradually away from animistic thinking—in which unexpected events or experiences are accounted for by endowing an object with life—has been examined in several non-European communities. Piaget implied that culture could encourage or suppress animism, but not until the comparative study of children in five American Indian tribes did we know how significant the role of culture could be and how long

belief in immanent justice could persist or even intensify.[44] Margaret Mead[45] found no evidence at all of animistic thought in Manus because, she explains, Manus speech scarcely deals in metaphors; the dangerous environment puts a premium on correct physical adaptation, and parents don't communicate beliefs about supernaturals to children. Piaget's contrasting stages of cognitive development have been criticized as being too sharply separated from one another. Children don't shift gears as abruptly as he claims, and two patterns of cognition may very well coexist, a child switching between them to suit different situations.

Genetic Commands. How an individual responds in development depends on the genetic material an individual has acquired in his conception, plus conditions he encounters while he lives. His physical, cognitive, and emotional capacities grow and alter to the extent that his hereditary potentials permit, as well as in whatever directions his experience allows. No one any longer sees much point in asking abstractly how much of an individual's personality comes through heredity and how much from experience or environment (though genetic psychology is trying hard to learn

⟪ For Hopi Indians Life Passes Through Four Stages[46]

Many people conceive of life as proceeding in ages or stages, Shakespeare's "seven ages of man" (*As You Like It,* II, vii) being very famous.

The lower line, in a sand painting which the Hopi Indians make preparatory to an initiation ceremony, executed in yellow, represents the road which the Hopi traveled when they emerged from the earth and went toward the rising sun. Every Hopi still travels this road in his lifetime. The four spots, executed in blue-green, symbolize the traveler's footprints. The four crooks stand for four stages of life: the longest, childhood; the next, youth; then manhood; and the shortest one, old age, when a man grows small again and walks by the aid of a stick in a stooped position.

which human variations stem primarily from environment and which depend mainly on the action of genes). Everything that happens to a person, whether primarily ascribable to experience (like learning to speak Chinese or coming down with sunstroke) or mainly genetically controlled (like a man's inability to distinguish the flat colors of red and green), depends on his hereditarily based capacity to react. Genes, which the individual derives from both parents at the moment of conception, carry and transmit instructions that cause the developing human entity to grow and react in certain specific ways. Each individual (unless he is an identical twin) possesses an individual combination of genetic instructions. Some of these are strict and uncompromising; they can be carried out in only one way—for example, in building one type of blood rather than another. Perhaps research will some day demonstrate temperament to be largely in this category; I myself assume it will. More often, and less finally, the genetic instructions operate within broad latitudes so that the genes, acting jointly with the environmental conditions that a person encounters, influence, say, his height, age of puberty, caries, interests, abilities, intelligence-test scores, predominant defense mechanisms, personality disorder, and longevity. Whether in the course of development the genes act flexibly or as strict commands, they always require an environment in which to express themselves. Any environmental factor— say, a mother's nurturance or an enlightening book—can act only because the person's genetic potential allows him to utilize that experience in a certain way.

THREE PRINCIPLES

Concepts used in one pursuit of knowledge can be successfully borrowed or analogized by another and, like a hybrid strain, often promote a fresh, productive spurt of growth. The concept of stress and strain taken over by social science from engineering illustrates very well what I mean. I see a correspondence between certain principles of development applicable mainly to embryological unfolding and the postnatal development of human personality. Those principles—which I call *cumulative influence*, *critical experience*, and *critical age*— can, I believe, be usefully generalized beyond the cellular level.[47]

Cumulative Influence. The first principle of development states that the way an individual responds in a given situation depends on all previous events in his life which held significance for him. John Dollard[48] expressed this idea several years ago when he advised social scientists interested in biographical methods never to lose sight of the continuous character of an individual's life. The person is a temporal whole whose earlier meaningful experiences are connected to later experiences (not that everything earlier has equal significance, as you will learn when I come to the principle of critical influence).[49] In Chapter 1, where I reviewed briefly the biography of Gregorio, the Navaho Indian hand-trembler, I pointed out certain of his experiences that, taken together, made a diagnostician's career attractive to him, though they can hardly be said to have determined his profession. Early experiences can for a long time neutralize what under other circumstances would be a shock. Early in life a U.S. child develops an image of the President as a benign, protective figure. This image strongly backs his continued faith and respect for the office itself, despite the debates and conflicts that periodically rage over the man holding it.[50] The principle of cumulative influence doesn't claim that early events determine what happens later; far more modestly it asserts that significant events influence and limit what a person later becomes. One way events gain their power to act is by becoming part of the dynamic inner world of meanings which a person draws upon to appraise later situations; such meanings guide him to pick his later course of action, by which, in turn, he modifies his personality anew. Earlier experiences persist subjectively or motivationally, in the way that the individual himself consciously or unconsciously perceives them. Many scientific studies, however, which deal simultaneously with data reported by hundreds or even thousands of subjects assume that some culturally standardized way of treating a child or an early traumatic experience—say, a broken home—bears the same general significance for each individual. Though this approach has been useful, it doesn't encompass the unique way each individual himself perceives and embodies his experiences and doesn't take into account what he makes of it. I say "makes" deliberately, using the present tense. Memories come to be reinterpreted and refurbished as they undergo the influence of subsequent events which alter former meanings and give them vastly different implications for guiding behavior.[51]

Two problems arise. First, how can we know when an experience is significant for an individual, especially if he is an infant who can't tell us and is presumably unable to make fine discriminations in his environment? Second, how can the precise relationship of earlier to later events be validly traced and determined? The next two principles of development will partially help in ascertaining what are significant experiences, whereas theories of how socialization operates, including the psychoanalytic theory of instincts (to be examined in Chapter 8), purport to explain how certain early experiences acquire their power to motivate. Remember that the past doesn't operate from the past, like a physical force continuously extending into the present. The past is gone and currently can do nothing except as its traces continue here and

now to act in the minds and bodies of men or through social arrangements, the way former friendships live on in lasting continuing alliances.

Critical Experience. The second principle covers what social scientists mean when they call attention to especially "important" conditions of learning. For example, Abram Kardiner deems some patterns of culture to be basic in personality formation.[52] In that category he places family organization; the character of the disciplines applied to sex, anal behavior, dependence, and aggression; experiences gained in coping with things and with people; rules, values, taboos, and myths that are especially emphasized for each new generation, and cultural ideals in general. Almost anything may be a critical experience for learning some behavior or other. Psychoanalysts believe that what happens in a child's oral, anal, and sexual systems of behavior possesses far-reaching consequences. Social psychiatrists predict that events which block important strivings of an individual and chronically upset a person's equilibrium can induce enduring forms of strain or personality disorder in one so disposed. Circumstances replete with anxiety have been held critical in the sense that behavior acquired in them is relatively easily lost.[53] Relationships with parents are clearly of crucial importance in role-learning and for creating a sense of identity. While the principle of critical experience tries to establish what experiences are likely to be especially significant in cumulative development, it amplifies the first principle in only a very general way. Hence we still face the question, How can the precise relationship of a significant earlier experience to a later one be validly traced? For that, we need good theories that explicitly isolate critical events and explain how they exert their crucial influence.

Critical Age. The final principle of development calls attention to critical periods, times of life crucially important for certain learning.[54] It is best exemplified in imprinting (which I'll go into later in this chapter), through which, for only a brief interval after birth, some animals establish a quite irreversible conditioned response to whatever object significantly enters their environment, which includes human beings. No critical age in personality formation has been established with similar precision and fixed importance. The idea of a "critical period" has often taken the form of regarding early childhood as the most, or at least a very highly, important time for acquiring significant personality characteristics. In comparison, the rest of the life cycle has remained practically ignored, with the possible exception of attention paid to adolescence in European and American society, when teen-agers must choose a career and develop a sense of mature identity.

Investigators have dealt with critical ages in two ways. Deductively, some have justified why one period of life is more important than another, then proceeded to observe what basic learning occurs in it; psychoanalysis illustrates this method. More inductively, observers have empirically and statistically worked out what particular age periods are crucial for certain kinds of learning. For example, John W. M. Whiting[55] demonstrated how the age bracket during which adults institute certain kinds of training constitutes an important factor in engendering later-life guilt feelings. Critical age levels differ for one kind of training or another. He worked with data about 75 culturally different communities and had judges rate each on the degree to which members who become ill blame themselves for their illness; for example, by regarding their illness as stemming from a "sin" they have committed.[56] Whiting thereby made the degree of a patient's sense of responsibility for his own illness an index of guilt feelings (or of superego strength). A strong sense of personal responsibility for one's own illness, he reasoned, would very likely be traceable back to anxiety aroused in early years by adults on whom the child depended for affection and security. Acting on this theory, he proceeded to find out as best he could at what age certain kinds of behavior become socialized. He found that superego strength (represented by degree of patient's responsibility for his own illness) stood highest when weaning came between 1 and 3 years. That relatively long interval seems to be a critical period for the oral system of behavior. Toilet-training proves to have two critical ages: one between 1

⟮ An Intellectually Curious Thirteenth-Century Emperor, Frederick II, Designs an Experiment That Failed

. . . he wanted to find out what kind of speech and what manner of speech children would have when they grew up, if they spoke to no one beforehand. So he bade foster mothers and nurses to suckle the children, to bathe and wash them, but in no way to prattle with them or to speak to them, for he wanted to learn whether they would speak the Hebrew language, which was the oldest, or Greek, or Latin, or Arabic, or perhaps the language of their parents, of whom they had been born. But he laboured in vain, because the children all died. For they could not live without the petting and the joyful faces and loving words of their foster mothers. And so the songs are called "swaddling songs," which a woman sings while she is rocking the cradle, to put a child to sleep, and without them a child sleeps badly and has no rest.[57]

SALIMBENE

John W. M. Whiting's reasoning, showing the chain of events that leads from critical age levels to superego strength, the latter being indicated by the degree to which people blame themselves for their own illnesses.

and 2.4 years and a second between 3 and 4, the latter correlating even higher with guilt feeling. Superego strength is found to be high when modesty training comes between 3 and 4 years, when training in heterosexual inhibitions occurs between 4 and 6, and when training in independence takes place between 2 and 4. Another inductive investigation into critical age involved a long-term follow-up of the same U.S. children as they grew to maturity. It showed the first four years of school, the period from 6 to 10 years of age, to be critical in the formation of such personality characteristics as social spontaneity, the degree to which a person becomes involved in mastering tasks, and the degree to which a person becomes interested in things traditionally linked with his or her own sex.[58] During those four early school years, the child identifies with his parents, attempting to adopt both their values and overt responses. He also encounters a peer group, to whose expectations and evaluations he becomes very sensitive and to which he accommodates his behavior. He may develop a lasting sense of ineffectiveness and social anxiety if peers at this time reject him.

Developmental Crises. Those times when a person in the normal course of life passes from one status to another one that demands altered role-playing, when he grows from one level of responsibility to a greater one, or when he must relinquish a vital role in order to play less forceful parts present

him with a serious adaptive challenge—however welcome a particular social move may also be.[59] The ensuing discontinuity calls on him to make resourceful changes in personality. Difficulty follows from the very abruptness with which some changes are demanded, social systems perhaps too poorly mitigating problems of growth through preparatory training. On the other hand, there is inherent pleasure in transiting to many challenging new roles and tasks, for, as our experience tells us, growth offers recurrent opportunities for self-actualization and for satisfying more needs. Yet inertia opposes new demands that appear too strenuous; insecurity holds a person back from risky adjustments; and the unpleasant definition of a new status repels individuals the way Manus youth were repulsed by the hopelessness of their future adult roles.[60]

Developmental crises begin in the inescapable hazards of infancy, including birth itself. The new baby must learn to suck, manage to avoid over- and under-stimulation, and to differentiate itself from its environment.[61] Some crises, like those confronting U.S. adolescents and mature men in Western society who face retirement, are long-term and take a considerable time to resolve. Another kind of crisis is short-term and recurrent, like changing roles from one season or pleasurable activity to another, and it generates twinges of depressive nostalgia as strong emotional anchors are torn free. Learning a new way of life in which one must master new nuances of role-playing constitutes a developmental crisis for immigrants, cultural anthropologists, and diplomats. Seven years after he became Ambassador to India, Chester Bowles vividly recalled the confrontation between Bombay and his family and himself:

. . . the smiles we had managed to produce for the reporters, photographers and other welcomers gradually faded as we drove from the airport to downtown Bombay. This ride is a disheartening introduction to the new Indian Republic, especially on a dark and sultry night.

The strange new smells, the grim miles through one of the world's worst slums, the sidewalks covered with tens of thousands of sleeping people, some on cots but most of them lying on the hard pavement, the ever-present poverty, misery and squalor, were impressions which we each absorbed silently and apprehensively.

No more reassuring was the fantastic old hotel. . . . Its enormously high ceilings, the many turbaned servants, its air of elegance and luxury were in shocking contrast to the streets through which we had just passed. . . .

At the risk of losing face with the servants who assigned us to our respective and distant beds, we soon reassembled in one room, where we slept on beds, sofas and window seats. All of us needed consolation in these strange new surroundings.[62]

REINFORCEMENT AND OTHER KINDS OF LEARNING

[Theorem XII] Organisms capable of acquiring anticipatory goal reactions will strive to bring about situations which are reinforcing.[63]

CLARK L. HULL

Hull's Theorem XII contains the nucleus of his theory about learning. It predicts that people will repeat acts and other behaviors that experience has proven gratifying, those behaviors becoming established as enduring characteristics of personality. I shall continue occasionally to use the words "learning" and "socialization" nearly synonymously, even though to do so overlooks the special significance that the term "learning" possesses in modern psychology. Learning is a very thoroughly investigated, though as yet incompletely understood, process by which animals through interaction with environment lastingly modify their behavior according to whatever degree of reinforcement (reward) or punishment they encounter. Henceforth, when I refer to learning in this restricted sense I shall speak of *formal learning theory*, though the plural "theories" would be more correct.[64]

The acquisition of some personality characteristics can be well accounted for with a formal theory of learning, like Clark L. Hull's, B. F. Skinner's, or Edward C. Tolman's. Using a formal theory of learning based on Clark Hull's ideas, but devised by Neal E. Miller and John Dollard[65] to explain the acquisition of social habits (as distinct from habits mastered by animals in highly controlled, laboratory situations), John W. M. Whiting[66] showed how adults among the Kwoma in northeastern New Guinea transmit culture to their children. Whiting assumed that a person learns when drives impel him to act in ways that earn reward or punishment. Learning begins when drives of sufficient intensity have been activated and a person makes one or more responses suited to environmental cues. Cues are stimuli (like a sounded gong or the sight and smell of cooked food) that stimulate as much as they guide a person's response. The feast, spread out for all to see and smell, directs guests to satisfy their hunger drive by eating. Suitable rewards then reduce the drive's intensity: Food quells hunger; orgasm stills sexual desire. Subsequently, as Hull's Theorem XII affirms, when the organism again experiences the same drive in the presence of the same cues it will, as a result of having previously been rewarded, tend to make the same response in order again to experience peasurable reinforcement. A person who is intelligent and adaptive will also learn to avoid a response for which he has previously been punished. Important organic drives that direct social learning include hunger, thirst, sex, colon and bladder distention and pain. Even more important for social personality formation are acquired drives that must first be learned. Fear, anger, and appetites for special foods or particular kinds of sexual partners illustrate common acquired drives, and so do wishes for power, money, affection, and responsibility. A person will learn behavior that gratifies the acquired wish, thereby reducing the intensity of the impelling stimulus. Many acquired drives are learned through the process whereby organic drives win satisfaction. For example, mothers who quiet their children's hunger by nursing them become needs of the child. Their presence alone is reinforcing. Books, money, and academic freedom, and other social needs presumably acquire their urgency through similar learning. Note that acquired drives differ from one social system or social stratum to another, which is partly what is meant by saying that different social personalities arise through socialization. In their turn, acquired needs become a basis for still further learning. A need for his mother makes a child sensitive to her threat to withdraw her love if he does wrong. If she decides to employ this threat to accomplish socialization (mothers don't do so equally in all communities), then he will heed her, thereby internalizing social norms very strongly and developing a strong conscience.

By this formal learning theory, Whiting proposed to explain not only the source of habits like eating and sex but identifications with parents and other models and superego formation. Were he repeating his work today, he would no doubt recognize that behavior may be acquired even without consistent reinforcement. Most people find some social skills—for example, mountain climbing and learning to write professionally—hard and painful to acquire. The inadequate rewards and pain attending them may actually serve to enhance their value and hasten their mastery.[67] Learning among the Kwoma or in any other community isn't wholly a matter of trial and error. A pupil—child or adult—has other people to guide and direct him. As a result, he doesn't learn only habits that happen accidentally to reward him but also many which others in his community have traditionally deemed good and for which teachers employ techniques that arouse drives, constitute clear-cut cues, and insure rewards at strategic moments. Teachers try to heighten the pupil's motivation and reduce his effort by leading, instructing, demonstrating, and providing guidance. Through scolding they arouse the acquired drive, fear, in order to forestall undesirable responses.

Whiting's theory of learning is, like other learning theories by Yale psychologists of the 1940s, deliberately lean. A gratifying outcome is deemed sufficient to create in a person an enduring tendency to repeat a response whereas punishment leads to the behavior's extinction. It seems most improbable that human beings learn even motor habits so mechanically, without the use of thought and insight. In fact, laboratory experiments by some psychologists interested in learning allow them to conclude that even rats build up insight into learning situations. Figuratively speaking, experience enables then to create cognitive maps in which to store up information useful for future action. Subsequently, they consult such maps in order to compare a novel situation with previous ones and to adapt to it with responses that proved successful in the past.[68]

The promise of a single systematic theory that would explain all learning in all societies impressed few anthropologists as either desirable or useful. Consequently, not many followed John Whiting's example. Most anthropologists studying psychological problems found formal theories of learning too lean and abstract to grasp fully what goes on in a culture, and preferred to explain socialization in terms of the special circumstances attending it in particular cultures and situations. The criticism that formal learning theory accounts for behavior mechanistically and by exaggerating what others or outside experience puts into a person, is also relevant, though anthropologists, like other social scientists, never have

paid much heed to a person's dynamic properties or felt constrained to emphasize his active propensity for socialization. As to whether formal learning theories, which grew up in laboratory settings where they were put to the task of accounting for hundreds of learning experiments involving mice and rats, can ever account for human behavior in complex social situations, the answer is that they can undoubtedly account for a good deal.[69] However, they best satisfy someone who prefers a selective, schematic account and who doesn't care about the full psychological and social reality that learning situations possess for teachers and pupils.[70]

Naturally, such theories can't explain everything. What reinforcement does the highly punishing belief in ghosts provide for children who learn to believe in them on the Micronesian island of Ifaluk?[71] They

⟨ Drive, Response, Cues, and Reinforcement Promote Kwoma Learning

During childhood a Kwoma boy learns to avoid the house tamberan while ceremonies are being held. The drive in this case is anxiety (he is warned that he would die if he did so); the response is avoiding the house tamberan; the cues are the sound of the gong rhythms, the statements of others that a ceremony is being held, the sight of his father, uncles, and older brothers decorating themselves; the reward is escape from anxiety. In adolescence a boy learns to carry on secret love affairs with adolescent girls. The drives are sex, sex appetite, and anxiety (sex impells him to seek girls, sex appetite leads him to choose a girl culturally defined as attractive, and anxiety impells him to do so secretly); the response is the complex of behavior which leads to and includes sexual intercourse in the bush; the cues are the sight of an attractive girl, verbal permission from her, the environmental scene which has both public and secluded spots, etc.; the reward is sexual orgasm, satisfaction of sex appetite, and anxiety reduction. The adult habit of beating gongs against sorcery when a relative becomes ill may be used as a final illustration. . . . The man's drives in this case are fear that he, too, may become ill unless the sorcery is stopped, fear that his relatives may die, and anger at the sorcerer; the response is going to the house tamberan and beating the gongs in a particular way; the cues are those which indicate that a relative is sick; and the reward is a reduction in fear and anger. Thus, although the habits become more and more complex . . . as the individual matures, the four essentials of learning and performance pertain to the behavior of individuals of all ages.[72]

JOHN W. M. WHITING

acquire their strong fear of ghosts—harbingers of illness and death—not so much through direct teaching as on occasions when a frightening noise sounds on the roof, a stone falls, or a person becomes ill and the cause is attributed to a ghost. Melford Spiro explains children's acceptance of this explanation by hearkening back to earlier experiences that taught them to perceive their world as threatening and so prepared them to believe in the existence of malevolent beings. Their dismal perception of life originated in daily cold baths and in their abrupt displacement once a sibling was born. The same adults who protected the child also harmed it, just as ghosts act both for good (curing illness) and evil. That malevolent spirits are female is no coincidence, for so was the parent who mainly nurtured but also harmed the child. The socially standardized, traditional belief in ghosts, when he encounters it, confirms the Ifaluk child's already established view of the world. Therefore he learns the belief, even though he isn't impelled to it by any basic or acquired drive or confirmed in it through some kind of reinforcement.

Imprinting. Anthony F. C. Wallace[73] offhandedly suggests that social scientists borrow the ethologists' theory of imprinting to see if it helps to explain human socialization. According to that theory, an unknown, innate releasing mechanism (IRM) in an animal prompts it to respond to key stimuli it receives from its environment.[74] It is as if the animal were selectively tuned in to a few key signals. The jungle fowl, for example, will not brood any chick which lacks the typical wild color pattern on its head and back. That pattern calls out her brooding behavior. In jewelfish, the male's dark ruby-red throat coloring constitutes a key signal that releases fighting activities in a rival. IRM's break down in certain conditions; for example, when an animal is ill. Imprinting represents a particular type of IRM, one which a variety of stimuli can arouse. Within a very brief time period, the IRM succeeds in establishing an enduring conditioned response to an object. For example, a newborn greyleg gosling shortly after birth will respond to an amazingly wide range of objects; it will not only follow its mother but hens and human beings as well—and even rowboats. Since such acquired responses are typically quite irreversible, they are termed "imprinting." A similar IRM lastingly attaches monkey infants to dummy mothers.[75] Imprinting, which in ethology itself doesn't explain much behavior, can't yet be successfully applied to complex human learning. One thing it fails to account for is an animal's appreciation of specific objects (particular human beings), something probably acquired in other ways than through imprinting.[76]

Explicit and Inexplicit Learning. Anthropologists are disinclined to employ a single, general theory of learning to explain personality formation. What they have done is call attention to various kinds of experience through which people internalize particular aspects of culture or personality. Take, for example, the distinction between explicit and inexplicit learning. The first calls attention to deliberate instruction, the kind that directs children to wash their hands before eating, to observe caution in crossing busy streets, and instills multiplication by drill. The advice a person receives or sequence he follows is self-conscious, or highly explicit. In the course of such instruction, additional, unanticipated learning *in*explicitly occurs, growing out of the very conditions and context of the instruction, like moods unintentionally provoked by listening to music. The pupil acquires a specific attitude toward dirty hands or street traffic. The experience inexplicitly teaches him to learn more efficiently or saps his inclination to assert himself actively in learning. The pattern of interpersonal relations between teacher and pupil itself communicates information that each learns; in some cultures the pattern is such that it encourages complementary passivity toward persons in authority or, it symmetrically calls forth more of the same quality that the teacher himself displays. The universe may come to be conceived in terms resembling the context in which learning occurs, with the result that an observer who attends carefully to that context receives clues to a community's world view—its *Weltanschauung*.[77] A key feature of inexplicit learning is its lack of manuals and codes; it is quite opposite to the highly programmed learning, responsibility for which we assign to teaching machines.[78]

It is reasonable to expect that most learners of appropriate age will give foremost attention to the significance of whatever is presented to them as being central in a particular learning context. When a father is teaching his son to drive, for instance, how the older man shifts gears, not his flinging a match out of the window, is the important point to be learned; and it is so understood. However, what a teacher and his society ideally deem to be the central lesson isn't always communicated to those who are learning. Inexplicitly, an unintended message may be stressed, even one contrary to social norms or the lesson's central point.[79] The high level of normlessness (anomie) penetrating North American life at almost every level is so learned. Every social system provides its members with goals worth striving for, at the same time instructing them in acceptable and unacceptable means for reaching those worthwhile ends. Some means, like fraud and force, are ruled out as immoral and illegal while others receive strong endorsement. In many subtle ways, Euroamericans in the United States and Canada learn implicitly to emphasize the importance of goals and achievement above means, and consequently means come to be invested with disproportionately slight significance or emotion.[80] As a result many people in those countries (and in others too), without becoming outright criminals, learn to adapt by short-circuiting their principles adeptly. Now and then they pull a fast one when the result is highly worthwhile—that is, to sacrifice a bit of their integrity in order to achieve some highly desirable end, and compromise their moral values for the sake of getting something important done. We learn to utilize expertly, without strong pangs of conscience, almost any technically efficient means, even if it runs counter to our loosely implanted moral values. The results, distressing consequences of anomie, confront us in gerrymandering, in legislatures making decisions without open hearings or votes that go on record, in cheating by athletes and by other hard-pressed college students, and in government officials scandalously favoring themselves or their friends. We are quite able to tolerate a considerable amount of some such deviance, allowing it to go unpunished for a long time, perhaps until concerned citizens who can afford it enlist the courts for legal action.

Direct and Indirect Learning. A teacher, human or machine, formally (as in the classroom) or informally (as on a nature walk through the woods), directly transmits information, attitudes, and skills for the manifest purpose of promoting some kind of change in the pupils. Indirectly, pupils as well as teachers (the human teacher, at least) are also always learning simply because life is full of casual opportunities for him who is ready to perceive them. Plainly, not everything that one learns is intentionally taught; Durkheim[81] has pointed out that "indirect effects on the character and faculties of men [are] produced by things having quite a different objective: by laws, by forms of government, the industrial arts, and even physical phenomena. . . ." Simply living with things, sounds, and people; under government or among machines, teaches something about the strength of authority, the impenetrable nature of matter, and so on. Participation in certain social relations indirectly confesses a sense of identity as well as knowledge of one's status and its importance. Even an ax, hoe, dress, or painted pot contains lessons available to anyone who can decode them, not merely lessons pertaining to using those objects but also information about discriminating between patterns, colors, materials; guidance in discovering the limits of one's strength or size, and so on. Much learning that currently inheres in tools, fasteners, buildings, toys, and countless other artifacts would utterly cease if those things suddenly disappeared from culture.[82] Speech and writing provide the major media for lifelong direct learning. It follows that inadequate skill in using language sharply limits or rigorously directs what an individual will learn.[83] The restricted speech repertory of working-class children compared with that of middle-class children definitely hampers them in profiting from school instruction, even when both groups enjoy equal educational facilities.[84] Play, by contrast, richly furnishes opportunities whereby much youthful learning takes place, including muscular habits and the meaning of significant social roles —often long before children can realistically utilize those habits or play the roles.[85] Sometimes it is hard to tell whether a lesson is directly learned or comes as a byproduct. Are children's prejudicial and other ethnocentric attitudes derived from parents who teach them consciously, just as they teach religious beliefs? Or do children displace on persons whom they evaluate as socially inferior the frustration, resentment toward authority, and hostility that harsh, authoritarian parental treatment arouses in them? No doubt it works both ways, but psychologists can't yet say which is primary.[86]

Active and Passive Learning. My examples have shown that learning takes place passively almost as often as it does under circumstances where a pupil actively rehearses his lessons. We see the distinction afresh among Eskimo, where boys encouraged by adults actively practice hunting and building snow houses whereas girls, who acquire the same skills and in an emergency can execute them, though a little less skillfully,[87] do so mostly by watching and listening when the opportunities arise. I am reminded of an incident that occurred among the Kaska Indians, where girls are also not expected to learn actively to hunt. One day in late fall my wife and a Kaska Indian companion, Clara, were walking to a nearby settlement when 19-year-old Clara spied a porcupine up in a small tree. She seized her ax (without which northern Indians never travel in cold weather), cut down the tree, dashed in pursuit of the fleeing animal, caught up with it, and efficiently dispatched it, exulting, "I'm as good as a man!" An American professional man's wife often learns her husband's role passively, yet well enough to be able to advise and help him without openly practicing it. Akin to the active and passive distinction in learning is that between autogenous and sociogeneous learning. An individual learns some forms of culture autogenously, or by himself—giggling is an example—without aid or direction while other learning he undertakes with active social support.[88]

Other Learning Experiences. All communities enjoin some deeds but negative learning means that someone is taught never to carry out certain behavior because of its undesirable significance or its inappropriateness to one's rank, which may be either too high or too low, compared with that of the people who regularly perform such behavior.[89] Samoan girls shy away from prematurely emulating adult women's roles because to do so would carry a forbidden note of presumption.[90] Through negative learning, some social systems maintain a mosaic type of social structure, the many, various social categories being identified by sharply delimited occupations, hair or beard styles, and forms of dress.[91] In the Sindhi-speaking village of Pat, West Pakistan, where I lived, members of the landlord stratum never learn crafts or repairs, because labor with one's hands is a social blemish so disreputable that the deed would be held against the family for a long time, blocking its claim to high prestige.[92]

Socialization utilizes learning that proceeds via empathy, imitation, and identification, three processes that overlap and mix with one other.[93] Empathy allows a person to adopt and enact feelings and muscular states that have been conveyed to him. You can observe its operation in children who imitate the posture of a bystander or pretend to drive a speeding, swaying vehicle. Margaret Mead notes the typically feminine stance and posture adopted by 10-11-year old Iatmul boys who prior to their initiation spend much of their time among women. Identification that also uses imitation is present in the medical student who emulates an admired professor whose role he is himself mastering. How an individual shall identify himself—by the age, sex, or some other quality possessed by the model—will be pressed upon him through the vocabulary others use to him, the dress he wears, and the expectations voiced by his admonishers. U.S. teachers using such forms of address as "children" or "class" stress age identity, whereas use of personal names would emphasize individuality and might enlarge each pupil's capacity to learn from a greater variety of role models. We also acquire some behavior absorptively, through a kind of psychic osmosis or behavioral contagion.[94] Not merely food preferences or aversions and speech habits are "caught" from others—perhaps from family members with whom one identifies consciously or unconsciously—but also ways of falling ill, symptoms of illness themselves, and ego-defense mechanisms.

Communities make unequal use of various modes of learning, of all of which people are by birth presumably capable. Java and Bali, where babies are limp and soft and keep their neonatal flexibility, heavily rely on kinesthetic learning, especially for classical dancing. In one famous Javanese school in Jogjakarta, boys and girls chosen for their aptitude imitate a teacher who stands with her back to them.[95] Not a word is spoken as occasionally an assistant will move a child's arm into a different, desired position. The only sound is the orchestral music of gongs, strings, and xylophones. In Bali the teacher stands behind his pupil and pulls the young body into prescribed positions. Balinese also put a premium on a child's passive acquiescence to other forms of behavior. A mother expects her baby to go limp, and embodies this expectation in every movement she makes while handling it. Being flexible, the baby in turn reactivates the mother's expectation and maintains it through feedback. When looked at in a wider context, the Balinese use of kinesthetic learning turns out to be quite suited to the culture's overall design of socialization, in which adults consistently maintain, and rely on, the young learner's passive acceptance.[96] Although Balinese children partake of heaven a little more than adults do, they aren't regarded as at all equal to adults in their ability to participate fully in the community's social life. To make a child ready, adults who hold and move him literally put him through a series of appropriate habits. Monotonously his carrier pulls back his left hand and extracts the right to accept something, for nothing must ever be taken with the left hand. At every turn his teachers place a premium on passively allowing others to shape one's behavior into desired forms, just as the dancing master does. A child is passed from hand to hand in a company of girls and women, who all assume responsibility to keep him from

In Bali a teacher standing behind a dance pupil, manipulating his body into prescribed positions, illustrates the use Balinese make of kinesthetic learning. (Indonesian Information Office)

unacceptable activities. If he seizes a forbidden object, it is taken from him and replaced by a substitute. If he wanders, he is pulled back. From all this the child learns to associate a pleasant mood with conformity to social expectations, whether in etiquette or dancing. Deviation from the customary pattern creates a sense of distrust. Although the Manus utilized kinesthetic learning far less than the Balinese do, it was also apparent in this lagoon world where the people lived in pile dwellings reached by rickety ladders. A year-old child learned to clutch his mother firmly around her neck; whenever his grip slackened she reseated him with a decisive, angry gesture, communicating to him the necessity to hold on tightly.[97]

Disciplines. With learning goes enforcement or discipline, both positive and negative,[98] though dictionary usage has made

negative discipline so much the more familiar of the pair that the idea of discipline being positive has all but disappeared. Instead of interfering with behavior, positive discipline enlists rewards and promises of reward to instigate adaptation and expression. In childhood, positive sanctions stimulate a child to identify with his parents or other adults and to imitate heros and other social models. Discipline positively considered urges a person to exploit his resources for growth and directs him to mine his environment for satisfactions of which he and his community approve. Positive discipline begins in infancy when a baby is put to the breast to nurse and thereby achieves a dependable sense of relaxation, enterprise, and confidence on which his ego thrives. This prototypal situation of learning accomplished through help will be repeated throughout life whenever social arrangements hold up, as their primary object, growth rather than suppression. Soon tangible rewards (candy, gold stars, money) as well as such incentives as praise or a pleasant mood that allies a child with his mother come to be added to the repertory of positive reinforcers. Communities and subdivisions within them have their own values governing what sanctions to emply. U.S. mothers in a New England town felt unhappy about rewarding children materialistically for good behavior. To do so, they felt, would teach them to be good merely to obtain candy or another prize, not for the sake of being good itself. They much preferred incentives like praise or maintaining a loving relationship with the child. Many American mothers present models to the child, themselves or a neighbor's youngster, to illustrate what they want him to be and not to be. Middle-class mothers, especially, are prone to reason with a youngster; in effect, they label a preferred course of action, thereby outlining it very explicitly, and explaining its probable outcomes versus what to expect if some other line is followed. Reasoning increases in use as a person matures, being very readily employed in adult socialization. However, it has special problems when employed with children. Even when the parent has a sufficient stock of clear reasons suitable to a child's understanding, it is time-consuming and leads to arguments should the youngster brightly counter with his own reasons for adhering to a different course of action. In small-scale, homogeneous social systems, reasoning is unlikely to be heavily employed, because there people don't ordinarily reflect on why anyone should follow traditional behavior.

Negative sanctions threaten, or actually bring, punishment, the variety of which is almost infinite. Western man's complex structure of law, the sting of shame and contradiction, the loss of social support, the illegal sanctions of discrimination and "justice" by night-riders are only a few culturally familiar examples drawn from the huge panoply of devices that man has utilized to control the behavior of his fellows. For children, Euroamerican mothers favor techniques like distraction, chastisement, ridicule, and the kind of isolation that occurs when they withdraw their affection from a child to indicate their displeasure with his behavior. "I love you very much when given a chance," F. Scott Fitzgerald[99] wrote to his daughter, Scottie, after she had disappointed him several times. He was trying to impose one of the subtlest of all punishments, implying that by being good she could keep a happy, loving relationship extant between them. Parents often withdraw affection more by lack of responsiveness than by any direct act or statement. They look coldly at the child, banish him in a separate room, or refuse to listen to what he says. Sometimes they threaten him with separation or say that he is making them unhappy, as Fitzgerald in one period many times told Scottie in his letters. In the United States, at any rate, evidence suggests that even physical punishment controls behavior less by the pain it inflicts than through the blow it delivers to the child's self-esteem and by the way it interrupts the free flow of parental love and affection. Some children find the parental disapproval it signifies very hard to bear. From the young person's perspective, a warm, affectionate parent inflicts more severe punishment by spanking than a cold parent, in whom there is little affectionate behavior to be interrupted. This explains why lower-class children who grow up in crowded and relatively loveless households can't be controlled even by parents who use much physical punishment. In other communities, where parents are so warmly affectionate that they prefer to leave threats and whippings to strangers, masked gods, and other impersonators, such punishments should be much less painful than they would be if they wrecked the gratifying character of the parent-child relationship. Formal learning theory steps in to warn that although punishment often succeeds in eliminating children's undesirable behavior, in itself it lacks direction and doesn't teach any alternative behavior. It may even arouse hostility, or create some other emotional state that blocks the child from learning.

Some social systems favor ridicule as a punishing device. Frequently Euroamerican grade-school children, who never hear one of their well-trained teachers ridicule a pupil's failure, employ it themselves in the classroom, tittering at one another's shortcomings when called on to recite or to answer a question.[100] American Indians found ridicule as handy as praise, and incorporated both practices into flexible naming customs that allowed them to substitute a ridiculous sobriquet in place of a praise-laden one when somebody grossly blundered.[101] Ridicule makes a person highly sensitive to others' opinion and instills a quick sense of shame or concern with losing face. In one respect shaming works on personality like "psychological discipline" that relies on a mother abruptly cutting off her customary warmth and affection. Where love-oriented discipline prompts a child to make the mother's demands his own, lest by neglecting them he again earn the unbearable loss of her love, shame in conjunction with a weak or vulnerable ego creates fear lest others discover one's deficiencies and offenses and once again release their crushing ridicule.[102] In either case, the external sanction is internalized, so that it comes to operate autonomously, from within the person.

Punishment is neither randomly nor accidentally chosen by members belonging to a given social system; it follows traditional lines, adheres to general values, and is governed by sympathies for the person being disciplined. It may possess complex unconscious meanings for persons who practice it, relating, for example, back to the parents' own childhood and their experience with negative disciplines.[103] In a socially stratified community, the character of discipline varies with the family's class or caste position. Middle-class mothers in a New England town, compared with working-class mothers, demonstrate greater affectional warmth to youngsters and use ridicule less as a form of punishment. But they more often deliberately withdraw their love or warmth to discipline the child. Some people believe that youngsters in small-scale communities rarely dissent in the course of their socialization and that therefore negative discipline is unnecessary for them.[104] My own experience in several small-scale northern-Canadian Indian and Eskimo communities supports the thought that negative discipline may be infrequently used, but what I say is based largely on impression. The hypothesis deserves much more serious testing.

FURTHER READING

A number of general readings which I am about to recommend for this chapter carry over into treating social agents of cultural transmission, like the family, parents, and school, a topic which forms the body of Chapter 7. This is true of an early work by W. D. Hambley, *Origins of Education Among Primitive Peoples* (1926), a book now mainly of historical interest. Franz Boas broadly reviews socialization under the title "Education" in *Anthropology and Modern Life* (1932: ch. 8) as do Gerald H. J. Pearson under the still more restrictive title "The Psychoanalytic Contributions to the Theory and Practice of Education" (1959), and Margaret Mead in her encyclopedia article "Education, Primitive" (1931). I also suggest an attentive reading of chapter 3, "Criteria of Experience," in John Dewey, *Experience and Education*

(1938). Jules Henry has compiled "A Cross-Cultural Outline of Education" (1960) that could serve as a guide in field-work on socialization, and Jean Floud and A. H. Halsey examine sociological and anthropological approaches to "Education and Social Structure: Theories and Methods" (1959). "Culture and Socialization," by David Aberle (1961), reviews "causes" and related matters pertaining to the process; W. H. Sewell covers "Some Recent Developments in Socialization Theory and Research" (1963), while, under the title "Socialization," (1954) Irvin L. Child gives theories and surveys a somewhat earlier literature on the same topic. Methodologically directed, Child is especially concerned with the use of correlation studies that relate parental behavior to the later behavior of the child, including his own work with J. W. M. Whiting, *Child Training and Personality* (1953). *Research on Children*, published regularly by the U. S. Children's Bureau Clearinghouse for Research on Childlife, contains abstracts of much current research on many aspects of child development, including socialization. The active role a person himself plays lifelong in socialization forms the main theme of chapters 1 and 2 in Ernest Becker, *The Revolution in Psychiatry* (1964). Without much recognition of cultures other than his own, Daniel A. Prescott summarizes how "The Individual Shapes Himself," in *The Child in the Educative Process* (1957: chap. 11). J. Rouart, "Développement de la personnalité" (1957), presents a very useful summary of developmental and related psychological theories. David P. Ausubel devotes chapter 3 of his *Theory and Problems of Child Development* (1958) to heredity in relation to environment. For a more substantial account, see Amram Scheinfeld, *Your Heredity and Environment* (1965). Theodosius Dobzhansky reiterates the degree to which culture and personality depend on a genetic base; see his "Cultural Direction of Human Evolution—a Summation" (1964) and *Mankind Evolving* (1962: chap. 3). A symposium in the *Merrill-Palmer Quarterly* for October, 1963 (vol. 9, no. 4), considers the "Contributions of Piaget to Developmental Psychology." Piaget's work is also appreciatively summarized in chapter 5 of Roger Brown, *Social Psychology* (1965), and in Henry W. Maier, *Three Theories of Child Development* (1965: chap. 3). J. P. Scott reviews research on "Critical Periods in Behavioral Development" (1962), mostly directed to nonhuman vertebrates. Many topics connected with development are examined in Robert I. Watson, *Psychology of the Child* (1965), along with pertinent empirical studies and the methods they used. In "The Psychology of Social Learning" (1949), Edward C. Tolman shows how all of personality structure, including the cognitive maps by which men act, can be accounted for with formal learning theory. The wide applicability of formal learning theory is further demonstrated by Albert Bandura and Richard H. Walters, *Social Learning and Personality Development* (1963), while Robert A. LeVine describes some applications of "Behaviorism in Psychological Anthropology" (1963a), referring to Hull's formal learning theory.

REFERENCES

1 Dewey, 1938: 4, 5.

2 de Beauvoir, 1948: 40.

3 I follow Kardiner (1939: 124), who obtains his data from Bogoras (1909). Compare Bogoras' account of the Chuckchee with Syomushkin's novel *Alitet Goes to the Hills* (1952) and with the account by Antropova and Kuznetsova (1964: 825–835).

4 M. Mead, 1951c: chap. 5.

5 J. W. M. Whiting *et al.*, 1966.

6 M. Mead, 1954b.

7 M. Mead and Macgregor, 1951: 18.

8 M. Mead, 1954c: 404.

9 Bredemeier and Stephenson, 1962: 86–89.

10 M. Mead, 1947d.

11 J. W. M. Whiting and Child, 1953: 107–109, 116–117.

12 M. Mead, 1956c: 363–369.

13 Herskovits, 1948: 37–45, 626.

14 M. Mead, 1963b.

15 Lucian, 1711: iv, 156.

16 Locke, 1959, I:140.

17 Cooley, 1902.

18 Dewey, 1922.

19 G. W. Allport, 1955: chap. 2–3. Note a similar disparity of views at the 1964 Social Science Research Council meeting on socialization, reported in M. B. Smith, 1965: 18.

20 Thomas and Thomas, 1928: 572.

21 Dewey, 1887: 382–386; in what follows I also draw on Dewey, 1922; Kostiuk, 1961; E. Becker, 1964: 14, 25–26, 38, 42, 172, 173.

22 Myrdal, 1965.

23 I. Honigmann and Honigmann, 1953.

24 R. D. Hess, 1963.

25 Sartre, 1956: 409–411.

26 Piaget, 1932: chap. 1.

27 Bredemeier and Stephenson, 1962: 72.

28 Hentoff, 1964.

29 Sapir, 1932 and 1934a.

30 Stern, 1938: chap. 4.

31 Hambly, 1926: 212.

32 A. F. C. Wallace, 1961b: 116.

33 W. Bruce Cameron, personal communication.

34 Leites, 1948: 110–112.

35 On many points in this paragraph I take leads from Ausubel, 1958: 4–5, 106–107, 116–119.

36 Gesell and Ilg, 1943 and 1946. See also Walters and Parke, 1965.

37 M. Mead and Macgregor, 1951.

38 M. Mead, 1947e.

39 Ibid.

40 Havighurst, 1952; L. B. Murphy, 1962: 293 and 1964.

41 Piaget, 1929 and 1932. For a historical note on Piaget's life and work, see John H. Flavell's chapter in Kessen and Kuhlman, 1962. See also the critique by R. I. Watson, 1965: 492–494.

42 Piaget, 1932: 104–170

43 Ibid., pp. 196, 250–261.

44 Havighurst and Neugarten, 1955: chap. 6. See also research in West Africa by G. Jahoda, 1958a and 1958b.

45 M. Mead, 1932b.

46 Voth, 1901: plate LII, following p. 94.

47 Cf. R. I. Watson, 1965: chap. 3.

48 Dollard, 1935.

49 Angyal, 1941: chap. 10.

50 R. D. Hess, 1963: 552.

51 Horney, 1939: 42–46.

52 Kardiner, 1939: 21.

53 J. Henry, 1948.

54 R. I. Watson, 1965: 62–66.

55 In Tanner and Inhelder, 1956–1960, II:185–197.

56 J. W. M. Whiting and Child, 1953: chap. 11.

57 In Ross and McLaughlin, 1949: 366–367.

58 Kagan and Moss, 1962: 272.

59 Ausubel, 1958: 103–106; R. Benedict, 1938.

60 M. Mead, 1956c: 368.

61 L. B. Murphy, 1962: 308–312.

62 Bowles, 1954: 7.

63 Hull, 1937: 26.

64 Cf. Hilgard, 1956; Wolman, 1960: chap. 4 and 435–438.

65 N. E. Miller and Dollard, 1941. See also Kunkel, 1965.

66 J. W. M. Whiting, 1941.

67 Festinger, 1961; D. Lawrence and Festinger, 1962.

68 G. W. Allport, 1960b; Apple, 1951–1952; Tolman, 1948.

69 Cf. Bandura and Walters, 1963.

70 A. F. C. Wallace, 1961b: 115; Sutcliffe, 1952.

71 Spiro, 1953. I strongly suspect that a formal learning theorist would find much

less trouble than Spiro does in explaining how a belief in ghosts requires reinforcement. See also Noam Chomsky's critical look at B. F. Skinner's claim to be able to explain complex, real-life behavior with his formal learning theory. This appears in Chomsky's review of *Verbal Behavior* in *Language*, 1959, 35: 26–58.

72 J. W. M. Whiting, 1941: 176–177. By permission of Yale University Press.

73 A. F. C. Wallace, 1961b: 115.

74 Lorenz in Tanner and Inhelder, 1956–1960, I.

75 Harlow and Harlow, 1965a and 1965b.

76 Margaret Mead in Tanner and Inhelder (1956–1960, I:207) makes a negative statement about human learning apparently consistent with imprinting. Thumb-sucking, she claims, is absent in every group where somebody feeds the baby within an hour of birth. Such prompt feeding, she hypothesizes, avoids some kind of deprivation.

77 Bateson, 1942–1943: 77–79.

78 M. Mead, 1964a: 107.

79 *Ibid.*, p. 80.

80 Merton, 1957: chap. 4.

81 Durkheim, 1956: 61.

82 M. Mead, 1964a: chap. 5.

83 *Ibid.*, chap. 6.

84 Bernstein, 1964: 67.

85 G. H. Mead, 1934.

86 Mosher and Scodel, 1960.

87 M. Mead, 1964a: 61

88 M. Mead, 1946: 673; she credits Wayne Dennis with the distinction.

89 M. Mead, 1964a: 62, 72.

90 M. Mead, 1928a.

91 Coon, 1951: 2–6.

92 J. J. Honigmann, 1960.

93 M. Mead, 1964a: chap. 4.

94 Du Bois, 1949.

95 Unsigned article in *The Times Literary Supplement*, July 16, 1964. See also M. Mead, 1940–1941.

96 M. Mead, 1940–1941.

97 M. Mead, 1930b: 23.

98 Kardiner, 1939: 25–29, 44. Much of what follows draws on Sears, Maccoby, and Levin, 1957.

99 Fitzgerald, 1963: 40.

100 J. Henry, 1960: 286.

101 Pettit, 1946: 59–74.

102 M. Mead, 1961a: 494.

103 Wolfenstein, 1955e.

104 Nathan Miller, 1928: 260.

Socialization and Cultural Context

7

The human mind is of a very imitative nature; nor is it possible for any set of men to converse often together, without acquiring a similitude of manners, and communicating to each other their vices as well as virtues.[1]

DAVID HUME

. . . the nature of the end implies, in part, that of the means. When society, for example, is oriented in an individualistic direction, all the educational procedures which can have the effect of doing violence to the individual, of ignoring his inner spontaneity, will seem intolerable and will be disapproved.[2]

ÉMILE DURKHEIM

GROUP MEMBERSHIP AND PERSONALITY

If in certain respects every man is like all other men, like some other men, and like no other men, then men must everywhere be influenced by inescapable, similar conditions; by experiences they share only with certain other men, and, finally, by combinations of heredity and experience unique from one individual to another.[3] What most interests me are cultural phenomena that lead a person to behave in ways resembling the ways of people who belong to his own community, social stratum, or organization. I recognize the inevitable fact of individual uniqueness and am concerned with how it fares in culture, and I am also concerned with why some behavior refuses to conform to even the most insistent social norms. But mainly I want to know how it is that many of the same human potentials—like the ability to love, fear, and project; the determination to resist ambiguity; and the capacity to reach out toward further growth —come to express themselves differently in each culture.

Mainly, though by no means exclusively, cultural influences reach personality through social relationships, both those that involve direct face-to-face interaction and those in which contact is impersonally mediated through books, movies, teaching machines, and other artifacts. To be sure, people also shape their ways of thinking, feeling, and acting through activities in which they engage and through their experience with artifacts. Oscar Lewis[4] speaks of "the brutalizing, isolating nature of the farmer's work" and its "far-reaching effects on his personality" in Tepoztlán. Equally good evidence indicates how greatly the airplane and radio have altered Western man's conception of time and distance, and how with television a whole generation has grown up convinced that "seeing is believing."[5] In fact, social interaction doesn't occur by itself but in context with other activities and with the support of physical things—tables, chairs, rooms, and machines —that channel it. Nevertheless, I believe it proper to accent human links as the most important channel of socialization. From the standpoint of socialization, the most significant, sustained, and systematic human relationships work themselves out in enduring groups, like the family, a lasting peer group, or a closely bound neighborhood, though occasionally even a chance acquaintance or an author pulled at random from a shelf exerts a lasting social influence, even if he is but momentarily known. When a person is socialized in plural groups that possess radically different characters, he is simultaneously or alternatively exposed to a variety of experiences in response to which he modifies his behavior. Such diversified social relationships don't necessarily produce troublesome results for personality development; after all, the groups' expectations may be wholly compatible, or else the person segregates what he learns, vigilantly keeping it in its proper time and place. He reserves one vocabulary for the street and another for the classroom, one set of attitudes for his friends and another for his teachers.[6]

FAMILIES, INDEPENDENT AND DEPENDENT

The family is undoubtedly effective in enlisting young members' cooperation in a broad range of socialization, and its influence probably lasts longer than that of any other group. Founded by parents who mutually perceive advantages in a constant supply of love, sex, and economic goods and services, the family skillfully uses those resources as it induces its members— mainly children, but to some extent also adult members—to modify their behavior according to norms that it transmits and enforces as an agent of society. Practically everywhere, within the family the mother controls the key events that affect children's personalities, though her degree of importance varies culturally. The father's key roles, again making allowance for cultural variation, largely go to facilitate his wife's maternal services and, in manifold ways, to protect and sustain the mother-and-child pair. Family relations are compounded of more than mutual help, gratification, love, harmony, and devotion. Each actor in the domestic circle also feels hate, disappointment, anger, frustration, and selfishness, and the long-term balance between positive and negative emotions profoundly affects psychological development. When expected behavioral modifications fail to appear or when norms lose their hold, the family may apply stern sanctions to compel conformity. If they should fail, or conflict becomes too great for the family to master, it dissolves, imperiling each member's welfare. Dissolution is much more likely should the group consist only of two parents with their offspring and lack the buttressing of authoritative grandparents or helpful siblings of parents. The continued presence of those other relatives may help keep the group together even if the parents themselves would like to separate.

Personality formation hinges on the household's structural features, such as the number of children present, inclusion of other persons in addition to the parents and their children actors' relationships to one another, the group's atmosphere, as well as on the members' temperamental and other personality characteristics. Where two parents independently rear children in comparative isolation from other relatives, a child can hardly escape responding to the crucial emotional importance of parents in his life. Nobody can replace them, no one else shares the time and responsibility that they devote to his early rearing. Hence the orphan's grievous plight. A child reared under the concentrated affectivity of the small, independent family gains an extreme sense of personal responsibility and a strong, clear feeling of identity. He learns to perceive himself as vital in any chain of action in which he engages.[7] Those things happen in a household consisting of a single biological family, a unit so familiar to many readers that they regard it as "natural."

Yet in many social systems the nucleus of two parents and their children doesn't exist independently; it is embedded within a larger cluster of similar nuclei that form a household. Parts of India and Mexico have several brothers living together around a common courtyard with their wives and children, the whole group perhaps standing under the authority of the brothers' father if he still lives. Hopi Indians expect married sisters and their husbands to remain in the maternal household, as the Kaska Indians also prefer; this arrangement makes a number of "mothers" readily available to each child. In Africa south of the Sahara, a man often installs his several wives in separate houses within a compound dominated by his father or some other patrilineally related elder. A newly formed Samoan nuclear family buds in a household that contains either the husband's or wife's parents, and other relatives living in the village also remain ready to care for the couple's children. The Samoan youngster, who has half a dozen adult women ready to care for him and to dry his tears, and half a dozen males possessing degrees of authority over him, doesn't find his own parents to be as crucial as they are to U.S. children. He diffuses his affection and patterns his emotional attitudes after a host of kinsmen. The developmental effects of his parents' distinctive personalities on his own are consequently mitigated, and he becomes endowed with a broad basis for adaptation.[8] Grandparents living in the same household with parents and their children double the ambivalence normally kindled between parents and children. Small children in such families are treated with an extra generous share of gratification (degree of infant indulgence in a culture is roughly proportional to the number of adults regularly occupying a single household), but the training they receive with respect to sex, dependence, and aggression is also quite severe when grandparents are on hand to lend added support to social values in which they have had a long commitment.[9]

I don't speak of children briefly visiting indulgent grandparents who lack formal authority over the small biological family. I am describing a social system like that found among the Sioux, Cheyenne, and other Plains Indians, wherein the parents' parents possess formal childrearing roles which they exercise daily. In such a setting the older generation acts as a conservative force that brakes people's readiness to change, and anchors each subsequent generation firmly to tradition. There, in historian Marc Bloch's words, the most malleable is joined "to the most inflexible mentality."[10] Among the Omaha Indians a grandfather warned a girl, saying: "If you do not learn to do these things and abide by the teachings of the elders you shall stop at a stranger's house and your place will be

A Kaska Indian grandfather plays with his daughter's child.

near the kettle pole, your hand shall rest on the kettle pole and without being told to go you shall go for water, and when you have brought the water you shall look wistfully into the door of the lodge, and they will tell you to open a pack so that they may do their cooking."[11] The Plains Indians were and remain culturally very conservative. They have struggled to perpetuate their culture with as little modification as possible, even after such mainstays as the buffalo and war disappeared, the shack displaced the tipi, and much of their land slipped into the hands of avaricious frontiersmen from the East.

COLLECTIVE CHILDREARING

From time to time, men have experimented with social inventions intended to attenuate parents' roles in socialization, or even as far

as possible to eliminate them. Robert Owen, founder of a nineteenth-century Wabash utopia that failed, believed that the community should rear children past the age of three, in order to prevent them from perpetuating their parents' wrong ideas.[12] Equally idealistic European Jews who founded Kiryat Yedidim, an Israeli kibbutz that Melford E. Spiro and his wife studied in 1951, planned through communal childrearing to uproot unwholesome parental authority and free women from the yoke of domestic service by eradicating the traditional, capitalistic, male-dominated Western family.[13] They created the kibbutz, a revolutionary social form designed to prevent the growth of economic classes and to end man's exploitation of his fellows. To perpetuate kibbutz life, with its twin ideals of communal work and common ownership, they planned for children to be reared collectively. As early as possible their care would be taken over by trained socializers —nurses, nursery-school teachers, and other educators—who represented the kibbutz and wholly embodied its ideals.

Collective childrearing in Israel, and in residential nurseries found in Soviet Russia and other East European communist countries, is sometimes mistakenly identified with the depriving institutional care given, with shocking psychological consequences, to motherless children.[14] In countries where women's roles approximate the responsible social roles of men more closely than they do in the United States, children are not separated from their mothers as completely as if they were in an orphanage. Nurseries simply relieve mothers of many childrearing obligations, leaving them free to work for the country. Even institutions that care for youthful clients who lack biological mothers need not be the psychologically deadly and emotionally starved places they have sometimes become. The most severe, adverse effects on development occur when childrearers fail to provide

Melford Spiro

youngsters with substitute maternal care, because they are too busy to mother children individually and because they repeatedly expose young children to traumatic separations from mother figures with whom the youngsters have formed deep emotional attachments.[15] A well-run institution that makes conscientious, nurturant surrogate mothers available can be a better place to grow up in than a home where a mother severely rejects and inadequately mothers her own baby. In Kiryat Yedidim, a nursing mother visits her baby many times daily during the six months' vacation she enjoys before resuming work. Afterwards, parents may drop into the nursery or youngsters' dwelling as often as they like, though generally they get together with their children in the evening when work is over. At that time they voluntarily supplement the nurses' caretaking and training duties, something that runs counter to the philosophy of communal education, which holds that after a child is two years old parents should only be responsible for loving the child. In response to the nurturance and comfort that nurses and nursery teachers extend, the children manifest strong love and dependence toward those caretakers, though the adults' disciplinary roles also generate hostile feelings, just as the parents' would. Unwittingly, a child sometimes calls a nurse "Mother" and deliberately puts her in the parent's place. His desire to keep the nurse's approval makes him obey her, probably as often as he would obey his mother. By 1951, the kibbutz's system of communal socialization had produced comparatively few young adults to observe for the long-term results of the system and Spiro's brief return to Israel in 1962 allowed him time to do little more than register a few impressions. They were, however, favorable impressions. The young people he had known in 1951–52 struck him as having developed into mature, purposeful individuals endowed with responsibility and good humor.

THE WORLD INTRUDES

I picture the family as forming a bridge across which society introduces its norms and values, as well as its resources and opportunities, to the child all the while that he remains dependent on adults' protective care. Traffic is heavy across the bridge, for the child learns about the world from many kinds of messages that his perceptive parents, who experience it much more fully than he does, carry to him. What his parents or their surrogates do in the realm beyond the household very much colors their interaction with the child, and significantly affects his socialization. In Frobisher Bay, Eskimo parents who are most firmly integrated in town life through steady jobs, committee memberships, and house ownership put more pressure on children to attend school than parents less actively involved in town affairs and busier making a living off the land. In a social system where people accumulate food through farming or animal husbandry, small children are too ineffectual to play productive roles; but precisely in such communities they experience the strongest pressure to be responsible and obedient. On the other hand, there they are somewhat spared from the necessity to achieve and become self-reliant or independent, for farmers and cattle-breeders don't insist very forcefully on those particular virtues, which appeal more to hunting and fishing people.

Apparently each type of social system cultivates those personal attributes which its technological system demands for successful adaptation.[16] We who demand moral responsibility in education, business, and personal conduct also expect it early in a child's maturation; hence we regard as moral backsliding even his failure to drink neatly from a cup after he has once mastered that skill. To take a somewhat different example of technological roles influencing personality formation, an Alorese infant in his tropical, mountainous country makes no garden in the wet season. Yet, Abram Kardiner claims, he never in his life escapes from the psychological consequences of the fact that his mother does so and, as a result, frequently leaves him hungry during a critical period of his life.[17] Where mothers have few economic obligations and are required to play only small parts in ceremonial life, observers rate their maternal behavior as more indulgent toward their infants than in places where tasks load them down.[18]

A complex chain joins the U.S. father's family role with conditions that he experiences daily in his work-place. A man subject to heavy subordination and supervision on his job, who receives much disparagement and little respect or esteem from society at large, becomes endowed with a large fund of hostility to direct against his wife and children.[19] That is one reason why children in lower-class families generally experience more hostility, greater severity, and less warmth than their middle-class peers. Remember that such conditions in early socialization also encourage a relatively weak superego which exerts little anxiety or guilt when a person fails to live up to social norms. It is as if lower-class men who win little approval from the world find themselves short of approval to use in rearing their children. The way such men are apt to compensate for their daily bitter frustrations and other social difficulties—for example, by overvaluing physical power—brings the family into still more distress. A man who compensatorily exercises his strength on his helpless wife and children, persons whom he can safely control, creates a serious problem for his son. The boy won't be inclined to admire or resemble someone who terrorizes him. Since the father in such a family often withdraws considerably from his family, spending much time away from home in other groups, he isn't even physically available as an object of his son's identification. Hence the boy turns to his mother for emotional support and identification, only to find himself subsequently hampered by that sexually inappropriate choice and forced to rebel violently against it. This he does, aided by all manner of culturally provided symbols of aggressive masculinity, and with few pangs of conscience. An obvious way of redirecting this unwholesome chain of events would be to enhance the social esteem and security which lower-class men receive for their work. However, Americans (who identify income and esteem) are neither wise nor willing enough to distribute social esteem and respect generously. Nobody is entitled to approval unless he first gives proof of having acquired socially valued skills. If in such circumstances the son's superego and other motives turn out to be too weak to induce him to delay his own gratifications, so that he drops out of school before he has learned sufficient skills to raise his social value to the level which his community demands, he will likely grow up to reenact his father's role in his own family and to rear his own youngsters for failure.

Childrearing in the middle-class family likewise reflects the father's status in the world beyond the household, whether he derives his income from owning and operating his own enterprise in the "old" middle-class manner, or follows the "new" pattern of working for a bureaucratic corporation.[20] The new mode of middle-class life

❨ Who Are A Child's Most Important Moral Surrogates?[21]

Answers for this question can be obtained by asking a child what he considers to be good and bad things for someone of his age to do and who would praise or blame him for doing each. Compare children's answers given in Kiryat Yedidim, an Israeli kibbutz; in four American Indian tribes, and in the midwestern United States. The figures show the percentage of children who mentioned parents, educators, groups, etc., as sources of praise or blame. (Percentages total less than 100 because I have not included all types of socializers.)

I

Percentage of children mentioning

	Age category	Parents	Educators (nurses, teachers)	Groups (peers, kibbutz as a whole or other group)	Self
Kiryat Yedidim	6–11	18	32	32	0
" "	12–17	13	20	58	1
" "	18+	5	0	76	11

II

Percentage of children mentioning

	Age category	Family	Teachers	Age mates	"Everybody"	Self
Papago Indians	8–18	73	4	5	8	1
Hopi Indians	8–18	49	6	11	14	1
Zuni Indians	8–18	75	11	3	2	1
Sioux Indians	8–18	39	12	9	13	—
Midwestern Euroamericans	10–18	45	16	9	14	3

The kibbutz relegates parents to a minor role. Furthermore, in the child's opinion their importance declines with his age (along with the importance of nurses and teachers), while the power of other group members and of the individual himself increases. Papago, Hopi, and Zuni Indian children mention the family more often than Euroamerican children do, which suggests that those southwestern Indians invest the family with moral authority more exclusively than do Euroamericans.

emerged in America toward the end of the last century. In place of being responsible for a private enterprise and resolutely facing the risks of the marketplace, a man in the "new" middle class works in a large, protective organization; adheres to its highly codified rules of procedure, and benefits from its many security and welfare provisions. Detroit mothers belonging to the "old" middle class, in the way they rear their children for self-control and personal reliance—as though for the responsibilities of private entrepreneurship—are individualistically oriented. They are significantly more likely than bureaucratically oriented mothers to feed their babies on schedule and to begin urinary training before the child is 11 months old. Much less likely are they to respond immediately to a baby who cries when "nothing is wrong with him." They reveal less permissiveness, and demonstrate an inclination to teach the child that he must be ready, if necessary, to change himself to adapt to society. More strongly than "new" middle-class mothers do they dissuade the baby from finding pleasure playing with his own body, and they are also readier to leave it at home in a competent person's care while the mother shops. These entrepreneurially oriented mothers appear to be communicating to the child that if he can't change, he should be strong enough to exercise his power of will rather than to remain simply passive.

Not only does what parents do in the world outside or the social virtues they uphold intrude on socialization. Technological innovations in culture quickly seep into the household to transform traditional modes of childrearing. This happened among Winnebago Indians when diapers, training pants, and wooden floors came along and moved formerly highly permissive mothers to hasten toilet training.[22]

Parents, by utilizing their more extensive experience in society; their greater knowledge of its demands, opportunities, and pitfalls, and even their disappointments and failures, try consciously to prepare children for successful social participation. They encourage skills they know to be rewarded, encourage habits likely to succeed, and warn against personal traits that can only bring disapproval. "I don't want you to live in an unreal world," F. Scott Fitzgerald wrote to his daughter, "or to believe that the system that produced Barbara Hutton can survive more than ten years, any more than the French monarchy could survive 1789. Every girl your age in America will have the experience of working for her living. To shut your eyes to that is like living in a dream."[23] Thus, a boy or girl is guided toward success and warned from danger by parents who dearly want him or her to taste, as fully as possible, satisfactions that the world offers. Obviously, the more parents know about their society, the better they can ready the child to participate in it. Any particular family, however, can screen only selected aspects of the world. What parents perceive depends on the range of their own experience, roles they have played, the breadth of knowledge they have attained, and the sensitivity they have cultivated to social demands. Those assets, you know, depend very closely on the social stratum which the family occupies. Well-informed parents never forget that the world outside is always changing. They don't want to give their children a dangerously out-of-date image of life, or information as useless as an ancient road map would be in a suburban area newly built up on the margins of a freeway.

The importance attached to the family's cultural composition, meaning the degree to which it refracts a reasonably complete image of the social system which the child will some day enter, is nicely shown by comparing two types of households found among North Dakota Mandan Indians.[24] In an all-Indian household, which contains little Euroamerican cultural influence, a child internalizes a fully Indian character structure. Experience teaches him to get along with whites, but he never becomes like them. "Just like lizards that change their colors," an Indian explains, "with whites we act one way and . . . with Indians we act another way." The presence of a white model in the family, resulting from an Indian man's marriage to a woman of European descent, alters the group's cultural composition. Most Mandan children who grow up in such mixed families adopt (even overadopt) Euroamerican cultural standards. Having been well prepared to live in a world conforming to white values —even speaking English at home—they find it comparatively easy to quit the Indian community and move toward wider participation in Euroamerican society. Judging from the existence of two highly divergent modes of child training in the United States —one exercised by entrepreneurially oriented mothers who emphasize control, hardening, and strictness, while the other, practiced by bureacratically inclined mothers, leans toward encouragement, reward, and affection[25]—U.S. parents deliberately choose methods they believe suited to achieve what their experience indicates to be desirable personality characteristics. Since our social system isn't wholly agreed about what method is best to follow or what type of personality is most desirable, American parents carrying out their childrearing roles face much conflict and uncertainty. The very discrepancy between diverse parental standards in a social system is a condition that influences personality, contributing to a relativistic and tentative approach to life from which some people recoil with hardened resolve and intensified rigidity.

The family forms a bridge which messages from the world outside reach children. In the other directions, the family sends out members it has prepared for roles in the larger society. Not that parents teach everything that has to be known. Espe-cially, they can't complete a child's education in a large-scale, complex, heterogeneous social system. Take political roles, for example. Compared to growing up with family and lineage elders—kinsmen who also form public authorities—U.S. domestic life provides scarcely any preparation for playing roles in the country's political system.[26] In a world like ours, where political, occupational, and other roles differ widely from roles the individual learned to play in the family, many additional learning situations become essential to round out his training. Even so, a person is more apt to choose political and other attitudes that harmonize with what his parents' believe than he is likely to choose contrary to them, and in that way early training does carry over.[27]

INSTABILITY THROUGH TIME

Like other cultural phenomena, beliefs and customs connected with socialization change with time. Indeed, if socialization means the process whereby people embody their culture and prepare themselves to realize social expectations, then it must be sensitive to many social phenomena as they change. Especially marked and well documented are the changes that have crept into ideas and practices connected with childhood socialization in European and American culture during the last two or three centuries. We smile unbelievingly at John Locke advising parents in 1693 to maintain discipline over children as firm as that which they would keep over a dog or a horse, "creatures [not] half so wilful and proud . . . as man."[28] Some variations in socialization are doubtlessly matters of random cultural drift,[29] but during the last half-century in America some changes have occurred in response to our new conceptions of human nature and as a result of our heightened regard for play.[30] American parents who can't shake their disapproval of infantile thumb-sucking and childhood masturbation are carrying over attitudes belonging to a day that believed children to be endowed with unshakeable, dangerous impulses needing to be vigilantly and firmly controlled so that children wouldn't hurt themselves. By the middle of the present century, childhood had been bowdlerized and the baby transformed into an almost completely harmless creature whose erotic impulses, infant-care manuals said, should be ignored. One can almost see the new spirit becoming entrenched. The *Ladies' Home Journal* of 1920 advises parents to avoid "any act tending to produce in after years, what the psychoanalysts call infantile fixation."[31] During early childhood, it warns, "command and exhortation are worse than no avail. . . . the child should be encouraged to tell his fears . . . to unload unpleasant emotions from [his] soul" lest they accumulate with dangerous later consequences. Release, not self-control and suppression is recommended.

Parents who obeyed such advice no longer regarded the enjoyable as synonymous with the wicked and deleterious. Gratification has become virtuous, at least in some things.[32] Playing with a baby, instead of "spoiling" it, has become an aid to its development and acknowledges one of the child's inherent needs. In a culture where not to have fun is cause for suspicion, where impulse gratification has become a matter of duty, parenthood itself is idealized as a joy; not a matter of stern, moral virtue. All this keeps pace with other changes in culture, like our shortened workweek, longer vacations, and increased means for enjoyment. A "fun morality," stressing gratification in place of puritanlike inhibition and denial has emerged, influenced by the subtle action of profound technological and social changes, including greater economic productivity and increasing urbanization.[33] In cities, the family has grown smaller and thus able to devote more attention to individual members; it doesn't have to fend so much for itself, leaving members more time to have fun. Even in the country, automobiles and modern roads have brought families close to towns and regularly draw many timesaving urban services to the kitchen door. Cities have facilitated revolt against traditional morality by switching over child care from one set of principal socializers—parents who earnestly guard tradition—to teachers. Children spend much time away from home, especially among peers, thereby accentuating their separation from parental control and the traditional morality parents guard. In fact, parents' ability to control their children has virtually collapsed in some parts of the city, giving rise to high delinquency rates in those neighborhoods.[34] Increasingly, the world, since World War I, has favored an experimental, nontraditional approach to life, and greater responsiveness to

⟨ Advice in Infant Care, A U. S. Government Publication, Grows Increasingly Mild and Permissive[35]

Severity in the handling of	1914 to 1921	1921 to 1929	1929 to 1938	1938 to 1942–1945	1942–1945 to 1951
Masturbation	*Decreases*	*Decreases*	Constant	*Decreases*	Constant
Thumb-sucking	Constant	*Decreases*	Constant	*Decreases*	*Decreases*
Weaning	Increases	Increases	Constant	*Decreases*	Constant
Bowel training	Increases	Increases	*Decreases*	*Decreases*	*Decreases*
Bladder training	Increases	*Decreases*	*Decreases*	*Decreases*	*Decreases*

inclination, not merely in childrearing but also in economics, government, literature, art, and other areas of culture.

If Bateson[36] is right that the child who learns by punishment sees one world and the child who learns by reward perceives a different one, then a substantial new *Weltanschauung* must have been created for many twentieth-century Americans and other inhabitants of the Western world.[37] American and English parents, apart from learning to respect a child's needs more, and to show more consideration of his wishes in respect to his eating habits, toilet accidents, dependence, and freedom of movement outside the home, also resort to physical punishment less than they used to. For discipline they make more use of reasoning with a child or else deprive him of some measure of their warmth when he has done wrong.[38] These changes are most marked in the middle class, though they have also begun to reach toward lower levels in stratified communities. Protectiveness of girls has declined and comradely affection between father and child, especially father and son, has intensified, the man's role becoming much less authoritarian than it had been. This is not to say that discipline has become less compelling, or—contrary to what some critics say[39]— less effective. Discipline has become surer and much more persuasive in its ability to induce youngsters to embody adult standards and values. Modern disciplines urge a child to identify with his socializers, which in turn creates in him a highly sensitive superego. However, shortcomings have also been found in modern childrearing methods by people who value qualities like masculine accomplishment, competitiveness, and self-assertion. Something in the modern family has led boys to neglect cultivating self-assertion, independence, and leadership. What is that "something"? Probably the fact that their socialization has become more like girls' has traditionally been. It

seems that boys acquire such qualities (which, after all, may have been more important in an entrepreneurial than in a bureaucratic culture) when the father rather than the mother acts as the main disciplinarian—that is, in a patriarchal context—not where fathers are affectionate pals to their sons.

But cultural changes rarely please everyone. Some people, pleased as they are with their current way of life, remain nostalgic for selected bygone virtues, even though such remnants of the past have lost their appropriateness for contemporary conditions. To counteract such laggards, governments lend their power and deliberately increase their totalitarian span of control, to the point where they try to alter socialization so that it, and the social personality it will hopefully produce, keep up with other revolutionary changes. This happened in the Soviet Union, where Bolsheviks recommended that teachers and parents swing over to western European types of childrearing and education.[40] Postrevolutionary parents did adopt new patterns which, they expected, would better suit their children for the kind of world they expected to build.[41] For example, they largely abandoned religious training and gave up trying to preserve tradition. They made achievement-drive and the cultivation of personal values, like security and self-expression, target goals for a young person to attain.

OTHER AGENTS

Social relationships apart from those enacted in the family, through the norms they present and the models they hold forth for imitation and identification, also pattern personality, particularly in the later years of childhood and throughout adulthood. Keep in mind that in all human relations, the influence people possess over one another stems less from what they are, objectively speaking—or think they are—than it de-rives from the meaning that one actor assigns to the other. Such meanings, whereby persons in interaction literally interpenetrate one another,[42] depend in part on ego's previous experience, in part on the other's manifest role behavior, and in part on the situation wherein both actu-ally confront each other—a situation whose own contours become meaningful accord-ing to the way ego perceives it. In Hume's[43] still apt phrasing, members of a group enter deeply into each other's senti-ments, causing "like passions and inclina-tions to run, as it were, by contagion, through the whole club or knot of compan-ions."[44] It must not be supposed that mu-tual influences proceed equally back and forth and that each group member pos-sesses identical intellectual, moral, or phys-ical power to affect those with whom he interacts. A person who identifies with an-other—say, a parent—or who surrenders himself to a generalized other—a reference group—puts himself on the receiving end of socialization. Attracted by the other's imposing image (as he perceives it, of course) or irresistably impressed by the persuasive authority emanating from group norms, and guided by his own needs, anx-ieties, and other traces of previous experi-ence, the learner incorporates the other per-

⟨ English Mothers Describe Changing Trends in Child Care[45]

Miner's wife: "Well you try to do a bit more for them, don't you? I always think you try to do just a bit more than you think was done for yourself."

Scaffolder's wife: "I'm bringing them up better. They used to stick to routine too much. They weren't allowed to have their freedom. You know, play and do things. I wasn't allowed to do things like playing with soil and things like that, like Lynn does —I wasn't allowed to ever get dirty. I was never allowed to make a mess."

Warehouseman's wife: "They've got more freedom, haven't they, today, kiddies have, than what we had. I mean, when I was young we didn't have so much money; and another thing, we had to go to Sunday School, I mean we *had* to go; I mean, it wasn't just put up to you, oh you please yourself, we'd *got* to go. On a Sunday you used to have your best clothes on, didn't you, and you used to have them on all day . . . I mean, we used to have to look after our clothes, but today they don't seem to bother, do they?"

Garage-owner's wife: "We're a bit more free and easy; I mean, Sundays, when we were young, meant best clothes and no toys and sit still, but my children wear jeans on Sunday and we go up to the allotment [individual plot of ground for growing family food] and get really messy. They did go to Sunday School for a bit, but Brenda said 'It's nothing but standing up and sitting down, we'd rather come to the allotment with you.' "

Driver's wife: "I think there's a much closer relationship between parent and child —of course, I was one of a big family—but I notice it with my older children; they can talk to me a lot easier than ever I could with my mother—even though she was a real good mother, I mean she was a wonderful person really, but you just couldn't get through to them in those days. I don't think, same as mine do to me. I think they're better for it, they want to be able to confide in you now and again; mind you, times have altered—there seems to be a greater pace altogether these days, they grow up very quickly."

son's expressive style, the group's standards or the model's characteristic ways of thinking and feeling that reach him as if by contagion.

Don't misunderstand me to say that under some circumstances socialization can act wholly from outside the person. Even when influence flows only one way, socialization amounts to more than slavish copying, passive obedience, or total surrender. A personality is always patterned thanks to the cooperation of the model-taker, who, perhaps unintentionally, utilizes this avenue to realize his potentials.[46] It may be the only avenue a poor person's straitened circumstances, a political prisoner's rigorous confinement, or a child's powerless situation allows, but, whether he is aware of it or not, the decision to comply behaviorally is his.

Social scientists, despite the respect they pay to subjective definitions of situations ("If men define situations as real, they are real in their consequences"[47]), are quicker to note objective characteristics of socializers. It is not surprising that they do, for where a thousand subtly different meanings might attach to grandparents, objectively they are grandparents, and by virtue of their anchorage in the past are apt to exert a conservative force in socialization. At least, that interpretation of their influence is a convenient hypothesis to explain the way some people, like the Plains Indians, have held on to their language, ways of thought, and memories of a past enduring like hot glowing embers. In other communities, notably in Polynesia, the youthfulness of primary agents of child care proves to be significant. Whereas grandparents introduce a child to matters over which they assert full command and assurance, a child-nurse who has barely begun to learn her own culture gives her charge a special kind of license to be himself. Injunctions are implanted lightly, reflecting their shallow roots in the teacher's own personality, and social

responsiveness is encouraged as the pupil implicitly learns that he and his nurse must avoid irritating elders who have charged a monitor with his care. Still another objective set of conditions exists when parents who stand at the pinnacle of their careers directly rear their own children. Middle-class Euroamericans, Manus described by Margaret Mead, and the Eskimo I knew in the Baffin Island town of Frobisher Bay, all fit in this category. Just as the parents expectantly face a relatively new and uncharted world, so their children learn to look toward the future curiously, "as though it were an unwritten chapter in an unfinished book," Margaret Mead says; a book they are being prepared to read.

The rise of influential new agents of socialization, in accompaniment with other historic cultural changes, will impinge on social personality. In America, beginning quite early in childhood, everyday companions who possess the same strengths and weaknesses as oneself have joined parents to become major sources of cultural learning. The change has been adaptive, for as parents fell out of touch with a rapidly changing world they needed help adequately to introduce that world to a growing child. Particularly immigrant parents arriving in the New World, confronting a culture whose details they themselves had to master, lacked preparation to serve as effective models and teachers. School-age children even became the sometimes impatient educators of their elders. The increased importance of peers in socialization has resulted in attenuated self-respect, led to increased reliance on conformity, and to some extent substituted the comfort of crowd approval for individual moral autonomy. The force of guilt has weakened, while shame to a great degree has taken over the superego's function of controlling behavior.[48] That conclusion, however, brings us face to face with an apparent contradiction. Earlier, I reported on U.S. mid-

Eskimo children in Frobisher Bay are started in life by alert and confident parents facing an as yet uncharted world. They, in turn, approach their future as if it were "an unwritten chapter in an unfinished book."

dle-class patterns of socialization which, through the calculated use they make of love-oriented techniques of punishment, whet the effectiveness of a superego that has firmly embodied adult social norms. Now, however, I say that under the influence of peer groups, conformity based on shame is replacing the importance previously possessed by guilt. Possibly there has been no shift from guilt to shame. The contradiction disappears if it can be demonstrated that contemporary conditions promote intensified social awareness along with a heightened sense of personal responsibility. If this interpretation is true, then it follows that nowadays people will be conflicted between inner-directed commands strongly sanctioned by guilt and other-directed pressures firmly backed by shame. Thus, both shame and guilt will be heightened in effectiveness.

The role peers play, of course, extends beyond childhood. It operates especially powerfully whenever persons, like college students or army recruits, are confronted with an unstable culture to which they must constantly, quickly, and surely adapt. In such impersonal situations, the good opinion of peers counts for a great deal, which allows mastery of social standards to be effectively harnessed to their reinforcing attention and approval. Peers don't only cue the newcomer to what authorities formally expect; it is of even greater consequence that they are able firmly to set the unofficial limits within which a newcomer learns to carry out formal expectations. The peer group's informal expectations may deviate widely from official norms, but only rarely does any question arise as to which set of standards will prevail. When conflict does arise and an individual, like the rate-buster, adopts official norms in favor of the peer group's demands, he becomes deviant in his fellows' eyes and may be punished by them to the extent their power allows. In Viet Nam we saw what happens if the peer group perceives the official norms under

Home from school, this girl trudges up to her mountainside home in the Austrian Alps.

of ideas, skills, patterns of relationship, and complicated artifacts. They can also afford to pay for the specialists' training and upkeep. In them, formal education becomes essential for survival, though by no stretch of the imagination is everything taught in the schools equally vital. Schools also help generate new ideas and lead to combining in novel forms existing skills or knowledge, and so they enrich still more the social system's complexity, and intensify its need for schools, teachers, and the professional middlemen who mediate culture. Unfortunately, everything a middleman handles loses something of its freshness or immediacy, and in the classroom the relevance to life of even the most vital ideas or skills often grows pretty dim, becoming just more dull facts.[50] Our schools largely fail to apply known methods of retaining the meaningfulness, fullness, and richness that accompany learning in real life, where pupils learn by doing things in circumstances that endow those acts with meaning and good sense. There, learning is also apt to be much more pleasurable than in the classroom, because it captures a larger share of the pupil's interest, motivation, and alertness. In the confining atmosphere of most schools, with their enforced, prolonged passivity and heavy proportion of negative discipline, young people fail to understand the relevance and practicality of much that they are taught and, especially in a heterogeneous community, can't relate it to the kind of life they will live.

Much that a child learns is useless to him for the good reason that in his eyes it plainly lacks the lustrous values with which the teacher or textbook idealistically surround it. Children mark the school's artificiality. Even more painfully, they experience its deadly boredom, against which they withdraw; for example, by dropping out or by organized rebellion.[51] Drop-outs, you know, face an unenviable future. The value we put on schooling so all-pervades con-

which it operates to be attacked by outsiders. In response to dissonant antiwar sentiments voiced back in the United States, the enlisted men intensified their commitment to war with all its dangers and discomforts, and didn't lose morale as some concerned citizens feared they might.

For good reason, schoolteachers and similar, trained, highly specialized agents of deliberate instruction—cultural middlemen —who teach the child in a setting sundered from his normal surroundings thrive mainly in large communities that possess considerable technological and social complexity.[49] Communities of such scope need instruction on a higher level than the family or peers in order to maintain their huge stock

temporary American culture that many jobs and on-the-job training possibilities remain firmly closed to a youth lacking high-school or college training, no matter how alert or motivated he may be.[52] Without trying to insure that everything school offers will be useful for life and for a job, Americans make a safe, full passage through the school system a prerequisite for enjoying many adult cultural advantages. Those who get off before the eighth, twelfth, or sixteenth year of schooling are considered unfit for all the privileges the social system has to offer, and, since labeling is a form of self-fulfilling prophecy, unfit they too often duly become. They find no desirable jobs; don't move up the class ladder; on the incomes they earn or welfare payments they receive, they can't buy the goods which in our society give visible proof of social worth; they lack the manners, speech, and tastes that win people wide acceptance, and are unable to cope knowledgeably with many areas of life in a complex social system. We refuse to use our ingenuity to find a mutually satisfactory place for so-called uneducated people. Hence we doom them to what they and we recognize to be an inferior life.

MATERIAL PROPS FOR LEARNING

Not all the agents of socialization are personal. Man-made products also play a significant role in socialization, especially in literate social systems where the printed word efficiently communicates the hoarded information of centuries. Vehicles, tools, weapons, and other material apparatus are props as indispensable for certain types of cultural learning as is the laboratory apparatus of our universities. Some countries have strenuously debated the unintended consequences of mass media, especially the influence of movies, TV, and comic books on childhood. Whether or not their role is critical remains unclear, mainly because too

much has been claimed for them. A sociologist hypothesizes that such mass media mainly reinforce existing attitudes in American youth but don't themselves create such attitudes.[53] Undoubtedly they contribute a great deal to setting local fads and even international behavioral trends, but these mostly remain on a peripheral level of personality.

Children's school readers carefully pored over daily in many classrooms probably influence considerable childhood learning, even though they may not be the sole instillers of the attitudes they foster.[54] Stories in third-grade readers used in U.S. schools repeatedly show effort or work rewarded; they extol self-assertion as an effective means of reaching desirable goals. Like the morals that parents and teachers point up, these school readers reiterate the importance of acquiring skills and of learning well; but they don't praise intellectual activity as such. Children read that it is good to gather more and more isolated bits of information, especially from persons in a superior knowledgeable position, but they aren't encouraged to acquire understanding. Unrealistic optimism prevails in these children's books; failure rarely occurs, and goals are quite easily attained. Reflecting a poorly concealed bias in American society, central characters in the stories are male more than twice as often as they are female. Surely this confirms the reader's belief that one sex is more important than the other, even if that isn't the only way he finds it out. Stories frequently differentiate male and female roles, just as our culture does. They generally leave female characters to display affiliation and nurturance and to flee danger; rarely do girls display traits of activity, aggression, achievement, or construction; seldom do they win recognition. In other words, girls are pictured as kind, timid, inactive, unambitious, and uncreative. Furthermore, characters in the story who are nurtured by a central charac-

Comic books portray unheard-of adventures to these Frobisher Bay Eskimo children.

ter are mostly female, suggesting that females are likely to be in a helpless position.

Here is an excerpt from a third-grade reader. Note the way the story presents male and female roles:

"I was playing here and the door closed and I can't open it!" said Amy from inside the closet.

"Push that thing above the doorknob," Stuey told her.

"I can't! I can't!" Amy was crying. "It won't push! Oh, Stuey, get me out. It's so *dark* in here!"

Stuey grabbed the doorknob. He turned it and pulled with all his might. But the door did not open.

"Amy!" he said. "I'll go and get Mother to unlock the door. She has the key on her key ring. It won't take long."

Amy let out a scared squeal and began to cry even harder. "Oh, don't leave me all alone. It's so dark!"

.   .   .

Then Stuey had an idea.

"Listen, Amy," he called to her. "I'm going to fix a light for you—kind of like a flashlight. I'll drop it down to you through the transom. Then I'll get Mother. O.K.?"

He could hear Amy crying. "All right," she said doubtfully. "But hurry up, Stuey. I don't *like* it in here."

Stuey got several things from his do-it-yourself box in his room. Then he began to work quickly and seriously at something he had often done for fun.[55]

The school readers portray males as bearers of knowledge and wisdom, and also as the persons through whom knowledge reaches a child. Strangely enough, the narratives frequently represent children as better socialized than adults. That is, children conform more closely than adults to socially approved behavior. This raises the interesting possibility that if young readers should be tempted to identify with those adult characters, they may be induced to pattern themselves after disapproved behavior.

SOCIALIZATION FOR DEVIANCE

The same general process of socialization that equips near-ideal members of society helps the deviant to embody nonconformist, even illegitimate, versions of culture. Deviants strikingly remind us that socialization acts not like a mechanical cutter that turns out dozens of pieces of cloth tailored to the same proportions, but selectively, by fusing an individual's dynamic potential with social expectations, skills, and other resources. Consequently, as I have already said, no two individuals ever develop identical personality characteristics; social or status personality are abstractions, useful only so long as we don't reify them. In deviance, individuation has reached an extreme with respect to conspicuous or socially crucial personality characteristics. Basically, the deviant has missed firmly enough internalizing certain social norms by which others judge him. He has missed them because environmental circumstances prevented the norms from fully or clearly reaching him, because he couldn't comprehend their meaning, or because, for one reason or another, he rebelled and withdrew his endorsement from them.

However, to act deviantly is also learned directly, just as a person learns to farm, to choose the right objects for a trousseau, and to do long division. Some neighborhoods constitute literal schools for deviance; they are replete with suitable models inviting identification, and practically devoid of negative sanctions that operate against deviant learning. As a result, an apt pupil not only succeeds in learning what the larger social system regards as wrong, but his learning is even reinforced through positive discipline, as when boys who emulate adult gangster types win approval from peers and from the flattered models themselves.[56] Deviance sometimes comes through mastering perfectly acceptable social habits, like literary craftsmanship, marksmanship, or accurate knowledge of a city, which are then put to idiosyncratic and unwelcome uses. In any case, the underlying process by which the deviant comes to modify his behavior in response to socially patterned experiences is identical with the socialization of persons who cannot be regarded as deviants: Biological resources, including a given heredity, develop in interaction with society, perhaps aided by discipline. Even the family advances deviant socialization, occasionally directly but often indirectly; for example, when a stressful home tests to the breaking point an individual's capacity to adapt. Everyone has such a breaking point. As domestic poverty, parents' poor mental health, and harsh parental disciplines pile up stress, its weight comes to reach a point where it triggers off unwholesome, deviant reactions, like depression, protective withdrawal, or hostile acting-out against society. A society's deeply ingrained system of allocating prestige and other rewards, whereby it confines certain people to crowded slums and condemns unskilled workers to fruitless poverty, similarly engenders stress that can lead to deviance.

The crucial step in building a stable deviant career comes with publicly labeling a person a troublemaker, failure, drug addict, homosexual, or delinquent.[57] This step may come implicitly when others withdraw a job and friendships or otherwise destroy the person's normal, everyday life, as happens in a so-called correctional institution. Once the deviant accepts the public's label, the prophecy it implies begins to fulfill itself. Increasingly he shapes up to the image people hold of him, perhaps joining a deviant group in which his identity is readily justified, where he learns to operate with a minimum of interference. He may even rationalize his status with the aid of socially standardized beliefs borrowed from social sciences: "We are sick, sick, sick!" the youthful gang sings in *West Side Story*. Like other learning, deviants often develop their special proclivities with little or no conscious awareness of what they are doing. One object in counselling them is to intensify their awareness of their own development, to show them the track onto which they have switched their behavior, with the aim of halting the trend they have adopted.

STUDYING SOCIALIZATION, PARTICULARLY CHILDREN'S

Whatever contributes to socialization acts, as I have often said, in a cultural setting wherein it derives a large measure of its meaning and effectiveness. Hence, properly to study the process requires paying attention to the artifacts, persons, and conditions (like a group atmosphere or some intolerable ambiguity) that socialize *in* the setting wherein the agents operates.[58] I need to inform myself about what the pupil brings into the situation, his readiness and attitudes, as well as what the agent brings or possesses. Assuming I am dealing with a personal agent of society rather than books, tools, and other objects, to understand his influence I want to know his position in society and the conceptions he holds of himself, of his role, of his pupils, and of the material which he transmits. Those almost certainly relevant bits of information I want to perceive in as full a cultural background

as necessary. But how much is it necessary to know about the cultural background? And theory I find available for understanding personality formation is too general to allow me to tell precisely what elements in a particular culture impinge on an educative relationship between two or more persons. The result is a challenge to be as imaginatively creative as possible, to consider practically everything as potentially relevant—economy, ecology,[59] political organization, philosophy, religion. The greater the pattern of unexpected connections and ramifications that I can discover in a social system between background factors and the actual business of socialization, the more insight I gain into personality. The primary rule to follow is not to be so bound by existing theories, psychoanalytical or others, that presume to explain personality formation, that the potential significance of additional formative elements to which the theories are blind will be overlooked.

In Chapter 2 I said that field-going anthropologists, in contrast to psychologists and sociologists, tend to follow a characteristic method when they collect information about culture and personality. The divergence extends into the way each discipline studies socialization. To be sure, the approaches overlap more than I indicate, and mutual influence between them appears to be increasing; at least, anthropologists are trying to adapt the more precise research techniques of the other two disciplines. Nothing should prevent such diffusion, though it would be tragic if somehow it led anthropology to abandon totally its characteristic fieldwork methods. Quite properly, in what follows I spend most time on children because their socialization has pretty well monopolized the attention of investigators.

Into a New England town, psychologists sent interviewers who queried nearly 400 mothers about topics connected with childrearing, many of the questions being de-lineated in such a way that answers given to them could subsequently be treated quanti-tatively.[60] In each home they visited, the interviewers inquired about the degree to which a mother used reward, punishment, and other disciplinary techniques; her per-missiveness for behavior that stemmed from the child's hunger, eliminatory needs, de-pendence, sex, and aggression; her severity in trying to eradicate undesirable activities in those five behavioral areas, and her modes of inculcating desirable habits through values or goals held up to the child or through demands and restrictions placed upon him. The interviewers also gauged the mother's temperamental qualities, her warmth, affectionateness, and level of self-esteem, as well as other feelings and atti-tudes communicable to children.[61] Such are the topics—"dimensions," the New England study calls them—frequently studied by psychologists and sociologists who do research on childrearing. The New Eng-land study abstracted such dimensions from the web of interpersonal relations engaging adult and child. When time or children's age didn't permit the visitors to observe or question the youngsters themselves, the mothers were requested to provide informa-tion about how the youngsters responded to their warmth or preferred type of discipline. The investigators who drew up the research prepared the interview schedule in which they carefully assembled points on which information would be collected. Then they employed trained interviewers who went out, not to observe directly, but to ask a great many parents what they regularly do or did in relation to a specific child—say, at two years of age.

In contrast, the anthropologist acts as if he had all the time in the world as he goes off to collect his own information while liv-ing in the community whose childrearing practices he is studying. He stations himself where he can witness for a prolonged pe-riod of time what a relatively small number of parents and children do, as well as what they claim to do. He seeks their reasons for acting and for rationalizing their acts; he notes their goals and their frustrations. He pays as much attention to those who behave normally (according to expected pattern) as he does to those who by deviating from ideals sometimes cast the expected pattern in sharper outline. Though he may carry with him A *Field Guide to the Ethnological*

⟮ *Observe Child Training in Cultural Context!*

Our message and advice to those who follow us is that studies of child-training practices should not be conducted without a careful description and analysis of the environment that forms the context of these studies. This analysis should include a census of the number of children in the family and their ordinal position; a careful study of the mother's total role requirements for her family and community; a description of the father's role as husband, child caretaker, and model bread-winner and determiner of family status; some designation of the position of the family in the community and its relationships with neighbors and relatives; an account of the influence of nonparental caretakers on the child and the amount of time that the child spends with them; an estimate of variation in child-training techniques brought about by the use of various caretakers with varied requirements, and a measurement of the living space available to the family and a description of the way that it is utilized.[62]

LEIGH MINTURN AND WILLIAM W. LAMBERT

Study of Child Life,[63] and dip into it now and again to be reminded or freshly alerted, no schedule dictates what he must look for, or acts as the sole skeleton on which he must hang all his observations. Instead of lifting abstract dimensions of behavior from the intercourse of mother and child, the anthropologist keeps them embedded in their natural contexts as he describes the situations in which mothers actually act warmly, coldly, severely, or permissively. He keeps the total culture in mind, referring as much of it as necessary to the particular situation being described. That is, if mothers alarmedly recall small children from a swift riverbank, he makes clear how it came about that the children managed to get near the water and what the mothers were doing at the time.

Because sociologists and psychologists usually work with a comparatively small number of measurable variables at one time, they have adopted considerably more rigorous standards to govern their research than have anthropologists. They also usually select questions likely to be definitely answerable. They are more likely to examine the influence of childrearing procedures *on children* rather than tracing their influence further into adult life, as psychoanalysts and anthropologists frequently do. They carefully give the proportion of mothers who receive specific scores on affectional warmth or severe sex training, and who utilize love-oriented techniques of punishment. With such measures they confine their speculation; correlation and other mathematical techniques allow them to state precisely the degree to which mothers who practice one dimension of behavior report specific responses in their children.

By contrast, anthropologists' accounts are highly generalized, speaking of "the" Kaska Indian or "the" Alorese mother, as though in those social systems all women and children were alike. Sometimes they leave no way of discovering whether they are reporting a cultural ideal, a statistical mode, or a randomly selected pattern of behavior. You may ask why anthropologists

⟨ *Rating New England Mothers' Interviews for Affectional Warmth*[64]

A mother who scored high for affectional warmth, when asked what things she enjoyed in her daughter, Sally, said: "Well, I like her sweetness, and the way she speaks and the way she wants to do something to please, and her interest in things. She is very interested in everything, and of course, very anxious to learn to read, and she will very often get one of her books and read me a story, which is just laughable, but very serious to her, so we listen to it very carefully; and she likes to go and play records for me, and she loves to draw pictures for me, and of course, we make much of that sort of thing—neither one of them can draw worth two cents, but they love to draw. But just as funny as some of these things are, of course, I think they are all wonderful —all of their little accomplishments—and we hang them up on the kitchen wall."

This mother scored low in affectional warmth on her response to the question "What sort of things do you enjoy in Peter?" "Well, I don't enjoy too many things in him because at the rate he's going, well, he doesn't mind too well; he's got a mind of his own. I don't enjoy too many things. Like sometimes if I want to read or sing to him, he doesn't care to, he doesn't even want to sit down. Sometimes if I want to watch television for a half hour, and rest my brains, he starts annoying me. He doesn't want that, or else he wants me to go to bed with him. So I really don't enjoy too many things that he does because they're not worth enjoying."

don't also choose more readily answerable questions and equally specific fieldwork procedures, tactics that seem well suited to the goal of sound knowledge. Such a question can't be easily answered. To adopt those strategies would drastically redefine the objectives of cultural anthropology. Each discipline judges good work by its own standards and operates with its own, relatively autonomous conventions, which need not coincide with those of another field. I have learned to appreciate anthropological reports for their sense of immediateness, for the fullness with which they report a hundred details of context, and for their hunches concerning personality formation. In sociologists' and psychologists' reports, on the other hand, I admire the thoroughness with which research was designed long before questioning a single interviewee began; the quantitative presentation of specific facts, some statistically treated to bring out further significance; the tested hypotheses, and the interpretative sections in which the authors build new theory by reaching beyond the facts they have in hand.

Investigators belonging to any discipline may also try to gain information from children through projective tests, unfinished stories to which each subject fits his own ending, and cleverly contrived tasks susceptible of success, failure, or frustration. Such instruments are intended to tap children's perceptions and sentiments or to sample the youngsters' coping techniques and other personality characteristics. Obviously, investigators always secure as much personal information as necessary, like parents' ages, the duration of their marriage, education, the husband's occupation and income, and whatever else their research plan (which is based on previous research) defines to be theoretically significant. Such data allow other facts to be more meaningfully interpreted. For example, a U.S. husband's occupation, income, and education can be

used to locate his family's position in the social-class hierarchy. Such information can be used to enhance the significance of mothers' statements about their childrearing practices, which become additionally significant by being matched against the women's social-class position. Doing this had revealed the extent to which permissiveness and other dimensions of Euroamerican mother-child behavior vary from one social-class level to another. An investigator starting out on a relatively new problem may be totally unaware of what personal data are likely to produce valuable insights. In such a case, he may begin by undertaking an exploratory study which he executes in anthropological fashion to look for likely controlling variables, like income, education, or ethnic background. Later, he takes the hypotheses he formulated and incorporates them into a carefully constructed, pretested interview schedule, following which he probes to discover how often and how strongly the variables control the behavior in question.

CROSS-CULTURAL EXPERIMENTS

Although anthropologists still believe that all experiences which significantly affect a child influence the adult he becomes, the introduction of carefully controlled statistical procedures in anthropology has led to more delimited, experimental attention to specific events in early life and to how they enter personality formation. Such experiments treat cultures as though they constituted controlled laboratory conditions that can be manipulated, so that they will differ with respect to only a few preselected variables at a time. Then the cultures are compared, to learn whether, generally speaking, the presence or absence of some early experience, or the intensity and importance with which adults present some experience to a child (here we are dealing

with antecedent variables), make a difference for the presence or absence of some
adult personality characteristic or the relative degree to which some adult behavior
(the consequent variables) appears.

Let's be specific. In cultures where mothers turn their love on and off to discipline
children, do children grow up with over-
bearing superegos? In cultures with prolonged oral gratification, do adults throughout life continue to associate the mouth
with comfort and assurance? The pacemak-
ing investigation of this type, *Child Training and Personality*, by John W. M. Whiting and Irvin L. Child, uses a sample of 75
cultures (on which ethnographers have
written monographs) to investigate relationships between specific antecedents in
childhood and equally specific consequences in adults. (The terms "antecedent"
and "consequence" in a work using statistical techniques of correlation do not mean
cause and effect.) Since I shall return to
Whiting and Child's work and treat it quite
fully in a later chapter, I'll be brief here.
They find that in communities where childhood socialization is severe with respect to
weaning, people tend to be anxiously preoccupied with the oral zone. Presumably,
severe weaning led persons into their anxious, or negative, fixation on that zone; at
least, the theory on which Whiting and
Child base their work so assumes. Actually,
their method only tells the investigators that
indigenous medical theory in communities
practicing severe weaning is more likely to
trace illness to the oral passage than it is
likely to do so in communities that permit
oral indulgence. In many communities with
severe weaning, people believe that illness
results from eating and drinking magically
poisoned foods, from verbal spells, and
from sorcerers' incantations. We must assume that such medical beliefs validly indicate an anxious fixation on the oral zone,
which is in turn linked to severe weaning.
Another cross-cultural study using correlation discovers that communities in which
parents discipline children harshly tend to
believe in an aggressive, harsh spirit world.
That's all the correlation reveals. Theory,
however, allows us to fill in by reasoning
that people who grow up under harsh
parental discipline form aggressive parental
images in their minds which they later
project on supernatural figures about which
they learn, in much the same way that people who take projective tests release their
motivational states into the figures they perceive in ambiguous inkblots or drawings.
Even though such cross-cultural studies
each attend to only a few antecedent variables, that doesn't deny that many experiences exert a cumulative influence on personality.[65] When Whiting and Child
consult dozens of ethnographies to isolate
crucial childhood events and rate the force-
fulness of abstract dimensions of early
experience, they travel much the same path
taken by the psychologists who interviewed
the 400 New England mothers concerning
their childrearing habits. It so happens that
both undertakings have a common background and stem from similar interests
shared by the social scientists, some of whom
were once close colleagues.[66]

Most field-based anthropological studies
of socialization have been cross-sectional;
that is, an investigator observes the influence of child-training practices by simultaneously looking at small children who
are being socialized, at adolescents, and
at adults, who are not only doing the
socializing but represent fully socialized
human beings. He observes the effects that
follow by comparing one group with the
other. The fieldworker regards adolescents
and adults as the groups in which early
experiences have had a sufficient time to
work themselves out. To follow this strategy, however, he must be sure that the culture hasn't drastically altered since the parents themselves were reared, and that the
parents were in fact reared by the same

training practices they now apply and whose educative impact he is studying.[67] Data secured through the cross-sectional method may be considerably augmented by life histories and other retrospective accounts of earlier years provided by adolescents and fully mature adult informants. One hopes that their memories won't distort the past too much, and that subjects will cooperatively provide full information frankly and candidly.[68]

A rare anthropologist and a number of psychologists have carried out longitudinal studies of development, following the same youthful subjects for days, months, or years. Periodically they treat the children to observations and tests and utilize written sources of information, such as school and health records. Longitudinal methods can be employed to gauge the influence of earlier experiences on later personality or they may be used simply to trace, step by step, the emergence of changes in personality organization.[69] Visits by an anthropologist to a community that he or another person has studied earlier can be converted into longitudinal research provided that the previous investigators' field notes contain detailed information about clearly identifiable persons whose subsequent development may be retraced. The method can also be used with unspecified persons. Provided that no significant migration into or out of the community has occurred, one then looks to see how the same anonymous individuals who lived the culture on an earlier occasion have developed to the time of the second field trip. Those who once paddled canoes to the fish nets are observed cranking and repairing outboard engines; women who learned to cook in canvas tipis are studied as they keep house in three-room frame dwellings. When Margaret Mead[70] returned to Manus after being away 25 years, she recalled many of her informants by name and through their photographs. Yet her restudy deals mostly with a continuing group of largely anonymous people who successfully modernized their culture.

FURTHER READING

This chapter has devoted major attention to the social agents of cultural transmission or to what Clyde Kluckhohn and Henry A. Murray, in their important paper "Personality Formation: the Determinants" (1953), call "group-membership determinants" of personality. They present some readings dealing with those and the other determinants in a book which they edited with the collaboration of David M. Schneider, *Personality in Nature, Society, and Culture* (1953). Several chapters in Talcott Parsons and Robert F. Bales, *Family, Socialization and Interaction Process* (1955), refer to topics covered in this chapter, and James H. S. Bossard and Eleanor S. Boll, in *The Sociology of Child Development* (1960), give exhaustive attention to the family's manifold tasks. For another kind of communal education to place alongside the kibbutz material, see Monica Wilson, *Good Company* (1951), which describes the youth villages of the Nyakyusa. Good literature exists on schools as agencies of cultural transmission. See: Margaret Mead, *The School in American Culture* (1951d); Frederick G. Gruber, *Anthropology and Education* (1961); George F. Kneller, *Educational Anthropology* (1965); Bryan R. Wilson, "The Teacher's Role—A Sociological Analysis" (1962); and Ruth Landes, *Culture in American Education* (1965). In *Some Modern Maoris* (1946: chaps. 5 and 9) Ernest and Pearl Beaglehole discuss the difficult adaptation of Maori to the New Zealand school system; Melford E. Spiro examines distinctive patterns of an Israeli school, in *Children of the Kibbutz* (1965: chaps. 11 and 12); Gerhard Lenski points out some consequences of attending Catholic schools in the Detroit area, in *The Reli-*

gious Factor (1963: 267–280); and Murray L. Wax and others appraise *Formal Education in an American Indian Community* (1964)—the Pine Ridge Sioux, whose children are also the subjects of Gordon Macgregor's *Warriors Without Weapons* (1946). Books on child care socialize parents who, in turn, socialize their children. For a discussion of such literature, see Part III in Margaret Mead and Martha Wolfenstein, eds., *Childhood in Contemporary Cultures* (1955). Zevedei Barbu, *Problems of Historical Psychology* (1960), is concerned with historical changes and their impact on personality. Margaret Mead summarizes anthropological methods of "Research on Primitive Children" (1954b). All the projective *Methods for the Study of Personality in Young Children* examined by E. Lerner and L. B. Murphy (1941) may not be applicable to anthropological fieldwork situations but many deserve consideration. Jane Ritchie writes on the use of doll and plasticine play in *Childhood in Rakau* (1957: 105–133). David Ausubel, *Theory and Problems of Child Development* (1958: chap. 5), describes many ways of studying personality development, a topic that forms the substance of Paul H. Mussen, ed., *Handbook of Research Methods in Child Development* (1960), in which chapters 14, 21, and 22 directly concern personality. I must specially note "Contributions of Anthropology to the Methods of Studying Child Rearing," a review by John W. M. Whiting and Beatrice B. Whiting (1960), which forms chapter 21 in Mussen's book. This may be the most appropriate place to call attention to selected literature *Linking Social Class and Socialization,* which happens to be the title of a conceptually rich "workgroup report" edited by Harold Proshansky (n.d.). In chapters 9–11 of *Social Stratification,* Harold M. Hodges (1948) sums up studies of class-linked patterns of socialization and personality. William H. Sewell also appraises studies and assumptions bearing on "Social Class and Childhood Personality" (1961), while Urie Bronfenbrenner in a somewhat broader context covers "Socialization and Social Class through Time and Space" (1958).

REFERENCES

1 Hume, 1898, I:248. First published in 1748.
2 Durkheim, 1956: 132.
3 C. Kluckhohn and Murray, 1953.
4 O. Lewis, 1951: 296.
5 M. Mead, 1965b: 268.
6 Polgar (1960: 230 ff.) refers to a similar phenomenon by the term "biculturation."
7 M. Mead, 1942a and 1948b; J. J. Honigmann, 1946: 94, 148; Langner and Michael, 1963: 444–447.
8 M. Mead, 1928a: chap. 13.
9 J. W. M. Whiting and Murdock, 1951: 27–30; J. W. M. Whiting, 1961: 358–359.
10 Bloch, 1953: 40; M. Mead, 1951a: 14 and 1965a: 152; Deetz, 1965: 97.
11 Fletcher and La Flesch, 1911: 333. The Potawatomi, described by Searcy (1965: 92), still give grandparents prominent roles to play in socialization.
12 Owen, 1927: 280.
13 Spiro, 1963: chap. 3 and 1965. See also Rabin, 1958 and 1961.
14 Ribble, 1943; Spitz, 1945.
15 Ainsworth *et al.,* 1962: 142.
16 Barry, Child, and Bacon, 1959.
17 Kardiner, 1945b: 147.
18 J. W. M. Whiting, 1961: 358.
19 McKinley, 1964.
20 D. R. Miller and Swanson, 1958: chap. 4.
21 Spiro, 1965: 488; Havighurst and Neugarten, 1955: 117–118.
22 Oestreich, 1948: 91; *cf.* J. J. Honigmann, 1959: chap. 16.

23 Fitzgerald, 1963: 36.
24 Bruner, 1956b; see also his 1961 account of Mandan culture change.
25 D. R. Miller and Swanson, 1958: chap. 1; *cf.* Sears, Maccoby, and Levin, 1957: 434.
26 LeVine, 1960: 293.
27 Hyman, 1959.
28 Locke, 1880: 35.
29 Herskovits, 1948: chap. 34.
30 Wolfenstein, 1951, 1953, 1955c, and 1955d.
31 Stendler, 1950: 130.
32 Leslie and Johnsen, 1963.
33 Y. A. Cohen, 1961: 107–112; Newson and Newson, 1963: 243.
34 Faris, 1944: 744.
35 Wolfenstein, 1953: 129.
36 Bateson, 1944: 729.
37 *Cf.* Newson and Newson, 1963: 183, 201, and chap. 13.
38 Bronfenbrenner, 1958 and 1961; Hodges, 1964: 178–180; Newson and Newson, 1963: chap. 13.
39 LaPiere, 1959.
40 M. Mead, 1951e; Matthew, 1959.
41 Inkeles, 1955.
42 Teilhard de Chardin, 1959.
43 Hume, 1898: 248.
44 Social stimulation serves more ends than socialization. Extreme isolation and sensory deprivation grossly distort perception, disturb feelings, promote anxiety, lead to visual hallucinations, and foster delusions. Experimental evidence of those results warrants the conclusion that man depends on continued commerce with his social environment to maintain a high level of functioning. *Cf.* Solomon *et al.*, 1961.
45 Newson and Newson, 1963: 239, 240, 241, 244. By permission of George Allen and Unwin, Ltd., with acknowledgement to International Universities Press.
46 G. W. Allport, 1955: chaps. 8–9.
47 Thomas and Thomas, 1928: 572.
48 M. Mead, 1940–1941; Riesman, 1950; Lipset, 1961.
49 Herzog, 1962.
50 Hazell, 1965.
51 Coleman, 1961: chap. 11; see also Friedenberg, 1963.
52 Dexter, 1964.
53 Hodges, 1964: 193.
54 Child, Potter, and Levine, 1946.
55 Robinson *et al.*, 1964: 196–197. Originally from Moore, 1960: 71–72. Copyright 1960 by Lilian Moore. Reprinted by permission of Random House, Inc.
56 Glaser, 1962.
57 H. S. Becker, 1963: 31–39.
58 Geertz, 1959: 235.
59 Edgerton, 1965; *cf.* M. Mead, 1965a: 149.
60 Sears, Maccoby, and Levin, 1957: 12–17.
61 *Cf.* Minturn and Lambert, 1964: appendix III.
62 Minturn and Lambert, 1964: 292. By permission of John Wiley and Sons, Inc.
63 Hilger, 1960.
64 Sears, Maccoby, and Levin, 1957: 54, 55. See how similar ratings taken from systematically collected anthropological data are used in Minturn and Lambert, 1964.
65 *Cf.* Y. A. Cohen, 1961: 382.
66 Dollard, 1964.
67 M. Mead, 1954b: 759–762.
68 *Cf.* M. R. Yarrow *et al.*, 1964.
68 A. A. Stone and Onqué, 1959; C. Kluckhohn and Rosenzweig, 1949.
70 M. Mead, 1930b and 1956c.

Childhood in Culture

8

We must remember how we acquire our manner of acting and thinking. From our earliest days we imitate the behavior of our environment and our behavior in later years is determined by what we learn as infants and children. The response to any stimulus depends upon these early habits. Individually it may be influenced by organic, hereditary conditions. In the large mass of a population these vary. In a homogeneous social group the experience gained in childhood is fairly uniform, so that its influence will be more marked than that of organic structure.[1]

FRANZ BOAS

APPROACHES TO CHILDHOOD

In childhood, children learn not only to be adults but also to be children in whatever way adults define that status and with whatever rights, rewards, and responsibilities they endow it.[2] Children in every culture possess a distinctive status, and socialization, though it varies tremendously, in each carries its special pleasures and vicissitudes. This view is quite different from the untenable assumption which holds the child's life to recapitulate the evolutionary development of mankind, or regards Western children's attitudes, games, drawings, and thoughts to parallel the thinking, painting, and religion of contemporary adult "savages."[3]

Some accounts of child life in various countries and social classes cover in careful natural-history fashion how adults behave to their children and how the youngsters respond. They don't infer much of what happens psychodynamically or attempt to trace the long-term consequences of particular childrearing practices. Other reports, of which the investigation of the Maori made by a team of psychologists will provide a good illustration, devote themselves to the covert, psychodynamic processes of personality formation and say rather little about the day-to-day cultural context in

214

which those processes occur and are manifested. Such studies, which consider primarily the effects that certain adult practices have on children, have been a central interest in anthropological and psychoanalytic culture-and-personality research. Represented, then, in the reports that follow are two or three major ways of carrying out socialization research. The first concentrates on *how* socialization occurs, the second on *consequences* that can be credited to specific childrearing practices. A third approach, already alluded to, asks what leads adults to use one kind of rearing practice rather than another and searches for the answer in history, culture, and the adults' personality characteristics. Those questions I take up in Chapter 9.

Note in the accounts of childhood that follow another difference in the way they treat their subject. Most of them, like the one dealing with Egypt, adhere closely to a common-sense level of discourse. They present people whom we can understand and empathize with as they nurture and teach children and launch them into responsibility and independence. The children, too, seem familiar, even though they learn to behave in ways culturally very different from our own. The Maori study is conspicuously different. Enveloped in a mantle of psychological concepts, the account often so transmutes the child's experiences, and departs so far from a common-sense level of description and explanation, that we perceive concepts far more than real people in action. Such accounts are highly analytical and, in the popular sense of the word, "theoretical," though I insist that *all* observation, no matter on how rudimentary or common-sense a level, is informed by some theory.

Each of the following accounts that deals with an exotic setting (the so-called "anthropological" accounts)—Egypt, the Hopi Indians, the Maori, and a village in northern India—follows its own outline. If they cover the same subjects they do so in nonparallel ways; for example, the anthropologists who report on the North Indian village scarcely mention sex training. Sometimes such differences are due to the fact that the cultures dwell unequally on different aspects of childrearing. That is, some people put out special effort to promote independence training, the learning of sex roles, or superego formation, while other people deemphasize those ends. But differences also arise because fieldworkers hold different interests and operate with unequal standards of what they feel is important to treat detailedly. On some topics, also, no matter how important they regard them to be, they may have difficulty getting sound information in particular communities. The dearth of observations concerning sex training in the North Indian village stems from more than the fact that the account stops before children reach puberty; it undoubtedly reflects the severe taboo on sex in Hindu India compared, say, to tribal India.[4]

Yet the anthropological accounts possess a common character that sets them off from sociologists' studies of child life in various U.S. and Canadian classes. The fact that the latter all deal with Euroamerican culture, in which the observers were themselves probably reared, isn't the only reason why they possess a similar quality. Their authors also tend to play down early nursing, weaning, and anal training, interests that psychoanalysis bequeathed to anthropologists. Or else the sociologists encompass those subjects within broader topics, like the severity or permissiveness of parental actions in general. They are also apt to omit attention to familiar things, for they tacitly accept the cultural context including a household in which parents exert the predominant influence over children. Each of the following reports of childhood in culture covers a relatively brief moment in the history of those communities and social strata. They scarcely acknowledge that childhood has not always been that way. A number, however, recognize changes to be contemporarily under way and speculate about consequences they will have.

SUBMITTING TO ADULTS IN AN EGYPTIAN VILLAGE [5]

Rural life in hot southern Egypt alters little from one day to the next. Every morning most of Silwa's 3,500 people rise early, some literally at the crack of dawn to the meuzzin's chant as he loudly praises God in the day's first call to prayer. Sixty percent of the villagers live by farming, and sunrise sees men and boys from peasant families treading paths to the fields. Later in the day, when women and girls go to fill their waterpots in the Nile, they leave the village nearly deserted. Land irrigated by the river forms Silwa's major source of existence; it constitutes the great good, to sell which is about the worst thing that could happen. Everybody works, even children, who become economically ever more valuable as they approach the time when they will afford leisure to their aging parents. Economic interest, however, is far from being the only incentive to work; people are too socially conscious for that. The great care a man bestows on his most visible fields betrays how much social approval counts in what people do. Proverbially they call contentment an inexhaustible treasure, and to the extent that they don't strive competitively to accumulate wealth for its own sake they seem to live by the proverb. But a relatively undeveloped technology, as well as a weak achievement drive also lurk behind the village's unexpanding economy, for Silwa has benefited little from ambitious government plans to modernize agriculture and introduce conveniences. As a result, change has been slow enough to preserve considerable continuity between generations. Pride in family and lineage, respect for seniority, and undivided loyalty to the kin group (should it face threat) are paramount values. Out of deference, a son won't dare to smoke or even sit in his father's presence. The sense of sexual distinctiveness is so great that men and women scarcely look at one another, and a job that traditionally belongs to one sex will never be executed by the other. Women walk the village lanes self-effacingly, hugging the house walls and leaving the center of the walk to men. In the same spirit, spouses never betray public intimacy, certainly not before their own children. A woman won't even refer to her husband by name. The man holds family authority, but his wife manages the house and carries the storeroom keys. Children find it easier to achieve a comfortably warm relationship with their mother than with their father, through whom descent is traced, and with the mother's relatives more than the father's. Five daily public calls to prayer; God's name reverently murmured when starting a new task; heavy quoting from God's word, the holy *Qur'ān* (Koran), and respect due to men of piety and saintly ancestry keynote Islam. Such observances charge the culture with an almost tangible aura of sacredness. Even illness is partly explained by religion, if only by recognizing it as a God-sent, Job-like test of endurance and patience. However, Silwans don't unreservedly love their rural life or find complete contentment through its values. Juniors on occasion challenge seniors; kin-group solidarity sometimes cracks; pious religious scholars command less authority than they would like, and villagers with wider experience beyond Silwa disparage the village's satisfactions, unfavorably comparing them with those obtainable in cities.

Throughout pregnancy a woman has many ways ritually to express concern for her unborn child.[6] She keeps her state secret during the first month, thereby protecting the highly susceptible embryo from the baleful evil eye; she avoids ridiculing or criticizing anyone, lest the fetus be molded in that person's image, and she doesn't overexert herself. Her food cravings even enlist her husband in the business of reproduction; for him to help her satisfy them does her condition good. At the same time, the cravings, like the avoidances, enhance her social importance. Villagers say that "money and children are the joy of this life," and among those joys, boys rank first. Boys are a capital investment for both parents, and from birth they heighten a father's prestige. Swaddled in the parents' old clothes, a newborn baby is displayed alongside its mother's jewelry to show that to her its value outranks those precious things. During the next 40 days, angels themselves entertain the infant and guard it against evil spirits. Just the same, the mother rarely leaves its side, not even during the naming ceremony at which (as in other rites of passage, like circumcision, marriage, completing memorization of the Qur'ān, and returning from a pilgrimage to the holy city of Mecca) blood flowing from a sacrificed ram confers a blessing. After 40 days the woman quits confinement to resume her normal life. Stocked with gifts, she takes her baby to visit relatives, thereby ritually introducing it to the portion of society that counts.

Personality characteristics which a baby evinces are presumed to have been inherited from its mother's relatives through her milk. This doctrine, however, doesn't indicate a fatalistic readiness to accept whatever the child becomes, for parents concern themselves very much with directing children's moral development. Some engage a so-called "good" man or woman to call and "teach" the baby moral virtues. The tutor, after praying, transmits his goodness quite tangibly by giving the baby a sweet to suck, on which he himself has first nibbled. Since experience is also believed to set personal-

ity, it must be managed for a child; for example, by avoiding long-extended nursing, which a father fears will induce undue compassionateness and "darken" the child's mind. At first the mother nurses a supine baby, turning to it helpfully with her breast; but quite soon she encourages it to sit up for feeding as well as on other occasions. Although she offers her breast whenever the child is hungry, she conceives of nursing to be compassionate as well as purely alimentary. By feeding the baby she also in her mind sets up obligations for it. Some day she may pointedly recall them, telling a boy how "I enveloped you for nine months and . . . fed you with my breast." Reciprocally he owes her the duty of obeying and helping her. Somewhat earlier weaning for a boy (at about 18 months) than for a girl literally accelerates his growth, for which parents indeed wish. The earlier onset of weaning in one sex also recognizes different role qualities to be appropriate for men and women; women may safely be allowed to grow more compassionate. Silwans admit that weaning constitutes a conflict. It does so even for the mother herself, who believes both that a child has a right to nurse as long as he wishes (otherwise he will turn obstinate or disobedient) and that she should terminate nursing if she wants to conceive again. Knowing that a child only gives up the breast with difficulty, she begins to wean him early, gradually, and without severity. Mainly she tries to distract him, for instance by encouraging him to become interested in other activities. Toilet training has already begun by this time. A mother, sensing when a baby as young as 4 months must defecate, purposefully straddles it between her outspread legs. Then, with walking, a child receives instructions to signal its needs, and at the age of 3 or 4 he must leave the house to toilet. Throughout babyhood, siblings and other relatives attend to a little boy and girl affectionately and playfully, caressing and tickling them, throwing them into the air, and otherwise showering them with stimulation. Only older siblings deliberately encourage them to walk, and everybody remains most casual about sleeping hours, so that children learn to sleep anywhere and through anything.

Age 4 brings a sharp curtailment in maternal care, and reverses the pattern of gratification and "compassion" hitherto linking adult and child. For one thing, a younger sibling is born and displaces the older child from its central position in the household. Villagers not only expect sibling rivalry to occur; they deliberately exacerbate it; for example, by invidiously praising a younger to an older child. Without the test of rivalry, they believe, a boy would grow up too slowly and weakly; jealousy hurries him toward independence. Sometimes jealousy becomes excessive, whereupon the tormented, rivalrous child is propitiated by being permitted to regress a bit to an earlier form of gratification. Seated on his mother's lap, he is fed a special dish designed to enable him to bear up under the strain of rivalry. He needs much of such fortitude, for from now on rivalry of one sort or another will constitute one of his strongest incentives to appropriate behavior. Growing independent ushers the youngster into play groups of peers where, under rigorous sanctions of bullying, teasing, and ridicule, he is socialized into such cultural values as modesty. Under such circumstances, children acquire a strong sense of the meaning of social approval. Around the age of 5 or 6, boys publicly undergo circumcision, and girls, in full privacy, another genital operation, cliterodectomy. Circumcision signifies that a boy has attained a responsible religious status; it fits him for prayer. Less explicitly, the mutilation in each case symbolically identifies the individual's sex. In girls, the operation is also supposed to reduce sex excitement, thereby protecting them against temptation into premarital unchastity. Informally, cir-

cumcision and cliterodectomy carry a punitive connotation, for mothers threaten disobedient children with these operations. At the same time women prepare a son for circumcision by playfully manipulating his little penis while musing aloud over his future as a man among men. According to psychoanalytic premises, children around age 5 are strongly aware of their genitals and enter the Oedipus complex, whose confused emotions are likely to incite boys to worry about castration and girls about their lack of a penis. By this theory, threatening young children with genital mutilations, and then actually carrying this out, could be construed as taking advantage of a developmental stage to intensify and exploit such worries in order to enforce docility.

Silwans conceive of growing up as requiring strong restrictive disciplining of children, thereby insuring their conformity to adult standards of decorum, and making them subservient and afraid. Parents want to produce a docile child who won't bring shame on the family and a son who won't challenge the authority held by his father and other elders. Toward this latter end, a man gradually reduces his intimacy with his son, leaving him to discover greater warmth and permissiveness among his maternal kinsmen, who possess little disciplinary authority over him. Directly and indirectly, elders instill fear in youngsters. They create terrifying imaginary figures; point out danger inhering in sacred places, like a saint's tomb; threaten with snakes or even more dreaded scorpions, and encourage fear of God. Yet, increasingly as boys grow older they must suppress fear lest it betray that they are deficient in an important manly virtue, courage. In an uncommon interpretative passage, Hamed Ammar, who studied Silwa, hazards the hypothesis that fear aroused in children, together with the jealousy engendered by younger siblings, motivates the undercurrent of tension and suspicion that prevails in the village, and condition adult rigidity and cautiousness.[7] Prior to a child's adolescence, Silwan parents apply physical punishment readily and harshly, without regularity or consistency, and often while they are in a bad temper. They also discipline by sharp scolding, bitter sarcasm, and outright cursing, and leave the child no opportunity to justify his misdemeanors or mistakes. Parents have no ear for such explanations because if socialization "fails" they blame only themselves. Silwans seldom talk of their own childhood and have trouble recalling it, partly no doubt because little about it is pleasant to recollect and partly because a sharp antithesis separates that period from adult life. For example, adults are too conscious of their dignity to play games, and show no interest in children's play.

Children secure considerable relief from domestic pressure in play groups where they form friendly identifications and also vent aggression, either directly or through rough games. From 6 to 7 they rigidly segregate themselves in games according to sex, boys' and girls' play having distinctly different characteristics. Boys' games develop motor skill and coordination. They are aggressive and require considerable exertion, assertion, competitiveness, and brute strength, qualities that form part of the male image. Some even require the loser to confess that he is a woman. Girls play more quietly and less violently, in ways that frequently reproduce female occupations. Where boys settle differences with blows and wrestling, girls spit, pinch, bite, and vituperate. Much more than girls, boys color their games with sexuality. Clearly, play enables children of each sex to identify with their culturally defined sex roles. It also gives them a chance to exercise the highly valued principle of seniority, for leadership in a group always goes to the seniormost child, who consequently acquires power over his or her fellows. Adults, who like to see children progres-

sively wean themselves away from idle play, likewise regard children's stories as useless, demonic, to be discouraged. But surreptitiously at night, children recount expressive tales that, by all indications, go far to compensate them for their tensions, frustrations, and submissive status. Three general themes predominate in stories: first, good things that are eaten, enjoyed, hidden, won, and always abundant; second, masculinity, power, and authority; and third, revenge, retaliation, chicanery, and trickery. The latter subjects are reminiscent of how children resort to lies and deception to escape adults' ire. Stories also dwell on humiliation, fear of being outdone by others, powerlessness, and vulnerability. They release fantasies without disguise as they depict weak, ordinary people becoming powerful, superior, and heirs of good fortune.

Silwa has two kinds of schools: a relatively new national school at which attendance, though irregular, is ideally compulsory, and no less than six traditional religious schools that teach from the *Qur'ān* and encourage the book's memorization. Although learning the scripture brings God's special blessing it also occasions severe corporal punishment, which teachers aren't slow in administering. People voluntarily send sons to learn the *Qur'ān*, at least until they are old enough to work, but they don't cooperate as closely with the national school, despite the fact that it too includes religion in its curriculum. Its aim of abolishing illiteracy and its methods for doing so strike villagers as largely irrelevant. They may be right, since some people who attended and learned to read have subsequently relapsed into illiteracy.

With physiological adolescence, boys and girls have become conforming enough to be trusted to fulfill their adult responsibilities on the farm and at home. Adult tasks and topics of village interest gradually crowd out time for stories and games. Physical punishment becomes rare and boys' freedom greater. Adolescent girls, however, find their movements much more heavily curtailed as, out of concern for modesty, they adopt a veil and become confined to the home and its immediate neighborhood. Puritanical ideals, which young people hitherto escaped, now descend in full force. Shame controls what adolescents wear and attaches to the way their pubescent bodies develop. Boys very carefully urinate only in private. Any pleasurable reference to sex or sexual attraction is inhibited, though not utterly denied, for boys form singing groups in which they express romantic interests through song. Religious attitudes are fully implemented as boys accompany adult men to the mosque for prayer and join mystical brotherhoods to participate in ecstatic evening rituals. Adolescents in this homogeneous community aren't overwhelmed by storm and stress; nor do they yet become fully self-assertive, sexually practicing adults. They mostly remain timid, apprehensive, and withdrawn—qualities that excellently complement the power that elders continue to wield as they go about contracting a boy's or girl's marriage.

The Hopi way of socialization [8]

The school attended by Hopi Indian children on their desert reservation in northern Arizona had ended and most of the youngsters had already departed when four children, brothers and sisters 5 to 13 years old, approached their teacher and asked for permission to stay in the building until evening. The teacher was surprised. Usually children didn't linger but hurried home as soon as classes finished. What was the matter?

"Oh," said the oldest girl, "it is because our grandmother is dying, and we do not want to become sad."

Hopi children learn early to control their feelings and thoughts by avoiding oc-

casions of sadness, anger, and all that is evil. Such discipline is part of a larger pattern of strong control that has enabled the Hopi to survive in an environment full of danger from enemies, drought, famine, illness, and white strangers. The ideal man in such an environment remains "Hopi"—peaceful, good, happy, strong, self-controlled, intelligent, wise, and physically powerful. Poised and tranquil, he keeps a "good heart," concentrates on good thoughts, and avoids anxiety. In his social relationships he stays peaceful, modest, cooperative, unselfish, and law-abiding. All opposite, deviant tendencies are lumped in the concept *kahopi*, and are personified in the evil "two-heart," or witch.

How do children become more "Hopi" than *kahopi*?

The First Five Years. Hopi children are born in the same house where the mother has been at home since her childhood and where her husband came to live when they married. A child spends practically all the first three months of his life supine on a cradleboard, which is never hung or stood up vertically. Thereafter, for another 3 to 9 months, the cradleboard serves him as a place to sleep until, at his desire, it is finally discarded. Being cradled probably gives him a sense of security; it may even communicate the expectation of restriction and control, a message often repeated as he matures. A baby receives the breast whenever it wants, and it may suck until satisfied. In the extended family many arms convey security and comfort. Not even when a child is asleep need he find satisfaction only within himself, for he sleeps in a room with others. Hence, from infancy he becomes familiar with interdependence as his white American peers learn the importance of individualistic self-sufficiency. Weaning occurs gradually and early; it is usually completed by age 2, and undoubtedly brings with it the first lesson in independence. Yet, in one sense, a Hopi is never completely

(A Hopi Boy Recalls Happy Preschool Years[9]

"Mother: (The propeller-like noise of a toy 'bull-roarer' is heard.) Naquima!
Naquima: (now 4 years old) What?
Mother: Stop twirling that flat stick with the string and making that noise, or a bad wind will come.
Naquima: What bad wind?
Mother: The neighbors will talk about you, you'll disgrace the whole family, if you make a strong wind come. That is not Hopi.
Naquima: Oh, listen what a loud noise it makes, Mama!
Mother: I'll let the Spider Woman catch you in her web, or a coyote get you, or a Navaho, if you don't stop. *(The bull-roarer is abruptly stopped.)*
Naquima: I've stopped, Mama. You won't let the Spider Woman get me?
Father: No, come here, Naquima. I won't let anything get you.
Naquima: (now 18 years old) If anyone threatened or punished us, there was always somebody else around to comfort us so that we were never frightened or hurt for long.
Mother: (Naquima a child again) Don't touch the fire, Naquima. It's hot. It'll burn you.
Father: Don't go near the edge of the cliff, Naquima. You might fall over.
Naquima: (18 years old) Those were the only two really big don'ts in my life when I was very small. And I didn't hear them very often. Someone was always with me— my big sister or my mother—to see that nothing did happen to me. My childhood was very happy. And full of wonder. My grandmother telling stories filled the days with wonder.

. . .

Father: (speaking as a Katchina with a heavy, menacing voice through a mask) Where is Naquima?
Mother: Naquima, the Katchina wants you!
Father: Where is he? Are you his mother?
Mother: Yes, what do you have for him? He has been hoping for a fine bow and arrows.
Father: No, he has been bad. I am going to take him away and eat him.
Naquima: That was enough for me. I scurried into the house and hid under one of the couches. The Katchina had a terrible face. I could still hear them.
Mother: No, don't take him away.
Father: Yes, he has been bad. Fighting with the other children and killing chickens. Where is he? *(shouting)* Naquima!
Grandmother: I am his grandmother. Please, don't take him away.
Father: We always eat the bad Hopi children.
Mother: If we give you some food, won't that do?
Father: No, I want Naquima.
Grandmother: Katchina, why don't you take my old man instead? He's not much use to me any more. Take him and leave Naquima.
Father: Which is your old man? This dried-up old fellow?
Grandmother: Yes.
Father: No, too tough. I want Naquima. *(bellowing)* Where is he?

Mother: Please, Katchina, he will be good, I promise you. His uncle will see that he is. He didn't mean to be a bad boy, and he won't be any more. Take this food, and leave Naquima with us. Please!

Father: (dubiously) He will be good from now on?

Grandmother: We will all promise that he will be a good boy, his mother, his uncle, his grandmother and grandfather. Take this food.

Father: All right, I'll let you keep the boy. Give me that basket of food. And since Naquima is going to be a good boy from now on, give him this bow and arrow.

Mother: Thank you, Katchina. I'll go and find him and give them to him."

weaned: All his life he continues to feel bound up with members of his extended family. At 15 months, with the onset of walking and speech, the child begins to be toilet-trained, something that also comes gradually and without shock. Nocturnal bladder control, however, isn't expected until past age 2 and enuresis may persist much longer, until 6 or 7. The fact that a cold-water dousing is institutionalized treatment for boys' persistent bedwetting suggests that it may be more common in them than in girls, just as thumb-sucking, temper-tantrums, fighting, and stealing are known to be. What is special about boys? Whereas a girl grows up in a house where she expects to remain even after her marriage, the boy when he is only 4 or 5 begins to break away, spending more and more of his time in the fields, on the range, or in the kiva—the ceremonial chamber. Apparently difficult expectations connected with a man's adult role are communicated early to a boy and underlie his behavior problems. His adult role will be harder; he will have to leave his natal household and marry into a group of strangers, where his status will be marginal and he will hold major responsibility for coping with the natural and supernatural environments. It is, therefore, not surprising to find Hopi men practicing transvestism and reversing their sex role, something women never do. By age 5 girls begin to feel more restricted than boys. When the latter can break away from home, girls must stay to help their mother.

Now they, too, express their difficulties in the form of temper-tantrums, stealing, and fighting, but in a less pronounced fashion than boys.

Until age 6 the principal childrearers are the mother and other females in the matrilocal extended family. Older siblings, boys or girls between 5 and 12 years old, also care for small charges, taking them along wherever they go to play or work. In keeping with the mother's disciplinary role, children in personality tests cite the father as a main source of happiness. The mother and her brother (when he visits) may, if necessary, spank an unruly child, whereas other disciplinarians mostly scold. In the more traditional villages, kachinas, who impersonate supernatural beings, help out with disciplinary roles. Gift-giving kachinas bestow rewards for good behavior and cannibal kachinas threaten to abduct bad children, for whom parents then plead. Displacing discipline on the masked beings allows parents to avoid arousing hostility in a child that might be turned against them. It also reinforces the youngsters' love for the parents, who protect him from the terrifying supernaturals. Where supernaturals punish, parents remain mostly the authors of good things without inconsistently also becoming frequent sources of frustration and other painful experiences. Although the child soon discovers that the masked beings are only neighbors and kinsmen, he continues to believe that the gods themselves possess great power over his life.

Looking down from a roof top, across Hotevilla, the most conservative Hopi village. (Soil Conservation Service)

In general, adults make the first five years of childhood quite permissive. It is a period when learning depends much on imitation and experiment, carried out by children who are treated as important and integral members of the household group. In play they emulate their future roles; girls build houses with wet mud, make pottery, and grind; boys make believe they farm and herd, shoot with small bows, and run races. Both sexes enjoy pets, such as rabbits and prairie dogs, but treat them roughly. The youngsters are firmly controlled for the sake of their physical safety; protected against such supernatural dangers as witches, evil spirits, and illness of supernatural origin, and guarded against strangers or nonkinsmen. So it is that even before he is six, the Hopi child, though he has been kindly and permissively reared, perceives that the world in which he lives is extremely hazardous. Psychological tests show youngsters of this age to be more relaxed and spontaneous than older children. After all, they are not yet fully disciplined. Tests also reveal the girl's inner life to be

somewhat simpler than that of the boy, who has become quite introverted and beset by a pervasive vague anxiety which his behavior problems confirm.

Initiation. A heavy measure of adult responsibility, ceremonial as well as secular, is introduced to children between 6 and 10, a period marked by very intense learning, especially in the religious domain. Now adults reiterate and drive home the lesson that if *all* Hopi behave properly, keeping a "good heart," then the kachinas will send life-giving rain and other blessings. Myths and folktales reiterate in varying contexts the importance of the inner man relative to outer appearance.[10] An initiation ceremony held in a kiva every four years symbolizes the transition to greater responsibility that this age period brings. Depending on the ceremonial sodality the child joins, the initiation may being a ritual whipping carried out by the godly impersonators, which will be much more painful for the stripped boys than for the clothed girls. Don Talayesva describes his: "I struggled, yelled, and urinated . . . Blood was running down over

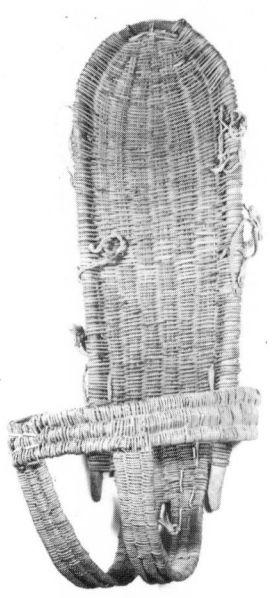

Diapered and wrapped in a blanket, a Hopi infant is bound on a cradleboard like this, a piece of cloth cushioning his head. Binding insures that he will develop a straight carriage. (Southwest Museum, Los Angeles)

Kachinas dancing in the plaza of Walpi, another Hopi village. (Smithsonian Institution, Bureau of American Ethnology)

my body." The next morning the sheepskin on which he had slept stuck fast to his lacerated skin.[11] The ceremony reaches its climax when the kachinas unmask for the benefit of the initiates, revealing they are not really deities but relatives and neighbors. "They were not spirits, but human beings. I recognized nearly every one of them and felt very unhappy, because I had been told all my life that the Katchinas were gods . . . I felt the worst when I saw my own father."[12] One girl grew "all mixed up" and "mad at my parents. . . . 'These people have made me silly,' I said to myself, 'and I thought they were supposed to like me so good.' "[13] Although unsettling, the discovery doesn't wholly disillusion the child. Rather, it builds up his identification with the system of beliefs, whose real nature he now comprehends. The girl I just quoted later saw the kachinas as "the most *important thing in life* . . . children can't understand these things. . . . It takes a while

to see how wise the old people really are." After all, the ceremony had advanced her prestige; to believe is reassuring, and, furthermore, no acceptable alternative belief system exists.

Following initiation, public opinion to a considerable extent replaces the matrilineal household as the main sanction limiting and guiding the Hopi child. His father and paternal kin retain their positive role, but the larger community becomes a source of fear, anger, and shame, leaving home as the place where he can look for praise and other rewards. Both boys and girls now join one or more secret sodalities, each with its own initiation. Especially for the boy, these memberships carry weighty new ceremonial duties that he must execute responsibly. They also compensate him for his tenuous link with the household group and more and more draw him into the kiva, out of the company of women, affiliating him with men. In the company of his own sex he learns to spin, weave, make moccasins, and participate in ritual. Economic tasks also grow heavier as a boy is called into the fields to help men, put to the duty of guarding orchards, and set to herding. Somehow boys and girls still find time for school, an experience particularly liberating for the housebound girl. Most children attend for about four years, though the regularity of their presence varies in the face of competing economic and ceremonial duties. The English and other things children learn are far removed from their lives. So strongly are children insulated from the world of strangers and nonkin that they obey teachers only superficially, without committing the inner core of their persons. As one Hopi put it, "You just wait till you can go home." Nor do parents value the contributions of the school.

Late afternoon and evening leave time to play popular team games featuring competing groups that put little emphasis on scoring or winning. Children find gratification in playing itself, though some games have magical point to them, like archery that promotes crop growth. Girls, with fewer organized games, utilize their play groups to polish their skill in verbal aggression, their mutual criticism developing an objective attitude to another's performance. At home, a girl's duties continue to increase, cutting seriously into her mobility and leisure. Between 10 and 12, intensified seclusion restricts her still more; from then until her marriage she is not supposed to go out unless chaperoned. First menstruation brings a passage rite and a new name; formerly at the time of the puberty ceremony, her hair was done up in a special pattern that she retained until marriage.

Another Transition. Although middle childhood has expanded both sexes' range of social contacts and aroused girls from their simple, unquestioning walled-in existence, the trend toward spontaneity and extraversion is quite short-lived. (It may be

Economic duties confine girls to the home more than boys. (U. S. Public Health Service)

merely an artifice of the psychological test on which the observers relied, rather than a true shift in personality.) Just before puberty, boys and girls withdraw into themselves, terminating much of their lively responsiveness to outside stimuli. When, however, the first, still vaguely defined sexual impulses rise to consciousness, quite without any connotation of evil, they halt the introversive trend and facilitate an outlet for emotional impulses. Both sexes are prepared: From childhood they have received matter-of-fact, natural education in sex, a subject about which the Hopi speak plainly; and they participated in mutual masturbation and other kinds of sex play. Don Talayesva recalls how his aunts teased him when he was still uninitiated by calling him their sweetheart; how he and his friends attended closely to animals' sexual doings and had fun playing housekeeping with girls, and how he heard men in the kiva joke and

([Pandemonium in the Kiva

*The dreaded moment which the candidates have so often been told about and of
which they stand in such great fear has arrived. They are about to go through
the ordeal of being flogged. Presently a loud grunting noise, a rattling of turtle
shell rattles and a jingling of bells is heard outside. The two Ho Katcinas and
the Hahai-i have arrived at the kiva. . . . They first run around the kiva four
times at a rapid rate, then dance on each side of the kiva a little while,
beat the roof of the kiva with whips, jump on it, constantly howling the word
u'huhuhu and finally enter the kiva. The two Ho Katcinas take a position
on the east and west side of the large sand mosaic, the Hahai-i at its southeast
corner, the latter holding a supply of whips. The children tremble and some
begin to cry and to scream. The Ho Katcinas keep up their grunting, howling,
rattling, trampling and brandishing of their yucca whips. All at once someone
places a candidate on the sand mosaic, holds his (or her) hands upward and one
of the Ho Katcinas whips the little victim quite severely. . . . It is said that four
strokes are supposed to be applied, but the Katcinas do not always strictly adhere to
this rule. The girls have their usual dress on, but the boys are entirely nude.
The persons holding them are also nude except for a scant loin cloth, and they
wear their hair loose, as is customary in all Hopi sacred ceremonies. When one
child has been flogged another one is at once brought forward and beaten and
then another and so on until all have gone through the ordeal. One is flogged
by one Katcina, the next one by the other, the two Katcinas constantly changing
about. When a whip is worn out it is handed to the Hahai-i Katcina who
exchanges it for a fresh one. Some of the children go through the process with
set teeth and without flinching, others squirm, try to jump away and scream.
Occasionally a "sponsor," pitying his little ward, presents his own hip, snatching
the child away, and receives a part of the the flogging in the child's stead,
in which case, however, the flogging is usually very severe.*

*With the crying and screaming of the candidates men and women mingle
their voices, some encouraging them, others accusing the Katcinas of partiality,
claiming that they whip some harder than others; in short, pandemonium reigns
in the kiva during this exciting half hour. But the scene has not only its
exciting, but also its disgusting features. As the whips are quite long they
frequently extend around the leg or hip of the little nude boys in such a manner
that the points strike the pudibilia, and the author noticed on several occasions
that the boys, when being placed on the sand mosiac, were warned to protect
those parts, which they tried to do by either quickly freeing one hand and pushing
the pudenda between the legs or by partly crossing the legs. It was also noticed
on several occasions that some of the boys, probably as a result of fear and
pain, involuntarily micturated and in one or two cases even defecated.*

*When all the children have been flogged the Hahai-i Katcina steps on the
sand mosaic, bends forward, raises the ceremonial blanket and is then severely
flogged by both Katcinas, after which the two latter apply a thorough
scourging to each other in the same manner, to the great satisfaction of the
little novitiates who have just been so cruelly treated by these two personages.*[14]

H. R. VOTH

(Chicago Natural History Museum)

Hopi children learn at 6 or 7 that their behavior helps to control the rain and other blessings that kachinas can give or withhold. (Santa Fe Railway)

emotions. Instead of responding emotionally, they are apt to approach situations intellectually and imaginatively, though without wholly abandoning themselves to fantasy. Far from being puritan, they recognize that the world has many pleasures and attractions, but that these have their due place and that knowledge tones down their exuberance. The dangerous world they construe, together with the limits they impose on their emotions, desires, ambitions, and especially on hostile feelings, generates "inside pressure" for which they find no adequate outlet. Consequently, the Hopi Indian often feels an uncomfortable, vague anxiety that he doesn't understand, that originates in his own overdisciplined self, and that he learns to project outward as he suspects others of influencing him unfavorably through witchcraft. Thereby he adds to his sources of fear. One area of personality remains relatively unaffected by discipline and untouched by shame or conscience: the instinctual urges, particularly sex, that a person has since childhood been conditioned to accept.

boast about sexual intercourse.[15] An adolescent boy finds his sexuality much easier to gratify than does a girl, who is forbidden to roam and is watched lest she become boy-crazy. A second initiation ceremony is especially significant for boys, whom it pushes fully into the responsibilities and privileges of manhood. Formerly a youth would then start his career as a warrior, and he still serves the community at large by going on dangerous salt-gathering expeditions that possess religious significance. Out of his sexual liaisons he meets a girl to marry, the partners themselves selecting one another with their parents' consent.

Adolescents are adults in personality as well as responsibility. Socialization has left them deeply disciplined, cautious, restrained, and highly selective toward their

CONFORMITY AMONG POLYNESIAN NEW ZEALANDERS [16]

In northern New Zealand, a group of psychologists ("ethnopsychologists" they call themselves) carried out one of the most ambitious investigations of early personality formation through field work ever organized.[17] Their research on the Polynesian Maori is notable not only for the detailed attention special investigators, using a variety of tests, paid to different periods of childhood, but also for the experiment they devised to validate observational data with Rorschach test results.

In the wild, mountainous country of North Island lies a 2-mile-wide and 5-mile-long pocket of comparative fertility, Rakau Valley. At the valley's southern end, located

40 miles from the nearest towns, is the small community of Rakau inhabited by *pakeha* (white) and Maori families. About half of the seventy Maori families receive their incomes directly or indirectly from the world's largest planted forest, which is located near Rakau. Other employed adults farm, drive transport, and do construction. The average wage is about $27 weekly but low rents or owned homes, vegetable gardens, and allowances for dependent children help to avoid a very low standard of living. Though households comprise only parents and children, families are large and houses small and therefore crowded with an average of seven persons to each one. Most of the Rakau Maori claim descent from the great twelfth-century migration which, they believe, carried their ancestors to New Zealand from Central Polynesia. Then, in the mid-nineteenth century, Europeans arrived to confront the warlike tribes, their influence quickly transforming many aspects of traditional Maori life. Yet even today language, claims to ancestry, names, and lineage associations keep alive a strong sense of Maori identity.

The First Five Years. A Maori mother who tells an interviewer that "a home is not a home without children" reveals a genuine Maori value. Even parents with large families don't resent the arrival of another infant. Most babies enter the world in a town hospital so that only after it reaches home can friends and relatives crowd around to admire it. For four months or so the infant is breast-fed by most mothers whenever it wants, because, a mother explains, she can't bear to hear it crying. Although weaning comes early, being gradually achieved with the aid of a bottle, the Maori nevertheless permit considerable early oral indulgence. Three psychologists, using a rating scale devised for cross-cultural comparison which permits a top score of 21 on oral gratification, awarded the Rakau Maori an average of 15 points. Some small-scale communities

have been rated higher; the Arapesh, Comanche Indians, and Copper Eskimo scored 16 points each on the "satisfaction potential" estimated to be developed in the body's oral zone by socially standardized early-feeding practices; a few people have earned 18, and the Hopi Indians only 14.[18]

Until the next child comes along, the new Maori baby occupies its own bed in the parents' bedroom; later it will share a room with siblings. The first two years constitute an extremely permissive period. We aren't told at what age toilet training begins, but it must be fairly early. It is achieved through only mild discipline and with so little fuss that, in the mothers' opinion, it comes quite "automatically." Three judges rated the Rakau Maori quite high on the degree to which they permit early anal gratification, giving them 18 out of a possible 21 points. Children receive little positive encouragement in walking or talking. Care comes from a number of people who indulgently grant a youngster almost every wish and pet him to his heart's content. Fathers also find time after work to play with a baby. Gradually the toddler weans himself from his mother's supervision as he ventures into the yard following his elder siblings, backed by privileges of food, attention, and leniency that those older youngsters already lack.

Recall that at age 4 among the Egyptians of Silwa a sharp curtailment of maternal care starts that reverses the pattern of gratification and "compassion" that has linked mother and child since the first days of life. Among the Kaska Indians, if you can remember back to Chapter 1, the age between 2 and 3 marks the crucial time when a mother, who has been the child's primary source of affective stimulation, withdraws herself emotionally, becomes typically remote, and reacts disinterestedly even when showing her appreciation. In Rakau the reversal in almost unlimited gratification comes even earlier. As soon as the next child arrives, usually when the previous

In Rakau it is mainly older children who care for youngsters. (Ans Westra; A. H. and A. W. Reed)

youngster is only about 14 or 18 months old, the golden period of childhood halts and privileges favoring him above his older brothers and sisters cease. From this time on, though he may cling to his mother's skirts, his dependence receives little gratification. Firmly he is pushed to join the children outdoors without any thought of compensating him for losing his favored place and the lion's share of attention which now go to the new baby. Sibling rivalry is not exacerbated as in Silwa but disregarded, with confidence that the youngster will soon overcome it. A child dethroned from his former high priority may try to regain parents' attention by amusing or helping them, but even if they respond, it only adds to the inconsistency and capriciousness which their attitudes toward him have assumed. Punishment follows the same inconsistent pattern, leaving the child to figure out his parents' mood in an effort to predict how

they will react. Anyway, he isn't much in care of parents after the birth of a new sibling because from then on his supervision tends to be almost exclusively delegated to older children. Young girls find a more secure role to play than boys, for they can help their mother tend to a new baby, thereby winning approval and feeling wanted and needed. To be sure, parents continue to love their children and to continue their education. By age 4, if not earlier, Maori children have explicitly learned to respect property; to share their toys with others in the family, and not to be rude, tell lies, break things, or fight. Training to inhibit aggression, which follows a period of relative tolerance for aggression, comes with marked insistence; the total score, representing three judges' ratings of the severity with which control of aggression is inculcated, reaches 16 out of a possible 21 points. Demands for sexual modesty are imposed more lightly, the total severity score for sex training being only 11.

The likely psychological repercussions of the curtailed time and attention devoted to young children following the birth of a sibling have received due attention. One consequence of the Maori mother's emotional rejection is counterrejection by the child. Although this leads to the youngster's further isolation, and aggravates his need for love, it does encourage self-assertion. Another trend encouraged by shearing strong parental interest in the youngster is independence; this follows simply because his further dependence becomes practically impossible. At the same time, his personality receives an other-directed set. A tendency toward compliance develops as a way out of the pressing emotional problems that have suddenly filled his world. Finally, due to the unpredictability of his parents' reactions, a Rakau child learns caution in a variety of situations and to look carefully before he acts. Jane Ritchie[19] deduces 12 themes that characterize the 5-year-old

For the Rakau girl, the mother's direct socializing influence is more important than it is for a boy. (Ans Westra; A. H. and A. W. Reed)

Maori child's personality. She discovers that those themes anticipate in a general way 15 out of 20 deductions made by another psychological fieldworker about Rakau social personality (to be described later). Hence it would seem that the first five years set the mold for most of the personality that follows. From now on, little except sex will occur to modify basically the individual's style of life.

Middle Childhood, from 6 to 13. Though by 6 the Rakau Maori child has overcome the "major obstacles" in his socialization, he has much more to learn. Children in the middle years look very much to siblings for this learning, just as, in their turn, they guide still younger household members. True, the older siblings are as capricious in the way they award and punish as the parents, or even more so; but a child can more easily establish contact with them than with his disinterested parents. Since the older children understand little more than their charges about the world into which they are growing, and have no clear conception of the goals toward which they are heading, or why, learning in middle childhood can't be guided by many explicit or certain standards. Much of the child's time is spent in large, sometimes sexually mixed, groups of friends. Playing at rather unimaginative games in such peer groups, where terms of behavior are almost entirely set by children without adult interference, he encounters his happiest experiences. The sense of security which peers furnish largely motivates him to conform to their demands, in strong other-directed fashion. Aspiring too high is especially likely to be cut down by the ridicule of peers. Praiseworthy and blameworthy actions, rather than meeting the standards of parents and being done to retain parents' warmth and affection, are carried out because other children demand them.

Judging from the Children's Apperception Test (which didn't work very well with Rakau youngsters), a child remains very conscious of his parents—though it may be that the pictures stimulated him to think of them more than he otherwise might have. But he views his parents neutrally, as physically present in the world without his being emotionally related to them. Yet the Maori child would like to make a positive approach to his parents and to experience a warm, close relationship with them. While children admit aggression in the test, they control other desires constrictedly, though not because they are afraid of environmental sanctions. When desires are released, disruptive anxiety appears, as if the child were saying: When I try to get what I want, everything goes wrong, so I'll stop trying . . . and wanting too. Presumably he took the decision to live warily during that early, crucial time in his life, after a sibling had displaced him from the focal point of affection and attention. The personality of middle childhood contains nearly all 12 themes deduced from the 5-year-old's behavior, including caution, isolation from family members, love needs, compliance, insecurity, and independence. The earlier trends don't retain exactly the same form they took in the 5-year-old, but show up in ways

appropriate to the new life situation. Once more it seems "that the roots of the personality characteristics of these children lie in the early years of childhood."[20] Another check on the continuity of Maori personality comes by comparing the behavior of the 6–13-year-old with the social personality deduced by another fieldworker using older as well as younger children. Once again the fit is good. The children's primarily "miserable" adjustment, which the Children's Apperception Test indicates, makes the researchers momentarily dubious. Do the youngsters really carry the "signs of mental ill health" suggested by the test? Do more positive features of child life exist? The psychologists confess that they neither found any evidence of a more satisfactory inner life or any reason to suppose that greater satisfactions in fact exist and that they had missed them.

Adolescence. Almost as soon as the Maori child was old enough, the New Zealand psychologists began to rely on tests rather than on observation of situational behavior to understand its development. For adolescents, the Thematic Apperception Test provides nearly all the psychologists' insights.

TAT results reveal that home and parents gain renewed value for youngsters at puberty. Now the child's growth renders the adult world less remote, and parents in their turn regain interest in the children, awarding them greater prestige as well as further obligations and restrictions. Contrary to younger children's resentment of household tasks, such work carries newly conceived rewards in adolescence, though implications of drudgery linger. The role of peers declines, partly on account of youngsters' orientation to and identification with adults, and partly because newly emerging impulses and heightening competition create disharmonies among peers. This isn't to say that adolescents compete amongst themselves for scholastic achievement or success in jobs; Rakau youngsters don't aspire that high. Even though youths tend to model themselves on older persons, peers continue to exert socializing influences, notably with respect to dress, speech, and job choice. Rekindled parental interest in the children is considerably founded on the adolescents' awakening sexual impulse and the possibility that they will misbehave sexually, with pregnancy resulting. The young person knows very well that external controls oppose his personal desires but, without serious inner conflict, he accepts the desires themselves. He reveals no strong superego. Nor would we expect any, given the fact that in earlier life no affectionate parents made any zealous efforts to implant moral standards by encouraging the child's identification with them. The adolescent's two most conspicuous defenses are a tendency to overconform to social expectations and affective neutrality; he still eschews close emotional involvement.

Adult status comes gradually; it is signified by the youth openly smoking, quitting school, and taking a job preparatory to assuming responsibilities of marriage and parenthood. Marriage attracts boys and girls as an arrangement that will provide them with sexual opportunities, a parent surrogate who will satisfy their affective needs, and enhanced prestige. Boys, however, are a bit afraid that they won't be able to meet responsibilities entailed by marriage and that they will find difficulty in coping with a relationship emotionally more intense than any they have been accustomed to.

Validation. The unique element in the New Zealanders' venture into culture and personality is their experimental use of the Rorschach test—administered to 41 boys and 37 girls between 9 and 17—to validate data obtained from other sources. First, on the basis of two summers' observation, James Ritchie[21] set down how personality develops in Rakau, going up to the threshold of adulthood. Since he drew on findings of the other fieldworkers and traversed the same ground that I have already covered, I shall omit most of his descriptive findings. I do want to single out a few further consequences of the very young child's broken affective relationship with his parents that Ritchie stresses and which I have left out. The snapped affective ties of early childhood, he says, generate hostility and aggressive tendencies that must be carefully controlled lest their expression imperil the person's integration into the peer groups on which he depends so strongly for security. Into young adulthood the Maori brings considerable repressed hostility masked beneath surface geniality, physical agility, and an intense round of activity. Some hostility gets deflected against the self, with the result that the lighthearted Maori whom *pakeha* see is actually a somewhat depressed person when viewed from within. Other hostility and derived anxiety periodically find expression in overt behavior, including drunken acts (for which personal responsibility can be disowned), scapegoating, gossip, and manufactured grievances. Occasionally the last-mentioned expression reaches almost paranoid intensity, but people do manage to maintain their stability.

In the experiment's next phase, James Ritchie[22] formulated "Basic Personality in Rakau." Since he intended his account to be validated by Rorschach-test data, he couched it partly in the argot of Rorschach analysts. The result is a fairly abstract formulation divided into three parts: mental approach, intellectual level, and emotional life. In his mental approach, the person in Rakau reflects his limited physical and social environments. Contact with the intrusive world of *pakehas* has not really expanded the Maori's social personality. In some ways, unfamiliar experiences have driven behavior into more restricted and stereotyped channels than was the case aboriginally (judging from earlier, far

Omnipresent group life in Rakau protects the individual from fear of social isolation. His self-esteem and sense of personal competence derive from others' responsiveness. (Ans Westra; A. H. and A. W. Reed)

less psychologically informed, accounts of bygone Maori life). The social personality is nonassertive, nonexperimental, and prosaic. People tend to be cautious and vigilant in the face of new experience, tolerant of novelties only if they come in limited quantities. If new experience promotes threat that can't be ignored, the person takes flight into physical or psychological withdrawal. A few individuals who are deviantly oriented to achievement, find satisfaction in abstract conceptual activity, but most confine themselves to easily achieved, familiar goals. The intellectual level reflects not what a child has learned in school but a person's out-of-school environment. The familiar and practical form the largest part of a Maori's conceptual repertory, with the result that his intellectual functioning is reduced to a level far below his real ability. In its emotional life, the social personality appears outwardly poised, supple, and confi-

dent. These qualities belie an inner life filled with struggle for control, tension, unfulfilled desire, and self-doubt. Although direct gratification, especially in sex, allays some anxiety, and the permissive warmth of group life temporarily masks hostility and aggression, the pinnacles of emotional life are trimmed down. Individuals spend much energy trying to satisfy their needs for love and esteem, but with emotionality little directed outward. The egocentric Maori seeks, but without a complementary ability to give. Yet he heeds outer reality as he vigilantly seeks safe places for, and safe responses to, his truncated feelings and needs.

Now Ritchie[23] is ready to predict more specifically what the Rorschach test should reveal. He does so in 20 hypotheses in which he predicts the composite Rorschach record that should be forthcoming from his sample if his hypotheses are correct. If his subjects should give the responses he predicts, then the acceptability of his hypotheses would be enhanced. Among the hypotheses we find familiar themes, for, as I pointed out, subsequent investigators reached many conclusions similar to Ritchie's. For example, he infers that the early years with their indulgence will predispose Maori toward a pattern of "direct satisfaction," while parental emotional rejection will sharply interrupt that trend. Fear of further rejection, he expects, will remain a permanent character trait, and personality will become endowed with strong love needs, as well as with a pattern of noninvolvement as a defense against further rejection. He infers a high degree of insecurity and anxiety, mild extraversion, and submerged aggression and hostility. Aggression, he believes, will be used against the self in sadomasochistic fashion, producing hypochrondriasis, and depression. Sexuality will be freely expressed, accompanied by neither fantasy or interpersonal involvement. He also hypothesizes an early tendency for people to dichotomize into achievers and nonachievers, with the majority strongly conforming to nonachieving norms. He expects intellectual ability to be reduced to a level of crude generalization, and perception to be limited to concrete persons and things. He infers that people are far more concerned with themselves in relation to others than with material goods, on which they place relatively little value. Men, he predicts, are less rigidly patterned than women, capable of more emotional expression, and therefore less prone to emotional problems of control.

Ritchie expressed these hypotheses in terms of expected Rorschach indicators, constructing a hypothetical, scored Rorschach test protocol of a typical Maori between 9 and 17 years old. When he completed this composite protocol, to which actual records would be matched, he had already begun to collect Rorschachs in Rakau, and this, he admits, may have slightly contaminated his predictions. To reduce this effect he invited another psychologist to duplicate his translation of the inferences into specific Rorschach indicators, and discovered that the two hypothetical protocols agreed at many points. On a few points they disagree, often because of oversimplifications in Ritchie's inferences that misled his colleague.

It is worth glancing at a few of Ritchie's translations into Rorschach argot. His hypothesis that early indulgence will predispose personality in favor of patterns of direct gratification results in the specific prediction that responses to color cards, compared with responses to black-and-white cards, will be faster and more direct and that subjects will score *FC* (form dominant over color) more frequently than *CF* or *C* (in which color overwhelms the subject so that he doesn't attend to the inkblots' form). Ritchie expects the reversal in direct gratification instituted by early rejection to show up in a high frequency of form responses and in frequent anxiety indicators. Submerged hostility and aggression will manifest themselves in a high frequency of inanimate and animal movement along with low human content. He even predicts that his Maori sample will take a long time in formulating each response.

Ritchie and another psychologist independently interpreted the 78 actual protocols obtained in Rakau. The second psychologist possessed far less knowledge about Maori culture than Ritchie, so in a sense he worked blind. Both treated the protocols as referring collectively to a single typical Maori from whose record the Maori social personality could be interpreted. I forbear reporting in detail the not wholly unambiguous results; they can be read.[24] Instead, I will sum up how Ritchie sees the fate of his hypotheses. Undoubtedly critics could present the case more unfavorably than he does; yet, if they attach any credibility to the Rorschach, they would have to agree with him that a number of his deductions are borne out—some, as he recognizes, more strongly than others. In fact, all but one hypothesis gains support, though a number do so only with qualification. One inference—that of mild extraversion—he must reject entirely, for the sole Rorschach indicator comes out just oppositely to what he had predicted. Some of his previous statements he feels must be modified; for example, the Maori is not anxious about particular problems; rather, he experiences a diffuse feeling of inadequacy and dread from which he generally manages to escape. Aggression turns out to be below what the level of frustration would suggest, and isn't at all directed inward toward the self in the form of depression. Ritchie believes that the depressive individuals he encountered during fieldwork must have been atypical Maori. Why he so unreservedly trusts the Rorschach findings, putting them above conclusions based on his clinical observation of people in their life situations, he doesn't explain. I suppose that mostly the test's capacity to bring forth specific, measured, personality characteristics recommends it to him as a validating instrument. Undoubtedly he believes that the test has sufficiently demonstrated its transcultural ability to gauge personality.

Two conclusions from the experiment strike me as especially worth noting. First, Ritchie criticizes his fieldwork for the way it led him to underestimate the significance of peer groups as a source of individual security. He admits that he paid too little attention to the day-to-day social setting accommodating personality. Second, he agrees that he overestimated the importance of "unpropitious" feelings, chiefly because he failed to note how adjustively the Maori fit into group life. His approach was heavily critical rather than appreciative, deriving from too strong an interest in psychopathology. His expectation that rapid

technical development and the influence of Europeans in Rakau would upset Maori adjustment proved unwarranted. As I have already maintained, the bias of pathology to which Ritchie subscribed is very common, if not dominant, among social scientists.[25]

Comparative. Rakau Maori childhood and social personality recall closely similar features reported for another Polynesian people, the Samoans of Ta'u. In Samoa's very highly ordered social system, much depends on a person knowing his position and attendant roles. In certain areas of life and in certain relationships, which take all one's attention and allegiance, no room remains for nonconformity, individualism, or originality. Rorschachs collected from Samoan adult men bear out that Samoans conformingly suppress originality, just as the test confirms similar trends among the Rakau.[26] A difference appears in the way conformity is culturally accounted for between the two people. In Samoa it is said to be patterned by an elaborate and highly formal culture pattern,[27] whereas among Rakau Maori, peer groups' powerful expectations are held to be responsible for maintaining adherence to tradition.

Both the Rakau Maori and the Samoans of Ta'u are emotional suppressers, but in somewhat different ways. Margaret Mead says that the Samoans, an emotionally level people, expend little emotion on anything. She documents this assertion by referring to their unintense personal loyalties, lack of commitment to causes, and absence of deep, vivid emotions or sexual attraction and explains those characteristics configurationally.[28] They follow, she says, from the emphasis Samoans put on formal pattern in certain areas of life, thereby avoiding situations of strong choice capable of creating powerful emotions. The people of Rakau express feelings readily, but inhibit deep and lasting emotional involvement or commitment, a state they distrust.[29] Psychologists working in Rakau see inhibition of emotional ties primarily as defensive and rooted in the child's earliest traumatic experiences, not as patterned by the cultural configuration.

Two childrearing practices occur in partly similar and partly different forms on Ta'u and in Rakau: the use of child care-takers and children's exclusion from adult interest. Both have similar consequences in personality formation. In Samoa, care of young children by only slightly older ones who still lack defined personalities perpetu-ates a low level of individuality. The gifted man may rise to the top, but he doesn't influence his children or pass on to them his personal qualities, because he so rarely comes into intense contact with them. Chil-dren enjoy very limited opportunities to identify with adults. Margaret Mead calls attention to the care Samoan child-nurses take to escape adult attention by not allow-ing their charges to outrage convention or to get hurt; otherwise, the nurses will be punished. Children learn not what our chil-dren learn—namely, to be good for a re-ward or to escape punishment—but to keep quiet, sit still, and conform to rules in order to be let alone and stay where they like. Such a setting, where transgression and nontransgression become matters of expedi-ency, provides little opportunity to learn to feel guilt.[30] In Rakau, the child's emotional rejection, socialization by siblings, and firm incorporation into a peer group duplicate in a general way the mode of childrearing found in Samoa and give rise to a very simi-lar lack of originality or individualism, to a weak superego, and to a strong responsive-ness to group expectations.[31]

Polynesians in the Cook Islands, particu-larly Aitutaki, resemble at least New Zea-land Maori in being highly sensitive to group judgments.[32] Fear of shame in the Cooks constitutes a powerful incentive to conform, though Christianity has brought with it a greater measure of guilt than for-merly existed. Rorschach records from Aitutaki reveal children to be emotionally constricted, anything but broad and expan-sive in their approach to the world, and devoid of almost any imagination or indi-viduality. For anyone to think up novel ways of doing things is certain to earn dis-approval. Clearly their personality resem-bles that of the Samoans on Ta'u and of Rakau Maori children.[33]

SOCIALIZATION IN A RAJPUT VILLAGE [34]

The final ethnographic study is centered on childhood in a north Indian village and re-sumes the natural-history type of approach that characterized Ammar's account of Egyptian rural socialization. It was exe-cuted, however, in a far more carefully planned, systematic fashion.[35] In that re-spect, it blends the anthropological ap-proach with what, toward the end of the last chapter, I identified as sociologists' and psychologists' interests in socialization. Be-fore going to India, the two anthropologists who did the work, together with four other two-person teams that would make com-parable investigations in Mexico, Kenya, the Philippines, Okinawa, and New Eng-land, were instructed in what specifically to look for and how to schedule their field-work. Each team packed along a mimeo-graphed field guide designed to insure com-parable coverage of a large series of variables and topics.[36]

South of the Himalaya Mountains in the Ganges valley of the state of Uttar Pradesh is Khalapur, one of India's half-million vil-lages, surrounded by its irrigated fields. Five thousand people live in its greyish, sunbaked adobe and whitewashed brick homes located near a Hindu temple. The two anthropologists concentrated their re-search on one neighborhood composed en-tirely of Rajput landowners, excluding any representatives of the Washerman, Gold-

Men's quarters of a Rajput house. (Patricia J. Hitchcock; Cornell University South Asia Program)

A lane in Khalapur. (Leigh Minturn Triandis; Cornell University South Asia Program)

An outdoor class of the primary school. (Patricia J. Hitchcock; Cornell University South Asia Program)

Rajput women in their courtyards. (Leigh Minturn Triandis; Cornell University South Asia Program)

smith, Leatherwork, Brahman, and other village castes. Rajput men idealize themselves as potential rulers or warriors, and as being stronger and more virile than other castes. Their self-image, with its touchy sense of honor, causes many to feel markedly ambivalent about their present heavy, direct involvement in farm work, which they see as rather demeaning and as depriving of ample leisure. If they could afford it, they would prefer to supervise laborers, who would do the actual plowing, watering, and reaping of their fields. Women and children concentrate their life in the courtyard of the woman's house, while men and adolescent boys gather in the men's house or, rather, on its platform. Separate houses for men and women in parts of India and Pakistan accommodate the custom of purdah (already mentioned in connection with Muslim Egypt), whereby women rigorously seclude themselves from any unrelated man's gaze. Physical separation allows the patrilineally related men of a family to spend nearly all their leisure in the company of other male villagers. The wives of brothers, together with their unmarried daughters and young sons, married sons' wives, and sons' children—two or three generations, or an average of about seven women and children—commonly share a courtyard. A definite code of etiquette governs the women's company as much as the men's. Women's rank within a courtyard stems from that of their husbands, which, in turn, depends heavily on the men's relative seniority. As brides, these women came as strangers to Khalapur, where they will probably stay until their death.

Infancy. For a married Hindu woman to bear children is important for her and her husband to carry out their lives properly. Since a man jeopardizes his salvation should he die without a son, and because boys will some day strengthen the family's productive manpower, sons are preferred to daughters and much more elaborate cere-

monies mark their birth. A girl, because of the handsome dowry that should accompany her at marriage, confronts her family with a financial liability. Yet girl babies arouse a pronounced sentimentality in mothers that seems to contain a tender regard for the fact that some day girls will be lost when they go away to their husbands' homes. Among the Hopi, remember, a boy's childhood foreshadows *his* eventual departure at marriage and generally harder future life.

Although God himself resides in a newborn child, the high infant death rate makes his health a matter of considerable concern. In addition, parents worry about supernatural dangers, evil eye, and whether the child will grow up adequately to fulfill his roles. Protective charms and other magical precautions, one even assuring that boys won't grow up to be sexually impotent, apparently afford parents some security. Despite other women's presence in the house, much of the infant's early care rests with the mother, who nurses it whenever it seems inclined to suck. She also sleeps with the baby at night, a custom she may continue with girls until they are 8 or 9 years old. From about the age of one year, an infant regularly receives solid food; irregularly, however, such feeding started considerably earlier, and quite without any thought of weaning it from the breast. Casual attention paid to urination and only slightly more to defecation keep toilet training from becoming in any sense problematic. The mother's vigorous and not too gentle handling during sponge baths, however, shapes that situation into a real daily struggle, so that it becomes virtually the only situation injecting a note of stress into the infant's bland daily life. A Rajput mother, thoroughly familiar with babies since her own childhood, doesn't dwell on her baby's uniqueness, hail its first smile, or drop everything to rush to its comfort when it cries. For other reasons, a visitor skirts

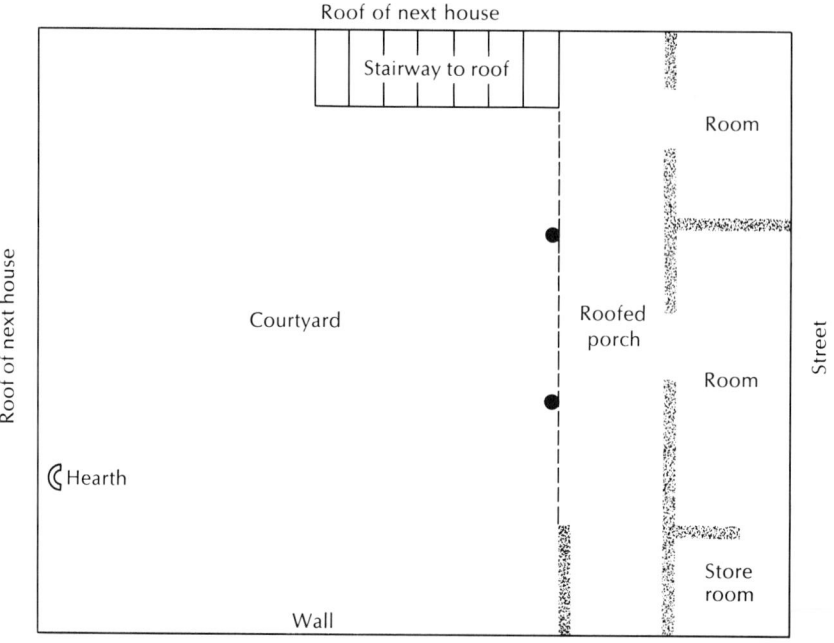

In Khalapur the way a mother in an extended family rears her children is related to her life spent with other women in a woman's house and courtyard, like those shown here. Unlike other courtyards, this one (for which a latrine or drain and an exit to the street have been omitted) apparently lacks a cattle compound for cows and buffaloes. Family cooking is done on the U-shaped mud hearth, which stands about 6 inches high.[37]

openly praising and admiring a baby; he knows that doing so brings bad luck and raises the suspicion that he is throwing an evil eye.

Preschool Years. Considerable passivity and casualness keynote the first two years of life, in which nobody does much to challenge a Rajput youngster to exert himself. When speech appears, indicating that he is becoming teachable, he gets some directions and, if he fails to heed them, punishment; but adults believe that he learns best through observing and imitating life around him. Without being pushed and with time variation from one child to another—for the age at which something in a child's de-

velopment should happen doesn't interest Indian mothers—he gradually participates in an increasing range of daily life. Should a new sibling displace him from his mother's bed, he may later return to it and to his other siblings, who also sleep there. Sibling rivalry is strikingly absent, no doubt because all during its preschool years a child never feels his security threatened in the household. The first real demands, usually in his second or third year, appear with weaning. Mothers now insist that during the day he use a proper place in the courtyard or street to urinate and defecate. Neither weaning nor toilet training presents anybody with serious problems. Likewise, the anthropologists noted no feeding problems, probably because in this consistently casual setting nobody bothers unduly about a child's eating habits. Similarly, very slight pressure calls for neatness and cleanliness; in fact, a well-groomed child is in danger of drawing a serious variety of evil eye. Mothers do little positively to guide their children's behavior by reasoning with them or by explaining why something should be done or avoided. Hence, children do in fact learn much through observation and imitation, at first from women and then, after they have been weaned and toilet trained, from men, whom they join on the men's house veranda. Other children also act as models, particularly in like-sex play groups, where activities are patterned after adult tasks. As yet, Rajput children receive little real training in work, responsibility, or self-reliance. If a youngster falls into trouble, he is not expected to cope with it by himself; he runs to adults (rather than to peers). A child, therefore, makes many requests of adults without receiving proportionate encouragement to comply with others' requests. Yet preschool children's obedience and passivity are two of the most valued personality characteristics, and they are counted on to rule out such troublesome qualities as anger, fighting, disrespect for seniors, overexcitement, and others that plague adults. Despite the ideal, children (incidentally, like adults) don't readily comply with directions, especially not if the directions happen to fall outside customary or habitual obligations. In response to disobedience, mothers shout, scold, and lose their temper. Their anger, however, doesn't last; the storm quickly passes, the event is forgotten. Having abundant opportunity to witness anger and quarreling, children readily learn to vent their own anger, even against their mother, and often it succeeds, winning them their own way. Men, in accordance with their more exalted rank, are obeyed much more quickly than women.

Amongst themselves, children do much bickering and teasing, and occasionally fighting, gaining practice in quarrelsomeness of a type reported for several Indian villages.[38] All adults shrink from praising their own children directly or too strongly lest it make them unamenable to control. They may, however, extol other, absent children, holding them up as models. In the balance, punishment occurs much more frequently than tangible rewards offered for good conduct. Scolding, which takes such forms as cursing, insults, or ridicule; threats of physical punishment, and appeals to fear (of ghosts, for instance) is far commoner than physical discipline, which, when it does occur, usually consists of nothing more than a slap. Mothers, for reasons that will soon be clear, ignore trying to capitalize on their warmth and affection in discipline. Derogatory statements like "They will say you are a dirty boy," since they threaten the child with loss of social support, come closest to love-oriented techniques of punishment. Erring children are mostly punished by their own mother, particularly if she is conveniently nearby. Otherwise, a senior woman in the courtyard might issue a reprimand, but rarely would a woman dare strike someone else's child. Older children show no such reluctance to administer chastisement but fathers, who generally remain stern and remote figures to their children, are deterred by the respect due to their own seniors from disciplining even their own children when a patrilineally related older man happens to be present.

Raters who compared Rajput mothers in Khalapur with mothers in four other communities that had been studied with the same frame of reference rated the Indian mothers lowest in maternal warmth, meaning that they cater very little to children who fuss or demand attention, and that they even scold children for crying.[39] Being regularly undemonstrative, they can't turn their warmth on and off, as they would have to do if they used affection in a disciplinary way. (From my reading of the anthropologists' account, I see the mothers as emotionally responsive, but in a rather casual, unintense way.) Their lack of emotional expression springs from the value they place on emotional control for the children themselves and communicates to the child that his mood-swings won't be tolerated. Rajput mothers tend to be more hostile and punitive to boys, the preferred sex, than to girls, which is in keeping with their early, sentimental regard for daughters. Significantly, a daughter has even fewer chores to perform at home than a son, because, women explain, in her own house a daughter is a guest. After her marriage, they add, as a daughter-in-law in another house, she will have much work to do and her life will be hard.

Khalapur mothers rank below the mean of the five communities in the amount of time they spend with babies and children. This doesn't mean that other women and children relieve them greatly of the burden of caretaking; compared with some of the other communities, older children in Khalapur play very slight roles caring for children. Nor is that duty delegated to other adults. The Rajput mothers, compared with mothers in the other four communities, rank lowest in responsibility training, and are about in middle position in the severity with which they discipline children who fight with their peers. The mothers do, however, punish peer aggression more severely than they punish aggression toward themselves, one possible reason being that children's quarrels in the courtyard might involve the mothers and disrupt relations among the women who must live together. The fact that a Rajput mother spends most of her time in close contact with other women and their children, hardly ever leaving the house, also explains her intolerance for her children's moods, fussiness, and other signs of troublesomeness that would promote minor confusion in the crowded courtyard if they went unchecked. Yet these mothers rank low in the consistency with which they impose demands for obedience, which to some extent nullifies their effort to control peer aggression.

School and Work Years. As a child grows older, responsibility for his care falls more and more to the parent of the same sex. Simultaneously, modesty training, clothing, and hair styling dramatically identify a boy or girl with his or her appropriate sex role. Boys now encounter much stricter discipline from the father than before, and are taught masculine values by him. Yet they retain the possibility of using the mother as protection and comfort against the father's wrath. The mother's coercive influence over boys declines to practically zero, and respect shown to her also drops, some boys becoming downright rude, as they would never dare be to their father. In an adult masculine group, with its talk of real, potential, or merely fanciful "enemies," a boy learns new attitudes toward aggression, especially the importance of self-defense should he or his kin be attacked. Games at this age provide training in dominance patterns as senior children direct the younger; they also feature mild competition, but leave winning an unimportant goal. School for boys and somewhat increased economic responsibilities for girls, as well as for boys who don't go to school, curtail time available for play, especially in a household of modest means or one without daughters-in-law. Girls' tasks, like spinning and weaving, teach her skills useful for a rural woman to know. Since school attendance depends largely on a boy's inclination, it tends to be irregular. Furthermore, as in Silwa and among the Hopi Indians, the Rajput parents, who are mostly illiterate, provide little help for the young scholar and confer only meager recognition on him for good scholarship. They offer equally little praise or other reward for good work

An exceptionally hostile mother of a 5-year-old boy:
"Q. When Mahender was a baby and crying at night, how quickly would you try to tend to him.
 A. It is not in my hands. If a person is bent on crying he will go on crying. When he is crying I pick him up and nurse him and if he is hungry, I give him something to eat.
Q. Do you feel that children should express their feelings? How about laughing?
 A. When the child is laughing useless with no reason, I have to scold him.
Q. Tell me about the last time he learned to do something by himself.
 A. He has not learned anything; he is mad. He does not know anything. . . . Those children who are clever, they do work but he is mad.
Q. What do you do when Mahender does not obey immediately?
 A. I beat him. I have no patience. I beat him with a stick. . . . Mahender is a shameless boy. I have to tell him a thing four times and then he does it. Other children do it when you ask them once and you feel so happy.

· · ·

Q. Sometimes children get angry with their parents when they are being scolded. How do you handle this?
 A. Still he is not old enough to be angry like this but when he is angry with one of us he goes to the others.
Q. What do you do?
 A. I love him and make him sit near me, what else?
Q. What if he should kick or beat you?
 A. If he beats he will get a beating in return. . . .

· · ·

Q. When he is good, do you praise him?
 A. When he does something good we have to praise.
Q. What do you say?
 A. I do not say anything to him or pamper him too much.
Q. You do not praise?
 A. No."

A mother of a 5-year-old girl:
"Q. Sometimes children get angry with their parents when they are being criticized or scolded. How do you handle this with Reeshmii?
 A. What to do? I console her and make her sit near me. When her father gets angry with her I feel very bad. If someone scolds her and she cries, I say 'What do you want? Do you want food?'
Q. When she is naughty, how is she usually punished?
 A. I set it right by scolding and saying 'Don't fight, don't do anything.' I don't slap her, I just frighten her. She gets frightened very soon and starts crying.
Q. You just threaten to slap her?
 A. Yes, she starts crying very soon.
Q. Do you praise her, when she is good?
 A. I praise . . . I say 'You look very nice like this.' I love her very much then."

that girls and boys do at home. Parents do, however, quickly become impatient with inept performance, all the more so because they judge by adult standards. Hence, it is not surprising that children should be slow in quitting their fundamental passivity to become notably self-reliant or conscientious about their duties at home or in school. Fortunately, demands made of them are seldom arduous.

Comparative. One village doesn't sample a subcontinent that contains an estimated half-million villages—more, if East and West Pakistan are counted. Dispersed over a vast terrain, the village economies, crops, dress, and houses are adapted to diverse climatic and other environmental conditions; they contain speakers of 12 to 15 major languages, and their customs embody the values of half a dozen major religions, not to speak of tribal religions and customs. Variety even thrives in a single village. The anthropologists reporting on Khalapur describe only Rajput socialization; for the most part, they ignore thirty-two other castes living in the community. With so much diversity, socialization must follow extremely different lines from one rural part of South Asia to another. Each individual fieldworker, with his special interests, problems, and concepts, in his own way adds to the diversity. Thus one investigator reports that his south Indian village values mastery of human relationships; this trait is neither indicated nor disproved for the Rajputs of Khalapur. Perhaps Rajputs hold the same value, only the concept didn't occur in the research design guiding the anthropologists who worked that village. Should similar personality characteristics be reported under different terms, comparison becomes difficult and the impression of diversity is misleadingly enhanced.

Pervasive concern with controlling human relationships has been reported from Gopalpur, a small village in Mysore containing about fifteen castes.[41] Lacking

conspicuous poverty, the villagers feel themselves to be masters of their physical environment, and they have deflected their attention from the management of things to the control of social relations. This concern appears in a childhood that, like Khalapur's, encourages little self-assertion, thereby calling the child's attention to how important other people are. A little later, lack of toys and books turns social play into the most satisfying play, especially between siblings, who also care for and train each other. "Everything conspires to turn the child away from manipulation of its physical environment towards manipulation of its social environment," the investigator observes. The youngster learns that through crying, begging, and compliantly doing tasks that parents desire he can wield a relatively powerful social influence. As a result his aim becomes the same as that of his elders, who seek to retain control over an unreliable social world containing people who break promises, steal, lie, and kidnap. (Unreliability of people is also apparent in Khalapur where, despite the ideal of obedience, neither children nor adults comply with directions that fall outside of customary of habitual obligations.) Quite directly, Gopalpur children perceive their parents' concern with social relations: They witness how people press on one another as individuals and depend on one another through the caste structure, whose hereditary groups perform indispensable ritual and economic duties in the community. Mother-child relations, filled with bargaining and threat, provide daily lessons in social management. Witness this sequence that began when a boy old enough to wander around the village by himself came home and announced, "Mother, I am hungry."

This is the moment of entrapment, the only time during the day when the mother is able to exercise control over her child. This is a time for bargaining, for threatening. The mother scowls at her child, "You must have worked hard to be so hungry." The mother serves food and says, "Eat this. After you have eaten it, you must sit here and rock your little sister." The child eats and says, "I am going outside to play. I will not rock my sister." The mother says, "You eat so much; where do you go; why won't you stay home?" The child replies, "I have a stomach-ache, I cannot rock my little sister." The child finishes its food and runs out of the house. Later, the child's aunt sees it and asks it to run to the store and buy some cooking oil. When it returns, the aunt says, "If you continue to obey me like this, I will give you something good to eat." When the mother catches the child again, she asks, "Where have you been?" Learning what occurred, she says, "If you brought cooking oil, that is fine; now come play with your sister." The child says, "First give me something to eat, and I will play with my sister." The mother scolds, "You will die of eating, sometimes you are willing to work, sometimes you are not willing to work; may you eat dirt." She gives it food and the child plays with its sister.[42]

The passage is interesting for more than the extraordinary role played by food, the reciprocal note in the boy's relationship to his mother, and the latter's use of bargaining to obtain compliance. It recalls features of maternal and child behavior in Khalapur in northern India, especially the mother's low maternal warmth and the hostile tenor of her scolding, particularly in the curse "May you eat dirt!" The same ambiguity surrounds responsibility in both places; obedience is greatly valued, but demands for it aren't so zealously followed up that it ever becomes highly achieved.

The report on socialization in Khalapur hardly concerns itself with how the child psychodynamically perceives socialization. A psychoanalytical account of personality formation in another north Indian village applies Melanie Klein's theory to reveal how childrearing there brings into existence two unconscious nuclear fantasies, one based on the mother's role, the other on the father's.[43] The village is Deoli in the foothills of Rajasthan state, the same place where the researcher G. Morris Carstairs, a physician, had spent his own childhood playing with Indian children and speaking their language. In 1951, when Carstairs went back, the community contained thirty-six castes, but he devoted himself to relatively high-caste ("twice-born") Hindu men, many of them Rajputs. He told his subjects, usually in Hindustani, "I am trying to learn what sort of a man I should be now if I had been born in your family and been brought up as one of your community." Through life histories, dreams, and responses to Rorschach and other psychological tests they told him, baring their conscious and unconscious strivings. From such data Carstairs derived the two nuclear fantasies that form the cores of behavior.

The first fantasy, derived from the maternal relationship, conceives women to be, on the one hand, selfless, dutiful, subservient, kind, feminine, and modest and, on the other hand, as demanding, repulsive (in menstruation), and destructively weakening to a man (through sexual relations). The terrible, bloodstained goddess Kali epitomizes the second (bad) feminine image. An infant learns the first part of this fantasy during its nursing period, when it is fully indulged and becomes acquainted with no frustrating experiences. Weaning between 18 and 24 months traumatically cuts the child off from exclusively possessing his mother, and instills the first indication that women are bad. Throughout childhood, experiences consistently reinforce the ambivalent fantasy concerning women, which, in turn, later motivates such adult personality characteristics as easy optimism, mistrust of people, and a deep regard for world renunciation, symbolizing a longing to regress to the all-gratifying period of infantile orality. The second fantasy has to do with the father, a commanding authority who shows no affection, and to whom a boy must utterly submit by eradicating every sign of competition. Rooted in this second nucleus are such passive, adult characteristics as a pliant, subservient, and ingratiatory attitude to all authority (could this overlap with the Gopalpuri concern over controlling human relations?) and distrust of one's own masculinity (symbolically expressed through idealizing chastity, and feeling worried about each loss of precious semen through masturbation and sexual intercourse).[44]

Pervasiveness of social class

"There are as many different kinds of education," said Durkheim,[45] "as there are different milieux in a given society." Childhood varies between social milieux within a community almost as much as it does between communities. Class in particular influences socialization, and does so in many ways, including through family life and the physical setting where home and neighborhood are located. Social-class membership influences personality through classbound customs, values, and general mode of life that are directly and indirectly, explicitly and inexplicitly, communicated by adult and peer models. However, far from being closed entities, classes are readily affected by what transpires in the larger social system of which they form integral parts. Hence, pertinent attitudes, expectations, and stereotypes that reach a person from members of other classes in society, including the way he is regarded and treated by virtue of his class membership, contribute

powerfully to patterning his behavior. Discrimination and disparagement are hard to bear, but that doesn't prevent them from being internalized.[46] For convenience in what follows I shall describe class socialization in oversimplified terms, practically ignoring the fact that families constituting a class are far from identical. Families that embody versions of behavior discrepant with the prevailing patterns followed in the class or neighborhood are apt to socialize their children in deviant patterns. Thereby they begin to set the course for their children's subsequent mobility up or down from whatever level they themselves occupy. Although occasionally I introduce a real community to illustrate childhood in various class contexts, most of the time I generalize for the United States as a whole. Dealing with types obviously limits the applicability of my descriptions, but it cues one regarding what to expect in describing actual upper- or middle-class ways of life or cultures of poverty. If my examples come mainly from the United States and Canada, that's because we know relatively little about class-linked styles of life abroad.

The unknown uppers

The folkways and mores of upper-class life and childhood have evaded the inquiring social scientist. Families of high social standing guard their privacy too well to permit an observer to station himself in their homes or private schools, and they somehow escape questionnaires.[47] The spacious homes and grounds where children of upper-upper-class families grow up and the privileged conditions under which they attend school, travel, and recreate develop an appreciation of seclusion and privacy and foster a strong sense of individuality. These children have little experience with crowds, and become extremely sensitive to the manners of their own kind. Carefully selected governesses, guards, and tutors supervise many of their activities, help to pattern their emotional life, and, like parents themselves, avoid excessive demands for obedience. If anything, such caretakers overemphasize their employers' class-bound values,[48] thereby probably not implanting the same kind of superego that parental upbringing promotes in middle-ranking social strata.[49] Identity in the upper class comes to be shaped and buttressed by ancestors and a glorious past vividly maintained by genealogies, portraits, and other symbols. Identity also rests very firmly on economic well-being and socioeconomic security, as well as on the father's indubitable occupational importance or even his indispensability. This gives upper-upper-class people a sense of self-confident assurance. Their relative seclusion exposes them to a highly uniform series of cultural experiences that consistently reinforce one another. More than in any other social class, upper-class American children learn dutifully to observe the ritualistic nuances of public behavior. Tone of voice, subject of conversation, dress, posture, and body care come to be carefully watched and cultivated according to classbound standards. Etiquette soon becomes automatic, and contrary to what a person with more casual habits might believe, quite satisfying. Functionally, it guides upper-class young people in selecting friends, and eventually a spouse, from among people who possess the same expressive style. On this class-level education need not be pursued as a tool leading to a career, for these children will inherit wealth. Contrary to behavior in more median strata, an upper-class boy accepts his father as a model to be emulated rather than as someone whom by his own achievements he must surpass.[50]

Lower-upper Class. Much of the deportment and values of upper-upper-class life are emulated by "lower-uppers" and taught to their children. Here, just below the top stratum, socialization lacks the props of tradition and ancestry; lower-upper-class people know not only the social distance between them and lower orders of society but also the gap sundering them off from the topflight level. Money is especially valuable because it has power to buy the costly educational advantages of private schools (which used to be reserved for the elite alone), where lower-upper-class children in pursuit of upward mobility can make contacts and identify with their upper-upper-class peers. Lower-upper parents value formal education especially for the way it prepares boys for social advantages and constitutes an indispensable avenue to a professional or managerial career.

MIDDLE-CLASS DEMOCRATIC AND RATIONAL AUTHORITY [51]

Although the middle-class mother is apt to approach maternity happily and seriously, being quite delighted with her pregnancy and fully prepared to meet domestic adjustments that she knows a new baby will bring, she is nevertheless uncertain about how best to rear her child. She and her husband believe that they have assumed a tremendous obligation, that much depends on their behavior as parents; but what is the right way for them to act? In girlhood she never had to adopt the "little mother" role with her siblings that in some cultures teaches girls the traditional, indisputable lore of motherhood. She realizes, too, how drastically childrearing has changed since her mother's day. A cardinal rule insists that her role be rationally attuned to the child's needs, but small children often fail clearly to communicate their needs. To solve her dilemma, the middle-class mother relies considerably on guidance from informed experts, whose recommendations ideally have only the children's welfare in mind. She becomes a student of Spock, Gesell, and similar popular sources of childrearing advice. Other-directed in many ways, she also evaluates the route her child's development takes by comparing him with her neighbors'. Nothing would more distress her than to discover that her youngster is falling behind, or that she is unwittingly neglecting something she should be doing to meet his needs or promote his healthy growth.

The middle-class family's small, planned size favors children. Homes so created may not be wholly child-centered, but the conscientious adults who run them do so with an eye to furthering the child's happiness and wholesome development. For example, they guard against favoritism for one youngster over another, deny any sex preference, and unlike Silwans try to forestall sibling rivalry by devoting extra consideration to the older child when he is in danger of being displaced. Parents' studied respect for one another, which often stems from true mutual esteem, is extended to the children. Parents treat them as individuals with specific rights and duties, and they come to think of themselves as distinct identities, sharply differentiated from their environment. Obvious evidence of social success makes the parents, especially the father, very acceptable to the children, whose sense of self-esteem consequently thrives. Baby books, scrapbooks, family photo album, birthday parties, and verbal approval frequently expressed by adults go far to develop children's sense of identity and the feeling or possessing value and importance.

The small household, however, places the middle-class child at a serious disadvantage by restricting his opportunities for independence. It fosters a degree of dependence about which both parents and children become anxious. Furthermore, the youngster

finds his gratification limited. Absence of siblings to compete for toys, love, and attention doesn't mean free and unstinted provision of those goods. Parents carefully ration and control their love, attention, and other rewards, using them to develop in the child desirable personality characteristics, such as self-reliance and a motive to achieve. The family's small size, plus the climate of respect that engulfs children in the middle-class household, encourages them to develop close and intense emotional ties to their parents and to form very strong identifications with them. This emotional dependence parents subsequently exploit as the basis of important learning, learning that in lower social strata depends on physical punishment or threats of punishment. Due to the closeness binding the middle-class mother and child, any withdrawal of her affection provokes extreme anxiety. Yet she deliberately provokes that anguished response to enforce discipline, precisely timing her behavior so that the child perceives his reinstatement in her good graces to occur as soon as he complies or makes restitution. Such love-oriented, or "psychological," discipline fosters a strong, self-regulatory superego that, with the aid of idealized parental images that have been internalized, operates very capably without adults' physical supervision.

I have suggested that the rational manner in which middle-class parents exercise authority and impose discipline succeeds in closely binding their children to them. Parents have other ways of earning and keeping children's love and respect. They disbelieve in trying to impose respect by showing greater strength or, as Silwan and Hindu fathers do, by virtue of their seniority. A middle-class father earns his children's respect through his occupation, the income from which controls the family's social rank and other advantages. Signs of success constantly enter the home, thanks to his occupation, his dutiful work habits, and his training. Parents also count on their fairness and their democratic, egalitarian attitudes to keep children's respect.[52] In the home's democratic atmosphere, where middle-class adults avoid arbitrarily stressing obedience for its own sake, children can freely disagree and argue with their elders. They have a right to be shown why a course of action should be followed. Should a child misbehave, ideal procedure calls for discovering why he acted as he did, and henceforth as much as possible helping him to avoid similar circumstances. Indulgence and permissiveness hardly mean that the child is left unbridled.[53] As a matter of fact, diligent attention to his development, close supervision, and love-oriented punishment restrict and tame him beyond anything known among his lower-class peers. He is clearly "oversocialized" with respect to sex and aggression. Sex is always wrong before marriage or betrothal, and one may fight only if unfairly provoked to do so by another person who is equally matched or stronger.

Middle-class socialization shows no signs of producing irresponsibility, as critics of its relative permissiveness have feared. From a very early age one of its aims is to strengthen independence and responsibility (although, as I have pointed out, the milieu also encourages dependence). The child learns to control himself and becomes conscious of how heavily his own efforts count toward attaining desirable goals, ranging from mother love to good grades. At home he learns to mute his exuberance, wipe his feet, wash his hands before eating, clean his teeth, hang his clothes, and do his homework. Rewards, like the movies or television are given only on condition that he fulfills his responsibilities. Bedtime is firmly regulated, just as his health-conscious mother very carefully plans his meals; for health, she believes, underlies doing well in school.

Duty and effort possess high value, as do earning one's own way and postponing immediate satisfactions for the sake of long-range goals. Middle-class children grow up in a highly ordered, rational world where the future is always present as a series of predictable ends that can be attained through modifying and controlling present behavior.[54]

The middle-class family devaluates physical labor and deplores physical aggression, but it puts a premium on verbal skills and cultivates them with the aid of considerable resources that it possesses. Reading aloud, reasoning with a child as though he were an adult, and fantasy play which adults often originate provide further practice in communications skills. Thanks to such preparation and to their broad range of social experiences, middle-class children learn to control language earlier than children of lower socioeconomic status. The former also manage to express their inner states more effectively and to speak with less redundancy. They come to appreciate how subtle arrangements of words and sentences convey determinable shades of meaning. A complex use of language, in turn, acts on the middle-class child's perception, guiding him to note many cues and relationships in his environment. Consequently, he grows up in a relatively complex world that further patterns his personality.[55] For example, it focuses his attention on himself so that he becomes preoccupied with finely discriminated inner states of being, sometimes to an extent that interferes with his adaptation. Language skills augment his adaptive resources. He finds that he can manipulate people through words and carefully expressed attitudes, a skill his parents cultivate in relation to him in preference to dominating him through strength and authority. His expressive skills demonstrated at home and in school help create a favorable sense of identity, as well as an attractive social image which brings him recognition and other rewards.

What I have said indicates that middle-class parents regard formal education as indispensable. A boy's career and earnings depend on school, while formal education will help a girl find an economically and otherwise well-suited husband. Education is believed to make better mothers. Hence, parents bend their efforts to insure that their children will find school tasks manageable and meaningful. They see to it that the community provides good schools. At many points school and the middle-class home reinforce each other, teachers encouraging the same norms, values, and skills that parents first began to sanction. Obviously, children from such homes have

❪ English Parents in 5 Classes Report on Their Practices in Childrearing[56]

	Percentage in occupational class				
	I and II	*III–WC*	*III–Man*	*IV*	*V*
Breast-feeding: at 1 month	60	50	50	51	34
Breast-feeding: at 3 months	39	34	24	22	12
Breast-feeding: at 6 months	20	12	11	11	7
No bottle after: 6 months	10	9	4	1	1
No bottle after: 12 months	50	47	29	21	15
Pacifier: at some time	39	53	71	75	74
Pacifier: still at 12 months	26	38	55	57	46
Bottle or pacifier to go to sleep	23	36	47	52	51
Bottle or pacifier if wakes	24	36	40	47	42
Bedtime: 6:30 P.M. minus	47	31	29	24	31
Bedtime: 8:00 P.M. plus	7	12	20	23	26
Sleeps in room alone	54	42	20	18	3
Potty training not started (12 months)	12	16	17	13	23
Of those started, never successful	36	38	46	42	79
Genital play checked	25	50	57	69	93
No smacking	56	38	32	42	35
General smacking	39	53	60	54	58
Frequent tantrums	9	8	14	15	23
Father's participation:					
high	57	61	51	55	36
little or none	19	6	16	18	36
Baby-sitting: once or less	25	36	42	42	59

Percentages are based on a survey of 700 mothers of one-year-old children, made in the prosperous city of Nottingham, England. The authors describe Classes I through III–WC (white-collar) as "middle class" and Classes III–Man through V (manual workers) as "worker class." In I and II, professional and managerial specialists, like doctors, clergymen, teachers, nurses, and police officers, have been classed; III–WC contains clerical workers, foremen, shop assistants, and tradesmen in one-man businesses. Class III–Man includes skilled manual workers and drivers; IV contains semi-skilled machine operators, bus conductors, window-cleaners, porters, and so on; V has unskilled laborers, such as refuse collectors, cleaners in industry, messengers, as well as the persistently unemployed. Nottingham, England's eighth largest city, housed 312,000 people at the time of study.

a big edge in mastering tasks set by teachers. They find teachers understandable and appealing role models, much more so than Hopi Indian children do. Middle-class children take advantage of extracurricular activities; outside of school they participate in the Boy Scouts, Girl Guides, Sunday School, and other church events. In the closely supervised activities of those associations youngsters demonstrate their personal popularity, a characteristic on which they and middle-class parents set great store.

Middle-class adolescence stretches out for a prolonged time without any official lifting of the blanket taboo on sex. In typically self-controlled fashion, however, middle-class adolescents manage to find sexual gratification, mostly through masturbation and petting. Sexual intercourse, or even the contemplated loss of virginity, becomes a momentous event, especially for girls. With the teen-age years, peer groups increasingly promote a series of values and activities that exist outside the official adult norms of middle-class society. Parents and other adults may disapprove of such behavior, and even indicate their disapproval, but in practice they tolerate it and actually help young people to acquire it, for example by providing them with spending money. Clothing and coiffure styles, sports cars, and a specially cultivated language are conspicuous attributes of teen-age youth culture; other practices; like use of marijuana, drinking, drag-racing, and mischief-making remain subterranean. Even police tend to tolerate middle-class youthful delinquency, recognizing such acts and their authors as different from what occurs in a lower-class cultural setting.[57]

Late in his teens comes an event for which the middle-class young person has been waiting and preparing for many years —he goes to college, the most popular one that will have him. Although a college education is almost indispensable for a career,

or for a husband who is successful by middle-class standards, ostensibly a youth goes to college to benefit from the liberalizing and broadening effect that higher education will have. Some adolescents, however, become weary, disappointed, or disenchanted with the last four years of their 16-year-long educational program. Some would like more time for the friendship and fraternity (or sorority) life than college permits. Others, if the "Berkeley Rebels" of 1965 can be believed, find that too many of the faculty, and other deadly campus features, neither broaden nor liberalize their spirits. Undoubtedly, college does influence American, middle-class status personality, but to what extent, remains to be seriously and competently studied.[58]

Comparative. I spoke of American middle-class socialization as permissive. Sixth-grade, middle-class, U.S. children in Dryden, New York, might not entirely agree. At any rate, compared to sixth-grade, middle-class youngsters in Cologne, Germany, the Americans more often perceive their parents as punitively depriving them of privileges or verbally rejecting them through nagging, scolding, and yelling.[59] Conversely, the German children report parents to be considerably more nurturant. In Dryden, middle-class parents frequently explain why they punish a child or ask him to do something, but in Cologne parents in an equivalent social stratum do so even more. Judging from what the youthful informants say, apparently truthfully, German mothers and fathers call for significantly more responsibility and exercise stronger supervision; for example, they demand to be told how the child has spent his money and insist that he get their permission before he goes to some entertainment. They use physical punishment more readily, but less often do they goad their children to do better than other children or to get good marks in school. In other words, they less often urge achievement on the child. Fa-

❨ *Certain New England Middle-Class Mothers Tend Quite Consistently to Rear Children More Permissively and Less Rigidly, and More Often with Pleasure and Less Often with Rejection, than Working-Class Mothers*[60]

Scales	Middle class	Working class	p
Median age at completion of bowel training	18.8 months	16.4 months	.01
Percentage rated *high* on:			
Severity of toilet training	15	26	.01
Permissiveness for dependency	42	29	.02
Punishment and irritation for dependency	44	56	.02
Sex permissiveness	53	22	$<.01$
Permissiveness for aggression toward neighborhood children	38	31	n.s.
Permissiveness for aggression toward parents	19	7	$<.01$
Severity of punishment for aggression toward parents	36	51	$<.01$
Amount of restriction on the use of fingers for eating	66	81	$<.05$
Pressure for conformity with table standards and restrictions	23	39	$<.01$
Restrictions on care of house and furniture	65	78	$<.01$
Pressure for neatness and orderliness	43	57	$<.01$
Strictness about bedtime	28	38	$<.05$
Strictness about noise	28	38	$<.05$
Keeping track of child (frequency of checking whereabouts)	26	33	n.s.
Extent of father's demands for instant obedience	53	67	$<.05$
Importance of child's doing well at school	35	50	$<.01$
Use of praise if child gives no trouble at table	49	63	$<.05$
Use of ridicule	31	47	$<.01$
Deprivation of privileges	34	42	n.s.
Use of physical punishment	17	33	$<.01$
Amount of caretaking of infant by person other than mother or father	18	11	n.s.
Mother's warmth to child	51	37	.01
Father's warmth to child	60	56	n.s.
Percentage showing some rejection of child	24	40	$<.01$
Percentage of mothers "delighted" over pregnancy	73	65	.05
Percentage in which family authority exercised primarily by:			
Father	29	25	n.s.
Both equally	62	59	n.s.
Mother	9	16	n.s.

Note that the father plays a greater role in middle-class than in working-class socialization. As the last column shows, the probabilities are high that many of these differences do not arise from chance alone ($p = 0.5$ or less). Although some are not significant (n.s.), statistical considerations of another sort warrant keeping them.

thers don't play as prominent a role in U.S. childrearing as they do in the German household, where they even surpass mothers in imposing responsibilities and in supervising youngsters.

CHILD-CENTERED CRESTWOOD HEIGHTS [61]

Four thousand Canadian parents in Crestwood Heights, on the outskirts of Toronto, extol their upper-middle-class suburb as ideally suited for rearing children. They have contrived a community in which every family, in order to maximize everyone's happiness, accumulates all that is best and latest in ideas, values, experiences, and material things. .With those resources the community turns out highly independent, achievement-oriented adults who are acutely sensitive to interpersonal expectations. Though they fall a bit short of their own ideal expectations of happiness, they are very much inclined to perpetuate their way of life. Crestwood Heights viewed in the 1950s hardly represents what North America in general has achieved, but it does fulfill what some middle-class people dream American life should and some day will be like: endowed with space for growing children, within easy reach of the father's office in the teeming city, and superabounding in comforts and economic security. Here a child in his playpen looks out into an arduously furnished home, which to an observer is reminiscent of a department store, charmingly arranged ("the broadloom jungle") but without the homely litter proclaiming that people actually "live" there. The child learns that some of those furnishings are for use and others for display. For all, he must show concern and respect. Mindful of the home's precious contents, parents fear and resent children's boisterous behavior; yet, in theory, this is

the one corner of the world where each member of the family may be himself. Obviously, the house is more than a place to live; proudly it proclaims the parents' social maturity, including their excellent biological and social adjustment to each other. Some day the child, if he correctly fulfills his promise, will also have his own home, on the same style as this or better. In Crestwood Heights hardly anyone looks back to ancestry, tradition, or history. Present health, current happiness, and immediate security are the outstanding values on which children thrive as they are directed by an optimistic vision toward their future careers. Their success is taken as practically inevitable or, as they see it, for granted. The emphasis on career appears almost as soon as a child can walk. Jokingly, adults ask what he will be when he grows up, and if necessary they inform or correct his choice. He comes to feel that life's opportunities extend nearly without limit. When the time come to choose, really he does so without too greatly fearing the energy, struggle, and competition that any given career demands.

The forethought and planning characteristic of Crestwood Heights extends to family planning; parents arrange to have children as they arrange to finance a car or a trip to Europe. Following birth in a hospital, the baby is immediately launched upon a series of separations from its mother as technically trained people move in to care for its needs. Many times in a child's early life he learns to part with his mother as she must bear to part with him, he for his own sake and she for hers, otherwise her undercurrent of frustrated resentment might break through and grossly distort her maternal role. She knows that motherhood calls for loving the child and providing him with security so that his mental health won't be threatened, but her actual role is difficult due to the lack of agreed-upon rules for childrearing. Her sense of responsibility wars with her uncertainty, driving her to seek help wherever she can find it. In the family, where every individual owes respect to every other, conflict —symptoms of malfunction—must at all costs be avoided because it might injure the child. Explosive pressure must also be avoided, but covert pressure is relentless as parents seek to win and coax the youngster, whom it is wrong ever to overwhelm.

Around 3 the child enters the professionally staffed nursery school, whose aims are to reinforce his emotional and physical independence from his mother and to teach him social and physical skills. In this setting, where he discovers that time for him and for any single activity is scarce and strictly rationed, his mother hopes he will learn to get along well with other children. Social adjustment is already a matter of considerable importance. She further trusts that the nursery will correct any "problems" that she may have noted in the child. With the Crestwood Heights father away at work, day-to-day authority falls very much on the mother, who carefully shores up his image so that his symbolic importance remains undiminished. Siblings have no formal right or duty to discipline young children and what supervision they offer is strictly informal.

From nursery school, boys and girls in equal proportion graduate to the state-supported school system and start 13 or 14 years of serious general training for their adult roles. School is followed by Scouts and dancing lessons. The whole schedule of activities in the school years is such that parents know at almost any moment where their children are and what they are doing, and youngsters learn the importance of time and punctuality. Progress through school takes them through a series of numbered age grades, further divided, on the basis of intelligence and performance, into achievement levels. A child's current grade

becomes an important source of identity; those grades above him represent the future into which he must win promotion by effort and hard work.

Whatever contribution these children make at home is less significant for the help it provides than for the way parents see it forming character. The fact that fathers play their roles outside the home limits a boy's opportunity to learn the masculine role from him, and other male role models are also lacking. By being separated in school and camp, each sex learns from peers to follow a different demeanor; girls' more refined, and boys' rough and noisy. The degree of their separation isn't too great, however, for wholesome development is thought to require each sex to take a moderate interest in the other, an early interest that anticipates preadolescent dating. The years from 6 to 12 similarly rush other experiences at the child, with the result that when puberty arrives few novel means are left with which to validate near-adult status. Boys have already begun to wear long pants and girls to fix their hair in adult fashion and to have dates.

In high school and throughout the teen-age years boys and girls become preoccupied with dating, summer jobs, choice of their life's vocation, and their sex roles. As pressures intensify for responsibility and achievement, both sexes look for a likely career, though a girl knows that for her a job will be only a way stop en route to marriage and motherhood, plus a guarantee of economic security should her marriage break up. She is kept in school and sent on to college because parents and the rest of society believe that education adds to her popularity and will help her find a suitable husband. She receives no formal instruction in the arts of child care or homemaking. Rather, she learns to place great emphasis on her charm and physical attractiveness, attributes on which her ability to captivate boys depends. In grooming and dress styles both sexes follow the lead of their peers rather than of adults, and they weigh adult values much more carefully than hitherto before internalizing them. As the time for a career choice draws nearer parents, despite their profound interest, resolve not to intervene in the child's process of selection. For one thing, they recognize how little they can do to push a child who has been trained in independence, especially in a direction where he doesn't feel inclined to go. With the teen-age years, the mother loses some of her power to discipline, especially where boys are concerned, and the father comes into control of certain important privileges, like access to the family car. Between 16 and 19, the adolescent's experiences with his peers sharpen the conflict between his age group's norms and parental standards. From being merely weighed, adult values come to be critically and even rebelliously examined, but rarely do Crestwood Heights young people seriously act out their rebellion. From high school, boys and girls pass into college. Though intellectually skilled and emotionally independent, they are still almost totally unequipped to start a career. But they understand more or less clearly what will be expected of them in the years ahead and in college proceed to acquire more of the necessary skills.

WORKING-CLASS BOSTON VILLAGERS [62]

Crestwood Heights domiciles people who are in the upper reaches of the middle class. Boston's West End (now demolished for urban renewal) is home for Italian-Americans who form part of America's working class, people whose culture shades into the lower-class way of life. Economical rents, convenience to work, and a feeling of belonging attach these New Englanders to their spotlessly clean apartments in a high-density slum neighborhood. The crowdedness of the West End disturbs them little,

for they don't demand the privacy that upper- and middle-class families so deeply value and pay for, nor do they convert housing into a boastful status symbol. With only a grade-school education plus a couple of years of high school, the Italian-Americans mostly work in skilled and semiskilled jobs that in 1957 brought them about $80 a week. Yet the wage earners aren't all of a kind. Some seek routine; they try to maintain a stable way of life, economic and social security, and regular friends. Others are action-seekers who move from one adventurous episode to another looking for thrills. To some extent during socialization young people, especially boys, pass from action-seeking to increasing routinization. As adults they look back with nostalgic memories to their action-packed years.

Children begin life in a single-family household which the mother's married daughters, other relatives, and parents' peers often visit, but where they rarely see grandparents, for West End Italian-Americans neither cherish nor greatly respect that older generation. Family authority belongs to the husband. Somewhat as in Egypt's Silwa and in India, separateness rather than social togetherness prevails between husband and wife. A couple rarely shows any visible sign of emotional closeness. Child-rearing belongs to the mother, who routine-orientedly runs the household first of all to satisfy adult wishes, for the family remains adult-centered even after children are born. As quickly as children can, they must conduct themselves as miniature adults, doing what parents want them to do. The mother uses her husband as a model of masculinity and authority, after whom a boy is to pattern his behavior. She readily lets the boy know when his behavior departs from masculine ideals. Her daughter she shows how clever women can get around men if they have to. Physical and verbal punishment control children, but without impinging on the feelings that parents love them. Much

Working-class boys as they grow up appear at home less and less; in action-seeking peer groups, however, they come alive. (U. S. Department of Labor)

more rarely do youngsters win rewards for obedience. Boys and girls tend to be raised impulsively and nonrationally, being told what to do with little thought given to how they might interpret directions. Parents don't behave self-consciously toward children or try to see things from a childish perspective. As a result, in the home a child gets no training in taking another's point of view or in learning to see himself objectively and self-consciously as he appears in the eyes of others. No firm or clear sense of identity emerges in early or in later childhood. Parents also don't try to prepare a child for some predetermined goal; they lack any clear image of what his future job or other status is likely to be. West Enders primarily want for the little adults what they want for themselves: security and other people's acceptance. They acknowledge that formal education is good, but without pushing children toward that goal.

Whereas at home a child must behave as

a little adult, with peers—whom he joins on the street long before he goes to school—he can act his age. From early years, the West Ender spends his life, except for a temporary break shortly after marriage, with one or another peer group. Soon after his marriage, an action-seeking man returns to his street-corner gang, while the majority of men, in more routine-oriented fashion, form new peer groups that include family members as well as friends. When these meet in members' homes, the sexes usually congregate in separate rooms. As her children leave to play in the street, the mother tries to impress on them norms of proper behavior that differs little from those held in the middle class. The child, however, soon discovers that those official norms clearly diverge from rules of the street, and learns to act adaptively according to the rules of whichever situation he finds himself in. He becomes able to subvert official norms without experiencing burdensome guilt. Children learn the morality imbedded in stated rules without actually internalizing much of it. The rules, however, are always available, to be used if convenient to measure the extent of someone's deviation from them. Some deviation from ideals is regarded as inevitable, and this comforting thought allows a person to justify a certain proportion of failure and disappointment. Youthful peer groups provide many opportunities for children to assert their superiority, special skills, physical strength, and repartee. On the street they may display themselves as individuals to win approval in ways they never could at home. Nevertheless, they must adhere to group norms, or else, as in Rakau, they will feel their peers' sharp, stinging criticism. Boys as they grow toward adolescence appear at home less and less. Their relationship to parents becomes exceedingly tenuous and often conflictful, for they find the adult-centered, routine-oriented household's norms increasingly onerous. Girls, who from 7 or 8 have been helping mothers in household tasks, achieve considerably less freedom. In adult company, the adolescent remains extremely lethargic and sullen, but in the action-seeking peer group he comes alive. Games, athletic contests, fighting, sexual adventures, and mischief-making attacks on the conventional world sometimes raise him to a state of quasi-hypnotic, almost drugged excitement, which enables him to feel that he is really in control of his life. Adolescents think little of their future as adults or of ultimate success goals. They have little motivation to study and to learn in school, whose values bear little relationship to the intense life they are living with one another. Greatly as they admire the material trappings of modern life, especially cars, they won't have any of society's annoying impositions. As in Rakau, the West End peer group frowns on educational and occupational mobility and questions the masculinity of someone who does well in school. Socialization emphasizes becoming person-oriented rather than being directed toward impersonal goals, such as a career, income, knowledge, or prestige. In time, West Enders do take on impersonal goals, like jobs, but all through life they pursue them outside the peer group. Friends and groups remain ends in themselves and not instruments. A West Ender's mobility in the class system hinges on anything that pushes or pulls him out of his peer group, or any talents or psychological needs that propel him into the wider world and encourage him to strive for impersonal goals, and on teachers or social workers who succeed in drawing him away from his street-corner friends.

BEYOND THE REACH OF OFFICIAL NORMS

It takes considerable effort and deliberately cultivated doubt to write about the patterns of childrearing of the lowest social class without too flagrantly betraying one's own classbound attitudes. Too many sociologists treat the culture of people living on the ground floor of society as though it were fraught with unrelieved deprivation and stress. The anthropologist Oscar Lewis laces his view of the culture of poverty with a few relieving glimpses of people enjoying themselves, but these are brief; mostly he dwells on its harshness.[63] It is by imagining what lowest-class life is *not* that these authors are enabled to see the suffering it imposes. To the degree that lower-class people compare themselves to other, relatively more fortunate social strata, such as the working-class Boston villagers and the child-centered suburbanites of Crestwood Heights, they too conceive of a better way of life and hope to alter their present patterns. I really doubt that lower-class life is so nearly totally bleak and filled with unrelieved misery as most often pictured. Yet I can't say much more, because, as I said, firsthand views of lower-class experience are pretty generally written from middle-class perspectives.

The lower-class youngster grows up in a behavioral realm that, as he well recognizes, includes many practices running directly contrary to society's official values. As a result, his world becomes bifurcated into "we" and "they," and from "them" he remains thoroughly alienated. He learns, however, that the values and behavior patterns of the large society rank as somehow superior to certain of his own; he therefore finds it useful to rationalize his disinclination to measure up to them.[64] Sometimes he attacks the official norms symbolically through delinquent acts as if, in a society well-schooled in the language of force, he were resolved to assert his own power. The fact that neither the family nor the child's peer group (which he joins early) demands commitment to all official values leaves the lower-class child to internalize those values

very poorly, which of course makes the possibility of flaunting them that much easier.
His parents identify money, not mobility, as
the key to sheer existence and fun. Hence,
where the middle-class youngster learns to
value school for the sake of his future
career, the lower-class child comes to appreciate the desirability of getting a job and
earning money in order to enjoy more of
the good things that society will otherwise
keep out of reach. Impelled by zest for immediately having these good things, he
drops out of school early, thereby ruling
himself out of many possible jobs. Since the
father's occupation doesn't allow him regularly to provide good things for his family,
the child's perception of his father isn't
magnified. Instead, guided by society's official values, lower-class youngsters perceive
the father as a failure, thereby stripping
him of potential authority to socialize his
children through their respect for him and
for his achievements. Relieved of considerable pressure generated by conscientiously
pursued, internalized parental norms, lower-
class children remain subject to considerable socialization by threatened and actual
physical punishment. The child's inability,
in a society that values achievement, to
identify with parents who are models of
social and economic success lowers his self-
esteem and blocks growth of a satisfactory
self-image. So does the large family, which
requires that children share their toys and
wear hand-me-downs. Children at home are
reacted to as a relatively undifferentiated
group, not as individuals, and they get little
chance to express their views or to initiate
action.[65] A lack of warmth and demonstrated affection in the lower-class home
bars those feelings from being employed as
"psychological" forms of discipline. Sometimes tangible rewards appear—money, ice
cream, and presents—but good behavior
more often goes unnoticed. Parents tend to
be authoritarians who emphasize their om-
niscience and strength to secure the child's

obedience, assigning his wishes a very low
priority compared to their own. They see
little need rationally to defend their directions or to explain why one line of conduct
is better than another. Punishment tends to
be erratically and severely meted out when
the child draws attention to himself through
misbehavior. This has several consequences: first, punishment and misconduct
aren't predictably connected in the child's
mind; second, he learns to adapt by con-
cealing what he has done; and third, it leads
to a relatively mild superego because not
only does punishment fail to coincide with
misconduct, but with time the disapproved
act less and less threatens any warm emotional bonds linking child to parent, bonds
on which the growth of conscience depends. Warmth increasingly dissolves and
in its place the severe punishment which the
child receives generates hostility toward
parents that spreads even to the norms they
try to inculcate.

Peer groups possess the same importance
for lower-class children that they do for
working-class West Enders. Children in so-
called deprived neighborhoods spend much
of their free time playing in the streets,
where they remain well beyond the range of
adult supervision and where peers' values
take over to an extent that parents scarcely
recognize. One lesson the child learns from
peers reinforces what he also learns at
home; namely, to fear and avoid authority
rather than to respect it. Now, however,
those attitudes are directed against police,
teachers, and all adults outside the home
from whom he expects interference and
punishment rather than warmth and permissive respect.

Compared with middle-class children,
lower-class youngsters' sexual and aggressive impulses remain comparatively under-
controlled. From parents and neighbors
who fight and from the mother who fears
her husband's physical power, they receive
direct training in the importance of physical

strength and violence, adaptive learning that the streets and peer groups reinforce. The children, who have not strongly internalized guilt in connection with sex and so often play beyond the range of adult supervision, find it easy to experiment with sex. By late adolescence a far larger proportion of lower-class than middle-class boys have had sexual intercourse and much more frequently secure sexual gratification in that manner, usually with prostitutes, than through masturbation or petting.[66] Neither the home or peer group equips the lower-class child for school, whose values at many points depart from those of his family and friends. The language he has learned to use at home and in the street limits him in communicating nuances of meaning, in expressing feelings, and in differentiating precisely between qualities of experience—skills that school rewards.[67] In his notions of the future, chance plays a great part, and he gives correspondingly slight attention to how connections between events work themselves out. Furthermore, his span of anticipation is short, leaving him heavily present-oriented. Since parents themselves hold realistically low expectations of how far their children will go in school, and remain vague about boys' ultimate occupational level, they do little to motivate the youngsters, and can't induce them to attend much beyond the age when they become legally free to quit.

FURTHER READING

Das Kind in Brauch und Sitte der Voelker, by Hermann H. Ploss (1911–1912), is one of the earliest ethnological surveys of childhood in culture, dating to late nineteenth century. *The Child in Primitive Society*, by Nathan Miller (1928), covers similar ground, making many generalizations that modern scholarship no longer finds acceptable. *Childhood in Contemporary Cultures*, edited by Margaret Mead and Martha Wolfenstein (1955), is in some respects a modern counterpart to those books, though not as systematic and organized. In *Four Families*, a film released by the National Film Board of Canada, Margaret Mead comments on childhood in India, France, Japan, and Canada. As the title indicates, *Educational Ideals in the Ancient World*, by William Barclay (1959), is given over to values that governed learning in biblical times and in ancient Athens, Sparta, and Rome. Many books and articles follow children's development in particular cultures. For the Caribbean area, David Landy examines a *Tropical Childhood* (1965) in Puerto Rico; A. A. Campbell, *St. Thomas Negroes—A Study of Personality and Culture* (1943); Madeline Kerr, *Personality and Conflict in Jamaica* (1952); and Yehudi A. Cohen, "Structure and Function: Family Organization and Socialization in a Jamaican Community" (1956), " 'Adolescent Conflict' in a Jamaican Community" (1955a), and "Character Formation and Social Structure in a Jamaican Community" (1955b). Africa is represented by O. F. Raum, *Chaga Childhood* (1940); Barrington Kaye, *Bringing Up Children in Ghana* (1962), and Margaret Read, *Children of Their Fathers* (1959); Marie-Thérésè Knapen, *L'Enfant mukongo* (1962), Meyer Fortes, *Social and Psychological Aspects of Education in Taleland* (1938), Benjamin Kidd, *Savage Childhood* (1906), and Robert A. LeVine and Barbara B. LeVine, "Nyansongo: A Gusii Community in Kenya" (1963). For European childhood we have Eric Dehn's short, comparative "Fashions in Discipline" (1964); L. Bernot and R. Blancard, *Nouville, un village français* (1953); and a preliminary sketch of personality and socialization in an Austrian village by John J. Honigmann in the *American Philosophical Society Year Book, 1963* (1964: 418–421). P. Ariès' *Centuries of Childhood* (1962) confines itself to France and the *ancien régime* while Magdalen King-Hall takes her account of *The Story of the Nursery* (1958) from the Middle Ages through the Victorian era. That European outlier, Israel, has been studied mainly from the vantage point of the kibbutz, the best source being Melford E. Spiro, *Children of the Kibbutz* (1965). The volume of material on Asia and the Pacific islands is great; it includes Edwin Terry Prothro, *Child Rearing in Lebanon* (1961); Verrier Elwin, *The Muria and Their Ghotul* (1947), and Géza Róheim, "The Western Tribes of Central Australia: Childhood" (1962). Several studies come from the Philippine Islands: Ethel Nurge, *Life in a Leyte Village* (1966); George M. Guthrie, *The Filipino Child and Philippine Society* (1961); Marianne F. Dozier, "North Kalinga Personality Configurations and Child-Rearing Patterns" (1963), and William F. Nydegger and Corinne Nydegger, "Tarong: An Ilocos Barrio in the Philippines" (1963). Thomas W. Maretzki and Hatsumi Maretzki cover child training in "Taira: An Okinawan Village" (1963). For Javanese childhood we have Kurt Danziger, "Parental Demands and Social Class in Java, Indonesia" (1960b); the same author's "Independence Training and Social Class in Java, Indonesia" (1960a); and two titles by Hildred Geertz, "The Vocabulary of Emotion" (1959) and *The Javanese Family* (1961). Gregory Bateson and Margaret Mead use photographs heavily in *Balinese Character, A Photographic Analysis* (1942). Margaret Mead's most popular books refer to the Pacific island area, notably *Coming of Age in Samoa* (1928a), *Growing Up in New Guinea* (1930b), and *Sex and Temperament* (1935). In their company I would put Thomas Gladwin and Seymour B. Sarason's *Truk: Man in Paradise* (1953). Concerning New Guinea, see John W. M. Whiting, *Becoming a Kwoma* (1941); H. Ian Hogbin, "Education at Ontong Java, Solomon

Islands" (1931); and the same author's "A New Guinea Childhood: From Weaning till Eighth Year in Wogeo" (1946). Everett E. Hagen, in *On the Theory of Social Change* (1962: chap. 8), analyzes personality formation in Burma and Java, basing his work on other sources. "Culture Pattern and Adolescent Behavior," by F. L. K. Hsu, B. G. Watrous, and E. M. Lord (1961), compares Chinese, Hawaiian, and mainland U.S. adolescents. American Indian children are described in Inez M. Hilger's three monographs: *Chippewa Child Life and Its Cultural Background* (1951); *Arapaho Child Life and Its Cultural Background* (1952); and *Araucanian Child Life and Its Cultural Background* (1957). Studies of the Navaho include those by Dorothea C. Leighton and Clyde Kluckhohn, *Children of the People* (1947); Clyde Kluckhohn, "Some Aspects of Navaho Infancy and Early Childhood" (1947); and Louise Lamphere, "Loose Structuring as Exhibited in a Case Study of Navajo Religious Learning" (1964). Irma Honigmann and John J. Honigmann report on "Child Rearing Patterns among the Great Whale River Eskimo" (1953), while in Alaska, Margaret Lantis collected material for *Eskimo Childhood and Interpersonal Relationships* (1960). *Pre-School Children of the Hare Indians* is a small monograph based on observations which Hiroko Sue (1965) made in a series of summer and winter camps of those far northern Athapaskan people. Frederica de Laguna reconstructs aboriginal "Childhood among the Yakutat Tlingit" (1965), and Ann McElroy Searcy covers both *Contemporary and Traditional Prairie Potawatomi Child Life* (1965). Dipping below the border, Kimball Romney and Romaine Romney studied "The Mixtecans of Juxtlahuaca, Mexico" (1963). From culturally closer to home come two studies of Midwest communities: Robert J. Havighurst *et al.*, *Growing Up in River City* (1962) and A. B. Hollingshead, *Elmtown's*

Youth (1949). *Children of Bondage* by Allison Davis and John Dollard (1940) traces the personality development of urban Negro youths, many of whom John H. Rohrer and Munro S. Edmonson follow half a generation later in *The Eighth Generation Grows Up* (1960). The plight of lower-class youth in modern America is grippingly presented by Arthur Pearl in "Youth in Lower Class Settings" (1965). A brief view of class and socialization in Australia appears in chapters 8 and 9 of *Social Structure and Personality in a City*, edited by O. A. Oeser and S. B. Hammond (1954). James H. S. Bossard and Eleanor Stoker Boll review many topics of American child life in *The Sociology of Child Development* (1960). In anthropological fashion, John L. Fischer and Ann Fischer cover "The New Englanders of Orchard Town, U. S. A." (1963).

REFERENCES

1 Boas, 1932: 56.

2 *Cf.* M. Mead, 1964a: 64–65.

3 Schurtz (1903: 178) takes this view, for a detailed rebuttal of which see Hallowell, 1939.

4 *Cf.* Elwin, 1947.

5 From Ammar, 1954. Hamed Ammar, who studied the village in about 1950, had full command of the Arabic language.

6 Radcliffe-Brown, 1952: 149–151.

7 For a discussion of mutual suspicion in peasant cultures, see G. M. Foster, 1960–1961.

8 My main source is L. Thompson and Joseph, 1944. I have also consulted P. Beaglehole, 1935; Dennis, 1940 and 1955; Eggan, 1943 and 1956; Simmons, 1942; Goldfrank, 1945; Aberle, 1951. Mostly those sources describe the Hopi as they were around 1942 and somewhat earlier.

9 Peterson, 1954: 55–57. By permission of Beacon Press.

10 Postal, 1965.

11 Simmons, 1942: 83.

12 *Ibid.*, p. 84.

13 Eggan, 1956: 360.

14 Voth, 1901: 103–104.

15 Simmons, 1942: 76–77.

16 My account of the Rakau Maori study uses summaries written by Jane Ritchie, 1957; Earle, 1958; Mulligan, 1957; James E. Ritchie, 1956 and 1963; E. Beaglehole and Ritchie, 1961. Ernest Beaglehole, a long-time Maori student and an anthropologically well-informed psychologist, directed the Rakau research when it began in 1953.

17 In its scope the Rakau project calls to mind the Indian Personality and Administration Research, set up in the United States in 1941. See L. Thompson, 1951.

18 J. W. M. Whiting and Child, 1953; 50–52, 341–343; Jane Ritchie, 1957: 178–179.

19 Jane Ritchie, 1957: chap. 8.

20 Earle, 1958: 107.

21 James E. Ritchie, 1956: chap. 2.

22 *Ibid.*, chap. 3.

23 *Ibid.*, chap. 4.

24 *Ibid.*, chap. 5.

25 A reviewer, Ralph Piddington, detects that Ritchie tends to think unilinearly about culture change among the Maori, regarding it as a process in which the Maori adopt European-derived culture patterns. Ritchie doesn't allow for culture change being the progressive emergence of behavior patterns that derive both from European and Maori cultural traditions, Piddington says in his review of *The Making of a Maori*. For the review, see the *Journal of the Polynesian Society*, 1964, 73: 86–87.

26 Cook, 1941–1942 and 1942.

27 M. Mead, 1930c: 80–87.

28 M. Mead, 1928a and 1928b.

29 See also James E. Ritchie, 1963: 152.

30 M. Mead, 1930b: 141, 232, and 1940–1941: 97–98.

31 Jane Ritchie, 1957: 143; Earle, 1958: 80.

32 E. Beaglehole, 1957: 226–235.

33 As part of the Rakau Maori study, the investigators compared Rakau personality characteristics with those of other Maori groups. See Jane Ritchie, 1957: chap. 9. For another psychologically oriented Maori study, see E. Beaglehole and Beaglehole, 1946. The latter two authors also describe socialization in Pukapuka, another Polynesian community; see E. Beaglehole and Beaglehole, 1941.

34 Based on Minturn and Hitchcock, 1963; Minturn and Lambert, 1964: chap. 15. More information about the village, Khalapur, which was studied for information about socialization in 1954–1955, will shortly be available. Meanwhile, see Hitchcock, 1959. He has also done a fine ethnographic film *North Indian Village*, which centers around the caste system in Khalapur.

35 B. B. Whiting, 1963: 2–13.

36 J. W. M. Whiting *et al.*, 1966.

37 B. B. Whiting, 1963. The figure is reprinted by permission of John Wiley and Sons, Inc.

38 *Cf.* Srinivas, n.d.

39 Minturn and Lambert, 1964: chap. 15.

40 *Ibid.*, pp. 312–314. By permission of John Wiley & Sons, Inc.

41 A. R. Beals, 1963, who carried out 14 months of fieldwork in 1959–1960. Narain, 1964, summarizes other studies; see also his 1957 book as well as W. S. Taylor, 1948; Cormack, 1953.

42 A. R. Beals, 1963: 19–20. By permission of Holt, Rinehart and Winston.

43 Carstairs, 1957.

44 Morris Opler, who reviewed Carstairs' book, doesn't believe very strongly in the theory and also finds grounds for disagreeing with some of the latter's observations. The exchange between the two men can be followed in the *American Anthropologist*, 1959, 61: 140–142; 1960, 62: 504–511.

45 Durkheim, 1956: 67.

46 *Cf.* C. C. Hughes *et al.*, 1960: 250–251, 295–296.

47 O. W. Ritchie and Koller (1964: 53), whom I follow in this section, call attention to the importance of biography for knowledge about upper-class life.

48 Baltzell, 1961: 280.

49 M. Mead, 1930b: 141; Bateson, 1942–1943.

50 McArthur, 1955.

51 Bronfenbrenner, 1958; Langner and Michael, 1963: chap. 16; O. W. Ritchie and Koller, 1964: 56–58; Sears, Maccoby, and Levin, 1957.

52 *Cf.* Elder, 1962.

53 *Cf.* LaPiere, 1959.

54 Bernstein, 1958.

55 Bernstein, 1958 and 1964.

56 Adapted from Newson and Newson, 1963: 152–153, 229. By permission of George Allen and Unwin, Ltd., with acknowledgement to International Universities Press.

57 Myerhoff and Myerhoff, 1964; E. A. Smith, 1962.

58 Sanford, 1964.

59 E. C. Devereux *et al.*, 1962.

60 Adapted from Sears, Maccoby, and Levin, 1957: 426–427. © 1957 by Harper & Row, Publishers, Incorporated.

61 My material comes from chapters 1 through 7 of Seeley, Sim, and Loosley, 1956; see also Robert Olson, 1957.

62 Based on Gans, 1962; he lived in Boston's West End for 8 months in 1957–1958. See also Whyte, 1955 and 1964.

63 O. Lewis, 1959 and 1961.

64 Sewell and Haller, 1959.

65 Elder, 1962.

66 Kinsey, Pomeroy, and Martin, 1948: 347–349.

67 Bernstein, 1958.

As the Twig Is Bent

9

'Tis Education forms the common mind,
Just as the Twig is bent, the Tree's inclin'd.[1]
ALEXANDER POPE

How important is early learning?

In 1693, John Locke,[2] who styled himself a humble "under-labouror" clearing rubbish from the path to knowledge, wrote that "little, or almost insensible Impressions on our tender Infancies, have very important and lasting Consequences." Nearly two hundred years later the Victorian savant Herbert Spencer,[3] who normally pondered schemes of vaster, evolutionary development, noted human nature to be "more modifiable by early training" than by anything else. Then Freud came along. During the first half of the twentieth century, the question of the lasting consequences of the pristine epoch of childhood unbridled the most fervid support as well as some of the bluntest and most vulgar expressions of disbelief ever heard in the social sciences. The full truth of the controversial matter, I hasten to add, remains definitely unsettled.

Locke, Spencer, and many psychoanalysts all imply that personality characteristics acquired early limit the personality's subsequent maneuverability, or are themselves irreversible. The deep embedment of early learning together with the fact that it occurred without reflection are often cited to explain its persistence.[4] As a result, some anthropologists predict, behavior internal-

263

ized without choice in infancy and early childhood will better survive in a culture changing under foreign influence than behavior learned late in life.[5] Like the inner core of an onion, early experiences will be the last to peel off during culture contact.[6] Consequently, culture change must be uneven, vast sections of behavior altering without disturbing the early-laid foundations of social personality. Among the Mandan-Hidatsa Indians of North Dakota, the kinship system persists along with customs of women gardening and keeping house. The former age-grade system, however, which a Mandan or Hidatsa entered when he was already 8 years old and didn't seriously participate in until he was 10, has vanished. So has the aboriginal religion, which he didn't fully learn until he was 30.[7] Similarly, when change struck the culture of Manus, the people readily abandoned their ancestral cult and its auxiliary activities, aspects of culture in which children had received minimal indoctrination and practice.[8]

Such reasoning obviously doesn't claim that early learning renders personality utterly rigid and totally unmodifiable. What it assumes is that early learning, without being completely irreversible or decisive, possesses a high degree of finality, a conclusion that some people resent because in no way do they want to be bound by, or compelled to overcome, what they learned during the highly plastic period of childhood.[9] Psychologists looking for evidence that early learning endures have repeatedly observed, tested, and interviewed the same U.S. subjects, with the result that the influence of early learning has turned out to be a more complex question than Locke and Spencer suspected.[10] Some behavior in their subjects did indeed persist from early life through the school years to early adulthood. Certain maternal practices concealed sleeper effects; their delayed action required several years before showing up in a child's behavior, by which time the

mother had probably changed her practices. There were also instances in which a child transformed his early responses when faced with the demand to conform to roles appropriate to his or her own sex. Some undifferentiated early behavior of boys, like general passivity, became expressed in young men through more highly differentiated forms like noncompetitiveness, sexual anxiety, and social anxiety. Early rage reactions that had been manifested by small girls gave rise not to aggressiveness or easily aroused anger—personality characteristics poorly fitting the American, ideal feminine role—but won later expression in less strongly disapproved traits like intellectual competitiveness and a preference for masculine interests. Women who had vented early rage quite freely also gave evidence of being conflicted over dependence and tended decidedly to model themselves on adult males, who in America are allowed to display more aggressiveness than women. Apparently girls learn early, even as young as 5 years, the American stereotype that men are more aggressive and less nurturant than women. Several childhood traits—compulsiveness, irrational early fears, working persistently at tasks, and excessive irritability in the early years—also gave little sign of stability or of continuing in a recognizable way into later behavior.

APPROACHES TO SOCIALIZATION

For the time being let's leave the importance of early learning and turn to the process, or processes (since opinion there too is divided), of socialization involved in the first few years of life. I will have more to say about the relative importance of that period when I revive the critical barrage unleashed against the "early learning theory" and when I consider the views of people committed to paying greatest attention to later learning. In the meantime, I propose to examine in some detail three major viewpoints that account, each somewhat differently, for how early childhood experiences structure personality. These are, first, the psychoanalytic viewpoint, emphasizing developmental influences emanating from libidinous bodily organs or erogenous zones; second, a viewpoint associated with anthropologists like Margaret Mead and Geoffrey Gorer, which uses the concept of communication to understand the formative impact of certain patterns of child care; and, finally, a highly pragmatic, somewhat eclectic viewpoint common in much contemporary psychology and sociology. Roughly, the three views parallel the recent history of social scientists' interest in early learning. At first, psychoanalysts of orthodox persuasion ascribed the origin of nuclear personality characteristics to transformations of bodily drives pressing for gratification through the mouth, anus, and genitals. Caretakers of a child in varying ways and degrees encouraged or discouraged instinctual expression in those bodily zones, with predictable consequences for emerging personality. A reaction to this orthodox psychoanalytic doctrine was led partly by anthropologists, sociologists, psychologists, and psychoanalysts influenced by those social sciences.[11] Without wholly ignoring the dynamic role of the bodily zones, they enlarged the theory to allow greater scope to culture in determining the vicissitudes of the instincts. Also, they more prominently feature the role of the ego.[12] Abram Kardiner and Erik Erikson did much to promote the second period. In what follows I am not writing history; therefore I am not bound by chronological succession nor required to mark even each important shift in theory. I shall include Kardiner and Erikson with the psychoanalytic viewpoint, along with Sigmund Freud himself. Despite the important innovations the first two introduced into the theory, their orientations remained basically similar to Freud's as they followed him in his pioneer conception: that personality arises through the socially accomplished transformation of somatic drives. (Some people accuse Freud of ignoring society and accounting for personality solely in terms of bodily instincts. If they really believe that, then they don't know his work.) Kardiner and Erikson put considerable stress on variations occurring from one culture to another in the way a child's caretakers act toward him, thereby influencing his emerging personality. Margaret Mead's approach has likewise been comparative, but in a special way she significantly reoriented socialization theory from the lines laid down by Freud and followed by later psychoanalysts. Hence, I have singled out her ideas for examination. More recently in the history of socialization research, psychologists and sociologists, joined by an occasional anthropologist (like John W. M. Whiting), freshly attacked the subject. Eclectic in the cordiality they extend to any potentially useful theory and any childrearing practices, they have so far worked mostly in the United States. Here they use social classes in much the same way that anthropologists compare Samoa, Manus, Hopi, or other world cultures. That is, they work from one social level to another to discover under what circumstances or with what consequences childrearing practices alter in determinable ways. Their research bears another significant, identifying feature: They reject the assumption that all parents or families in a community homogeneously adhere to the same patterns of socialization. Instead, they prepare themselves to find intracommunity variability by noting differences between classes and, occasionally, ethnic groups. Increasing adoption of this approach by anthropologists going further afield to do research in exotic social systems where sufficient intracultural variability exists is bound to enrich our understanding.

Despite differences between the three viewpoints, none of the three conflicts with the basic conception that socialization occurs because an individual is propelled to modify his behavior as he interacts with his society and culture. A child grows into a constantly unfolding realm of objects, situations, and social relationships. Impelled by needs and aided by his developing potentialities, he ever increases and differentiates his responses to those aspects of the world that present themselves to his attention. In responding, he creates an accumulating set of meanings about himself and the world, which he tests by letting them guide his future responses. In all this, language plays a profound role. It allows the child to name and categorize experience, and furnishes the wherewithal for communication, through which he enlists help; solves social problems; learns about ideals, values, and expectations; and tests his growing stock of meanings against consensus. Each of the three viewpoints emphasizes the infant's immaturity and helplessness, conditions that make care, love, security, and stability profoundly important for development. Though all three deemphasize prenatal socialization, intrauterine learning remains a possibility, especially if, as some people allege, the fetus actually responds to the mother's distress, fatigue, and other emotional states. Few students of socialization concern themselves with personality formation in the womb, and the overwhelming majority also ignore the learning significance of birth, despite all that has been written about the birth trauma and the lasting anxiety accompanying separation from the mother at birth.[13]

THEORY OF THE INSTINCTS [14]

"The theory of the instincts," Freud held to be, "so to say, our mythology," meaning that instincts constitute postulated ("mythical") entities of the kind any maturing science uses, though they can never be directly verified by inspection. Aided by this theory,

psychoanalysis traces far-reaching, deep-seated consequences ensuing from the way children are reared during the highly plastic period of infancy and the ensuing early years of childhood. The key for understanding those consequences lies within the body, in the sexual instincts and their energy, libido. Energized from within by libido, an instinct in pursuit of maximum satisfaction exerts a constant force, at least until satisfaction actively or passively achieved through some person or object temporarily quells it. The satisfaction itself is held to be akin to adult sexual pleasure, regardless of whether it is attained through oral, anal, or genital zones. Instincts being highly plastic, both their aim of gratification and the objects by which they attain it can be substantially altered, deferred, or inhibited and repressed. Genitality, for example, can be gratified in the aim-inhibited guise of tenderness, or forthrightly, through masturbation or sexual intercourse with persons of either sex, or with various objects. Genitality may even merge with the insinct of orality and be partially satisfied through eating. Too much suppression of instincts, however, won't work, for libido is bound to escape and the form it then takes might be a neurotic symptom.[15]

The three main avenues of instinctual expression—oral, anal, and genital—are (as their names imply) each associated with a specific bodily zone. There, starting at a very early age, each impulse comes pleasurably alive. In doing so, it also promotes a response from other persons, and by virtue of that response it experiences the impact of social patterning. The zones can hardly help bringing even a baby into early and intense interaction with its social environment. What happens as a result will vary according to the culture of the persons by whom it is reared. Infants and children who, by virtue of belonging to the same community, class, or caste, undergo similar oral, anal, and genital socialization are affected similarly and in consequence acquire similar social characters.[16] Whether the biologically given impulses are more important than culture, or vice versa, is a futile argument, for one presupposes and cannot operate without the other.[17] Therefore, critics are wrong who claim that psychoanalytic instinct theory unduly emphasizes the role of biology in personality formation. In themselves the instincts lead to nothing. Character structure arises through the way a person, impelled from within, interacts with agents of society who encourage, restrict, or regulate instinctually motivated behavior associated with each of the three bodily zones. Thereupon the principle of cumulative development operates, earlier experiences influencing the way in which the person perceives later instinctual gratification. An anally dominated person, for example, experiences sexual intercourse quite distinctively, investing it with characteristic compulsiveness and sadism, keeping records of the frequency with which he has orgasm, and so on. Hence, objectively similar behavior is differently perceived or experienced from one person or culture to another, depending on the type of character in which it is embedded. The analyst's task is to use all clues at his disposal to identify the individual character structure or social character in question.

Activation of the erogenous zones follows a fixed temporal order of succession—a "long journey," Freud calls it—from the oral, to the anal, to the genital, followed by several quiescent years in which genitality lies latent until its reinstitution at puberty. Each stage persists into a later organization of personality, or, to say it better, the mode of adaptation learned at each stage carries over and continues to serve throughout a person's life. In Erik Erikson's terms,[18] at the breast the baby first learns to adapt by mastering the mode of getting; then comes taking; with the anal stage he learns releasing and holding on, and genitality brings

Erik Erikson

the earliest learning concerning intrusion or, for girls, inclusion. Mastery of each new mode brings the child a partially new identity as it alters his social role. By each developmental step he advances toward the goal of full, adult genitality, assuming he doesn't seriously regress to an earlier level or remain fixed at a pregenital stage so that an early mode of adaptation persists in marked form. As Erikson puts it, in childhood any of the basic modes can be overdeveloped or underdeveloped, such distortion being carried along by the person as he matures.

Motivated by his energized instincts and aided indulgently or frustratingly by his caretakers, the infant and child carve out for themselves overt and covert patterns of behavior. For example, a well-fed baby learns to get and take food from its mother and develops an optimistic attitude about the world with its bountiful resources. As a child learns to control his sphincter muscles, thereby temporarily deflecting the anal instinct from its aim of achieving pleasure through evacuation, he sublimates that aim into a culturally valued character trait, orderliness (assuming that history has made this trait available in his community). In a homogeneous community, the attitudes he learns are synchronized with his later responsibilities and roles. For example, among the Sioux Indians, generous feeding creates people capable of acting as bounteous mothers or as generous hunters and strong, confident warriors. Subsequent experiences throughout life are apt to reaffirm early lessons. Religion, in an illustration Erikson offers, at every turn "collectively annotates" the sense of early trust (or mistrust, should that have been the case).[19] A heterogeneous social system doesn't allow early learning to be as closely attuned to later-life roles, but makes it likely that both individual and community will suffer from an ill fit between character structure and culture. Character traits carved out through the interplay of the instincts and society go back in time much before a particular person's infancy. Yet the theory has evolutionary implications for culture history. Erikson implies that over time a homogeneous community through trial and error selects those childrearing procedures that integrate well with its culture and best prepare children to meet expectations and attitudes attached to the adult social roles they will some day play.

Chiefly instrumental in whatever socialization occurs through the instincts are satisfactions and deprivations that a child encounters at each stage of his development.[20] Satisfaction not only reinforces learning, and deprivation not only provides punishment to eradicate socially undesirable responses, but the total balance between early satisfaction and deprivation also influences emerging personality characteristics. Too much early deprivation and ensuing anxiety result in crippling strain that persists to handicap the individual in his later life, whereas a balance favoring satisfaction

enhances psychological strength and adaptive skill. Except that there can be too much of a good thing! Good maternal care (for the young child, that is) can sow bad effects that show up in later life.[21] Psychiatrists trace unfortunate consequences to early indulgence, the technical equivalent of what is also called "spoiling." Such indulgence handicaps a child by failing to endow him to weather harsh realities in later life. Such consequences ensue not because indulgence itself cripples personal resourcefulness, but because it hardly suits the difficult nature of human striving in practically any social system.*

Each erogenous zone, as I have said and shall demonstrate more fully, possesses its specific consequences for personality development while the social attention paid all the zones taken together results in a balance of satisfaction and deprivation that further influences personality formation. In what follows, I propose to look at each zone-anchored stage of psychological development explored by Freud and his followers, examining the influence that has been claimed for it. Bear in mind how behavior associated with the zones puts the child into close, regular physical contact with other persons with whom he consequently identifies and toward whom he channels affection, hostility, and ambivalence. These mechanisms are also highly significant in fashioning his world of meanings and in carving out a style of life.[23]

Oral Stage. Throughout life the mouth remains an important organ of adaptation, though never again as exclusively as during the period of infancy, when it provides the sole means for coping. An individual's first regular interaction with the world occurs primarily through his mouth, as it draws in comfort and nourishment. Thereby he learns to get, and in the process fashions a

---

* The Arapesh and Great Whale River Eskimo both illustrate handicaps imposed on personality through indulgent childrearing.[22]

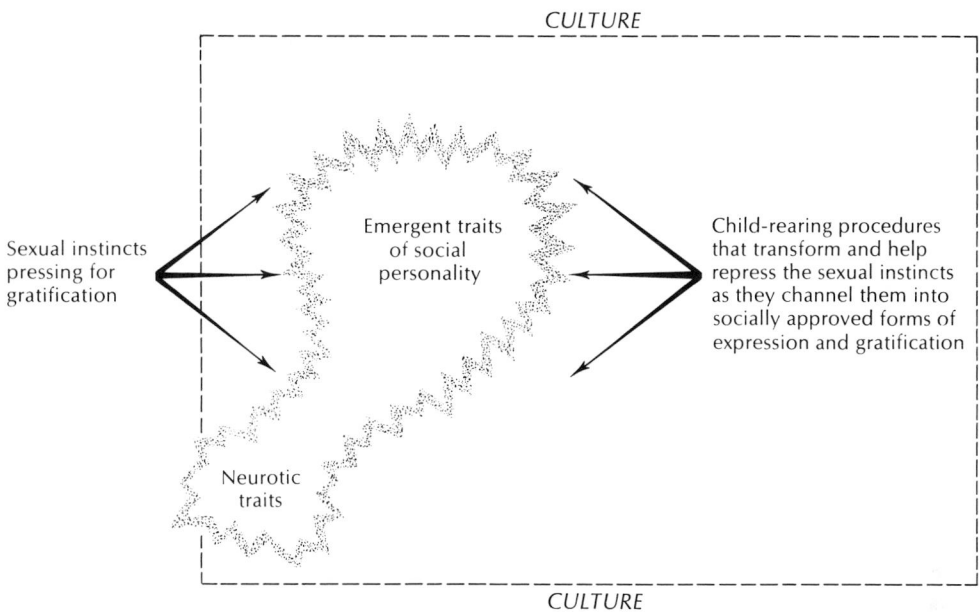

The psychoanalytic, or instinct, theory of socialization.

long-lasting stock of meanings that define both himself and the world into which birth only lately launched him. Undisturbed, highly pleasurable sucking, theory claims, brings a deeply rooted conviction that everything will always be well. Aided by nurturance that a bounteous mother freely extends, the baby (who has succeeded in getting someone to do pleasurable things for him) develops a feeling of trust in the world, a belief that people are good and generous, and a sense of mastery. From such fundamental attitudes no personality wholly escapes. Identity in the oral stage comes to be formed around self-esteem, on the theme "I can." The regular conjunction of pleasurable feeding and the mother's close presence leads the baby to perceive her as good. She thus becomes his first apprehension of social goodness. Oral gratification may be strong enough to convince a person that there will always be a representative of the mother to care for him and provide what he needs, or that some day,

on earth or elsewhere, he will enter a bountiful paradise. Such optimism can as readily render him inactive and passive as it can endow him with tremendous energy and self-confidence. Niggardly nursing and undependable early experiences with the mouth teach different lessons. The world becomes conceived as unreliable and the individual's sense of mastery becomes tinged with uncertainty and anxiety. Instead of optimistic confidence in his ability to succeed, a person whose basic trust in the world has been badly shaken by early oral deprivation assumes a lifelong burden of unsatisfied wanting. Due to this truncated sense of mastery, he tends to rely more on duress or fantasy than on active doing. No fuller record of long-term psychological and cultural consequences of oral deprivation has ever been made than in Alor. The Alorese ego in its early years gets no assistance in forming adequate executive capacities to deal with the outer world, including dealing with other persons. The people not only lack a grip on the world, but also any emotional basis for effectively relating with one another. Kardiner visualizes their culture as completely immobilized due to their stunted ego development.[24]

In the later phase of the oral stage, as other organs augment the child's adaptation, growth equips him to assume a more active and directed approach to his environment. He adds to his personality a mode of taking, along with simply getting. His eyes improve their focus; he learns to use his ears to discriminate and localize sounds; his hands reach out to grasp with increasing purposefulness, and his teeth erupt. Simultaneously, his caretakers inhibit his indiscriminate taking, just as they restrain his biting, so that he encounters his first serious difficulties in coping with the world (unless his oral experiences have already been traumatic). Mother and other agents of society now see to it that "good" and "bad" acts become meaningfully differentiated in his experience, with the result that he acquires his first apprehension of the nature of sin and wrongdoing. Now, too, sadistic instincts come to the fore. Should they fuse with the oral impulse, they will create an aggressive, malicious character structure in which the mouth becomes a primary vehicle of attack and injury. Erikson,[25] assisted by his theory, discovered how infantile oral learning that coincides with the biting stage fortifies the Yurok Indians to carry out their historically derived cultural practices. Salmon fishermen, acorn gatherers, and formerly traders in shell money and woodpecker scalps, the Yurok live along the Klamath river in mountainous northern California. Among them a child quickly reaches the end of his period of generous and frequent breast-feeding, for weaning begins at 6 months, around the same time as teething. Early weaning not only accelerates independence, but also provides a serviceable psychological groundwork for these Indian fishermen, who as adults set nets for prey but believe that only by behaving themselves and saying "please" in appropriate ritual fashion will fish be caught in them. Throughout life they maintain a fervent "please" toward the supernatural, a petitionary attitude for which their early, forcible disengagement from the mother prepared them by implanting an irrevocable residue of nostalgia for her. A good Yurok is able to weep when he prays to the food-sending, invisible powers, but he must avoid being too eager to take what they send or the supply will elude him. It is as if premature weaning during the biting phase of his development, in addition to instilling a sense of nostalgia for the breast also kept him from learning to take forcibly. Early weaning, therefore, doesn't handicap the Yurok. It provides a characterological foundation for behavior, like wanting without showing it too frankly, that the Indians' culture comprises.

The evidential quality of the proof put forward for the prepotent role of the oral instinct in early socialization receives some setback when confronted by experimental evidence of child development. Infants' attachments to adults, for example, and their social responsiveness are less tied to feeding than some psychoanalysts believe. In fact, Erikson clearly saw the extent to which maturing organ systems other than the mouth structured an emerging personality independently of the oral system of behavior. An infant demonstrates an early, very likely innate potentiality to seek attention and to take note of interesting environmental stimuli that have little connection with feeding or with the mother's nurturant role.[26]

Anal Zone. As far back as 1908, Freud confessed that he could no longer say on what precise occasions he first received the impression that a systematic relationship exists between a person's type of character and the functions of a bodily organ. "But," he assures the reader, "no theoretical anticipations of mine played any part in producing this impression." Of the three relationships that so irresistibly struck him, none provoked opponents of psychoanalytic theory more than that tracing the psychogenesis of stinginess, meticulousness, extravagance, and other traits to the anal zone. Without showing outright disgust for the idea that pleasure could be generated by a full bowel or through its evacuation, the opponents mostly chose more scholarly ways to express their surprise, shock, and utter disbelief. After half a century of fulminating, they still haven't succeeded in completely dislodging Freud's inductively formulated hypothesis.

Toilet training, by demanding that a child cease to evacuate as freely as he pleases, curtails instinctually rooted impulses pressing for gratification. Though he gives in to his caretakers' demands, a child's inclination is to continue to find pleasure by bowing to no regulatory discipline and by freely indulging his own autonomy. Should he do so, however, he will be punished. As a compromise between his impelling instincts and unrelenting adult disciplines, his ego institutes a number of skillful defensive maneuvers, including reaction formations, that become enduring personality characteristics. In one such reaction, the child doesn't merely give up securing gratification through unrestricted defecation. He goes to an extreme: He becomes inordinately compulsive, stingy, meticulous, and anxiously distrustful of everything spontaneous, traits that pave the way for a later passion for indexing, classifying, listing, planning and programming, regardless of whether they lead to any productive results. Or sublimation helps him to mount another defense against anal interests; unconsciously he deflects them into generosity, extravagance, obligatory gift-giving, or potlatching. Thereby people continue through life to experience pleasure unconsciously bound up with uninhibited defecation. Physiology as

well as cultural expectations cuts short pleasure furnished by a gorged colon, but, symbolically, people do manage to cling to such gratification as they zealously maintain order, are unable to tolerate the smallest thing out of place, and won't allow the least disturbance to routine—behaviors appropriate for a bureaucratic state. Toilet training calls on the child to comply in other things than evacuating in suitable fashion. Adults teach him the kind of attention he may pay to feces, channelling his interest along wholesome, or at least socially normal, lines. They forbid him to play with fecal matter, except as he sublimates the temptation creatively in cooking, sculpture, and other plastic arts. A community's strong distaste for dirt or its passion for cleanliness, represents highly valued reaction formations against the discountenanced, pleasurable interest that children take in fecal matter they have emitted. If all these derived anal-character traits sound familiar, they should, for they name virtues, compulsions, and obsessions familiar in Euroamerican society. Speaking in a more general, less culturebound fashion, a child's anal stage of development gives him experience in alternating such forms of mastery as withholding and expelling, letting go and holding on. Compliance with parents' wishes at this critical time, which presents life's earliest demands for obedience, also strengthens a child's sense of responsibility. As his capacity to pursue pleasure turns out to be limited by powerful adults who insist on curtailing his libidinous strivings, he learns that something of his own autonomy must be surrendered in living with others. But his understanding of what personal autonomy and its partial surrender imply is informed by the early trust he gained during his oral stage. Finally, the challenge of anal training creates his first strong experience with shame and doubt, feelings amplified by his caretakers' attitude and their disciplines. "Can I do it?" he in effect asks himself as he struggles with the not yet fully mastered sphincter, rehearsing a question that will test his self-esteem many times in years to come. To be sure, every social system introduces those early learnings differently and with unequal amplitudes, patterning them to suit other elements in its culture.

Proof of the lasting influence of early experiences associated with the anal, or indeed with any, bodily zone is largely evidential. The clinician guided by the theory unravels the twisted skein of his troubled patient's life, tracing back personality characteristics to early anal training that the person recalls. A psychoanalytically minded anthropologist uses the theory similarly when he cross-sectionally compares ongoing training with personality characteristics manifested by adults and older children in the community. Essentially by such methods has an anal character structure been revealed to predominate in Western culture with its Protestant, capitalistic values—the setting where Freud first detected it.[27] During the wartime years, anthropologists belonging to the allied powers thought they found it, together with evidence of unusually severe anal training, in Japanese culture. The anal character, they thought, lay behind the Japanese people's neatness, orderliness, perfectionism, ritualistic cleanliness, conformity to rule, pedantry, love of scatological obscenity, and other elements of their national character.[28] Because of the war, the investigators took their facts from literature and from Japanese whom they interviewed in the United States, many of them in internment camps where they had been moved from their West Coast homes. Those who disagreed with the wartime anthropologists, whose conclusions could well have been motivated by unconscious wartime bias, offered alternative interpretations of the evidence, brought forth new data, and stimulated considerable critical discussion.

Where the matter rests is well stated by one expert on Japan, who predicts that the true story of Japanese character structure will be learned only after an investigator spends "years, not months" in Japan itself.[29]

Genital Zone. Little time elapses after birth before children begin to take interest and find pleasure in their genitals, including the way the organs function in urination. Between the years 3 and 5 the other erogenous zones become erotically subordinated to the expanded libido invested in the genitals, those relatively small, inconspicuous body parts on which depend not only all of human and cultural survival but also a big share of personal happiness and interpersonal adjustment. In themselves they may be commonplace, but their intense eventual erotization makes them the most emotionally significant bodily zone, and for society the hardest to discipline. In the third main stage of development their erotization seriously begins. Simultaneously, a child normally rids himself of earlier, more primitive, libidinous rootings that threaten to interfere with his mature social role and block his course toward fully genital, adult status. Only unexaggerated traces of pregenital libido remain and, like anal endurance and orally rooted enterprise and energy, fortify adaptability. It is through pleasure-giving genital behavior that a child obtains the deep inner satisfaction that he formerly realized through eating, defecation, and retention. As in the former stages, long-term consequences follow from early genital gratification, which aid growing up and complete emotional weaning from the mother, hitherto the child's chief source of pleasure. Genital gratification—a duty that some communities specifically prescribe and allocate to young children's caretakers —lays a foundation for later sexual adequacy as it inculcates a positive attitude toward sex.[30] Through alleviating tension, it inspires self-esteem and self-confidence, encourages a confident attitude toward the world, and communicates to the child knowledge about his sexual identity and his eventual sexual role.[31] If masturbation is free of conflict and guilt in early childhood, it can offer youngsters who need it compensation for harshness and deprivations that they encounter in other areas of life or that they experience by virtue of their inadequacy and powerless vis-à-vis adults.[32] Interference with early genital pleasure promotes quite opposite consequences, fixing anxiety on sex, calling out timidity, intensifying dependence, and undermining the child's confidence.

As inevitably as development itself, the genital stage brings the culture's incest taboos into force and sets off one of the most crucial of early conflicts, the Oedipus complex. Much has been written explaining the Oedipus situation, criticizing psychoanalytic conceptions of it, reinterpreting it, and arguing whether it exists universally or inevitably as part of man's phylogenetic inheritance. Freud's own view certainly startles. He describes the genitally advanced boy continuing to make his mother the love object she has been for him since the oral stage. The youngster seems on the threshold of recapitulating the tragic destiny of King Oedipus who, in blindly slaying his father and marrying his mother, did something other people do only in their dreams. Freud said:

The little man wants his mother all to himself, finds his father in the way, becomes restive when the latter takes upon himself to caress her, and shows his satisfaction when the father goes away or is absent . . . the little boy shows the most open sexual curiosity about his mother, wants to sleep with her at night, insists on being in the room while she is dressing, or even attempts physical acts of seduction. . . .[33]

Affection for his father comes to mingle ambivalently with jealousy and hostility, though to be sure he can't clearly sort out his confused feelings. The father's excessive power far outweighs the child's, who is left to work out his agonizing conflict through irritability and in fantasy, as when he promises his mother how nobly he will treat her once he is grown up. Underlying the drama is the boy's anxiety lest he lose the organ whose erogeneity is so prominently in the foreground. He fears that his father will castrate him. At every opportunity he exhibits his penis to reassure himself that the danger hasn't materialized. The girl—who also realizes bitterly that her father is more powerful than she—to her alarm finds that she has already lost her penis—at least that's how she accounts for her disappointingly incomplete sexual make-up. Partially she resolves the Oedipus complex by substituting her father as a love object, but doesn't gain much through the exchange for now she confronts her mother as a rival for that man's affection. What helps more is for her to become as much like the rival as possible, and through identification she models herself on her mother's role, thereby preparing herself for her feminine career. Similarly, the boy identifies himself defensively with the rival father. Temporary repression of the sexual instincts as the years of latency begin helps to make such defenses workable and allows sublimated genitality to be invested in aim-inhibited love bonds that, instead of being destructive, maintain the family's unity.

Is the Oedipus Complex Universal? Whether similar phenomena of incestuous love and jealous hate emotionally affect young children in other than Euroamerican social systems has been closely examined. In one of the earliest psychological analyses of social structure, Bronislaw Malinowski[34] held the Oedipus complex to be functionally suited to Europe, where it stems from the combination of a puritan morality that condemns children's sex play; an overly strict father, especially in lower social

Bronislaw Malinowski (All rights reserved by Leslie A. White)

strata, who holds jural rights over his wife and child; and a timid mother who stands in awe and fear of her powerful husband. These factors drive husband and wife apart and emotionally divide the father from his children. Malinowski observed quite another family structure in the Trobriand Islands where matrilineal descent binds a child more closely to his mother's kinsmen than to his father. Under this arrangement his mother's brother, not his father, wields the greatest authority over him and his father is much less strict than his counterpart in Europe. His children idealize this kind, half-playful and half-protective parental figure and friend. They do, however, direct hostility on the disciplinarian, their maternal uncle, with the result that the Oedipus complex is absent. Psychoanalysts object to this conclusion. They point out that Malinowski is describing something else than

what they mean by an Oedipus complex. Contrary to what he suggests, a young child's status conflict with his father arises from deeper motives than simply resentment of paternal authority and discipline. A boy challenges his father for his mother's undivided sexual love, for her exclusive sexual possession. Abram Kardiner[35] realized this when, using many of Malinowski's same fieldwork data, he ascribed the absence of an Oedipus complex in Trobriand children to their many opportunities to indulge in sex. The islanders' nonpuritanical morality, Kardiner thought, helps them avoid exaggerated instinctual leanings on the mother and prevents her importance from being inflated in the child's eyes. Ernest Jones, a psychoanalyst, also reinterpreted Malinowski's data to show that Trobrianders don't after all escape the Oedipus complex which he, like other orthodox psychoanalysts, assumes to be universal.[36] In the Trobriands, the Oedipus complex is effectively disguised, and Malinowski, being psychoanalytically untrained, couldn't see through the disguise to observe that the Trobrianders' mother's brother symbolizes the father. Some years later, Géza Róheim, another psychoanalyst with highly orthodox leanings, thought he settled the controversy by discovering the classic father-child Oedipus conflict in the matrilineal Normanby Island, located about a hundred miles from the Trobriand group.[37] Later, to clinch matters, he accumulated much other evidence which he interpreted to prove that the classic Oedipus complex regularly occurs in communities with matrilineal social structures, where the mother's brother plays an important role in a child's life. He supported Jones, claiming that matrilineal descent itself acts as a clever, ego-constructed, ideological defense against universal Oedipal tendencies inherent in human nature. Yet Dorothy Eggan, carefully examining the matrilineal Hopi Indians, found nothing to indicate an Oedipus

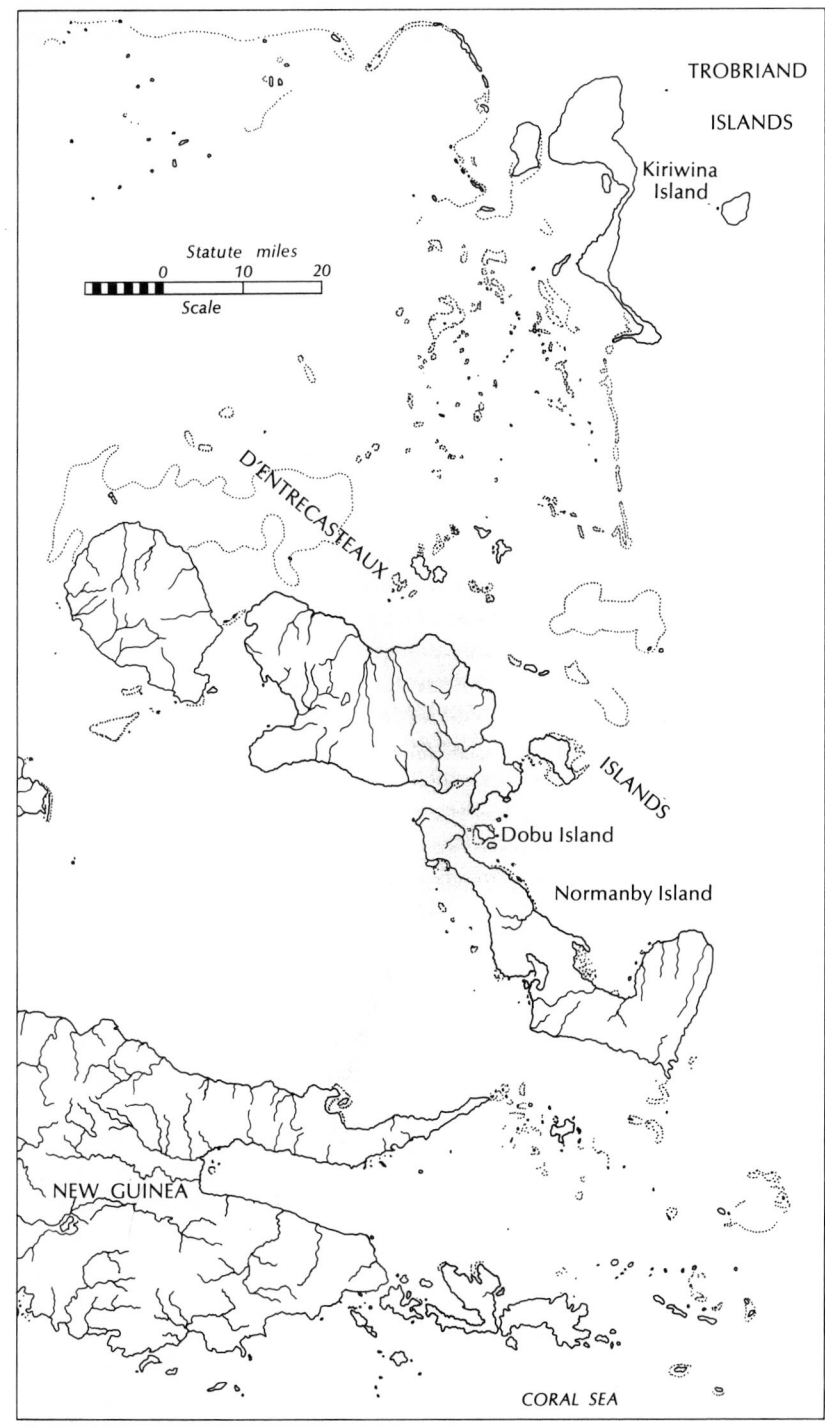

The Trobriand Islands, Normanby Island, and adjacent places in the
Southwest Pacific.

complex.[38] She ascribes its absence among those Pueblo people to the way they diffuse affection in a wide network of social relations, so that their social structure, unlike ours, doesn't concentrate intense emotional concern in parents.

Such inability to settle the matter can only mean that the universality of the Oedipus complex is one of those propositions that empirical facts alone can never prove or disprove. Adherents of the proposition find evidence for it in the very same data that doubters cite to disprove it. Most social scientists have become quite uninterested in whether the Oedipus complex is universal, culturally restricted, or given to assuming different structural guises. An increasing number do well without using the concept at all.[39]

LOST PARADISE OF ORALITY

When Erik Erikson visited the Pine Ridge reservation of the Sioux Indians in South Dakota in 1937, he found a people mostly untroubled by inner tension, personality conflict, or neurosis.[40] Psychologically the people didn't match up to such inescapable signs of "cultural pathology" as alcoholism, drunken brawls, petty thieving, pervasive apathy, and failure to create a culture adapted to the present-day world. The Sioux had not moved into the twentieth century psychologically, despite being urged ·by schoolteachers and Indian Service personnel to hurry up and do so. The Indians continued to be strongly oriented to the aboriginal past; they could not forget their former independence, finding few positive values in their contemporary existence and no basis of trust. Seemingly they were waiting for the Supreme Court to give them back the Black Hills with their vanished buffalo. Erikson inquired about former patterns of nursing and other instinctually related childrearing practices by which these

people had been reared and by which, he suspected, they remained anchored to their former style of life even though it had become perilously unadaptive. Grandmothers told him of the emphasis they had put on nursing, feeding the baby whenever he whimpered and continuing the practice for as long as 3 or even 5 years without making any systematic attempt at weaning. Since any lactating woman could provide any child with her breast, children had nearly unlimited privileges of oral indulgence; they enjoyed an unrestricted oral paradise. Out of this childhood came a very oral people characterologically well endowed to accept, and act on, the tribe's ethical ideal of generosity. The baby's rich experiences in getting furnished him with a good foundation for giving, which his later toilet training confirmed. Before he became toilet trained, however, the child, as his teeth erupted, began to be edged out of his paradise of orality. He tended to bite the breast with his newly developed organs, grandmothers recalled, and told with amusement how they would then thump his head so that the youngster flew into a rage. Thereupon mothers used to say, "Let him cry, it will make him strong." People thought they could recognize a future good hunter in the strength of a baby's infantile fury. Erikson sees in those teeth and rage experiences a possible foundation for the hunter's and warrior's ready ferocity—good preparation, he calls it, for aggressive stalking, catching, encircling, killing, stealing, taking. In the women he met and interviewed, he observed a fixation on biting, shown by the way they used their teeth for work and to play with. The discontinuity between the unlimited gratification of the first oral phase and the punishment administered for biting in the second also provided the Sioux with a "sense of badness," which their religion subsequently tapped by requiring strong hunters to humble themselves for supernatural help. They made themselves small and helpless again, equivalent to an infant in the first oral phase who still retained free access to paradise. Erikson insists on being clearly understood:

We are not saying . . . that their treatment in babyhood *causes* a group of adults to have certain traits—as if you turned a few knobs in your child-training system and you fabricated this or that kind of tribal or national character. . . . We are speaking of goals and values and of the energy put at their disposal by child-training systems.[41]

Such values, Erikson points out, like anything in culture persist only as long as they "work." He doesn't mean that they will vanish once they no longer work economically. Sioux Indian values long ago failed to work happily under reservation conditions, and they conflict with new values urged upon the Indians by people surrounding them. So long as the values possess psychological and spiritual utility, they will "continue to be anchored, generation after generation, in early child training." Toilet training allowed the Siouan child to reach by himself gradual compliance with cleanliness standards. Older children, rather than powerful disciplinary adults, played large roles in setting the youngster an example. Easy anal training consistently supported the tribe's loose property values, and many Sioux still see no inherent goodness in accumulating possessions. They "let go" easily. It was quite compatible with the value placed on generosity. In the genital stage, learning introduced strict object taboos rather than attacking the sexual aim itself and branding it as dangerous or evil. Around age 5, brother and sister began to avoid each other, and each sex began to play in its own peer group. At this age, boys took (and still take) special delight in handling 3- or 4-inch bones called, according to their shape, horses, buffalo, and bulls. These toys probably served as a medium to cultivate competitive and aggressive daydreams at a critical time in development, a time when older brothers were starting to introduce the youngsters to values inherent in hunting. In this way "phallic aggression" became equated with the ferocity expected of men in pursuit of game.

In 1946 a large-scale study of Sioux Indian children described them as growing increasingly apathetic and passive. "The picture of Dakota child personality which emerges from the [psychological] tests," this study concludes, "is one of weakness of natural drives and spontaneity resulting from repressive forces set in action early in the child's life. . . . Dakota child personality seems crippled and negative, as if it rejected life."[42] Although Erikson observed the same apathetic trends in adults back in 1937, he demurs to the diagnosis of their source. Early childhood can't be blamed. "Early childhood among the Dakota, within the limits of poverty and general listlessness, is a relatively rich and spontaneous existence which permits the school child to emerge from the family with a relative integration—i.e., with much trust, a little autonomy, and some initiative."[43] Emotional withdrawal results once the child, in school and on the reservation, discovers that he won't be able constructively to use the character structure with which his early rearing endowed him. He can't develop a sense of identity meaningful in terms of his earlier experiences, whose enduring traces he continues to bear. ". . . absence of goals for initiative," Erikson continues, "leaves unused and undiverted the infantile rage which is still provoked in early child training. The result is apathy and depression" rather than constructive taking and aggression. The Siouan child perceives the world as hostile because he projects on it his own unused, inner rage. ". . . the Dakota child now *projects* where in his old system he *diverted*."[44]

TESTING THE IMPORTANCE OF
EARLY CHILDHOOD
CROSS-CULTURALLY

Proof for the psychoanalytic theory of the sexual instincts is almost entirely evidential in nature. Unquestionably the theory works for psychiatrists who use it in their clinical practice and for social scientists who, usually in modified form, apply it to cultural data. One ambitious attempt has been made to test, in a more rigorous fashion, hypotheses related to the theory, though those hypotheses can't be called lineal descendants of it.[45] Results obtained through this attempt, by John W. M. Whiting and Irwin L. Child, go far in confirming that early childhood is indeed critical for some personality characteristics, but whether the results also support the theory of which I have been writing is another question, so drastically did Whiting and Child revise the psychoanalytic concepts with which Freud and his followers worked.

The two authors, an anthropologist and a psychologist, entertain two propositions: First, through the medium of socially standardized, widely shared patterns of childrearing, culture in each social system produces a social personality type; second, a social personality type, in turn, expresses itself through patterns of culture; through the things that people do, say, think, feel, and make. In their experiment, Whiting and Child select beliefs about illness and therapeutic practices as patterns of culture which express certain social personality characteristics brought about through oral, anal, genital, and other training. The individual thus becomes a link in a chain whereby one aspect of culture, childrearing, leads to other cultural patterns, like adults' medical beliefs and practices. By no means does childrearing *cause* the later cultural patterns, which are historically rooted whether they have been locally invented or borrowed from other cultures. Childrearing,

through the balance of early gratification and deprivation, causes only definite fixations and anxieties. These, in turn, become characterological bases for meaningfully carrying out traditional culture patterns. Fromm's words fit nicely: "It is the function of the social character to shape the energies of the members of society in such a way that . . . people . . . find gratification in acting according to the requirements of the culture."[46]

Whiting and Child would just as soon avoid the word "instinct," with its several meanings. Instead, they talk of five behavioral systems, using "system" as a convenient label to cover the hidden drive, as well as the activity and covert behavior organized around the drive. The *oral system* is a concept wide enough to cover not only infantile sucking but beliefs and practices related to nursing and weaning as well as those having to do with eating, drinking, spitting, and vomiting. Defecation, urination, and ideas and practices relating to cleanliness and orderliness are classed in the *anal system*. The *sexual system*, as Whiting and Child call it, includes overt and covert behavior related to masturbation, sex play, sexual intercourse, exhibitionism, and even pornography. Beliefs, practices, and values associated with the wish for succorance and nurturance—getting help, love, and attention—comprise the *dependence system*. The aboriginal Sioux Indian's stance as he solicited supernatural patronage, including his tears, reveal dependence (weeping is one of the earliest forms of showing dependence), and so do touching and holding onto objects for affection. Acts like fighting, brawling, property destruction, insulting and cursing, and their associated beliefs fall into the *aggression system* of behavior. Guided by psychoanalytic and formal learning theories, Whiting and Child assume that indulgence (reward) experienced during the early socialization of any of those five systems would instigate

John W. M. Whiting (Harvard University)

positive fixation on behavior making up that system. That is, a person who had been so gratified would be conditioned to expect good things to happen to him henceforth through the indulged system, his happy outlook enduring long past childhood. Such a person, or organized aggregate of people, would very likely make much use of the system; for example, employing it in something highly desirable, like therapy. On the other hand, children who had predominantly encountered frustration in a given system would develop no sanguine outlook connected with that system. Negative fixation would instill an enduring expectation of anxiety. He would expect unpleasant consequences, like illness, to occur to him through the system.

Further productive work with this theory required that the researchers find some way to measure the degree of early indulgence

or frustration encountered in each behavioral system by children in actual communities. That would allow the investigators to gauge the corresponding level of positive fixation or, in the case of frustration, anxiety. To make their test they used published ethnographer's descriptions of childrearing and of children's reactions to it. Three judges ranked the cultural practices associated with each behavior system for the degree of initial satisfaction and initial anxiety they engendered. Statements in an ethnography indicating prolonged early indulgence in oral or anal behavior, or relatively great freedom to exercise genital sexuality or dependence, constituted evidence of potentially high initial satisfaction. If after only a brief period of early indulgence, severe punishment came to be applied to a behavior system in order to promote new learning, the raters ranked that cultural practice high in its ability to promote initial anxiety.

Another task required the investigators to determine, on sound theoretical grounds, how to detect the existence of positive and negative fixation in adult personality. As I said, they chose therapy and explanations of illness to serve as indicators of the extent to which early indulgence and frustration endured. Therapy performed in a way that involves any of the five behavior systems they regarded as indicative of positive fixation on that system, while an explanation tracing illness to a system they viewed as evidence of anxiety bound up with that area. Oral-performance therapy, consisting in swallowing something helpful—either food or medicine—involves the oral system. Defecation and urination regarded as possessing therapeutic value represent therapy linked to the anal system. Therapeutic use of sex occurs rarely; Whiting and Child found only four communities holding coitus to be therapeutically useful. The dependence system is involved in therapy that makes use of prayer which, theoretically speaking, reveals dependence on supernatural beings analogous to a child's dependence on adults. Aggression appears in therapy that consists in destroying something held responsible for illness, or in tricking or commanding a supernatural being, undermining its power to cause illness. Going on to explanations of illness that betray anxiety fixed on a beharioral system: Oral explanations claim that the patient ate something bad for him, or ascribe his disorder to other's verbal spells. Anal explanations of disease hold defecation to be somehow related to illness, or else trace disease to a form of sorcery that employs feces, hair clippings, or other exuviae. On theoretical grounds Whiting and Child also group the healing use of charms, curses, spells, and rituals with anal explanations. A sexual attribution of illness claims sexual acts and sexual excretions, including menstrual blood, to be responsible. Disease accounted for by flight of one's soul or by possession by a foreign spirit—soul and spirits being agents who also play succoring roles—represents a dependence explanation. Disobedience to spirits, for which they visit

punishment on the patient, stands as an explanation involving the aggression system, as does an act of outright aggression by a member of society that carries sickness as its punishing sanction.

As the two investigators predicted, socially patterned therapeutic practices often do employ the behavior system that in early childhood had been conditioned to yield high levels of satisfaction. Psychoanalytic theory gains a measure of support when 40 communities that treat illness by oral means turn out to average 14.2 for degree of potential, early oral satisfaction, whereas 21 communities that make no healing use of the oral zone average only 13.6. Results, however, fail to run consistently in the predicted direction. Thirty communities that rely on the dependence system for curing, on having their ratings for early dependence satisfaction averaged fall *below* the rating obtained by 27 communities that lack such a form of therapy. However, for four out of five systems the differences in average ratings run in the right direction; that is, as had been predicted by the researchers. Often, how-

❡ *Explanations of Illness Depend on Whether Early Socialization Arouses Anxiety in Any of 5 Systems of Behavior*[47]

Average rating for communities where corresponding explanation of illness is:	Socialization anxiety in each system of behavior				
	Oral	Anal	Sexual	Dependence	Aggression
Present	12.22*	12.10	12.21	13.38*	14.82*
Absent	8.94*	11.00	11.21	11.71*	10.80*

* $p < .05$.

Socialization anxiety in corresponding system of behavior is:	Number of communities in which corresponding explanations are present or absent									
	Oral explanations		Anal explanations		Sexual explanations		Dependence explanations		Aggression explanations	
	Abs.	Pres.	Abs.	Pres.	Abs.	Pres.	Abs.	Pres.	Abs.	Pres.
High	3	17	5	6	7	7	7	8	4	12
Low	13	6	5	4	7	7	10	5	11	5

ever, the difference between averages is very, very small and statistically insignificant.

The hypothesis which predicted that early anxiety generated in a behavior system through severe training would endure into adulthood, and would recommend that system to be used in accounting for sickness, held up even better than the proposition covering positive fixation. For each of the five systems, the differences, though sometimes slight, ran in the predicted direction. In three areas (the oral, dependence, and aggression systems) the difference turned out to be statistically significant. The test of negative fixation, or of the enduring consequences of early deprivation, not only backs psychoanalytic theory but upholds currently popular stress theory, particularly the belief that traumatic experiences in early life leave lasting, scarlike traces in personality.[48]

Whiting's students and later associates, using practically the same method of cross-cultural comparison, ingeniously tracked down a number of other relationships between early socialization practices and adults' socially patterned behaviors that likewise reveal the enduring influence of early, critical experiences. Together, all these efforts provide impressive, statistically backed support for insights originally given by psychoanalysis and backed only evidentially. The cross-cultural experimentalists have learned that where children must cope with harsh parents, people frequently believe in a harsh, aggressive spirit world. This finding quite agrees with psychoanalysts, who assume religion to be the screen on which supernaturals represent projections of parents.[49] People highly indulgent to children take few pains to propitiate powerful gods but proceed, much more confidently and forthrightly, to control the spirit world through magic that compels supernaturals to act. Nor do such people dread ghosts, which, the theory says, are also fearful projections of parents. In an earlier chapter I recounted Abram Kardiner's theory, inspired by Freud, which holds that harsh, traumatic early experiences implant lasting emotional traces in personality, which subsequently motivate defensive, compensatory projection in the domains of religion, art, and folklore. This theory obtains support from the findings I've just sketched, as well as from a cross-cultural investigation of pictorial art.[50] Kardiner expected that projection would be intensely active in a basic personality containing strong emotional needs carried along from a highly stressful, anxiety-packed childhood. If complexity in pictorial art can be validly taken as an index of intense projective activity, and if such complexity can be measured (by such features as many repetitions of figures, enclosed figures, and lines oblique to each other) then, judging from data found in thirty cultures, projective activity does increase when accompanied by a stressful, early childhood marked by severe socialization. Especially when the oral and dependence systems of behavior have been subjected to heavy childhood frustration does the relationship between early stress and projective activity show up strongly. Apparently emotional deprivation encountered in those two systems is highly critical with respect to the psychodynamic use that people make of complex pictorial art.

CHANNELS FOR COMMUNICATION

. . . in a thousand details of the way the body is handled, the sequences in which events are learned to occur, the culture is communicated to the child, and his character becomes an embodiment of it.[51]

MARGARET MEAD

Psychoanalysts working with the instinct theory, psychologists using a formal theory of learning, and ordinary folk warning against teaching a child bad habits all expect that experience will directly influence the way children come to behave. Saying that experience teaches means that it possesses clearly recognizable, even measurable consequences: Oral indulgence builds optimism; parental harshness leads people to fear supernaturals; picking up the baby when it cries, some people believe, causes spoiling; and so on. Margaret Mead claims that direct learning does not exhaust the significance of early life.[52] She shows how early experiences are also indirectly instrumental for teaching something. Events occurring to an infant as early as his first days of life constitute channels that mediate communication between it and its caretakers. Communication between a child and his culture begins long before any verbal skills make their appearance. Such messages can be decoded by a skillful interpreter, who possesses requisite abilities* and knows the cultural context in which the communicators live and their social personality, to reveal how culture is being embodied by the community's youngest members. Even very early messages will be repeated in coming weeks, months, and years, being communicated in other contexts and reinforced through many channels, like a message that we want to make sure of, and so both phone it and then confirm in writing.

An observer who would use Margaret Mead's approach, which for brevity I am going to call a communication theory of socialization, will have to pay close heed to the smallest details of childrearing. It is of little use to note simply that babies are swaddled. Precise context and the form of swaddling, including attitudes behind it, have to be delineated, for swaddling isn't the same when, for example, Great Russians or East European Jews do it. Mead[53] firmly rejects the usefulness of comparing swaddling in different cultures the way Whiting and Child compare socialization in the oral, anal, and other systems of behavior to see if early indulgence or frustration will have the same consequences for social personality formation. It won't, Mead confidently promises, first, because in form and detail no childrearing practice will be the "same thing" from one culture to another, and, second, because the messages adults invest in such practices will be different. So, too, with bathing babies, nursing, weaning, and other details of child care.* In place of doing as did Whiting and Child, abstracting a few common elements from behavior in various cultures (like harshness or leniency), Mead urges attention to the subtle characteristics of childrearing practices that are pregnant with meaning for children in a particular community. To gauge such features fully and accurately, it will pay the observer to familiarize himself with the way similar practices are executed in neighboring communities within the same culture area. Doing that will bring out clearly the subtle characteristics in which culturally distinctive meanings are embodied and communicated to the child. The communication approach to socialization is configurational because it assumes that total context contributes to meaning. What bathing babies in one culture teaches depends on socially patterned attitudes held about chil-

---

* Alfred L. Kroeber praised Margaret Mead's "high order of intuitiveness, in the sense of her . . . ability to complete a convincing picture from clues." See his review of *Growing up in New Guinea* in the *American Anthropologist* (1931), 33: 248–250, p. 248.

* One can observe that bathing babies differs between cultures. First, find out something about childrearing and associated values in New Guinea Iatmul, Bali, and middle-class Hollywood. Then show the 16mm, silent, one-reel film produced by Gregory Bateson and Margaret Mead, *Bathing Babies in Three Cultures*.[54]

dren, on mothers' economic and other roles, as well as on beliefs about dirt and health.

Social Interaction. Communication theory applied to socialization regards a person's relationship to his parents or other socializers as a system of intercommunication in which both parties exchange information, often of a nonverbal sort. Let's for the time limit the matter to childhood and say that some messages originate from the child. Parents decode them according to the socially defined meaning they attach to children and children's action. From birth, children occupy a definite social status toward which parents hold definite expectations.[55] The child and his maturing behavior furnish cues that parents perceive and respond to in culturally designed fashion. In the way they respond, they influence the child's unfolding behavior, setting his personality. One culture visualizes a baby communicating helplessness while another sees it exerting strength; the mother behaves as if it were capable of setting up its own will and needs over against hers. The New Guinea Iatmul perceive a baby as strong. A few weeks after birth the mother ceases to carry it everywhere with her, but she places it at some distance, on a high bench, where it must cry lustily to assure her that it is hungry. Only then does she cross over to feed it generously. This is one of the first ways that an Iatmul child learns that if you fight hard enough, then something which treats you as strong as itself will yield; anger and self-assertion will be rewarded.[56] The meaning of the cues to which parents respond is historically unstable, and as they alter in response to changes in culture so do parents' responses to the child alter, thereby altering his personality. Adults communicate to a child through the behavioral style they adopt when they interact with him.[57] They may strikingly differentiate their status from his, or identify themselves with

him by emphasizing his and their basic similarity. Should they extend toward him the style of behavior customary between adults, he will have nothing to unlearn once he himself passes into adult ranks. But should they treat him as being in a special position—inferior, incapable, and powerless—then they will introduce a gaping discontinuity between his experiences in childhood and afterwards, a gap that he will have to cross successfully before he can assume full, adult status.

Adult-child relationships are symmetrical when parents or other grown persons respond to what a child is or does by acting similarly, or in their initial behavior expecting him to respond as though he were similar to them. They treat the youngster as if expecting him to grasp the situation fully as they, the adults, do. Even a baby is acted toward as if he were a true person, unfinished perhaps, but able in some degree to oppose his mother's will with his own and endowed with the same basic rights and capacities that she possesses. Mohave Indians, although they regard children as relatively incomplete people, extend them the same considerable measure of equality that they show to everyone, regardless of age. Symmetry in Mohave early interpersonal relationships, and the closely related fact that adults don't shut the Indian child out of a full, undress view of adult activities, probably contributes to a growing person's self-esteem, and facilitates his development without too much conflict and uncertainty.

Complementarity in relations between a child and adults occurs when they construe his behavior to fit in with different but complementary behavior of their own. The parent and child play different roles, the mother, for example, in her protective strength and succorance acting as though the child were helpless, fragile, and dependent. A British father illustrates complementarity when he self-consciously puts himself up as a model for his son, from whom he expects deference and other qualities that complement his assurance, strength, and knowledgeability. Competition for the floor between an American father and his son, each of whom with ill-concealed impatience waits his turn, makes for quite another type of situation, one that possesses overtones of symmetry. (Not that symmetry prevails in all U.S. parent-child situations—far from it!) When interpersonal relations incorporate exchanges between parents and child—love, trust, feces, and tears being treated like physical objects that can be bargained over, exchanged, and rewarded—then reciprocity prevails as a behavioral style. Reciprocal relationships occur frequently in the United States, where they carry over to children the adult pattern of "making a deal" from which each side expects to benefit.

Channels of Communication. More specific channels, like nursing, swaddling, and sexual training, carry messages to even very young children. Any sequence of parent-child behavior in a culture, including dressing or bathing the baby, keeping him in a playpen at a certain age, or using fear as a disciplinary technique, may carry culturally significant messages that contribute to personality formation or reinforce existing attitudes. Nor need every community transmit important information over the same channels, say nursing or toilet training.[58] In one place, sex training may convey lessons of great weight, while few flow through toilet or independence training; another social system emphasizes toileting but communicates little via the area of sex. The task can, of course, be shared among several avenues, the same information passing over each. Anthropologists studying communication will attend most closely to channels heavily utilized in a culture, without trying to devote equal time to everything that happens in childrearing, noting matters of importance rather than solely matters of fact.[59]

Through many avenues the French child comes to understand that it is essential that he maintain intellectual and emotional control which, he is promised, opens up prospects of happiness as well as of becoming a fully developed human being. He learns this trait of French national character from the way he is taught deliberately to enjoy food and drink, from his parents' almost constant admonishments to behave correctly, and from warnings they give him to manage his impulses, expecially open hostility. In all these channels, socializers are guided by the same prevailing attitude, one that informs French socialization in the *foyer* as well as in school: The child can't be left to grow but must be made into a proper person, just as a fruit tree must be cultivated by grafting, pruning, and training.[60]

Clues to Attitudes. The communication theory of socialization holds that sequences of parent-child behavior—feeding, holding the baby, or, much later, initiation—furnish clues to adult values and attitudes. The underlying attitudes also reveal themselves in proverbs, folktales, myths, and embody themselves in architectural features and toys with which a child comes into contact. Socialization communicates those attitudes according to which children are encouraged enduringly to shape their responses. Just as attitudes motivate the parent, so after being assimilated to the child's world of meanings they motivate him as well. What looks like the same kind of training in two cultures may in each possess quite unique significance for both parents and children, depending on the underlying substratum of attitudes and meaning. From slight clues an observer infers implicit, socially patterned attitudes, and then checks his deductions against behavior in other situations involving myths, toys, and so on. Sioux Indian mothers don't use colostrum, giving the reason that it is hard for an infant to extract it from the breast, and then, for all the hard labor, it is worth nothing to the infant.[61]

This hints that Siouan mothers seek to indulge and maximally gratify babies, a conclusion that their other acts bear out. A pregnant Yurok Indian mother, already by the way she rubs her distended abdomen to keep the fetus awake, expresses the emphasis she will put on accelerating the baby's postnatal development, which is exactly what Yurok childrearing does at many points.[62] In socially disintegrated communities of "Stirling County," Nova Scotia, self-demand feeding expresses something quite different from what it means to contemporary, middle-class North American mothers.[63] There it is used by cold, businesslike mothers who don't enjoy their sometimes illegitimate or unplanned babies. It communicates to an infant not respect for its autonomy, not maternal unselfishness in a child-centered household, but a message the authors don't attempt to decode except to note how such casual feeding promotes a baby's early participation in the characteristic disorderliness of everyday life that those communities allow. From the way an Arapesh mother claims to feed a child to "save it," yet feeds it irregularly because she neglected to plan for somebody else to do so if she arrived back home late, and from other imprecise adjustments that give Arapesh life a quality of clumsiness, Arapesh children learn a characteristic attitude.[64] They emulate their parents in accepting what is offered without discriminating accurately between the details of giving and taking. An Arapesh child's later experiences continue to pattern an essentially passive approach to environment and neglect to focus his attention outward on significant details of external experience.

Ruth Benedict[65] demonstrates hypothetically how in each of three European cultures swaddling has assimilated distinctive, important cultural emphases. In each it possesses characteristic values and mediates a range of attitudes. Augmenting communication that proceeds simultaneously as well as subsequently in other channels, swaddling builds up in a baby culturally specific identifications, security, or frustration. Great Russians swaddle most tightly and continue it longest, justifying the act as necessary for the infant, who otherwise "would tear its ears off . . . break its legs." Furthermore, mothers point to what to them must be a convincing explanation, "You couldn't carry an unswaddled baby." Swaddling probably communicates to a Russian infant a restriction on its movement rather than on its emotions, and its frequent opportunities to vent emotional release make that lesson even clearer. The physical isolation that tight swaddling entails also contributes toward the personal inviolability that Russian adults preserve in adulthood, though other experiences undoubtably augment the way this value is learned. Along with later cues, swaddling develops the eyes to become the main sensory organs for grasping the world, a central importance they retain throughout life. Poles say that an infant is so fragile that without supportive bindings it would break in two. If swaddling is painful (Poles believe it is), it also hardens a child and, like any suffering, helps to prove its worth. It provides the earliest lesson in hardening and, in company with being left to cry without attention and the implacable, sudden weaning to which a Polish baby is treated, hastens independence. Among Jews in eastern Europe swaddling also has distinctive properties. Loose bindings and a bed on a soft pillow almost tangibly reveal the Jewish mother's concern with her children's warmth and comfort. Even so, she regards the swaddled baby with pity, while yet believing that to swaddle is good because it insures straight legs. Among those Jews, as swaddling ushers a child into the warmth and close physical intimacy of the family, it communicates to him the importance of the succorance that he will some day owe to his own children, to the pitiable

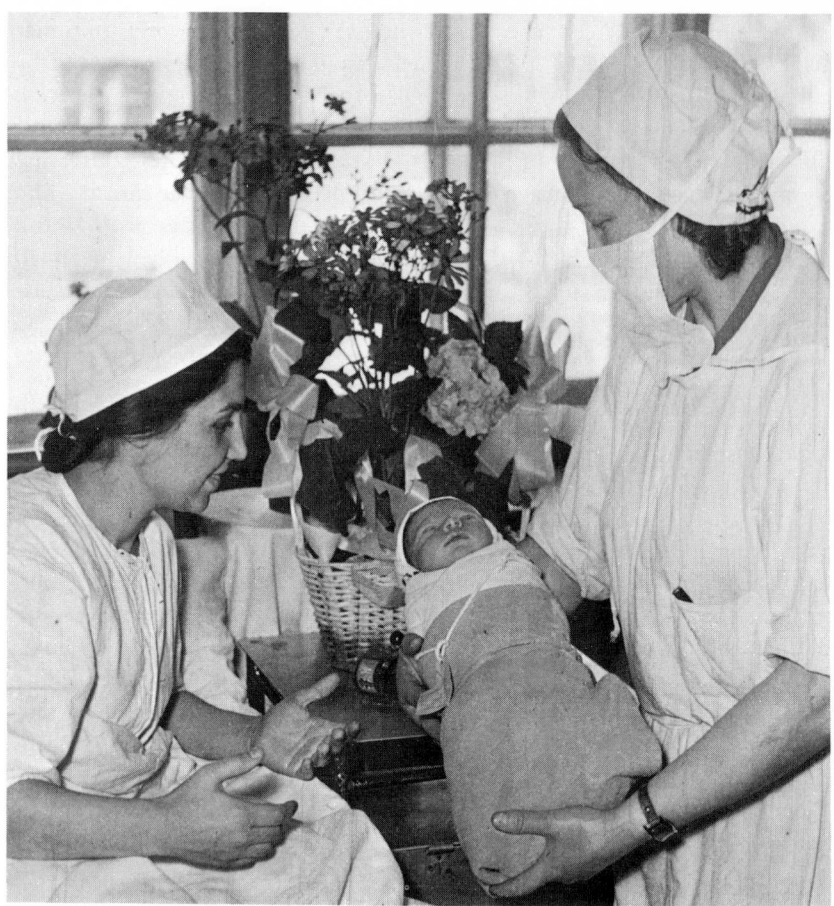

*Swaddling a baby, Russians explain, prevents it
from hurting itself. (Sovfoto)*

poor, and to the still unschooled.[66]
Whether as children Great Russians, Poles,
and East European Jews in fact receive
those messages from swaddling remains to
be ascertained by application of clinical or
experimental methods.

No childrearing sequence independently
communicates any attribute of personality
or, in off-on, switchlike fashion, sets any
behavior in motion.[67] Nor does the theory
any place voice the preposterous idea that
anything done to a child can originate a
culture pattern. Swaddling Great Russian
children doesn't cause the Russians to grow
up believing strong constraining authority
to be necessary, but it is one of the ways in

which parents communicate the self-protec-
tive value they associate with tight control.
How Jean or one hundred Jeans learn to be
French, a question that socialization research hopes to answer, isn't the same question as "How did French culture arise for
Jean to learn?" Conceive of socialization as
a circular, or self-regenerative, process. The
newborn child or an adult immigrant entering a new country, through his behavior
stimulates his socializers to act. As they
respond to him in traditional fashion, he
learns to modify his behavior in terms of
expectations he perceives in what they do
or say to him. But at the same time, he
reinforces their traditional perception of

him, and helps to perpetuate the customary attitudes and other behavior with which people respond to children or to immigrant adults. The culture pattern is already there when he arrives, has perhaps been there for centuries; now it is both communicated to him and simultaneously perpetuated in his socializers' personality as they act it out anew. Anthropologists studying socialization interrupt the circle at childhood, dwelling there extra industriously, because that happens to be a convenient place to learn how culture becomes embodied in persons, not because childhood is the only time of life in which culture is communicated.

Decoding. The communication theory of socialization provides no checklist of early attitudes and values likely to be communicated in early life; no panorama of channels to consult for important learning they mediate; and no rules for decoding the meaning of unspoken messages that pass between parent and child. Each culture and each situation are left to speak for themselves. No wonder they don't speak clearly to everyone, but only to someone highly capable of interpreting fleeting clues. To be more useful, the method must be accompanied by a few guidelines, which need not violate the configurational character of the approach or reduce it to the mechanical system of interpretation found in "dream books." The first rule to bear in mind is that unlocking the meaning of what is being transmitted over any channel of behavior within a particular culture depends on knowing more than whatever happens to be occurring in that channel alone. The investigator must be aware of the age at which a practice is instituted, the reasons for it, the extent of adults' emotional involvement, the nature and emotional magnitude of the goal they hope to achieve, and considerable about the context in which the practice occurs. "Early toilet training followed out for some casual reason of household arrangement will have a very different, and possibly almost negligible effect, while toilet training at an age when it might be conceived to be less traumatic . . . may, because of the weight given it by the adult, have far stronger effects."[68] A young working-class child who roams the neighborhood and attends movies alone reveals not his parents' child-centered permissiveness but the push out of an adult-centered household that they have given him.[69] Feeding a child whenever it cries shows less concern for the child's welfare when carried out by cold, businesslike mothers inhabiting socially disintegrated communities than it transmits a lesson in the disorder that characterizes such settings.[70] At first glance, the 2–3-month-long Arapesh initiation ceremony seems to mean exactly what it does in other cultures, where a group of jealous males grudgingly admits younger males and severs their dependence on women. But the form misleads. Arapesh perform the ceremony, in which novices receive no instructions to despise women, according to their central cultural value: to promote growth. The gauntlet run by initiates isn't administered in a spirit of cruel hazing but nurturantly, so that the novices will grow.[71]

Decoding is helped by knowing how people conceive of human nature, particularly of human emotions, since such knowledge governs their expectations in socialization and, as they become communicated, help to set the child's emerging repertory of responses. What potential emotional responses are actually emphasized? Which ones (shame, guilt, or respect) are deemphasized? The Javanese, for example, don't differentiate shame from guilt, and they fuse both with fear and respect.[72] The significance that a practice, injunction, or other experience holds for learning also depends on its relationship to significant events that have preceded it in the life cycle, or that accompany it at a given step in development. In the Egyptian village of Silwa, circumcision and cliterodectomy co-

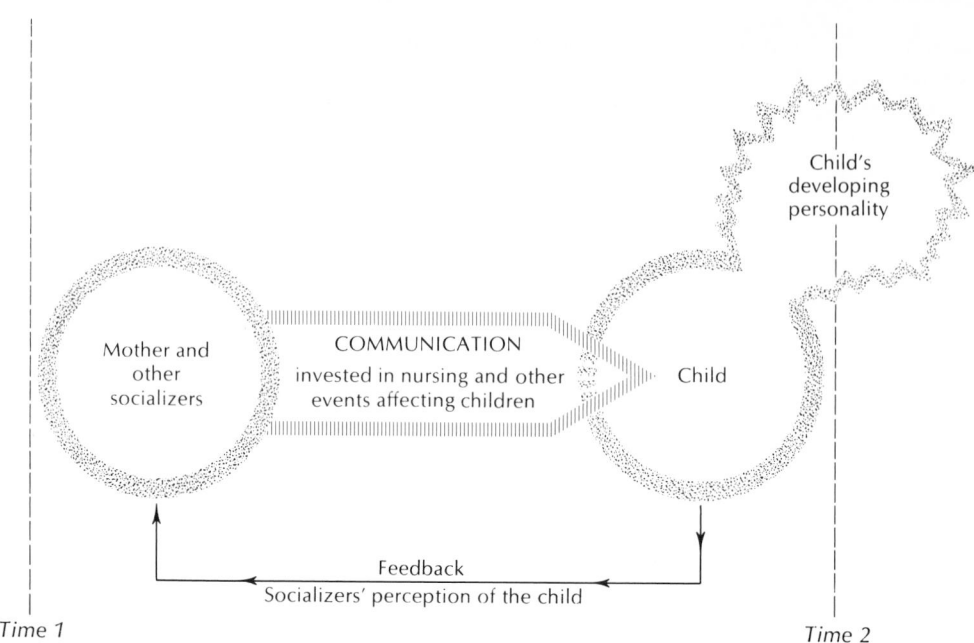

Time 1   Time 2

Early learning viewed as communication.

incide with the genital period of development, when the Oedipus complex brings about strong castration anxiety. This coincidence may endow the genital operations with heightened meaning for young Silwans.

The quality of children's affective relationship to those who monitor his experiences can also play a strategic role, now cushioning and now exacerbating an event of potentially traumatic significance. Always keep in mind that entering into the practice to influence personality formation are the attitudes with which it is both executed and perceived. Precisely here a most difficult question confronts the theory: To what extent is a child capable of perceiving attitudes that lie behind his caretakers' actions? Don't perceptual and cognitive immaturity tend to insulate the infant from parental attitudes?[73] The communication theory of socialization, without having faced this question squarely, relies on evidence indicating that some attitudes apparently do get through—even to an in-

fant[74]—and that far from being a neophyte as well as a neonate, an infant is sensorily and perceptively alert, acute, and discriminatory.[75] The approach must also be deflected from a fallacy on which it verges; namely, conceiving of parent-child communication to be analogous to genetic mechanisms that with slight change repeat their instructions from one generation to another.[76] Especially in a heterogeneous community, observers must bear in mind that parents don't merely replicate their own socialization or perpetuate the culture they embody; that altered circumstances of culture will affect children and prompt them to reinterpret what parents communicate, and that how reinterpretation occurs will alter from one generation to the next.

DIMENSIONAL APPROACH

Highly pragmatic and empirical though it is, the final approach to socialization that I am going to outline is hardest to identify, mainly because it avoids confining itself to a single set of clearly stated assumptions.[77] Unlike psychoanalytic instinct theory, which supposes that biological strivings turn into enduring character traits through the way they are gratified or frustrated, and unlike communication theory, which assumes that parent-child relationships and practices carry information concerning cultural expectations, the *dimensional approach* (to give it a terse, arbitrary label) holds no comprehensive, prior, guiding assumption for research to act on. (I chose the term "dimensional," because the word is widely used for separable elements of socialization, such as are often capable of being measured or of being correlated with other cultural variables.) Sociologists, psychologists, and anthropologists following this approach will utilize anything observable or reportable that happens in childhood —any caretaking or deliberate training behaviors; any interactions, actions, and attitudes involving parents and child, whether expressive of love or annoyance, even if not intended to teach children anything. Facts are especially sought that are susceptible to being utilized by already consistently supported social science theories, like formal learning theory. Combinations of facts are also attended to if they fit into a less strongly verified theory, say psychoanalysts, because the researchers see in the situation possibility of testing a crucial aspect of that theory. Well-tested theories serve them like proven tools that assure them that they will be able to work productively; doubtful theories are like troublesome, unresolved problems about which they hope to be able to do something. Let's see how this works. Psychologists examining socialization in a New England metropolitan area discovered weaning to be practically always frustrating, except under most fortunate circumstances. They knew that psychoanalytic theory claims a strong, compelling, tissue-rooted basis to exist for oral behavior. If

psychoanalysts are correct, they reasoned, then one could logically predict that early weaning would be more upsetting than late, because the tissue-rooted need had received very little gratification. Their facts, however, indicated the opposite: Late weaning proves to be more difficult. Formal learning theory, which asserts that drives become fixed by being rewarded, explains their facts better than psychoanalytic theory. Late weaning is emotionally more upsetting than early because the oral drive grows stronger with longer sucking, presumably by being prolongedly rewarded.[78] To take another example, this time from the theory of common sense, it would seem likely that the more mature a child, the better he is able to learn a new task, like bowel training. But inquiries made of 379 New England mothers showed this expectation to be highly doubtful. Toilet training upsets a child when begun too early—before he is capable of assuming the required degree of control—or too late, after his habit of casual elimination has been strongly reinforced. Data from the same mothers also refutes the popular belief that women compensate for their marital and personal difficulties by unloading warmth on their children. Rather, emotionally satisfied women who possess good self-esteem make the warmest mothers.

What I am describing is less a theory than a strategy, a way of studying socialization that ventures to commit itself deeply to few presuppositions. Like a walker using his knowledge of geography, woodcraft, and other clues to help him find his way in a strange countryside, the strategy employs any possibly helpful, theoretical ideas that enhance the meaning of data. The dimensionalists also intend to discover how certain antecedent variables pertaining to mother's personality, father's occupation, housing, or religion explain the child's developing personality. Note, I say the child's personality, for the object of these investi-

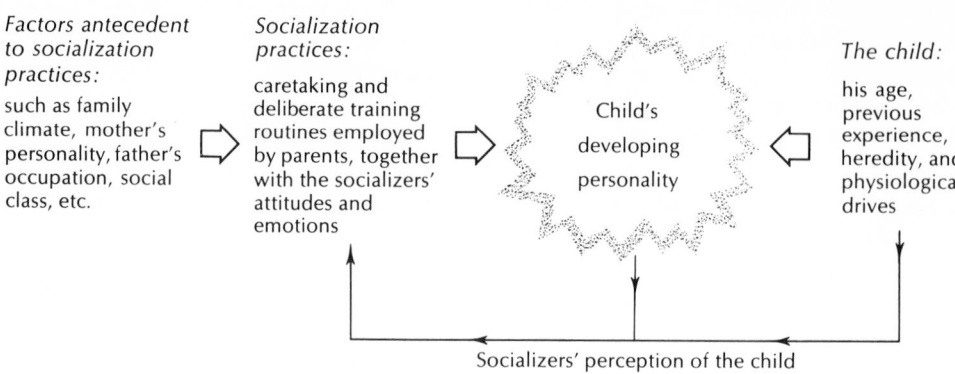

The dimensional approach and some of the variables it heeds. My object is to show the great importance that social environment possesses in this approach, compared to the potentialities and resources that the child brings.

gators is to proceed cautiously when it comes to making interpretations about long-term consequences of early childrearing. They much prefer a longitudinal method of examining the long-time course of socialization to cross-sectionally interpreting its consequences. Their approach adheres to the principle that socialization is integrally bound up with other aspects of culture. Pressures that impinge on a growing child are seen to be by-products of a horde of considerations that impinge upon the parents and influence their childrearing practices. Family size, the amount of energy and time mothers have available to care for children, and household composition exemplify such influencers.[79] A mother in Crestwood Heights alone in her own home, surrounded by neighbors with whom she has no close ties, faces different circumstances than does a Rajput mother confined to her crowded courtyard in Khalapur; in consequence the Crestwood mother treats her children differently. No more in the two theories I have previously described is the relationship between socialization and personality conceived to be simply cause and effect.

The dimensional approach doesn't assume that any parental trait implants a specific personality characteristic in the child. What happened earlier in the youngster's life can well vary the action of a later sequence. As in the communication theory, the mother responds to her child according to the way she perceives him, though the dimensional approach doesn't as strongly make the point that the perception of children is socially patterned. This means that her childrearing acts are first of all influenced by the child's behavior, which may embody the cumulative influence of a series of earlier, mutual responses that transpired between them. Hence, the generally low correlations found between specific childrearing practices and traits of child behavior reported by New England mothers. The poor coefficients indicate that the mothers' practices and attitudes have *some* importance, but they are far from being the only influence at work in personality formation. They may not even be the truly important ones. Although sociologists and psychologists theoretically recognize that many variables mutually determine one another in organismic fashion, they find this view hard to maintain in interpreting actual research findings. Therefore they often sound as if they are saying that what the mother does is independent of the child's behavior toward her as well as unrelated to other factors in the on-going situation and in the child's earlier life.

Accounting for Socialization. By way of countinuing with the dimensional approach, let me show it at work in a New England town as it exposes the manifold personal and cultural factors that influence maternal behavior.[80] Far from sharing a single pattern of childrearing, the town's mothers range along a continuum of interdependent attitudes and other dimensions of behavior. Those who took delight in finding they were pregnant, for example, demonstrated greater warmth to the infant after its birth. Many of the 379 interviewed mothers agree with psychoanalysis to the extent of indicating that weaning is difficult. The more severely a mother sought to enforce weaning, the greater the child's upset. A child's unpleasant early oral experiences, however, don't condition later feeding problems for him. Difficulties with eating appear to stem much more from other frustrations imposed later by mothers who practice severe toilet training, rarely permit the youngster to express aggression toward parents, become angry when he "unnecessarily" demands attention or nurturance, rely frequently on physical punishment, and demonstrate little warmth. Feeding contributes more to a baby's development than sheer survival. Together with the protection, play, comfort, and other gratifications that a mother provides, feeding elicits the child's firm, emotional attachment to her. Attachment in turn becomes the secure base from which he proceeds to explore the world; develops skills, knowledge, and eventually a con-

science, and becomes attached to persons other than his mother.[81] A mother's responsiveness is critical for learning what sort of behavior to expect from other human beings—loving and need-satisfying on the one hand; hating, rejecting, and anxiety-arousing on the other. As the child discovers other human beings, who in some ways differ from his mother, and gets over his initial unfamiliarity with them, he responds to them as he learns to respond to his mother. Whether he readily modifies his early response pattern and treats them differently from his mother depends on the amount of anxiety he transfers to them from his maternal relationship. In Alor, for example, great anxiety is engendered in children through early maternal neglect. Under such circumstances, as a child grows up and comes to know new persons, he fails to deal with them as significantly different from his mother. For a time at least, he goes on responding unrealistically to them, as if they were equivalent to her.[82]

The New England mothers, like other Euroamerican parents, identify urination and defecation with sex, apparently because all three functions involve a common bodily area and to some extent even utilize the same organs. The sexual anxiety of these women stands sharply revealed in their attempts to hasten toilet training, especially in girls. Toilet training *is* often difficult to master, but just as feeding problems are not themselves inherent in the oral zone but reflect frustrations encountered in striving for other satisfactions, so very upsetting experiences encountered in toilet training can be explained without wholly relying on the anal and genital drives themselves. Children of affectively cold mothers who underwent severe toilet training suffered more than those who were severely trained by emotionally warm mothers. Apparently the former used their severe training practices to communicate their coldness and so sharpened the youngsters' problem. What

([Emotional Control or Laissez-Faire?[83]

Statistical analysis of information obtained by interview about mother-child relationships in six culturally different communities shows Mexican and Indian (Khalapur Rajput) mothers to be significantly less warm than the others. They show relatively little warmth; use praise less; apply physical punishment more frequently and more intensively, and are intermediate on a scale that measures the hostility which mothers show to their children. Both the Indian and Mexican communities are also characterized by a common feature of social structure: In both, brothers and their families share dwellings that surround a common courtyard where children play with siblings and first cousins. Occupying such a multiple-family dwelling allows a minimum of privacy, and it is reasonable to suppose that people living in such close proximity easily irritate each other. Therefore, emotional control is essential for the group's survival. The mothers' coldness toward children who play in the crowded courtyard apparently disciplines the youngsters to restrain themselves.

	Factor scores for warmth of mother		Factor scores for warmth of mother
Okinawa	.62	United States	—.01
Philippines	.18	Mexico	—.34
Africa	.00	India	—.48

The data from the six cultures beg for testing on a larger scale, using more social systems. Is it predictable, due to reasons just cited, that whenever a nuclear family shares a courtyard with other families, mothers evidence more emotional control in relation with their children than mothers living in more private houses? That is, do they show less warmth, demonstrate more hostility, praise less frequently, use physical punishment more often, and generally reveal less permissiveness? Data from seventy-six cultures cast doubt on the hypothesis. Low maternal warmth *is* more common in communities where families live together than where they live alone and praise is also less frequently used by mothers in the former. But contrary to the hypothesis, mothers in multiple-family dwellings tend to be *less* hostile, use physical punishment *less* readily, and are frequently *more* permissive than those living in single-family households.

		Percentage of multiple-family dwellings	Percentage of single-family dwellings	n
Mother's warmth	High	59	74	23
	Low	41	26	12
Mother's hostility	High	37	48	17
	Low	63	52	22
Frequency of praise	High	57	63	26
	Low	43	36	17
Frequency of physical punishment	High	39	53	25
	Low	61	47	28
General permissiveness	High	66	55	34
	Low	37	45	24

When you think of it, doesn't that make good sense? If a family must live together with other families in crowded circumstances, isn't it best not to be too emotionally demonstrative or intense? It would seem wise to let children have as much rein as possible; otherwise the place will be constantly upset by anger, nagging, and crying youngsters. The researchers reach almost the same conclusion as they revise their original interpretation. They decide that the maternal syndrome of low warmth, slight use of praise, dampened hostility, and infrequent physical punishment that tends to be found in multiple-family households indicates a laissez-faire policy of childrearing rather than one of emotional control.

kind of mothers are especially severe in toilet training? Apart from refusing to tolerate the child's masturbation, to allow him to play sexually with other children, or to countenance any show of immodesty, New England mothers who admitted especially severe cleanliness training also sought most strongly to have their children conform to adult standards with respect to table manners, neatness, and orderliness; they expected children to help care for the house and furniture, to be quiet, and to do well in school. Forbidding any disobedience or aggression toward parents, they also relied on severe forms of punishment, like chastisement and depriving the child of his privileges. They felt little warmth toward themselves or toward their husbands and children, which may partly explain why they made no effort to reason with children while directing their socialization. Such characteristics define New England urban mothers who utilize severe toilet-training practices, but they don't account for those practices elsewhere in the United States or in other cultures. All we can say is that what occurs in one system of behavior is systematically related to other attitudes (like lack of warmth) which they succeed in further communicating to the child, and to other practices (like demanding conformity to adult standards) which they obviously reinforce.

"How much attention does X seem to want from you?" interviewers asked New England mothers, referring to a specific child and to dependence which isn't dictated by any actual need for help but which

children seek for its own sake. "How about following you around and hanging onto your skirts?" "How does X react when you go out of the house and leave him with someone else?" Responses to such questions showed that the mothers' tolerance for dependence was likewise related to definite qualities in their relationship to their children and to their husbands, as well as to attitudes they held toward themselves. Mothers who accepted dependence also showed affectional warmth for the child, were gentle about toilet training, and made little use of physical punishment. They tended to tolerate the child's aggression toward parents, held both themselves and their husbands in high esteem, and were permissive about sex. Their reports cast serious doubt on the popular notion that indulging a child's dependence will spoil him; that is, heighten his demands for nurturance when there isn't any actual need for it. Quite the contrary. Mothers who punished dependence more often reported children reacting with the very kind of behavior—dependence—that they, the mothers, had sought to prevent.

With regard to sex and aggression, some communities make no attempt to teach a child to recognize those impulses or to release them in socially patterned ways; they insist only that they be suppressed or controlled. That holds for New England mothers, but since I propose to discuss sex training in the next chapter I will now confine myself solely to aggression. Practically all social systems firmly prohibit in-family fighting as well as aggression directed against parents. How tolerantly they regard hostility displayed beyond the bounds of the household varies. New England mothers tended to be somewhat permissive about children fighting outside the home. Some even felt that youngsters must be encouraged to fight to protect their interests, but such permissiveness varied from one class to another. Surprisingly, lower-class mothers permitted less aggression, both toward parents and toward other children. They punished aggression toward themselves more severely than did middle-class mothers. On the whole, all the mothers took a less punitive approach toward their sons' aggressiveness outside the home than toward their daughters'. The psychologists who studied the New England town believe that in the sample they covered the average child received more actual punishment for aggressive behavior than for any other act. Despite the mothers' pronounced, nearly unanimous trend to suppress aggression, even here variability appears. The mode is to be severely restrictive, but the range includes some quite permissive mothers. With such severe sanctions directed against that system of behavior, youngsters could hardly escape becoming uneasy, uncomfortable, and anxious about aroused aggressive impulses, and they would, in all likelihood, be very cautious about expressing them. Yet both permissive mothers and restrictive mothers report children who display high aggression. The more severe the punishment intended to curb the behavior, the more aggressive the child. Aggression was most successfully curbed in families where mothers clearly communicated the attitude that fighting was wrong and would not be tolerated, and where they themselves managed with nonpunitive forms of discipline. Children in such a household perceived no aggressive models after whom to pattern their behavior and also had few opportunities to learn how satisfying it could be to act aggressively. Aggression, as the world

has ruefully learned, nearly always tends to evoke counteraggression, in the family as well as in the theater of politics and history.[84]

Permissiveness or strictness varies from one behavioral system to another.[85] Circumstances may force the most permissively inclined mother to become restrictive; for example, if she lives in a multi-family house with thin walls where she can't allow the same noise level that she would tolerate on a farm. Yet an over-all tendency with respect to permissiveness or strictness does appear in the New England sample. If a woman permits her child a fair amount of aggression, she will very likely also tolerate his sexual behavior, show leniency with regard to his table manners and neatness, and practice gentle toilet training. Mothers who insisted strongly on orderliness quite conformably showed themselves severe about toileting. What psychoanalysts call an anal character—a personality marked by orderliness, compulsiveness, and similar characteristics—may better be explained in a child as resulting from direct learning rather than being produced through sublimation or reaction formation.

My brief excursion into the empirical approach favored by a number of sociologists and psychologists brings out how little, compared to anthropologists, they try to identify a single, unified pattern of child-rearing in the community as a whole. Rather, they set out to grasp and explain the internal variability that exists, and to report it in frequency tables. A relatively homogeneous social system, the East African Ganda, where the approach has been tried on a small scale, shows the same variability in maternal practices and other caretaking routines.[86] With frequency tables one can statistically work up modal patterns, like the modal age of weaning or the modal mother's measured degree of warmth, but few investigators who do so regard such modes as typical practices by which to characterize the whole community. It is quite true that an anthropologist doing fieldwork also observes the behaviors of discrete individuals, which become bases of his generalizations. But he does so much less systematically, precisely because as a rule he isn't as interested in variability. He converts his discrete observations into abstractions, general patterns descriptive of what people in general regularly do. One method doesn't deny the other; one isn't finally right and the other totally wrong. However, where a high degree of variability exists, an observer might be wise to abandon the attempt to find a single pattern fitting almost everyone.

FURTHER READING

A good book to follow this chapter is Paul H. Mussen, John J. Conger, and Jerome Kagan, *Child Development and Personality* (1963: espec. chaps. 6, 7, 8, 11, and 12). The work summarizes a wealth of information about prenatal and early postnatal individual development. George De-Vos and Arthur E. Hippler review "culturally determined child-rearing practices" in 'Cultural Psychology' (in press), and Gregory Bateson writes more theoretically on "Cultural Determinants of Personality" (1944). Marie-Thérèse Knapen, *L'Enfant mukongo* (1962: chaps. 1–2) presents a brief, eclectic theory of the same subject which she then proceeds to utilize, and David C. McClelland, *Personality* (1951: chap. 10), examines some likely variables in early childrearing and ponders their possible influence on personality. Sexual instinct theory, Freud's and his students', is well presented in Edith Buxbaum, "Psychosexual Development: the Oral, Anal, and Phallic Phases" (1959), and critically reviewed in Gerald S. Blum, *Psychoanalytic Theories of Personality* (1953: chaps. 2–

5). In *The Interpersonal Theory of Psychiatry*, Harry Stack Sullivan (1953, pt. 2) recounts his own form of the libido theory and his ideas on early ego development. Several attempts, like the one William H. Sewell describes in "Infant Training and the Personality of the Child" (1952), have been made to try out instinct theory by testing children differently reared. Harold Orlansky, "Infant Care and Personality" (1949) reviews a wealth of such literature but not always wisely, claims Sidney Axelrad's rejoinder, "Infant Care and Personality Reconsidered" (1962). Melford E. Spiro reports on what data he could obtain about the Oedipus complex in *Children of the Kibbutz* (1965: chap. 10). In a difficult article, "Psychologic Weaning: Childhood and Adolescence," Margaret Mead (1949c) explains how early childrearing holds clues to future adult roles and how nursing and weaning situations are prototypes for later heterosexual relationships. In *Social Structure and Personality*, Yehudi Cohen (1961: chap. 11) tests cross-culturally the hypothesis that early, repetitive food gratification creates an emotional predisposition to share food in later life, whereas early, recurrent experience with deprivation encourages a tendency for adults to amass goods. Dorothy Lee's essays on "Individual Autonomy and Social Structure" and "Responsibility Among the Dakota," reprinted in *Freedom and Culture* (1959), glimpse parent-child relationships marked by great deference and respect for the youngsters. Jack L. Rubins takes a "A Phenomenological View of Early Development of the Child" (1962), and discusses how to gauge a young child's experience. Differences between Swiss and U.S. "Maternal Attitudes Toward Child Rearing," by Henry G. Jarecki (1961), deals mainly with problems encountered in child-rearing, like stuttering, masturbation, and lying. Additional significant psychological investigations of socialization in the United States include Alfred L. Baldwin, Joan

Kalhorn, and Fay Huffman Breese, *Patterns of Parent Behavior* (1945); William H. Sewell, Paul H. Mussen, and Chester W. Harris, "Relationships Among Child-Training Practices" (1955); and Vaughn Crandall and Anne Preston, "Patterns and Levels of Maternal Behavior" (1955). John and Elizabeth Newson, in *Infant Care in an Urban Community* (1963), apply the dimensional approach to an English city. Heavily ethnographic in scope, *Six Cultures* (1963), edited by Beatrice B. Whiting, reports on specific variables that had been set forth in detail for the ethnographers in John W. M. Whiting *et al.*, *Field Guide for a Study of Socialization in Five Societies* (1954). Leigh Minturn and William W. Lambert interpret certain responses of *Mothers of Six Cultures* (1964)—the same six cultures described in the Whiting volume mentioned above. Peter H. Wolff, in "The Natural History of a Family" (1963), looks observantly at mother-child behavior in a single, middle-class Boston family, and in "Research in Dimensions of Early Maternal Care" (1963) Leon J. Yarrow explains why he thinks that psychologists have too often considered the wrong variables in studying the very early part of life. My allegation that the dimensional approach adopts an eclectic attitude to theory is not really at variance with Henry W. Maier's title, "The Learning Theory of Robert R. Sears," which heads chapter 4 in Maier's book, *Three Theories of Child Development* (1965).

REFERENCES

1 Pope, 1963: 95. First published in 1734.
2 Locke, 1880.
3 Spencer, 1963.
4 Herskovits, 1948: 40.
5 Bruner, 1956a.
6 Spiro, 1955: 1249.
7 Bruner, 1956a and 1956b.
8 M. Mead, 1930b: 103 ff, 317–318; 1932, and 1956c: chap. 12.
9 M. Mead and Macgregor, 1951: 18–19; M. Mead, 1954c: 404.
10 Kagan and Moss, 1962.
11 Wolman, 1960: 330–336, and chap. 9.
12 As a result, "ego psychology" grew up. See Munro, 1955: 89 ff.
13 Rank, 1952.
14 Apart from specifically cited sources, I have drawn from Freud, 1924b, 1933, and 1938b; E. Jones, 1948: chap. 24, 26; Abraham, 1953: chaps. 13–15; Kardiner, 1939; Erikson, 1963. For summary statements, see Kardiner and Preble, 1961: 342–343, 353.
15 Freud, 1938b: 573.
16 Abraham, 1949a: 412–413.
17 *Cf.* E. Beaglehole and Beaglehole, 1941.
18 Erikson, 1963; Maier, 1965: chap. 2; Erikson, in Tanner and Inhelder, 1956–1960, IV:136–154.
19 Erikson, in Tanner and Inhelder, 1956–1960, III:171.
20 J. W. M. Whiting and Child, 1953.
21 Kardiner, 1945b: 347–348.
22 M. Mead, 1935: 49, 51, 56, 144; J. J. Honigmann and Honigmann, 1959: 12–13.
23 T. Parsons, 1961.
24 Kardiner, 1945b: 253–254.
25 Erikson, 1963: 175–180.
26 Walters and Parke, 1965.
27 Róheim, 1934b.
28 Gorer, 1943; La Barre, 1945.
29 Haring, 1953. Material dealing with Japanese national character and touching on anal training or related matters will be found in Haring, 1946 and 1953; Sikkema, 1947; Kerlinger, 1952–1953; Lanham, 1956; Norbeck and Norbeck, 1956. For a brief review of the literature, see Moloney, in Murdock and Whiting, 1951: 34–35.
30 Ariès, 1962: 100–104.
31 T. Parsons, 1961: 186.
32 Y. A. Cohen, 1956.

33 Freud, 1935; 291–292; Stephens, 1962; the latter reviews the Oedipus concept extensively.

34 Malinowski, 1927.

35 Kardiner, 1939: 481.

36 E. Jones, 1925.

37 Róheim, 1943a; 1950: chap. 3, and 1952.

38 Eggan, 1943.

39 See, however, Ernest Becker's (1961–1962: 494 and 1964: chaps. 6–7) reinterpretation of the notion.

40 Erikson, 1963: chap. 3.

41 Ibid., pp. 137–138. By permission of W. W. Norton and Co., Inc.

42 Macgregor, 1946: 209.

43 Erikson, 1963: 163. By permission of W. W. Norton and Co., Inc.

44 For two recent sources on the Pine Ridge and other Sioux, see Hagen and Schaw, 1960 (summarized in Hagen, 1962: 472–502); Wax et al., 1964.

45 J. W. M. Whiting and Child, 1953.

46 Fromm, 1949: 5.

47 J. W. M. Whiting and Child, 1953: 162, 164.

48 Other important evidence tending to confirm the same point comes from a mental health study conducted in New York City; see Langner and Michael, 1963: chap. 13.

49 See Spiro and D'Andrade, 1958; Lambert, Triandis, and Wolf, 1959; J. W. M. Whiting, 1959. For a more complete summary of these findings, see J. W. M. Whiting, 1961.

50 Barry, 1957.

51 M. Mead, 1952b: 422.

52 My account of her theory comes mainly from M. Mead, 1953b, 1954c, and 1955b; M. Mead and Macgregor, 1951: 27; R. Benedict, 1949.

53 M. Mead, 1954c: 398–399.

54 M. Mead, 1956b.

55 T. Parsons, 1961: 174.

56 M. Mead, 1949b: 69.

57 What immediately follows is mainly from Bateson, 1942–1943 and 1944: 728–729; M. Mead, 1948a and 1949b: 64, 74, 392.

58 M. Mead, in Tanner and Inhelder, 1956–1960, IV:150–151; also Mead, 1955: 8–9.

59 G. W. Allport, 1955: 41.

60 Métraux and Mead, 1954; Wolfenstein, 1955a; Dolto, 1955.

61 Erikson, 1963: 135.

62 Ibid., p. 175.

63 C. C. Hughes et al., 1960: 286.

64 M. Mead, 1952b: 422–423.

65 R. Benedict, 1949.

66 Zborowski, 1949.

67 M. Mead, 1951f: 74 and 1954c: 396–397.

68 R. Benedict, 1949: 349.

69 Sears, Maccoby, and Levin, 1957: 446.

70 C. C. Hughes et al., 1960: 286.

71 M. Mead, 1935: 75.

72 Geertz, 1959: 236.

73 Ausubel, 1958: 262–263, 265.

74 R. I. Watson, 1965: 204–208.

75 Kessen, 1963.

76 Cf. A. F. C. Wallace, 1961b: 112–113.

77 Mostly my remarks will refer to Sears, Maccoby, and Levin, 1957, a book I shall also designate as a study of New England mothers. See also Maccoby, 1961. Landy's (1965) Puerto Rican village study exemplifies the dimensional approach applied in anthropology; he uses the New England mothers as a control group with which to compare island mothers.

78 Cf. J. W. M. Whiting, 1954: 524–525.

79 Minturn and Lambert, 1964: 291.

80 What follows is mostly from Sears, Maccoby, and Levin, 1957.

81 Ainsworth, 1961–1963, II:103–104.

82 Ambrose, 1961–1963.

83 Minturn and Lambert, 1964: 64, 78, 167–168, 289.

84 Cf. Bandura and Walters, 1963: 118–133.

85 Cf. J. W. M. Whiting and Child, 1953; Prothro, 1960.

86 Ainsworth, 1961–1963.

Later Life Is Important, Too

10

*Men resemble their times more
than they do their fathers.*[1]

ARAB PROVERB

THE CRITICAL BARRAGE [2]

Psychoanalysts' and anthropologists' diligent inquiry into early socialization provoked a notably antagonistic response. Sharp and vigorous criticism, sometimes barbed with downright nasty ridicule, landed most forcefully on the theory of sexual instincts. Even a number of psychoanalysts backed away from the classic Freudian doctrine.[3] Critics also often included Margaret Mead in their attacks, but the dimensional approach remained beyond criticism of the sort that I shall relate (though in a different spirit, its professors have constantly raised constructive questions of their own method and interpretations, also pointing out contradictory information bearing on the same U.S. social classes[4]).

Plenty of evidence could be found to question Edward Bruner's thesis that what a person learned early persists to the extent of resisting substitutes brought in from a foreign way of life.[5] Babies learn very early to supplicate emotional support, and mothers reinforce such dependence, but most people outgrow extreme dependence and discard social supplication as a useful coping technique.[6] Some criticism, rather than outrightly condemning research on early socialization, proposed to reorient it, urging that, for the sake of greater comparability, anthropologists more consistently cover the same topics of early childrearing in different cultures and not provide a mass of detail on say, breast-feeding for one and practically nothing on the same subject for another. Margaret Mead[7] replied that fieldworkers are wise if they attend closely to those systems of behavior on which a social system itself focuses and through which it heavily channels communication. Then, too, sometimes an anthropologist can't get equal amounts of information on all topics of socialization due to his subjects' reticence and other fieldwork conditions.

Critics dwelt insistently on the weaknesses of instinct theory. Comparative studies of U.S. children don't consistently confirm that the balance of early gratification and frustration encountered, for example, in the oral zone affects learned personality characteristics. Confidence, self-assurance, or optimism don't consistently vary between children fed on demand or by schedule, or weaned early rather than late.[8] Psychoanalytic theory, according to the critics' criteria, lacks empirical foundations. It dwells too much on freely postulated, unconscious, nuclear personality states that, despite being difficult to verify, are held responsible for motivating a host of peripheral and overt behaviors. So enormous is the variety of peripheral behaviors ascribed to the same few nuclear motives, that practically anything an individual does, even the most contradictory acts, can be taken as evidence of the existence of those springs of action. Explanatory mechanisms employed to connect early and later behavior—like projection, compensation, reaction formation, fixation—are flexible enough to allow almost anything to be traced back to pregenital and genital instincts. The overextended use made of instinct theory endangers anthropologists' ability to understand culture, for the theory practically neglects the way culture patterns behavior. More

happens even in the first year of life than the Freudian theory acknowledges; as a result, social scientists who rely on it miss many important psychogenic processes of personality formation, including a substantial part of ego development.[9] Reliance on psychoanalytic theory causes researchers to explain behavior far more complexly than necessary. Isn't it likely that an Alorese man wants sexual intercourse because it is pleasurable, not because he is hunting for a satisfactory mother image? Critics point out that mere statistical correlations between antecedent childrearing practices and subsequent traits of adult behavior, no matter in how many cultures and with what degree of statistical significance they occur, says not a word about causality. John W. M. Whiting and Irvin L. Child agree, pointing out, however, that consistently positive correlations lend support to inferences about causality. Some journalistic critics, who knew they liked neither instinct theory nor the emphasis put on early learning in general, didn't trouble to find logical and methodological shortcomings in such theoretical approaches, but simply ridiculed them by coining the epithet "diaperology." A degree of opposition also arose from people who felt that early learning theories demeaned their historic culture by associating national character traits with swaddling or toilet training. People who resented tracing "everything" to sex may have been unconsciously repelled by the unpleasant connotation that sex possessed for them. Finally, some Americans, even though their middle-class homes are child-centered, can't believe that any significant or enduring learning takes place as early as infancy.[10]

Psychoanalytically minded investigators' failure to express early learning in terms of a generally acceptable, experimentally proven, formal learning theory greatly vexes some psychologists. They disapprove of the loose, nonexperimental way in which influences are ascribed to early childrearing, the baby's phenomenological experiences being gratuitiously assumed. They demand better grounds for maintaining that persons start to learn something as abstract as attitudes to authority through the way they are swaddled in infancy. Such statements should be offered much more tentatively than they are, and with an eye to how they might be verified (for example, by comparing children who had and had not been swaddled). I am mystified by the criticism that socialization theory has outrun available knowledge, which is too poor to permit conclusions about lasting influences exerted by early childhood experiences.[11] Quite likely too much *has* been claimed for childhood, but the purpose of theory is precisely to anticipate new and unexpected knowledge and boldly to outrun what is known. Of course, not all scientists are equally avid in stretching for original, new conceptions; some prefer cautiously to improve on what seems demonstrably true.[12] Theories themselves can never be proven immutably true or false; they remain well beyond the range of provable empirical data. Facts only offer distant support for continuing to hold a theory; when they cease to do that, the theory is usually abandoned.[13]

Views that ascribe personality formation to childhood can be censured for possessing the weakness afflicting all historicism; that is, they assume, contrary to evidence, that what a person becomes is fixed by what once happened to him. Much social science fails sufficiently to acknowledge the power of human consciousness to reflect, and by reflection to alter itself. Social science is too fatalistic. It traces behavior back to infancy and early experiences, or views culture as itself the fixed product of history. Those are the errors of historicism.[14] I acknowledge both the nearly mortal danger of thinking in such terms (the danger comes from the way it saps our will and confidence) as well as its nearly irresistible appeal. Yet I know of no critic who rejected completely a de-

velopmental approach in personality study, or who suggested that it would be more desirable to account for behavior by properties possessed at any given moment by persons and their situation, without trying to reconstruct how they got to be that way. Any developmental approach is a species of history, and very firmly do Western intellectuals believe a historical view-point to be almost indispensable for understanding behavior. At the same time, national character research has been charged with neglecting the influence of historical events. In societies rich in documentary materials, anthropologists should explain social personality not only by referring to details of child care, but also by examining other marks left by the past. The significance Americans attached to the expanding Western frontier, for example, has left its imprint on the American character, and we all still reveal the emotional impact made on our parents and grandparents by the Great Depression, just as we are still, in effect, all children of immigrants.[15]

It is beguiling to speculate about what would have been the fate of socialization research in anthropology, if, instead of adopting and modifying psychoanalytic theory, which drew the heaviest critical barrage, it had equally industriously strengthened and continued to apply the earlier configurational approach. As enunciated by Ruth Benedict in *Patterns of Culture* and polished by Margaret Mead in *Coming of Age in Samoa* and *Sex and Temperament*, this approach emphasizes unconscious patterning. Patterning means that what people do, think, feel, and make reflects general modes of conduct imputed to society, or conforms to pervasive, dominant emphases in culture as a whole, like Samoan formalism, Arapesh passivity and growth, or Kaska Indian emotional isolation.[16] Undoubtedly a configuration theory of patterning would have created its own difficulties. Especially when it sought to explain how personality becomes patterned—that is, assimilated to the whole's dominant characteristics—would it have run up against contemporary social science's inflexible empirical bias, just as psychoanalytic instinct theory does because, critics say, it isn't sufficiently objective or rigorously testable.[17]

LATER LIFE IMPORTANT, TOO

How can one claim, C. W. M. Hart[18] increduously demands, even for a homogeneous community that childhood experiences are at all uniformly standardized, and as a result capable of endowing everyone to respond in similar ways? Uniform learning only appears with puberty, he maintains, and then it is especially conspicuous in those social systems that in elaborate and dramatic fashion initiate youths standing on the threshold of adulthood. Initiation "schools" make very certain that a culture's whole value system contained in its myths, religion, philosophy, and self-justification will be formally and explicitly transmitted under highly emotional circumstances. At this point Hart sounds a bit like Lucien Lévy-Bruhl,[19] who accounted for the importance "primitive man" attaches to his emotion-filled, mystical collective representations by the fact that often they are acquired under vivid, exciting, ceremonial circumstances and periodically renewed under the same exhilerating conditions. Myths, religion, and philosophy, according to Hart, being learned late possess the greatest stability in culture, strongly resisting challenging alternatives when offered by another culture. The tenacity of later highly standardized learning compared to early learning can be illustrated by observing how people who readily take over newly introduced tools and appliances leave strange gods alone. Adults' readiness to adopt the white man's hoe, gun, and other implements is

consistent with how childhood unsystematically teaches a boy that for food-getting any tool is good, so long as it works. (Hart is actually illustrating how early inexplicit learning of a trait—call it adaptability—successfully carries over into adulthood.) Initiation, by contrast, attaches a youth firmly to specific, highly valued ideological elements of his social heritage.

I think we can question Hart's assertion that prepubertal learning is unstandardized, lacking pattern. I also demur from his generalization that people are usually readier to borrow technical traits than religious ideas or other ideologies. Modern idea systems, like parliamentary government and political self-determination, have diffused extraordinarily fast in the modern world, getting into some tribal areas far ahead of costly technology, which would be useless anyway without proper technical training.[20] Nor do people wait until puberty before teaching children basic ideas and values. Americans asked to judge the televised confrontation between the late Senator Joseph R. McCarthy and the U. S. Army in 1954 applied to that highly specific public issue very broad values they had learned in childhood.[21] They saw it to be a test of power between McCarthy joined by his supporters on the one hand and his opponents on the other. To judge the contest they employed such early learned values as the wrongness of lying, wasting time, exposing your own group to criticism, and disrespecting dignity; also, they judged by using early learned lesson that it is sinful to be evasive or inadequate.

Hart's main point, however, that substantial, enduring learning occurs in later life, can't be denied, for much evidence supports the assumption of later learning and illustrates the stability of what is learned beyond early childhood.[22] At the same time, who would deny that some early learning also persists in personality and in culture? Let's avoid being forced into choosing between those positions. Early life is important, but a person's world of meanings continues in significant ways to be formed and altered throughout his life, so long as he continues to interact alertly with other people and with things. Liberals interviewed in connection with the McCarthy hearings judged the two sets of opponents with other values in addition to the broad, general ones they had learned in childhood: They employed legal principles (it is wrong for one party to sit as judge, prosecutor, and jury) and referred to constitutionally guaranteed liberties like freedom of speech, that early parental discipline had done little to instill. In fact, such formally guaranteed liberties are constantly being denied to children undergoing socialization. Many U.S. parents use fear to make children conform, yet McCarthy's liberal critics claimed that it is wrong to use fear to induce conformity, just as it is wrong to impute guilt not actually proven, another point at which parents are likely to be careless. Such values begin to be acquired around adolescence, when U.S. children confronting broader social issues question the general applicability of values they learned in earlier years.

REVERSING EARLY GRATIFICATION

That later-life experiences count, sometimes enough to reform personality strikingly, has occurred to a number of anthropologists who in their fieldwork found that abundant infantile nurturance, protection, and gratification failed to influence personality as in theory they were supposed to. Other socializing events intervened and left their traces conspicuously evident.[23] Among Navaho Indians, stressful situations like school, with which a child must cope after passing out of his indulged early years, destroy his earlier poise and security and sow seeds of insecurity.[24] In the kibbutz Kiryat Yedidim, early child-training practices to a consider-

able extent gratify a child's initial impulses but subsequent shifts of nurses, changing physical environments, rejection by parents following birth of a sibling, emotional rejection by the collective as it devotes its warmest attention to younger children and temporary abandonment when parents make trips away from the kibbutz all painfully upset him.[25] Children's consequent insecurity motivates their hostility and withdrawal, and creates a strong demand for love. In New Zealand Maori, the primary character structure with its friendliness, generosity, and hospitality based on early gratification is never wholly obliterated, even though sudden reversal of early gratification accompanied by pressure to assume independence superimpose a sense of insecure loneliness on the earlier trends.[26] The Maori continues to be generous and friendly within the tribal community, but those behaviors are now directed by his attempt to assuage insecurity and bring him love and appreciation. A surprising number of communities reverse or discontinue early indulgence—sometimes, as with the Rakau Maori, as soon as the child can walk. Among the Kaska Indians, the same thing occurs when the mother ceases to respond warmly to the youngster.[27] Seemingly the discontinuity always exerts a hard push toward independence, even though it isn't consciously so intended. Among the Kaska, for example, it simply springs from a casual, laissez-faire attitude toward children, similar to what observers have also encountered in some U.S. mothers. In Java, the father changes his role when the child is about 5 years old, shifting from a display of affectionate warmth to distance and reserve.[28] By so doing he begins to teach one of the paramount Javanese values, respect. He is communicating that all social relations in Java are hierarchically ordered and that one must openly express that order. Upon the father's emotional withdrawal, the world beyond the family, with all its constraint, formality, and concern for status differences and respect fully enters the child's life. Like early nurturance and parental comradeship, emotional withdrawal isn't equally critical or traumatic in all communities. Among Hindu Tamils, for example, whose social structure rigidly prescribes a person's role behavior, emotional withdrawal apparently occurs without leaving any scar of insecurity or disturbing the child's emotional development.[29]

MORE FULLY AWARE AND INTENTIONAL

Modes of learning operative in early life continue to serve personality formation. Identification, for example, can be detected in the cognitive picture that a person forms of the boy or girl, the man or woman, he would like to be and the goals he would like to achieve. Once the model is implanted, whatever increases discrepancy between how a person currently evaluates himself and his goals provokes anxiety and is likely to be shunned. Whatever reduces discrepancy between himself and his model stands a good chance of being put into practice.[30] At times, familiar social types become models after whom to pattern behavior or serve as lessons of what to avoid in role playing.[31] In Mexico, the man who is *muy macho*—strong, virile, valiant, a "real man," good drinker, and good lover—presents a masculine ideal. Patriotic and religious heroes, as they are interpreted in a later age, can influence socialization in the same way, though apparently they don't do so in all places.[32] Just as identification becomes more highly defined and deliberate with age, so it becomes considerably easier to communicate in socialization as understanding grows and words mediate the largest part of interpersonal interchange. Attitudes to be communicated also grow more explicit and differentiated. The individual's

growing experience with his culture makes it easier for him to perceive others' attitudes from small cues and to adjust his modes of behavior appropriately. Subtle environmental features influence a child's personality, like the esteem that his parents or other socializers hold for each other or for him. He is sensitively aware of conflicting messages; for example, an acknowledgment of his independence accompanied by attempts to keep him relatively dependent. Socialization in later life operates through individuals who are more fully self-aware and intentional, deliberately choosing behavior to adopt and learning situations in which to participate. Although much learning continues to take place below the threshold of full conscious awareness, insight accumulates though not everyone brings it equally to bear on his experience.

DEVELOPMENTAL TASKS IN LATER LIFE

Changes in growth and capacities as they encounter social expectations continue to call on the person to master new developmental tasks through childhood's middle years, adolescence, and adulthood.[33] In his middle years, the child who, unlike the lower- or working-class youngster hasn't already received a firm push out of the home, gets it and enters peer-group life. A host of new physical and cognitive skills appears in his behavioral repertoire, enabling him to master new responsibilities that rapidly increase in volume as adolescence approaches. He learns to get along with age-mates, to build an appropriate sex role, and to develop suitable attitudes toward himself as a growing organism, a task that some cultures aid by passing him through a series of rituals which publicly measure his growth and achievements. Being promoted from one grade to another in a school system serves a similar function. Attitudes toward adult groups, from family to tribe and nation, also take form, as well as the meanings he holds for sacred objects and sentiments.

Adolescence. The years adjacent to physiological puberty bring a youngster up against the challenge to master masculine or feminine sex roles, to use his body (including the genitals) effectively, to achieve full emotional independence, and to strike out for economic independence by entering an occupation or at least preparing for one. Adolescence demands a readiness to take chances and to commit oneself to others, including in many cultures sexually, without fixation on pregenital stages of development. It is a time when a person carves out a substantially new social identity—an adult one—congruent with his earliest learning and character structure. Sometimes, to cite the modern Sioux Indians' predicament, a congenial role isn't to be found in a community that hangs back from fully endorsing the present. In some Western countries we find adolescents who confusedly withdraw from identifying with adult-controlled institutions, though without clinging to childhood and dependence. In fact, they may strain for greater independence than adults will permit. The hitherto relative smoothness of development is broken, as in a march when one enters an uncertain terrain across which one flounders in sad contrast to the confident way the going went earlier. Yet, everything we have learned since Margaret Mead's journey to Samoa confirms that, far from following the same course everywhere, the pattern of adolescence is culturally derived. In Israel, for example, although no marked difference shows up when kibbutz and nonkibbutz adolescents are compared, kibbutz adolescents show certain characteristics consistent with the socialization they have previously received.[34] Their consistent puritanical trend may be explicitly derived from rigid, adult-imposed rules on sex play

and premarital sexual intercourse. Their slighter emphasis on long-range goals and on specialized occupational aspirations reflects the fact that they have been socialized for kibbutz careers and hence need be less concerned with their future. They will take their places in the collective, which itself maintains a future outlook and assures them meaningful goals, much as the formal pattern of Samoan society does.

Discontinuity. Adolescence in the United States illustrates how disharmonious may be the transition that a person has to master from one point to another in his life cycle.[35] Discontinuity can't ever be entirely avoided in the course of traveling from birth to death, but cultures can go far to accentuate or soften it.[36] We exaggerate the contrast between childhood and adulthood when we hold that a child should be irresponsible, tractable, and sexless, but then, as adulthood approaches, expect him smoothly, firmly, and unerringly to assume mature responsibility, authority, and sexual competence. Not all people as sharply separate child and adult status. Papago Indians —in fact, many American Indians and Eskimo—encourage a reasonable degree of responsible social action and independence from a youngster's early years. Other of the world's people allow children to scream authoritatively at adults, testifying that they enforce no pattern of submission that will have to be abruptly cast aside once childhood is left behind. Many social systems tacitly recognize that children too have sex interests and more or less permit sex play and premarital sexual intercourse. We overlook these and similar sensible solutions to problems of growth as we contrive to overload adolescence with critical choices that a youngster must make abruptly and successfully, almost as though they were ordeals that qualified him for maturity.

Men in the course of evolving culture several times discovered means of overcoming discontinuity by forcefully jaculating youngsters into new, advanced roles, initiation ceremonies being one of the best solutions. Yet, initiation doesn't everywhere occur with equal intensity. If we overlook the possibility that some social systems may have elaborated initiation rites as dramatic ends in themselves and, as Yehudi A. Cohen[37] does, view those rites as strictly instrumental, then their high intensity in some communities indicates major discontinuities and anchorages. The rites are highly elaborated in order to deal with serious developmental problems. Where, precisely, might the discontinuity lie? In the emotional hold maintained by the immediate family; for initiation, in the course of promoting a child to advanced status, weakens his identification with his parents and siblings. It follows that small-scale social systems with extended kin groups that demand the growing individual's loyalty and responsibility would have clear need for dramatically propelled social launchings. Cohen finds that in fact they tend to have them, which is quite in accord with his

theory. Communities with extended kin groups arrange drastic initiatory procedures and stage them at the very earliest moment of puberty, roughly between 8 and 10 years, before profound physiological changes indicative of adulthood even begin to show. One way they push the boy toward wider social identification and obligations is by disrupting his customary relationships to his family, firmly dislodging him from the household, for example, by sending him to live in a youth house and activating a brother-sister avoidance that rigidly curtails social relations he formerly enjoyed with sisters. Initiation ceremonies and other treatment that arrests the inertia of customary behavior and pushes a person forward to new achievements in growth often appear harsh and painful to a cultural outsider, especially should he overlook how they may have been prepared for by earlier, nearly unrestricted gratification or how they usher in compensations for the person who grows through them.[38]

Adulthood and Aging. Following ado-

⟨ Samoa Patterns Continuity in Attitudes to Work

. . . our children are not made to feel that the time they do devote to supervised activity is functionally related to the world of adult activity. Although this lack of connection is more apparent than real, it is still sufficiently vivid to be a powerful determinant in the child's attitude. The Samoan girl who tends babies, carries water, sweeps the floor; or the little boy who digs for bait, or collects cocoanuts, has no such difficulty. The necessary nature of their tasks is obvious. And the practice of giving a child a task which he can do well and never permitting a childish, inefficient tinkering with adult apparatus, such as we permit to our children, who bang aimlessly and destructively on their fathers' typewriters, results in a different attitude towards work. . . .

So our children make a false set of categories, work, play, and school; work for adults, play for children's pleasure, and schools as an inexplicable nuisance with some compensations. These false distinctions are likely to produce all sorts of strange attitudes, an apathetic treatment of a school which bears no known relation to life, a false dichotomy between work and play, which may result either in a dread of work as implying irksome responsibility or in a later contempt for play as childish.[39]

MARGARET MEAD

lescence, growth calls the individual to meet important socially defined obligations: to select a spouse; start and maintain a family; rear children; adhere to satisfactory standards of family life; assume civic, military, or religious responsibilities, and, of course, execute his occupational role becomingly and successfully. Passing years bring the tasks of adjusting to middle and old age and accepting some degree of retirement, another serious discontinuity in some cultures. Characteristics of personality adopted much earlier contribute their influence to how adequately a person alters his behavior in aging and accepts the crises of aloneness, bodily change carrying loss of sexual vigor, and death. His identity changes as do even his recollections of the past.[40] In a community where the old are isolated, their aloneness allows them to adopt new personality patterns that sometimes are so far removed from social reality that they are taken as symptoms of mental illness. Observation of many aging people in an American city, all of whom enjoyed good health and had at least minimum funds needed for independence, reveals a mutual process of disengagement that detaches the aging person from others.[41] An engaged person interpenetrates his society and it enters him, defining and correcting his inner world of meanings and cueing his activities. He acts in many and quite varied roles, thereby successfully acknowledging social expectations. Disengagement frees him from society. Not only does he withdraw from playing many socially designed parts; society withdraws too as it relieves him of its norms and expectations—for example, favoring younger people for many powerful roles. The disengaged person relinquishes his achievement drive, which demands strong confidence in the future, and faces the task of finding attractive substitutes for the esteem and self-satisfaction that achievement earned him. Primarily he dis-

covers them in affectionate and expressive behavior to which others respond. Personal ties, especially to kindred, become more salient at the same time that distant and impersonal ties wane away. Because women throughout their life generally play more emotional and expressive roles than men, their transition to the expressiveness that comes with disengagement is easier. A woman can find more satisfactory role models for expressive acts among her own sex than her husband can find, for he is likely to see retired men—his principal role models—as tinged with failure. Everyone doesn't become disengaged in the same way, nor is the course followed by aging similar in every culture or for every person. Individuals who have participated intensely in roles that influence wide areas of society, or who possess rare skills, probably remain engaged longest.

Ego development

Ego development begins with birth, perhaps even before, its course being shaped by the balance of early gratifications and disappointments.[42] Fundamentally, ego strength rests on physical development, even on mundane physical endowments like vision, hearing, and mobility, capacities that allow the purposeful pursuit of things and people. It also depends on such acquired abilities as learning expertly to perceive and differentiate internal and external reality and communicating well, talents that strengthen the child's capacity to meet experience resourcefully. As the grows, his successful accomplishment of ever more goals heightens self-confidence, an asset which in turn endows him to meet further challenges. Throughout life, the ego's ability to manage reality depends on experiencing it; that is, on encountering actual situations that call for strength. A strong ego can thrive regardless of whether its owner is a hunter, farmer, warrior, or trader; it is independent of relative level of affluence, of degree of technical development, and of whether the social system is competitively, cooperatively, or individualistically organized.[43] A community, like that of the Zuni Indians or New Guinea Arapesh, that disallows self-maximizing tendencies simply cuts out achievement as a valid ego goal. On the other hand, a competitive social system provides the person with cultural mechanisms that communicate the psychological importance of achievement. Competition, however, isn't essential if an ego is to be patterned around achievement. The Ojibwa Indians and Eskimo, two individualistic and highly noncompetitive social systems, require as the price of ego development getting progressively out from under others' control and excelling in the use of supernaturally derived power (Ojibwa) or constantly polishing skill (Eskimo).

Superego control

Growing children learn to incorporate cultural values through example, as a result of positive and negative discipline applied by persons with whom they identify, and from their conceptions of the situations they confront. They also acquire a superego to insure that henceforth they themselves will live up to those values. The superego I have already described as a process whereby, when one has gone too far in accommodating forbidden impulses, moral pressure is directed against the ego in the form of pangs of conscience or shame. It includes a positive component, an appreciation for values that merit social approval, called the ego ideal. When the ego behaves in a manner conforming to the ego ideal, then it experiences a glowing feeling of pride transmitted by the superego. Biting shame

or guilt replaces pride when the ego, having defaulted and deviated from important values, falls short of its own image of goodness.

The strictness of the superego is held to depend on what happens in the family before puberty, chiefly in the first 6 or 10 years of life, with the sixth year being perhaps the critical one. Thereafter, the person subsumes more and more of his behavior in school, religion, politics, and economics under the earlier values he learned in his family.[44] Personally, I don't interpret this to mean that only values learned early in life are controlled by the superego. We internalize new values throughout life, and in that sense superego formation isn't once and for all completed. This gets at another aspect of superego formation; namely, its unintentional character. Many ego ideals are directly learned, but the superego in general is indirectly acquired by virtue of the context in which learning occurs; hence it varies from one culture to another.

Have you noted that in speaking about negative sanctions emanating from the superego, I carefully distinguished between guilt (conscience) and shame? I prefer to see both feelings as manifestations of the same process, though the dynamics of learning differ for each. Any circumstances that succeed in drawing children's attention to their own responsibility for making moral choices and require them to make restitution for wrongs they have committed encourage a quick sense of conscience. One very effective way of arousing such responsibility is to reason with a child and explain to him why an act is wrong, thus increasing his sensitivity to choose. Arbitrarily issuing demands to a child, unreasonably or authoritatively imposing orders on him, and using physical punishment when he has transgressed are more likely to instill strong fear of doing wrong than they are apt to stimulate him to make his parents' or the community's values his own.[45] Parents who themselves enjoy respect in the household, whose warmth and nurturance bind the child dependently to them, and who in his eyes can do no wrong, are better sources of conscience than nurses, governesses, or child-caretakers.[46] An affectionate, demonstrative mother encourages her children to identify with her and to become emotionally highly dependent on her. When she deliberately cuts off her customary warmth as a consequence of the youngster's disobedience, she painfully sanctions him for having deviated from her values. Thereby he learns to guard those values carefully and to manage himself vigilantly; he develops a strong, fully reliable superego. Things are otherwise in a colder, less permissive family where parents, due to their low-grade social and occupational statuses, are less idealized by their children. If severe physical punishment further counteracts the child's identification with such parents, then little urges him to make their values his own.[47]

Socialization may develop intense sensitivity to guilt, shame, or both.[48] In communities where only a few agents of socialization, like the parents, have charge of a child and directly punish him, people will have guilt-oriented superegos. Children learn to adopt the parents' moral role as well as the parents' values. Following a transgression they experience that role within themselves as condemnation. However, when a number of people take a hand in child's training or when his parents don't punish him directly but threaten that other agents, like masked kachinas, will do so, then he doesn't introject his parents' moral role. In place of guilt, his superego experiences painful anxiety lest other people who have witnessed or learn about his transgression will withdraw their approval. Observation and testing of children reared communally in an Israeli kibbutz by a series of changing nurses, teachers, and parents bear out the expected degree to which the kibbutz child perceives others in his group to be the most important agent of social con-

⟮ Social Personalities Vary in Ego Strength and Security[49]

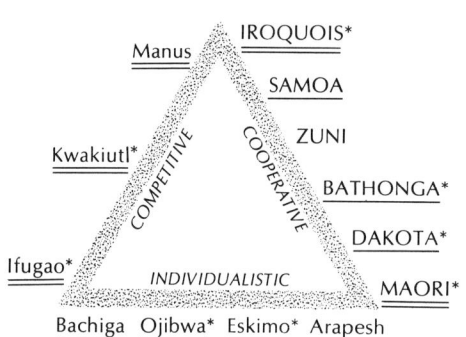

Double underlining shows high, or strong, ego development; single underlining, medium ego strength; no underlining, low ego strength. Capital letters indicate high psychological security; small letters, low security. (Note that all the cooperative communities are rated high in security.) An asterisk signifies that suicide is allowed.

Neither competitive, cooperative, or individualistic social structures bar development of a strong ego. Some people, like the competitive Kwakiutl and Philippine Ifugao, possess strong egos with limited psychological security whereas the cooperative Maori and aboriginal Iroquois Indians manifest both high ego strength and high security. Suicide is socially recognized as a valid means of coping under critical conditions in settings of both medium and high ego strength and high or low psychological security.

trol and fears their anticipated punishment. His superego evokes no burden of inner condemnation but dreads the disapproval and blame that his group will inflict.[50]

LEARNING TO DEFEND

The ego's resourcefulness in escaping conflicting pressures originates from within and without the organism, and depends partly on defensive mechanisms that it learns to employ. By age 6 Euroamerican children have autogenously developed most of the mechanisms employed by adults; that is, those that happen to be common to their culture.[51] Ensuing years enhance their ability to use them adroitly, skillfully, and not too obviously. How different defense mechanisms are learned has been revealingly explored through several experiments designed by a psychologist, Daniel R. Miller, and a sociologist, G. E. Swanson.[52] They studied the defensive techniques favored by early teenage, psychologically undisturbed boys in the seventh to ninth grades of schools located in the general area of Detroit. Also, they interviewed the boys' mothers to find out about earlier experiences on which adoption of favorite defense patterns might depend. Some defenses, the two men assume, require almost no previous skill, depend on responses present shortly after birth, but distort reality as the subjects ordinarily perceive it to a maximal extent. Mechanisms of this type have general applicability; that is, they are suited to all sorts of conflict, but, because of their high power to distort, their use creates serious social difficulties for the person who relies on them. Escape through fantasy and denial exemplify such easy defenses which Euroamerican society used mostly when other techniques prove unavailable. Another type of defense isn't so easy. It depends on having previously mastered complicated behavioral reactions, distorts reality less, and can be applied only

to specific kinds of conflict. A good example is displacing aggression against oneself when anger is really felt toward another person. Self-displaced hostility requires having first learned to appreciate being respected by others in a group which rigorously disallows aggression directed against its own members. Obviously, it is specifically limited to defending against conflict created by aggression, and its use in the U.S. middle class, at least, creates relatively few difficulties; in fact, by facilitating self-control it keeps a person from serious social difficulties. (Masturbation, conceived in somewhat unusual terms as sexuality displaced against the self, constitutes another nondistorting, advanced defense.) Miller and Swanson hypothesize that defenses of the first group will more often be favored by working-class boys and that middle-class youths will prefer those of the second type. Research, which cleverly utilized projective and paper-and-pencil tests, adequately bears our their expectation. Working-class boys in response to deliberately contrived, unavoidable failure on a paper-and-pencil test tended to deny they had erred, in that crude way defending against something worse that they feared might happen to them. Middle-class youths, on the other hand, tended purposefully to forget their failure, using repression as their characteristic type of defense. They accomplished the same end that they would have achieved through denial, but in a more acceptable way, without too seriously distorting reality. Middle-class youngsters asked to supply an ending to a story involving interpersonal conflict, showed much greater readiness to displace aggression from the original object to that character in the story to whom they identified. Their working-class peers, however, made less use of self-displacement as a technique of coping with hostility.

Why do different types of defense come to be favored in these two culturally different social classes? For one thing, middle-class families exact greater resourcefulness, initiative, and responsibility through socialization that relies heavily on identification and love-oriented techniques of punishment. They also demand more faithful adherence to an accurate perception of reality. Boys coming from this background have internalized a firmer ego-ideal, which they don't dare violate by directly venting aggression. Hence they seek a safe substitute for that disallowed tendency (something they are also likely to do in the case of sex), finding it in displacement. Likewise, they repress the knowledge that they did wrong rather than risk further disapproval by sloughing off responsibility and distorting reality through denial. Working-class boys are disciplined, often with the aid of harsh, corporal punishment, to obey parents' authoritarian orders. To escape punishment they readily deny wrongdoing, which is easy because their situation doesn't expect them to attend to reality as faithfully or as rigidly to inhibit aggression, the expression of which violates no egoideal and brings relatively little social disapproval.

ROLE BUILDING

Lifelong socialization, especially in a large-scale system, represents a long sequence of learning to play new roles appropriate to fresh statuses and to refurbish old roles as cultural conditions change. I have already recognized the importance of models in role building. It would seem that the larger and more shifting the array of persons who serve as models—the more mothers a girl sees, the more teen-agers a boy meets, the more physicians a medical student observes —the richer and more faceted will be his own respective role. Other components of a role require direct teaching: Somebody must instruct the teen-ager in a new dance and the would-be administrator takes a course in management. Roles also draw on

old learning and established habits first acquired in now outworn statuses but still helpful in enabling a person to cope in his new social niche. In addition to learning a role, people in a large-scale society must hear about available roles and the prerequisites they demand.[53] In small-scale homogenous communities practically all roles are socially inherited as a son follows his father's career; in the United States this happens with plumbing, for example, and in geographically localized careers, like coal mining. Other occupations, like boxing or dancing, recruit through the glamorous image with which they impress boys and girls, more strongly in certain social classes and ethnic groups than in others. Still other positions are filled by people drifting in from other jobs, which is how art students turn to teaching art. Technical development that expands the range of occupations in a previously homogeneous community—something that is happening among Eastern Arctic Eskimo—instigates this kind of secondary occupational recruitment, especially if requisite new skills can be learned through on-the-job practice. Schools in America recruit for many professions. Teachers arouse a student's interest in chemistry, anthropology, medicine, or biology; validate his talent; guide him to where he can secure further, professional training, and often help him secure financial assistance.

SEX ROLES

Socially patterned personality traits that distinguish men and women, Margaret Mead shows in *Sex and Temperament* and *Male and Female*, can be deliberately cultivated with their importance doubly underscored, or sex differences can be diminished and regarded as of practically no importance. The greatest differences in socialization between boys and girls occur in social systems where everyday occupations place a high premium on superior strength or superior development of motor skills.[54] Hunting large animals; grain rather than root-crop agriculture; domestication of large animals raised for themselves alone or for dairying, and nomadic pastoralism fall into this occupational category. Sex differences in socialization are also marked whenever people live in extended families that contain two or more generations, practice polygamy, or follow other customs likely to build up large, highly cooperative, composite households. However, when each nuclear family of husband, wife, and children lives alone, so that each spouse must on occasion be ready and able to assume the other's roles, then differences in the rearing of boys and girls go unemphasized. The contemporary United States possesses a highly mechanized technology that renders many tasks highly independent of physical strength. We also live in nuclear families isolated from other kin. Considering those two antecedent conditions, it follows that we should rear children with only slight regard for sex differences, especially in higher social strata where on-the-job brawn is seldom called for. Of course, we don't treat the sexes as precisely alike. The clothes boys and girls wear, interests adults encourage them to develop, attitudes parents teach, and occupations mentors hold out as most appropriate to one sex or the other communicate quite clearly that sex roles will in definite ways be different. Relatively small variations in early socialization begin to generate interests that lead to characteristic male and female styles of role playing. Play, for example, often affiliates a child with activities practiced by adults of his own sex.[55] Boys learn to be more assertive than girls if parents acquiesce when they refuse to do work their mothers and sisters do, and if, unlike girls who must return immediately from an errand or from school, they are allowed to tarry.[56] Household tasks en-

forced on small girls in many cultures begin to pattern their domestic interests, promoting their identification with women, and to restrict the situations available to them for wider learning.

SEXUAL IDENTITY

Sex typing, meaning visible differences in the conduct of boys and girls or men and women, rests on sexual identity. In a community that emphasizes sex differences, identification with one sex rather than the other usually begins to be learned very early, along with requisite attitudes for playing the appropriate sex roles. U.S. middle-class children however, especially girls, form their sexual identities more slowly than lower-class youngsters.[57] In fact, in some middle-class families, notably those where parents have had many years of schooling and in which parents don't portray themselves in highly contrasting sex roles, children shy away from adopting attitudes and interests traditionally appropriate to their sex and retain until adulthood their disinclination to do so.[58] Findings by psychologists confirm the uncertainty and diffuseness attached to learning a sexual identity in middle-class Americans, especially for boys.[59] Recently, however, we have learned of the special plight the lower-class Negro boy faces in a society controlled by middle-class values, and who grows up in a mother-centered, woman-dominated household.[60] To wean himself from the socially inappropriate identification formed with women, he adopts an exaggeratedly violent, ultramasculine stance that is apt to land him in other trouble. In an Israeli kibbutz, the communally reared boys also have little opportunity to observe adult males with whom they can identify. The adult males they most frequently see—their fathers—treat them little differently than do their mothers. Kibbutz girls also remain unclear about their sexual identities, though less so than boys. Apparently the lack of sexually different role models penalizes both sexes.[61] Feminine identification, the alluring attractiveness of the female role, in many parts of the world also confronts boys with a handicap that threatens their proper social development.[62]

I can't cite the frequency with which boys develop identity crises or compare them to girls' corresponding problems (like masculine protest) but I have facts to demonstrate that cultures likely to encourage boys' feminine identification also reveal traits, like frequent crime and theft and dramatic initiation ceremonies, that testify to boys' actual or potential conflicts over their sex identity.[63] In 48 social systems, as family arrangements likely to promote boys' feminine identification reduce opportunities for contact and identification between father and son, theft and personal crime (murder, rape, suicide, sorcery, and making false accusations) break out more frequently. The relationship traced in the United States between lower-class broken homes, in which the mother by herself rears her sons, and delinquency is consistent with that finding. The custom of a child sleeping with its mother for a year or so after birth, the father being ousted from his wife's bed, probably sets up a very strong identification of boys with their mother. Personal crime and theft occur more frequently where such sleeping arrangements are practiced. Potential conflict over feminine identification is also revealed by initiation ceremonies that take place at puberty, or shortly before, in which older males painfully haze a boy, perhaps mutilating his penis, while excluding women from the affair. Such ceremonies tend to flourish where an emotionally close relationship is fostered between mother and son; functionally speaking, they counteract boys' intense dependence on, and identification with, women.[64] Other devices also exist to wean the boy emotion-

ally; for example, he can be physically separated from his mother and put to live with a new male authority, like his mother's brother. Men's secret societies in Africa, Melanesia, Australia, and South America, whose hidden doings may never be seen by, or revealed to, women, periodically provide men with ceremonial opportunities to display their masculine identity, as if to assure them it is true.[65] Ceremonially, the society members express their opposition or antagonism to women, the musical instruments and secret paraphernalia they employ often possessing an unmistakably phallic character, through which they serve as props for the masculine ego. Myths allude to the time when men first asserted themselves, gaining their sexual identity at the same time that they escaped from female domination.

SEX

Freud[66] believes that following the phallic stage and on the heels of the Oedipus complex, sexual development comes to a standstill until puberty, though he admits that for development to stand still doesn't mean a complete loss of interest in sex or the total cessation of sexual activity. His admission is wise, judging from what anthropologists have learned. In the Trobriand Islands, for example, children before puberty actively engage in sexual exploration and experimentation, sex providing a major interest of the "junior republics" in which they play.[67] If they can't properly carry out coitus, even with initiatory help from an older companion, they can at least, directly and without disguise, pleasurably satisfy their curiosity and sensuality. No parent would dream of interfering in such amorous play so long as children show due discretion by not carrying it on in the house. In contrast to sexually permissive people like the Trobrianders, middle-class Euroamericans expect that sexual gratification will wait until marriage and actually contrive to make it difficult during the long premarital years. Whereas early sex play denotes a degree of symmetry between adults and children and encourages children's emotional independence, enforced sexual renunciation in the United States emphasizes a nearly unbridgeable gap between generations. For 20 years or more, from the cradle to college graduation, adults' watchful control over sex keeps young people mindful of their inferior power and supervised status. The psychosexual moratorium serves education, strengthening adults' power to establish whatever they want in children kept dependent and submissive for a long time.[68] Kiryat Yedidim, an Israeli kibbutz which deliberately preserves sexual freedom in early childhood, when adults candidly answer a child's sexual questions, strongly enjoins sexual intercourse in adolescence lest it distract the young people's interests and energies away from activities designed to prepare them for their future lives.[69] A child kept from gratifying his sexual impulses learns to look for gratification in other ways: by mastering things of which adults approve, by developing industriousness and application, and by devoting himself to the outside world.[70]

Whereas children in communities tolerant of sex play and premarital sexual relations learn about sex as they do about many activities, by playing at it and practicing it, in more restrictive social systems the period before puberty permits much more hidden learning, accomplished mainly through conversation with peers, humorous remarks, and pornographic pictures or graffiti.[71] Somehow such channels also manage to transmit favorite variations in sexual behavior that differentiate one social class from another, like a preference for nude intercourse, sexual relations only with the light out, or readiness to be erotically aroused by pictures of the sex act. Where people allow no sexual behavior until marriage, socialization in sex confronts parents with an unparalleled problem, for, since they are unable to offer any direct substitute form of gratification, their discipline must be entirely negative.[72] Euroamerican mothers don't even dare put a label on the behavior being socialized, on the emotional state of sexual arousal, or, in many cases, on the genitals. Since something named is easier to think and reason about and therefore to control, their muteness severely handicaps a young child who must learn to suppress his sexuality. Of course, youngsters soon devise their private labels, which often incorporate the conflictful idea that sex is dirty or allied with toilet functions. In a New England town, the strictest sex training came from mothers who were also severe or nonpermissive in other areas of behavior and, generally speaking, emotionally cold toward their children. Strongly antipathetic to childhood masturbation, they likewise severely toilet-trained their youngsters, frequently checked on their whereabouts, used physical punishment fairly often, tolerated little dependence, and emphatically demanded that a little girl adopt a clear-cut feminine role and a boy a masculine one. Somehow U.S. children nevertheless manage to learn from peers, books, movies, and even scholarly research that sex isn't only evil but "normal"—even glamorous and fun. By adolescence they have acquired a perception of premarital sex that doesn't unduly stress its dangerous consequences. Often with the tacit support of parents and other adults, and in spite of official morality, a number of young people in high school do have premarital relations, though not equally in all social classes.[73] Clearly, social values directed against premarital sexual gratification have not been well internalized by young people who decline any longer to postpone sexual gratification. What I have already said about dimensions of the parent-child relationship best calculated to implant a strong conscience is fully supported when it comes to sex. Girls with strong superegos, who are least likely to engage in premarital sex relations, incorporate conventional sexual norms introduced to them by warm and lenient mothers. The same norms taught by authoritarian parents or other adults who severely restrict a girl's freedom, who offer a minimum of warmth, and whose demeanor is rejecting are very poorly learned and don't suffice to restrain a girl from having premarital sexual relations.[74]

SERIOUS PLAY

Play, far from being a frivolous activity and passing time that might be more profitably employed, provides both children and adults with one of the most attractive methods of learning ever discovered. Through rulebound games as well as less rigorously regulated amusements, people assimilate values like giving and sharing, sharpen their ability to see themselves reflected in others' eyes, and win opportunities to try on the posture of leader as well as follower.[75] Imitative play gives children firsthand experience with enforcing and meeting adult values: "Don't be late!" "Be quiet!" "Be careful!" A child carves out his sex role through imaginatively enacting sex-typical adult statuses he has seen or heard about that serve his personal values. Play familiarizes the player with the huge inventory of a complex culture, allowing children from different backgrounds to experiment with unfamiliar heritages of experience that they never encounter at home.[76] Competitive sports teach competition, achievement, and hope, and give practice in dealing with victory, disappointment, and frustration. Games and play interpret life to a child, serving as models that replicate in understandable form the way his culture conceptualizes financial and other interpersonal relationships, strategies involved in war, and the nature of cultural differences (Indians *and* cowboys, Russians *and* Americans).[77] Many of my generalizations are illustrated in the single game of playing house, as actors mirror the dominant and submissive roles of parents and children; exert pressure to conform to parental values; practice buying, cooking, serving, and tasting food; care for children as nurturantly or impatiently as mothers at home; go to sleep and are aroused, and leave home to return with purchases or the rewards of labor.

Culturally significant activities that children pass over in their play provide insight into the emotional meanings attached to the culture for which they will some day be responsible. Manus children's activities in 1928 took few hints from admired areas of adult life.[78] Youngsters played like puppies or kittens: in rough-and-tumble fashion racing, punting, swimming, and playing tag or tug of war. They imitated the deliberate gestures of adults, hurled small wooden spears in imitation of adult warfare, and beat small drums. Mostly they followed unimaginative activities that taught them alertness, physical resourcefulness, and initiative, but that didn't feed thought or emulate adulthood. Children made little use of make-believe or pretense, except shortly after age 3 or 4, when boys were given little bows and arrows and small fish spears. Youngsters rarely sought to imitate adult ceremonies or other important elements in adult life. Rather than pushing to enter upon their future roles, they left those alone. When the time came for adolescents to assume adult responsibilities, they did so ungraciously and only under pressure of strong sanctions. Apparently the same hatred they felt toward the adult superstructure had led them as youngsters to refuse to reenact many adult roles, especially ceremonial ones. When Margaret Mead went back to Manus in 1953, she found youngsters' play much more imaginative.[79] She concluded that 25 years before, children's sense of an undesired, unlovable, and unfree future had oppressed and deterred them from emulating key roles in adult life. Since then, however, the Manus had built a new culture based on Western prototypes, in which children have acquired new zest and a sense of release which they reflect in their play.

Play is a projective activity, often consciously so, through which a person executes in fantasy what intrigues him or what he wants better to comprehend. When an adult does this—for example, trying out several openings of a talk he must give—any distinction between work and play dissolves. (For income-tax purposes it might be well not to admit too candidly when work is also a game!) Play acquires its projective potential because it isn't directly instrumental for survival and therefore need not adhere too closely to reality. Along with folktales, music, and religion, play belongs in the category of freely expressive behaviors, activities that nevertheless help persons to meet cultural pressures and conflicts.[80] Yet it doesn't wholly ignore reality but sensitively reflects changes in a way of life. In the Baffin Island town of Frobisher Bay I observed how teen-age and young adult Eskimo switched from an informal, individualistic form of baseball to another style that better reflected the newly created Eskimo townsmen's dependence on rules and formal organization.[81] In the traditional game, as many men and boys played on each of two sides as wanted to. Even boys 7 or 8 could claim a turn at bat and men in their forties joined in on Sunday afternoon. As each player took his turn, he swung at the ball as many times as he needed in order to get a hit. Nobody struck out. In fact, there was no umpire. After hitting the ball, unless it was caught before it bounced, the batter ran in a clockwise direction around the field from

A Frobisher Bay Eskimo girl seriously engrossed in play.

first, to second, to third base, and then home. To be put out of the game, he had to be tagged by the ball itself while he was off base, either when it was held in an opponent's hands or when it was thrown and hit him as he elusively dodged from the safety of one base to another. Each side played until all its players had been eliminated, after which, the other side finally got its turn at bat. Players kept no score, indicating that they didn't think of the sides as corporate groups that won or lost. When daylight failed or too many players had quit to meet some other responsibilities, the game ended. Contrary to the opinion of Eurocanadians who watched this game,

Eskimo ballplayers of Frobisher Bay.

"Eskimo baseball" had rules, but compared to official baseball they were few, broadly defined, and not strenuously insisted upon. In those respects, as well as in the game's tolerance of players of all ages, it reflected and taught the informality characteristic of traditional Eskimo culture. Once the young men began to play regulation baseball, rules became paramount. An official rulebook turned up, and the players referred difficult questions to it. They learned to respect the rules and tried to apply them faithfully, aided by an umpire. They learned to run in a counterclockwise direction around the diamond. Playing for the sake of playing and for individual success in escaping being tagged by almost any means gave way to playing in order that the team as a whole might score. The premium on skill converted ball playing into a relatively closed game, limited to nine men on a side Whereas formerly nobody evaluated a prospective player's skill, now the teams sought to recruit men with expertise. Youngsters of 8 or 9 could hardly compete with young

adults who had learned the game in southern schools or, in one case, a reformatory. A Eurocanadian umpire and coach criticized the players' skill, bringing to the playing field the dominant role Eurocanadians possess in administration, employment, and education. Plainly the formalism enveloping Eskimo who participate in town life had also entered a game that Eskimo long ago borrowed and reinterpreted to suit traditional values in their culture. Now it was once again transformed to give practice in other principles and values belonging to an evolutionarily new phase of that culture.

The extent to which play reflects culture shows up in the way competitive games systematically vary from one type of culture to another.[82] Games that encourage competition but limit it to agreed-upon rules fall into several classes. Some are games of physical skill; their outcome depends on the players' physical activities. Games of strategy, on the other hand, put a premium on choosing rationally among possible courses of action. Outcomes of games of chance rest wholly on smartly guessing, or simply on the throw of dice or the reading some other artifact gives. Games of physical skill don't correlate neatly with any particular kind of culture. Games of strategy, however, since they simulate social interaction (chess, for example, resembles war), tend to appear only in social systems complexly enough organized to offer something to be projected into play. Games of chance utilize prevailing ideas of supernatural power and feelings of dependence on that power. People whose deities are unpredictably benevolent or coercive favor games of chance. Both games of strategy and games of chance allow the escape of tension; in the first, tension engendered by the uncertainties of complex social interdependencies; in the second, by uncertainty as to deities' benevolence or coercion. Pressure and conflict created through socialization likewise express themselves, as if through safety valves, in specific types of adult games.[83] In communities where mentors demand achievement and punish nonachievement, games of physical skill that sometimes involve elements of strategy hold an important place. Baseball illustrates play of this sort. People prefer games of strategy in complexly organized social systems that, like the Hopi, strongly sanction obedience in child training. Finally, games of chance occur predominantly among people like the Samoans, who demand and reward responsibility, often for routine chores, and fear too much straining to achieve.

FURTHER READING

Orville G. Brim, Jr. reports on a conference deliberation on "Socialization Through the Life Cycle" (1964). Participants concluded that socialization after childhood often deals primarily with overt role behavior and attempts little to influence fundamental motives or basic values. See also Brim's recently published book on adult socialization (1966). In chapter 6 of *Revolution in Psychiatry* (1964), Ernest Becker reflects on the relationship of earlier to later learning. Several papers in the *International Social Science Journal* (vol. 15, no. 3) pertain to personality change in aging, as do many chapters in Richard H. Williams *et al.*, eds., *Processes of Aging* (1963), and Bernice L. Neugarten, *Personality in Middle and Late Life* (1964). For a fine guide to a variety of concepts pertaining to later learning, including ego formation and sextyping, see Boyd R. McCandless, *Children and Adolescents* (1961). Albert Bandura and Richard H. Walters, in *Social Learning and Personality Development* (1963), extensively review self-control learning; Robert A. LeVine, in "Political Socialization and Culture Change" (1963b), draws attention to the family's role in developing motives favorable to political stability, his data pertaining mainly to Africa; and Roger Brown devotes chapters 5–8 of *Social Psychology* (1965) to tracing the acquisition of intelligence, language, and morality. Problems connected with sex-role identification are reviewed in a symposium published in the *Merrill-Palmer Quarterly* (1964, 10: 3–50). "Youth and the Political System," by David Easton and Robert D. Hess (1961), examines the relatively untouched topic of political socialization, for which also see Fred I. Greenstein, *Children and Politics* (1965). *In Alienation and Freedom* (1964), Robert Blauner describes socialization at work in an industrial context—the factory, while Ernestine Friedl, in "Lagging Emulation in Post-Peasant Society," notes how Greek farmers adopt obsolescent, urban elite behavioral models. Stanley Elkins, "Slavery and Personality" (1961), reviews psychologically relevant literature dealing with personality in concentration camps. For other examples of such literature, see Bruno Bettelheim, *The Informed Heart* (1960), Elie A. Cohen, *Human Be-*

havior in the Concentration Camp (1953), and Primo Levi, *If This Is a Man* (1959). Many chapters in Philip Worchel and Donn Byrne, eds., *Personality Change* (1964), deal with personality formation and reformation in adulthood. Books describing the experiences of foreign students abroad provide much data into later-life socialization; see, for example: Ralph L. Beals and Norman D. Humphrey, *No Frontier to Learning* (1957), dealing with Mexican students in the United States; John W. Bennett, H. Passin, and R. K. McKnight, *In Search of Identity* (1958); Cora A. Dubois, *Foreign Students and Higher Education in the United States* (1956); Richard D. Lambert and Marvin Bressler, *Indian Students on an American Campus* (1956); Richard T. Morris, *The Two-Way Mirror* (1960), a comparative study; Franklin D. Scott, *The American Experience of Swedish Students* (1956); and John Useem and Ruth Hill Useem, *The Western-Educated Man in India* (1955). There is practically no end to the books that account for learning in later life in industrial, bureaucratic, hospital, and many other contexts of Euroamerican society.

REFERENCES

1 Cited in Bloch, 1953: 35.
2 In this section I have drawn heavily upon, and interpreted Inkeles, 1953; Inkeles and Levinson, 1954; Lindesmith and Strauss, 1950; Little, 1950, and G. D. Spindler, 1955: 182–183. See also Barnouw, 1963: chap. 10; J. J. Honigmann, 1961b: 125–128. For Soviet Russian reactions, see Dunn, 1965.
3 Horney, 1939: chap. 3.
4 *Cf.* Ericson, 1946–1947; Maccoby and Gibbs, 1954.
5 Bruner, 1956a and 1956b.
6 Sears, 1963.
7 M. Mead, 1955a: 8.
8 Orlansky, 1948 and 1949.
9 *Cf.* L. B. Murphy, 1962: 295–297. E. Becker (1962b) considers the same criticism directed against an aggressive drive, one I did not specifically consider in the previous chapter.
10 M. Mead, 1954c.
11 Brodersen, 1957: 98.
12 Kuhn, 1962; Polanyi, 1962: chap. 10.
13 Rogers, 1965.
14 Popper, 1957.
15 Potter, 1954; M. Mead, 1954c: 397 and 1965b: 3.
16 *Cf.* Sapir, 1929.
17 See Theodore D. Graves' review of Victor Barnouw's book *Culture and Personality* in the *American Anthropologist*, 1964, 66: 483–484; see also J. J. Honigmann, 1961b: 126–128.
18 C. W. M. Hart, 1955.
19 Lévy-Bruhl, 1926: 36–37.
20 Sahlins and Service, 1960: 89.
21 Wiebe, 1958.
22 Fenton, 1957; Leis, 1964.
23 Generalization based on Campbell, 1943; Goldfrank, 1945; Holzinger, 1961; and G. D. Spindler, 1955: 182–183. Other sources will also be cited.
24 D. C. Leighton and Kluckhohn, 1947.
25 Spiro, 1965: chap. 16.
26 E. Beaglehole, 1944; E. Beaglehole and Beaglehole, 1946.
27 Underwood and Honigmann, 1947.
28 Geertz, 1961: 116, 146–153.
29 Straus, 1954.
30 Kagan and Moss, 1962: 271.
31 Klapp, 1962 and 1964.
32 They don't among the Rajputs of Khalapur, for example; see Minturn and Hitchcock, 1963: 331.
33 Havighurst, 1952: chaps. 3–5.
34 Rabin, 1961.
35 R. Benedict, 1938; Kneller, 1965. See, however, the discussions by Bealer, Willits, and Maida, 1964; Josselyn, 1964.
36 J. Henry, 1960: 292–294.
37 Y. A. Cohen, 1964. For other psycho-

logical explanations of puberty and initiation ceremonies, see J. W. M. Whiting, Kluckhohn, and Anthony, 1958; Stephens, 1962; Young, 1962; M. Mead, 1949b: 88.

38 M. Mead, 1952b: 435.

39 M. Mead, 1928a: 227–228. By permission of William Morrow and Co., Inc.

40 Butler, 1963.

41 E. Cumming, 1963; E. Cumming and Henry, 1961.

42 Josselyn, 1955: chaps. 10–11.

43 M. Mead, 1961a: 485–496.

44 Sears, Maccoby, and Levin, 1957: chap. 10.

45 Shoben, 1963.

46 M. Mead, 1942a: 128–129; Whiting in Tanner and Inhelder, 1956–1960, II: 199–202; Bateson, 1942–1943: 78.

47 See Langner and Michael, 1963: 459–464.

48 Much of what follows derives from Spiro, 1965: chap. 15. See also M. Mead, 1961a: 494–505, 518–519; Piers and Singer, 1953; J. W. M. Whiting and Child, 1953: 262; Lynd, 1958: chaps. 1–2.

49 M. Mead, 1961a: 497.

50 Samoan children also appear to be less ruled by conscience than U.S. caucasoid youngsters, according to results reported by Grinder and McMichael, 1963.

51 Prugh, 1960: 280.

52 D. R. Miller and Swanson, 1960.

53 Strauss and Rainwater, 1962.

54 Barry, Bacon, and Child, 1957.

55 Mussen, Conger, and Kagan, 1963: 269–270.

56 Y. A. Cohen, 1956.

57 McCandless, 1961: 332–333.

58 Kagan and Moss, 1962: 171; *cf.* Sears, Maccoby, and Levin, 1957: 384–385.

59 Kagan and Moss, 1962: 171.

60 See, for example, Rovere, 1965; Rohrer and Edmonson, 1960: 160–162.

61 Spiro, 1965: 236–243. On the special difficulty boys face in establishing sexual identity, see Lynn, 1961.

62 *Cf.* Bettelheim, 1954.

63 Bacon, Child, and Barry, 1963.

64 J. W. M. Whiting, Kluckhohn, and Anthony, 1958. For additional work on initiation ceremonies in socialization, see J. W. M. Whiting's (1961) summary discussion and the references he cites. Also see Bettelheim, 1954; Norbeck, Walker, and Cohen, 1962; Y. A. Cohen, 1964; Turner, 1964; J. W. M. Whiting, 1964; Young, 1962 and 1965; DeVos and Hippler (in press). Girls' puberty rites apparently serve quite a different function from boys', judging from Central Africa where they correlate with matrilineal organization and glorifying the role of the nubile girl, therefore reinforcing her sense of feminine identity; see Richards, 1956.

65 R. F. Murphy, 1959.

66 Freud, 1935: 286.

67 Malinowski, 1927: 49–58.

68 J. Henry, 1949.

69 Spiro, 1965: 328, 333, 347–349.

70 Erikson, 1963.

71 Kinsey, Pomeroy, Martin, and Gebhard, 1953: chap. 16.

72 Sears, Maccoby, and Levin, 1957: chap. 6.

73 Vincent, 1961: 8–12, 244.

74 *Ibid.,* p. 181.

75 Cooley, 1902; G. H. Mead, 1934; *cf.* Erikson, 1963: 219 ff.

76 O. W. Ritchie and Koller, 1964: chap. 14.

77 P. Cooper, 1965.

78 M. Mead, 1934.

79 M. Mead, 1956c: 364–368.

80 Roberts *et al.,* 1959.

81 J. J. Honigmann and Honigmann, 1965.

82 Roberts *et al.,* 1959.

83 Sutton-Smith *et al.,* 1963.

Cultural Psychiatry

11

. . . it may be that they are luckier,
Now steeled by so impervious a trance
Against all searing passions that recur,
And the cold scrutiny of circumstance. . . .[1]

NATHANIEL THORNTON

Only in those cases in which the
environment acts with different intensity
or perhaps even in different directions
upon the organism may we expect
increased unlikeness under the same
environmental conditions. When, for
instance, for one individual the margin of
safety is so narrow that the environmental
conditions are excessive, for another one
so wide that adequate adjustment is
possible, the former will become sick,
while the other will remain healthy.[2]

FRANZ BOAS

"ILLNESS" IMPLIES TOO MUCH

Some time ago my reading confronted me with an important choice. I had to decide if mental illness was indeed "illness" in the usual sense of the word, or if the term simply provided a convenient, not very thoughtful label—possibly a metaphor—for disordered behavior, and didn't at all mean to place depression and chronic alcoholism in the same semantic category with tuberculosis, malaria, and cancer. Yet even metaphorically, consistently labeling conditions as diverse as chronic alcoholism, depression, and malaria "illness" might readily cause them to be regarded as all quite similar. Were they similar in any more significant way than conventionally warranting attention by a medical doctor? Semanticists, I recalled with something of a jolt, predict that when we give things the same name we soon tend to treat them alike, however different in fact closer examination would show them to be. I thought about this issue, listened attentively to arguments,[3] and decided, without firmly committing myself, to be wary of terms like "mental illness" and "psychiatric disturbance." My position, therefore, isn't as extreme as that of Thomas S. Szasz, a psychiatrist, who titled his book *The Myth of Mental Illness.*

Thinking about some forms of human

320

behavior as though they were illness obscures whatever may be a person's responsibility for them. His "responsibility," I believe, would be quite different if his psychotic actions were due to constricted arteries that failed to supply the brain with sufficient blood rather than due to having too often sought solace in drugs or alcohol; hence I unhesitatingly call the former state "illness." Like any categorization, labeling behavior as illness begins to explain; it sees the patient victimized by something that happened to him. Psychiatric theory makes very explicit the patient's passive role in "falling" sick and, sometimes, even in recovering. The interpretation many people attach to the label *illness* carries even more unfortunate implications. Implicitly and quite fallaciously we assume that someone who is sick can't be socially useful, and that what is a symptom doesn't deserve serious consideration. The label carries weighty consequences, some of which might be better avoided. It excuses ousting a nonconformist; if he is sick then we need not accept him as we would somebody who is well. Calling it illness allows a person troubled with dread to enter the security-giving confines of the sick role, permits a murderer to escape execution and one kind of imprisonment, and excuses certain ill-advised actions, thereby thankfully relieving the actor himself as well as his teachers, parents, and friends of responsibility and embarrassment. Clearly, such unintended blessings give the nomenclature advantages, though nobody wants to justify scholarly classification by extraneous public utility.[4] But the consequences might be outrightly undesirable. The illusion that he is ill may seduce an individual into socially negligent behavior or provide an easy rationalization for illegitimate deviance. "We're disturbed, we're disturbed, we're the most disturbed," sing the young delinquents in *West Side Story*. "We never had the love that every child oughta get." A diagnosis of psychi-

Thomas S. Szasz

atric illness carries a risk for the patient if it slows down his recovery from whatever troubles him by restricting his treatment to scarce medical specialists, by enforcing a passive role on him (after all, a patient with a high malarial fever *can't* do much for himself), and by esoteric therapeutic explanations that reduce his knowledgeable participation.[5] Viewing behavior as illness warrants hospitalizing the patient, whose treatment then takes place under highly artificial circumstances rigidly separated from his everyday social relationships. Yet, psychiatric disorder primarily exists in relation to such relationships, and the patient must somehow learn new behavior patterns that will enable his return to them. Is the hospital an effective setting in which to manage such new learning?[6]

Sometimes, in order to warn myself and

my readers away from undesirable connotations of the terms "illness" and "psychiatric disorder," I speak of "personality disorder." (That term, I hope, will not be confused with the psychiatric symptom pattern bearing the same name.[7]) "Disorder," an evaluative term, has its own shortcomings. Disorder seen from another vantage point becomes a highly personal kind of order, one unrelated to the requirements of the world, yet capable of easing life under loads of stress that the person can't handle in socially more acceptable ways. Or, as O. H. Mowrer says, personality disorder represents an unconscious effort to bring about personal change and growth.[8]

ECOLOGY AND EPIDEMIOLOGY

Fish, pine trees, and people cluster together more or less thickly and vary in other characteristics from one point in geographical space to another, though not always constantly through time. *Ecology* investigates such variability to learn why it occurs. Personality disorder wears a different look, changes its content, and varies in frequency from one point in social and cultural space to another. For example, in the United States if a psychiatrist ranks his cases by social class, he will more frequently recognize more seriously disturbed persons as he goes down the social ladder, in the process also encountering increasing poverty and shorn prestige. *Epidemiology*, which is actually a special type of ecology, counts cases and proposes to explain why such variability occurs and what may be its historical course.*

Cultural psychiatry (also known as social and transcultural psychiatry[12]) goes beyond counting, plotting, and statistically manipulating numerical data. It also looks for qualitative patterns of personality disorder: how in one setting depression and blame point inward against the self while in another blame and anger are paranoiacally turned outward against others; how under excessive loads of stress people unconsciously choose more or less respectable incapacities with which symbolically to appeal for help, or how through history strain manifests itself in various guises. Holding fast to an ecological approach, cultural psychiatry explains frequencies and patterns of disorder as consistently as possible in cultural terms, noting the cultural backgrounds of both psychiatrist and patients. The ultimate goal is etiology, knowledge of the factors, especially cultural ones, that influence the onset and course of personality disorders. Cultural psychiatry remains individual-centered even while exploring health-relevant conditions in society. Its aim is to discover cultural patterns that help or injure persons, affect individuals' performance, or encourage personality conflict. The investigators hope that their professional competence will lend them enough authority to make administrators, teachers, managers, legislators, and courts heed their recommendations. In a social psychiatric frame of action, social scientists helped strike down legal segregation in the

---

* Epidemiology employs two main measures: (1) By counting all persons who enter treatment or a hospital during an extended period of time, usually a year, it estimates the *incidence* of disorder in a community. (2) By counting all cases extant at a specific time, regardless of their duration, it estimates *prevalence* of disorder. Two main techniques allow prevalence to be gauged: (1) On a certain date take a census of all persons from the community being treated by private physicians, clinics, or hospitals, as was done in the New Haven study,[9] or (2) much more ambitiously, like the Midtown Manhattan study,[10] carry on a house-to-house community census that incorporates a diagnostic interview, thus obtaining information about actual, not merely treated prevalence. Understandably, researchers may count both actual and treated prevalence, which is precisely what the Midtown Manhattan group did.[11]

United States, and in other ways have contributed to cultural reforms in factories, institutions, schools, and local communities.

Logically, the extent and gravity of personality disorders in any social system depend on a judgment made by authoritative specialists, such as priests and psychiatrists. Broadly speaking, such judgments follow two courses. In the first, a diagnostician deals with symptoms and asks, In which ready-made disease category does the pattern of symptoms fit—schizophrenia, anxiety neurosis, or possession by devils?[13] New methods, standards, and categories for diagnosis—as well as a greater readiness to diagnose relatively mild disorders—and other differences in procedure between practitioners carry vast implications for epidemiology because they bring about apparent increases or decreases in the frequency of disorders.[14] If diagnostic methods vary between communities, then so will the frequency of disorders.[15] When authorities cease to call something illness, then that "illness" disappears from history, or at least it appears less frequently, as recorded occurrence of dysmenorrhea (painful menstruation) has declined since the century's early decades. Does this indicate that menstrual pain has also decreased? Or has it perhaps increased, despite the fact that it has become harder to draw official recognition to it? The second approach to judging personality disorder dispenses with nosology, (the classification of diseases). As currently exemplified, an existential psychiatrist refuses to impute properties to man. When his attention is drawn to a disorder, he seeks to understand it phenomenologically, that is, from the standpoint of the troubled individual. He takes into account the situation as the other conceives it, together with the goals for which the other strives. What is really happening in the subject, or going through him? How does he feel? Insofar as possible, disorder is apprehended from within the world of the other, personally rather than impersonally, and without prejudgments.[16]

SICK CULTURES?

Does psychiatry only investigate difficulties besetting individuals? Does it—can it—also conceive of disordered social systems, detect what historical forces have twisted their cultures, and then apply its knowledge through cultural reforms urged upon lawmakers? One highly psychoanalytical minded anthropologist assures us that we might as readily treat culture as a person, for both use symbol systems containing hypotheses about reality that function to allay anxiety, and both must, whether they like it or not, periodically test those symbol systems against the real world. Such testing will show that, despite their having arisen in response to concerted efforts to solve human problems, cultures contain suicidally lethal traits, inadequacies, ineptitudes, inhumanities, and hostilities that jeopardize the community's survival. Therefore, like mental patients, communities sometimes fail to live effectively; their cultures increase rather than allaying anxiety.[17] We know communities that have culturally perfected their abilities to maintain peak levels of hostility and anxiety: Dobu, Alor, the Stalinist Soviet Union, and Kaingang come immediately to mind. Harold Lasswell[18] sees nations fumbling through international dealings with impaired reality testing, uncertainty concerning their own strength, and anxiety revealed in paranoiac international suspicion.

Accepting such judgments, what can anyone do about disordered social systems, short of collecting them as dependencies (which may call for ruinous wars), with the intention of becoming their enlightened ruler? Perhaps Lasswell means that dangerous national styles of international relations are the collective products of individual personality disorder. Then questions follow fast: In whom is such disorder localized? In those alone who shape international policy or also in citizens who, having conferred authority on their presidents and foreign ministers, trust and obey the latter? Or in both? Is everyone equally disturbed? That won't be easy to prove, and it contradicts the fact that, unlike an impaired clinical patient, the national community manages many areas of life effectively. It gives evidence of some stable, happy individuals —or are we too blind to admit that? Even Richard Brickner in his alarming book *Is Germany Incurable?* (published in the emotional period following America's entry into World War II) warned that "When we speak of Germany as a paranoid society we do not mean that every German is paranoid." Simply lack of reliable, clinical evidence should restrain us from irascibly condemning cultural characteristics we deplore by ascribing them to psychiatrically disturbed people.[19] When we criticize culture in that way we shamefully betray the way we devalue and cast out the mentally ill, who, after all, are capable of enriching our lives.[20] Logically, we have absolutely no defense once we succumb to the eternally tempting fallacy of disposing of disputes over morality or aesthetics by branding as noble or ignoble the sources whence they spring. Our own standards may then be similarly impugned.

Following a more sophisticated theory, Erich Fromm[21] points out that every social system commits itself to a fateful choice when it selects from the broad range of possible human strivings a few that it makes dominant in its culture. Unfortunately, those chosen sometimes prevent the community's members from developing to full, human maturity, because they deprive people of realizing freedom, spontaneity, and general expression of self. A social-system that has chosen its major ends unwisely sows grave defects in many people's personalities. True, its culture will probably

also provide immunizing patterns of behavior that allow living with those defects, which consequently don't always show up as serious neurotic or psychotic symptoms. Nevertheless, they warp and cripple so that members never achieve optimal mental health: That is, people lack ability to love and to be creative; they can't emancipate themselves from "incestuous ties to clan and soil"; they suffer from want of a true sense of identity based on experiencing themselves as the subjects and agents of their own powers; and they fall short in developed objectivity and reason. Persons of great sensitivity and integrity feel unsatisfied with such immunizing patterns. A sane society's culture, Fromm claims, corresponds to the true, objective needs of man (not necessarily to what he feels to be his needs, because even the most pathological aims can be felt to be desirable). That our society is unhealthy he sees proven by the high rates of psychiatric disturbances and homicide and the way our prosperity leaves people fundamentally unsatisfied, because their basic human strivings—those enumerated above—have been neglected. Fromm calls attention to two important topics: first, to the cultural sources of personality disorder; and, second, to cultures so designed by their makers that they forestall adequate satisfaction in many areas of life. Fromm and other humanistic social critics[22] perpetuate this stream of thought while other social scientists emphasize poverty and similarly objective noxious conditions that make up socially disintegrated communities, and that by forestalling human happiness likewise have repercussions in personality disorder and other forms of deviance.

PSYCHOTIC, CHILD, AND PRIMITIVE

We move by degree from what we unhesitatingly call "normal" to what everyone would agree is unmistakably a disordered

Since the paranoid emotional core has been growing in German culture for at least five generations, many of its spokesmen who will testify here have been dead a long time. That, however, does not damage the value of what General X, Professor Y, and Journalist Z said. The emotional content of a paranoid patient's conversation with his psychiatrist—checked with the reports of the patient's associates—is ample data for identifying his trouble. The patient may be counted on to make it symptomatically clear how he gets on with others.

It does not matter in the least whether Nietzsche, Wagner, Wilhelm II, and von Treitschke were paranoids as individuals, although at least three of them "feel" most suspicious. The point is that, using the emotional idiom steadily developing in their environment, they were both expressing and adding fuel to tendencies that, however often present as sporadic deviations in other cultures, had become *fundamental* in the German culture.

Remember that the diagnosis of paranoia must depend strictly on descriptive data—on what the patients says, what he indicates he would like to do, what he actually does. It is no less accurate for all that. These Germans' testimony is *illustration* of a tendency—a tendency finally so strong that, for any reader who has made the acquaintance of the individual paranoid, only one conclusion is possible.

Listen, for example, to the voice of Johann Gottlieb Fichte, first Rector of the University of Berlin, sometimes called "Germany's first nationalist": ". . . neither law nor right exists except the right of the strongest. These relations place in the hands of the prince responsible to Fate the divine right of the Majesty of Destiny and of the Government of the world and exalt him above the precepts of individual morality into a superior moral order." Fichte makes no bones about his opinion as to who deserves the rights of the strongest: "If you [the German people] sink into the depths, the whole of humanity sinks with you without hope of eventual restoration."

To von Treitschke, weakness is "the most abject and the most despicable" of all political crimes—"the crime against the Holy Ghost of politics." Since the state cannot recognize any power above itself, it is morally justifiable for it to sign all treaties with this mental reservation.

That bourgeois morality with its conception of the rights of other nations must never stand in the way of Germany's triumphal progress was quite overtly recognized. Joseph Reimer, the Pan-German, expressed it ominously in 1905: "Do not say that every people has a right to its existence, its speech, etc. By making play with this principle, one may put on a cheap appearance of civilization, but only as long as the people in question does not stand in the way of any more powerful people."

Ernst Hasse, a Reichstag deputy, "master mind" of the Pan-German League and editor, wrote in 1907 that Germany needed war because she was "encircled by enemies! That's what we have been since the beginning. We have suffered more from this situation than any other people in Europe." Paranoids have always suffered more than anybody else.

This encirclement motif struck a fundamental chord in the hearts of paranoid-tending Germans, as it well might, considering the fundamental nature of its paranoid appeal. It follows from paranoid reasoning that all nations are potential, if not yet actual, enemies. Evidence of secret hostile plots is constantly being unearthed.

The outside world is well acquainted with the Nazis' use of projection. At the time of the Czech crisis, for example, the Berlin papers shrieked: "BLOODY REGIME —NEW CZECH MURDERS OF GERMANS, EXTORTION, PLUNDERING, SHOOTING—CZECH TERROR IN SUDETENLAND GROWS WORSE FROM DAY TO DAY!" And at Poland's eleventh hour: "ANSWER TO POLAND, THE RUNNER-AMOK AGAINST PEACE AND RIGHT IN EUROPE!" "WARSAW THREATENS BOMBARDMENT OF DANZIG!" "UNBELIEVABLE AGITATION OF THE POLISH ARCH-MADNESS . . . !"

personality. Somewhere along the road we encounter transitory, paranormal states, tolerated or even cultivated in otherwise normal people as they erupt from the flat plain of ordinary existence. I speak of trances, episodes of possession, and paranormal states deliberately stimulated by fasting, alcoholic intoxication, psychedelic drugs, and other mind-changing substances. Often such states form integral parts of ceremonies, serving simultaneously as both emotional outlets and socially integrating devices.[24] A vivid mystical experience in which a believer harbors a divine presence or confronts a power-conferring vision is no ordinary event, but neither does it conform to the persistent, emotional, and cognitive impairment found in personality disorder.

Some elements in personality disorder superficially resemble certain commonplace customs of small-scale exotic cultures and the thinking processes of children: Objects possess life or dreadful potency; strangers are enemies; and magical talismans quell anxiety. Far from having gone unnoticed, such analogies have been inflated into a theory claiming that psychotics idiomatically misrepresent the world because they share with children a too unrestrained readiness to fall into a "paleological" mode of thought such as comes down to us from early man.[25] Small-scale, non-Western people, the theory explains, never having felt the power of Aristotelian logic, still regularly think that way. Western man,

recognizing that A cannot be non-A and A simultaneously, generally organizes his thoughts along evolutionarily more advanced, logically sterner lines. This theory fails to recognize that most people are capable of dealing with the same facts on different levels; by using different concepts they show up other aspects of the same reality, just as changing one's physical position reveals surprising shapes belonging to the same mountain. A woman can be a man's mother-in-law at the same time that she is a witch given to secret nocturnal visitations and mischief. When a Melanesian calls her a witch, he no more follows a unique logic than does the cartoonist who depicts the stereotyped mother-in-law as a termagant. Neurotic or psychotic thinking is clearly something else. Nor can the mental patient be said to have regressed to childhood.[26] Though his helplessness approaches that of a child, his life is based on infinitely richer experiences.[27]

A DIFFICULT JUDGMENT

Communities vary in how they recognize and deal with personality disorder. In Euroamerican society, judgments of mental illness are complex, upsetting, and for emotional reasons often difficult to make. Such a decision can hardly be formulated without implying that the person whom it covers has behaved undesirably as well as abnormally.[28] Depending on circumstances, relatives and friends greet the decision with varying degrees of readiness, worry, pity, annoyance, morbid fear, disgust, relief, or an ambivalent mixture of such emotions. It is as if we perceive an insidious threat in unconformity, especially in the fact that it destroys a measure of social consensus. We have extraordinarily little tolerance for private reaction patterns; they affect us the way a schoolboy's Beatle haircut annoyed teachers to the point where they secured court orders to enforce conformity. We welcome at the same time that we deplore the disordered person's removal to an institution, and we console ourselves (without knowing all the facts) that there he will be protected from injuring himself and others while receiving treatment. The remote location of such institutions, away from population centers, symbolizes the degree to which we cast out such nonconformists from society. Very likely, a patient who perceives the unpleasant consequences that such a judgment concerning him entails, won't concur in it, and his refusal creates a threat to his liberty that further complicates an already difficult matter. Hence the complicated process of commitment, resembling the trial whereby society ascertains a criminal's guilt before putting him in a penitentiary. As in criminal proceedings, sufficient wealth and legal talent enable some people successfully to refute society's professionally informed judgment that they are "mentally sick."

Mostly, we entrust a psychiatrist with power to judge personality disorder, and courts, families, and social agencies call on him to confirm their suspicion or allay their anxiety. In his diagnosis he relies on specialized knowledge and consults a clinical psychologist, who, striving for as high a degree of objectivity as possible, administers a battery of tests presumed to be reliable tools for measuring the subject's position on either side of the line that separates normality from mental illness. Such tests, however, aren't as objective or valid as one might think. Most disquietingly, middle-class persons often score better on them—that is, farther from the point registering serious disorder—than lower-class persons; sometimes appreciably so. This hints that clinical testing like intelligence testing (both are often combined) embodies subtle middle-class prejudices of what constitutes appropriate emotional and social behavior. After the psychiatrist has examined the person, consulted the psychologist's report, and talked to the person's associates, he renders his professional judgment, a judgment that can hardly hide persuasive cultural standards of what is normal and abnormal. Once again, as I shall demonstrate, middle-class subjects tend to fare better, more frequently emerging with less serious grades of disorder than people of lower social standing. The psychiatrist's judgment possesses manifold meanings—including frightening ones that he doesn't intend to convey—for the subject, his family, the court or agency to which the psychiatrist reports, and society at large.[29] Because people act in terms of such meanings, using them to confer a new status on the patient, they can have great impact on his welfare, including his therapeutic progress.[30]

Although I used the word "abnormal" in the preceding paragraph, I don't identify all abnormality with psychiatric disturbances. Quite the contrary! Abnormal in a general sense designates any and all deviant behavior that fails to conform to norms in some specific social system or that transgresses approved limits.[31] Whether such behavior also indicates personality disorder is often difficult to say, despite the glib, rash way some Americans call whatever they dislike or disagree with "sick." The same outward act of illegal deviance may be motivated by profound inner disequilibrium—in which case we call it evidence of strain and view it as symptomatic of personality disorder—or by quite other inner states. An adolescent's reckless, illegal mischief, for example, may be indicative of strain, expressive of new-found strength, or a resourceful retaliation for a slight. Homosexuality, like premarital sex relations, is deviant, but not necessarily "sick." It ruins the meaning of mental illness to lump together under that label all deviance. A prophet or the man who lives intimately with God acts in statistically abnormal ways, but whether he reveals psychiatric disorder requires that we know his behavior's psychodynamic wellsprings and other antecedents. That knowledge, I repeat, is often difficult to obtain, especially if we start by believing that aberrant acts like prophecy, homosexuality, and suicide could never be carried out by anyone but a psychiatrically deeply disturbed person.

The problem

Personality disorders rise from three antecedent sets of conditions: *heredity, physiology*, and *life experience*. We want to know how socially patterned—that is, cultural—factors entering any of these influence the onset and course of disorder. Sometimes one antecedent predominates, without, however, being a single cause; for example, physiological tissue defects are critical in the delirium of advanced cerebral arteriosclerosis. But heredity, which always predisposes what the body does, and life experience are also implicated, the latter perhaps in the person's socially patterned eating habits that contributed to his blood vessels becoming impaired. We can't be sure that disorders whose etiology we today confidently assign predominantly to one of these three antecedents won't soon, as theory advances, be better explained on some other grounds. Every living discipline faces such uncertainties regarding the fate of its current knowledge; nevertheless, we have no alternative but to go ahead with what we believe to be true until something better appears.

I shall no longer delay the question, What is personality disorder? To answer it I could borrow a psychiatric diagnostic manual and venture a deictic definition,[32] one pointing to the assorted phenomena belonging under that rubric: anxiety more or less directly revealed; neurotic reactions of phobic fear; obsessive and compulsive elaborations which if omitted plunge a person into panic; disproportionate sadness and discouragement; hypochondriacal worry about illness; perpetual, neurasthenic fatigue; protective amnesia along with conversion reactions, in which the person may "forget" how to use a part of his body or a sense, like hearing. All these indicate psychoneurotic disorders whose predominant antecedent is probably life experience. Going on, I could point to pervasive—to a significant extent probably hereditarily founded—personality disorders, like affective swings from gloom to gladness and back; extreme suspiciousness, unstable temper, and ineffective excitement set off by the slightest pressure; also to sociopathic disorders, whose symptoms—such as alcoholism, sexual aggressiveness, and insensate hostility—bother, even victimize, other people. Nor could I omit psychosomatic disorders, expressed in high blood pressure, migraine, asthma, peptic ulcers, and other ailments promoted, instigated, or advanced by emotional disturbances. Generally adjudged to be graver than any of the disorders I have so far pointed to are affective psychoses marked by extreme and pervading disturbances of mood, emotion, perception, and thinking; psychotic depression so black that the person can't eat, sleep, or work; manic-depressive psychoses, whose fantastic imaginings and ceaseless energy render the individual a problem to himself no less than to others; and schizophrenia, indicated by spectacular disturbances in cognition. Rounding off my list of what the term personality disorder designates are hereditary mental deficiency, indexed by

HEREDITY		
Predominant in	*Plays some part in*	
Personality disorders (inadequate personality, schizoid or paranoid, aggressive type, etc.) Psychotic disorders Mental deficiency	Neuroses* Psychosomatic disturbances Brain disorders	
PHYSIOLOGICAL FACTORS		
Predominant in	*Play some part in*	
Brain disorders	Neuroses Sociopathic disorders (antisocial or dysocial reactions) Psychosomatic disturbances Psychotic disorders Mental deficiency	
LIFE EXPERIENCE		
Predominant in	*Plays some part in*	
Neuroses Psychosomatic disturbances	Personality disorders Sociopathic disorders Mental deficiency Brain disorders	Likely influence of culture (social patterning)

*Some psychiatrists believe that as many as 30 percent of people suffer from "deeply embedded" and "subclinical" neurotic symptoms that are not severe enough to call for medical attention. Such people are prone to develop full-blown neuroses that remain intractable even when therapeutically treated.[33]

Probable etiology of personality disorders.[34]

poor intellectual and learning ability, and physiologically founded brain disorders, including senile changes of the sort I mentioned in the previous paragraph.

Another answer to my question states general conceptions that define personality disorder.

Personality disorder involves a person's capacity for performance, or endows his performance with special qualities. He may be more or less disabled or intellectually subnormal and therefore incapable of making socially adequate judgments and discriminations. He may bring to his role an intensity, enthusiasm, or perspectives at variance with what is expected; or, on the other hand, his apathy and diminished ability to feel anything may be so extreme that he can barely muster enough interest to live. If the disorder is not present from

birth but sets in after a period of normal life, then he and his associates experience a change in his personality (not necessarily a change for the worse; personality disorder is not all equally impairing). Some psychiatric disturbances are expressed via consistent immorality; at least, the individual seems bent on injuring or seriously annoying others with whom he lives and on whom he may be dependent. His superego is so dampened that social norms and injunctions scarcely touch him. In other cases, unsure of his own powers, a person is unable to relate his behavior to any likely future outcome, perforce living wholly encapsulated in the present. He may lack ability to choose or control his feelings or cravings which, consequently, overwhelm him. Often cognition is perceptibly affected. Private values control the system whereby he receives messages, interprets them, and transmits his reactions back to his environment.

Withdrawal from the external world does not automatically hamper adaptation to reality. However puzzled and distressed the disturbance may leave a person, his impairment can possibly be prevented if society can accommodate him, perhaps by viewing his personality as now possessing special talents that can be incorporated in a socially desirable, useful role. The individual himself may be wisely able to capitalize on his behavioral trend, socially and beneficially exploiting certain elements in it. Personality disorder can even be put to work in the service of the social system, thereby protecting the person with personality disorder from the grave consequences that often follow such impairment. If personality disorder is to be socially accommodated in greater degree, society must transcend the limits it currently imposes on behavior. It must increase its ingenuity for incorporating diversity by leaving places for as great a variety of temperaments and proclivities as possible.

Both physiologically founded personality disorders and those deriving predominantly from life experience consist of relatively private, idiomatic ways of reacting to the world and self. Either resources with which to follow normal behavior patterns are lacking (due to congenital or physiological impairment) or else an idiomatic way has been learned as the best means of organizing experience and to serve some personal, precious end. Viewed in this way, personality disorder is clearly a matter of degree because all of us constantly react idiomatically to what engages us and our fellows. So long as we can get others to reaffirm our private meanings, so long as people's private sectors overlap or we think they overlap, we are safe. But at a point, private reactions cease to be socially affirmed, become lost to "that thorough community of life, where each wanted support in the feeling that he was among people he knew, and where one so carefully got on together in the comprehensible."[35] The more we try to preserve the private system from destruction, the more we withdraw from an impossible world.[36]

Some serious personality disorders dramatically exemplify idiomatically fostered withdrawal. Schizophrenics exemplify this when they employ highly individual patterns of speaking, using very personal idioms not easily decoded that apparently reflect equally idiosyncratic, metaphorical ways of thinking.[37] In certain forms of schizophrenia, the person misreads even commonplace things that others say.[38] He enters a hospital canteen, and the girl waiting on him inquires: "What can I do for you?" Unlike most of us, the schizophrenic ignores obvious cues of the situation and so doesn't perceive this message as a polite readiness to serve him. Does she, he wonders, imply something about doing him in? Is she inviting him to have sexual relations with her? At times we all err in separating the levels on which experience reaches us. At first glance the bold "STOP!" on a highway sign arrests me, and I take it as an official command. Then context shows it to be part of an advertisement and I confidently go on, paying it no further heed. Television viewers occasionally send cough medicine and gifts to characters in soap operas; apparently they interpret the dramatic level as equivalent to the reality level on which newscasters report. But for one consistently to make experiences conform to highly private assumptions, so that jokes, greetings, commonplace expressions, and appurtenances aren't what others take them to be, but confirmatory evidence and apparatus, say, of a dastard plot against which paranoid vigilance must constantly be maintained, is another matter, and quickly alarms one's associates. The neurotic, too, expresses private premises about the world when he anxiously cringes under omni-present, undefined danger; phobically shuns elevators or cellars, and repeatedly scrubs his well-soaped hands to keep them sanitary. Because his private sector is smaller, his reactions strike others as less bizarre than the psychotic's. To put it differently, he shares more of what his contemporaries say or do; what they tell him he generally understands as they intend he should.

This private reaction pattern, or clinical picture, is what we need to understand culturally. What cultural factors pattern personality disorder differently from one social setting to another; affect the frequency with which its diverse forms appear; lend it different meanings; and influence its course? Theoretically, one could ask these questions about primarily physiologically founded disorders, such as mental deficiency,[39] as well as about so-called functional disorders, reorganizations of behavior wherein experience predominates etiologically. However, it is mostly the functional disorders that have been studied culturally, and to them will go the lion's share of attention.

THE CHARACTER OF DANGER

. . . people fall ill of a neurosis as a result of frustration . . . [of] their libidinal desires.[40]
SIGMUND FREUD

A good theory of functional disorder in cultural psychiatry does two closely related things well: Utilizing the latest relevant facts uncovered in research, it specifies life experiences that lead to personality disorder. In doing so, it makes explicit place for culture—socially patterned events and arrangements that lead to such disorder. No theory is perfectly satisfactory; on closer inspection, each reveals loopholes or adumbrated connections that it becomes the business of subsequent theories to correct.

New theories, which in most cases merely modify their predecessors, naturally throw up their own lacunae and with time reveal new limitations. The more we know, the more ferocious our hunger for knowledge, and the more demanding our standards. Individuals vary in the standards by which they appraise theory in social science. One man will be left unappeased by an explanation that quite contents another. In such cases we speak of "rival" theories. But in biology, rivals compete for the same environmental niche, whereas rival theories are actually often specialized to appeal to different niches; that is, to people holding different assumptions or preferring to proceed with different methods. Someone who holds the early psychoanalytic view that childhood and early family relations harbor the seeds of many disorders will find little sustenance in Alexander H. Leighton's synthesis,[41] which I now propose to review, unless he first reorients his basic thinking. Leighton doesn't ignore early life, but he pays it less heed than others believe it deserves.

A Relatively Steady State. An illness model prevails in Leighton's theory, symptoms of psychiatric disturbance being regarded as unfortunate goal-directed activities which, like fever, help the organism cope with stress. The particular modes of coping are usually (but not always or equally) unfortunate because they endanger the individual, interfere with his life, add to his stress, or alarm his associates. His symptoms help even while they hinder, and thereby they create a dilemma out of which he seeks guidance. Behind such thinking is the familiar concept of homeostasis, which I shall briefly review.[42]

When an organism is injured or its internal condition becomes upset, it automatically institutes certain activities that operate to retrieve its previous state, or at least try to retrieve it. As a wound seriously drains blood from the body, the spleen begins

Alexander H. Leighton (Blackstone-Shelburne New York)

countervailing efforts to release stored material that helps replenish the blood supply. If hard work or infection rockets body temperature, countermeasures try to dissipate as quickly as possible the heat generated and thus return the body to its previous temperature. Homeostasis is a general term for those corrective processes that function to preserve biological equilibrium. Equilibrium in this context doesn't mean perfect balance, but designates a dynamic state that is always being upset and then restored, a constant process of come and go that closely resembles the way a thermostat starts and stops a furnace to preserve an approximately steady room temperature. Homeostasis is at work when a disturbed psychological state leads to unpleasant feelings and then to ensuing, corrective behav-

ior. Man's consciousness allows him to predict upsetting consequences of behavior with some accuracy. Reasoning on the basis of what he has learned, he not only anticipates danger but deliberately takes steps to avoid it. Hence, his psychological equilibrium isn't, like a constant room temperature, automatically preserved. But he can err. He thinks to preserve his vital balance but in so doing actually imperils his adaptation. Someone who has learned since childhood to expect only a raw deal from life may be wrong when he treats every situation as equivalent to those that previously brought him suffering. Subjectively, he is convinced that he is acting homeostatically in his own best interests, but life constantly changes, and as a result behavior that guaranteed equilibrium in the past no longer assures it; in fact, it threatens it. The physical body benefits from automatic homeostasis, but in a changing world, where equilibrium is constantly being upset by new conditions, behavioral rigidity is fatal. Man's creative consciousness and freedom allow him to transcend his immediate environment in grasping for a steady state; he isn't dependent only on the people and resources that his current situation contains. But those very capacities also spell trouble if they lead him to create too many, highly private meanings unshared by his society.[43]

When Striving Is Blocked. Few men create an original theory. Most take cues offered by their predecessors and contemporaries, combine them with insights born of their own experience, test the results as carefully as they can, and offer the product for criticism. The revealing chapter notes appended to the theory that A. H. Leighton developed and tested in the Cornell Program of Social Psychiatry testify to his indebtedness. His conception of mental illness as a response to danger especially recalls Hans Selye's theory explaining how stress spurs the organism to mount emergency, biologically adaptive responses.[44] When those responses are prolonged, Selye discovered, they produce shock that reinstates the initial stress phase, thus starting the cycle over again.

Under certain conditions, striving—a fundamental process in personality—fails and engenders personality disorder.[45] Striving (to review what I said in an earlier chapter) begins even before birth; parturition itself constitutes an act of becoming in which, as in other growth, an individual surmounts interfering conditions. Childhood promptly introduces a long series of socially patterned interferences that continue through the rest of life as a person seeks to attain or maintain what he perceives to be desirable, and to avoid or repel what is undesirable. His perception, in turn, obeys meanings that are defined ever more sharply by each act of striving and dealing with the world. Considerable variation in socially patterned meanings among individuals, social strata, and social systems obviously channels striving toward a multiplicity of incommensurably ranked objects. Some objectives, however, given the nature of human nature, are more salient than others. Such vital ends—their specific forms are legion—can be categorized under physical security; sexual satisfaction; opportunity to express hostility; giving and receiving love; recognition from others; opportunity for spontaneity or creativity; orientation of oneself to others, and of others with respect to oneself; a sense of identity; membership in a definite human group; and some consistent map, mazeway, or sense of a moral order that instills a feeling of being unambiguously right in what one does and experiences.[46] The particular forms in which people in a given culture pursue such salient ends matter less, if mental health is to be protected, than that they find them, even if those forms are socially deviant.[47] The "corner boy" finds recognition in his delinquent peer group; the college youth finds it in his fraternity, if not on the cam-

pus at large. The goals need not even all be found externally, through adjustment to culture, but may lie in oneself,[48] though psychiatrists fear lest too great reliance on fantasy, like reliance on drugs or alcohol, merely mask one's failure to attain satisfactory, salient goals.

From time to time, striving to attain or maintain vital ends inevitably fails, with distressful consequences for the person's equilibrium (which Leighton calls essential psychical condition, and Karl Menninger refers to as vital balance). When his goals are blocked, the striver's condition becomes upset, a fact that registers in unpleasant feelings, such as disappointment, depression, anxiety, jealousy, and others, whose function is to mobilize the person to do something that will restore his steady state.[49] Sometimes such feelings occur without any tangible cause to which the sufferer can ascribe them, suggesting that they stem from unconsciously experienced interference. A certain amount of stressful interference with vital striving is inevitable, and the unpleasant feelings it promotes are mild, unintense, or brief; equilibrium merely fluctuates before the person retrieves his vital balance. Resourcefully he substitutes one goal for another; finds a different job or girl friend; retakes the test he failed, or paints another picture with which he is better satisfied. However, there may be no substitute. Some goals, like love or sexual potency, are hard to replace and not everyone is ingenious or flexible enough to shift his goals. It requires a variety of talents to make painting a substitute for satisfying social relations, and capital or at least a good credit rating is needed to start a new business. A man with less than a grade school education enjoys little scope for switching jobs. Masking the disagreeable feelings with bourbon, a trip to the South Seas, or sexual excitement won't be of permanent help, because such efforts leave the fundamental threat unaffected and invite further interference that intensifies distress. When interference continues unabated, reaching a given magnitude, quality, or duration, distress becomes extraordinary. Equilibrium fails to be recovered or, having been recovered, promptly becomes upset again in fresh circumstances. The person begins to show the strain under which he labors. To use language from engineering, stress has begun to deform the human material on which it relentlessly bears. To mitigate his persistent or intense distress, a person tries various, to some degree socially patterned, solutions for handling his strain. Some of those solutions produce such bizarre alterations in his overt behavior—incapacitating fear, suicidal depression, or widespread suspicion and mistrust—that others judge him to be neurotic, or even insane. His disturbed emotions may also express themselves physiologically, through hypertension, headache, or peptic ulcers whose pain drives him to doctors who never seem to help.

Personality disorder exists simultaneously on two levels of personality, the same two that we have repeatedly encountered in describing normal personality. Overtly or physiologically we have symptoms that publicize themselves in a compulsive or chronic habit, sensory disturbance, paralysis, paranoid suspicion, or hypertension. On the covert level, inferred from what the person says and from his actions, is the underlying disequilibrium born of a sense of threat. Many times, overt symptoms don't automatically restore the vital balance because the threat created by interference with vital strivings remains unabated and strain continues. In fact, the very symptoms may add stress and strain, intensifying the downward spiral, as in the alcoholic who loses his job and alienates his friends, or the depressed person struggling with his bleak outlook. Some symptoms, however, actually aid a person to strive toward salient ends and interference with them that isn't compensated for adds to

strain. This happened to certain obsessive-compulsive men who found themselves in the army and at the front, where military culture failed to accommodate their particular form of deviance. Their inability to indulge their obsession with orderliness, or their compulsion to keep meticulously clean by frequent bathing, stressed them so much that they became depressed.[50] Not everyone betrays his inner disturbance through signs that the community judges to be bizarre or abnormal or that prove maladaptive. Nagging guilt may actually be respected as a sign of saintliness; worry and fussiness, although laughingly taken as eccentric, may in fact be regarded as indicative of conscientiousness; and psychosomatic illness may be used to exact valuable secondary compensations from other people. Hence, socially speaking, personality disorder does not necessarily interfere with adaptation.

Sources of Interference. The settings in which we act possess great instability, changing from day to day as well as registering more momentous, long-range mutability. Hence, the conditions in which we pursue vital ends constantly alter. Loved ones die; friends leave; new responsibilities pose fresh challenges; hopes explode; dreams sag; well-fitting old roles become useless; and our cognitive maps must be refurbished to agree with the latest rules and discoveries. In some communities, change churns along especially heavily, leaving a great wake of far-reaching consequences and a rich swell of dilemmas. By itself, change signifies nothing for personality disorder; what counts is whether it multiplies interference with salient strivings. The fact that change enriches experience and makes life more entertaining, comfortable, and leisurely, doesn't extirpate all opportunities for salient goals to be blocked. In fact, the most advantageous innovations can deprive people of earlier fulfillments and value. Opportunities for interference are truly ubiquitous. Since striving often implicates other people, they naturally take an interest in the objectives we pursue and in how we maneuver to attain them. Lest a person's actions imperil others' goals, every society imposes limits around how he strives, regulating the process legally, conventionally, and logically.[51] All communities are to some extent prescriptive, and prohibit, or at least disapprove strongly of, particular deviant kinds of striving—homosexuality, for example. But some cultures facilitate striving by tolerantly incorporating a considerable range of alternatives, allowing people of diverse temperaments and socioeconomic status to pursue congenial paths to salient ends. Another source of blockage arises when objectives once attained turn out to possess unexpected shortcomings or limitations. College isn't only the sociable place that an unscholarly high-school student pictured; a wife won't be the mother figure a man unconsciously seeks, and the role for which one diligently qualified himself turns obsolete due to rapid cultural change. The goals toward which we strive may have defects of another kind. A parent encourages a child to make assumptions about how he expects the child to behave, but after the child acts according to those assumptions he indicates that he didn't at all want that kind of response. The child is put in a double bind. He can form no consistent pattern of action to meet the wishes of somebody who plays a most important role in his life.[52] Striving for mutually incompatible ends—say, popularity *and* authority, both of which can't be enjoyed simultaneously—further bars goal achievement. Personal inadequacy, including inept physical and social skills, mental deficiency, age, and emotional instability, inevitably close off access to some vital goals. Excessive timidity, lack of sex drive, and an inability to accept and give love deprive people of salient experiences. In fact, goals fail because in themselves they don't confer satisfaction; they must be appropriately used in order to serve a personality. The most highly paid, powerful, creative, or glamorous career withholds a satisfactory sense of identity to someone whose standard of reference remains far beyond himself. Disasters like a tornado, flood, or bombing interfere with the striving

❨ Progress of a War Neurosis[53]

Phase one: In the initial phase the person, an airman just inducted into the role of flyer, pursues salient strivings; his personality is in equilibrium.

Phase two: Moved to the theater of war, he begins to experience stress and strain in his role, but for a time manages to ward off any serious disturbance to equilibrium by muscular exertion and rough-and-tumble play. Strain, however, visibly appears in his restlessness and his extensive use of alcohol and sexual outlets. Such masking avails little, for with repeated missions stress and strain continue to mount, in time reaching a point where they seriously disturb him. He shows his disturbance in constant tremor and apprehension, in his startled reaction to sudden noise, and in battle dreams that involve aircraft. He can't even look at aircraft without developing intense, phobic anxiety. No plane feels safe to him.

Phase three: His major symptom, phobic anxiety, conflicts with his own definition of his role, and that conflict further interferes with his pursuit of a favorable self-image and favorable recognition from others. He meets ʰthis new interference with a new symptom, depression, which involves strong feelings of unworthiness and failure. In effect, he blames himself. He tries to overcome these feelings by returning to flying, only to surrender anew to fresh anxiety. His effectiveness as a flyer has disappeared.

of thousands of victims, erasing the fruits of long work. Nor is a near-miss much less shocking. Still, being in a disaster together with other people mitigates much of its stressful impact.[54]

Like other cultural psychiatrists in recent decades, Leighton emphasizes disintegrated social conditions as an important source of mental illness.[55] Under such structural conditions, containing elements so strongly noxious for personality that more benign cultural factors cannot mask or neutralize them, vital strivings are frequently blocked, and people try to resolve loads of stress too great to bear, so that personality disorder results. How can we recognize such noxious environments? Naroll[56] points to suicide voluntarily committed in a manner that brings it to public notice as a type of protest; homicide defiantly committed and deliberately brought to public attention; drunken brawling; and deaths attributed to malevolent witches in the community. His approach, however, doesn't identify the stressful conditions which would predict those behaviors. Leighton[57] deictically defines a disintegrated community or neighborhood by its high frequency of broken homes; few or only weak formal and informal associations; few and weak leaders; scarce patterns of recreation; frequent hostility, crime, and delinquency, not all of which can be discovered by inspecting the police blotter, and weak or fragmented networks of communication (the neighborhood is cut off through lack of roads, telephones, and social networks joining it to the wider society). In Émile Durkheim's terms, people feel little sense of cohesiveness, and share hardly at all in the larger social system's values.[58] A disintegrated community, Leighton believes, will also show associated phenomena—none of them necessarily disruptive, though dangerous when they occur rapidly, one after the other—like a recent history of disaster; widespread ill health; extensive poverty; confusion occasioned by the coexistence of

two or more cultures that have no ordered relationship to each other; widespread secularization, meaning an absence of religious sentiments; extensive in-or-out migration; and recent widespread cultural (e.g., technological) change.[59] Persons with long and extensive exposure to adverse conditions in disintegrated communities are more likely to have disordered personalities than individuals who have lived under more favorable circumstances, not only because disintegrated communities increase interference with vital strivings but also because they are less equipped with resources to which a disturbed individual can turn for help in relieving this upset condition. In the next chapter I shall present some of the evidence that supports this hypothesis.[60]

Don't assume that social disintegration causes personality disorder. It is wiser to assume that reciprocal bonds link the two variables. While disintegration contributes experiences that interfere with a person's striving and thereby promote serious, prolonged personal disequilibrium, the considerable proportion of disordered people in a disintegrated social setting themselves contribute to that noxious condition. In such a reciprocal state of affairs it is difficult to isolate one factor as cause and another as effect. The same warning holds when serious personality disorder occurs more frequently among a population of low socioeconomic status.[61] The relationship may at least partly stem from the fact that an unknown number of disordered people have, as a consequence of their personality state, drifted into poverty.

The Character of Danger Socially Patterned. What interferes with vital strivings varies from one culture to another. This supports the possibility that the amount or degree of interference likewise varies, making some cultures tougher than others.[62] For example, some cultures define success of one sort or another as chronically limited, or social arrangements consistently funnel the bulk of advantages to a few.[63] Our schools have made grading into something that menaces personal welfare. One might at least expect college professors in their classes to refuse to tolerate a system that urges everybody to aspire to the top but invariably keeps the majority from getting there. Only about four out of 40 students are allowed to win A, eight or so may earn B; the majority must be content with C. Many people who must live with such arrangements as well as with constant threats of war, poverty, social disparagement, and cultural confusion, intelligently find ways of adaptively coping with them. The culture itself provides some patterns for getting along with its own stringent demands. For example, campus culture keeps students safe from the frustration of grading by making it quite respectable to land only a C.[64] In similar fashion, lower-class people shrink their area of striving in a world they know they can't conquer.

Family life in each U.S. social class contains its own interferences that block vital strivings.[65] New Haven's socioeconomic Class III consists of people who enjoy job security and five- or six-room houses located in good neighborhoods; belong to

⟪ Social Integration and Disintegration Contrasted

. . . Slashtown, the backwoods collection of some twenty-five shacks where Rose Chiason lived and had her babies, can be regarded as disintegrated. . . . Here one can see a gravel road as the only straight and tidy thing in a landscape of spindly trees, alder clumps, shallow soil, and granite outcroppings. The houses tend to be at a distance from each other, reflecting the social isolation, furtiveness and suspicion of the people they contain. A general air of dilapidation or of unfinished building also parallels in concrete terms the broken family life and the low and unstable economic base. The red flare of geranium in a rusty can at a window, or a one-armed teddy bear alone in the mud of a yard, serves to highlight the general absence of decoration and play, of the materials for the creation and development of human capacity for enjoyment and sharing. It is a place where both leadership and followership are weak, where channels of communications are deficient, and where the sentiment patterns are confused and, except for hostility, lacking in affective strength. From the overcrowded dwellings, little paths lead into the swamps and the woods.

In contrast to all this is a fishing village of Cap Aux Anges . . . [that] can be regarded as integrated. . . . It lies boldly about a cove, looking part of the landscape rather than, as Slashtown, like an artifact thrown away and forgotten in the weeds. The comparatively large houses bright in paint, the several roads and the network of paths which run from dwelling to dwelling, reflect the solid family units and the busy interactivity and interdependence of the people. There are gardens and white picket fences, a two-story school with a flagpole in front, numbers of stores, a Masonic Lodge, a recreation hall where amateur shows are occasionally presented, a ball field, and, in the center of all, a white church with square tower and sturdy spire. The boats in the cove and the fish plants on the shore indicate the main subsistence base while the fields and the woods provide certain supplemental resources. The whole is a social system with relatively clear and functioning sentiments, with well-marked patterns of leadership and followership, and with highly effective means of communication.[66]

ALEXANDER H. LEIGHTON

community organizations, and look toward a future in which things will be even easier. Mental patients from this stratum experienced danger of a special character in earlier life. Their mothers, rigid perfectionists and powerful family figures, enforced discipline and compliance in order to promote the children's development. Effectively, they withheld affection to control the child, for they were ambitious on behalf of this individual who apparently offered them another chance to achieve their own slow success. Psychiatric patients in Class V—people with lower earnings, facing the ever-present problem of securing enough money to meet necessities, living in the city's worst slums, isolated from formal organizations, resigned to a hard life, and viewing the future with faint optimism—experienced a different pattern of stress. Class V patients remember rebelling against physical punishment inconsistently administered in childhood. They recall the father as the dominant household figure, as a punitive person who quarrelled and fought with his wife, and as someone who viewed the patient's maturation as a threat to his own strong family position. School onerously burdened Class V patients; they failed frequently and their teachers hardly urged them to stay. Subsequently they regarded their parents as failures whom they couldn't respect or identify with. They disliked their jobs and couldn't find better ones. In general they felt trapped. Hostile to authorities by whom they felt exploited, they brought their hostility along to the clinic and promptly earned the therapist's dislike. In contrast, Class III patients quickly shed anxiety and hostility toward therapy and won the therapist's liking.

Choice of Symptoms. If in response to interference that blocks salient strivings individuals express their resultant disturbance symptomatically, why do symptoms vary? Remember, psychological anthropology is concerned with how personality becomes socially patterned, and in cultural

psychiatry this interest attaches to how people learn to respond to stress.[67]

Choice of symptoms can be explained in particular cases. Generally speaking, a symptom is predominantly rooted in a specific hereditary or physiological condition, so that it appears in an organ system that has been chronically unstable; in a pattern of behavior learned earlier, like the need to be clean or to avoid sin; or in some cultural feature—like alcohol, intense religiosity, or a high frequency of violence—characteristic of a community. In roots of the latter type, with which I am primarily concerned, a person utilizes his culture as he strains to cope with stress. Anthropologists inquire into the cultural appropriateness of symptoms, like the legitimacy accorded to depression by the Hutterites, a religious enclave in the western plains of Canada and the United States.[68]

The Hutterites, a simple, prosperous people, consider themselves chosen by God to live the only true form of Christianity, a way of life that entails sharing of goods, cooperative production, and other forms of communal living. Hutterities strictly limit one another's aggressive, acquisitive, and sexual impulses. Their insistence on conformity parallels the Hopi Indians' in quite suppressing individuality, creativity, and originality. Outsiders, however, see no emotionally flat, compliant, submissive people, but rather a complacent, self-satisfied, vigorous, assertive, and somewhat stubborn group. In their two paramount values, religious conformity and impulse control, we have the center that shapes the modal form taken by serious personality disorder among them. Depression marked 74 percent of all cases of psychotic personality disorder out of a total of 53 cases uncovered in the lifetimes of 8,500 individuals. What seems to have happened in that majority of cases is this: Sexual or aggressive impulses in this puritanical, cooperative community interfered with a person's satisfactory image of himself. Disequilibrium

Manitoba Hutterite women, members of a communal settlement that lives out its faith. (National Film Board of Canada—Chris Lund)

resulting from threat to that image found a traditional channel of socially patterned expression, called *Anfechtung*, that not only protected the person's public standing and preserved the community's unity, but also won him understanding and emotional support. Where the psychiatrist sees a certain type of depression, Hutterites perceive the devil's hand; the victim is suffering because he succumbed and questioned basic religious beliefs. (Though he might wonder when he could have done so!) The person accepts the diagnosis. He believes he has sinned and ruminates endlessly on his religious unworthiness, thus fully incorporating the community's interpretation of his disorder. Neighbors come to his aid with far from punishing, nurturant, and sympathetic responses; they remind him that confession will restore him to God's favor. By confessing, regardless of whether he recalls committing the offense, he further affirms the

group's interpretation and integrates himself more firmly into its supportive structure, thereby helping his depression to dissolve. As a symptom, depression accords closely with Hutterites' social character; that is, with their strong passive, dependent, and submissive motives. Symptoms commonly associated with schizophrenic and aggressive sociopathic reactions, which possess none of the congruence with Hutterite culture and personality that depression exhibits, would be wholly illegitimate in this social system and would threaten rather than bolster its values and beliefs.

Symptoms that express inner disturbance may be clearly symbolic, as if deliberately devised to communicate something that the person wants to broadcast. Paralysis during World War I asked that a soldier be excused from the mortal risk of battle. A dread-ravaged soldier cowering beneath blankets or under a bed reacts the way he was taught to protect himself during bombardment. Vomiting dramatizes an intention to reject something. Recalling consciously or unconsciously how sleep or alcohol brought surcease from disagreeable feelings, a person installs fatigue or drinking as chronic modes of coping under heavy strain. Objects (like drugs or alcohol), beliefs, and habits that form a normal part of a culture are utilized to construct convincing symptoms, though the person does so in incomprehensible, private ways and in behest of personal strategies of living. The paranoid in Africa dreads witches or evil spirits—real dangers that everyone acknowledges to exist, though in not quite the same way. Hence his neighbors soon recognize something amiss in his contrivance, just as we do when someone complains that he is being secretly influenced by radio waves. So heavily are symptoms under the control of a person's external situation that they may be suppressed. Through reading or college courses in abnormal psychology and mental hygiene, a person may gain enough insight into a psychodynamic processes to inhibit neurotic and psychotic symptoms, at least for a time. There are fashions in symptoms; they change as other conditions in culture alter. In Chapter 13 I talk about how in certain social statuses people are predisposed to definite expressions of mental illness that conform to their general style of life.

PERSONALITY DISORDER SOCIALLY APPROVED

A person obviously possesses an adaptive asset if he is able to express his disequilibrium through symptoms of which his community approves, and to which people assign positive meaning. Such a talent might even suit him for a highly prestiged social status. Catalepsy in some social systems marks spirit possession; extreme masochism

A Chuckchee (Siberian) shaman. (American Museum of Natural History)

is one indication of being a saint; and callous, antisocial personality disorder (in the clinically delimited sense of the term) confers leadership ability and earns considerable respect.[69] A number of anthropologists believe that shamans are in this category, coming from the ranks of the mentally deranged, and being either neurotic, psychotic, or probably most often hysteric.[70] Kroeber[71] more cautiously surmises that some communities allow this respected status to be acquired only by someone who has experienced conditions which by our

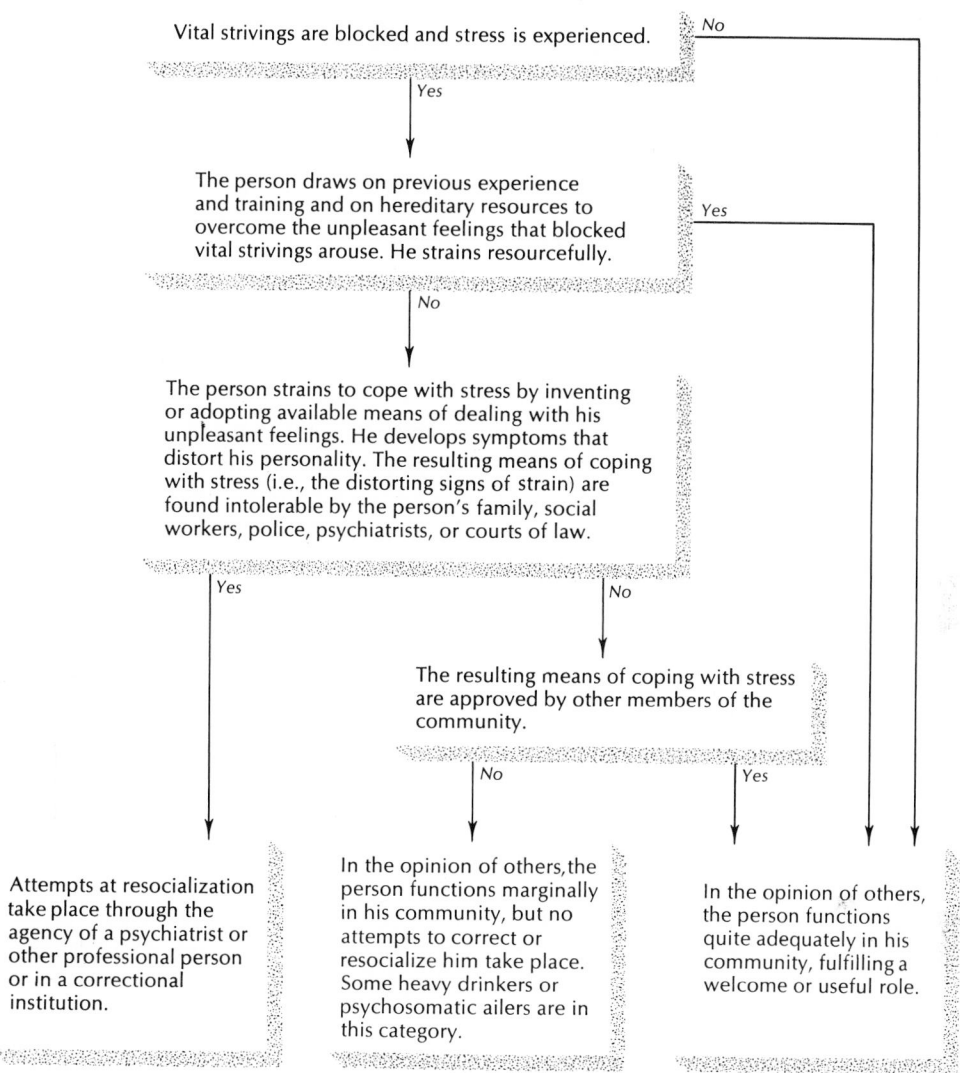

Vital strivings are blocked and stress is experienced. — No

Yes

The person draws on previous experience and training and on hereditary resources to overcome the unpleasant feelings that blocked vital strivings arouse. He strains resourcefully. — Yes

No

The person strains to cope with stress by inventing or adopting available means of dealing with his unpleasant feelings. He develops symptoms that distort his personality. The resulting means of coping with stress (i.e., the distorting signs of strain) are found intolerable by the person's family, social workers, police, psychiatrists, or courts of law.

Yes — No

The resulting means of coping with stress are approved by other members of the community.

No — Yes

Attempts at resocialization take place through the agency of a psychiatrist or other professional person or in a correctional institution.

In the opinion of others, the person functions marginally in his community, but no attempts to correct or resocialize him take place. Some heavy drinkers or psychosomatic ailers are in this category.

In the opinion of others, the person functions quite adequately in his community, fulfilling a welcome or useful role.

Outcomes to blocked vital strivings vary, depending on the means a person uses to adapt to stress and on how his resulting behavior is socially evaluated.

cultural norms would be labeled psychotic; he avoids saying that those experiences necessarily indicate severe personality disorder.

My inclination is to doubt the claim that shamans in general are likely to be markedly disturbed people.[72] I find too little evidence to support the contention. To resolve the problems calls for nothing less than good, clinical data secured from shamans themselves, material of the sort that John Gillin collected from half a dozen curers in the Guatemalan community of San Luis Jilotepeque.[73] While those professionals obtained their power from dreams, usually following a crisis like illness, they did not display the flamboyant behavior typical of shamans, who, for example, take flight to the spirit world and publicly engage in physical struggles with spirits.[74] Nevertheless, it is interesting to note that four out of six Guatemalan curers provided Rorschach protocols that in another setting could label them schizoid. They reveal an upsurge of "primitive material" which the ego hardly scrutinizes. "Primitive drives" predominate in their personalities and they but poorly comprehend common, everyday problems. But unlike schizophrenics diagnosed in clinical practice, the curers organize their thoughts well and, in contrast to San Luis laymen, from whom Gillin also collected Rorschach records, they manifest little inner tension and rigidity. They even surpass other Indians in intelligence and creative productivity. The Rorschach record of the last practicing woman shaman among the Alaskan Nunivak Eskimo offers no definite sign of pathology (except possibly for some paranoid trends that are doubtlessly related to her competitive, jealous, overt demeanor).[75] But a retired shaman and cripple in the same community—a man of average intelligence—in his responses to the test more clearly suggests personality disorder.[76] High anxiety stems from his relations with other people as well as from his own felt incompetence; he gives evidence of strong sex conflict, and his possible pathology seems to be organized around suspicion and impulsiveness. An Apache Indian shaman studied through interviews and the Rorschach test gave indications of character disorder, of infantile features in his personality, and of being confused about his sexual identity.[77] Studies like these are provocative, but they are still far from sufficient to demonstrate that shamans, for all their florid, expressive role behavior that sets them apart from laymen in their community, regularly differ from their nonprofessional contemporaries by being psychiatrically disordered.

RESPONSIBILITY

Is an individual responsible for the symptoms that express his severely disturbed equilibrium? Leighton skirts this issue, though in the way he represents personality automatically reacting to blocked striving by disequilibrium, which in turn gives rise to symptoms, he leaves as little room for responsibility as for rationality.

One way of answering the question is to draw an analogy between the symptoms of personality disorder and those of disease. Obviously, no malaria victim elects to fight invading microorganisms by purposely selecting his ravaging fever as the weapon. A part of him adapts purely automatically to his condition by fever, the function of which is curative. Similarly, the analogy goes on, a disturbed person automatically responds symptomatically to his inner state, and little choice is involved. This argument, it seems to me, falls down once we realize that it omits taking into account several facts. It doesn't recognize that symptoms of personality disorder, unlike many symptoms of bodily disorder, vary with culture; psychiatric symptoms differ from one social system, social class, and ethnic group to another. In fact, they are part of culture and like culture can be changed. Shedding neurotic symptoms in psychotherapy isn't as wholly passive and automatic as the analogy with medicine comfortingly suggests. It frequently requires laborious learning and strenuous willing. These considerations suggest that a high element of responsibility governs many expressions of personality disorder, though it is true that a person often chooses his response largely unconsciously, adopting his symptoms without being fully aware. Conventionally we absolve unconscious choice from responsiblity, or, speaking more accurately, our society disagrees on the degree of responsibility to assign to specific behaviors unawarely performed. Freud himself argued that the unconscious is not beyond responsibility. "One must hold oneself responsible" even for the content of one's dreams, he maintained, for they are "part of my own being."[78] The diagram shows the alternatives, as I see them, in Western culture. Much personality disorder of a functional kind falls near the middle range, between conscious purposeful action (point A) and automatic, goal-oriented bodily responses (point B). Where do responsibility and freedom stop? The decision is for you and me to make. Talking of responsibility reintroduces the question of whether it is wise to call personality disorder an illness. I have already suggested several consequences that might follow from that habit of labeling, and Thomas S. Szasz[79] holds forth others when he terms hypochondriasis, conversion hysterias, and certain schizophrenic delusions "impersonations" of bodily illness. They are undertaken—of course not as consciously planned strategies —for the gain they bring, especially in a civilization where Christian and medical values strongly favor someone who is weak and apparently helpless. Such people are not, as they seem to be, ill; rather, they are frustrated, unhappy, and perplexed due to social and other difficulties. To win help they engage in a private form of communication whose symbols can be decoded as readily as they can be learned. In fact, the person himself must master a new, better language if he is to be helped. Like some deviants, a disturbed person ignores legal means and socially accepted rules in his striving, pursuing his ends with any means at his disposal; he plays the game as he wills. Such people confront a psychiatrist with social and ethical problems. They should be treated as seriously as possible for the activity in which they are engaged; nothing less is consistent with democratic respect for the individual. To treat a patient's moral dilemmas as illness is to fail to regard him as a responsible human being and to ignore the moral implications of his behavior.

Ernest Becker[80] calls mental illnesses *ways of life founded on cultural and individual stupidity.* They are alternative searches for meaning undertaken by those who have been crippled by experiences that have interfered with the growth of better meanings for coping effectively. Schizophrenia is created by hobbling a child when he seeks meaning in the world and value in himself. He grows up inept at using his potential powers, inept in social relations, and withdraws to a realm of fantasy exclusively, where his power grows to extreme proportions. At the same time that reveries answer his questions concerning his identity, they further inhibit him in gaining knowledge of the real world. As a result, he grows stupid about those things that facilitate social interaction, even lacking in a sense of humor. Schizophrenia often occurs in lower socioeconomic strata where cultural circumstances hinder learning, where identification creating a sense of self is weak, and where hardship and stress encourage withdrawal.

Depressive states likewise signify ineptness. Just as we become temporarily depressed upon losing an object that validated our identity and value, so lasting depression follows a sharp change in the world wherein we once found sufficient meaning and validation. To blame oneself when that happens via self-accusatory depression is a way of restoring meaning in a frustrating situation, but it is a poor, stupid way of doing so. Yet it may be the only one available to somebody like an American woman who has been reared with such limited horizons that she can't discover new interests when old ones change—for example, when children are married and aging begins.[81] Depression often also occurs among successful people in higher socioeconomic strata who feel guilty when their comfortable life no longer yields all they believe it should.

Personality
disorder
frequently is
assigned to
this area

Purposeful action
which we can
launch by saying,
"I will do so-and-so"

Unconscious,
goal-oriented
behavior

Automatic,
goal-oriented
bodily responses,
such as fever

A — B

Traditionally Euroamerican society regards freedom and
responsibility as decreasing from A to B.

O. Hobart Mowrer strikes a somewhat different note when he traces personality disorders to conduct of which a person is ashamed and guilty; he has violated his high set of ideals and values, and now needs people who can help him adopt right conduct that will bring him approval rather than guilt.[82] Call his condition "sin" rather than "illness," Mowrer urges, and you convey to him hope and a vision of new potentialities, rather than pessimism and confusion. You will also be helping him to blame himself, for in fact he is largely resonsible for his predicament, and can do something to help bring about a change in it. The secret of Alcoholics Anonymous lies in its demand that the alcoholic who seeks redemption admit his true guilt; thereupon he enters on a group-supported program of good works and restitution. Mowrer and others who take this point of view, or call the interest taken in mental illness a social movement that substitutes irresponsibility and exculpation for individual responsibility, substitute moral theory for the illness model.[83]

Without agreeing with all that Szasz, Becker, and Mowrer say, I think we should allow for some degree of personal choice even in personality disorder. Whether we call the behavior in question illness, self-deception, stupidity, or sin, its redirection is often a difficult task and calls for help. The most effective helper is someone with compelling qualities, like love, faith, and hope. Those qualities, regardless of the scientific theory he employs, augment the disordered

person's own capacities, aiding him to reorient himself more happily. Reorient himself to what? Not necessarily to the demands of society, for they may be so poorly defined, contradictory, inhuman, and in conflict with individual temperaments and proclivities that they are truly insufferable.[84] On the other hand, to think only of individual adjustment or of realizing personal strivings and potentials ignores the fact that one lives in, and must adapt to, a society. Therapist and patient face a tremendously creative task: synergically to integrate personality and culture, sacrificing the needs and opportunities of neither, while constantly trying to make culture more richly satisfying to a greater range of distinctively endowed people.

AS-YET-UNIDENTIFIED FACTORS

My review of current theory in cultural psychiatry accurately reflects, I believe, the extent to which social science disciplines primarily account for personality disorder in terms of life experience and culture. Anthony F. C. Wallace[85] argues that cultural factors can be admitted to such explanations while giving much more attention to physiological facts than has customarily been the case. His biochemical approach to schizophrenia, by which I propose to show his reasoning, begins by stating the problem: Schizophrenics are people who once carried on culturally organized lives. How did they become so incapable of executing situationally appropriate behavior that society has extruded them to an institution? He rejects as illogical the possibility that schizophrenics' disarrayed meanings occurred through experiences they encountered in their lives, and as the only remaining plausible explanation advances a physiological foundation for their condition. Of course he knows that, in spite of diligent searching, no organic lesion has ever been located for schizophrenia. Undeterred, he assumes an as-yet-unidentified "biochemical insult" that occurs sometime in the future schizophrenic's life, usually during his middle adolescence, and reduces his capacity to orient himself meaningfully to his world. Just as a brain-damaged patient strives to save himself from his handicap,[86] so the schizophrenic's symptoms represent desperate efforts to correct catastrophic consequences which he perceives to accrue from his desemantization and from his persistent feelings of unreality, which one ex-patient described as being like waking in a strange room, "except that I had lived in the room for months."[87] He establishes private ways of reacting, but ever-increasingly they demonstrate his social inadequacy, finally earning him the abandonment of society, precisely what he has dreaded. Culture becomes involved in the process by patterning the form taken by the symptoms. Wallace also postulates an as-yet-unidentified physiochemical factor to underlie the sudden recovery of a previously highly disturbed person, who becomes the prophetic leader of a successful revitalization movement.[88] Similarly, Wallace accounts for hysteria and for a culturally specialized psychosis, Eskimo *pibloktoq*, by postulating a calcium deficiency, though once again without biochemical evidence to support his theory.[89]

AN IDEAL CONCEPTION

Despite many efforts to detect, measure, and repair personality disorder, we rarely ask what a human personality is like that functions at peak effectiveness, and several people who have identified good personal functioning find that there is little clinical use for their discoveries. But then, that isn't so strange when you recall that medicine, which sets the model for thinking about mental hygiene, also deals with illness without giving much thought to explicit criteria of health. A physician, despairing of defining "wellness" in positive terms, regards it simply as freedom from troublesome symptoms. Several provocative characterizations of positive mental health have appeared, however, that don't identify wellness with the kind of person who, obeying the law of Samuel Butler's *Erewhon*, rigidly suppresses all signs of illness.[90] And they decline to define normality relativistically, making it whatever the greatest number of people conform to in a given community. To do so would mean regarding both ends of the graph—the 18 percent of the New York City population that are symptom-free and the 23 percent that are impaired—as unhealthy, compared with the larger proportion troubled by "normally" mild or moderate symptoms.[91] Characterizations of positive mental health don't even purport to be limited to Euroamerican culture, but in effect represent ideal conceptions of personality which might, with only a few modifications, apply anywhere in the world.

What kind of person represents the ideal of personal well-being and peak effectiveness?[93] He is a self-accepting person, someone who can live with both his potentialities and his limitations and, assuming he is adult, accepts his limits with proper detachment. He continues always to actualize himself, to whatever degree his potentialities permit, as he moves progressively closer to his own goals. He is able to relax. Various aspects of his personality work together integratively, with the result that he experiences himself as a coherent whole. Conflicting or divergent trends are coordinated rather than allowed to flourish in

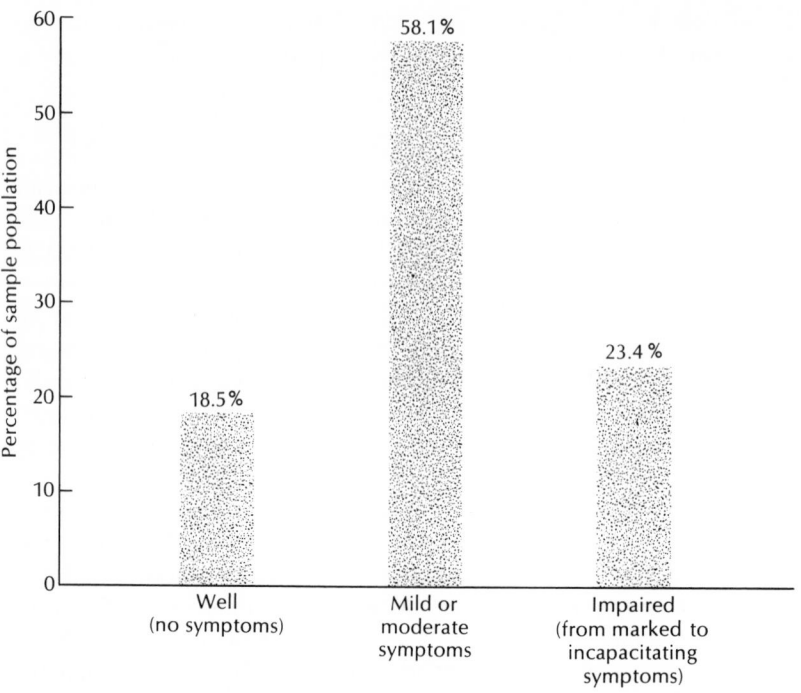

*Distribution of symptoms revealed by a sample
of 1660 Midtown New Yorkers.*[92]

warring partnership. Stress doesn't skip an integrated personality, which is, however, resilient enough, like a strong young tree, to bend under it and can cope effectively with strain so that the individual stays out of serious trouble. Partly he manages to do so because his richer personality possesses a greater variety of ways of handling situations, including difficult ones. An effective person treasures his autonomy, makes discriminations independently, and regulates his behavior internally, according to his own values. Yet most of the time his perception of reality accords with the world as others see it. Autonomous leanings still permit him to relate to others, trusting them, loving, and being loved. He meets situational requirements dependably and efficiently. Also remarkable is his capacity to play social roles synergically, satisfying personal needs at the same time that he fulfills social obligations and meets others' defini-

tion of the situation. On this criterion many U.S. working-class people who hold unsatisfying jobs and can't find more agreeable ones fall down badly.[94]

Some characterizations of wellness ring with strong ethical overtones, insisting, like Zeno and other Greek stoics, that to be effective a person must utilize those elements in his nature that separate him from the rest of creation and distinguish him as a human being. Evolution has endowed man with an enormous capacity for consciousness and the fully well person employs it in living. He controls himself for the sake of future goals—rationally forgoing opportunities for immediate gratification.[95] In the same vein Diogenes Laertius, paraphrasing Zeno, says that "desire is irrational." Good men are austere and vigilant for their own improvement.[96] Erich Fromm[97] identifies himself with the same tradition when he claims that full maturity requires adherence to needs inherent in human nature. Fromm[98] also finds that human nature demands a sense of freedom; a sound capacity for objectivity; use of reason, the endowment through which humanity controls the world; spontaneity; a capacity to live intensely in a fully awake manner; and genuine expression of self, including the ability to love and create.

All such beliefs, which discover what *should* be in what merely *is*, commit the normative fallacy. What is a healthy, effective, or integrated personality must always be a subjective judgment, which we can't escape by sloughing it off on the supposed authority of human nature or evolution. Such beliefs also verge on the cultural fallacy: establishing what should be for all men by what the philosopher's or psychiatrist's own middle-class culture idealizes. Prescriptions of high-level wellness must be seasoned with a stronger dose of cultural relativism. Somebody should look for how wellness is actually patterned and manifested in various social systems and in culturally different social strata within the same social system. I also fear that definitions of high-order personal effectiveness smuggle in the notion that normality means adjustment *to* something, to culture, and therefore make wellness synonymous with conformity. For Abraham H. Maslow,[99] well-being requires an appetite for privacy, meditation, and contemplation, as well as an appreciation of noncognitive, nonrational, and unconsciously motivated mythological thought. If we try only to master the world, he warns, we cut off the possibility of full being. He is repeating an old, old lesson that Asian teachers have taught for well over a millennium. On the other hand, how many people actually want to achieve psychological well-being that involves transcendence of environment and a high degree of detachment from conventions? In the Bhagavad-Gita,[100] Krishna speaks of "the conflict between right and wrong [as] the sickness of the mind."[101] Few people

actually try to escape from that prison to achieve a degree of transcendence wherein he is, like a lotus leaf that rests unwetted on water, in the world of action yet free of it, accepting feelings of pleasure and pain with an even mind that remains unmoved and serene.[102]

If high-level wellness means not simply absence of symptoms, then it can exist independently of them, even in conjunction with illness and personality disorder. A severely impaired patient in a mental hospital could still possess a significant degree of positive mental health, despite the fact that psychiatrists find his behavior so unwholesome or destructive that he must be locked away.

FURTHER READING

The *International Journal of Psychiatry* covers subjects discussed in the preceding and the next two chapters, for which *The Sociology and Anthropology of Mental Illness,* by Edwin D. Driver (1965), provides a useful bibliographic guide. In Cultural Psychology: Comparative Studies of Human Behavior" (in press), George De Vos and Arthur E. Hippler review the field. "Social Psychiatry," by H. Warren Dunham (1948), provides a short history of the topic, while his "Methodology of Sociological Investigations of Mental Disorders" (1957) concisely presents assumptions and concepts. Both are reprinted in his collection *Sociological Theory and Mental Disorder* (1959). Paul Hoch (1961) and Thomas A. C. Rennie (1955–1956) introduce "Social Psychiatry," as do Alexander H. Leighton in *An Introduction to Social Psychiatry* (1960), and Marvin K. Opler in chapter 2 of *Culture, Psychiatry, and Human Values* (1956). See also Opler's introduction "The Cultural Backgrounds of Mental Health" in the volume he edited, *Culture and Mental Health* (1959b), and his paper, "Anthropological

Aspects of Psychiatry" (1959a). Jane Murphy's "Social Science Concepts and Cross-cultural Methods for Psychiatric Research" (1965) is an elementary introduction to anthropological concepts applicable to investigating personality disorder in culture. Morton Beiser, writing from the perspective of Leighton and the Cornell Program in Social Psychiatry, summarizes the confluence of "Poverty, Social Disintegration, and Personality" (1965). Robert N. Rapoport, "Social Anthropology and Mental Health" (1963) describes anthropology's collaboration with psychiatry, a subject also treated in Clyde Kluckhohn, "The Influence of Psychiatry on Anthropology in America During the Past One Hundred Years" (1944), and Margaret Mead, "Psychiatry and Ethnology" (1961c). In "The Relevance to Psychiatry of Recent Research in Anthropology," Ernest Becker (1962b) uges new efforts in that collaborative relationship. D. D. Reid describes a number of "Epidemiological Methods in the Study of Mental Disorders" (1960); John A. Clausen and Melvin L. Kohn review "The Ecological Approach in Social Psychiatry" (1954–1955), and with others Dorothea C. Leighton covers "Ecology and Epidemiology" in the first chapter of *The Character of Danger* (1963). R. J. Plunkett and J. E. Gordon find many limitations in their survey of *Epidemiology and Mental Illness* (1960). Donald A. Kennedy comprehensively introduces "Key Issues in the Cross-Cultural Study of Mental Disorders" (1961), together with summaries of work done toward resolving those issues. Raymond G. Hunt admits how little we know about "Socio-Cultural Factors in Mental Disorder" (1959). For one of the few empirical studies of mental health, see Theodore A. Kotchen, "Existential Mental Health: An Empirical Approach" (1960). Clemens E. Benda discusses the implications of "Existentialism in Philosophy and Science" (1960–1961), including psychi-

atry. I have given little thought to defining illness in itself, but Aubrey Lewis, "Health as a Social Concept" (1953), goes into the matter in some detail. Karl Jaspers appraises "The Explanatory Theories—Their Meaning and Value" in chapter 11 of *General Psychopathology* (1963).

REFERENCES

1 *The New York Times*, May 1, 1961. Copyright 1961 by The New York Times Company. Reprinted by permission.
2 Boas, 1932: 47.
3 By people like Adams, 1964; E. Becker, 1963 and 1964; Mowrer, 1960 and 1961; Szasz, 1960 and 1961. See also Jaspers, 1963: 779–790; Laing, 1960: 33; Ausubel, 1961b.
4 *Cf.* Mandelbaum, 1954: 22.
5 Szasz, 1961: 255.
6 McPartland, 1960.
7 D. C. Leighton *et al.*, 1963: 99–100.
8 Mowrer, 1961.
9 Hollingshead and Redlich, 1958.
10 Srole *et al.*, 1962.
11 *Cf.* Manis *et al.*, 1964.
12 Margetts, 1965; A. H. Leighton and Murphy, 1965; Wittkower and Fried, 1959–1960; Srole, [1965].
13 Jaspers, 1963: chap. 12.
14 Taylor and Chave, 1964: chap. 17.
15 *Cf.* Wortis, 1950: 181–187, 226–227; Szasz, 1961: chaps. 2–3; D. C. Leighton *et al.*, 1963: chap. 2.
16 Laing, 1960: 28–33; Jaspers, 1963: 55–56. Marvin K. Opler (1963) contrasts existential psychiatry with "scientific" work in the field.
17 La Barre, 1954: chap. 13; *cf.* Marvin K. Opler, 1956: 157.
18 Lasswell, 1951.
19 See Montagu, 1961.
20 E. Becker, 1964: 7; Jaspers, 1963: 730.
21 Fromm, 1955.

22 R. Benedict, 1934b: chaps. 7–8; Sapir, 1924. See also M. Mead, 1928a: chaps. 13–14 and 1935: chap. 18 and Conclusion.

23 Abridged from Brickner, 1943: 158–192. Margaret Mead's introduction places Brickner's book in proper perspective when, very kindly, she says that "because we live in an emergency for the whole of civilization, because every ounce of disciplined competent thinking, every spark of intuition and insight that we can muster is needed, Dr. Brickner has written this book. And because . . . there are still many in the world who would rather convict a brother scientist of a typographical error than take the time to find out what he is talking about, Dr. Brickner has been unusually brave to write it" (p. 10). Caroline E. Playne (1925) probably had less at stake when, this time in retrospect, she diagnosed the German and French "group minds" at the time of World War I and found them both equally alienated from sanity. She cites evidence: passionate nationalism, chauvinism, contagious hero worship, glorification of the military, and suicidal acceptance of war as inevitable.

24 E. C. Parsons, 1945; Brant, 1950: 220; Zingg, 1942.

25 Arieti, 1956; *cf.* Freud, 1959.

26 *Cf.* E. Becker, 1964: 82–87; Hallowell, 1939 (reprinted under another title in Hallowell's collected writings, *Culture and Experience*, 1955: chap. 2).

27 Engelmann, 1963.

28 Lemert, 1962.

29 Jaspers, 1963: 780.

30 E. Cumming and Cumming, 1957.

31 Wegrocki, 1939; Savage, Leighton, and Leighton, 1965: 24–25. *Cf.* Schwitzgebel, 1964: 24–27.

32 What follows is based on A. H. Leighton, 1959: chap. 4. See also *Diagnostic and Statistical Manual of Mental Disorders* by the American Psychiatric Association, 1952; Stengel, 1959; Menninger, 1963: chaps. 8–11; Savage, Leighton, and Leighton, 1965. Also see the different approach of Jaspers, 1963: chaps. 1–3.

33 Taylor and Chave, 1964: 168–170.

34 Based on A. H. Leighton, 1959: 122; A. H. Leighton, Lambo, *et al.*, 1963: 59–79. Recognition of genetic, physiological, and experiential factors simultaneously operative in psychiatric disorders is part of the "multifactorial view." The number of factors and their names vary slightly among different writers; *cf.* Plunkett and Gordon, 1960: chap. 4.

35 Rilke, 1949: 89.

36 Sapir, 1932; Lévi-Strauss, 1950: xvii; Jaspers, 1963: 281–282; E. Becker, 1961–1962.

37 Grant, 1963: chap. 9.

38 Bateson, 1955.

39 *Cf.* Sarason and Gladwin, 1958.

40 Freud, 1950: 323.

41 A. H. Leighton, 1959.

42 Stagner 1951: *cf.* Sluckin, 1954: chaps. 1 and 4.

43 Menninger, 1963: chap. 5.

44 Selye, 1953 and 1956.

45 A. H. Leighton, 1959: chap. 5; *cf.* Menninger, 1963: chap. 7. There are echoes of William McDougall in Leighton's concept of striving as well as in his use of sentiment as an analytic concept.

46 The vital strivings are mostly as A. H. Leighton gives them, with identity added following Becker's (1964: 112 ff.) discussion. On freedom from ambiguity, see A. F. C. Wallace, 1961b: 16, 125.

47 Shoben, 1962: 770.

48 Maslow, 1962; this is similar to Menninger's (1963: chap. 5) view that man's freedom and consciousness allow him to transcend his immediate environment in maintaining homeostasis.

49 Menninger, 1963: 293–295.

50 Grinker and Spiegel, 1943: 73.

51 G. Wilson and Wilson, 1945: 49–58.

52 A. H. Leighton, 1959: 151–157; for the double-bind theory, see Bateson, Jackson, et al., 1963; Watzlawick, 1963.

53 From Grinker and Spiegel, 1943: 115–121. I use the theory of A. H. Leighton, 1959: 149–150. Contrast with the theory of Mowrer, 1961: 151.

54 Janis, 1958.

55 A. H. Leighton, 1959: 157–160 and chap. 6. For an early version of the same view, see Faris and Dunham, 1939: 10–11; cf. Polgar, 1962: 162.

56 Naroll, 1959.

57 A. H. Leighton, 1959: 318–319. See also A. H. Leighton, Lambo, et al., 1963: 180. Analogous markers could be used to define a disintegrated family or other groups and organizations.

58 Durkheim, 1951.

59 A. H. Leighton, 1959: 320–323.

60 See also J. M. Murphy, 1962.

61 Srole et al., 1962: 200–201.

62 Naroll, 1959; Arsenian and Arsenian, 1948.

63 Such cultures have been examined by Ruth Benedict, n.d.

64 Cf. J. Henry, 1963: chap. 6.

65 Myers and Roberts, 1959.

66 A. H. Leighton, 1959: 313. From My Name Is Legion, © 1959 by Basic Books, Inc., Publishers, New York.

67 Marvin K. Opler, 1956: 192.

68 My account is from B. Kaplan and Plaut, 1956: chap. 5. See also Eaton and Weil, 1953 and 1955; Siegel, 1955.

69 R. Benedict, 1934a and 1934b: chap. 8.

70 Devereux, 1956b; Czaplicka, 1914: 169, 172; Hambly, 1926: 217–222, 258; Freeman, 1965.

71 Kroeber, 1952: 310–317; but note the inconsistency between his 1940 and 1952 positions; he may, of course, have changed his views.

72 See the debate between George Devereux and Marvin K. Opler in the American Anthropologist, 1961, 63: 1088–1093.

73 Billig, Gillin, and Davidson, 1947–1948.

74 Eliade, 1964.

75 Lantis, 1960: 113–127, 182–183.

76 Ibid., pp. 131–147, 183–185.

77 Boyer, 1961, 1962, and 1964; Klopfer and Boyer, 1961.

78 Freud, 1952; Mullane, 1965.

79 Szasz, 1961 and 1963.

80 E. Becker, 1964.

81 E. Becker, 1963; cf. M. J. Field, 1960: 38–39.

82 Mowrer, 1961: cf. Menninger, 1963: chap. 15.

83 Hartung, 1963.

84 Fromm, 1955: 72, 193.

85 A. F. C. Wallace, 1960, 1961b, and 1961c.

86 Goldstein, 1940.

87 Hackett, 1952, cited in A. F. C. Wallace, 1960: 704.

88 A. F. C. Wallace, 1956a and 1961b: 153.

89 A. F. C. Wallace, 1961c.

90 Ellenberger, 1960: 165–169.

91 Shoben, 1957.

92 Srole et al., 1962: 138.

93 What follows adheres closely to M. Jahoda's (1958) summary, but also introduces some other material.

94 Fried and Lindemann, 1961: 95–99; Kornhauser, 1962.

95 Shoben, 1957.

96 T. V. Smith, 1934: 560–561.

97 Fromm, 1961: 69.

98 Fromm, 1955: chap. 2.

99 Maslow, 1960.

100 Bhagavad-Gita, 1954: 45.

101 Watts, 1957: 115.

102 Bhagavad-Gita, 1954: 45.

In Defense Against Stress

12

Mental abnormality . . . must be defined in terms of the relationship between actions and situations. But it is not always easy to say exactly what the actual situation is. . . . The external world of physical reality is always transformed by the person; he reacts not to the world but to his conception of it.[1]

ROBERT E. L. FARIS

H. WARREN DUNHAM

Cultures that consistently maintain a resistive or regretful attitude toward all manifestations of psychopathology may be rated as having progressed beyond those that tend to induce certain kinds of psychopathology by rewarding them. . . .[2]

A. L. KROEBER

"SOCIAL CAUSES" OF SUICIDE

Statements about personality disorder become statements of personality in culture when the frequency of, or the form taken by, the disorder can be related to cultural conditions that antecede or accompany it. Only then can we possibly understand the social reasons why, for example, during World War II many young Americans were rejected as unfit for military service because of poor mental health. With such information we are also likely to find etiological blueprints by which to act to at least diminish the flow of patients to psychiatric clinics and hospitals.[3] I have indicated that one of the most promising ideas with which social scientists have explored the social bases of personality disorder is that of stress engendered by society's social arrangements. Cumulative stress, they claim, takes its toll in personal wear and tear as the person strains to adapt. Alexander Leighton[4] merely offers a refinement of this hypothesis, making blocked striving for salient goals the threat that engenders stress and provokes strain.

Many investigations that fall within the area of cultural psychiatry have fruitfully used the concept of social stress, including Émile Durkheim's famous study of *Suicide*, a work first published in 1897.[5] He em-

351

phatically states his intention to look for social conditions that favor ("cause," he says) suicide, but he doesn't wholly disregard the individual in favor of the social environment where, he believes, the real "productive causes" of suicide reside. Regularly he steals a glance at the motivating states of personality engendered by social conditions in order to show how the latter actually affect people.[6] This is precisely the task of psychological anthropology and the point of Edward Sapir's advice to study culture in the locus of the person. Altruistic suicide, undertaken from a sense of duty or so that others may live is not symptomatic of strain, nor is all egoistic suicide self-destruction taken as a private right when the power of society over the individual atrophies or weakens. However, even suicide as a result of stress is easier where a person sees no reason to endure his sufferings. Because Protestantism possesses fewer common beliefs and ritual practices than Catholicism, it dominates individual judgment less and therefore integrates its followers more loosely than does the Catholic Church. Hence, Durkheim explains, Protestants face greater risk of suicide than Catholics, and Jews less than both. In fact, "suicide increases with knowledge," not because one learns to destroy oneself but because knowledge undermines commonly accepted opinions and therefore frees the individual from dogma, whose roots are social. Any factor that emancipates men from social domination and throws them on their own resources favors suicide.[7]

Of all four types of suicide that Durkheim discusses—altruistic, egoistic, anomic, and fatalistic—he explains the motivational basis of egoistic suicide least well, probably because egoistic suicide isn't a type of suicide at all, but rather designates a kind of social climate in which prohibitions on taking one's own life are easily ignored.[8] Some people undoubtedly do find difficulty in bearing extreme freedom and individualism

that slackens the bond connecting person and society, and to them the term "egoistic suicide" might apply. Such people remind us of Margaret Mead's[9] advice that we educate for the choices that face us in our modern, large-scale world, where we have gained enhanced possibilities of choosing. Altruistic suicide, illustrated by the Hindu widow who immolated herself on her husband's funeral pyre,[10] the Eskimo oldster who went on the ice to freeze in order to save his group a mouth to feed, and the soldier who deliberately offers his life in war, is clearly psychologically motivated. Its sources, however, are not dismay, fear, or other unbearable feelings, but hope, enthusiasm, and faith.

Two of Durkheim's types of suicide—anomic and fatalistic—are, according to his own reasoning, founded in stress (though he doesn't use that word). Anomic suicide accompanies economic crises, even "fortunate crises" that enhance a country's prosperity. Why does he claim that every disturbance to social equilibrium, even if it achieves greater comfort, is an impulse to voluntary death? Because in such crises the regulatory role of society breaks down with serious personal consequences. Normally society helps men rein their wants, needs, and passions; it sets extreme limits to human ambitions beyond which people don't aspire. It sets an end to desire, one of course varying with social position. The result, generally speaking, allows people to live in harmony with their conditions, even with poverty. They desire only what they may legitimately hope for as the normal reward of their acts. But when economic disaster strikes, it stressfully forces men suddenly to reduce their wants and learn greater self-control, and eradicates their customary comforts and social advantages. Painful adjustments are required which some people can't manage to achieve. In economic growth, on the other hand, restraint on ambition disappears; customary relations are disrupted; desires increase; and rules lose their compelling hold as people who eye abundance grow impatient with control. Stress mounts when demands cease to be regulated or grow too inordinate to be fulfilled. "How," under such anomie "could the desire to live not be weakened?"[11] Should religion in a community lose its regulatory hold and government become the servant rather than the master of industry, then anomie becomes not merely the acute concomitant of crisis but a chronic state. From top to bottom of the social ladder aroused greed remains unsated; thirst for novelty and pleasure is endless; nobody sees any reason to endure the least reverse; and rules cease to be binding.

Anomie, a cultural condition that encourages people to pursue culturally valued goals so intently that they pay relatively minor attention to the legitimacy of the means they use to attain those goals, has become an important explanatory concept in social science.[12] For a community implicitly to condone the use of illegitimate but technically efficient means to win a game or make a quick pile of money hardly stresses someone who fails to notice the dissolution in values, but the anomie is felt as it interferes with his vital strivings. Hence, in Alexander Leighton's theory, anomie together with Durkheim's egoistic type of social structure (in which the bonds holding individual to society have slackened) represent two indicators of social disintegration, a general condition likely to block striving and upset personal equilibrium. Recall some other earmarks of social disintegration: frequent hostility and violence, widespread ill health, extreme poverty, and cultural confusion accompanying cultural change. Taken together, those features resembled a social environment to which Durkheim ascribes his fourth type of suicide, fatalistic suicide, which is the outcome of chronic frustration, excessive regulation, "futures pitilessly blocked and passions violently choked by oppressive discipline."

ALCOHOL DISSOLVES ANXIETY

Half a century after Durkheim's *Suicide*, Donald Horton[13] delved into what Durkheim would have called the social causes of excessive drinking. Viewing personality and culture as two sides of the same phenomenon, Horton reasons that difficulties inherent in a way of life will be registered in individual conflicts and anxieties. To resolve their distress, individuals will use suitable forms of behavior that they find or innovate in their culture. Drinking alcohol to allay anxiety is an instance of stress-reducing behavior. Under certain conditions, therefore, drinking constitutes a sign of strain. Paradoxically, drinking may arouse new anxieties, because intoxication releases forbidden aggressive and sexual impulses. Socially patterned conventions erected around drinking and tested through time provided some protection against anxiety aroused through drinking. They allow people to drink safely; that is, to dissolve their anxieties through moderate amounts of alcohol taken in standardized ways without risk of punishment. This theory equips Horton to understand drinking psychologically. Using a large number of anthropologists' accounts of drinking in culturally different communities, he proposes to find out whether aggressive and sexual impulses are released following heavy drinking; whether the general level of anxiety in a community controls the degree of drinking (that is, whether drinking is a response to stress), and, finally, whether threat of punishment for drunken behavior restricts drinking. Published ethnographic data assure him that all over the world alcohol releases aggressive and sexual impulses, and that the untrammeled release of these during intoxication is usually dreaded. Available information also shows that the degree of drinking varies cross-culturally with the amount of stress—Horton calls it anxiety—that people experience. However, judging the level of anxiety from publications can be done only by finding easily apparent, logically defensible indicators for it. Horton hits on subsistence insecurity as such an indicator. He reasons that in communities which regularly face subsistence insecurity, male insobriety will frequently be high (as indicated by descriptions in ethnographies like "excessive" drinking, "complete drunkenness," and "terribly given to drunkenness"). Contact with another way of life suggests itself as another indicator of anxiety, for anthropologists' accounts frequently describe contact with another way of life as severely disorganizing. He finds just what he predicted: Heavy drinking correlates with subsistence insecurity, and every case of recent culture contact he examined also includes extreme insobriety. His evidence also suggests that he is on the right track in expecting that strong negative reactions to aggression and sexuality will restrain insobriety, though here he ran into special difficulties with his method. In the end he concludes that people in many parts of the world use alcohol to reduce anxiety. Drinking, in other words, furnishes a means of adapting to socially engendered stress. Intoxication, to be sure, threatens a community with further stress, but threat of punishment limits insobriety. In his too great readiness to see deficiency motives, like anxiety, at the source of heavy drinking, Horton demonstrates a prevailing bias in psychological anthropology to which I have already called attention. His reasoning that culture contact intensifies stress, hence the heightened drinking, is questioned by the possibility that recent contact may have introduced alcohol to people who don't appreciate its potency and lack established drinking conventions; therefore they frequently drink to the point of terrible drunk-

enness. That happened after the Eskimo in Frobisher Bay received legal drinking privileges, but judicial punishment imposed for drunkenness soon led a large proportion of drinkers to rectify their conduct.[14]

ALL THAT IS WRONG WITH CULTURE

Psychosis is the final outcome of all that is wrong with a culture.[15]

                              JULES HENRY

Such culture traits as private homes that shield us from relatives' and neighbors' interference; the tough-guy private eye who combines violence and love; and our highest-in-the-world standard of living that allows our homes to be flooded with deep-pile carpeting, stereo sets, and electric kitchen gadgets aren't inherently stressful. But they can interfere with vital strivings and keep a person, perhaps a child, in a state of chronic disequilibrium, leading to severe personality distortion.[16] Jules Henry spent 500 hours observing in the homes of U.S. families that had a psychotic child to learn how parents used their version of American culture to lay the foundations for insanity. Let me make it clear that he did not study people in disintegrated pockets, but visited hard-working, law-abiding, moral folk who lived in good neighborhoods where they were popular. The stresses encountered there are outcomes of standard U.S. culture and national character, not by-products of promiscuity, drunkenness, poverty, and other elements of disorganization.

Adult Americans can adjust to one another's lack of involvement, insincerity, struggles for dominance, and an emphasis on strength that excludes tenderness as shameful or feminine. Children, however, can't prosper under the care of self-centered, impulse-dominated, detached, and confused people who fear being exploited in their parental role or by their employer,

Jules Henry (Washington University Photographic Service—Herb Weitman)

who yearn for achievement and project it on the child, and whose commitment to toughness comes out in stubbornness and callousness to even a baby's needs. When people are confused about their own identities and in conflict over their role being "merely" that of housewife and mother, they produce joyless, confused homes that lack tenderness and generosity. They fail to regard the needs of children as separate from their own. The most comfortably furnished home in the country can't compensate for the barriers to early striving its culturally nurtured climate poses. We have engineered it so that in America babies remain a strictly private enterprise. Nobody oversees parents in our impersonal society,

with the result that even lethal care becomes possible. Parents with personalities marked by shallowness of involvement, a tendency to read life off in terms of a struggle for dominance and submission (in which the child, too, must be cowed lest it gain the upper hand), and a readiness to substitute strength for tenderness can become pathogenically entangled with their children. Emotional disorder in children results as "the product of underlying, culturally determined psychological conditions, different in all parents, but ramifying hideously . . . until the entire psychic apparatus of the child is invaded by the cancer of emotional illness."[17]

The more conflict around basic tasks like eating, sleeping, crying, and elimination, the greater will be the tension engendered in the growing youngster. No other culture than our own has transformed each of these tasks into a battleground whereon we daily replicate our general cultural orientation toward struggle and survival. Our culture provides for no extended social responsibility to care for young children. Hence, all responsibility is put on the mother regardless of her emotional and intellectual readiness, or unreadiness, for the role. Our houses allow mother and child to be separated in relatively very distant rooms, thereby further reducing approaches between them. The higher the standard of living in the home, the more obstacles come between a Euroamerican mother and her baby. The combination of love and violence, so common in our movies, gets buit into our family relations too, entering with fathers for whom roughness and toughness do the work of love. Only in that way can withdrawn men who fear tenderness bring themselves into contact with children, especially boys. Strength becomes not simply a means of having fun, but also acquires the purpose of "strengthening" the child and "making him into a man." Parents also construct delusional systems around their children which enable them. to half believe that the youngsters aren't present. Sometimes the result is psychosis; the child's sense of identity becomes completely destroyed as he tries to adapt to the stressful conditions he daily encounters in his home.

Exposed to Unequal Stress

Social classes in the United States provide controlled conditions necessary to test the claim that heavy, cumulative stress disorders persons exposed to it. Each class, despite practicing its own alternative forms of behavior, shares the same general culture and belongs to the same larger social system. Each, theory holds, also stands exposed to unequal amounts of stress. If, as theory predicts, a person strains in adapting to stress, then evidence of such strain in the form of more, and more severe, personality disorder should show up in social strata where stress is more pronounced. We should encounter more of the most distorted personalities in the most highly disadvantaged neighborhoods of our great cities. Ambitious investigations in New Haven and Manhattan support such reasoning. However—and the subsequent chapter will make this more clear—stress alone doesn't produce the severe distortion noted among lower class personalities. More complex factors accompanying the cultural diversity of modern, American stratified society, including differences in values and style of life among different social classes—quite without regard to any stressful impact they may have—influence the picture of the poor mental health that disadvantaged people present to psychiatrists.

The New Haven study, which confidently concluded that cultural conditions in different social classes, including stress, influence the development of personality disorder, began in 1950.[18] Previously, nobody had ever adequately studied the proposition,

often asserted, that the presence of mental illness differed from one social class to another. To discover the extent of personality disorder in the city's population, a Yale University team of sociologists and psychiatrists sought to locate all persons from the community who, between May 31 and December 1, 1950, were in treatment with a psychiatrist or under psychiatric care in a clinic or hospital. They called on and wrote to private practitioners of psychiatry as far away as New York City and to well-known, private treatment centers as distant as Canada, Florida, and Kansas. Twenty private practitioners understandably refused to cooperate, but 75 "treatment agencies" agreed to furnish data on patients from New Haven. Once patients had been located, the investigators used each patient's neighborhood of residence, occupation, and education to determine his class position; the same criteria were employed to stratify the city population of 239,000 people. The investigators found it convenient to divide New Haven's approximately 72,000 households into five social classes. Wealthy people, including highly educated business and professional leaders, living in the most exclusive neighborhood and constituting about 3 percent of the city's strength, make up the top social bracket, called Class I. Upper-middle-class families of men occupying high managerial and professional roles and frequently college-educated, about 8.4 percent of the total population, constitute Class II. The next stratum accommodates small proprietors, white-collar office and sales workers, and skilled manual workers. People on this level, about 20.4 percent of the city's total, make up Class III and are predominantly high-school or business-school graduates. In Class IV are the families of semiskilled factory workers and some white-collar workers who have at least a grade-school education; they make up 49.8 percent of the city's total. Semiskilled factory workers and unskilled laborers, most of whom never finished elementary school, and their families comprise the lowest stratum, Class V which amounts to 18.4 percent of the city.

When the New Haven study proceeded to compare the number of psychiatric patients, it discovered them to be considerably underrepresented in classes I–IV but grossly over-represented in Class V. Class I constitutes 3 percent of New Haven's population but only 1 percent of the patients in treatment come from this social level. Class V accounts for 18 percent of the town, yet 38.2 percent of the located patients belong to this stratum. In Class V, men especially risk personality disorder. Constituting 17.9 percent of the population, they represent 43 percent of patients in treatment, whereas women, who account for 18.9 percent, furnish 33.2 percent of the patients. Negro or white, the proportion of people with personality disorder increases as class standing drops, indicating that class, not color, is the potent factor. Somewhat in line with what Durkheim leads us to expect, Catholics and Jews seem slightly better protected from mental illness than Protestants.[19] However, in the most disadvantaged sector of town —Class V—religion matters little. There Protestants and Catholics both face great risk of mental illness, though Jews remain a bit better off. When patients' disorders are divided into two types, neuroses and psychoses, it appears that each type tends to predominate at a different end of the class spectrum. In classes I and II, some 65 percent of the professional men and members of their families who become mentally ill are diagnosed as neurotic. In Class III, only 45 percent of the disordered white-collar and skilled manual workers, small proprietors, or their close kin are so judged. The proportion drops to 20 percent in Class IV and to only 10 percent in Class V. With respect to psychoses, the prevalence becomes greater moving down from Class I to Class V, though the magnitude varies from

one type of disorder to another. Organic disorders (meaning mental illness due to traumas or to infections, such as syphilis) show the largest increase from higher to lower strata.

Do classbound cultural factors influence the high prevalence of psychoses in lower-ranking social strata? Perhaps psychotics at the bottom of the status ladder had drifted down in class as a result of their illness, hence the greater proportion of psychoses there. The New Haven study offers no proof for the hypothesis of downward mobility. Using schizophrenics to test the hypothesis shows that only 1.3 percent of schizophrenic patients stand in a class below that of their parents, whereas 4.4 percent have been upwardly mobile in their lifetimes. A very large proportion obviously come from the same social level in which they have been born and reared, indicating that pathogenic cultural factors influencing personality disorder probably originate in the social setting from which the patients come.

The New Haven study does not try to test hypotheses designed to track down the precise, socially patterned, pathogenic factors that contribute to more and more serious personality disorder in the lower social strata. It does, however, draw on already available theoretical insights to point a tentative finger in the direction that later etiological research has taken to discover the cultural dynamics of psychiatric illness.[20] For example, the presence or absence of traumatic experiences in early infancy may differ from one social class to another. A loveless infancy, such as is theoretically more likely to occur in Class V families, could institute lifelong dependence as well as states of dejection, apathy, and lack of trust in others. In later childhood, in the lower class, neglect of training in orderliness, rigidity, punctuality, and perfectionism may prepare the way for relatively more severe later-life conflicts. Blocked sex-

role identity formation and uncertain dominance feelings in early childhood may also
occur more frequently in lower-class than
in middle-class families. A defective superego may be encouraged by the way children
in Class V are reared. In later life, in the
lower class, a disturbed superego together
with a tendency to act out disturbances in
identification aggressively may call for a
diagnosis of serious psychiatric disorder. "It
is not coincidence that the public psychiatric clinic for children in this community
is filled, in large part, with Class V boys
and girls sent there by the juvenile court or
school authorities," or that the state prisons
are filled by a disproportionately large
percentage of young adults from classes IV
and V.[21] Lower-class people continue to
face stronger threats throughout their adult
life, as well as qualitatively different ones
than those confronting the higher classes.
Upward mobile individuals, who naturally
come from the lower ranks, encounter particularly intense conflicts and emotional
trauma. Growing old is more difficult for
class IV and V persons, who lack adequate
insurance or pension plans and are continuously threatened by the fate of becoming
dependent.

The New Haven investigators, as I have
said, deal very tentatively with the psychological and social genesis of mental illness. They favor quite another order of explanation to account for the fact that personality disorder occurs disproportionately
more frequently in the city's lower class,
finding the answer in the unequal way patients from different social classes are psychiatrically treated. Despite America's
stress on social equality, the kind of psychiatric treatment its citizens receive depends
to some extent on their social class, depending not only on their ability to pay, but on
their ability to understand psychotherapy

⟨ *Psychiatric Care of Schizophrenics Varies with Patients' Social Class*[22]

As the following table (which refers to 1950) shows, upper-class schizophrenics in
New Haven receive higher-grade therapy than those in the lower class:

| | Percentage under treatment receiving | | | |
Class	Psychotherapy	Organic therapy	Custodial care	Number of patients
I–II	51.7	24.1	24.1	29
III	20.5	48.2	31.3	83
IV	15.3	47.7	36.9	352
V	9.1	33.7	57.2	383

Psychotherapy includes forms of treatment, such as psychoanalysis and group therapy,
undertaken with the assumption that a patient's difficulties may be eliminated through
discussion and reeducation. *Organic therapy* is directed principally toward a bodily
organ and assumes that the patient's symptoms may be eliminated, or at least controlled, by some form of chemical or physical intervention. Lobotamies, electrocon-
vulsive, and insulin-coma therapies belong in this category as does treatment through
sedation and physiotherapy. *Custodial care*, which hardly constitutes treatment in the
proper sense of the word, rests on the assumption that little can be done for a mental
patient beyond providing him with a place in which to eat, sleep, and exist until he
recovers spontaneously, or dies.

and to arouse a positive response in the psychiatrist who treats them. Upper-class patients diagnosed to have neurotic symptoms receive psychotherapeutic treatment by private practitioners. The lower the class the greater the likelihood of finding neurotic disorders treated medically or surgically, including by shock. Among psychotic patients, schizophrenics show the most marked divergence in therapeutic methods. More than half (57.2 percent) of Class V schizophrenics languish in understaffed state hospitals year after year, receiving primarily custodial care. About half (51.7 percent) of classes I–II schizophrenics receive psychotherapy and only 24.1 percent have been abandoned to mere custodial care. As a result, a large number of chronic schizophrenic patients from Class V remain in state hospitals year after year, thereby disproportionately swelling the prevalence of mental illness on this level. Culture enters the analysis because the very cultural background of neurotic lower-class patients handicaps them for treatment by some kind of psychotherapy. Their values and understandings diverge so much from those of professionally trained psychiatrists that they are able to receive little help from insights he provides. Considerable modifications in psychotherapeutic techniques will be necessary in order effectively to bridge the cultural gap between psychiatrists and the poorly schooled, unskilled and semiskilled neurotic laborers of the lowest socioeconomic level, or members of their families.

JUDGING FROM 120 SIGNS AND SYMPTOM ITEMS [23]

In Manhattan's Midtown area, research set out with the conviction that different cultural conditions in childhood and adulthood influence differences in a population's mental health. The family plays an especially important part, for it presents a bridge for cultural influences, transmitting them to children during the most impressionable years of life. The 175,000 largely adult people who made Midtown home in 1954 constituted a heterogeneous lot. Socioeconomically, the neighborhood runs from a gold coast to slums. Ethnically, it contains a large proportion of European immigrants coming from nearly every country in central and western Europe. Three out of ten American-born inhabitants arrived in this area from beyond New York City's borders. Not everyone who flocked to Midtown finds Manhattan a satisfactory place to live, but the more achievement-oriented people remain because the city gives them opportunities, leave them poised to climb, and lets them keep in touch with others who can help them. Here they can organize their leisure time and social activities around their career. Midtown's cultural climate corresponds to the hustle, frantic speed, hypercompetitiveness, personal anonymity, indifference, and even brutal harshness of Manhattan as a whole. Institutionally, the neighborhood accommodates a very large proportion of medical specialties, an especially large number of hospitals, several private and public schools, many churches (which most Midtowners don't frequent), and a plethora of associations, including ethnic-group societies of the *Gesangverein* variety. Trouble likewise thrives. Juvenile delinquency is half again higher than in the rest of New York City's white health areas, and cases of tuberculosis are double what they are among whites in other boroughs (though similar to the rate in the rest of Manhattan). As is only to be expected, these pathologies aren't equally distributed; together with personality disorders they concentrate in a belt of blocks covered by five- and six-story tenements that house the poor. For closer analysis, the Midtown research project drafted a probability sample of 1911 persons, aged 20 to 59, drawn to

Midtowners live within easy travel distance of New York's central business section.

Whole blocks of tenement housing stretch toward the river and the upper reaches of Manhattan Island.

Small in floor space and catch of sunlight, most of the dwellings offer little play area for children, who are drawn to the cement and asphalt streets.

The large variety of churches gives little clue to the slack vitality of religion in the lives of most Midtowners.

Local institutions in Midtown Manhattan reflect the ancestral culture of the neighborhood's many foreign nationalities.

The dozen public schools, like this one, and many private and parochial schools cater to the neighborhood's heterogeneous families.

Largely residential in character, Midtown's high-density housing forms an almost unbroken wall of brick, mortar, and glass.

replicate in miniature the neighborhood's composition. As many as 1660 persons in this sample were actually interviewed to obtain information about their education, occupation, total family income, and rent. By means of these data the sample could be stratified in socioeconomic levels that provide the controls through which the cooperating sociologists, anthropologists, and psychiatrists tested their theory that cultural conditions make a difference in mental health. But perhaps the disordered person drifted down in the class structure once impairment began to interfere with his adaptation. Recognizing this possibility, the study worked out each respondent's parental socioeconomic status, using as indicators his father's schooling and occupation at the time the respondent was 18 or 19 years old.

At that age, when the person was very likely about to launch his career, his father had probably reached the middle of his own work history.

The Midtown study undertook a treatment census which, like that of the New Haven study, enumerated Midtown residents being treated in a standard psychiatric facility on May 1, 1953, the survey's prevalence day. Major attention, however, went to discovering the over-all frequency of personality disorder whether treated or not. Interviewing the sample constituted a census ambitiously designed to enumerate validated signs and symptoms of mental health and illness in a cross section of a large population. The task of eliciting intimate information about people's past and present mental health in a single interview session,

([Some Items of Information Used To Judge Midtown Respondents' Mental Health[24]

Hands damp often. Sometimes.
Hands tremble often. Sometimes.
Smoke too much.
Bothered by sour stomach several times a week.
Often have hard time making up my mind about things I should do.
Childhood health poor.
Childhood fears of:
   Strangers.
   Being left alone. Little. Much.
   Being laughed at. Little. Much.
Is worrying type.
Never change mind.
Always be on guard with people.
Prefer to go out by myself.
Feel somewhat apart even among friends.
Personal worries get me down physically.
I rarely make a mistake.
No right and wrong, only easy and hard ways to make money.
Interviewer's Observations:
Respondent's tension level at start: Nervous. Sporadic nervous.
   Mostly relaxed.
Respondent's attitude: Hostile. Suspicious. Friendly. Solicitous.
Alertness-intelligence: Dull. Slow. Average. Above average.

using a 65-page mimeographed schedule, proved to be a delicate task, even for the trained psychiatric social workers, clinical psychologists, social caseworkers, and social scientists who did the questioning. Subsequently, two psychiatric judges read a summary of the answers given to the 92 structured questions relating to symptoms of malfunction during recent adulthood, consulted information obtained about 28 selected signs of childhood disturbance, studied the interviewer's observations concerning the respondent's behavior during the interview, and took note of certain other data. The highly skilled judges complained that they couldn't make valid assessments of mental health simply from the schedule's 120 signs and symptom items without also knowing something about each respondent's attitudes toward society, as well as his physical health, age, and marital status. Informed on those points, and leaning away from judgments of illness whenever in doubt, the psychiatrists rated each interviewee's degree of symptom formation in six categories: "well (symptom-free)," "mild," "moderate," "marked," "severe," or "incapacitated." Persons in the last three categories received a rating of "impaired."

Nearly One Quarter Impaired. The treatment census enumerated 864 Midtown patients who had been in public and private psychiatric hospitals five years or less, another 290 on the rosters of psychiatric clinics, and 959 more under treatment by cooperating psychotherapists. These figures yield a total prevalence rate on the census day of 1,290 per 100,000 population, a figure considerably over the crude rate of 798 discovered three years before in New Haven.[25]

Only 18.5 percent of the 1660 persons aged between 20 and 59 interviewed in their Midtown homes turned out to be symptom free. Concerning the rest of the sample population, the two psychiatrists rated 36.3 percent mild, 21.8 percent moderate, 13.2

percent marked, and 17.5 percent severe. They judged 2.7 percent of the persons to be incapacitated, even though they were not in hospitals. Combining the marked, severe, and incapacitated ratings brings to nearly one quarter (to be exact, 23.4 percent) the impaired proportion of Midtown's adult population. Their personalities have been distorted to the point where, in the judges' opinion, they need professional help. (Yet psychiatric facilities were currently giving attention to only 5.4 percent of them.) Adding the number of patients in hospitals raises the proportion of impaired to 23.9 percent, indicating a mental morbidity rate of 239 per 1000.* The psychiatrists judged most of the impaired to be probably neurotic or marked by character disorders (67.8 percent). They deemed about one quarter (26.5 percent) to suffer from psychotic-type and 5.7 percent from organic-type disorders. Keep in mind the tentative character of these judgments, which the psychiatrists reached from studying the results of the interviews, and remember that they did not personally confront the subjects. Probable neurosis and character disorders, psychoses, and organic-type disorders double their frequencies from ages 20– 29 to 50–59, which no doubt means that Midtowners susceptible to personality disorder find considerable difficulty in meeting the stresses of adult life and approaching old age. In no age bracket is one sex at greater risk of personality disorder than another. Single women, of which disproportionately many find Midtown's central location and small apartments convenient, show impairment neither more nor less frequently than wives. On the other hand, single adult men at all ages more often reveal signs of impaired mental health than single women. Religion favors the mental health of neither

---

* Different survey methods have revealed morbidity rates of 232 per 1000 (aged 65 and over) in Syracuse; 333 in Salt Lake City; 138 in New Jersey and 108.6 in Baltimore.[26]

Catholic nor Protestant Midtowner, which may be related to the casual attention he pays to such matters. Jews, however, show a remarkably low frequency of impairment; their symptoms tend mostly to be mild or moderate.[27] Jews of low socioeconomic status especially tend to be at low risk from psychiatric impairment. Whatever the reason—and the result may be connected with religious orthodoxy, which is probably strongest among poor Jews—the favorable position of Jews in this respect is clear enough to warrant suspecting the operation of some as yet unknown impairment-limiting mechanism that counteracts or partially contains the stress they experienced during childhood.

Disarticulated, Wearing Assaults. When respondents' class position is measured by their parents' socioeconomic level, the proportion of well people recedes gradually from the highest to the lowest stratum (see Table), whereas the impaired rate mounts from 17.5 percent in the highest level to 32.7 percent in the lowest. To explain these different frequencies, the Midtown investigators resort to the familiar theory of stress, and refer back to their conviction that different cultural conditions reaching children in the family affect mental health. Disarticulated, wearing assaults on the lower-class child's mind and body, they believe, render him more defenseless to crises and therefore more susceptible to personality disorder than the child who enjoys more

privileges. Judging from the way even subjects in the 20–29-year-old category vary in mental health as their parents' socioeconomic level varies, the seeds of disturbance must have been sown in preadult years rather than in adulthood. Evidence substantiating these conclusions came when the Midtown project examined those parts of the interview that probed for stressful experiences in childhood and adulthood.

To learn about stress in childhood, interviewers asked a number of searching questions that probed for whether the respondent had experienced such forms of unhappiness as living with parents who themselves had psychiatric difficulties or were of the worrying type.[28] In their school years, had they even felt that their father spent too little time with them, that their mother had wanted to run their lives, or that their parents didn't practice what they preached? Positive answers to these three latter items revealed that they had held a negatively colored perception of their parents' character. Information about parental quarrels, economic deprivation, parents' poor physical health, and broken homes in childhood constituted further evidence of preadult stress. Analysts scored each factor 2, 1, or 0, according to whether the respondent admitted that such stressful experiences had often, sometimes, or rarely/never been the case. A person whose parents died before he reached 7 received a score of 2 on that

(*Percentage of Impaired Midtowners Increases as Socioeconomic Levels Based on Father's Occupation and Education Decline*[29]

	(highest) A	B	C	D	E	(lowest) F
Well	24.4	23.3	19.9	18.8	13.6	9.7
Impaired	17.5	16.4	20.9	24.5	29.4	32.7
Number	262	245	287	384	265	217

Columns do not total 100 percent because people with mild and moderate symptoms have been omitted. Class differences with regard to those ratings are slight.

factor; if he also reported that his step-parents had often quarreled, he was given 2 more points, bringing his childhood stress score to 4. The investigators computed childhood as well as a total stress score; in the latter they included stresses that troubled adults at the time of their interview, such as poor physical health, work worries, and lack of neighbors, close friends, or membership in organizations and clubs.

Analysis brought out the importance of sheer number with respect to stress factors. Risk of personality disorder increases as the number of admitted stress factors mounts, so that persons with any two generally show greater psychiatric impairment than those with only one; and those with three, still more. No single source of stress by itself acts so erosively that it distorts all individuals who have had such an experience. No single traumatic event is so severe that it must impair everyone's later-life adaptation. Also no particular number of stresses constitutes a breaking point beyond which symptoms cripple virtually all persons with that number. Individuals vary considerably in their capacity to accumulate stress without breaking under the load. Childhood stresses differ in their noxious influence with attendant circumstances. Persons who were between 7 and 16 years old when their homes dissolved through divorce, separation, or desertion have come through the experience no worse off than persons who

grew up in unbroken homes. But individuals whose homes broke up *before* they reached 7 generally have worse mental health. Poor mental health of parents isn't all of a kind. Mothers troubled with psychosomatic ailments, for example, are more dangerous for their children's well-being than psychosomatically troubled fathers. Worrying parents tend to have worrying offspring, though a worrying mother bodes a little worse mental health than a worrying father. Economic deprivation in childhood is a factor of only moderate strength so far as mental-health risk goes; someone who grew up in a household where parents often quarrelled faces greater risk. Children who often disagreed with their parents are more likely to develop personality disorder. You are better off if in childhood you rejected (or felt yourself rejected by) only one parent rather than both.

The theory that charted the Midtown and similar epidemiological surveys maintains that piled-up stress produces strain. Results obtained from the Midtown study furnish no reason for abandoning that assumption, but neither do they specifically support the causal thinking embodied in the view. Statements that ascribe greater risk of personality disorder to some factor are ultimately correlational and not causal in nature. That some factor regularly produces (or causes) a given subsequent event—say, personality disorder or lung cancer—is very

(*Midtowners of Low Socioeconomic Status Report Somewhat More Childhood and Adult Stress than Persons Better Situated in the Class Structure*[30]

	Average stress scores by socioeconomic status		
	Low	Middle	High
Childhood stress score	3.13	2.94	2.65
Adult stress score	2.75	2.40	1.88
Combined childhood and adult stress scores	5.70	5.30	4.70

Individual stress scores run all the way from a nearly unbelievable zero to a high of 18.

hard to prove when working with human beings, for moral considerations prevent the scientist from experimenting on people as he does on fruit flies and rats. Furthermore, consciousness in human beings is much more complex than in animals. How can we demonstrate that a sample of young people brought up in broken homes will show worse mental health than a sample matched for heredity, experiences, and mode of perception reared in unbroken homes?

Does stress, as measured by number and by score, increase as we move from higher to lower socioeconomic status? The table reveals that it does, but not much. Interviewees of low socioeconomic standing on the average earned somewhat higher childhood, adult, and combined childhood and adult stress scores than persons in middle and high socioeconomic positions. Relatively low-ranking people earned an average combined stress score of 5.7 compared to 5.3 and 4.7, respectively, for the other two categories. The differences are obviously small. Contrary to what might have been expected, lower-class people did not report a notably or consistently more stressful childhood than middle and upper class. Experience with economic deprivation in pre-adult years varied sharply between socioeconomic levels, 30 percent of the lows reporting it and only 15 percent of the highs; but both highs, middles, and lows almost

equally frequently came from broken homes, had experienced poor health in childhood, had lived with mentally disturbed parents or parents in poor physical health, had heard parents quarreling, and had perceived parents negatively. An equal proportion of people in each main socioeconomic level—high, middle, and low—reported that they had perceived parents negatively, which means that parent-child relations in Midtown's lower class seem to be about as tension-laden or fraught with misunderstanding as in the middle and upper brackets. In fact, only 14.3 percent of respondents of low socioeconomic status (as measured by father's occupation and education) reported parents' often quarreling, whereas 16.1 and 14.8 percent of the interviewees in the other two categories did so. Only 10.2 percent of the lows admitted often disagreeing with parents, compared to 12.2 and 14.8 percent of the middles and highs. Here are proportions showing how some other specific childhood experiences are distributed from one socioeconomic level to another (respondents' status being judged from father's occupation and education):

Differences between socioeconomic levels with respect to adult life stresses are more sharply defined, persons of low socioeconomic status more often reporting a clearly

Percentage of responses by socioeconomic status

	Low	Middle	High
Parents the worrying type	52.0	54.9	51.0
Father's psychosomatic score			
2 or more	8.5	12.8	15.6
Mother's psychosomatic score			
2 or more	17.0	17.8	21.9
Mother worked outside of home	38.4	34.4	20.1
Poor physical health in early childhood	10.0	9.2	8.9
Mother didn't understand respondent	27.6	28.6	33.1
Parents didn't always show pride			
in children	14.5	12.7	17.9

more severe life than middles and highs. For example, 34 percent of the lows compared to only 11 percent of the highs gave their current health as poor or fair, and 13 percent of the lows but only 2 percent of the highs lived without close friends in whom to confide.

If average stress scores vary only a little from one socioeconomic level to another, does mental health (as measured by mental health ratings) also fluctuate but little? On the contrary! Mental health worsens far more rapidly from the high to the low socioeconomic level than stress increases. Lower-class people face a greater risk of relatively serious personality disorder even when they earn the same combined childhood-adult stress score as middle- and high-status people. A person chosen at random from all respondents of low socioeconomic status holding a combined stress score of 8, is three times as likely to be in worse mental health than someone randomly selected from people in the middle or high socioeconomic levels with the same stress score (see Table). I shan't go now into the prob-

able reason for this surprising fact revealed by statistical analysis of Midtown data, but in Chapter 13 I'll explore the problem.

The more serious plight of low- compared to high-status people can also be appreciated from the fact that the psychiatrists rating the interviews found only 3.6 percent of the highs to possess psychotic-type symptoms, but judged 13.1 of the lows to be marked by such relatively impairing traits. In contrast, 42.5 percent of the highs compared to only 24.5 percent of the lows were identified as probable neurotics. Therefore, in Midtown as in New Haven, highs tend to manifest less serious forms of personality disorder than lows, and, generally speaking, middles are in between.

Downward Drift and Mental Health. Evidence offered in the New Haven study furnished no grounds for holding that the high proportion of severely damaged people in the lower class resulted from drift downward of individuals psychologically too incapacitated to survive on higher social levels. Better techniques for measuring social mobility between generations in the

❨ Persons of Low Socioeconomic Status Carry Greater Mental Health Risk than Persons of Middle and High Socioeconomic Status, Even When Their Stress Scores Are Similar[31]

Adult-childhood combined stress scores	Average ridits by socioeconomic status		
	Low	Middle	High
4	.53	.46	.40
8	.78	.55	.53
12	.86	.76	.73
14+	.93	.79	.76

The Midtown study used ridits to calculate the risk of personality disorder faced in different socioeconomic categories. A ridit is a measure of chance or probability. The higher the ridit, the worse the mental-health risk of a category. Persons of low socioeconomic status with a stress score of 8 have an average ridit of .78 compared to .55 for middles and .53 for highs. One can say that for persons with a stress score of 8, there is a greater risk that an individual selected at random from the lows will have worse mental health than an individual selected at random from the middles or the highs. This doesn't say how much worse off; it only tells us that the "low" individual is about three times as likely to be worse off than one from the middle or high socioeconomic level.

Midtown study (like comparing a father's with his offspring's occupation) show that 21 percent of the sample's well, single men and women had climbed to higher rungs of the social-class ladder by moving into better jobs than their fathers'. Only 13.6 percent of the impaired, single men and women had moved upward. Of the unmarried wells, only 12.7 percent who occupied lesser occupations than their fathers' had experienced downward mobility compared to 30.1 percent of the unmarried impaired.[32] However, in the 1660-person sample as a whole, the downward mobile are little worse off in mental health than those who remained stationary, and only slightly worse than the upward mobile.[33]

How does mobility up or down in the occupational hierarchy hinge on mental health? Character disorders, especially alcoholism and an extremely passive-dependent make-up, often characterize the downward mobile, taking the sample of 1660 as a whole, perhaps because such behavior interfered with their jobs. Of course, it may also be that stresses brought on by having one's mobility aspirations blocked and having to adjust to a lower standard of living contributed to the symptoms that interviewers noted in persons who had drifted down. Upward mobile people frequently show such character disorders as obsessive compulsive traits, a symptom that must have greatly advantaged them in climbing closer to the top; they are also more apt to be schizophrenics. Even more frequently than the downward mobile, upward mobiles reveal a passive-dependent personality, perhaps because such persons readily complied with ambitious, low-ranking parents. Parenthetically, I must report that nearly half (49 percent) of the respondents holding low socioeconomic status reported that their parents had enjoyed higher socioeconomic status—a surprising discovery, given the American dream that each generation betters itself.

SOCIAL DISINTEGRATION IN STIRLING COUNTY

. . . here one sees through scattered clearings the sweep of bedraggled houses, some as small as play houses, a few large but ghostly with a sense of desertion. Here there is self-expression of a very different kind. Here is the face of a rejected community, built on pride of exactly the opposite values of the surrounding communities.

. . .

Are they unhappy in their poverty? One does not gain the impression that they are, so chained do they appear to their environment, as if the limitations of their horizon shielded them from caring. Young children can be beautiful on the road, the girls with tangled hair and fair clear skin and playful animal eyes, and the young boys with the simplicity and precocious bearing of the very poor. But as these children grow older they will press against the ceiling laid down upon them and lose themselves in the aimless and amoral world of their fathers and mothers.

. . .

It is a challenge to enter a home here. It is not they who rise to meet you; it is you who must brace yourself to meet them. No concessions are asked or given by these bedraggled people. You must like them or reject them on their own grounds. It is you who must sacrifice a part of your values to reach equality with them—and if you can do this, they will be your friends.[34]

JOHN COLLIER, JR.

A frank admission, these paragraphs, of the difficulty a sympathetic anthropologist encounters when he tries to understand, with his own humanitarian values, a class of people who embody cultural alternatives radically different from his own. If the author sacrificed part of his values in order to reach equality with those poor, bedraggled

An English fisherman and his family relax in their Stirling County kitchen. (Cornell Program in Social Psychiatry; Basic Books)

people, the lines he wrote indicate it to have been a temporary sacrifice. He is describing his conflictful encounter with a depressed area in "Stirling County," pseudonym for an actual place in the Canadian Maritimes, where Alexander H. Leighton and his co-workers went to see if social disintegration upsets personal equilibrium by chronically interfering with vital strivings and produces manifest signs of strain.

The New Haven and Midtown studies used urban classes to locate people who presumably live exposed to different amounts of stress and therefore stand at differential risk of mental illness. Investigators in predominantly rural Stirling County selected communities presumed to differ in the balance of noxious and benign conditions to test the claim that mounting stress (they speak of "persistent inter-ference with strivings") disorders persons exposed to it. Predominantly noxious conditions, Leighton[35] predicted, would create a high risk with regard to vital strivings for physical security, sexual satisfaction, expression of hostility, expression of love, securing love, obtaining recognition, expression of spontaneity, orientation in society, membership in a human group, and a sense of belonging to a moral order. Outstandingly noxious social settings would foster personality disorder rather than healthy forms of adaptation.

The Communities. For years the sea has brought Stirling County food and given it a highway to the world. Fishermen's boats and equipment in the coves testify to the continued economic importance of fishing. The woods furnish material for another basic industry, lumbering. (Recall how

*This house stands at the edge of an English
fishing community. (Cornell Program in Social
Psychiatry; Basic Books)*

Longfellow, who never visited Nova Scotia, ponderously begins *Evangeline: A Tale of Acadie* with: "This is the forest primeval. The murmuring pines and the hemlocks.") Between forest and sea, small farms given over to dairying and mixed crops also yield timber that provides a good share of a farmer's cash income. The county carries on a variety of commercial, clerical, and service enterprises, from movies to plants that pasteurize milk. The bulk of the people (speaking of 1950) maintain an average style of life. They own their own spacious but not expensively furnished homes and either own a car or carry life insurance, but not both. Some families stand above the average while others, who fall below it, neither own a car nor carry life insurance. In certain sections live predominantly French-speaking, Roman Catholic Acadians, descended from the first permanent settlers in North America. For not all Acadians were expelled when, in Longfellow's bitter description,

. . . on the falling tide the freighted
  vessels departed,

Bearing a nation, with all its household
  gods, into exile,
Exile without an end, and without an
  example in story.

English-speaking people who trace their heritage to the British Isles make their homes in other sections, where

Still stands the forest primeval; but under
  the shade of its branches
Dwells another race, with other customs
  and language.
Only along the shore of the mournful
  and misty Atlantic
Linger a few Acadian peasants, whose
  fathers from exile
Wandered back to their native land to
  die in its bosom.

From 1948 to 1950 fieldworkers infiltrated the county in search of data about kinship, leadership, religious life, associations, communication, language, education, and other matters. They studied its culture to a degree far exceeding what the New

A house in one of the depressed areas of Stirling County. (Cornell Program in Social Psychiatry; Basic Books)

Haven and Midtown studies had attempted to do. The data found their way to Cornell University where, having done their part in helping to complete a three-volume report, they rest in the form of 200,000 5-by-8-inch file cards.

In 1951 key informants and housing surveys helped to locate within the county communities that contrasted with one another in terms of three likely indicators of social disintegration: poverty, cultural confusion (defined primarily in terms of ethnic mixture), and secularization. As a result of these inquiries, six communities were chosen for special attention. By those three diagnostic criteria, Lavallée, an Acadian lumbering and commercial village of 300 people, and Fairhaven, a conservative English fishing village with 450 people, are relatively well-integrated communities. Four collectively designated depressed

areas, together holding slightly more than 350 persons, represent disintegration: Loomervale, Monkeytown, Northwest Jonesville, and The Bog. Armed with a schedule covering family life, interviewers questioned 1015 representative male and female household heads in the six selected communities. Interviewees spoke about their occupation, material styles of life, reading habits, ethnic identifications, language, strength of religious behavior, moves from place to place, and illness. They also provided information relevant for estimating the prevalence of personality disorder among them. With respect to poverty, the survey showed that in Lavallée and Fairhaven 94 percent and 76 percent, respectively, of the family heads follow average material styles of life, but that in depressed areas fewer than 10 percent do. In Lavallée 91 percent of household heads are Acadian and show pronounced ethnic identification; for example, by strong religious participation or a preference for the French-Acadian language. Fairhaven is homogeneous in the sense that 92 percent of the family heads report no Acadian ancestry. In the depressed areas of the county, however, cultural mixture and confusion for the most part prevail. For instance, in The Bog two thirds of the interviewees report Acadian ancestry but nevertheless are non-Catholic, or don't think of themselves as Acadians; 22 percent report no Acadian ancestry. Secularization is a phenomenon similar to Durkheim's notion of becoming emancipated from social domination by acquiring freedom from strong religious beliefs. In three out of four depressed areas, religion promotes slight social integration. Lavallée, where 81 percent of the family heads participate vigorously in religious behavior, shows little secularization. In Fairhaven 45 percent of the interviewees profess religion strongly. But in all the depressed areas, except Loomervale, only a quarter of the respondents do so.

Lavallée[36]

We Acadians are a separate ethnic group, and we have survived through a miracle willed by Providence.

The survival of the Acadians as a separate group is of fundamental importance.

The Catholic religion and the French language are integral parts of Acadian culture and must be preserved.

The Acadian group is superior to others in spiritual things, but is weaker in economic and political matters.

Having many relatives and friends is a very important thing in life.

The family must be kept strong.

Men and women have clearly different roles in life.

Although the most important thing about the community is that we are all the same, there are some people who are better off than others.

In the past, Acadians received very unjust treatment at the hands of other people.

Other types of people are different, some better than we are in certain things, some far inferior to us, and we Acadians have to judge carefully.

Acadian leadership must be developed.

Leaders must demonstrate their interest in the Acadian group.

Material success is highly desirable and can be achieved through work.

Fairhaven[37]

Fairhaven is the dominant village in this region and its way of life is superior.

Fairhaven is declining and may cease to exist as a going community.

Although Fairhaven is still the best place to live, there are a lot of things threatening its way of life.

Young people must migrate if they are to make anything of themselves.

Fairhaven is less homogeneous now and people are not so close to each other as they used to be.

Although its purposes and proper activities cannot all be spelled out exactly, the family is still very important.

The roles of men and women are clearly different, but traditional expectations cannot always be maintained.

The flexibility of the present is better than the rigidity of the past.

Fairhaven's leaders are effective, but their actions should always be evaluated.

Individualism and self-sufficiency are what give a man self-respect and respect from others.

Work is good in itself and something which should be done regularly and methodically.

Education should be a strict inculcation of "fundamentals."

The Baptist Church is the best guide to understanding God, the world, and man's place in it.

Depressed Areas[38]

People here are mentally and morally inferior.

It is good to be with people but you have to watch your step.

People are changeable and shifty, and you have to stand by yourself in life.

People in authority should not be trusted, but you have to show them respect to their faces.

A good way to distinguish yourself is by knowing something that nobody else knows.

Self-improvement is practically impossible.

Work should be avoided if possible.

A person shouldn't show himself better than his neighbors.

The supernatural world is strange and a man has to face it by himself.

The best thing to do in life is escape from your problems as quickly as possible.

New things should be looked at with considerable suspicion.

Lavallée

The Acadian educational system must be developed.

Personal success should be shared with others.

Religion is the most important thing in life.

Planning and working for long-range goals is more important than being preoccupied with the present.

The "good man" is one who works hard and enjoys his job, is a fervent Catholic and fulfills religious duties, and participates in community activities.

New experiences and innovations should be regarded with some caution.

Fairhaven

The management of one's acts, feelings, and beliefs must reflect dignity and control.

One should be frugal and make the most of material things.

One should be cautious about accepting innovations.

In the previous chapter I noted that Alexander Leighton deictically defines a disintegrated community by its high frequency of broken homes; few or weak associations; few or weak leaders; scarce patterns of recreation; frequent hostility; high rates of crime and delinquency, and weak, fragmented system of communication. In contrast to these seven diagnostic features, poverty, cultural confusion, and secularization, although they may help to spot a disintegrated community (as they did in Stirling County), don't define one. By the truly diagnostic criteria just listed, are Lavallée and Fairhaven relatively integrated and Loomervale, Monkeytown, Northwest Jonesville, and The Bog largely disintegrated? Thirty-nine man-months devoted to their close study confirmed the expected conditions, but warranted Loomervale's elimination from the disintegrated set because it showed too strong evidence of integration. One way now to proceed would be to summarize studies which the Stirling County researchers completed, thereby eth-nographically identifying each of the integrated villages and the depressed areas. You would then see what benign cultural factors predominate in Lavallée and Fairhaven, and how noxious social elements prevail in Monkeytown, Northwest Jonesville, and The Bog. But that would take a vast amount of space. Instead, I have set down in three parallel columns only the distinguishing sentiments (or values) of Acadian Catholic Lavallée, Protestant Fairhaven, and the "county pariahs."[39]

Since social disintegration represents a most crucial variable in the study, I should carefully point out how the depressed areas manifest that condition, thereby blocking vital strivings. Containing around 23–25 households, the depressed areas stand mostly on submarginal land. They are less than fifty years old, being products of changing cultural and economic tides that, when they turned, left relatively unwanted people with outworn skills on the beach. Each of those neighborhoods was described by one or another informant as positively "the worst place in the county," and each backed up his disparagement with obviously exaggerated references to laziness, drunkenness, fighting, sexual immorality, criminal activity, irreligion, and interbreeding resulting in poor heredity. Clergymen say that the people have lost their religion. The inhabitants incorporate many of the attributes that outsiders lavish on them and accept themselves as different. They support themselves through low-paying and intermittent jobs that require little skill and rationalize their low living standards by claiming that long-range goals and striving after betterment are useless. Some people have a stable family life, attend church occasionally, and retain their jobs, but they aren't sufficiently numerous for the authors to alter their conception of the neighborhoods as demoralized and disrupted. A lack of associational life is notable. Interpersonal relations are divided by antipathy and strained through wife- and child-beating. Formal offices of leadership do not exist, nor do informal leaders make their power felt. Illegitimate behavior frequently occurs, especially violations of liquor laws, and drinking usually brings out hostility among family members. Childrearing lacks the warmth found in Lavallée and Fairhaven. In the depressed areas almost half the mothers tend to be cold and businesslike; they rarely play with or cuddle infants. In comparison with the integrated villages, the infant is more often fed when he demands it, which, the authors say, indicates that the baby is already beginning to participate in the characteristic disorderliness of adult daily life. Mothers in the four depressed areas are less consistently concerned with differentiating between masculine and feminine behavior; that is, in providing training for sex roles. They are more lenient in making demands on the child and hold lower, more permissive standards of neatness, orderliness, cleanliness, and school performance. In

general, parents direct more aggression to children than in the integrated communities. Mothers make relatively little use of words and example to control children's behavior and don't rely on deprivation as a form of coercion. People themselves cite physical punishment as the preferred technique of childhood discipline, though actually they more often employ ridicule.

Culture and Personality Disorder.[40] Canadians who live in the depressed areas are economically underprivileged, socially disparaged, and politically powerless. Such restrictive conditions, social scientists hold, are likely to instigate social disruption and deviant behavior. Social disintegration won't affect everyone the same way, partly because in some persons its stressful action is furthered or countered by predisposing hereditary conditions, or eased through physiological strain brought on by malnutrition and infection. Where, for whatever reason, favorable ground is found, the stressful impact on vital strivings of broken homes, hostility, cultural confusion, and general disruption chronically upsets a person, so turning him to deviant modes of adaptation. That people in Monkeytown, Northwest Jonesville, and The Bog frequently select such forms of adaptation is indicated by the fact that signs of psychiatric disorder are appreciably more prevalent in those depressed areas than in Lavallée and Fairhaven.

The epidemiological survey, conducted by Dorothea C. Leighton and associates, estimated prevalence from 1010 interviews conducted with family heads. They scanned each interview record, looking for any sign of psychiatric disorder, any evidence that if the respondent had sometime in his adult life been thoroughly examined by a psychiatrist, he would have been diagnosed as suffering from some specific psychiatric condition. The research group attempted to diagnose the specific psychiatric conditions, and also rated each interviewee on a 4-point

Dorothea C. Leighton

Women in the county face a greater risk than men, though their symptoms are disabling to about the same, or to only a slightly greater, extent. As a matter of fact, since men have fewer symptoms than women, those that do have any are probably more frequently and more severely impairing. The period of peak risk comes earlier for men than for women—between 30 and 39 compared to between 40 and 49, respectively. A second peak in the 60–69 decade coincides for both sexes. Stress, therefore, promotes its greatest ravages in men as they make the transition from adolescence to adult life. They apparently find difficulty in altering their roles and attitudes and in coping with new dangers that beset striving in this growth period. Breaking away from one family to form another and problems of work and economic independence doubtlessly also create masculine uncertainty and conflict. At 60 men face another major transition in which noxious factors weigh heavily, probably because they see opportunities and alternatives diminishing and their capacities faltering. Women find it easier to move from adolescent to adult roles, but find the years of menopausal change and the actual or symbolic loss of their childbearing ability difficult to face. Between 60 and 69 their problem parallels men's. Why mental health should improve after 70 in both sexes isn't clear. The best explanation may be that individuals learn better with age to weather stress and to contain their strain.[41]

Contrary to what Durkheim might lead us to expect, in Stirling County religious involvement doesn't consistently favor mental health. Women who measure high in religious values turn out to have the worst mental health, and the order tends to be reversed for men. Yet, evidence that social integration in Durkheim's sense is prophylactic does show up. When Catholic, French-speaking Acadians in Stirling County are compared with the Protestant,

scale. He received an A rating if almost certainly he had been a psychiatric case in adulthood (e.g., if he had even been to a mental hospital or suffered a nervous breakdown); on evidence of only probable psychiatric disorder (e.g., ulcers, hypertension, or sociopathic behavior), he was rated B; on evidence of merely possible disorder, he got C; and if absolutely no evidence of disorder showed up, D. From their data, the psychiatrists estimate 57 percent of the county's population to be or to have been psychiatric cases. How sick is sick? The investigators appraised average degree of impairment due to all psychiatric symptoms revealed by an interviewee. Once more projecting their data, they estimate that 24 percent of the people of Stirling County have suffered from significant impairment in their lives, while 33 percent have experienced psychiatric disorder without significant impairment.

English-speaking men and women, the former category tends to be somewhat healthier than the county average while the latter is somewhat less well off. When Acadian-Catholic Lavallée is compared with Protestant-English Fairhaven, differences in A, B, C, D ratings even more sharply favor the former. Not religion alone, then, but the heightened integration brought about by a distinctive language and traditional sentiments —values behind Quebec Province's recent "nationalistic" upsurge—appears to support mental health.

All these interpretations are preliminary to the main question: Is personality disorder more likely to occur in the four depressed areas than in the two relatively integrated communities?* Comparing 33 respondents from Lavallée, 49 from Fairhaven, and 69 from Monkeytown, Northwest Jonesville, and The Bog indicates that the average mental health of the people in the two integrated communities is almost exactly the same as that of the Stirling County as a whole. In the relatively disintegrated neighborhoods, women are more inclined to personality disorder than women of comparable age in the county population, and men very much more so. The likelihood of finding personality disorder increases steadily from Lavallée to Fairhaven to the depressed areas. Degree of impairment also increases from integrated to disintegrated communities. In the depressed areas at least half the adult population needs psychiatric attention—for significant rather than severe impairment, it is necessary to add. Among the varied symptoms present in the disintegrated neighborhoods, compared with Lavallée and Fairhaven, are high proportions of sociopathic disorder (like alcoholism combined with dissocial or

* In making their tests to answer this question the investigators controlled for age, sex, and occupational position.

antisocial behavior), psychoneurotic patterns (periodic or constant maladjustment of varying degree throughout adult life), and mental deficiency.

Again the question: Did the psychiatrically disordered people in the depressed areas move to those neighborhoods after stresses experienced in other social settings had worn them down to where they could no longer adapt according to those other communities' norms? Or are the stresses of the depressed areas responsible for the mental health picture? Theory points to the latter alternative. Actually, the Stirling County study did not plan well to test the possibility that historically more effective people may have moved out of the depressed areas while less well-functioning people moved in. It is true that people who have spent only a small part of their lives in a particular depressed area show a slight tendency toward worse mental health than those who have lived there nearly all their lives. But what do we know about their level of functioning in the communities from which they came, or even the level of integration in that community?

One surprising discovery turns up. An advantageous occupational position or more years of schooling makes little difference in mental health in the depressed areas. This discovery is extremely meaningful. Giving a person from a relatively disintegrated community a better job or more schooling isn't sufficient to counteract the noxious life conditions that, operating as a total complex, disturb his personal equilibrium. A population's well-being is a function of the total cultural configuration, a response to a complex number of interrelated factors that form a whole, and it cannot be significantly altered by piecemeal tinkering that leaves the cultural whole largely unaltered. This comes remarkably close to what Ruth Benedict and Margaret Mead said more than thirty years ago when they viewed personality as patterned by

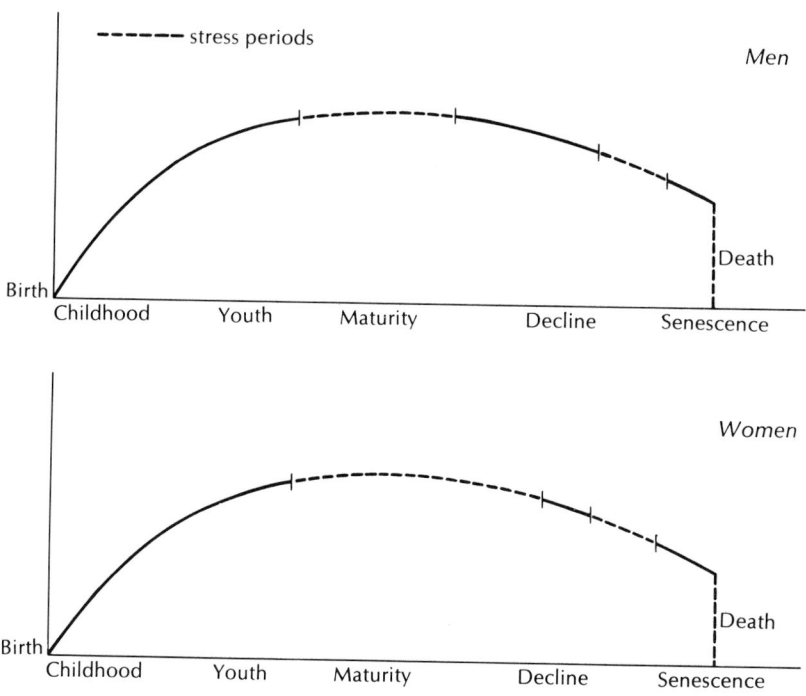

- - - - - - stress periods

Men

Birth

Death

Childhood   Youth   Maturity   Decline   Senescence

Women

Birth

Death

Childhood   Youth   Maturity   Decline   Senescence

These charts illustrate how apparent periods of increased psychiatric risk vary between men and women in Stirling County.[42]

dominant emphases in a cultural whole. A six-year study conducted in Manhattan, which found individual counseling of potentially delinquent vocational high-school girls to be largely ineffective for improving their school behavior or reducing dropouts, reinforces the same conclusion.*[43] Girls who gave signs of becoming delinquent received intensive social-work services, as a result of which three fifths changed "a little" and more than one third "hardly at all." A major objective sought to prevent girls from dropping out of school. Compar-

ison of those who had received social-work counseling and those who had not, revealed that an identical proportion of each graduated from high school, and that no consistent or significant differences characterized the attendance records of either group. Counseling and other kinds of tinkering don't even try to alter the society's social structure and culture, out of which poverty, low social status, and other dangerous conditions grow.[45] Studies like those I have just cited suggest that society as well as individuals needs attention if human behavior in response to social disintegration is to be better controlled.[46]

In Stirling County, and presumably elsewhere, disintegrated communities harbor a predominantly noxious environment that interferes with achieving vital goals, such as love, recognition, spontaneity, the sense of belonging to a moral order, and the sense of

* Robert Rice's[44] more informal report of an attempt to rehabilitate nine young drug addicts from Manhattan's Lower East Side leads to the same conclusion. The insurmountable difficulty was that so long as the young men stayed close to their neighborhood "they were subjected daily to the temptations that had helped to undo them in the first place."

being right in what one does. The action of whatever benign forces they contain is largely lost. The Midtown and Stirling County studies agree that the psychiatrically dangerous effects of noxious environments probably begin very early in life, when the child's urges for security, love, and approval first meet with inconsistency and lack of fulfillment. What he experiences during his first few years in the family anticipates most of what he later encounters outside the home. Environments high in social disintegration are extremely poor in providing help through which the emergence of personality disorder can be avoided. People in a relatively integrated setting, like Lavallée or Fairhaven, can find substitutes for which to strive, and they also get much help in avoiding psychiatric illness from tradition, religion, books, and compassionate advice. In the depressed areas of Stirling County there isn't much to encourage a person whose equilibrium is seriously disturbed. He is left to withdraw, to develop paranoid systems of thought, to sink into depression, and to mask his anxiety by alcohol, sex, fighting, and other forms of excitement.

Integration and disintegration in West African Yoruba [47]

That prolonged, wearing stress leads some people to strain conspicuously wins support through research carried out in Manhattan's Midtown and in Stirling County. However, both those communities belong to a single cultural sphere; their people embody a relatively common cultural tradition derived from Europe. Perhaps the same results won't turn up where culture has roots in a different past.

In 1959 Alexander H. Leighton carried his ideas to southwestern Nigeria, to the small community of Aro where T. Adeoye Lambo, a Yoruba psychiatrist, had devel-

oped a psychiatric hospital which employed modern, Western facilities and also drew on the healing services of traditional, Yoruba religious leaders.[48] The two men agreed on an exploratory program that would be carefully designed, first, to discover the prevalence of personality disorder among a small section of the Yoruba people, and then to identify cultural factors directing the origin, course, and outcome of such disorder. The latter aim embodied the familiar idea that socially disintegrated communities place their members at high risk of psychiatric disorder. Would this relationship hold, even in a non-Western society? How validly could a psychiatrist use Western diagnostic criteria on people with a radically different culture, whose conceptions of reality deviate strikingly from his own? These and other questions could be answered in the course of conducting one of the first modern prevalence surveys in a non-Western community, the results of which would also indicate whether rates of psychiatric disorder in Western communities grossly exceed rates in more traditional social systems.

Unfortunately for those problems, the Yoruba aren't one of Africa's most traditional people. Leighton and his associates from Cornell University and elsewhere studied a tribe of more than three million individuals which had responded to Western-derived change with considerable alacrity. The historical origin of the Yoruba and of the subtribe, Egba, to which the study primarily refers, remains unknown. Although primarily rural, the people have achieved some anthropological renown for their cities, some with more than 200,000 persons; in fact, about a third of the tribe lives in densely aggregated settlements of 20,000 and more persons. So large and concentrated a population has enabled trade to reach important proportions in economic life. Politically the tribe comprises a number of autonomous kingdoms, and its religion is also somewhat fragmented, being carried out in many cults or worship groups directed by various orders of priesthoods. Witchcraft and faith in the power of curses maintain firm hold over all but the most westernized.

Fieldwork. Armed with the appropriate questionnaire, psychiatrists with interpreters to act as mouthpieces interviewed 416 persons drawn mostly by sampling from 15 villages and eight sections of Abeokuta city, the lightly urbanized hub of the villages they studied. Cooperative subjects carried the interview through to the end, but a sizeable proportion resisted and seemed to withhold or give unreliable information. While the psychiatrists interviewed their cooperative and uncooperative respondents to identify psychiatric symptoms and consequent degree of impairment, social scientists scurried around each village observing. Later they intensively queried a proportion of the individuals who had supplied data to the medical researchers. Men with knowledgeable authority, like village headmen, provided auxiliary information about particular villagers' abilities to adapt, their dissocial activities, and other matters. A few sample questions from the psychiatric questionnaire, many of them copied from questions used in Stirling County and elsewhere, will show what cooperative subjects told about and resisting ones objected to revealing. (For each item the interviewer ascertained whether it occurred often, sometimes, or never.)

Does your food ever seem tasteless and hard to swallow?
Do you ever take weak turns?
Is this severe enough to impair your consciousness?
Do you feel in good spirits?
On the whole do you feel that most of your wishes are fulfilled?
Do you sometimes feel hopeless despair?
Are you bothered by short temper?

Are you sure of yourself?
Do you ever hear or see spirits or other things?
Do you think anyone is using "juju" [bad medicine] on you?
Do you think you are troubled by witchcraft?[49]

A planned, routine medical check of each respondent had to be abandoned as unfeasible, because it threatened completion of other parts of the survey.[50] Nevertheless, knowledge that low-grade anemia underlies much ill health in Nigeria led the examiners to solicit a drop of each interviewee's blood. They also treated some unearthed nonpsychiatric illness. Two or more psychiatrists evaluated the psychiatric status of respondents according to highly specific instructions. They identified the pattern of symptoms manifested, estimated degree of impairment, and assigned A, B, C, D ratings as in Stirling County. A subject received an A rating if he almost certainly appeared to be a psychiatric case; B, if probably; C, if possibly; and D if no evidence of such likelihood showed up. Prevalence in this survey again means lifetime prevalence, the psychiatrists being told to "make the ABCD rating of 'caseness' on the basis of all the symptomatology reported, past as well as present." During the evaluation process the raters a few times encountered words and acts that, because they belonged to another culture, proved difficult to interpret. This most often came up in distinguishing between a delusion and a culturally accepted belief. All in all, though, only 21 times in going through 385 usable protocols did cultural differences halt the psychiatrists. The authors admit, however, that they may have erred in understanding some of the information originally recorded.

In order to discover clear-cut, contrasting integrated and disintegrated social environments the social scientists working in

Yorubaland collected social, economic, and medical facts about 25 villages. Later, 15 of these were chosen for interviews, closer anthropological study, and (with the exception of one) classification along a continuum as integrated, intermediate, and disintegrated. Poverty, cultural confusion, and secularization—the same three indicators, somewhat redefined, that served in Stirling County—were used to determine whether a particular Yoruba village was integrated or disintegrated. To give an example of such redefinition: formal education, no indication of cultural confusion in Stirling County, became one in Yorubaland where, researchers assumed, educated persons would exercise a disruptive influence in essentially traditional communities. In addition, evidence of migration from a village suggested a threat to integration. The investigators expected that degree of integration would be manifested by the incidence of stable families, respected leaders, strong and active associations, tolerant and cordial interpersonal relations, law-abiding conduct, and an effective communications network. These are culturebound criteria only in the sense that all the rubrics used by anthropology to classify people—as matrilineal, as matrilocal, as constituting states, as fearing witchcraft, and so on—are culturebound. Such criteria imposed cross-culturally can be tolerated only so long as they work by producing understandings which the profession regards as worthwhile and logically defensible.

It is of some interest to note that more men in the two integrated Yoruba villages possess some Western education than do those in seven intermediate or five disintegrated villages. (The average size of those communities is small, only 61 people.) The proportion of people who spent money on Western education is high in integrated and low in disintegrated Yoruba communities. In both types of villages, a third of the people had spent their life in one or two places. By contrast, the intermediate villages show the greatest stability. I mention these points to show that, unlike what we expect in America, traditionalism and stability in another culture are not necessarily correlated with such high-priority indicators of integration as economic security, frequent religious worship, and family stability. Generally speaking, the indicators of integration used in Stirling County failed to work with equal facility when applied to the Yoruba. Hence, I personally doubt that disintegrated villages among the Yoruba have a stressful impact resembling that which Monkeytown, Northwest Jonesville, and The Bog are said to have.

Findings. Out of the 1010 respondents surveyed in Stirling County, 57 percent received A or B ratings; that is, they were judged likely to be or to have been psychiatrically disordered. Thirty-three percent of the respondents were deemed to be significantly impaired.* In 15 Yoruba villages (262 interviewees) the proportions are 40 percent highly likely psychiatrically disordered and 15 percent significantly impaired. Abeokuta city differs little from the rural communities; 34 percent of its 64 respondents received A or B ratings and 19 percent showed significant impairment. Stirling county had 17 percent in the probably well category; the Yoruba villages have 25 percent and Abeokuta city the same proportion. The Yoruba reported more symptoms than did the people of Stirling County, though the psychiatrists' failure to give a medical examination leaves the possibility that they mistook some signs of physical disorder for evidence of personality disturbance.

* This figure, 33 percent, is the proportion of respondents significantly impaired in Stirling County. Earlier, I spoke of 24 percent as the proportion of the adults estimated on the basis of the survey to be significantly impaired in Stirling County.

By certain indicators, women show significantly more evidence of strain in Stirling County than in the Yoruba villages, where men seem to be at greater risk. Modernization, the authors say, is affecting Yoruba men (especially young men) more than women, who continue secure in their traditional ways. The pressures of the modern era, however, have finally caught up to the women of Stirling County where men have been exposed to it long enough to find compensations and establish a new equilibrium. Women also seem to be at more risk in other parts of the world, perhaps for the reason that culture generally provides richer psychological satisfactions for men than for women, to the latter's psychological detriment.[51] Among Eskimo, for example, parents indulge children's dependence regardless of sex. But girls more than boys later assume traditional roles in which they encounter rapidly diminished gratification of dependence. This paves the way for a considerable prevalence of hysteria in women.[52] Norman Chance, using the Cornell Medical Index for interviewing in a North Alaskan Eskimo community subject to intense change from a nearby DEW-line site, found women to be worse off than men.[53] Men more easily than women could achieve satisfactory new roles, prestige through their jobs, and psychological benefits from their work contacts with Euroamericans. Among these changing Eskimo, the traditional sources of prestige for women have to a large extent been lost and little new has taken their place. Furthermore, lacking much experience with Western culture, women don't understand their altered situation.

As in Stirling County, where the prevalence of personality disorder increases with social disintegration, level of integration correlates directly with mental health among the Yoruba, their best mental health also occurring in the best integrated communities. Among the Yoruba, however, dis-

integration takes its heaviest toll in women; in fact, its "effect'" appears to be chiefly confined to women, for the likelihood of encountering a psychiatrically disturbed man increases much more moderately from integrated to intermediate villages and actually declines in fully disintegrated communities. The authors conclude that women of the integrated villages live in an environment highly congenial to their personalities, one that provides them with rich satisfactions. Quite a contrary condition, one full of disorientation, confusion, and uncertainty, promotes strain in women living in disintegrated communities. Men, however, in this rapidly modernizing, new nation must cope with turmoil and change in all kinds of communities. Their problems differ little between integrated and disintegrated social settings; hence their mental health also doesn't vary greatly. Yet change itself isn't the noxious factor either in their lives or in women's. The authors say this because mental health remains constant when, by a further process of comparison, changing integrated villages are compared to stable (traditional) integrated ones. Even when changing *disintegrated* villages are compared to stable disintegrated ones, mental health isn't worse in either.

The investigators hoped that in Nigeria they would encounter communities in which most people stayed put for their lifetime and between which there would be little geographical mobility. Thus they would establish whether social disintegration precedes personality disorder (as Leighton's theory predicts), or whether disintegrated communities attract psychiatrically disturbed people. Instead they discovered considerable population movement and couldn't after all test the hypothesis. However, they believe that migration in those Nigerian villages isn't "of such a nature as to suggest strongly that persons with psychiatric disorder cluster together to create disintegrated communities."[54] I find it worth noting that the Midtown, Stirling County, and Yoruba studies all worked with an almost purely ahistorical, synchronic theory to explain phenomena found in slums and other disintegrated communities. Cultural psychiatry obviously isn't ready seriously to explore the possibility that disintegrated communities are primarily historically created through some kind of funneling process. To be sure, the anthropologists and sociologists who cooperated in those impressive research undertakings found data supporting their ahistorical theories and hypotheses. Yet, if they had worked in a more historical frame of reference they would surely have industriously collected better information about migration and so might have discovered support for the theory of drift, which they reject.

How Culturebound? To what degree might the psychiatrists' evaluations of Yoruba mental health be culturebound? The

◖ Social Disintegration Threatens Mental Health[55]

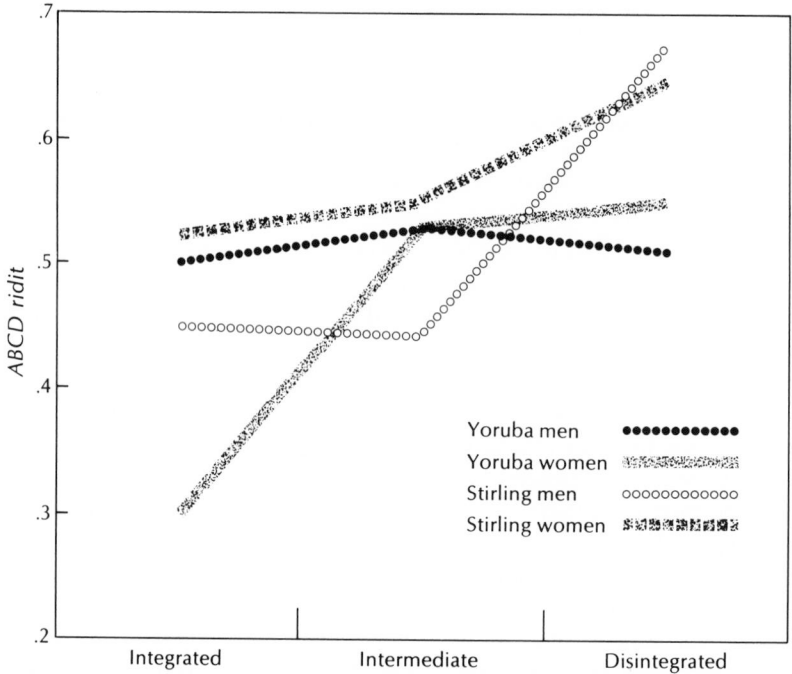

In both Stirling County and in Yoruba villages the best mental health occurs in the best integrated communities. In Stirling County both men and women show considerably worse mental health from integrated to disintegrated communities. Men are better off than women in the integrated communities and worse off in the disintegrated. Yoruba men show only slightly worse mental health from integrated to disintegrated villages, whereas women are markedly better off in integrated as compared to disintegrated villages. Women are better off than men in the integrated villages and worse off than men in the disintegrated.

The higher a group's ridit, the greater the probability that an individual selected at random from that group is worse off than another individual selected at random from the reference population. For Stirling County the reference population is the entire county sample; for Yoruba it is the total sample obtained in 15 Yoruba villages.

discipline of psychiatry, after all, developed in Europe and America; hence, when its practitioners categorize disorders and evaluate impairment in a culturally different social system they must be imposing their own imported cultural screen. How likely is it that the psychiatrists' views of personality disorder will coincide with the Yoruba's? Do the Yoruba even admit the existence of psychiatric disorder?

Yoruba culture does recognize personality disorder and even delineates a limited number of types of disordered behavior marked by disturbed feelings, ways of thinking, and patterns of activity. Whether the Yoruba regard such disorders as being equivalent to other illness, a pertinent question in view of Szasz's and Mowrer's recent critiques, is apparently more assumed by Leighton and his associates than critically investigated. The authors do speak of native "healers" who treat mental illness, but they don't explain what the concept of healer connotes to the Yoruba themselves. Symptoms recognized by native healers ring familiarly, for they resemble behavior that used to be commonly seen in public mental hospitals of America before modern treatment. To be sure, Yoruba diagnostic categories are less refined and discriminatory than the psychiatrists'. The healers also pay less heed to signs indicative of neuroses, sociopathic disorders, or senility. They are not prepared to admit that chronic tension, aggressiveness, sleeplessness, spendthriftness, or extreme shyness constitute treatable disorders. Childishness in the aged, being in "the natural course of events," remains untreated. Extreme aggressiveness and malice don't strike them as ailments; some people are simply born that way. In other words, Yoruba recognize mainly psychosis and, in agreement with Euroamerican psychiatry, evaluate it unfavorably. Many laymen in the United States would join them in feeling that the symptoms of neuroses and personality disorder don't lie within the range of illness and, as I have reported, some psychiatrists would on other grounds agree. Yoruba healers also don't heed signs of phobia, obsessive-compulsiveness, and depression as a subjective state, though they know that some people complain of sapped vitality, cry continuously, worry extremely, and lose their interest in life—significant signs of depression to a Western-trained psychiatrist. At any rate, it appears that many of the psychiatric disorders recognized in Euroamerican practice also turn up in Yorubaland, though Yoruba healers don't attend to them. Compulsiveness is one psychiatric symptom much less common among the Yoruba than in Stirling County. Of course, Yoruba have their own notions of causality for the disorders they recognize. They hold supernaturals, witchcraft, the magical intervention of other people, heredity, contagion, and even stress to be responsible for such behavioral disturbances.

FURTHER READING

In "A New Cross-Cultural Study of Drunkenness" (1962), Peter B. Field maintains, contrary to Donald Horton, that drunkenness in small-scale communities is "determined" by weak and diffuse social organization (an earmark of social disintegration), rather than by socially derived anxiety. Preliminary results analyzed by William Mangin show no direct link between "Mental Health and Migration to Cities" in Peru (1960). Melford Spiro, on the basis of his research on Ifaluk, demonstrates a connection between culturally induced stress and personality disorder in his chapter "Cultural Heritage, Personal Tensions, and Mental Illness in a South Sea Culture" (1959). A few other examples of stress theory applied to exotic cultures and personality data are: George A. De Vos and Horace Miner, *Oasis and Casbah—A Study in Acculturative Stress* (1959); Bingham Dai, "Obsessive-Compulsive Disorders in Chinese Culture" (1959); A. Irving Hallowell, "Fear and Anxiety as Cultural and Individual Variables in a Primitive Society" (1938), and Herbert H. Williams, *Some Aspects of Culture and Personality in a Lebanese Maronite Village* (1958). For a critique of the New Haven study, see S. M. Miller and Elliot G. Mishler, "Social Class, Mental Illness, and American Psychiatry: An Expository Review" (1964). Richard A. Cloward and Lloyd E. Ohlin, in *Delinquency and Opportunity* (1960), question whether neighborhoods of lower socioeconomic status are equivalent to socially disintegrated neighborhoods. They show that some slum neighborhoods are well integrated. W. Godfrey Cobliner, in "Social Factors in Mental Disorders" (1963), claims family disruption to be the main source of personality disorder, and Esther Milner offers stress and class as major related determinants in "Some Hypotheses Concerning the Influence of Segregation on Negro Personality Development" (1953). *Trapped: Families and Schizophrenia,* by Lloyd H. Rogler and August B. Hollingshead (1965), points out costs of schizophrenia in lower-class Puerto Rican lives. John A. Hostetler's paper "Persistence and Change Patterns in Amish Society" (1964) indicates that even a tightly integrated community can't counteract all stress and strain, especially if the community is a minority enclave surrounded by a society with many contrary values. H. Warren Dunham takes a critical look at several studies of "Social Structures and Mental Disorders" in an article subtitled "Competing Hypotheses of Explanation" (1961). Annual reports published by the Cornell Program of Social Psychiatry, directed by Alexander H. Leighton, reveal how research continues to be built on findings and problems brought out in Stirling County,

Midtown, and Yorubaland. Regarding possible applications of our knowledge concerning the relationship of the cultural environment and personality disorder, see Adam Curle's perceptive "A Theoretical Approach to Action Research" (1949).

REFERENCES

1 Faris and Dunham, 1939: 156.
2 Kroeber, 1952: 319.
3 Facts like those can be gleaned from the report of the Joint Commission on Mental Illness and Health, 1961.
4 A. H. Leighton, 1959.
5 Durkheim, 1951.
6 *Cf.* Inkeles, 1963: 322–325.
7 *Cf.* D'Andrade, 1961: 320–327.
8 See the suggestive study by Mintz and Schwartz, 1964.
9 M. Mead, 1928a: chap. 14.
10 J. A. Dubois, 1906: 355 ff.
11 A. F. Henry and Short (1954) demonstrate as false Durkheim's prediction that suicide increases in prosperity.
12 Thanks largely to Merton, 1957.
13 Horton, 1943.
14 J. J. Honigmann and Honigmann, 1965b.
15 J. Henry, 1963: 322.
16 *Ibid.,* chap. 9.
17 *Ibid.,* p. 350.
18 Hollingshead and Redlich, 1958.
19 *Cf.* Gurin, Veroff, and Feld, 1960: xx.
20 Hollingshead and Redlich, 1958: chap. 12; Myers and Roberts, 1959: 249–257.
21 Hollingshead and Redlich, 1958: 363.
22 *Ibid.,* p. 289.
23 Based on Srole *et al.,* 1962; Langner and Michael, 1963. Photographs used in the present chapter were made in 1966; hence they do not picture Midtown as it was in 1954 when the study was done.
24 Srole *et al.,* 1962: 388–390.
25 Hollingshead and Redlich, 1958: 210.

26 Plunkett and Gordon, 1960: 90.

27 Jews also show a low rate of alienation in a study reported by Meier and Bell, 1959. See also the resistance Jews show to alcoholism, which I reported in Chapter 1.

28 Langner and Michael, 1963: 104–105.

29 From Srole *et al.*, 1962: 213.

30 Langner and Michael, 1963: 380.

31 *Ibid.*, p. 381.

32 Srole *et al.*, 1962: 226.

33 Langner and Michael, 1963: 426

34 Cited in C. C. Hughes *et al.*, 1960: 245–246. From *People of Cove and Woodlot*, © 1960 by Alexander H. Leighton, Basic Books, Publishers, New York. Most of what follows, unless it is otherwise referenced, draws on *People of Cove and Woodlot* by C. C. Hughes *et al.*

35 A. H. Leighton, 1959: 178.

36 C. C. Hughes *et al.*, 1960: 140–160.

37 *Ibid.*, pp. 215–240.

38 *Ibid.*, pp. 295–308. Similar sentiments turn up among town-dwelling Navaho Indians, according to S. Parker and Sasaki, 1965.

39 A. H. Leighton explains his concept of sentiment in *The Governing of Men* (1945: 383–388) and *My Name is Legion* (1959: chap. 7 and p. 325).

40 From here to the end of my summary of Stirling County findings, I follow mainly D. C. Leighton *et al.*, 1963.

41 *Cf.* Gurin, Veroff, and Feld, 1960: xvii–xviii.

42 From D. C. Leighton *et al.*, 1963: 275, 278.

43 Meyer *et al.*, 1965. See also Witmer, 1951: chap. 29.

44 Rice, 1965.

45 *Cf.* Spergel, 1964: 187.

46 J. J. Honigmann, 1965.

47 Based on A. H. Leighton, Lambo, *et al.*, 1963.

48 Lambo, 1964.

49 For a device used to screen psychiatric symptoms among Alaskan Eskimo, see J. M. Murphy and Hughes, 1965.

50 As a result, symptoms of malnutrition may have been read as signs of psychiatric disorder. See Raymond Prince's review in *Transcultural Psychiatric Research Review and Newsletter*, 1964, 1: 48–51.

51 Langner, 1965.

52 S. Parker, 1962: 89–90; *cf.* J. J. Honigmann, 1949: 291–294, 313.

53 Chance, 1960, 1962, and 1965: 381; Chance and Foster, 1962.

54 From A. H. Leighton, Lambo, *et al.*, 1963: 280.

55 *Ibid.*, p. 234.

The Long Reach of Patterning

13

. . . we are not interested in what A or B may feel qua individuals, . . . we are interested only in what they feel and think qua members of a given community. Now in this capacity, their mental states receive a certain stamp, become stereotyped by the institutions in which they live, by the influence of tradition and folklore, by the very vehicle of thought, that is by language.[1]

BRONISLAW MALINOWSKI

The slum area populated by heterogeneous foreign-born elements forms a chaotic background of conflicting and shifting cultural standards against which it is quite difficult for a person to develop a stable mental organization.[2]

ROBERT E. L. FARIS

H. WARREN DUNHAM

WITH CONSCIOUS CONTROL RELINQUISHED

As some plants and animals—for example, the Peppered Moth in soot-polluted industrial areas[3]—blend protectively into their environments, so personality disorders sometimes dress in forms congruent to their cultural settings, as if hoping to escape quick detection. Whether such protective dress aids the disordered person's survival and social adjustment, as protective coloration helps biological survival, has to my knowledge never been examined. One could take an opposite point of view and say that when others reinforce a person's delusions, they actually restrict his recovery. The symptoms' protective dress and the social support they muster could counteract his capacity, or even need, to recover.[4] I already spoke of personality disorder assuming a form congruent with culture when I described the tolerance and understanding with which Hutterites accept depressive reactions. The choice of depression as a symptom is fortunate for a Hutterite because it rallies helpful support to the victim rather than earning him isolation and rejection. Phenomena like drunkenness, dreaming, preternatural experiences, and behavioral epidemics—like the tropistic surges of Crusaders to the Holy Land and the devilish struggles of

⁅ Did Her Community Hinder Caribou's Recovery by Reinforcing Her Delusions?

One day in April, 1941, while her father was away at his traps, Tooktook [Caribou] was drying fox skins for him. She placed some of the skins outside and immediately the dogs proceeded to tear one up before she could save it. Rather than face her father's rage, she replaced the skin by stealing one from a neighbour, Analic, who, though he noticed his loss, said nothing.

The incident passed without mention, and shortly thereafter, Tooktook married a man who was thirty years her senior. . . . She made a good wife, serving her husband well in sewing, making boots and cooking. Two years passed with nothing unusual happening. In December, 1943, Tooktook [then 21] gave birth to their first child. At the time the child was born, the patient complained of a feeling that something else was inside her after the baby had been delivered and afterbirth removed. She asked the women in attendance to feel her stomach, and they later reported that they could feel something inside her. Despite this, she was up and about the next day, in accordance with the Eskimo practice. On the third day, however, she was back in bed with complaints of stomach pain, and an old woman was called in to help. . . . She looked at the patient and explained to her that the pains were due to contractions of the womb. This seemed to quiet the patient for about two more days. Then, at night, she aroused her husband and some children who were sleeping in the tent to say that a fox had got into the tent and that its barking was disturbing her. He got up and looked around, as did the children, but they found nothing. Tooktook then said the fox had entered her. The next day the old woman returned to visit the patient, and when she was told what had transpired during the night, she told the patient that this occurrence was due to a sin that the patient had committed and that she had better confess. At first the patient refused to do so but two days later when the stomach pains were worse, and when an additional symptom appeared—a peculiar feeling of itchiness on her back—the patient proceeded to tell about the fox-stealing incident. On hearing this story, the old woman said that this was the cause of her complaint and that it was too bad that Tooktook had failed to confess earlier.

From this time until the spring of the next year, when she was removed, a period of about four months, the patient manifested a good deal of unusual behaviour. She began to act like a fox, her voice becoming more and more fox-like. She would lie in bed and bark like a fox. She lost control of her bowels and bladder and she had to be fed like a child. She stayed in bed most of the time, constituting a total loss to her husband since she could no longer look after his needs. . . . She had auditory hallucinations, hearing sounds that no one else heard, such as knocking at the door, an airplane and men talking. . . . She talked incessantly, jabbering especially about the poor treatment she had received from her father. . . . There was a good deal of imitative behaviour. She imitated the women chewing sealskins; she imitated the smiles and movements of others in the tent. She tried to imitate vocal sounds but her voice had become so hoarse from barking like a fox that she could not do this successfully. . . .

Tooktook complained that the fox was moving higher in her body to a point where she could feel its fur in her mouth. When she stretched out her feet, they appeared to the people to look like fox paws that had been skinned. This was accepted as a manifestation of the fox spirit which had entered the patient because of her stealing.

.   .   .

Her illness was explained as follows: When Analic, from whom Tooktook had stolen the fox, was born, an uncle pledged his services to help him fend off misfortune and enemies. As a result, when Tooktook stole the fox from Analic, his power resulted in the evil spirit of the fox entering her. Although she confessed her sin and also confessed having stolen other things, it was too late and the fox could not get out. Her father returned a fox to Analic but this, too, was of no avail. A group of elders prayed for her, but this was also in vain. She was in the clutches of the bad spirits and could not be released. Analic was powerless to help her since he dared not rebuke his guardian.[5]

MORTON I. TEICHER

possessed nuns in Loudun—also show how society provides the blueprint for minds that have lost full, conscious deliberate control. In drunkenness and sleep, when the threshold of consciousness sinks, as in personality disorder, behavior continues to abide by group norms, to follow customary methods of perception and defense, and to deal with familiar topics however distorted they become. Drugged, drunk, or dreaming, the person remains in touch with socially defined reality, for the simple reason that it is nowhere but within him. Preoccupations with weighty social concerns continue to run through psychotic delusions and confabulations, however idiomatic their meaning, while paranoia and depressive reactions represent exaggerated versions of defenses for protecting the ego.

Intoxication. Culture doesn't change the chemical nature of alcohol or the way it is metabolically assimilated in the body, simultaneously both inhibiting and exciting the nervous system. Though alcohol and its chemical action remain the same, drunken behavior varies with culture, particularly because people drink in diverse, socially patterned ways and with different expectations of what alcohol does. Intoxication, therefore, varies with styles of drinking that

prescribe the preferred beverage, subtly regulate the amount taken at any one time, effectively govern the speed with which it is consumed, and even anticipate specific consequences.

Kaska and Navaho Indians drink relatively unceremoniously and quickly, partly to avoid being interrupted by police or by unwelcome visitors who will demand some of the limited supply.[6] As a result, they become heavily intoxicated, in contrast to guests in a rural Austrian tavern who slowly sip beer or eighths of wine as an accompaniment to much talk.[7] Classes in a stratified community also follow alternative styles of drinking that likewise condition different modes of intoxication.[8] Whereas the French adhere to a time-tested style of wine drinking that permits even alcoholic addiction without evidence of drunkenness,[9] devastating consequences have followed the sudden arrival of alcohol to people who never established drinking customs.[10] The violence that brandy unleashed in some American Indians probably owes more to their lack of time-tested customs for using liquor and of knowledge regarding its dastardly effects than it can be blamed on their high levels of hostility and anxiety[11] suddenly undammed.

If control over behavior almost inevitably declines when alcohol is drunk, why do individuals who drink approximately the same amount over roughly the same period relinquish their self-control unequally? Some drinkers clearly refuse to compromise their dignity or firm sense of self-esteem by venting such familiar drunken traits as quarrelsomeness, heightened sexuality, and boisterousness; they fear the inner or outer sanctions that uninhibited release would rouse. Where there is much to lose through unrestrained drunkenness, intoxicated behavior will for as long as possible be guarded. In an experiment, men holding a central position in a group drank as much as social isolates, but showed much less disagreement, antagonism, tension, and self-assertion than the isolates did.[12] The former had won their social position because they lived up to group expectations, and they continued to do so even when drunk. Mohave Indians don't become heavily intoxicated chiefly because they fall asleep soon after they begin drinking.[13] As hysterical blindness and paralysis resolve a soldier's conflict between duty and mortal fear, so ego and superego combine to put a Mohave drinker to sleep, thereby defending him against eruption of disallowed, dreaded impulses, especially aggression. As a consequence of their alert defensiveness, intoxicated Mohave so long as they remain awake act pretty much the same as Mohave do when they are sober: affectionately, unaggressively, and with their customary flair for humor. Yet they brood about the dead, in spite of knowing that such thoughts are dangerous and invite illness. In Chichicastenango, a prosperous Guatemalan town,

⟨ Two Styles of Drinking

An Austrian tavern provides alcohol to accompany sociability. Guests drink because it stimulates pleasant feelings and gaiety, but one shouldn't become immoderately intoxicated. Most villagers agree and drink slowly and cautiously.

The men in the other picture have made their own brew, storing it in used bottles. Impatiently they waited for it to ripen so they could have "a little fun." Each drinker gulps large amounts without removing the bottle from his lips. Speed of drinking picks up as intoxication increases, and even extreme drunkenness is tolerated so long as it doesn't threaten anybody.

*Chichicastenango's many fiestas converge upon
the town's central plaza, dominated by the
whitewashed Spanish-colonial church.
(Guatemala Tourist Commisson)*

heavy drinkers find that market-day and fiesta drinking relieves some of the tension that their especially conflict-laden life generates, but in the process they also pile up more anxiety. Drinking is itself a sin, yet they carry on with it, and when intoxicated become quarrelsome and amorous, all at the cost of considerable later guilt, which they try to stave off by avoiding the return to sobriety. Consequently, they are apt to wake up with terrific hangovers. Quite the reverse happens in Chamula, a Mexican town, where heavy drinkers remain on the whole peaceable, incur no guilt-feelings, and also suffer no hangovers.[14] We know, too, that seventeenth-century Iroquois Indians drank without shame to attain complete, abandoned insobriety of a most Dionysian sort, from which they also recovered without hangovers.[15] Just how social patterning reaches into the human organism

to immunize against hangover remains a mystery.

How one learns to think about alcohol and drinking governs to some extent the risk of becoming addicted. Orthodox Jews make sobriety a specifically Jewish virtue and stereotype gentiles unfavorably as excessive drinkers, thereby identifying heavy drinking with non-Jewishness. Only at the risk of throwing away his religious identity can an Orthodox Jew use alcohol to the point of drunkenness.[16] A person who grows up familiar with alcoholic beverages and even uses them frequently, though in moderation is unlikely ever to rely on them to "slip away from the oppression of reality and find a refuge in a world . . . where painful feelings do not enter."[17] His protection seems to lie in learning early to use alcohol unemotionally, without ambivalence, as neither good nor bad but something normal—precisely the qualities lacking in alarmist temperance propaganda.[18]

Dreaming. When Freud laid down laws of dreaming, like the one that all dreams of the same night return persistently to the same problem troubling the dreamer, he didn't have enough evidence to say whether such laws applied everywhere, regardless of culture. He did, however, believe that dreams condense their message into similar symbols, regardless of culture, due to the basic unity of mankind's unconscious imagination.[19] Whether dream symbolism is cross-culturally similar has never been definitely settled, nor is it ever likely to be finally proven or disproven. We can only employ it as a working assumption—that is, as long as it works. If uncertainty wraps itself around such psychoanalytic views, nothing conceals the clarity with which social experience enters the dream world to structure both the dream images and the problems with which those images cope.[20] Surely, people have available as dream material only what waking hours have made familiar. A dreamer who never traveled by dog team isn't likely to find himself in sleep carefully fixing a sled in order to surmount the special problems connected with spring travel.[21] Like worrying, dreams recurrently turn over problems created for people who occupy certain statuses in a particular community. A Zulu woman must bear children early in her married life; yet she is quite unlikely to, since migrant labor keeps her husband away from the village for as many as ten months a year. In one study, many Zulu women who dreamed of "a baby" were in this dilemma; they were young, married, under considerable social pressure to prove their fertility. If they had already borne children they had lost many.[22] Their dreams portray their wish, which arises out of a difficult situation, and to that extent the dreams are socially patterned. Zulu women frightened by nightmarish dreams in which danger from a flooding river threatens them, confront a different predicament. They have had considerable experience with childbirth and have come intensely to fear further deliveries, despite pressure on them to continue bearing children. Their dream mirrors their socially engendered conflict and is therefore also socially patterned, like the dreams accompanying a traumatic neurosis, in which one again and again in the most vivid way relives a terrifying experience. Even when a dreamer gratifies his lightly censored wishes, he continues subliminally to recognize prohibitions on sex and aggression. Hence he feels guilt or shame. In one set of dreams that frankly involved incestuous sexual intercourse, the libidinous dreamer was repeatedly saved by being unable to complete the conflictful act. Timely interruptions, defects in the woman's sexual organs, and other obstacles kept him from fully violating the strong rule against incest.[23]

Dreams of a standardized sort are sometimes prescribed for a person who reaches a certain age or status, and the person usually manages to dream as he is expected to. Dreams of American Indians which, like their visions, formerly allied them with guardian spirits, fall in this category. So do the patterned dreams of Plains Indian youths that relieved them from playing highly prestiged male roles which, quite possibly, they didn't admire and felt disinclined to enter. They knew they had only to dream of the moon or a hermaphroditic buffalo to be exempted from the high-risk career of a warrior and become berdaches.[24] A person stimulated himself for a guardian-spirit by fasting, isolating himself in a lonely place, and concentrating on what he wanted to bring about—contact with supernaturals. But even so, some, like the young Kaska Indian man who resignedly told me, "Nothing see me . . . something don't want me," failed to reach the goal of the quest.[25] What Indians dreamed under such circumstances differed from ordinary dreams that occurred adventitiously.[26] Here is an example of a successful "culture pattern" dream told by an Ojibwa Indian:

I dreamt that I was alongside a lake and had not had anything to eat for some time. I was wandering in search of food for quite a time when I saw a big bird [loon]. This bird came over to where I was staying and spoke to me, telling me that I was lost and that a party was out searching for me; and that they really intended to shoot me instead of rescuing me. Then the bird flew out into the lake and brought me a fish to eat and told me that I would have good luck in hunting and fishing; that I would live to a good old age; and that I would never be wounded by a shot-gun or rifle. This bird who had blessed me was the kind that one rarely has a chance of shooting. From that time on the *majg* [loon] was my guardian spirit.[27]

Once the aboriginal cultures of the American Indians disintegrated (or should one say "evolved"?), dreams that formerly brought about supernatural power came to be interpreted like ordinary, every-night dreams; that is, with reference solely to the individual's experience.[28]

A modern interpretation of dreams, compared to the older view I've just given, strikingly reveals how culture and personality have shifted ground both in theory and method. Where the former, older view saw such dreams conforming to focal cultural interests embodied by the dreamer who responded to social expectations, the new interpretation sees social patterning to operate much less straightforwardly. Dreams are a form of defense mechanism that enable people unconsciously to adjust to stressful social conditions. Roy G. D'Andrade[29] adopts this view when he reasons that in social systems wherein individual anxiety

revolves around isolation and being on one's own, people will "emphasize" reassuring dreams that bring and control supernatural power, more so than will people who don't incur such anxieties. By what signs can one recognize communities wherein isolation and self-reliance provoke anxiety? One suggestive indicator is the custom of a son at marriage moving from his parents' home to live elsewhere. Such a shift, D'Andrade reasons, could well raise anxiety over isolation and being on one's own. He examines a world-wide sample of social systems and discovers what he predicted. The farther a boy is required to move at marriage, the more likely it is that his community uses dreams to seek and control supernatural power. Eighty percent of the 21 communities in which a boy on marriage goes to live in a different local group recognize the value of dreams about supernaturals who promise aide or information. In such communities, among which are the Kaska Indians, experts rely on dreams to help them cure and diagnose illness, and stereotyped dreams constitute prerequisites necessary before one can enter upon some roles. Hence, people deliberately induce dreams through fasting, drugs, or isolation. Only 40 percent of the 25 communities in which the newly married boy continues to live in the same village as his parents use dreams (with somewhat less emphasis than the former category), and only 27 percent of the 11 in which he stays in his parents' household. (Oddly enough, no particular emphasis is put on dreaming when a daughter moves following marriage.) Since food-gathering communities like the aboriginal Kaska Indians and Eskimo, where people gain a livelihood through hunting and fishing, are known to encourage independence, self-reliance, and achievement in children,[30] D'Andrade assumes that they will also inculcate anxiety concerning isolation and being on one's own. Consequently, according to his theory, they should emphasize dreams about supernatural helpers more than social systems that practice agriculture and animal husbandy in which, as we happen to know, childrearing stresses obedience, responsibility, and nurturance rather than independence and self-reliance. Acting on these clues, a check of 64 social systems reveals that 80 percent of food-gatherers (including the Kaska) use dreams to solicit or control supernaturals, compared to only 25 percent of communities gaining livelihoods through both agriculture and animal husbandry. The theory that such dreams defend in some measure against anxiety over isolation and self-reliance is again sustained. One might expect that people who rely either on agriculture or animal husbandry but not both will fall in between, experiencing more anxiety over isolation and self-reliance than those who practice both techniques. It seems they do. At any rate, they are clearly in between, with 60 percent recognizing the value of dreams to procure supernatural help, advice, and support.

Preternatural Experience. In the same way that drunkenness and dreams adhere to cultural guidelines, though they are beyond fully conscious control, so visions, specters, and related experiences demonstrate social patterning unmediated by fully aware volition. Social expectations can prepare people to leave what they recognize to be the everyday plane of reality, and urge them into extraordinary experiences. These experi-

❨ *Two Styles of Mescaline Intoxication*[31]

Peyote, a cactus that grows wild in the Rio Grande Valley and further south, produces a woody disc containing mescaline, which is eaten sacramentally as part of American Indians' modern religious ceremonies. Non-Indians characteristically experience mescaline intoxication differently from Indians; in fact, the former respond to it with quite unpleasant feelings.

Euroamericans	*Indians*
Their mood varies and shifts from agitated depression and anxiety to euphoria, depending on the stage of intoxication and the psychological characteristics of the individual.	The Indians' mood is at first stable. Then religious anxiety follows and enthusiasm, with a tendency toward feelings of religious reverence and personal satisfaction once the vision appears.
Social inhibitions frequently break down; sexual and aggressive behavior is shamelessly displayed.	They retain proper behavior even if they show revivalistic enthusiasm (which is proper in the situation).
The intoxicated person becomes suspicious of others around him.	No report of suspiciousness.
Unwelcome feelings of loss of contact with reality occur; depersonalization; meaninglessness, and "split personality."	Peyotists experience welcome feelings of being in contact with a more meaningful, higher order of reality.
Idiosyncratic hallucinations take hold.	Hallucinations occur, patterned by the Peyote religion's doctrines.
No therapeutic benefits or permanent change in behavior known.	Marked therapeutic benefits earned; chronic anxiety reduced; the Indian's sense of personal worth climbs, and his life contains more satisfaction.

ences hold special interest for us because they closely approximate a familiar element in personality disorder, hallucination. The American Indian's stereotyped vision, which, like his culture-pattern dream, brought him into conversational touch with spiritual guardians, reveals how cultural tradition structures paranormal experience. The pattern of such visions varied little across a big continent.[32] Indian prophets' supernatural revelations, some of which prompted profound political and social consequences, also stemmed out of the people's socially patterned readiness to enter immediate contact with a realm existing beyond the everyday frame of reality.[33] "I saw three men standing by the house who appeared like angels," the Seneca prophet who founded a new religion reported in 1799. "They told me . . . the great Spirrit knew not only what people was always doing but even their very thoughts . . ."[34] As Durkheim[35] wrote, the believer who enters such communion with divinity doesn't merely see new truths of which the unbeliever remains ignorant; "he is a man who is *stronger*." He comes to be forcefully endowed to conquer the world's miseries. If he doesn't achieve the social revolution he preaches, at least he is powerful enough to threaten the social edifice against which he launches his inspired attack.

Many Colombians believe in specters but not as unanimously as in Aritama, a village where nobody heeds Robinson Jeffers' warning that

The eye's tricks are strange, the mind has
    to be quick and resolute or you'll
    believe in them
And be gabbling with ghosts.[36]

As a result all in Aritama live in permanent fear of the illness and death that such apparitions bestow.[37] Some specters possess human form, like El Caballero who rides a deformed horse, his spurs and chains clanking in the night; or La Montuna, a dwarf-like, beautifully featured woman who moves over the ground with a groaning, rhythmical noise. Others are animal beings, like El Burrucoco, who tears out people's eyes and carries off small children. These uncanny manifestations show up at night; suddenly appearing out of nowhere surrounded by a faint glow, they are so well known that they can be immediately recognized. Wordlessly gesticulating, they command their victim, usually a man, to go in whatever direction they wish until he loses his trail. Practically every Aritama adult knows from firsthand experience the terror of encountering such apparitions, which, the authors explain, express early but unforgotten trauma produced when children witness parental coitus. Indians in northeastern North America also alarmingly detect at night prowling, visionary strangers, *otcibweak*; but these are not really supernatural, just extraordinary. The strangers are never observed properly to enter the area, hence their mysteriousness. On the east coast of James Bay, at Rupert House, mysterious prowlers suddenly encountered are white men spying on the Indians and waiting for a chance to steal children. At night they frighten people by knocking on doors, clumsily stumbling across tent ropes, and upsetting woodpiles.[38] Further north at Great Whale River on Hudson Bay, Indians report having physically grappled with nocturnal visitors and overhearing them converse in a strange tongue or make a spraying sound with their lips.[39] On James Bay's marshy west coast, in Attawapiskat where I worked, otcibweak out to steal children take varied forms: they look like surveyors, resemble explorers floating along streams in collapsible rubber boats—and even show up in the guise of anthropologists with cameras strung around their necks! Sometimes they rouse sleeping Indians by surreptitiously peering into cabin windows or through tent

Spirits like these, which Iglulik Eskimo shamans see in patterned dreams and visions, promise them help and information.[40]

openings. Such fantasies, I suspect, project anxieties aroused by the occasional presence in those small, isolated Indian communities of powerful, compelling, Euro-canadian visitors. The visitors' administrative and other official duties intrude on the Indian's autonomy, and the Indians don't fully comprehend their aims. Encounters with otcibweak are like frightening dreams in traumatic neurosis; they bespeak Indians' strain. In that sense, as well as in the forms they take, otcibweak are socially patterned.

Behavioral Epidemics. In 1632, the 30-year-old prioress of a French Ursuline convent in Loudun felt that demons had, in her own words, "insinuated themselves into my mind and inclinations" and "made of me one and the same substance with themselves."[41] Dwarfed and overconscious of her misshapenness, Sister Jeanne had talents for dissimulation and hypocrisy that had won her the compensatory satisfaction of a priorship. Classics of spiritual life, which her rudimentary education allowed her to read, gave her a taste for mysticism. A no less avid appetite for earthly gossip kept her informed about town affairs outside the gloomy old convent. Particularly, she knew about the doings of the young,

handsome new priest, Father Urbaine Grandier, who had already gotten one local young woman with child and now was ardently pursuing a retiring, saintly orphan girl. He having captivated Sister Jeanne's imagination, she tried to win his consent to become the convent's spiritual director; when that failed she conceived a confused, ambivalent mixture of hate coexisting with passion. In dreams he caressed and tried to seduce her, and when she related these dreams to the other nuns they promptly began to dream of importunate priests whispering indelicate propositions in their own ears.

A behavioral epidemic had begun. It took final form when a hoax, convincing the 17 nuns that the convent was haunted, allowed a crafty enemy of Father Grandier to persuade the nuns that their ghosts, as well as their nightly dream visitants, were real and probably satanic. Soon it became public knowledge that devils possessed the sisters of Loudun and that Father Grandier had done it. The curé himself shrugged off the charge, little realizing that this one sin he hadn't committed would give his many enemies their chance to prevail and send him to the stake. For the sisters, months of exorcism converted into public spectacles followed. Sister Jeanne, "bereaved of sense and reason," rolled on the floor, howling and grinding her teeth as devils blasphemed through her mouth, till enemas of holy water for a time dispelled them. Sister Agnes, young, slender, and lovely to look at, also fell in convulsions at the feet of the friar seeking to exorcise her. Other nuns, some the daughters of noble families, followed the prioress' example. The exorcisers, recognizing the cues for what their training had taught them they were, confirmed the nuns' belief that they were possessed. Such a belief can't truly be called a delusion, for it conformed very well to reality as socially defined by seventeenth-century French society. In all Europe many people at that time believed in the reality of devils, possession, and the Holy Spirit working deep in the mind. Man as well as God could launch forces that transformed the person in whom they lodged. A magician in league with Evil could wherever he wished install the Devil, whose working was sometimes scarcely distinguishable from the effects of divine grace. The law itself prescribed death for anyone who deliberately dealt with the Fiend. True, some educated people had their doubts, but it was the Church's official attitude that to disbelieve amounted to heresy. Illustrious theologians and illiterate believers, therefore, supported the collective possession of Sister Jeanne and her Ursulines.

Thirty thousand people thronged Loudun for the spectacle of Father Grandier's execution. They saw him go to "that just and fearful judgment to which," as he warned the priest lighting his pyre, "you too must soon be called." Sister Jeanne's possession, however, didn't immediately stop after Grandier's execution. It even infected her newest exorciser, Father Jean-Joseph Surin, who later recalled what it was like to accommodate "four of hell's most malignant devils," one of whom remained on duty day and night. It was as if he had two souls, "of

which one is dispossessed of my body and the use of its organs, and keeps its quarters, watching the other, the intruder, doing whatever it likes. These two spirits do battle. . . . At one and the same time I feel a great peace, as being under God's good pleasure, and on the other . . . an overpowering rage and loathing of God. . . ."

The devils of Loudun were undoubtedly real, as real as our electrons and protons, given the seventeenth-century climate of belief and its faith in the Church's ability to recognize empirical signs of possession. A small group of women could easily become infected by one another's fancies and by a confessor who authoritatively advised them that Satan had taken over their house and bodies. People supported one another in such beliefs; some encouraged the nuns to reveal the in-dwelling Fiend and to name his earthly agent; others confirmed one another in recognizing him even when, in keeping with the sisters' limited education, he spoke bad Latin.

"Epidemic" is, perhaps, a rather loose word to apply to phenomena of this sort. Yet it suits the qualities that Hecker[42] emphasizes when he describes the dancing manias of fourteenth- and fifteenth-century Europe as "diseases which are propagated on the beams of light—on the wings of thought; which convulse the mind by the excitement of the senses, and wonderfully affect the nerves, the media of its will and of its feelings." He finds it worth while "to place these disorders between the epidemics of a less refined origin, which affect the body more than the soul, and all those passions and emotions which border on the vast domain of disease, ready at every moment to pass the boundary." Why don't Europe and America today have epidemics of devil possession? Obviously because ideas have changed; culture has altered; patterning has no stock of ideas on which such beliefs can validly draw. Support for such epidemics wouldn't be forthcoming. They would flicker out almost as soon as they arose, just as witchcraft accusations began to dwindle in the seventeenth century when people would no longer go along with them and trouble to suppress them. The less something like devil-possession or witch-craft is believed in and its victims perse-cuted, the less it thrives to propagate. Today neither churchly nor secular authori-ties will credit witchcraft or devil posses-sion. Television cameras would roll all right but only to report foolishness, not some-thing credible. Few people want to be held up as public fools.

A steady chain of behavioral epidemics runs through medieval and modern his-tory:[43] prophecies foretelling the end of the world inspired mass terror; crusades offering passports to heaven set out to rid the Holy Land of Turks; witch manias boiled over from Europe into New Eng-land; flagellants scourged themselves, and Christian pogroms massacring Jews culmi-nated in the recent mass murders officially ordered by the German Nazi government. In the nineteenth century, U.S. and English religious revivals led thousands ecstatically to roll and jump on the floor, or to crawl, bark, or growl like dogs, and repeat what-ever they were told.[44] In 1938, Americans panicked in unison when they heard that Martians had invaded the Earth.[45] Organ-ized hunts for witches in Africa (very much resembling those aggressively undertaken in ·Germany in 1484 under a papal bull by two inquisitorial "dogs of our lord"[46]) recently purged soon-to-be independent nations.[47] On a smaller scale, certain small sects still await the end of the world,[48] and all across the nation college students suddenly were irresistibly challenged to see how many could crowd into a telephone booth. Re-cently, too, we had McCarthyism, when congressmen sought out communist poison as undeterred by skeptics as the exorcists of Loudun. Aldous Huxley says that after the seventeenth century radical Evil ceased to be patterned in metaphysical terms but be-came political and economic. "Radical evil now incarnates itself, not in sorcerers and magicians . . . but in the representatives of some hated class or nation."[49]

ETHNIC DISORDERS

In west Greenland an Eskimo hunter about to slip into his slim, skincovered kayak re-acts like a wartime, stress-torn pilot; his anxiety mounts so high that he involun-tarily urinates in his trousers. In a poor fish-ing village at the outskirts of Malacca in Malaysia, a feeble 70-year-old woman jumps at the slightest noise and compul-sively imitates a dog's bark. On a boat steaming along the Amur River in eastern Siberia, passengers amuse themselves by pretending to throw things overboard, whereupon one man, compelled to keep up with them, divests himself of everything loose and throws it into the water. These are three instances of socially patterned, ethnic disorders, forms of mental illness re-ported from particular ethnic groups. Are they unrelated to disorders that turn up in a Euroamerican psychiatrist's practice? I shall consider that question along with in-quiring into how such disorders assume their relatively stereotyped forms.

Kayakangst. Kayak phobia is well known in western Greenland and has also been known to affect Eskimo on the island's east coast and in the extreme northwest. Alone on a mirror-calm sea the kayaker suddenly becomes confused or dizzy; he can no longer gauge distances between ob-jects; the boat's bow blurs; his desire to move and squirm is counteracted by morbid fear that he may capsize; the lower part of his body chills, convincing him that his craft is flooding. Unless he snaps out of his state, anxiety will intensify and may para-lyze him so that he won't be able to paddle. If these terrifying attacks repeat themselves, a man will do all in his power to avoid them, even to abandoning kayaking. Zachary Gussow[50] points out that the dizziness and confusion are quite expectable consequences of isolation and sensory deprivation; aviators flying alone have reported similar reactions, as have European kayakers. Most aviators, once they understand the experience, manage to bring their anxiety under control, but among Eskimo nothing prevents the *Angst* from intensifying and becoming more frequent. Once it reaches phobic proportions it virtually ends the sea-hunter's career. Kayakangst, then, resembles crippling phobias encountered elsewhere, but is distinctively patterned in that it attaches itself to an Eskimo's traditional occupation. Also, Eskimo are culturally quite ready to respond in phobic fashion because of their socially standardized readiness generally to use withdrawal as a mode of coping with stress, phobic fear, of course, being an extreme, immobilizing form of withdrawal.[51] Finally, nothing in Eskimo culture intervenes to prevent anxiety encountered in kayaking from reaching phobic proportions; unlike the aviator, the sea-hunter lacks professional resources to help him check his rising terror and to restore his equilibrium.

Pibloktoq.[52] Much has been written about another Eskimo syndrome, *pibloktoq*, in which adult individuals, mainly women, become completely oblivious of their surroundings and strongly agitated. They strip themselves of clothing and become uncontrollably violent and talkative until they run down and collapse exhaustedly. An individual's exact behavior varies greatly, each instance of pibloktoq drawing from a pool of symptoms which together make up the disorder. Sometimes loss of consciousness subsequently removes any memory of the attack; often the victim flees across the snow or ice, nude or clothed, and wanders deep into the hills or mountains. She even climbs the rigging if on board a ship. Throwing oneself into snow or water has also been reported, as well as throwing things around. The victim of an attack may sometimes injure herself, but unlike some maniacal disorders (e.g., amok), pibloktoq doesn't result in harm to others. Etiologically, it has been credited to the depressing, monotonous, melancholy, long, dark, cold Arctic winter, but that explanation probably only reveals how a non-Eskimo perceives the climate that an Eskimo takes without resentment. Traumatic events, like extreme fright, a relative's death, sudden panic at discovering oneself far from home, and alarm at an impending crisis like starvation, also precipitate attacks. The seizure, Gussow[53] believes, restores the ego's balance in the face of threat. In her excitement the individual dramatically denies fear or threat, thereby compensating for her real feelings of helplessness. Her attack also wins her social support and attention. However psychologically primitive such an appeal for help may be, it is congruent with the Eskimo areal personality's strong dependence needs, to which I shall return. So, from one point of view, pibloktoq represents an ethnically specialized, highly flamboyant pattern of hysteria geared to the contours of Eskimo character structure.

From quite another perspective, A. F. C. Wallace[54] accounts for pibloktoq by a complex etiological chain in which culture and, to a somewhat larger extent, environment are initially responsible for a low calcium concentration in the blood, which, in turn, produces the symptoms. Physicians in Euroamerican practice recognize neurological symptoms (muscular spasms, convulsive seizures, and cognitive disturbances) similar to pibloktoq that follow from calcium deficiency, and several clues indicate that hypocalcemia actually occurs among Eskimo, particularly in Greenland. For example, reports claim slow coagulation of bleeding wounds in Eskimo. Nutritional surveys undertaken in Greenland and

Alaska attest to low calcium intake there. The low-lying summer sun and long winter darkness in the high Arctic also probably prevent the human body from synthesizing much vitamin D_3, a substance necessary to utilize dietary calcium efficiently. At the same time, the rarity with which Eskimo infants are afflicted with rickets militates against a calcium-deficiency theory for pibloktoq. Note that the hypocalcemia and hysteria theories both make provision for social patterning. The former subsumes culture under natural environment; the latter regards hysteria, specifically pibloktoq, as a congenial way for a relatively unsophisticated, dependent person to appeal for help. Both theories are speculative and the slim available evidence prohibits choosing between them until more investigations are carried out.

Pibloktoq is disappearing much as conversion hysteria has been dropped in Europe and America in favor of other symptoms, such as anxiety reactions.[55] Such swings in style of personality disorder following changes in people's total ways of life must themselves be regarded as socially patterned. Today, Euroamericans and Eskimo are both less simple than they were. With increased sophistication they outgrew such relatively crude and gross manifestations of personality disorder as hysterical blindness, paralysis, or convulsions, at the same time shedding a type of disorder that allowed dramatic, miraculous cures in which all symptoms quickly vanished. It would be very interesting to learn whether depression and anxiety have appeared more often among Eskimo since the breakdown of their isolation and their conversion to Christianity.

Wiitiko Psychosis. Cree and Ojibwa Indians living in northeastern Canada talk with nearly infectious conviction of that solitary, man-eating giant with heart of ice, the Wiitiko, who wanders naked through the forest devouring his own lips in his rampant lust for flesh. A person meeting him at once becomes his prey; but a shaman, enormously fortified by supernatural helpers, can magically overcome the Wiitiko and return to camp to relate his exploit. These Indians also believe that people can acquire the Wiitiko's repulsive

❲ Pibloktoq Attacks A Polar Eskimo Woman

In July 1909 I was witness of such an attack in the woman Inadtliak. It lasted 25 minutes. She sat on the ground with the legs stretched out, swaying her body to and fro, sometimes rapidly sometimes more slowly, from side to side and tortuously, whilst she kept her hands comparatively still and only now and then moved her elbows in to her sides. She stared out in front of her quite regardless of the surroundings, and sang and screamed occasionally, changing the tone, iah-iah-iaha-ha . . . , now and then she interjected a sentence, e.g., that the Danish had at last come to them, and again the great happiness this gave her now in the glad summer-time and so on. Her two small children sat and played about her, whilst the members of the tribe scarcely looked at her during the attacks; they seemed to be very well acquainted with such things. She recovered quite suddenly and only some hectic, red spots on her cheeks indicated anything unusual. Without so much as looking about her or betraying a sign of anything unusual she began, literally with the same movement, to give her youngest child milk and then went quickly on to chew a skin.[56]

H. P. STEENSBY

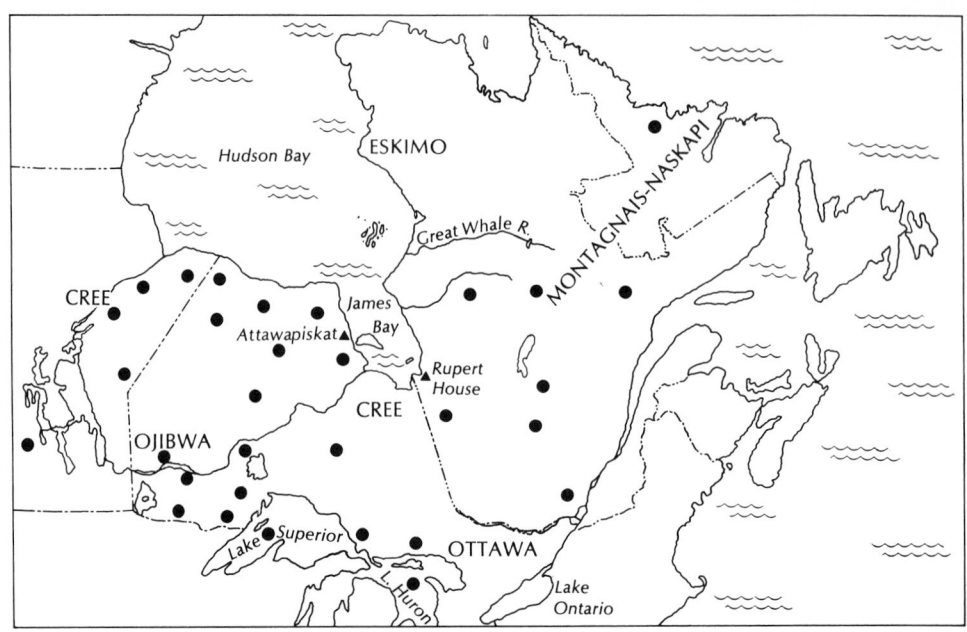

*Each black circle indicates approximately where
one Wiitiko case occurred. Place names also
refer to the previous discussion of otcibweak in
this chapter.*[57]

craving for human flesh. More accurately, perhaps, individuals become unhappy prisoners of the obsession that they may commit cannibalism, like a Wiitiko, and so turn into a Wiitiko. Persons who through cannibalism escaped death from starvation are dreaded lest they have acquired the Wiitiko's exclusive appetite for human flesh. Cannibalism, then, revolts the Cree and Ojibwa not only because it is an inhuman deed, but also because it doubly threatens others by converting the cannibal into a confirmed Wiitiko. Obviously a number of distinct but not necessarily unrelated ideas thread themselves around the Wiitiko concept. It refers to a powerful, manlike, folkloristic being to whom an ordinary person can fall victim. It also contains the idea that somebody can be obsessively dominated by the Wiitiko's cannibalistic appetite, or by his spirit. Finally, there is the idea that a person who through necessity gave in to cannibalism has become fixed in

the Wiitiko's appetites. I am afraid that serializing these concepts doesn't clarify what precisely is meant by the term "Wiitiko psychois," so confidently used in cultural psychiatry. At a minimum we can say that it designates an obsessive-compulsive state which can reach such extreme proportions that it immobilizes the victim, as it did the Cree Indian woman visited by Father Saindon somewhere in the James Bay region. Neighbors told him she was fighting "against the obsessing idea that . . . [she] wished to kill and she didn't wish [to]. . . . As a solution of her conflict, she fled from reality and took the stand of not wishing to see anyone or to speak with anyone."[58] Unfortunately, when the priest entered her tent he didn't give her a chance to describe her symptoms; so there went a rare opportunity for an inquirer with a good knowledge of Cree to interview a victim of Wiitiko disorder.

Morton Teicher[59] has most industriously

ranged through travel and other literature and solicited anthropologists who have worked in northeastern Canada to go through their unpublished field notes for every available word about Wiitiko disorders. With that information he set down some seventy cases of what he calls "windigo psychosis" (using the Ojibwa rather than, as I do, the Cree appellation). Some of his cases describe individuals whom famine had driven to cannibalism, but who felt no emotional compulsion to eat human flesh and came away from their desperate act without suffering any notable personality disorder. They can hardly be considered victims of Wiitiko disorder, regardless of what their neighbors darkly suspected. As for the other cases, I can't find one that satisfactorily attests to someone being seriously obsessed by the idea of committing cannibalism. By "satisfactory" I mean a trustworthy observer's eyewitness report of a person who in his own words or by his own actions clearly admits to a compulsion to eat human flesh. All cases on record fall short of my standard. Often they recount what others told a writer, sometimes an informant whose creditability itself remains in doubt. Sometimes, as I have already said, such hearsay evidence simply reports uncomplicated famine cannibalism. Other hearsay accounts describe people being killed, perhaps at their own behest, for their dangerous preoccupation with cannibalism, but the reporter didn't himself hear their admission. Hence I can't help but wonder if in those executions the Indians, rather like Euroamerican witch hunters, didn't simply suspect the victims, in conformity with their firm belief about compulsive cannibalism. Some instances are court cases involving men tried for murder, but the trial accounts don't clearly prove obsessive-compulsive behavior.

A good deal of speculation has delved into the alleged disorder's etiology and social patterning.[60] Obviously, the symptoms reflect a Cree and Ojibwa folklore charac-

❨ Rescue of a Woman Turning into a Wiitiko

One winter all the Indians of a certain settlement became excited because an old woman several miles up the river was said to be turning wihtigo. The missionary heard about the case and asked one of the Indians to go to her camp and bring her out to the main settlement. He refused because he said he would need fifteen men, and since most of the Indians were away hunting, he could not collect this number. Finally, one of the Indians I know very well, offered to go. He found the old woman in camp with her husband. She had not eaten for days and refused food which he offered her. She told him that if she became a wihtigo she would be as tall as the trees and nothing could stop her. . . . The old lady cried a great deal of the time. Her husband watched her day and night. He was very much afraid of her. My friend finally persuaded the old woman to come with him and after a few days in the settlement she began to eat again and soon recovered.

. . . The woman was around sixty years old. Her illness developed during the winter, about 1900. She was living at Poplar River when her symptoms developed. Her face swelled; she looked wild; she could not sleep; she refused to eat; she claimed that she could hardly keep from shouting; she was convinced that she was becoming a windigo; and she cried a good deal. She was finally brought to the settlement . . . where she recovered.[61]

                                                                A. IRVING HALLOWELL

ter, though we shall probably never know which historically came first, the obsession-compulsion or the notion of a forest-dwelling Wiitiko. The way the disorder revolves around cannibalism also has its roots in cultural reality, for necessity in the North does sometimes drive desperate people to eat human flesh.[62] Ruth Landes,[63] speaking for the Ojibwa Indians specifically, sees the disorder rooted in the conjoined fear of envy and sorcery that she uncovered in Ojibwa life. Using an epidemiological approach, she perceives Wiitiko disorder to affect primarily dominant or assertive men and women who by virtue of their personality are likely to be successful providers and skillful in other roles. These qualities mark them for their neighbors' envy and sorcery, which they seriously fear. Insecurity thus becomes the price Ojibwa pay for success. The Wiitiko psychosis with its partially disguised, retaliatory aggression symptomatizes the strain under which successful men labor.

WIITIKO DISORDER AND PIBLOKTOQ COMPARED [64]

Something more can be learned about how social patterning operates in personality disorder if we pause to note the difference between the self-preoccupation and depression associated with Wiitiko disorder compared with the more flamboyant, acting-out associated with Eskimo pibloktoq. Ojibwa Indians seem to favor disorder marked by morbid depression; the Eskimo on the other hand have typically reacted with convulsive hyperexcitability, "freezing behavior," and temporary loss or clouding of consciousness; that is, by uttering hysterical calls for help. To explain this difference, Seymour Parker heeds the way children in each ethnic group are reared, as well as certain features in the social characters arising through early socialization. Taking his cue from

psychiatrists whose Euroamerican practice indicates hysterical symptoms to prevail in people who have experienced highly nurturant, early socialization that allowed them richly to gratify dependence needs, and that demanded no early demonstration of independence and achievement, he notes that Eskimo socialization fulfills similar conditions. Eskimo adult social life reveals considerable mutual aid and cooperation—behavior calculated to encourage continued dependence and to provide nurturance, much as early life did. Childhood gratified the person's dependence and adult interpersonal life persists in nurturing him. Among the Ojibwa, however, the child's dependence strivings encounter early and severe frustration that prepares him for a high degree of self-reliance and individualism, such as his culture requires.[65] As a result, he retains his unsatisfied craving for dependency and nurturance all through life, expressing it, for example, in his religious attitudes when he begs (sometimes masochistically) for supernatural support or pity. Eskimo religion neither demands humiliation nor expects pity; nor is it as individualistic as the Ojibwa's. Eskimo religious avoidances and rules link the individual closely to his community as they warn him that doing wrong will affect not merely himself but others too. More than among Eskimo, witchcraft sunders Ojibwa from one another, thereby reinforcing individuality, providing little basis of trust, and blocking mutual aid as well as other nurturant relationships. The result is an atomistic social system that keeps people apart, and that intensifies longings for dependence and nurturance.

Returning now to the two patterns of personality disorder: Hysteria fits a social system like the Eskimo, where people are able freely to indulge their dependence; in a crisis it enables a stressed person dramatically to summon help and support. Morbid depression, with its admission of aloneness

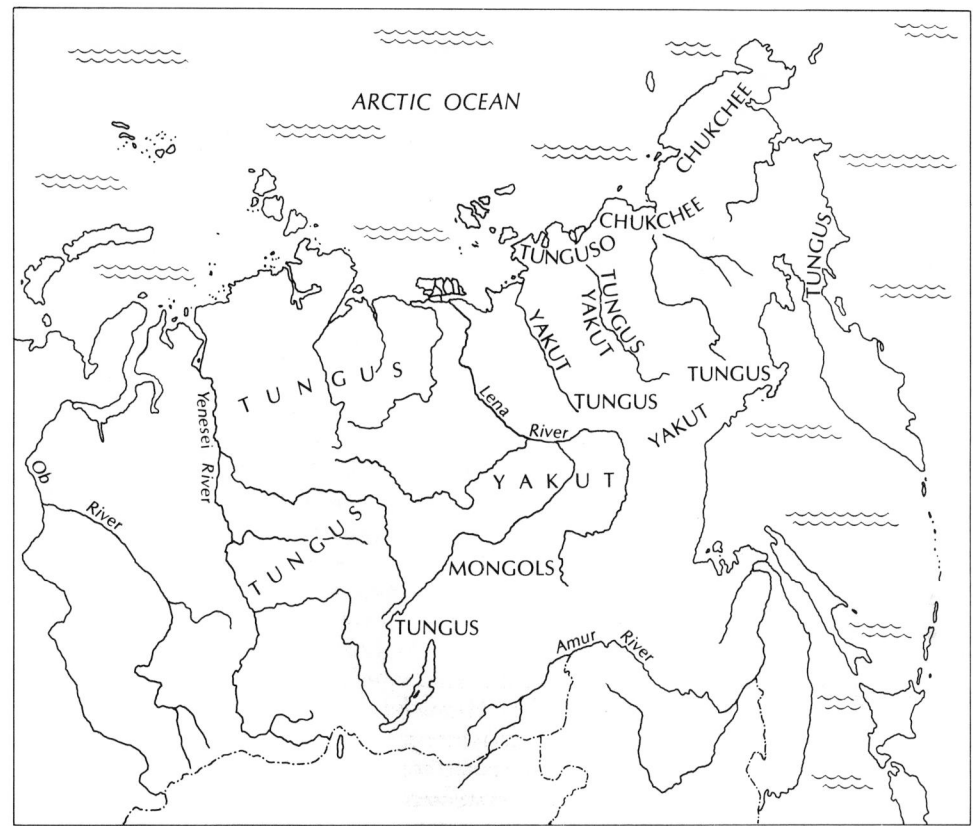

*Country of the Yakut, Tungus, and adjoining
people, where Arctic hysteria has been
reported.*[66]

and hopelessness, fits a different social
character, the Ojibwa, that recognizes no
reasonable ground for trying to summon
nurturance to win support in a crisis. Going
a step further and examining the content of
the Wiitiko disorder, the frightful Wiitiko
may well symbolize the mother who frustrated the child's dependence, as well as all
others in society who leave unfulfilled a
person's need for support.[67] Dependence
cravings mixed with rage generated by frustration burst forth in the Wiitiko psychosis,
the person in his fantasies threatening to
destroy frustrating objects in his environment by eating them.

The case for Parker's theory would be
greatly strengthened if he could also find
personality disorder involving morbid self-

preoccupation among the more westerly
Athapaskan Indians, like the Kaska, where
childhood also fails fully to satisfy dependence and provides only limited nurturance.[68]
There Wiitiko disorder doesn't occur. I
must also report that among eastern Arctic
Eskimo I have observed several instances of
depression and morbid guilt that assumed
severe proportions.[69] Conceivably, depression here represents a new mode for revealing strain, one inadvertently encouraged by
a more sophisticated way of life and devotion to Christianity. In a number of places
in the world Christianity accompanies guilt
and self-depreciation as usual forms of
depression.[70]

Arctic Hysteria and Latah. Depressed
economic conditions, intense cold, a mo-

notonous landscape, and the long winter night are offered to explain the etiology of Arctic hysteria, a disorder reported (once again, too often from hearsay) by travelers among the Yakut and Tungus in northeastern Asia.[71]

In one form, *ämürakh*, which is especially likely to affect women, the afflicted person is irresistibly driven to imitate gestures and sounds, sometimes a whole group or village becoming affected by such compulsive reactions. Other symptoms include shouting, violent actions, and profound fear. The second form, *menerik*, affects chiefly shamans and is brought on by shock or sudden pain, though the symptoms may thereafter return periodically. The victim also shows spasms and becomes strongly excited so that he howls, dances, and even attacks others. By appeasing evil spirits who send this disorder the shaman obtains relief.

First reports of *latah*, which P. M. Yap[72] calls a "fright neurosis," are credited to nineteenth-century European travelers visiting the Malay archipelago. Malayans themselves use the word to describe what they perceive to be a curious behavioral quirk or aberration—normal, yet not quite so, but certainly not a disease. It is another disorder primarily affecting women, especially those past their prime, though its onset may come considerably earlier. Typically, but not always, latah appears following a sudden, unexpected shock, but it can also be provoked by tickling. The original reaction may be flight, immobile collapse, or tremor. Thereafter, in varying degree, the disorder, like *ämürakh*, shows itself in automatic obedience to commands, compulsive imitation of actions and words, and anxiety. In Malaya as in Siberia, people so afflicted prove amusing and they may be invited to perform at weddings. P. M. Yap, trying to ground latah in cultural conditions, perceives congruence between the disorder and insecurity in social personality,

stemming, in turn, from rudimentary technological development. He notes that Malayans affected with echolalia and echopraxia tend to be shy, unaggressive, naive, retiring, self-effacing, colorless, and endowed with little individuality. Timorousness makes them fearful, and against fright they have only inadequate resources of defense. Latahlike behavior, called *imu*, also occurs among the Ainu, aboriginal inhabitants of the Japanese islands, where again victims are mostly women.[73] Here, too, a sudden stimulus, perhaps only a sharp word or loud interruption, ushers in the disorder with wild preliminary aggression or sudden, panicky flight. Thereupon more chronic reactions set in, the person echoing what he hears, automatically complying with commands, or else becoming stubbornly negativistic. Nobody really recovers from imu; he simply grows progressively more seclusive, shy, and fearful. No doubt latah, imu, and imitative Arctic hysteria follow a single pattern, one also reported for the central-Asiatic Mongols and from North Africa, the Middle East, Lapland, the Philippines, Thailand, and French-Canadians in Maine.[74] Accordingly, we aren't at all dealing with an ethnic disorder. David Aberle[75] analyzes the pattern into two major kinds of symptoms: first, imitative reactions in which the individual compulsively imitates what others do and say, especially someone with authority, but sometimes even animal sounds; second, startle reactions that express strong fear. The startled person may jump, freeze, flee, utter obscenities, or attack by violent, aggressive behavior. One can view both the imitative and startle reactions as attempts to defend against being overwhelmed by either the outside world or by urgent, inner motives. In one reaction, defense takes the form of identifying with the danger, via imitation; in the other, safety is sought in fleeing, abusing, or attacking the frightening stimulus. Women's socially patterned timidity makes them

⟮ Arctic Hysteria in a Yakut Forest

Once ... travelling in the Viluy district of the Yakut region, I stopped for the night in a forest yurta with some Tungus. On lying down to sleep I was disturbed by the piercing shouts and cries of a woman. When this had gone on for about half an hour, I rose and went to see what was the matter. On entering the yurta from which the cries proceeded, I found a Tungus man sitting beside the sleeping-place of his wife and holding her wrist. Her hair was all dishevelled so as to cover her face completely, she was nodding her head violently in all directions, and crying and howling like a dog. I could not see her face, but her husband's expression showed that he was quite accustomed to this sort of thing. He told me that these attacks were of frequent occurrence, and came on by day or by night. I remained in the yurta about half an hour, and during that time none of my interpreters was able to make anything of the sounds the woman was uttering. After I returned to my hut, her cries continued for some time longer. I was told afterwards that the violence of these attacks subsides gradually, the patient sighs deeply, becomes quiet, and begins to speak quite normally.[76]

R. MAAK

⟮ A Severe Case of Latah

A seranee *woman (i.e., of Malay-Portuguese extraction), aged 70, and feeble, whose husband was an ex-fisherman, living in a depressed fishing community on the outskirts of Malacca.*

She was a meek and senile woman. .... She jumped at the slightest noise, and at the same time repeated it, e.g., a noise made in imitation of a dog bark; also when she was spoken to abruptly in a loud and commanding voice she would show typical echolalia. Any aggressive movement made towards her, including attempts to tickle her would bring about confused and incoherent talk, with ineffectual efforts to escape. She never exhibited coprolalia. After some time she did not have to be constantly stimulated to show these symptoms. She imitated movements of the arms made in front of her, and contortions of the face, though without any exactitude. All simple and direct commands she promptly obeyed. She became tired, rubbed her eyes repeatedly, said she was mabok *(drunk), and begged me to desist because she wanted to be well, and attend mass that night. ....*

When composed she was fully oriented, could tell her age, and informed me that she had had four sons, all of whom had died.[77]

P. M. YAP

*Gururumba dancer imitating a "wild man,"
with mixed frightening and humorous effects on
his audience. His movements include agitated
bursts of activity and mock attacks that always
prove unsuccessful; thereupon he displays mock
rage by collapsing, kicking the ground, and
tearing at plants. At other times he holds
himself rigid or slowly rotates his body.*[78]

more vulnerable to anxiety and so to defensive ämürakh, latah, or imu.

Amok. Destructive, maddened excitement called "amok" occurs in Malaya, Indonesia, and New Guinea. Although its course has been traced through three stages, beginning with depression and followed by a period of brooding and withdrawal, the disorder is typified by the final mobilization of tremendous energy during which the "wild man" runs destructively beserk.[79] One of the earliest anthropologists to spot

congruence between personality disorder and social personality, Charles G. Seligman,[80] regarded attacks of wild excitement, threat, and assault among so-called Papuans of New Guinea and Melanesia as suitable forms for their characteristic impulsiveness and suggestibility to take.[81]

Amok not only provides emotional release; in at least one community it also discharges the individual from onerous social responsibilities without costing him social support.[82] Hysterical patterns of communication, in other words, need not be stupid (as they have been called in Euroamerican culture[83]); they may convey positive meaning and in an acceptable way enable an individual to adjust. Among the Gururumba, isolated until recently in the Eastern Highlands region of New Guinea, men between 25 and 35 (exclusively) demonstrate wildman behavior. Men in this age category have just begun to assume serious adult responsibilities and have taken their place in a network of economic entanglements. Frequently they find it difficult to meet all the financial obligations on which their rise in power and prestige depends. Running amok partially resolves the young men's frustrations, for it provides them with a permitted outlet for their strain. "Culture . . . supplies a pattern of action suited by its form to the individual's needs." The people, to be sure, account differently for the disorder, reasoning that ghosts unrestrainedly ruled by aggressive impulses have bitten the man running berserk, or that he is temporarily a ghost. Excused in this manner, the wild man expects no recriminations for what he does, and faces no demand for indemnity to cover damage he causes. He won't even be reminded of the episode. But people continue to talk about him in a way indicating that they have fixed him with a new identity, one different from what most men possess. His behavior has given evidence that he is less capable than others of withstanding pressures of social life. Hence, neighbors reduce their expectations toward him, not pressing him to pay his debts promptly and not extracting from him prior commitments to provide food for feasts. He doesn't become an outcast, and he realizes that he can't withdraw altogether from economic affairs, but he also knows that he must limit his participation. In that way the Gururumba incorporate amok in their design for effective living. Thanks to its socially assigned function, which resembles the gains secured by a Plains berdache dreaming of the moon or of a hermaphroditic buffalo, it allows a person, if he is so inclined, to escape in some degree from fulfilling the most highly valued cultural goals.[84]

Koro.[85] Known mostly from east and southeast Asia, particularly from Chinese cases, *koro* is no longer to be regarded as strictly areally delimited, for it has also been reported from the eastern Sudan and elsewhere. The person afflicted becomes anxious and even panicky in his concern that his penis is disappearing into his abdomen and that he will die. His genital organ feels cold, numb, remote, and depersonalized. Such feelings only too clearly betray their meaning to people like the Chinese, who closely identify vitality with sexuality and have long been intensely preoccupied with the vital properties of semen.[86] Because semen represents a store of vital essence and bodily energy, its loss through nocturnal emissions, masturbation, or frequent copulation can be dangerous. It hardly comes as a surprise to learn that masturbation and coitus can trigger koro. In China, the disorder's name, *suo-yang*, denotes a defect in yang, the principle present in all nature that symbolizes heaven, firmness, hardness, God, and maleness. Koro fits neatly into a culture with this complex of beliefs and fears; whether its patterning in other cultures will be explicable along similar lines remains to be found out.

Susto. Anthropologists working in Hispanic America have collected considerable information about *susto* (or *pasmo* and *espanto*, in addition to other names by which it is called in different localities).[87] The disorder, however, by no means afflicts only Spanish-speaking persons, but occurs equally commonly among individuals who speak Indian languages. Underlying susto is the assumption that a human being comprises a corporal substance plus one or more immaterial, detachable souls. Free to leave the body, a soul may wander, as it sometimes does, for example, during sleep or in consequence of an unsettling, frightening experience. An errant soul forms the major element of susto. As a result of being forsaken by his soul, a person becomes restless in sleeping, listless during his waking hours, and disinterested in personal dress; he loses his appetite, feels depressed, and becomes introverted. All symptoms don't blossom in the same person, or even turn up in a single locality; they make up the symptom pool by which susto is defined. Cure begins with diagnosis, in which causes of the ailment are ascertained, and proceeds with efforts to coax back the soul. Just how this folk illness that mainly centers around depression suits Middle American culture hasn't yet been explained. Epidemiologically minded anthropologists, such as Arthur J. Rubel, have been more concerned with establishing the circumstances in which susto will appear. He hypothesizes that it quite selectively favors people who have been traumatized through a social episode in which they have failed to meet vital age- and sex-role obligations of their community. Although susto is a response to social frustration, Rubel doubts that it will afflict someone who is blocked in becoming identified with a community or social stratum not his own; for example, an Indian who wants to be accepted by his mestizo contemporaries.

How Many Disorders? Ethnic disorders, the term under which I group kayakangst,

⟪ A Susto *with Complications in the Rio Grande Delta of Texas*

Mrs. Benítez is a thin, distraught woman of about 45 years of age. For the past six years she has been suffering from attacks brought on by an asustada condition. Mrs. Benítez's aura consists of severe, painful headaches, and a strange tingling sensation as if she were being pierced by numerous pins and needles. Following the aura she "goes out of her senses" and although able to hear those attending her, is unable to respond. Her limbs become taut and convulsive in movement, the jaw clamps shut, and the teeth clench in ironbound fashion. Upon regaining her senses she has no recollection of the seizure but is exhausted and has an overpowering urge to be completely free from the social world about her. Although Mrs. Benítez has several times been advised by physicians that she is an epileptic, her own diagnosis and that of her friends run counter to medical opinion.

Mrs. Benítez traces her condition from the vexatious (mortificada) period during which she lived with her husband, a man who has since deserted her and the children. "When I lived with my husband he used to beat me at regular intervals. On some mornings following a beating I could not lift my arms to eat with or in order to do the housework. I lived in an upset state all of the time [vivia asustada]." The first seizure she recalls caused her to go to an old man then living in Mecca with a local reputation for his effectiveness in the cure of susto. . . .

In December of 1958, Mrs. Benítez suffered a particularly severe seizure occasioned in general by the presence in her one-room apartment of the troubled relationship between her daughter and the daughter's husband, and in particular by an altercation between herself and the son-in-law. One night in an angry mood the young man came home in search of a revolver which he had left in the care of his mother-in law. The young man was quite intent on murdering a drinking companion with whom he had had words at a local bar. Mrs. Benítez refused to relinquish the weapon, which further incensed the youth. The son-in-law then proceeded to assault the informant verbally, at the same time knocking his wife about the house. On the following morning, in the early pre-dawn hours, Mrs. Benítez suffered a severe headache which awakened her, presaging the terrible seizure which followed. The violence of the scene during the night had caused her a susto nuevo which, combined with her older susto, created the very dangerous susto complicado or susto pasado.[88]

ARTHUR J. RUBEL

⟪ Rosa Castro Treats a Young "Patient" for Susto[89]

The curer, Rosa Z. Castro, was born in Monterrey, Mexico, 54 years before she posed for the photographs shown here. While her husband was sharecropping in Isola, Mississippi, two old women taught her the art of healing. Although her husband prefers that she treat only relatives (she counts up to 30 grandchildren), she willingly extends her services to any neighbors in San Antonio, where she lives, who request them. "I won't allow a person to die," she promises.

First, Rosa Castro holds some of the materials used in treatment; the cup contains a piece of blessed palm and the water in which she boiled it. Next, using a spoonful of lime, she makes a cross on a piece of paper, over which the "patient" will lie to be swept by a piece of *ruda* bush and prayed over. Then the young "patient" reclines on the paper, which is spread over a blanket, and, finally, is swept by the branch. (all John Avant)

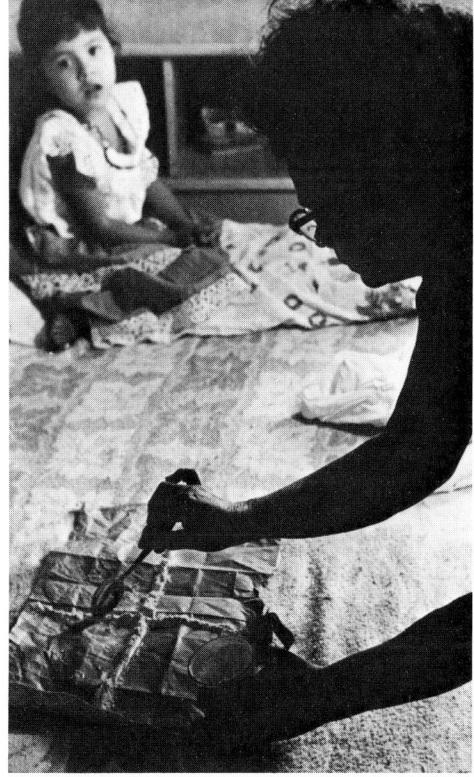
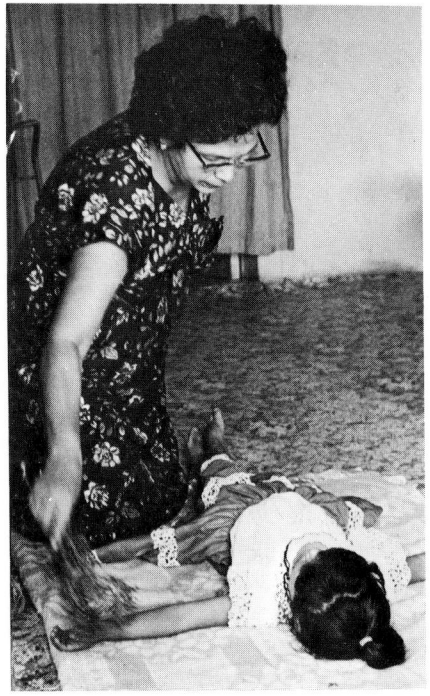

latah, and the other syndromes just discussed, isn't too apt, for such disorders aren't as culturally or areally delimited as the term suggests. Their hysterical, obsessive, anxious, or schizophrenic identities make them widely recognizable, sometimes in virtually the same symptomatic garb (like fear of a disappearing penis). Apparently the number of objectively distinguishable units of personality disorder is limited.[90] Such phenomena as gastrointestinal disturbance, depressed mood, uncontrollable rage, nonrational fears, compulsive imitation, or chronic suspiciousness can combine and recur in varying settings, taking more specific forms, like kayakangst, latah, schizophrenia, or other diagnostic categories. Karl Menninger[91] holds mental illness to constitute a single, unitary phenomenon which merely takes different channels of expression in individuals and cultures. Words like schizophrenia or paranoia refer to classes of unit symptoms that are relevant for appropriate treatment but that don't identify specific diseases.

Symbols that kill

Can sorcery kill? Can a person who believes in a sorcerer's power sicken and die once he suspects or, more terrifyingly, realizes that he has been selected as the victim? Anthropologists, dubious about informants' accounts of successful sorcery, are advised by a physiologist to believe their sources.[92] Social patterning achieved through intense and enduring fear may extend to severe physiological disturbance. Furthermore, in a community holding faith in the power of malevolent magic, the victim's neighbors and kin will confirm his belief that he is in mortal danger. Knowing any kind of support to be in vain, they withdraw from him, admitting their helplessness against the sorcerer's unleashed power. In effect, they abandon the victim to his depleted re-

sources with dreadful finality.[93] To be sure, the theory has its critics, who warn that nobody has actually observed sorcery to be obediently followed by illness and death.[94] They note that reports of thanatomania (death madness) aren't clearly authenticated, smack of hearsay, omit the possibility of an effective poison having secretly been used, and don't rule out organic disease or starvation as causes of death.

From the Eastern Highlands of New Guinea, a region where the first anthropologists arrived only in the middle 1930s, come reports of kuru, an ailment that people regularly attribute to sorcery.[95] Its symptoms, said to resemble the coarse tremor that seizes the extremities in Parkinson's disease, affect mainly women. In this part of New Guinea, sorcery constitutes a recognized means of redressing wrongs, with the result that most deaths, regardless of the physical cause that kills, are ascribed to one of its thirty-four named varieties. One of these magical means, also called kuru, requires the magician, who is usually a man, to obtain a piece of food or clothing that has been associated with his potential victim and in prescribed fashion to treat it, with the intention of provoking injury or death. People say he soon observes his victim to lose control over her limbs, take leave of her reason, and manifest erratic behavior—for example, making inappropriate sexual advances. Her sores won't heal, maggots fester in her skin and spread, dysentery appears, and she dies. Cases of kuru observed by visitors to the Highlands may not show all those alleged symptoms, but they regularly do reveal partial paralysis and lack of muscular control, attacks of which become increasingly frequent and strong. In the district where kuru appears to be centered, the illness prevails in 1 percent of the population at any one time. As a degenerative illness affecting the central nervous system, the ailment undoubtedly possesses a physiologi-

A kuru victim in an early stage of the disease. (R. M. Berndt)

mania and of the potency of magic in general would be enormously strengthened should the future fieldwork of epidemiologically minded anthropologists answer that question affirmatively.

Whether sorcery kills or not, fear is undoubtedly a psychological consequence of living in its presence. This fearful culture trait, however, doesn't thrive equally under all cultural conditions. Unlike quite another phenomenon, witchcraft—by which I mean an automatic, mystical propensity in someone to promote evil[96]—sorcery flourishes in social systems that lack clear-cut political authorities with power to punish offenses committed against individuals.[97] In such acephalous communities, sorcery constitutes a significant weapon whereby some individuals, at least, may effect control. By its nature it also aggravates the atomistic social state, increases the necessity for self-reliance, and makes it difficult for people to collaborate or to create political authorites.[98]

PSYCHOTIC PREOCCUPATIONS

I have discussed disorders possessing relatively unfamiliar forms, seeking correspondences between them and the rest of the culture in which they are found and looking to see how they come to be patterned. Social patterning also shows its hand in disorders like schizophrenia that retain a familiar structure, though different cultural components modify their delusions, hallucinations, confabulations, and other contents.[99] I propose to employ the word "delusions" as an over-all term to cover hallucinations and confabulation as I turn to exploring their patterning.[100] Delusions are vivid symbols that refer to particular cultural contexts internalized in a highly personal way by deluded individuals.[101] I am not so much concerned with how a person under private pressures distorts reality in

cal basis and to some extent implicates heredity. My interest centers on the degree in which kuru might also stem from emotional turmoil initiated when a person knows that he or she has become the object of creditable sorcery. It is possible that such emotion isn't involved at all, but that New Guinea Highlanders merely find it convenient to *explain* the illness in terms of sorcery. Hence, a most important question to be answered is: Do victims of the disease believe themselves to have been sorcerized *before* their paralysis and muscular noncoordination sets in? Theories of thanato-

his delusions as I am with how his delusions continue to adhere to reality, just as such symbolic products as proverbs, prayers, and dreams do. People especially utilize potent cultural values in their delusions as well as those natural channels—food and eating—which the community prefers for mediating social relationships. In the Virgin Islands, for example, French and Puerto Rican families are closely united through eating. They define family roles by the acquisition, dispensing, and consuming of food; mark changes in status by altered food habits; observe rules governing what and what not to eat and with whom one may eat, and abstain from food on certain occasions out of moral and religious duty. Among them, national dishes symbolize the community itself. No wonder that their delusions frequently incorporate food. On the other hand, religious delusions involving God or Jesus characterize British Virgin Islanders, quite in accordance with the Church's predominant position in their lives, its service as a powerful source of identity, and their tendency to express their feelings and moral values in religious terms.[102] The highest incidence of delusions in native Virgin Islanders involves children, as one might expect from a people who express their needs and feelings in terms of children and perceive even their environment as if it were a good or bad child. The high value placed on offspring also appears in some men's delusions that they are impotent and sterile.

We have abundant proof that as cultural values change, so do the private patterns by which psychotic people order their thinking. A tabulation of the schizophrenic content in Japan covering 20 years reveals that before and during World War II patients often claimed to be or to have met the emperor. In the postwar years such beliefs declined, the ruler's place being filled by such prominent features of the new times as Americans, the Communist party, and radioactivity.[103] A similar comparison of

schizophrenics at two points in English history, the mid-nineteenth and mid-twentieth centuries, shows that in the Victorian period religious figures much more often permeated their thoughts; not surprisingly, for religion played a greater part in life and a larger proportion of people attended church.[104] Patients who heard God's voice promising retribution or threatening the fires of hell brought to the hospital a personality that had been formed in religiously saturated homes and schools. Occasionally sex and religion intertwined in schizophrenic preoccupations, echoing a Puritanical insistence on sexual self-discipline and self-control. Sexual preoccupation became more common in the twentieth century than it had been in the nineteenth, not so much because prudish Victorian record-takers had avoided noting such evil concerns, but because sex became less suppressed and so more freely available for use in psychosis. Nineteenth-century hospitalized schizophrenics were also more disturbed. Partly, this seems accountable to the culture of the hospital, more humanized conditions of institutional care being known to exert soothing effects. Yet perhaps more than this is involved, for startling forms of violence seem to have continuously diminished in English culture through the latter quarter of the nineteenth century and into the twentieth, the trend paralleling changes in social values.

Italian and Irish Styles of Schizophrenia

More than delusions change with culturally different settings. The whole psychotic pattern, including the hidden psychodynamic states motivating the disorder, conforms to the general style of behavior followed in the patient's community.[105] Two sample groups of New York schizophrenic men, one of Irish, the other of Italian, parentage, matched for age (30–32) education (about 10 years), I.Q. (slightly over 100), and religion (Roman Catholic), and both predominantly lower-class, reveal how schizophrenia assumes a culturally distinctive pattern in different milieus. Practically all the Irish cases show traces of latent homosexuality but only about one third of the Italians do so. While not itself evidence of personality disorder, such traces in the Irish indicate the ambivalent anxiety, fear, and hostility promoted against female figures in a family where the father proved to be evanescent and unavailable as a figure with whom the boy could identify. Hostility toward the mother incorporated by Irish patients is deeply repressed, compared to the light repression of the hostility that Italians typically incorporate toward the father and that they easily ventilate. Just as the Irish are famous for sexual repression, for a pervasive concern with sin and guilt, and for protracted betrothals, Irish schizophrenics are more involved with guilt feelings centering around sex. Contrasting Italian norms allow much more direct expression of sexual impulses, as well as freer emotional expression in general,[106] and patients carry over this style of behavior into the hospital. With their spontaneous emotionality they give greater trouble to nurses and attendants; more of them than of the Irish tend to be assaultive, suicidal, destructive, and given to outbursts of temper.

Toward authority, Irish patients manifest the same compliance they learned to show to the central family authority figure, the mother. Italian patients, in a fashion consistent with their less passive make-up, more often reject authority, just as they learned to be repelled by an authoritarian father and punitive elder siblings. Irish schizophrenics, in conformity with the cultural readiness for fantasy, more often construct fixed and systematic delusions. Italians, who generally indulge little in fantasy, tend to create only fleeting schizophrenic

delusions, and mostly act out. In greater proportion than in the Irish, somatic and hypochondriacal problems occupy them, revealing Italians' more realistic conception of the body compared to the greater fantasy with which the Irish approach it. Alcoholism, present in 10 out of 30 Italian men, prevails in as many as 19 out of 30 Irish men, for whom it bolsters inadequate ego structures and serves oral-aggressive needs nurtured in close, early maternal relationships. In each ethnic sample, schizophrenia bears the imprint of a distinctive culture and of different social personalities created under contrasting systems of early socialization. Significantly, in three Irish patients from families in which the father occupied a strong, central position "the entire pattern of illness shifted over to the Italian model in every detail."[107]

THE GRAVITY OF LOWER-CLASS DISORDERS

In the previous chapter I reported on several studies carried out in the United States and Canada that showed gravity of personality disorder to increase as social class declined.[108] To be sure, different indicators of social class are used in New Haven, Midtown, and Stirling County, but one general conclusion can safely be drawn: North America is a continent whose communities and classes enjoy far from equal mental health, as psychiatric ratings and interviews conventionally measure that attribute. A plausible accounting for the relationship between low social status and serious personality disorder holds that poverty and other noxious conditions endemic in the lives of people in lower-ranking social strata induce heavy, cumulative stress that wears some people down until they show impairing signs of strain. At present, however, I am not concerned with such etiological explanation but with the question whether the form taken by personality disorder between lower and higher ranking social strata can be related to cultural differences between the levels. Evidence presented by Thomas S. Langner and Stanley T. Michael[109] indicates that such a relationship does exist. The characteristic pattern of disorder in persons of lower social status incorporates aspects of their culture just as the pattern higher up gives evidence of another style of life. In other words, strain is differently patterned on various social levels so that, to resume the image with which the chapter opened, it blends with its cultural setting just as the Peppered Moth blends into its soot-polluted environment. In the case of the socially disintegrated community, culturally distinctive features like a high frequency of violence, crime, and delinquency easily channel the vital strivings of persons under stress, providing a direction for strain to take.

The Facts. You will recall that the Midtown study secured information by means of interviews with 1660 persons aged 20–59. Psychiatrists later rated the information obtained from those persons on a 7-point scale. In making their professional judgments, they considered the interviewee's mental and emotional attitudes, physical health, age, marital status, as well as psychiatric symptoms that the trained interviewer managed to spot. The raters, however, did not at first consider actual social functioning or socioeconomic status in rating the respondent's mental health.* Of the 1660 respondents, 18.5 percent could be considered symptom-free or well; 36.3 percent went into the category of persons with mild symptoms; 21.8 percent were considered to possess moderate symptoms; 23.4

* In a second rating they took actual social functioning into account, including such matters as whether a respondent received welfare assistance or had appeared in court. As a result, 20 percent of the subjects received a worse mental health rating, and 5 percent a better one.

percent were called impaired.[110] At this point, bear in mind that the rating reflects the psychiatrist's standards. His professional values and the criteria he uses to gauge mental health screen reality and thereby create cases. Reduce the rigorousness with which rating is conducted, and the number of psychiatric cases grows smaller; increase it, and the frequency of mental illness is shown to be greater. Operationally speaking, the extent of mental illness in a community depends on standards which the psychiatrist employs.[111]

Midtown respondents were also classified into six socioeconomic levels (which I shall sometimes call classes), A being the highest and F the lowest, investigators judging a person's class by considering his father's occupation at the time the person was about 18 years old. The lower the socioeconomic level, the smaller the proportion of well people and the greater the proportion of those who are impaired. As the eye travels *up* the class ladder, from F to A, the proportion of people without symptoms increases while the prevalence of impairment almost halves. So far, facts accord with the prevailing hypothesis, which sees stress as especially severe in lower socioeconomic strata, where it wears people down to the point that a relatively large number show serious signs of disorder. To check this hypothesis further, the Midtown investigators also measured stress which, they predicted, would be heavier on lower socioeconomic levels. There it would correlate directly with measurably poorer mental health. Things failed to turn out wholly in expected fashion. Each of the 1660 Midtowners respondents received a stress score based on such reported factors as the amount of economic deprivation and poor physical health he had experienced in childhood and whether or not he came from a broken home. The investigators doing the scoring also noted his adult physical health; whether he worried about work or overwork, about getting ahead, and about the cost of living; and whether or not he enjoyed but few social affiliations with neighbors or close friends, and belonged to few organizations.[112] Imagine their puzzled amazement when they discovered that stress scores didn't vary much between socioeconomic strata—not as much as did extreme mental-health ratings. The failure of stress scores and mental-health ratings to move together with a good semblance of proportionality led to another calculation. Statistically, the investigators learned how much of a relationship actually existed in their data between severity of symptoms, stress score, and membership in socioeconomic strata, expressing this relationship in terms of ridits.[113] (A ridit measures the risk that a person from one class will win a worse mental-health rating from psychiatrists who study his interview and know something about his actual social functioning than a person from another class.*) The larger a class's ridit, the worse its members' mental health; the smaller the ridit, the better off they are. A mental-health ridit of .60 compared to another of .40 says that in the former category an individual is about twice as likely to be worse off than in the latter.

Another surprising discovery resulted. Persons of low socioeconomic status who in their lifetime had experienced any of the scored stress factors—regardless of how many!—run a greater risk of coming through a psychiatric screening with a worse mental health rating than persons of higher status. Regardless of difficulty in their lives, lower-class Midtowners run a risk of developing more serious personality disorder than those in middle- and upper-class positions. To be sure, the more stress

* In this phase of the study, investigators used mental-health ratings constructed with knowledge of respondents' socioeconomic level, of whether they received relief, and of other facts about actual social functioning.

they suffer, the greater the risk they run. But because of the subject of this chapter, I am much more impressed with the fact that as stress increases, risk for lows increases even faster.

Why Are the Lows Worse Off? Something in addition to stress influences the gravity of personality disorder in lower-class persons, judging from the way psychiatrists assess their mental health. Compared to persons of higher social rank and income, lower-status persons are judged to react with more severe symptoms and impairment to what, objectively speaking, appears to be the same amount of stress. The question is, Why?

Life Styles and Mental Illness. In 1939, Robert E. L. Faris and H. Warren Dunham published one of the first epidemiological studies of personality disorder in America, and related mental illness to socioeconomic status.[114] They discovered a high prevalence of schizophrenia in Chicago neighborhoods characterized by high mobility and occupied by a large proportion of foreign-born persons and Negroes. Guided by then prevailing sociological theory, which held the social group to be the source of human nature,[115] they concluded that the schizophrenic's hallucinations, delusions, inappropriate actions, and generally deteriorated behavior came about as a result of the slumdweller's isolation from many subtle forms of social control that create and maintain normality. Furthermore, the fragmented social setting of the slum gives rise to a parallel, fragmented consciousness: "The slum area populated by heterogeneous foreign-born elements forms a chaotic background of conflicting and shifting cultural standards against which it is quite difficult for a person to develop a stable mental organization."[116] Whether the slum neighborhood is actually disjointed or unstable doesn't matter, for a "person reacts not to the world but to his conception of it."[117] The form of the slumdweller's mental ill-

❲ Persons of Low Socioeconomic Status Have a Greater Mental-Health Risk than Persons of High Socioeconomic Status, Even When the Number of Their Life Stresses Is Similar[118]

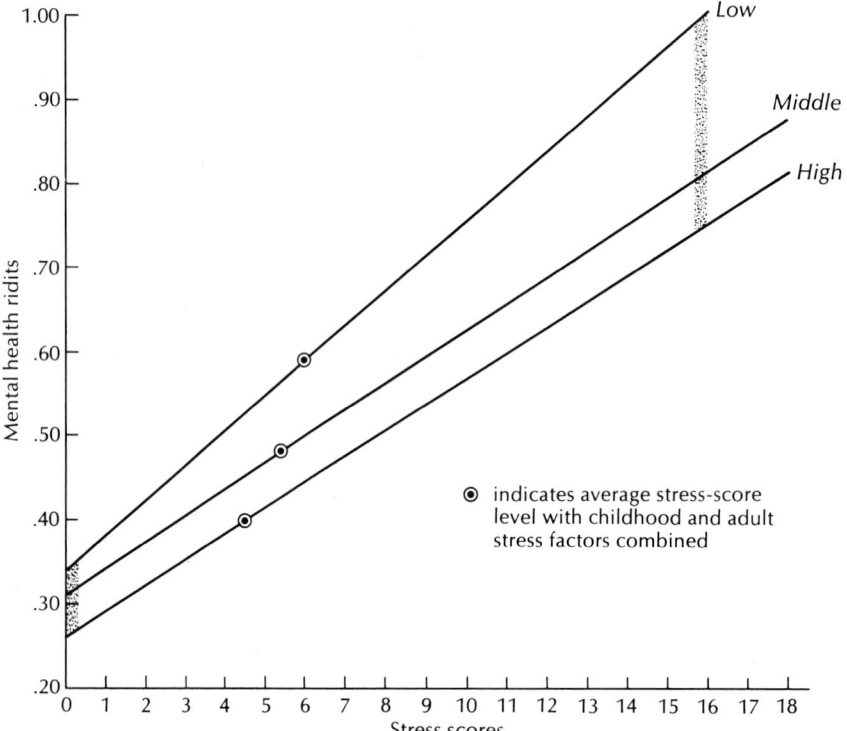

The most significant information given in this chart is conveyed by the relatively steeper slope of the line marked "low," meaning Midtowners of lower socioeconomic status. That line rises much more steeply than the lines designating persons of middle and high socioeconomic status. This means that the average mental health of lower-class people grows worse more sharply as stress scores increase. Already at stress score 1, lows start out with poorer average mental health than middles or highs who report the same amount of stress. By the time lows reach stress score 16, the difference has more than doubled, as you can tell by measuring the height of the hatched bar. The unmistakable conclusion is: Low-status people in Midtown fare disproportionately worse in mental health as their stress scores increase.

ness blends into the chaos, conflict, and instability of his cultural setting, and is created within a private world insulated from
wider social influences. Without corroborat-
ing all that Faris and Dunham say, subsequent research shows them to have been on
the right track in viewing mental illness as
patterned in conformity with class-linked
variants of culture. The Midtown study,
with its focus on fundamental units of personality disorder, such as the depressed
mood and chronic suspiciousness of schizophrenia, neurosis, and other symptom
constellations, also acknowledges social patterning to operate in mental illness. Obviously, to speak of social patterning in this
manner by no means denies the role that
stress may play in instigating personality
disorder. The Midtown investigators regard
higher-status people as learning to react to
stress in predominantly neurotic ways so
that characteristically they become nervous,
restless, and obsessionally worried; they develop upset stomachs or sleeplessness, and
find their hands trembly or damp with anxiety.[119] Despite their unhappiness and suffering, they actually strain in a rather effective way, one that spares them from getting
into serious social and economic difficulties.
They hold themselves in, harbor their problems closely, and continue to act responsibly in tightly controlled ways consistent
with their middle- and upper-class norms.
Some of their signs of strain actually serve
them well, helping them to fulfill their social roles carefully, and allowing them to
stay in upper-income brackets. Were they
to develop very disintegrative symptoms—
uncontrolled rage or chronic suspicion of
their office-mates and friends—they would
lose their jobs, alienate associates, and deprive themselves of many advantages. Soon
they would chute to a lower socioeconomic
level, where they would meet many people
with similar disabling and disruptive symptoms. People of low socioeconomic status
have learned to strain in relatively psychotic

fashion, which is consistent with their class-
linked style of life and compatible with the
futility, isolation, passivity, dependence,
mistrust, and social inadequacy they feel in
a "world they never made." Many of their
symptoms exaggerate socially normal alternatives, just as the higher-status person's
neuroticism exaggerates his customary
capacity for detail, concern with duty and
order, and sense of responsibility. Low-
status people, being more action-oriented,
act out, rather than hold in, their strain,
discharging their emotions explosively and
accusing others of being against them.
Their generally poor ability to take on others' roles, coupled with their concrete style
of thought, allows their paranoid delusions
to run free and uncontrolled.[120] For days,
weeks, even months, strain immobilizes
them so that they can't get going, and thus
fail to perform expected roles. Their way
of straining is so ineffectual that it intensifies society's rejection, causing them to lose
their jobs or to land in trouble with the
police. However, should a lower-class person be ambitious and identify with higher
socioeconomic roles, he then will very
likely learn a different way of straining, one
that protects him against serious personality disorder. He gets sick more effectively.[121]

My main point so far has been that a
person who becomes psychiatrically disturbed, in his effort to adapt to critical
stress exaggerates normal behavioral traits
and tendencies.[122] Schizophrenia, sociopathic behavior, and paranoia in lower-class
people not only represent a sharpening and
accentuation of customary elements in their
style of life; they are directly facilitated by
certain learned cognitive and emotional
traits, beginning with a lax and inefficient
superego that internalizes few social inhibitions.[123] Such people externalize their conscience and blame others when things go
wrong, an attitude ideally suited to paranoid delusions. Being more fatalistic, they

explain poverty and ill health in terms of luck or God rather than as amenable to personal effort. Because in the lower-class home emotional communication tends to be inhibited, the predominant style of behavior, normal and abnormal, is outward, away from personal control or accountability. Love as well as hate are directed outside the family. Unable with their weak egos effectively to cope with disturbing or unpleasant situations, these people flee from danger or else, blind to social consequences, respond aggressively. Their life permits or at least expects aggression, which may be quite adaptive in the neighborhoods where they live. Their sexual and dependent impulses also suffer relatively little control. Action-oriented, they rely less on words or concepts to test and manipulate reality; hence, they demand less logical consistency in their world view, and more quickly find evidence that social ideals and promises are not actually like they sound, which makes it easier for them to react to the world in private fashion, disregarding what others tell them.[124] Often such people feel low in spirits, pessimistic, and alone, reactions that intensify in schizophrenia and paranoid disorders. In their world nobody seems to care what happens to the next fellow. Armed with only minimal social and technical skills, they can't be sure of themselves; consequently, their self-esteem is low. In childhood they probably modeled their self-image on self-rejecting parents who had achieved few of society's values, however kind they may have been and whatever other fine qualities they possessed. No wonder they themselves are so sensitive to ridicule, against which they are prepared to retaliate with direct aggression. Negativism and suspicion color their social relations, particularly their relations toward authority. Almost totally powerless in fact, they remain politically apathetic even after they have climbed some rungs on the status ladder.[125] Their poor discriminatory ability, narrow range of experience, and limited use of compensatory fantasy can't aid them when, driven by stress, they succumb to personality disorder.

Persons of higher socioeconomic standing sharpen and exaggerate personal qualities of a different order to produce charac-

◖ The Slum "Pulls You Down"

More than five years ago, William Jenkins, a quiet and disenchanted Negro boy who had been born in West Harlem, had been reared there and had just been mugged there, joined the United States Army not strictly out of patriotism— but also as a way of escaping West Harlem.

Yesterday, having been discharged from the Army, William Jenkins was back on West 114th Street. It is still called a hustler's street by those who dwell there, and Jenkins said it was "depressing to be home."

"I have no ambition," he said. "Being born in this kind of neighborhood kind of pulls you down with it. I mean, nobody here likes to see you get any place."

He had no heroes as a youth; nor did he have any desire to finish school. He and his close neighborhood friends were never arrested by the police, he continued, "but this is because we were lucky—we could run faster than the others."

He still admits that he has "little ambition," but he hopes—and his friends hope—that 114th Street . . . may change so he will no longer have to say of it: "On 114th Street, there are no goals . . . nobody likes to see you get any place."[126]

                                                                                    GAY TALESE

teristic forms of personality disorder.[127] These people are so driven by ambition that they may convertly injure others to advance themselves. They restrict themselves by a sense of unflinching individual responsibility so strong that it easily reaches obsessive proportions. A demanding, relentless conscience keeps them obedient to social norms, and plagues them with a nagging sense of sin when they have transgressed those norms. They internalize and apply to themselves punishing feelings of guilt; in fact, they believe they should never blame others or depend on luck and circumstance. They even feel guilty when they find their life situation unacceptable; that is, when, despite their success, they still feel unsatisfied. At such times their depression testifies that they have nobody to blame but themselves and can find nothing by which to rationalize their predicament.[128] Higher-status persons' array of skills, especially verbal and social skills, not only helps them move in society but also provides weapons for defending themselves without resorting to physical force. Rational and much given to planning, they are quite capable of resolutely putting off immediate satisfaction for the sake of far-in-the-future goals that they hopefully expect to realize. Physical aggression and sexual behavior they rigidly curtail, with the result that those domains readily become matters of neurotic preoccupation.

Why the Lows Are Worse Off. Low or high, people in each class carry over into mental illness normal traits like those I have just described. Because middle-class values and norms in the status personality of the so-called highs dominate Euroamerican society, lows fare worse than highs as a result of using life styles maladaptively. Psychiatry endorses the higher-status norms, making that status personality the prototype of normality and a yardstick for evaluating personality disorder.[129] Logically, therefore, people who show strain by acting out or falling to pieces emotionally and cognitively, as lower-class people tend to do, *must* be judged as being in a worse state than people who worry, feel unworthy, or go to the doctor constantly with difficult stomachs. Even emotionally upset, higher-ranking people adhere closely to the norms by which their society is governed. Lower-class people, who are always at least a little outside the norms—that's why they are passed over in school and in many other situations—go too far in the way they strain. As a result, just as their normal style of adaptation subjects them to greater disabilities, so they suffer more through the way they bend under critical loads of stress.

It may be that these two status personalities correspond to personality types of much greater generality, types likely to be encountered in many places. Perhaps they correspond to two temperamental proclivities, each of which a different social stratum institutionalizes much as Margaret Mead in *Sex and Temperament* describes the Arapesh and Mundugomor as institutionalizing passive and aggressive tendencies respectively. Making allowances for variation in terminology and for features of behavior specially selected, doesn't Dostoevsky's "direct person" resemble the uninhibited lower-status person outwardly oriented? By that term, Dostoevsky[130] means someone who knows how to revenge himself and stand up for himself in general. He refers to people who

. . . when they are possessed, let us suppose, by the feeling of revenge, then for the time there is nothing else but that feeling left in their whole being. Such a gentleman simply dashes straight for his object like an infuriated bull with its horns down, and nothing but a wall will stop him. (By the way: facing the wall, such gentlemen—that is, the "direct" persons and men of action— are genuinely nonplused. For them a wall is not an evasion, as for us people who think and consequently do nothing; it is not an excuse for turning aside, an excuse for which we are always very glad, though we scarcely believe in it ourselves, as a rule. No, they are nonplused in all sincerity.)

Contrasted with a being of such forthrightness is the man of "acute consciousness," who, especially in the presence of his antithesis, thinks of himself as more mouse than a man. "Let us look at this mouse in action," Dostoevsky suggests:

Let us suppose, for instance, that it feels insulted, too (and it almost always does feel insulted), and wants to revenge itself, too. . . . Apart from the one fundamental nastiness, the luckless mouse succeeds in creating around it so many other nastinesses in the form of doubts and questions, adds to the one question so many unsettled questions, that there inevitably works up around it a sort of fatal brew, a stinking mess, made up of its doubts, emotions, and of the contempt spat upon it by the direct men of action . . . .

MODES OF DEFENSE [131]

If low- and high-status people possess alternative, nonpathological modes of adaptation that carry over into strain, they probably learn them at least partially in quite different conditions of early socialization and family life. A study conducted in Boston reveals how such learning may occur. The investigators examined not representative families belonging to two extreme social strata; they selected two types of psychiatric patients, one depressed and the other paranoid, and reconstructed their early development in what they ascertained had been distinguishable early domestic situations.[132] Each situation patterns a mechanism of defense suitable to protect the ego under the particular disciplinary pressures customarily applied to children.[133] Subsequently, stress bends and warps each form of defense in characteristic fashion, in the process giving rise to distinctive styles of personality disorder. Parents of depressed patients throw considerable responsibility on children, who are taught to anticipate what is expected of them. Punishment consists partly in advising a child that he should have known better; hence it emphasizes self-reliance. Mother represents the prime source of affection in the family, but her active role in exercising discipline somewhat widens the distance between herself and her children. A considerable distance separates father and child, though children come to know their father's pride in them even if he never directly expresses it. Theory suggests that a child who grows up in a family of this sort becomes highly sensitive to the parents' wishes, which he internalizes along with the parents' ego ideal; in effect, he becomes like the parents. He discovers that by manipulating his environment he can win his parents' approval and other desirable responses. Such learning together with the self-esteem it nurtures carries over into later life; the person continues to try to maintain harmony in his personal life and social relations through meeting demands imposed both by himself and others. Should he become emotionally upset, he turns his feelings inward; he feels badly that he did not, as he was taught to do, correctly anticipate what others expect. Introjection has become his major defense mechanism and on it he also relies when he is stressed.

In the typical paranoid patient's home the father rules by expecting his wife and children to carry out his orders without contradiction. He never suggests that they ought to anticipate his needs, and never shows pride in his children. Frequently he behaves so inconsistently and frighteningly that the mother has to act as mediator to preserve equanimity and to reassure the children. A considerable emotional distance separates the father from his children, whereas the lenient, affectionate mother, who puts few demands on them, remains very close. Growing up in this threatening setting sensitizes a child to parental hostility. Theory suggests that his paramount concern will be to defend himself from potential harm and to avoid arousing anger. He can't do so through controlling his environment; he can only try to avoid unpleasant events; for example, by denying responsibility for acts of which his father disapproves. In that way he discovers that denial and throwing blame elsewhere are effective means for protecting shaky self-esteem. Not only in the family but beyond, in instances where he fails correctly to anticipate the wishes of others, he continues to rely on projection as a mechanism to safeguard his ego's integrity, and he reacts with paranoid fears and beliefs when his equilibrium becomes seriously disturbed.

Burmese social personality tends to corroborate the model constructed to account for how Boston paranoids learn to favor projection as a major means of defense. In Burma, socialization also emphasizes fear and stresses parental dominance without recognizing the child's responsibility to anticipate adult wishes. Children are assumed to lack inherent responsibility for their actions and hence must be told what to do. A child hears few "oughts" in the family, where the weight put on seniority allows anyone who is older or greater in power and authority to act upon him, with the result that he gets little or no practice in acting on his environment. His father is not only dominant but also potentially dangerous; even his wife fears him. She and her children become allies, and often she interposes herself as an intermediary between her husband and her children. In this setting Burmese learn to utilize projection considerably for defense, to slough off responsibility and cast the fault on someone

else. Thieves, bad smells, evil spirits, rapists, and rivals are dreaded and blamed for misfortune, including illness. Each family is geared to defend itself from unrelated families presumed ready to take advantage of any show of weakness. A Burmese on the defensive, rather than acting contrite or apologetic, becomes angrier than those who vent their disapproval on him.[134] Significantly, suicide—aggression directed inward, against the self—rarely occurs in Burmese hospitals for the criminally insane. Homicide attacks, however, run high and sometimes succeed. Incidentally, the Burmese homicide rate stands as one of the world's highest.

FURTHER READING

By distinguishing between "Culture and Behavior," Clyde Kluckhohn (1954) is able to pick out manifold points at which individuality registers the imprint of society. De Vos and Hippler, under the title "Cultural Psychology" (in press), update Kluckhohn's article, and in the course of doing so review a number of forms of socially patterned, expressive behavior. Margaret Mead, relating "The Concept of Culture and the Psychosomatic Approach" (1947c), shows the extent to which patterning occurs. With addiction in mind, Donald D. Glad reviews "Attitudes and Experiences of American-Jewish and American-Irish Male Youth as Related to Differences in Adult Rates of Inebriety" (1947–1948), and M. L. Barnett reports on "Alcoholism in the Cantonese of New York City" (1955). Bronislaw Malinowski, in a chapter headed "Dreams and Deeds," in *Sex and Repression in Savage Society* (1927: 91–103) discusses the cultural sources of Trobriand Islanders, dreaming patterns, and George Devereux examines "Mohave Dreams of Omen and Power" (1956a). A. F. C. Wallace describes the extensive use

made of dreams for "The Institutionalization of Cathartic and Control Strategies
in Iroquois Religious Psychotherapy"
(1959b). South Italian tarantism, which is
either a behavioral epidemic or ethnic disorder, is reported on by Ernesto de Martino
in *La Terra del Rimorso* (1961). Nahum
Z. Medalia and Otto N. Larsen present a
study of "Diffusion and Belief in a Collective Delusion" (1958)—namely, the Seattle "windshield-pitting epidemic," which
mass media helped to spread. *Transcultural
Psychiatric Research* (formerly *Review and
Newsletter, Transcultural Research in Mental Health Problems*) should be watched in
connection with topics treated in this chapter. For a suggestion on how drumming
induces possession, see Andrew Neher's
articles, "Auditory Driving Observed with
Scalp Electrodes in Normal Subjects"
(1961) and "A Physiological Explanation
of Unusual Behavior in Ceremonies Involving Drums" (1962). Jane Belo's remarks
on trance in *Bali: Rangda and Barong*
(1949) bear closely on the subjects with
which this chapter opened. The many unsettled matters connected with trance are
admirably reviewed by Erika Bourguignon
and Louanna Pettay in "Spirit Possession,
Trance and Cross-Cultural Research"
(1964) and by Erika Bourguignon in "The
Self, the Behavioral Environment and the
Theory of Spirit Possession" (1965). Pro-
grammatically, Alexander H. Leighton and
Jane H. Hughes look on "Cultures as
Causative of Mental Disorder" (1961), and
Henri Ellenberger takes an equally comprehensive view of the "Cultural Aspects of
Mental Illness" (1960). See also Paul K.
Benedict and Irving Jacks, "Mental Illness
in Primitive Societies" (1954), and *Magic,
Faith, and Healing*, edited by Ari Kiev
(1964), which centers on non-western
forms of psychotherapy. Marvin K. Opler
discusses the cultural patterning of personality disorder in chapters 1 and 3 of *Culture, Psychiatry, and Human Values*

(1956). Neuroses connected with war
clearly illustrate the socially patterned nature of personality disturbance; see Roy R.
Grinker and John P. Spiegel, *War Neuroses
in North Africa* (1943: espec. pp. 236–
300). "Autobiographies of Former Mental
Patients," like those listed under bibliogra-
phies carrying that title prepared by Robert
Sommer and Humphrey Osmond (1960;
1961), or included in Bert Kaplan, ed., *The
Inner World of Mental Illness* (1964), provide an inductive basis for judging how culture and social structure enter personality
disorder. R. J. Plunkett and J. E. Gordon,
in their book *Epidemiology and Mental
Illness* (1960), raise a highly pertinent
question, "Is Mental Disturbance Communicable?" Parasop Ratanakorn rather
superficially examines cultural bases of
"Schizophrenia in Thailand" (1959–1960);
Carmi Schooler and William Caudill speculate about cultural factors governing "Symptomatology in Japanese and American
Schizophrenics" (1964); and E. D. Wittkower and others report on "A Crosscultural Inquiry into the Symptomatology of
Schizophrenia" (1960), but without relating findings to cultural factors. In *Social
Structure and Personality*, Yehudi A.
Cohen (1961: 477–485) demonstrates how
the total social structure affects a person's
world view and plays a special role in pre-
cipitating him into psychosis. Under the
title "Spirit Possession as Illness in a North
Indian Village," Stanley A. and Ruth S.
Freed (1964) present in detail a case of
hysteria with clearly socially patterned contours. See also N. S. Vahia, "Cultural
Differences in the Clinical Picture of
Schizophrenia and Hysteria in India and
the United States" (1963). Color and subordination are studied by A. B. Sclare as
"Cultural Determinants in the Neurotic
Negro" (1953); Georgene Seward looks at
social-class factors patterning breakdown
and treatment in chapter 5 of *Psychotherapy and Culture Conflict* (1956) and at

"Color and Conflict" in chapter 7; and August B. Hollingshead and F. C. Redlich raise the question of class and styles of neuroses in *Social Class and Mental Illness* (1958: chap. 8). "Goal-Striving, Social Status, and Mental Disorder," by Robert J. Kleiner and Seymour Parker (1963), suggests that the discrepancy between aspiration and achievement encourages lower-class personality disorder. By comparing *Racketville, Slumtown,* [and] *Haulburg* (1964), Irving Spergel shows delinquency to be patterned differently from one lower-class neighborhood to another, and John A. Clausen, in "Social Patterns, Personality, and Adolescent Drug Use" (1957), cites reasons for believing that drug-takers in urban slums possess faulty ego-defense mechanisms.

REFERENCES

1 Malinowski, 1922: 23.

2 Faris and Dunham, 1939: 158–159.

3 J. M. Smith, 1958: chap. 7.

4 Carpenter, 1953; Menninger, 1963: 290.

5 Teicher, 1954: 532–533; for another version, see Carpenter, 1953: 196–197.

6 J. J. Honigmann and Honigmann, 1945; Heath, 1964.

7 J. J. Honigmann, 1963b.

8 Dollard, 1945; G. P. Stone, 1962.

9 Jellinek, 1962.

10 J. J. Honigmann and Honigmann, 1965b.

11 Hallowell, 1946: 214–216; Horton, 1943: 299.

12 Bruun, 1962.

13 G. Devereux, 1948–1949.

14 Bunzel, 1940 and 1952: 254–260; *cf.* Mangin, 1957.

15 Carpenter, 1959–1960.

16 Snyder, 1958.

17 Freud, 1957: 31.

18 Lolli *et al.*, 1958; Devrient and Lolli, 1962.

19 Freud, 1938a; Kluckhohn and Morgan, 1951; D'Andrade, 1961: 299–302.

20 At this point I closely follow D'Andrade, 1961.

21 J. J. Honigmann, 1961a.

22 S. G. Lee, 1958.

23 D. Schneider and R. L. Sharp in D'Andrade, 1961: 311.

24 Erikson, 1963: 152.

25 J. J. Honigmann, 1949: 219.

26 Lincoln, 1935: pt. III.

27 Radin in Lincoln, 1935: 272.

28 Radin, 1936.

29 D'Andrade, 1961: 320–327.

30 *Cf.* Barry, Child, and Bacon, 1959.

31 A. F. C. Wallace, 1959a: 63–64. For Menomini Indians' experiences with peyote, see G. D. Spindler, 1952 and [1957].

32 R. Benedict, 1923; Norbeck, 1961: 41–45.

33 Howells, 1948: 268–279; A. F. C. Wallace, 1961a.

34 A. F. C. Wallace, 1952a: 341–342.

35 Durkheim, 1915: 416.

36 Jeffers, 1963: 66.

37 Reichel-Dolmatoff and Reichel-Dolmatoff, 1961: chap. 9.

38 A. J. Kerr, 1950: 125.

39 J. J. Honigmann, 1962: 73.

40 Rasmussen, 1929: 160, 208.

41 Aldous Huxley tells the story and identifies the leading characters in *The Devils of Loudun* (1953), the work I follow. See also Niau, 1887–1888.

42 Hecker, 1946: 85.

43 *Ibid.*; Zilboorg and Henry, 1941: 140–174; Gruenberg, 1957.

44 Yap, 1952: 520.

45 Cantril, 1940.

46 Zilboorg and Henry, 1941: 150.

47 Marwick, 1950.

48 Festinger *et al.*, 1956.

49 Huxley, 1953: 128.

50 Gussow, 1963.

51 *Cf.* J. J. Honigmann and Honigmann, 1965a: 244–245.

52 A large literature is summarized in Gussow, 1960; A. F. C. Wallace, 1961c.

53 Gussow, 1960.

54 A. F. C. Wallace, 1960 and 1961c: 262–270, 271–273. In the latter pages, other hysterias are explained with the hypocalcemia theory.

55 Chodoff, 1954.

56 Steensby, in Gussow, 1960: 222.

57 Teicher, 1960: 115.

58 Saindon, 1933: 11–12; *cf.* Teicher, 1960: 89–90.

59 Teicher, 1960.

60 Fogelson (1965), in one of the most recent analyses of Wiitiko disorder, delineates five types.

61 A. I. Hallowell, in Teicher, 1960: 64–65.

62 J. M. Cooper, 1933.

63 Landes, 1938a: 31–32. Her interpretation of Ojibwa culture and personality follows the model set forth for Dobu in Fortune, 1932. *Cf.* R. Benedict, 1934b: chap. 5. In Benedict's terms, both Dobuan and Ojibwa cultures exemplify low synergy and low deference. Each social system uses fear, suspicion, jealousy, hostility, and sorcery with the effect of fragmenting interpersonal relations.

64 Based mainly on S. Parker, 1962a; see also S. Parker, 1962b.

65 *Cf.* Landes, 1937.

66 Czaplicka, 1914: chap. 15.

67 S. Parker, 1960.

68 J. J. Honigmann, 1949: 181–182, 280–287, 307–308.

69 J. J. Honigmann, 1962: 35, 85; J. J. Honigmann and Honigmann, 1965a: 245.

70 H. B. M. Murphy, Wittkower, and Chance, 1964: 17.

71 I use the summary in Czaplicka, 1914: chap. 15.

72 Yap, 1952.

73 *Ibid.*, p. 523; Kumasaka, 1964.

74 Beard, 1880–1881.

75 Aberle, 1951–1952.

76 R. Maak in Czaplicka, 1914: 309–310.

77 Yap, 1952: 535.

78 Philip L. Newman kindly provided me with this information and with a color transparency from which the photo was made.

79 E. Beaglehole, 1938.

80 C. G. Seligman, 1929.

81 *Cf.* Worsley, 1957.

82 Newman, 1964.

83 E. Becker, 1964: 209.

84 Langness (1965) shows similar hysterical behavior to be differently understood and handled among the New Guinea Highland Bena Bena.

85 Based on Hsien Rin, 1963 and 1965; Yap, 1963 and 1965; Baasher, 1963: 52.

86 *Cf.* Gulick, 1961; Weakland, 1956.

87 Rubel, 1960 and 1964.

88 Rubel, 1960: 805–806.

89 Arthur J. Rubel arranged to have John Avant make the pictures and also provided information about the healer and her therapy.

90 D. C. Leighton *et al.*, 1963: 360, 364.

91 Menninger, 1963: 32–33.

92 Cannon, 1942.

93 Warner, 1937–1938.

94 T. X. Barber, 1961.

95 R. M. Berndt, 1958 and 1962: chap. 11; A. Fischer and Fischer, 1961.

96 Middleton and Winter, 1963.

97 B. B. Whiting, 1950.

98 Hallowell, 1946: 222.

99 *Cf.* Teicher, 1954.

100 Here I follow Weinstein, 1962.

101 *Cf.* Sapir, 1932.

102 C. Stainbrook (1955) reports similar information from Brazil.

103 Asai, 1964; Hasuzawa, 1964.

104 Klaf and Hamilton, 1961: 823.

105 What follows is from Marvin K. Opler and Singer, 1956.

106 *Cf.* Gans, 1962: 59, 86.

107 For a successful replication of this re-search, using 14 Irish and Italian schizophrenic women corresponding to the male sample, see Fantl and Schiro, 1958–1959.

108 Hollingshead and Redlich, 1958: chap. 7; Srole *et al.*, 1962: chap. 12; D. C. Leighton *et al.*, 1963: chap. 12.

109 Langner and Michael, 1963.

110 *Ibid.*, pp. 50–52, 76.

111 Rema Lapouse, in Pasamanick, 1959: 177–178; D. C. Leighton *et al.*, 1963: 45–55.

112 Langner and Michael, 1963: 148–149.

113 *Ibid.*, pp. 87–88.

114 Faris and Dunham, 1939.

115 I refer to theories like those of C. Cooley, 1902; G. H. Mead, 1934.

116 Faris and Dunham, 1939: 159–160.

117 *Ibid.*, p. 150

118 Langner and Michael, 1963: 152, 382.

119 From here to the section's end I follow mainly Langner and Michael, 1963: chaps. 15–16. Supporting material is included from Haggstrom, 1964.

120 Cameron, 1947: 440.

121 Gruening in Dunham, 1961: 269.

122 D. C. Leighton *et al.*, 1963: 14–15, 364.

123 The type of lower-class personality I describe is one from which individuals vary tremendously. It also ignores differences within the lower class itself. *Cf.* A. K. Cohen and Hodges, 1963.

124 *Cf.* Follett, 1924: 150.

125 Simpson and Miller, 1963.

126 Gay Talese in *The New York Times*, February 3, 1965. © 1965 by The New York Times Company. Reprinted by permission.

127 See also D. R. Miller and Swanson, 1958: chap. 8.

128 E. Becker, 1964: 129–130; *cf.* H. B. M. Murphy, Wittkower, and Chance, 1964: 9.

129 Hartung, 1963.

130 Dostoevsky, 1960: 186–187. Reprinted with permission of The Macmillan Company from *Notes From the Underground*, by Fëdor Dostoevsky, translated by Constance Garnett.

131 Hitson and Funkenstein, 1959. For a critical consideration of this work, see Morris E. Opler, 1959–1960.

132 *Cf.* Myers and Roberts, 1959; Marvin K. Opler and Singer, 1956.

133 *Cf.* D. R. Miller and Swanson, 1960.

134 See also Pye, 1962: chap. 13.

Bibliography

ABEGG, LILY. 1952. *The Mind of East Asia*. London.

ABEL, THEODORA M., JANE BELO, AND MARTHA WOLFENSTEIN. 1954. An Analysis of French Projective Tests. In: Rhoda Métraux and Margaret Mead, *Themes in French Culture*. Stanford, Calif.

ABERLE, DAVID F. 1951. The Psychosocial Analysis of a Hopi Life-History. *Comparative Psychology Monographs*, 21:1–133.

ABERLE, DAVID F. 1951–1952. "Arctic Hysteria" and Latah in Mongolia. *Transactions of the New York Academy of Sciences*, 14:291–297.

ABERLE, DAVID F. 1961. Culture and Socialization. In: Francis L. K. Hsu, ed., *Psychological Anthropology*. Homewood, Ill.

ABRAHAM, KARL. 1949a. Character-Formation on the Genital Level of Libido-Development. In: Karl Abraham, *Selected Papers of Karl Abraham, M.D.* Translated by Douglas Bryan and Alix Strachey. London.

ABRAHAM, KARL. 1949b. Contributions to the Theory of the Anal Character. In: Karl Abraham, *Selected Papers of Karl Abraham, M.D.* Translated by Douglas Bryan and Alix Strachey. London.

ABRAHAM, KARL. 1949c. The Influence of Oral Erotism on Character-Formation. In: Karl Abraham, *Selected Papers of Karl Abraham, M.D.* Translated by Douglas Bryan and Alix Strachey. London.

ABT, LAWRENCE E., AND LEOPOLD BELLAK, eds. 1950. *Projective Psychology*. New York.

ADAMS, HENRY B. 1964. "Mental Illness" or Interpersonal Behavior? *American Psychologist*, 19:191–197.

ADLER, ALFRED. 1927. *Understanding Human Nature*. Translated by Walter Béran Wolfe. New York.

AINSWORTH, MARY D. 1961–1963. The Development of Infant-Mother Interaction Among the Ganda. In: Brian M. Foss, ed., *Tavistock Seminar on Mother-Infant Interaction. 1st-2nd, London, 1959–1960. Determinants of Infant Behavior; Proceedings.* 2 vols. London.

AINSWORTH, MARY D., R. G. ANDRY, ROBERT G. HARLOW, S. LEBOVICI, MARGARET MEAD, DANE G. PRUGH, AND BARBARA WOOTTON. 1962. *Deprivation of Maternal Care*. World Health Organization: Public Health Papers, no. 14.

ALLPORT, FLOYD HENRY. 1924. *Social Psychology*. Boston.

ALLPORT, GORDON W. 1955. *Becoming*. New Haven.

ALLPORT, GORDON W. 1957. European and American Theories of Personality. In: Henry P. David and Helmut von Bracken, eds., *Perspectives in Personality Theory*. New York.

ALLPORT, GORDON W. 1960a. The Open System in Personality Theory. *Journal of Abnormal and Social Psychology*, 61:301–310.

ALLPORT, GORDON W. 1960b. *Personality and Social Encounter*. Boston.

ALLPORT, GORDON W. 1961. *Pattern and Growth in Personality*. New York.

AMBROSE, J. A. 1961–1963. The Concept of a Critical Period for the Development of Social Responsiveness in Early Human Infancy. In: Brian M. Foss, ed., *Tavistock Seminar on Mother-Infant Interaction*. 1st-2nd, London, 1959–1960. *Determinants of Infant Behavior; Proceedings*. 2 vols. London.

AMERICAN PSYCHIATRIC ASSOCIATION. 1952. *Diagnostic and Statistical Manual for Mental Disorders*. Washington, D.C.

AMES, DAVID W., AND BURTON R. FISHER. 1959. The Menominee Termination Crisis. *Human Organization*, 18:101–111.

AMMAR, HAMED. 1954. *Growing Up in an Egyptian Village*. London.

ANDERSON, BARBARA G. 1964. Stress and Psychopathology Among Aged Americans: An Inquiry into the Perception of Stress. *Southwestern Journal of Anthropology*, 20: 190–217.

ANDERSON, HAROLD H., AND GLADYS L. ANDERSON. 1961. Image of the Teacher by Adolescent Children in Seven Countries. *American Journal of Orthopsychiatry*, 31:481–492.

ANGYAL, ANDRAS. 1941. *Foundations for a Science of Personality*. New York.

ANTROPOVA, V. V., AND V. G. KUZNETSOVA. 1964. The Chukchi. In: M. G. Levin and L. P. Patopov, eds., *The Peoples of Siberia*. Translated by Scripta Technica, Inc.; edited by Stephen Dunn. Chicago.

APPLE, DORRIAN. 1951–1952. Implications of a Direct-Learning View of Personality. *Social Forces*, 30:49–52.

ARIÈS, PHILIPPE. 1962. *Centuries of Childhood*. Translated by Robert Baldick. London.

ARIETI, SILVANO. 1956. Some Basic Problems Common to Anthropology and Modern Psychiatry. *American Anthropologist*, 58:26–39.

ARSENIAN, JOHN, AND JEAN M. ARSENIAN. 1948. Tough and Easy Cultures. *Psychiatry*, 11:377–385.

ASAI, T. 1964. The Contents of Delusions of Schizophrenic Patients in Japan: Comparison Between Periods from 1941–1961. *Transcultural Psychiatric Research Review and Newsletter*, 1:27–28.

ASCH, SOLOMON E. 1952. *Social Psychology*. New York.

ATKINSON, JOHN W., ed. 1958. *Motives in Fantasy, Action, and Society*. New York.

AUSUBEL, DAVID P. 1958. *Theory and Problems of Child Development*. New York.

AUSUBEL, DAVID P. 1961a. *Maori Youth*. Wellington, New Zealand.

AUSUBEL, DAVID P. 1961b. Personality Disorder *Is* Disease. *American Psychologist*, 16:69–74.

AXELRAD, SIDNEY. 1962. Infant Care and Personality Reconsidered. A Rejoinder to Orlansky. *The Psychoanalytic Study of Society*, 2:75–132.

AXELRAD, SIDNEY. 1965. Juvenile Delinquency: A Study of the Relationship Between Psychoanalysis and Sociology. *Smith College Studies in Social Work*, 35:89–109.

BAASHER, T. A. 1963. The Influence of Culture on Psychiatric Manifestations. *Transcultural Psychiatric Research*, no. 15:51–52.

BACON, MARGARET K., IRVIN L. CHILD, HERBERT BARRY, III. 1963. A Cross-Cultural Study of Correlates of Crime. *Journal of Abnormal and Social Psychology*, 66:291–300.

BALDWIN, ALFRED L., JOAN KALHORN, AND FAY HUFFMAN BREESE. 1945. Patterns of Parent Behavior. *Psychological Monographs*, 58, no. 3.

BALIKCI, ASEN. 1963. *Vunta Kutchin Social Change.* Department of Northern Affairs and National Resources, Northern Co-ordination and Research Centre, publn. NCRC–63–3.

BALTZELL, E. DIGBY. 1961. The American Aristocrat and Other-Direction. In: Seymour M. Lipset and Leo Lowenthal, eds., *Culture and Social Character.* New York.

BANDURA, ALBERT, AND RICHARD H. WALTERS. 1963. *Social Learning and Personality Development.* New York.

BARBER, CARROLL G. 1959. Peyote and the Definition of Narcotic. *American Anthropologist,* 61:641–646.

BARBER, THEODORE XENOPHONE. 1961. Death by Suggestion. *Psychomatic Medicine,* 23:153–155.

BARBU, ZEVEDEI. 1960. *Problems of Historical Psychology.* New York.

BARCLAY, WILLIAM. 1959. *Educational Ideals in the Ancient World.* London.

BARNES, HARRY ELMER, AND HOWARD BECKER. 1952. *Social Thought from Lore to Science.* 2nd ed. 2 vols. Washington, D.C.

BARNES, J. A. 1954. Class and Committees in a Norwegian Island Parish. *Human Relations,* 7:39–58.

BARNETT, M. L. 1955. Alcoholism in the Cantonese of New York City: an Anthropological Study. In: Oskar Diethelm, ed., *Etiology of Chronic Alcoholism.* Springfield, Ill.

BARNOUW, VICTOR. 1949. Ruth Benedict: Apollonian and Dionysian. *University of Toronto Quarterly,* 18:241–253.

BARNOUW, VICTOR. 1957. The Amiable Side of "Patterns of Culture." *American Anthropologist,* 59:532–536.

BARNOUW, VICTOR. 1961. Chippewa Social Atomism. *American Authropologist,* 63:1006–1013.

BARNOUW, VICTOR. 1963. *Culture and Personality.* Homewood, Ill.

BARRY, HERBERT, III. 1957. Relationships Between Child Training and the Pictorial Arts. *Journal of Abnormal and Social Psychology,* 54:380–383.

BARRY, HERBERT, III, MARGARET K. BACON, AND IRVIN L. CHILD. 1957. A Cross-Cultural Survey of Some Sex Differences in Socialization. *Journal of Abnormal and Social Psychology,* 55:327–332.

BARRY, HERBERT, III, IRVIN L. CHILD, AND MARGARET K. BACON. 1959. Relation of Child Training to Subsistence Economy. *American Anthropologist,* 61:51–63.

BASOWITZ, HAROLD, HAROLD PERSKY, SHELDON J. KORCHIN, AND ROY R. GRINKER. 1955. *Anxiety and Stress.* New York.

BATESON, GREGORY. 1936. *Naven.* Cambridge, England.

BATESON, GREGORY. 1942–1943. Some Systematic Approaches to the Study of Culture and Personality. *Character and Personality,* 11:76–82.

BATESON, GREGORY. 1944. Cultural Determinants of Personality. In: J. McV. Hunt, ed., *Personality and the Behavior Disorders.* 2 vols. New York.

BATESON, GREGORY. 1946. The Pattern of an Armaments Race. *Bulletin of the Atomic Scientists,* 2 (no. 5):10–11, 2 (no. 6):26–28.

BATESON, GREGORY. 1955. How the Deviant Sees His Society. In: C. H. Hardin Branch, Ernst G. Beier, Richard H. Anderson, and Carroll A. Whitmer, eds., *The Epidemiology of Mental Health.* Mimeographed. Brighton, Utah.

BATESON, GREGORY, DON D. JACKSON, JAY HALEY, AND JOHN H. WEAKLAND. 1963. A Note on the Double Bind—1962. *Family Process,* 2:154–161.

BATESON, GREGORY, AND MARGARET MEAD. 1942. *Balinese Character, a Photographic Analysis.* Special Publications of the New York Academy of Sciences, no. 2.

BEAGLEHOLE, ERNEST. 1938. A Note on Cultural Compensation. *Journal of Abnormal and Social Psychology,* 33:121–123.

BEAGLEHOLE, ERNEST. 1944. Character Structure, Its Role in the Analysis of Interpersonal Relations. *Psychiatry*, 7:145–162.

BEAGLEHOLE, ERNEST. 1957. *Social Change in the South Pacific*. New York.

BEAGLEHOLE, ERNEST, AND PEARL BEAGLEHOLE. 1941. Personality Development in Pukapukan Children. In: Leslie Spier, A. Irving Hallowell, and Stanley S. Newman, eds., *Language, Culture and Personality*. Menasha, Wis.

BEAGLEHOLE, ERNEST, AND PEARL BEAGLEHOLE. 1946. *Some Modern Maoris*. Christchurch, New Zealand.

BEAGLEHOLE, ERNEST, AND JAMES E. RITCHIE. 1961. Basic Personality in a New Zealand Maori Community. In: Bert Kaplan, ed., *Studying Personality Cross-Culturally*. Evanston, Ill.

BEAGLEHOLE, PEARL. 1935. Notes on Personal Development in Two Hopi Villages. *Memoirs of the American Anthropological Association*, no. 44:25–65.

BEALER, ROBERT C., FERN K. WILLITS, AND PETER R. MAIDA. 1965. The Rebellious Youth Subculture—A Myth. *Children*, 11:43–48.

BEALS, ALAN R. 1963. *Gopalpur. A South Indian Village*. New York.

BEALS, RALPH L., AND NORMAN D. HUMPHREY. 1957. *No Frontier to Learning*. Minneapolis.

BEARD, GEORGE M. 1880–1881. Experiments with the "Jumpers" of Maine. *Popular Science Monthly*, 18:170–178.

BECKER, ERNEST. 1961–1962. Socialization, Command of Performance, and Mental Illness. *American Journal of Sociology*, 67:494–501.

BECKER, ERNEST. 1962a. *The Birth and Death of Meaning*. New York.

BECKER, ERNEST. 1962b. The Relevance to Psychiatry of Recent Research in Authropology. *American Journal of Psychotherapy*, 16:600–617.

BECKER, ERNEST. 1963. Social Science and Psychiatry: The Coming Challenge. *Antioch Review*, 23:353–366.

BECKER, ERNEST. 1964. *The Revolution in Psychiatry*. New York.

BECKER, HOWARD S. 1963. *Outsiders*. New York.

BECKNER, MORTON. 1959. *The Biological Way of Thought*. New York.

BEISER, MORTON. 1965. Poverty, Social Disintegration, and Personality. *Journal of Social Issues*, 21 (no. 1):56–78.

BELLER, E. KUNO. 1962. *Clinical Process*. New York.

BELO, JANE. 1949. *Bali: Rangda and Barong*. Monographs of the American Ethnological Society, no. 16.

BELO, JANE. 1955. Balinese Children's Drawing. In: Margaret Mead and Martha Wolfenstein, eds., *Childhood in Contemporary Cultures*. Chicago.

BENDA, CLEMENS E. 1960–1961. Existentialism in Philosophy and Science. *Journal of Existential Psychiatry*, 1:284–314.

BENEDICT, PAUL K., AND IRVING JACKS. 1954. Mental Illness in Primitive Societies. *Psychiatry*, 17:377–389.

BENEDICT, RUTH F. 1923. *The Concept of the Guardian Spirit in North America*. Memoirs of the American Anthropological Association, no. 29.

BENEDICT, RUTH F. 1934a. Anthropology and the Abnormal. *Journal of General Psychology*, 10:59–80.

BENEDICT, RUTH F. 1934b. *Patterns of Culture*. Boston.

BENEDICT, RUTH F. 1938. Continuities and Discontinuities in Cultural Conditioning. *Psychiatry*, 1:161–167.

BENEDICT, RUTH F. 1946. *The Chrysanthemum and the Sword*. Boston.

BENEDICT, RUTH F. 1949. Child Rearing in Certain European Countries. *American Journal of Orthopsychiatry*, 19:342–350.

BENEDICT, RUTH F. n.d. Unpublished Bryn Mawr 1941 lectures on synergy.

BENNETT, JOHN W. 1946. The Interpretation of Pueblo Culture: A Question of Values. *Southwestern Journal of Anthropology*, 2:361–374.

BENNETT, JOHN W. 1948. The Study of Cultures: A Survey of Technique and Methodology in Field Work. *American Sociological Review*, 13:672–689.

BENNETT, JOHN W., HERBERT PASSIN, AND ROBERT K. MCKNIGHT. 1958. *In Search of Identity*. Minneapolis.

BENNETT, JOHN W., AND MELVIN M. TUMIN. 1948. *Social Life*. New York.

BERDYAEV, NICOLAS. 1951. *Dream and Reality*. New York.

BERNDT, RONALD M. 1958. A "Devastating Disease Syndrome": Kuru Sorcery in the Eastern Central Highlands of New Guinea. *Sociologus*, 8:4–28.

BERNDT, RONALD M. 1962. *Excess and Restraint*. Chicago.

BERNOT, LUCIEN, AND RENÉ BLANCARD. 1953. *Nouville, un village français*. Paris.

BERNSTEIN, BASIL. 1958. Some Sociological Determinants of Perception. *British Journal of Sociology*, 9:159–174.

BERNSTEIN, BASIL. 1964. Elaborated and Restricted Codes: Their Social Origins and Some Consequences. In: John J. Gumperz and Dell Hymes, eds., *The Ethnography of Communication. American Anthropologist*, 66, no. 6, pt. 2.

BERTRAND, ALVIN L. 1963–1964. The Stress-Strain Element of Social Systems: A Micro Theory of Conflict and Change. *Social Forces*, 42:1–9.

BETTELHEIM, BRUNO. 1954. *Symbolic Wounds*. New York.

BETTELHEIM, BRUNO. 1960. *The Informed Heart*. New York.

Bhagavad-Gita. 1954. Translated by Swami Prabhavananda and Christopher Isherwood. Mentor Book ed. New York.

BIDNEY, DAVID. 1953. *Theoretical Anthropology*. New York.

BILLIG, OTTO, JOHN GILLIN, AND WILLIAM DAVIDSON. 1947–1948. Aspects of Personality and Culture in a Guatemalan Community: Ethnological and Rorschach Approaches. *Journal of Personality*, 16:153–187, 326–368.

BIRNBACH, MARTIN. 1961. Neo-Freudian Social Philosophy. Stanford, Calif.

BLANCHARD, WILLIAM E. 1961. Ce que l'incident diplomatique de l'U–2 nous enseigne de la mythologie nationale, du caractère national et de la politique nationale des États-Unis. *Revue de psychologie des peuples*, 16:134–146.

BLAUNER, ROBERT. 1964. *Alienation and Freedom*. Chicago.

BLOCH, MARC LEOPOLD BENJAMIN. 1953. *The Historian's Craft*. Translated by Peter Putnam. New York.

BLUM, GERALD S. 1953. *Psychoanalytic Theories of Personality*. New York.

BOAS, FRANZ. 1932. *Anthropology and Modern Life*. Rev. ed. New York.

BOGGS, STEPHEN T. 1956. An Interactional Study of Ojibwa Socialization. *American Sociological Review*, 21:191–198.

BOGGS, STEPHEN T. 1958. Culture Change and the Personality of Ojibwa Children. *American Anthropologist*, 60:47–58.

BOGORAS, W. 1909. *The Chukchee*. Memoirs of the American Museum of Natural History, vol. 11.

BONNER, HUBERT. 1961. *Psychology of Personality*. New York.

BOSSARD, JAMES H. S., AND ELEANOR STOKER BOLL. 1960. *The Sociology of Child Development*. 3rd ed. New York.

BOTT, ELIZABETH. 1957. *Family and Social Network*. London.

BOURGUIGNON, ERIKA. 1965. The Self, the Behavioral Environment, and the Theory of Spirit Possession. In: Melford E. Spiro, ed., *Context and Meaning in Cultural Anthropology*. New York.

BOURGUIGNON, ERIKA, AND LOUANNA PETTAY. 1964. Spirit Possession, Trance and Cross-

Cultural Research. In: Melford E. Spiro, ed., *Symposium on New Approaches to the Study of Religion.* Proceedings of the 1964 Annual Spring Meeting of the American Ethnological Society.

BOWLES, CHESTER. 1954. *Ambassador's Report.* New York.

BOYER, L. BRYCE. 1961. Notes on the Personality Structure of a North American Indian Shaman. *Journal of the Hillside Hospital,* 10:14–33.

BOYER, L. BRYCE. 1962. Remarks on the Personality of Shamans. With Special Reference to the Apache of the Mescalero Indian Reservation. *Psychoanalytic Study of Society,* 2:233–254.

BOYER, L. BRYCE. 1964. Further Remarks Concerning Shamans and Shamanism. *The Israel Annals of Psychiatry and Related Disciplines,* 2:235–257.

BRADBURN, NORMAN M., AND DAVID E. BERLEW. 1961. Need for Achievement and English Industrial Growth. *Economic Development and Cultural Change,* 10:8–20.

BRANDT, RICHARD B. 1954. *Hopi Ethics.* Chicago.

BRANT, CHARLES S. 1950. Peyotism Among the Kiowa-Apache and Neighboring Tribes. *Southwestern Journal of Anthropology,* 6:212–222.

BREDEMEIER, HARRY C., AND RICHARD M. STEPHENSON. 1962. *The Analysis of Social Systems.* New York.

BRICKLIN, BARRY, AND CARTER ZELEZNIK. 1963–1964. A Psychological Investigation of Selected Ethiopian Adolescents by Means of the Rorschach and Other Projective Tests. *Human Organization,* 22:291–303.

BRICKNER, RICHARD M. 1943. *Is Germany Incurable?* Philadelphia.

BRIM, ORVILLE G., JR. 1964. Socialization Through the Life Cycle. *Items,* 18:1–5.

BRIM, ORVILLE G., JR., AND STANTON WHEELER. 1966. *Socialization After Childhood.* New York.

BRODERSEN, ARVID. 1957. National Character: An Old Problem Re-examined. *Diogenes,* no. 20:84–102.

BRONFENBRENNER, URIE. 1958. Socialization and Social Class Through Time and Space. In: Eleanor E. Maccoby, Theodore M. Newcomb, and Eugene L. Hartley, eds., *Readings in Social Psychology.* 3rd ed. New York.

BRONFENBRENNER, URIE. 1961. The Changing American Child—A Speculative Analysis. *Journal of Social Issues,* 17 (no. 1): 6–18.

BROWN, NORMAN O. 1959. *Life Against Death.* Middletown, Conn.

BROWN, ROGER. 1965. *Social Psychology.* New York.

BROWNELL, W. C. 1888. *French Traits.* New York.

BRUNER, EDWARD M. 1956a. Cultural Transmission and Cultural Change. *Southwestern Journal of Anthropology,* 12:191–199.

BRUNER, EDWARD M. 1956b. Primary Group Experience and the Processes of Acculturation. *American Anthropologist,* 58:605–623.

BRUNER, EDWARD M. 1961. Mandan. In: Edward H. Spicer, ed., *Perspectives in American Indian Culture Change.* Chicago.

BRUNER, EDWARD M. 1964. The Psychological Approach in Anthropology. In: Sol Tax, ed., *Horizons of Anthropology.* Chicago.

BRUUN KETTIL. 1962. The Significance of Roles and Norms in the Small Group for Individual Behavioral Changes While Drinking. In: D. J. Pittman and C. R. Snyder, *Society, Culture, and Drinking Patterns.* New York.

BUNZEL, RUTH. 1940. The Role of Alcoholism in Two Central American Cultures. *Psychiatry,* 3:361–387.

BUNZEL, RUTH. 1952. *Chichicastenango.* Locust Valley, N.Y.

BURNOUF, DENIS. 1960. Thucydide ethnopsychologue. *Revue de psychologie des peuples,* 15:205–211.

BUXBAUM, EDITH. 1959. Psychosexual Development: the Oral, Anal, and Phallic Phases. In: Morton Levitt, ed., *Readings in Psychoanalytic Psychology*. New York.

CAMERON, NORMAN. 1947. *The Psychology of Behavior Disorders*. Boston.

CAMPBELL, ALBERT A. 1943. *St. Thomas Negroes—A Study of Personality and Culture*. Evanston, Ill.

CANNON, WALTER B. 1942. "Voodoo" Death. *American Anthropologist*, 44:169–181.

CANTRIL, HADLEY. 1940. *The Invasion From Mars: A Study in the Psychology of Panic*. Princeton. (Also Torchbook ed. New York.)

CARPENTER, EDMUND S. 1953. Witch-Fear Among the Aivilik Eskimos. *American Journal of Psychiatry*, 110:194–199.

CARPENTER, EDMUND S. 1959–1960. Alcohol in the Iroquois Dream Quest. *American Journal of Psychiatry*, 116:148–151.

CARSTAIRS, G. MORRIS. 1957. *The Twice-Born*. London.

CARSTAIRS, G. MORRIS. 1961. Cross-Cultural Psychiatric Interviewing. In: Bert Kaplan, ed., *Studying Personality Cross-Culturally*. Evanston, Ill.

CAUDILL, WILLIAM. 1949. Psychological Characteristics of Acculturated Wisconsin Ojibwa Children. *American Anthropologist*, 51:409–427.

CAUDILL, WILLIAM. 1958. Effects of Social and Cultural Systems in Reactions to Stress. Social Science Research Council, pamphlet 14.

CAUDILL, WILLIAM. 1962. Anthropology and Psychoanalysis: Some Theoretical Issues, In: Thomas Gladwin and William C. Sturtevant, eds., *Anthropology and Human Behavior*. Washington, D.C.

CENTERS, RICHARD. 1949. *The Psychology of Social Classes*. Princeton.

CHANCE, NORMAN A. 1960. Culture Change and Integration: An Eskimo Example. *American Anthropologist*, 62:1028–1044.

CHANCE, NORMAN A. 1962. Conceptual and Methodological Problems in Cross-Cultural Health Research. *American Journal of Public Health*, 52:410–417.

CHANCE, NORMAN A. 1965. Acculturation, Self-Identification, and Personality Adjustment. *American Anthropologist*, 67:372–393.

CHANCE, NORMAN A., AND DOROTHY A. FOSTER. 1962. Symptom Formation and Patterns of Psychopathology in a Rapidly Changing Alaskan Eskimo Society. *Anthropological Papers of the University of Alaska*, 11:32–42.

CHAPANIS, NATALIA P., AND ALPHONSE CHAPANIS. 1964. Cognitive Dissonance: Five Years Later. *Psychological Bulletin*, 61:1–22.

CHAPIN, STUART. 1947. *Experimental Designs in Sociological Research*. New York.

CHILD, IRVIN L. 1954. Socialization. In: Gardner Lindzey, ed., *Handbook of Social Psychology*. 2 vols. Cambridge, Mass.

CHILD, IRVIN L., ELMER H. POTTER, AND ESTELLE M. LEVINE. 1946. *Children's Textbooks and Personality Development: An Exploration in the Social Psychology of Education*. Psychological Monographs, 60, no. 3.

CHILD, IRVIN L., THOMAS STORM, AND JOSEPH VEROFF. 1958. Achievement Themes in Folk Tales Related to Socialization Practice. In: John W. Atkinson, ed., *Motives in Fantasy, Action, and Society*. Princeton.

CHINOY, ELY. 1955. *Automobile Workers and the American Dream*. Garden City, N.Y.

CHODOFF, PAUL. 1954. A Re-examination of Some Aspects of Conversion Hysteria. *Psychiatry*, 17:75–81.

CLAIRMONT, DONALD H. J. 1963. *Deviance Among Indians and Eskimos in Aklavik, N.W.T.* Department of Northern Affairs and National Resources, Northern Coordination and Research Centre, publn. NCRC–63–9.

CLAUSEN, JOHN A. 1957. Social Patterns, Personality, and Adolescent Drug Use. In:

Alexander H. Leighton, John A. Clausen, and Robert N. Wilson, eds., *Explorations in Social Psychiatry*. New York.

CLAUSEN, JOHN A., AND MELVIN L. KOHN. 1954–1955. The Ecological Approach in Social Psychiatry. *American Journal of Sociology*, 60:140–151.

CLINARD, MARSHALL B. 1964. The Theoretical Implications of Anomie and Deviant Behavior. In: Marshall B. Clinard, ed., *Anomie and Deviant Behavior*. New York.

CLOWARD, RICHARD A. 1959. Illegitimate Means, Anomie, and Deviant Behavior. *American Sociological Review*, 24:164–176.

CLOWARD, RICHARD A., AND LLOYD E. OHLIN. 1960. *Delinquency and Opportunity*. Glencoe, Ill.

COBLINER, W. GODFREY. 1963. Social Factors in Mental Disorders: A Contribution to the Etiology of Mental Illness. *Genetic Psychology Monographs*, 67:151–215.

CODERE, HELEN. 1956. The Amiable Side of Kwakiutl Life: The Potlatch and the Play Potlatch. *American Anthropologist*, 58:334–351.

COHEN, ALBERT K. 1955. *Delinquent Boys*. New York.

COHEN, ALBERT K. 1959. The Study of Social Disorganization and Deviant Behavior. In: Robert K. Merton, Leonard Broom, and Leonard S. Cottrell, Jr., eds., *Sociology Today*. New York.

COHEN, ALBERT K., AND HAROLD M. HODGES. 1963. Characteristics of the Lower-Blue-Collar-Class. *Social Problems*, 10:303–334.

COHEN, ELIE ARON. 1953. *Human Behavior in the Concentration Camp*. New York.

COHEN, YEHUDI A. 1955a. "Adolescent Conflict" in a Jamaican Community. *Samiksa: Journal of the Indian Psychoanalytic Institute*, 9:139–172.

COHEN, YEHUDI A. 1955b. Character Formation and Social Structure in a Jamaican Community. *Psychiatry*, 18:275–296.

COHEN, YEHUDI A. 1956. Structure and Function: Family Organization and Socialization in a Jamaican Community. *American Anthropologist*, 58:664–686.

COHEN, YEHUDI A. 1961. *Social Structure and Personality*. New York.

COHEN, YEHUDI A. 1964. *The Transition from Childhood to Adolescence*. Chicago.

COLEMAN, JAMES S. 1961. *The Adolescent Society*. New York.

COLLIER, REX MADISON. 1962. Independence: An Overlooked Implication of the Open System Concept. *Journal of Individual Psychology*, 18:103–113.

CONKLIN, HAROLD C. 1955. Hanunóo Color Categories. *Southwestern Journal of Anthropology*, 11:339–344.

COOK, P. H. 1941–1942. Mental Structure and the Psychological Field: Some Samoan Observations. *Character and Personality*, 10:296–308.

COOK, P. H. 1942. The Application of the Rorschach Test to a Samoan Group. *Rorschach Research Exchange*, 6:51–60.

COOLEY, CHARLES HORTON. 1902. *Human Nature and the Social Order*. New York.

COON, CARLETON S. 1951. *Caravan*. New York.

COOPER, JOHN M. 1933. The Cree Witiko Psychosis. *Primitive Man*, 6:20–24.

COOPER, MARTIN. 1965. Schopenhauer's Aphorisms. *The Listener*, 73:331–333.

COOPER, PETER. 1965. The Development of the Concept of War. *Journal of Peace Research*, [1965]: 1–17.

CORIAT, ISADOR H. 1940. The Structure of the Ego. *Psychoanalytic Quarterly*, 9:380–393.

CORMACK, MARGARET. 1953. *The Hindu Woman*. New York.

COULT, ALLAN D. 1962. An Analysis of Needham's Critique of the Homans and Schneider Theory. *Southwestern Journal of Anthropology*, 18:317–335.

CRANDALL, VAUGHN J., AND ANNE PRESTON. 1955. Patterns and Levels of Maternal Behavior. *Child Development*, 26:267–277.

CUMMING, ELAINE. 1963. Further Thoughts on the Theory of Disengagement. *International Social Science Journal,* 15:377–393.

CUMMING, ELAINE, AND JOHN CUMMING. 1957. *Closed Ranks.* Cambridge, Mass.

CUMMING, ELAINE, AND WILLIAM E. HENRY. 1961. *Growing Old.* New York.

CUMMING, JOHN, AND ELAINE CUMMING. 1962. *Ego and Milieu.* New York.

CURLE, ADAM. 1949. A Theoretical Approach to Action Research. *Human Relations,* 2:269–280.

CZAPLICKA, MARIE ANTOINETTE. 1914. *Aboriginal Siberia.* Oxford.

DAI, BINGHAM. 1953. Some Problems of Personality Development Among Negro Children. In: Clyde Kluckhohn, Henry A. Murray, and David M. Schneider, eds., *Personality in Nature, Society, and Culture.* 2nd ed. New York.

DAI, BINGHAM. 1959. Obsessive-Compulsive Disorders in Chinese Culture. In: Marvin K. Opler, ed., *Culture and Mental Health.* New York.

DALTON, MELVILLE. 1948. The Industrial "Rate-Buster": A Characterization. *Applied Anthropology,* 7:5–18.

D'ANDRADE, ROY G. 1961. Anthropological Studies of Dreams. In: Francis L. K. Hsu, ed., *Psychological Anthropology.* Homewood, Ill.

DANZIGER, KURT. 1960a. Independence Training and Social Class in Java, Indonesia. *Journal of Social Psychology,* 51:65–74.

DANZIGER, KURT. 1960b. Parental Demands and Social Class in Java, Indonesia. *Journal of Social Psychology,* 51:75–86.

DASGUPTA, AJIT. 1964. India's Cultural Values and Economic Development: A Comment. *Economic Development and Cultural Change,* 13:100–102.

DAVIS, ALLISON, AND JOHN DOLLARD. 1940. *Children of Bondage.* Washington, D.C.

DAVIS, KINGSLEY, AND WILBERT E. MOORE. 1945. Some Principles of Stratification. *American Sociological Review,* 10:242–249.

DEARDORFF, MERLE H. 1951. The Religion of Handsome Lake: Its Origin and Development. In: William N. Fenton, ed., *Symposium on Local Diversity in Iroquis Culture.* Bureau of American Ethnology, Bull. no. 149.

DE BEAUVOIR, SIMONE. 1948. *The Ethics of Ambiguity.* Translated by Bernard Frechtman. New York.

DE BEAUVOIR, SIMONE. 1953. *The Second Sex.* Translated and edited by H. M. Parshley. New York.

DEETZ, JAMES. 1965. *The Dynamics of Stylistic Changes in Arikara Ceramics.* Illinois Studies in Anthropology, no. 4.

DEHN, ERIC. 1964. Fashions in Discipline. *The Listener,* 72:85–87.

DE LAGUNA, FREDERICA. 1965. Childhood Among the Yakutat Tlingit. In: Melford E. Spiro, ed., *Context and Meaning in Cultural Anthropology,* New York.

DE LAGUNA, GRACE A. 1960. The *Lebenswelt* and the Cultural World. *Journal of Philosophy,* 57:777–791.

DE MADARIAGA, SALVADOR. 1928. *Englishmen, Frenchmen, and Spaniards.* London.

DE MARTINO, ERNESTO. 1961. *La Terra del Rimorso.* Milan.

DENNIS, WAYNE. 1940. *The Hopi Child.* New York.

DENNIS, WAYNE. 1955. Are Hopi Children Noncompetitive? *Journal of Abnormal and Social Psychology,* 50:99–100.

DE TOCQUEVILLE, ALEXIS. 1954. *Democracy in America.* 2 vols. Vintage Books ed. New York.

DEUTSCH, KARL W. 1953. *Nationalism and Social Communication.* New York.

DEUTSCH, M. A. 1949a. An Experimental Study of the Effects of Cooperation and Competition Upon Group Process. *Human Relations,* 2:199–231.

DEUTSCH, M. A. 1949b. A Theory of Cooperation and Competition. *Human Relations*, 2:129–152.

DEVEREUX, EDWARD C., JR., URIE BRONFENBRENNER, AND GEORGE J. SUCI. 1962. Patterns of Parent Behaviour in the United States of America and the Federal Republic of Germany: A Cross-National Comparison. *International Social Science Journal*, 14:488–506.

DEVEREUX, GEORGE. 1948–1949. The Function of Alcohol in Mohave Society. *Quarterly Journal of Studies on Alcohol*, 9:207–251.

DEVEREUX, GEORGE. 1951. *Reality and Dream*. New York.

DEVEREUX, GEORGE. 1952. Psychiatry and Anthropology. *Bulletin of the Menninger Clinic*, 16:167–177.

DEVEREUX, GEORGE. 1956a. Mohave Dreams of Omen and Power. *Tomorrow*, 4 (no. 3):17–24.

DEVEREUX, GEORGE. 1956b. Normal and Abnormal: The Key Problem of Psychiatric Anthropology. In: The Anthropological Society of Washington, *Some Uses of Anthropology: Theoretical and Applied*. Washington, D.C.

DEVEREUX, GEORGE. 1958. The Anthropological Roots of Psychoanalysis. In: Jules H. Masserman, ed., *Science and Psychoanalysis, Volume I. Integrative Studies*. New York.

DE VOS, GEORGE A., AND ARTHUR E. HIPPLER. [In press.] Cultural Psychology: Comparative Studies of Human Behavior. In: Gardner Lindzey and Elliot Aronson, eds., *Handbook of Social Psychology*.

DE VOS, GEORGE A., AND HORACE MINER. 1959. Oasis and Casbah—A Study in Acculturative Stress. In: Marvin K. Opler, ed., *Culture and Mental Health*. New York.

DEVRIENT, PIERRE, AND GIORGIO LOLLI. 1962. Choice of Alcoholic Beverage Among 240 Alcoholics in Switzerland. *Quarterly Journal of Studies on Alcohol*, 23:459–467.

DEWEY, JOHN. 1887. Knowledge as Idealization. *Mind*, 12:382–396.

DEWEY, JOHN. 1922. *Human Nature and Conduct*. New York.

DEWEY, JOHN. 1938. *Experience and Education*. New York.

DEXTER, LEWIS ANTHONY. 1964. *The Tyranny of Schooling*. New York.

DILTHEY, WILHELM. 1961. *Meaning in History*. Edited and introduced by H. P. Rickman. London.

DOBZHANSKY, THEODOSIUS. 1962. *Mankind Evolving*. New Haven.

DOBZHANSKY, THEODOSIUS. 1964. Cultural Direction of Human Evolution—A Summation. In: Stanley M. Garn, ed., *Culture and the Direction of Human Evolution*. Detroit.

DOLLARD, JOHN. 1935. *Criteria for the Life History*. New Haven.

DOLLARD, JOHN. 1945. Drinking Mores of the Social Classes. In: *Alcohol, Science and Society*. New Haven.

DOLLARD, JOHN. 1964. Yale's Institute of Human Relations: What Was It? *Ventures*, 3 (winter):32–40.

DOLLARD, JOHN, NEAL E. MILLER, LEONARD W. DOOB, O. H. MOWRER, AND ROBERT R. SEARS. 1939. *Frustration and Aggression*. New Haven.

DOLTO, FRANÇOISE. 1955. French and American Children as Seen by a French Child Analyst. Translated by Nathan Leites. In: Margaret Mead and Martha Wolfenstein, eds., *Childhood in Contemporary Cultures*. Chicago.

DOSTOEVSKY, FËDOR M. 1960. *Notes From the Underground*. Republished in: Avrahm Yarmolinsky ,ed., *Three Short Novels of Dostoevsky*, translated by Constance Garnett. Garden City, N.Y.

DOZIER, EDWARD P. 1955. The Concepts of "Primitive" and "Native" in Anthropology. In: W. L. Thomas, Jr., ed., *Yearbook of Anthropology 1955*. New York.

DOZIER, MARIANNE FINK. 1963. North Kalinga Personality Configurations and Child-Rearing Patterns. In: VI*e* *Congrès International des Sciences anthropologiques et ethnologiques. Paris—30 juillet–6 août 1960. Tome II. Ethnologie. Premier volume.* Paris.

DRIVER, EDWIN D. 1965. *The Sociology and Anthropology of Mental Illness.* Amherst, Mass.

DU BOIS, CORA. 1944. *The People of Alor.* Minneapolis.

DU BOIS, CORA. 1949. Attitudes Toward Food and Hunger in Alor. In: Douglas G. Haring, ed., *Personal Character and Cultural Milieu.* Rev. ed. Syracuse, N.Y.

DU BOIS, CORA. 1956. *Foreign Students and Higher Education in the United States.* Washington, D.C.

DU BOIS, CORA. 1960. *The People of Alor.* Reprinted with new prefatory material. 2 vols. Cambridge, Mass. (also 2 paperback vols. New York).

DUBOIS, J. A. 1906. *Hindu Manners, Customs and Ceremonies.* Edited and translated by Henry K. Beauchamp. 3rd ed. Oxford.

DUBOS, RENÉ J. 1959. *Mirage of Health.* New York.

DUFRENNE, MIKEL. 1953. *La Personnalité de base.* Paris.

DUNHAM, H. WARREN. 1948. Social Psychiatry. *American Sociological Review,* 13:183–197.

DUNHAM, H. WARREN. 1957. Methodology of Sociological Investigations of Mental Disorders. *International Journal of Social Psychiatry,* 3:7–17.

DUNHAM, H. WARREN. 1959. *Sociological Theory and Mental Disorder.* Detroit.

DUNHAM, H. WARREN. 1961. Social Structures and Mental Disorders: Competing Hypotheses of Explanation. In: Milbank Memorial Fund, *Causes of Mental Disorders: A Review of Epidemiological Knowledge,* 1959. New York.

DUNN, STEPHEN P. 1965. Some Preliminary Questions in International Anthropology. *Sovetskaia etnografiia,* 6:76–91.

DURKHEIM, ÉMILE. 1915. *The Elementary Forms of the Religious Life.* Translated by Joseph Ward Swain. London.

DURKHEIM, ÉMILE. 1938. *The Rules of Sociological Method.* 8th ed. Translated by Sarah A. Solovay and John H. Mueller. Chicago.

DURKHEIM, ÉMILE. 1951. *Suicide.* Translated by John A. Spaulding and George Simpson. Glencoe, Ill.

DURKHEIM, ÉMILE. 1956. *Education and Sociology.* Translated by Sherwood D. Fox. Glencoe, Ill.

EARLE, MARGARET JANE. 1958. *Rakau Children From Six to Thirteen Years.* Victoria University of Wellington Publications in Psychology, no. 11.

EASTON, DAVID, AND ROBERT D. HESS. 1961. Youth and the Political System. In: Seymour M. Lipset and Leo Lowenthal, eds., *Culture and Social Character.* New York.

EATON, JOSEPH W. 1964. Adolescence in a Communal Society. *Mental Hygiene,* 48:66–73.

EATON, JOSEPH W., AND ROBERT J. WEIL. 1953. The Mental Health of the Hutterites. *Scientific American,* 189 (no. 6):31–37.

EATON, JOSEPH W., AND ROBERT J. WEIL. 1955. *Culture and Mental Disorders.* Glencoe, Ill.

EDGERTON, ROBERT B. 1965. "Cultural" vs. "Ecological" Factors in the Expression of Values, Attitudes, and Personality Characteristics. *American Anthropologist,* 67:442–447.

EGGAN, DOROTHY. 1943. The General Problem of Hopi Adjustment. *American Anthropologist,* 45:357–373.

EGGAN, DOROTHY. 1949. The Significance of Dreams for Anthropological Research. *American Anthropologist*, 51:177–198.

EGGAN, DOROTHY. 1952. The Manifest Content of Dreams: A Challenge to Social Science. *American Anthropologist*, 54:469–485.

EGGAN, DOROTHY. 1956. Instruction and Affect in Hopi Cultural Continuity. *Southwestern Journal of Anthropology*, 12:347–370.

EGGAN, DOROTHY. 1961. Dream Analysis. In: Bert Kaplan, ed., *Studying Personality Cross-Culturally*. Evanston, Ill.

EIDUSON, BERNICE T. 1962. *Scientists: Their Psychological World*. New York.

ELDER, GLEN H., JR. 1962. Structural Variations in the Child Rearing Relationship. *Sociometry*, 25:241–262.

ELIADE, MIRCEA. 1964. *Shamanism*. Translated by Willard R. Trask. New York.

ELIOT, THOMAS D. 1955. Interactions of Psychiatric and Social Theory Prior to 1940. In: Arnold M. Rose, ed., *Mental Health and Mental Disorder*. New York.

ELKINS, STANLEY. 1961. Slavery and Personality. In: Bert Kaplan, ed., *Studying Personality Cross-Culturally*. Evanston, Ill.

ELLENBERGER, HENRI. 1960. Cultural Aspects of Mental Illness. *American Journal of Psychotherapy*, 14:158–173.

ELWIN, VERRIER. 1947. *The Muria and Their Ghotul*. London.

EMMET, DOROTHY. 1958. *Function, Purpose and Powers*. London.

ENGELMANN, HUGO O. 1963. The Non-Literate, the Psychotic, and the Child: A Reconsideration. *Anthropological Quarterly*, 36:27–33.

EPSTEIN, A. L. 1961. The Network and Urban Social Organization. *Human Problems in British Central Africa*, 29:29–62.

ERICSON, MARTHA C. 1946–1947. Child-Rearing and Social Status. *American Journal of Sociology*, 52:190–192.

ERIKSON, ERIK H. 1963. *Childhood and Society*. 2nd ed. New York.

FANTL, BERTA, AND JOSEPH SCHIRO. 1958–1959. Cultural Variables in the Behaviour Patterns and Symptom Formation of 15 Irish and 15 Italian Female Schizophrenics. *International Journal of Social Psychiatry*, 4:245–253.

FARIS, ROBERT E. L. 1944. Ecological Factors in Human Behavior. In: J. McV. Hunt, *Personality and the Behavior Disorders*. 2 vols. New York.

FARIS, ROBERT E. L., AND H. WARREN DUNHAM. 1939. *Mental Disorders in Urban Areas*. Chicago.

FENTON, WILLIAM N. 1957. Long-Term Trends of Change Among the Iroquois. In: *Cultural Stability and Cultural Change*. Proceedings of the 1957 Annual Spring Meeting of the American Ethnological Society. Seattle.

FESTINGER, LEON. 1957. *A Theory of Cognitive Dissonance*. Evanston, Ill.

FESTINGER, LEON, AND DANIEL KATZ, eds., 1953. *Research Methods in the Behavioral Sciences*. New York.

FESTINGER, LEON, HENRY W. RIECKEN, AND STANLEY SCHACHTER. 1956. *When Prophecy Fails*. Minneapolis.

FIELD, M. J. 1960. *Search for Security*. Evanston, Ill.

FIELD, PETER B. 1962. A New Cross-Cultural Study of Drunkenness. In: David J. Pittman and Charles R. Snyder, eds., *Society, Culture, and Drinking Patterns*. New York.

FISCHER, ANN, AND JOHN L. FISCHER. 1961. Culture and Epidemiology: A Theoretical Investigation of Kuru. *Journal of Health and Human Behavior*, 2:16–25.

FISCHER, JOHN L. 1958. Folktales, Social Structure, and Environment in Two Polynesian Outliers. *Journal of the Polynesian Society*, 67:11–36.

FISCHER, JOHN L. 1963. The Sociopsychological Analysis of Folktales. *Current Anthropology*, 4:235–295.

FISCHER, JOHN L., AND ANN FISCHER. 1963. The New Englanders of Orchard Town, U.S.A. In: Beatrice B. Whiting, ed., *Six Cultures*. New York.

FITZGERALD, F. SCOTT. 1963. *The Letters of F. Scott Fitzgerald*. Edited by Andrew Turnbull. New York.

FLETCHER, ALICE C., AND FRANCIS LA FLESCHE. 1911. *The Omaha Tribe*. Annual Reports of the Bureau of American Ethnology, no. 27.

FLOUD, JEAN, AND A. H. HALSEY. 1959. Education and Social Structure: Theories and Methods. *Harvard Educational Review*, 29:288–296.

FOGELSON, RAYMOND D. 1965. Psychological Theories of Windigo "Psychosis" and a Preliminary Application of a Models Approach. In: Melford E. Spiro, ed., *Context and Meaning in Cultural Anthropology*. New York.

FOGELSON, RAYMOND D., AND MELFORD E. SPIRO. 1965. Introduction. In: Melford E. Spiro, ed., *Context and Meaning in Cultural Anthropology*. New York.

FOLLETT, MARY P. 1924. *Creative Experience*. New York.

FORDHAM, FRIEDA. 1953. *An Introduction to Jung's Psychology*. Harmondsworth, England.

FORTES, MEYER. 1938. *Social and Psychological Aspects of Education in Taleland*. International Institute of African Languages and Cultures, memorandum 17.

FORTUNE, REO F. 1932. *Sorcerers of Dobu*. New York.

FOSTER, GEORGE M. 1960–1961. Interpersonal Relations in Peasant Society. *Human Organization*, 19:174–178.

FOSTER, GEORGE M. 1965. Peasant Society and the Image of the Limited Good. *American Anthropologist*, 67:293–315.

FREED, STANLEY A., AND RUTH S. FREED. 1964. Spirit Possession as Illness in a North Indian Village. *Ethnology*, 3:152–171.

FREEDMAN, LAWRENCE ZELIC, AND ANNE ROE. 1958. Evolution and Human Behavior. In: Anne Roe and G. G. Simpson, eds., *Behavior and Evolution*. New Haven.

FREEDMAN, DEREK. 1965. Anthropology, Psychiatry and the Doctrine of Cultural Relativism. *Man*, 65:65–67.

FRENCH, DAVID. 1963. The Relationship of Anthropology to Studies in Perception and Cognition. In: Sigmund Koch, ed., *Psychology: A Study of a Science*. Vol. 6. *Investigations of Man as Socius: Their Place in Psychology and the Social Sciences*. New York.

FRENCH, THOMAS M. 1944. Clinical Approach to the Dynamics of Behavior. In: J. McV. Hunt, ed., *Personality and the Behavior Disorders*. 2 vols. New York.

FRENCH, THOMAS M. 1954. *The Integration of Behavior*. Vol. II. *The Integrative Process in Dreams*. Chicago.

FRENKEL-BRUNSWIK, ELSE. 1952. Interaction of Psychological and Sociological Factors in Political Behavior. *American Political Science Review*, 46:44–65.

FREUD, SIGMUND. 1918. *Totem and Taboo*. Translated by A. A. Brill. New York.

FREUD, SIGMUND. 1924a. *Beyond the Pleasure Principle*. Translated by C. J. M. Hubback. New York.

FREUD, SIGMUND. 1924b. Character and Anal Erotism. In: Sigmund Freud, *Collected Papers*, Vol. II. Authorized translation under the supervision of Joan Riviere. London.

FREUD, SIGMUND. 1933. *New Introductory Lectures on Psycho-Analysis*. Translated by W. J. H. Sprott. New York.

FREUD, SIGMUND. 1935. *A General Introduction to Psycho-Analysis*. Rev. ed., translated by Joan Riviere. New York.

FREUD, SIGMUND. 1938a. *The Interpretation of Dreams*. Translated by A. A. Brill. In: A. A. Brill, ed., *The Basic Writings of Sigmund Freud*. New York.

FREUD, SIGMUND. 1938b. *Three Contributions to the Theory of Sex*. Translated by A. A. Brill. In: A. A. Brill, ed., *The Basic Writings of Sigmund Freud*. New York.

FREUD, SIGMUND. 1949a. *Group Psychology and the Analysis of the Ego*. Translated by James Strachey. London.

FREUD, SIGMUND. 1949b. *An Outline of Psychoanalysis*. Translated by James Stratchey. New York.

FREUD, SIGMUND. 1950. Some Character-Types Meet with in Psycho-Analytic Work. In: Sigmund Freud, *Collected Papers*, Vol. IV. Translated by Joan Riviere. London.

FREUD, SIGMUND. 1952. Moral Responsibility for the Content of Dreams. In: Sigmund Freud, *Collected Papers*, Vol. V. Edited by James Strachey. London.

FREUD, SIGMUND. 1953. *The Future of an Illusion*. Translated by W. D. Robson-Scott. New York.

FREUD, SIGMUND. 1957. *Civilization and Its Discontents*. Translated by Joan Riviere. London.

FREUD, SIGMUND. 1959. Obsessive Actions and Religious Practices. In: Sigmund Freud, *Standard Edition of the Complete Psychological Works of Sigmund Freud*, Vol. IX. Translated by James Strachey *et al.* London.

FREUD, SIGMUND. 1961a. *The Ego and the Id*. Translated and edited by James Strachey. New York.

FREUD, SIGMUND. 1961b. A Short Account of Psycho-Analysis. In: Sigmund Freud, *The Standard Edition of the Complete Works of Sigmund Freud*, Vol. XIX. Translated by James Strachey *et al.* London.

FRIED, MARC, AND ERICH LINDEMANN. 1961. Sociocultural Factors in Mental Health and Illness. *American Journal of Orthopsychiatry*, 31:87–101.

FRIEDENBERG, EDGAR Z. 1963. An Ideology of School Withdrawal. *Commentary*, 35:492–500.

FRIEDL, ERNESTINE. 1956. Persistence in Chippewa Culture and Personality. *American Anthropologist*, 58:814–825.

FRIEDL, ERNESTINE. 1964. Lagging Emulation in Post-Peasant Society. *American Anthropologist*, 66:569–586.

FROMM, ERICH. 1941. *Escape from Freedom*. New York.

FROMM, ERICH. 1949. Psychoanalytic Characterology and Its Application to the Understanding of Culture. In: S. Stansfeld Sargent and Marian W. Smith, eds., *Culture and Personality*. New York.

FROMM, ERICH. 1951. *The Forgotten Language*. New York.

FROMM, ERICH. 1955. *The Sane Society*. New York.

FROMM, ERICH. 1957. Symbolic Language of Dreams. In: Ruth Nanda Anshen, ed., *Language: An Enquiry Into Its Meaning and Function*. New York.

FROMM, ERICH. 1961. *Marx's Concept of Man*. New York.

FROMM, ERICH. 1962. *Beyond the Chains of Illusion*. New York.

GANS, HERBERT J. 1962. *The Urban Villagers*. New York.

GARRETT, HENRY E. 1960. Klineberg's Chapter on Race and Psychology: A Review. *The Mankind Quarterly*, 1:15–23.

GEERTZ, HILDRED. 1959. The Vocabulary of Emotion. *Psychiatry*, 22:225–237.

GEERTZ, HILDRED. 1961. *The Javanese Family*. New York.

GERTH, HANS H., AND C. WRIGHT MILLS. 1953. *Character and Social Structure*. New York.

GESELL, ARNOLD, AND FRANCES L. ILG. 1943. *Infant and Child in the Culture of Today.* New York.

GESELL, ARNOLD, AND FRANCES L. ILG. 1946. *The Child from Five to Ten.* New York.

GILLIN, JOHN. 1951. *The Culture of Security in San Carlos.* Middle American Research Institute, The Tulane University of Louisiana, Publn. no. 16.

GILLIN, JOHN. 1952. Ethos and Cultural Aspects of Personality. In: Sol Tax, ed., *Heritage of Conquest.* Glencoe, Ill.

GILLIN, JOHN. 1955–1956. National and Regional Cultural Values in the United States. *Social Forces,* 34:107–113.

GLAD, DONALD D. 1947–1948. Attitudes and Experiences of American-Jewish and American-Irish Male Youth as Related to Differences in Adult Rates of Inebriety. *Quarterly Journal of Studies on Alcohol,* 8:406–472.

GLADWIN, THOMAS. 1957. Personality Structure in the Plains. *Anthropological Quarterly,* 30:111–124.

GLADWIN, THOMAS, AND SEYMOUR B. SARASON. 1953. *Truk: Man in Paradise.* Viking Fund Publications in Anthropology, no. 20.

GLASER, DANIEL. 1962. The Differential-Association Theory of Crime. In: Arnold M. Rose, ed., *Human Behavior and Social Processes.* Boston.

GLUCKMAN, MAX. 1955. *Custom and Conflict in Africa.* Oxford.

GOFFMAN, ERVING. 1963. *Stigma.* Englewood Cliffs, N.J.

GOLDENWEISER, ALEXANDER A. 1933. *History, Psychology, and Culture.* New York.

GOLDFRANK, ESTHER. 1945. Socialization, Personality and the Structure of Pueblo Society. *American Anthropologist,* 47:516–539.

GOLDSTEIN, KURT. 1940. *Human Nature in the Light of Psychopathology.* Cambridge, Mass.

GOODY, JACK. 1962. *Death, Property, and the Ancestors.* London.

GORER, GEOFFREY. 1943. Themes in Japanese Culture. *Transactions of the New York Academy of Sciences,* Series II, 5:106–124.

GORER, GEOFFREY, AND JOHN RICKMAN. 1962. *The People of Great Russia.* The Norton Library ed. New York.

GOULDNER, ALVIN W., AND RICHARD A. PETERSON. 1962. *Notes on Technology and the Moral Order.* Indianapolis.

GRANICK, DAVID. 1960. *The Red Executive.* Garden City, N.Y.

GRANICK, DAVID. 1962. *The European Executive.* Garden City, N.Y.

GRANT, VERNON W. 1963. *This Is Mental Illness.* Boston.

GREENSTEIN, FRED I. 1965. *Children and Politics.* New Haven.

GRINDER, ROBERT E., AND ROBERT E. MCMICHAEL. 1963. Cultural Influence on Conscience Development. *Journal of Abnormal and Social Psychology,* 66:503–507.

GRINKER, ROY R., AND JOHN P. SPIEGEL. 1943. *War Neuroses in North Africa.* Prepared and distributed for the Air Surgeon, Army Air Forces, by the Josiah Macy, Jr. Foundation. New York.

GRINNELL, GEORGE BIRD. 1923. *The Cheyenne Indians.* 2 vols. New Haven.

GROSSACK, MARTIN M. 1956. Psychological Effects of Segregation on Buses. *Journal of Negro Education,* 25:71–74.

GRUBER, FREDERICK G., ed. 1961. *Anthropology and Education.* Philadelphia.

GRUENBERG, ERNEST M. 1957. Socially Shared Psychopathology. In: Alexander H. Leighton, John A. Clausen, and Robert N. Wilson, eds., *Explorations in Social Psychiatry.* New York.

GULICK, ROBERT HANS VAN. 1961. *Sexual Life in Ancient China.* Leiden.

GURIN, GERALD, JOSEPH VEROFF, AND SHEILA FELD. 1960. *Americans View Their Mental Health.* New York.

GUSSOW, ZACHARY. 1960. Pibloktoq (Hysteria) Among the Polar Eskimo. In: W. Muensterberger and S. Axelrad, eds., *The Psychoanalytic Study of Society*, vol. I. New York.

GUSSOW, ZACHARY. 1963. A Preliminary Report of Kayak-Angst Among the Eskimo of West Greenland: A Study in Sensory Deprivation. *International Journal of Social Psychiatry*, 9:18–26.

GUTHEIL, EMIL A. 1939. *The Language of the Dream*. New York.

GUTHRIE, GEORGE M. 1961. *The Filipino Child and Philippine Society*. Manila.

HACKETT, PAUL. 1952. *The Cardboard Giants*. New York.

HADDON, ALFRED C. 1901. *Head-Hunters: Black, White, and Brown*. London.

HAGEN, EVERETT E. 1962. *On the Theory of Social Change*. Homewood, Ill.

HAGEN, EVERETT E., AND LOUIS C. SCHAW. 1960. *The Sioux on the Reservations: The American Colonial Problem*. Cambridge, Mass.

HAGGSTROM, WARREN C. 1964. The Power of the Poor. In: Frank Riessman, Jerome Cohen, and Arthur Pearl, eds., *Mental Health of the Poor*. New York.

HAIRE, MASON, EDWIN E. GHISELLI, AND LYMAN W. PORTER. 1963. Cultural Patterns in the Role of the Manager. *Industrial Relations*, 2:95–117.

HALL, G. STANLEY. 1904. *Adolescence: Its Psychology*. 2 vols. New York.

HALLOWELL, A. IRVING. 1938. Fear and Anxiety as Cultural and Individual Variables in a Primitive Society. *Journal of Social Psychology*, 9:25–47.

HALLOWELL, A. IRVING. 1939. The Child, the Savage and Human Experience. In: *Progress in Scientific Research in the Field of the Exceptional Child*. Proceedings of the Sixth Institute on the Exceptional Child, Child Research Clinic of the Woods School, Langhorne, Pa.

HALLOWELL, A. IRVING. 1945a. The Rorschach Technique in the Study of Personality and Culture. *American Anthropologist*, 47:195–210.

HALLOWELL, A. IRVING. 1945b. Sociopsychological Aspects of Acculturation. In: Ralph Linton, ed., *The Science of Man in the World Crisis*. New York.

HALLOWELL, A. IRVING. 1946. Some Psychological Characteristics of the Northeastern Indians. In: Frederick Johnson, ed., *Man in Northeastern North America*. Papers of the Robert S. Peabody Foundation of Archaeology, vol. 3.

HALLOWELL, A. IRVING. 1950. Personality Structure and the Evolution of Man. *American Anthropologist*, 52:159–173.

HALLOWELL, A. IRVING. 1951a. Cultural Factors in the Structuralization of Perception. In: J. H. Rohrer and M. Sherif, eds., *Social Psychology at the Crossroads*. New York.

HALLOWELL, A. IRVING. 1951b. The Use of Projective Techniques in the Study of Sociopsychological Aspects of Acculturation. *Journal of Projective Techniques*, 15:27–44.

HALLOWELL, A. IRVING. 1952. Ojibwa Personality and Acculturation. In: Sol Tax, ed., *Acculturation in the Americas. Proceedings and Selected Papers of the XXIXth International Congress of Americanists*. Chicago.

HALLOWELL, A. IRVING. 1953. Culture, Personality, and Society. In: A. L. Kroeber, ed., *Anthropology Today*. Chicago.

HALLOWELL, A. IRVING. 1954. Psychology and Anthropology. In: John Gillin, ed., *For a Science of Social Man*. New York.

HALLOWELL, A. IRVING. 1954–1956. The Rorschach Technique in Personality and Culture Studies. In: Bruno Klopfer *et al. Developments in the Rorschach Technique*. 2 vols., vol. 2. Yonkers-on-Hudson, N.Y.

HALLOWELL, A. IRVING. 1955. *Culture and Experience*. Philadelphia.

HALLOWELL, A. IRVING. 1960. Self, Society, and Culture in Phylogenetic Perspective. In: Sol Tax, ed., *The Evolution of Man*. Chicago.

HALLOWELL, A. IRVING. 1963. Personality, Culture, and Society in Behavioral Evolution. In: Sigmund Koch, ed., *Psychology: A Study of a Science*. Vol. 6. *Investigations of Man as Socius: Their Place in Psychology and the Social Sciences*. New York.

HAMBLY, W. D. 1926. *Origins of Education Among Primitive Peoples*. London.

HANFMANN, EUGENIA. 1957. Social Perception in Russian Displaced Persons and an American Comparison Group. *Psychiatry*, 20:131–149.

HARING, DOUGLAS G. 1946. Aspects of Personal Character in Japan. *Far Eastern Quarterly*, 6:12–22.

HARING, DOUGLAS G. 1953. Japanese National Character: Cultural Anthropology, Psychoanalysis, and History. *Yale Review*, 42:373–392.

HARING, DOUGLAS G., ed. 1956. *Personal Character and Cultural Milieu*. 3rd rev. ed. Syracuse, N.Y.

HARLOW, MARGARET K., AND HARRY F. HARLOW. 1965a. An Analysis of Love. *The Listener*, 73:255–257.

HARLOW, MARGARET K., AND HARRY F. HARLOW. 1965b. Romulus and Rhesus. *The Listener*, 73:215–217.

HARRIS, MARVIN. 1964. *The Nature of Cultural Things*. New York.

HART, C. W. M. 1955. Contrasts Between Prepubertal and Postpubertal Education. In: George D. Spindler, ed., *Education and Anthropology*. Stanford, Calif.

HARTUNG, FRANK E. 1963. Manhattan Madness: The Social Movement of Mental Illness. *Sociological Quarterly*, 4:261–272.

HASUZAWA, T. 1964. Chronological Observations of Delusions in Schizophrenics. *Transcultural Psychiatric Research Review and Newsletter*, 1:27–28.

HAVIGHURST, ROBERT J. 1952. *Developmental Tasks and Education*. New York.

HAVIGHURST, ROBERT J., PAUL HOOVER BOWMAN, GORDON P. LIDDLE, CHARLES V. MATTHEWS, AND JAMES V. PIERCE. 1962. *Growing Up in River City*. New York.

HAVIGHURST, ROBERT J., MARIA EUGENIA DUBOIS, M. CSIKSZENTMIHALYI, AND R. DOLL. 1965. *A Cross-National Study of Buenos Aires and Chicago Adolescents*. Biblioteca "Vita Humana," Fasc. 3. Basel.

HAVIGHURST, ROBERT J., AND BERNICE L. NEUGARTEN. 1955. *American Indian and White Children*. Chicago.

HAWKES, CHRISTOPHER. 1954. Archeological Theory and Method: Some Suggestions From the Old World. *American Anthropologist*, 56:155–168.

HAZELL, MALCOLM. 1965. "He who can, does." *The Listener*, 73:703–704.

HEATH, DWIGHT B. 1964. Prohibition and Post-Repeal Drinking Patterns Among the Navaho. *Quarterly Journal of Studies on Alcohol*, 25:119–135.

HECKER, J. F. C. 1846. *The Epidemics of the Middle Ages*. Translated by B. G. Babington. London.

HELM, JUNE. 1961. *The Lynx Point People: The Dynamics of a Northern Athapaskan Band*. National Museum of Canada, Bull. 176.

HELM, JUNE, GEORGE A. DE VOS, AND TERESA CARTERETTE. 1960. *Variations in Personality and Ego Identification Within a Slave Indian Kin-Community*. National Museum of Canada, Bull. 190.

HENRY, ANDREW F., AND JAMES F. SHORT, JR. 1954. *Suicide and Homicide*. New York.

HENRY, JULES. 1948. Anthropology and Orthopsychiatry. In: Lawson G. Lowrey, ed., *Orthopsychiatry 1923–1948: Retrospect and Prospect*. Menasha, Wis.

HENRY, JULES. 1949. The Social Function of Child Sexuality in Pilagá Indian Culture. In: Paul H. Hoch and Joseph Zubin, eds., *Psychosexual Development in Health and Disease*. New York.

HENRY, JULES. 1960. A Cross-Cultural Outline of Education. *Current Anthropology*, 1:267–305.

HENRY, JULES. 1963. *Culture Against Man*. New York.

HENRY, JULES, *et al.* 1955. Projective Testing in Ethnography. *American Anthropologist* 57:245–270.

HENRY, WILLIAM E. 1951. The Thematic Apperception Technique in the Study of Group and Cultural Problems. In: Harold H. Anderson and Gladys L. Anderson, *An Introduction to Projective Techniques*. New York.

HENRY, WILLIAM E. 1960. Projective Techniques. In: Paul H. Mussen, ed., *Handbook in Research Methods in Child Development*. New York.

HENRY, WILLIAM E. 1961. Projective Tests in Cross-Cultural Research. In: Bert Kaplan, ed., *Studying Personality Cross-Culturally*. Evanston, Ill.

HENTOFF, NAT. 1964. Profiles: The Crackin', Shakin', Breakin' Sounds. *The New Yorker*, 40 (no. 36):64–90.

HERSKOVITS, MELVILLE J. 1948. *Man and His Works*. New York.

HERTZ, FRIEDRICH. 1925. Die allgemeinen Theorien vom Nationalcharakter. *Archiv fuer Sozialwissenschaft und Sozialpolitik*, 54:1–35, 657–715.

HERZOG, JOHN D. 1962. Deliberate Instruction and Household Structure: A Cross-Cultural Study. *Harvard Educational Review*, 32:301–342.

HESS, ROBERT D. 1963. The Socialization of Attitudes Toward Political Authority: Some Cross-National Comparisons. *International Social Science Journal*, 15:542–570.

HILGARD, ERNEST R. 1956. *Theories of Learning*. 2nd ed. New York.

HILGER, M. INEZ. 1951. *Chippewa Child Life and Its Cultural Background*. Bureau of American Ethnology, Bull. 146.

HILGER, M. INEZ. 1952. *Arapaho Child Life and Its Cultural Background*. Bureau of American Ethnology, Bull. 148.

HILGER, M. INEZ. 1957. *Araucanian Child Life and Its Cultural Background*. Smithsonian Miscellaneous Collections, vol. 133.

HILGER, M. INEZ. 1960. *Field Guide to the Ethnological Study of Child Life*. Human Relations Area Files, Behavior Science Field Guides. New Haven.

HINKLE, GISELA J. 1957. Sociology and Psychoanalysis. In: Howard Becker and Alvin Boskoff, eds., *Modern Sociological Theory*. New York.

HINKLE, LAWRENCE E. 1961. Ecological Observations of the Relation of Physical Illness, Mental Illness, and the Social Environment. *Psychosomatic Medicine*, 23:289–296.

HITCHCOCK, JOHN T. 1959. Leadership in a North Indian Village: Two Case Studies. In: Richard L. Park and Irene Tinker, eds., *Leadership and Political Institutions in India*. Princeton.

HITSON, HAZEL M., AND DANIEL H. FUNKENSTEIN. 1959–1960. Family Patterns and Paranoidal Personality Structure in Boston and Burma. *International Journal of Social Psychiatry*, 5:182–190.

HOCH, PAUL H. 1961. Social Psychiatry. In: H. W. Gruhle and W. Mayer-Gross, eds., *Psychiatrie der Gegenwart*, Vol. 3. *Soziale und Angewandte Psychiatrie*. Berlin.

HODGES, HAROLD M., JR. 1964. *Social Stratification*. Cambridge, Mass.

HOGBIN, H. IAN. 1931. Education at Ongtong Java, Solomon Islands. *American Anthropologist*, 33:601–614.

HOGBIN, H. IAN. 1946. A New Guinea Childhood: From Weaning Till the Eighth Year in Wogeo. *Oceania*, 16:275–296.

HOLLINGSHEAD, AUGUST B. 1949. *Elmtown's Youth*. New York.

HOLLINGSHEAD, AUGUST B., AND FREDERICK C. REDLICH. 1958. *Social Class and Mental Illness*. New York.

HOLMBERG, ALLAN R. 1950. *Nomads of the Long Bow*. Smithsonian Institution, Institute of Social Anthropology, Publn. no. 10.

HOLMES, LOWELL D. 1958. *Ta'u: Stability and Change in a Samoan Village*. Reprint of the Polynesian Society, no. 7.

HOLSTI, OLE R. 1962. The Belief System and National Images: A Case Study. *Journal of Conflict Resolution*, 6:244–252.

HOLZINGER, CHARLES H. 1961. Some Observations on the Persistence of Aboriginal Cherokee Personality Traits. In: William N. Fenton and John Gulick, eds., *Symposium on Cherokee and Iroquois Culture*. Bureau of American Ethnology, Bull. 180.

HOLZNER, BURKART. n.d. *Voelkerpsychologie*. Wuerzburg.

HOMANS, GEORGE C. 1950. *The Human Group*. New York.

HOMANS, GEORGE C. 1964. Contemporary Theory in Sociology. In: Robert E. L. Faris, ed., *Handbook of Modern Sociology*. Chicago.

HOMANS, GEORGE C., AND DAVID M. SCHNEIDER. 1955. *Marriage, Authority, and Final Causes*. Glencoe, Ill.

HONIGMANN, IRMA, AND JOHN HONIGMANN. 1953. Child Rearing Patterns Among the Great Whale River Eskimo. *Anthropological Papers of the University of Alaska*, 2 (no. 1):31–50.

HONIGMANN, JOHN J. 1942. An Interpretation of the Social-Psychological Functions of the Ritual Clown. *Character and Personality*, 10:220–226.

HONIGMANN, JOHN J. 1946. *Ethnography and Acculturation of the Fort Nelson Slave*. Yale University Publications in Anthropology, no. 33.

HONIGMANN, JOHN J. 1949. *Culture and Ethos of Kaska Society*. Yale University Publications in Anthropology, no. 40.

HONIGMANN, JOHN J. 1954a. *Culture and Personality*. New York.

HONIGMANN, JOHN J. 1954b. *The Kaska Indians: An Ethnographic Reconstruction*. Yale University Publications in Anthropology, no. 51.

HONIGMANN, JOHN J. 1959. *The World of Man*. New York.

HONIGMANN, JOHN J. 1960. Education and Career Specialization in a West Pakistan Village of Renown. *Anthropos*, 55:825–840.

HONIGMANN, JOHN J. 1961a. The Interpretation of Dreams in Anthropological Field Work: A Case Study. In: Bert Kaplan, ed., *Studying Personality Cross-Culturally*. Evanston, Ill.

HONIGMANN, JOHN J. 1961b. North America. In: Francis L. K. Hsu, ed., *Psychological Anthropology*. Homewood, Ill.

HONIGMANN, JOHN J. 1962. *Social Networks in Great Whale River*. National Museum of Canada, Bull. 178.

HONIGMANN, JOHN J. 1963a. Bauer and Arbeiter in a Rural Austrian Community. *Southwestern Journal of Anthropology*, 19:40–53.

HONIGMANN, JOHN J. 1963b. Dynamics of Drinking in an Austrian Village. *Ethnology*, 2:157–169.

HONIGMANN, JOHN J. 1963c. *Understanding Culture*. New York.

HONIGMANN, JOHN J. 1965. The Middle-Class View of Poverty Culture, Sociocultural Disintegration, and Mental Health. Paper presented to the University of Kentucky Centennial Conference on Cross-cultural Psychiatry and Psychoethnology.

HONIGMANN, JOHN J., AND IRMA HONIGMANN. 1945. Drinking in an Indian-White Community. *Quarterly Journal of Studies on Alcohol*, 5:575–619.

HONIGMANN, JOHN J., AND IRMA HONIGMANN. 1959. Notes on Great Whale River Ethos. *Anthropologica*, 1:106–121.

HONIGMANN, JOHN J., AND IRMA HONIGMANN. 1965a. *Eskimo Townsmen*. Ottawa.

HONIGMANN, JOHN J., AND IRMA HONIGMANN. 1965b. How Baffin Island Eskimo Have Learned To Use Alcohol. *Social Forces*, 44:73–83.

HONIGMANN, JOHN J., AND RICHARD J. PRESTON. 1964. Recent Developments in Culture and Personality. *The Annals of the American Academy of Political and Social Science*, 354:153–162.

HORNEY, KAREN. 1939. *New Ways in Psychoanalysis*. New York.

HORNEY, KAREN. 1945. *Our Inner Conflicts*. New York.

HORROCKS, JOHN E. 1964. *Assessment of Behavior*. Columbus, Ohio.

HORTON, DONALD. 1943. The Functions of Alcohol in Primitive Societies: A Cross-Cultural Study. *Quarterly Journal of Studies on Alcohol*, 4:199–320.

HOSTETLER, JOHN A. 1964. Persistence and Change Patterns in Amish Society. *Ethnology*, 3:185–198.

HOWELLS, WILLIAM. 1948. *The Heathens*. Garden City, N.Y.

HSIEN RIN. 1963. Koro: A Consideration on Chinese Concepts of Illness and Case Illustrations. *Transcultural Psychiatric Research*, October, no. 15:23–30.

HSIEN RIN. 1965. A Study of the Aetiology of Koro in Respect to the Chinese Concept of Illness. *International Journal of Social Psychiatry*. 11:7–13.

HSU, FRANCIS L. K., ed. 1961a. *Psychological Anthropology*. Homewood, Ill.

HSU, FRANCIS L. K. 1961b. Psychological Anthropology in the Behavioral Sciences. In: Francis L. K. Hsu, ed., *Psychological Anthropology*. Homewood, Ill.

HSU, FRANCIS L. K. 1964. Rethinking the Concept "Primitive." *Current Anthropology*, 5:169–178.

HSU, FRANCIS L. K., BLANCHE G. WATROUS, AND EDITH M. LORD. 1961. Culture Pattern and Adolescent Behavior. *International Journal of Social Psychiatry*, 7:33–53.

HUGHES, CHARLES C., MARC-ADELARD TREMBLAY, ROBERT N. RAPOPORT, AND ALEXANDER H. LEIGHTON. 1960. *People of Cove and Woodlot*. New York.

HUGHES, H. STUART. 1958. *Consciousness and Society*. New York.

HULETT, J. E., JR., AND ROSS STAGNER. 1952. *Problems in Social Psychology*. Urbana, Ill.

HULL, C. L. 1937. Mind, Mechanism, and Adaptive Behavior. *Psychological Review*, 44:1–32.

HUME, DAVID. 1898. Of National Characters. In: David Hume, *Essays Moral, Political, and Literary*. 2 vols., new impression. T. G. Green and T. H. Grose, eds. London.

HUNT, J. MCV. 1960. Experience and the Development of Motivation: Some Reinterpretations. *Child Development*, 31:489–504.

HUNT, J. MCV. 1965. Traditional Personality Theory in the Light of Recent Evidence. *American Scientists*, 53:80–96.

HUNT, RAYMOND G. 1959. Socio-Cultural Factors in Mental Disorder. *Behavioral Science*, 4:96–106.

HURWICZ, ELIAS. 1920. *Die Seelen der Voelker*. Gotha.

HUXLEY, ALDOUS. 1953. *The Devils of Loudun*. New York.

HYMAN, HERBERT H. 1959. *Political Socialization*. Glencoe, Ill.

HYMES, DELL. 1961. Linguistic Aspects of Cross-Cultural Personality Study. In: Bert Kaplan, ed., *Studying Personality Cross-Culturally*. Evanston, Ill.

INKELES, ALEX. 1953. Some Sociological Observations on Culture and Personality Studies. In: Clyde Kluckhohn, Henry A. Murray, and David M. Schneider, eds., *Personality in Nature, Society, and Culture*. 2nd ed. New York.

INKELES, ALEX. 1955. Social Change and Social Character: The Role of Parental Mediation. *Journal of Social Issues*, 11 (no. 2):12–23.

INKELES, ALEX. 1963. Sociology and Psychology. In: Sigmund Koch, ed., *Psychology: A Study of a Science*, Vol. 6. *Investigations of Man as Socius: Their Place in Psychology and the Social Sciences*. New York.

INKELES, ALEX, EUGENIA HANFMANN, AND HELEN BEIER. 1958. Modal Personality and Adjustment to the Soviet Socio-Political System. *Human Relations*, 11:3–22.

INKELES, ALEX, AND DANIEL J. LEVINSON. 1954. National Character: The Study of Modal Personality and Sociocultural Systems. In: Gardner Lindzey, ed., *Handbook of Social Psychology*. 2 vols. Cambridge, Mass.

JAHODA, GUSTAV. 1958a. Child Animism: I. A Critical Survey of Cross-cultural Research. *Journal of Social Psychology*, 47:197–212.

JAHODA, GUSTAV. 1958b. Immanent Justice Among West African Children. *Journal of Social Psychology*, 47:241–248.

JAHODA, MARIE. 1958. *Current Concepts of Positive Mental Health*. New York.

JAHODA, MARIE, MORTON DEUTSCH, AND STUART W. COOK. 1951. *Research Methods in Social Relations*. 2 vols. New York.

JAMES, BERNARD J. 1954. Some Critical Observations Concerning Analyses of Chippewa "Atomism" and Chippewa Personality. *American Anthropologist*, 56:283–286.

JAMES, BERNARD J. 1961. Social-Psychological Dimensions of Ojibwa Acculturation. *American Anthropologist*, 63:721–746.

JANIS, IRVING L. 1951. *Air War and Emotional Stress*. New York.

JANIS, IRVING L. 1958. The Psychoanalytic Interview as an Observational Method. In: Gardner Lindzey, ed., *Assessment of Human Motives*. New York.

JARECKI, HENRY G. 1961. Maternal Attitudes Toward Child Rearing. *Archives of General Psychiatry*, 4:340–356.

JASPERS, KARL. 1933. *Man in the Modern World*. Translated by Eden and Cedar Paul. New York.

JASPERS, KARL. 1963. *General Psychopathology*. Translated by J. Hoenig and M. W. Hamilton. Chicago.

JAY, EDWARD J. 1964. The Concepts of "Field" and "Network" in Anthropological Research. *Man*, 64:137–139.

JEFFERS, ROBINSON. 1963. *The Beginning and the End and Other Poems*. New York.

JELLINEK, E. M. 1962. Cultural Differences in the Meaning of Alcoholism. In: D. J. Pittman and C. R. Snyder, eds., *Society, Culture, and Drinking Patterns*. New York.

JOFFE, NATALIE F. 1949. The Dynamics of Benefice Among East European Jews. *Social Forces*, 27:238–247.

JOINT COMMISSION ON MENTAL ILLNESS AND HEALTH. 1961. *Action for Mental Health*. New York.

JONES, ERNEST. 1925. Mother-Right and the Sexual Ignorance of Savages. *International Journal of Psycho-Analysis*, 6:109–130.

JONES, ERNEST. 1948. *Papers on Psycho-Analysis*. 5th ed. London.

JOSEPHSON, ERIC, AND MARY JOSEPHSON, eds. 1962. *Man Alone: Alienation in Modern Society*. New York.

JOSSELYN, IRENE M. 1955. *The Happy Child*. New York.

JOSSELYN, IRENE M. 1964. Some Reflections on Adolescent Rebellion. *Children*, 11:122–123.

JUNG, CARL G. 1953. The Psychology of the Unconscious. In: C. G. Jung, *Two Essays on Analytical Psychology*. Translated by R. F. C. Hull. New York.

JUNG, CARL G. 1959. *The Basic Writings of C. G. Jung*. Edited by Violet Staub de Laszlo. New York.

KAGAN, JEROME, AND HOWARD A. MOSS. 1962. *Birth to Maturity*. New York.

KANN, ROBERT A. 1960. *A Study in Austrian Intellectual History*. New York.

KAPLAN, ABRAHAM. 1964. *The Conduct of Inquiry*. San Francisco.

KAPLAN, BERT. 1954. *A Study of Rorschach Responses in Four Cultures*. Papers of the

Peabody Museum of American Archaeology and Ethnology, Harvard University, vol. 42, no. 2.

KAPLAN, BERT. 1957. Personality and Social Structure. In: J. B. Gittler, ed., *Review of Sociology, Analysis of a Decade*. New York.

KAPLAN, BERT. 1961a. Cross-Cultural Use of Projective Techniques. In: Francis L. K. Hsu, ed., *Psychological Anthropology*. Homewood, Ill.

KAPLAN, BERT. 1961b. Editor's Epilogue: A Final Word. In: Bert Kaplan, ed., *Studying Personality Cross-Culturally*. Evanston, Ill.

KAPLAN, BERT. 1961c. Personality Study and Culture. In: Bert Kaplan, ed., *Studying Personality Cross-Culturally*. Evanston, Ill.

KAPLAN, BERT, ed., 1964. *The Inner World of Mental Illness*. New York.

KAPLAN, BERT, AND THOMAS F. A. PLAUT. 1956. *Personality in a Communal Society: An Analysis of the Mental Health of the Hutterites*. University of Kansas Publications, Social Science Studies, 1956.

KARDINER, ABRAM. 1939. *The Individual and His Society*. New York.

KARDINER, ABRAM. 1945a. The Concept of Basic Personality Structure as an Operational Tool in the Social Sciences. In: Ralph Linton, ed., *The Science of Man in the World Crisis*. New York.

KARDINER, ABRAM. 1945b. *The Psychological Frontiers of Society*. New York.

KARDINER, ABRAM. 1949. Psychodynamics and the Social Sciences. In: S. Stansfeld Sargent and Marian W. Smith, eds., *Culture and Personality*. New York.

KARDINER, ABRAM, AARON KARUSH, AND LIONEL OVESEY. 1959a. A Methodological Study of Freudian Theory: I. Basic Concepts. *Journal of Nervous and Mental Disease*, 129:11–19.

KARDINER, ABRAM, AARON KARUSH, AND LIONEL OVESEY. 1959b. A Methodological Study of Freudian Theory: II. The Libido Theory. *Journal of Nervous and Mental Disease*, 129:133–143.

KARDINER, ABRAM, AARON KARUSH, AND LIONEL OVESEY. 1959c. A Methodological Study of Freudian Theory: III. Narcissism, Bisexuality and the Dual Instinct Theory. *Journal of Nervous and Mental Disease*, 129:207–221.

KARDINER, ABRAM, AND MARGARET MEAD. 1959. Psychosocial Synthesis. *Science*, 130:1728, 1732.

KARDINER, ABRAM, AND LIONEL OVESEY. 1951. *The Mark of Oppression*. New York.

KARDINER, ABRAM, AND EDWARD PREBLE. 1961. *They Studied Man*. New York.

KARON, BERTRAM P. 1958. *The Negro Personality*. New York.

KATZ, DANIEL. 1961. Current and Needed Psychological Research in International Relations. *Journal of Social Issues*, 17 (no. 3): 69–78.

KAYE, BARRINGTON. 1962. *Bringing Up Children in Ghana*. London.

KEESING, FELIX M. 1958. *Cultural Anthropology*. New York.

KELLY, FRANCIS J., AND DONALD J. VELDMAN. 1964. Delinquency and School Dropout Behavior as a Function of Impulsivity and Nondominant Values. *Journal of Abnormal and Social Psychology*, 69:190–194.

KENNEDY, DONALD A. 1961. Key Issues in the Cross-Cultural Study of Mental Disorders. In: Bert Kaplan, ed., *Studying Personality Cross-Culturally*. Evanston, Ill.

KERLINGER, FRED N. 1952–1953. Behavior and Personality in Japan: A Critique of Three Studies of Japanese Personality. *Social Forces*, 31:250–258.

KERLINGER, FRED N. 1964. *Foundations of Behavioral Research*. New York.

KERR, A. J. 1950. Subsistence and Social Organization in a Fur Trade Community; Anthropological Report on the Ruperts House Indians. Typescript. Microfilm in University of North Carolina Library.

KERR, MADELINE. 1952. *Personality and Conflict in Jamaica*. Liverpool.

KESSEN, WILLIAM. 1963. Research in the Psychological Development of Infants: An Overview. *Merrill-Palmer Quarterly*, 9:83–94.

KESSEN, WILLIAM, AND CLEMENTINA KUHLMAN. 1962. *Thought in the Young Child*. Monographs of the Society for Research in Child Development, no. 83.

KIDD, DUDLEY. 1906. *Savage Childhood*. London.

KIEV, ARI, ed. 1946. *Magic, Faith, and Healing*. New York.

KING-HALL, MAGDALEN. 1958. *The Story of the Nursery*. London.

KINSEY, ALFRED C., WARDELL B. POMEROY, AND CLYDE E. MARTIN. 1948. *Sexual Behavior in the Human Male*. Philadelphia.

KINSEY, ALFRED C., WARDELL B. POMEROY, CLYDE E. MARTIN, AND PAUL H. GEBHARD. 1953. *Sexual Behavior in the Human Female*. Philadelphia.

KLAF, FRANKLIN S., AND JOHN G. HAMILTON. 1961. Schizophrenia—A Hundred Years Ago and Today. *Journal of Mental Science*, 107:819–827.

KLAPP, ORRIN E. 1962. *Heroes, Villians and Fools; the Changing American Character*. Englewood Cliffs, N.J.

KLAPP, ORRIN E. 1964. Mexican Social Types. *American Journal of Sociology*, 69:404–414.

KLEINER, ROBERT J., AND SEYMOUR PARKER. 1963. Goal-Striving, Social Status, and Mental Disorder: A Research Review. *American Sociological Review*, 28:189–203.

KLOPFER, BRUNO, AND L. BRYCE BOYER. 1961. Notes on the Personality Structure of a North American Indian Shaman: Rorschach Interpretation. *Journal of Projective Techniques* 25:170–178.

KLUBACK, WILLIAM. 1956. *Wilhelm Dilthey's Philosophy of History*. New York.

KLUCKHOHN, CLYDE. 1944. The Influence of Psychiatry on Anthropology in America During the Past One Hundred Years. In: J. K. Hall, G. Zilboorg, and H. A. Bunker, eds., *One Hundred Years of American Psychiatry, 1844–1944*. New York.

KLUCKHOHN, CLYDE. 1945. The Personal Document in Anthropological Science. In: Louis Gottschalk, Clyde Kluckhohn, and Robert Angell, *The Use of Personal Documents in History, Anthropology and Sociology*. Social Science Research Council, Bull. 53.

KLUCKHOHN, CLYDE. 1947. Some Aspects of Navaho Infancy and Early Childhood. In: G. Róheim, ed., *Psychoanalysis and the Social Sciences*, vol. 1. New York.

KLUCKHOHN, CLYDE. 1949. *Mirror for Man*. New York.

KLUCKHOHN, CLYDE. 1951a. The Study of Culture. In: Daniel Lerner and Harold D. Lasswell, eds., *The Policy Sciences*. Stanford, Calif.

KLUCKHOHN, CLYDE. 1951b. Values and Value-Orientations in the Theory of Action. In: Talcott Parsons and Edward A. Shils, eds., *Toward a General Theory of Action*. Cambridge, Mass.

KLUCKHOHN, CLYDE. 1954. Culture and Behavior. In: Gardner Lindzey, ed., *Handbook of Social Psychology*. 2 vols. Cambridge, Mass.

KLUCKHOHN, CLYDE. 1955. Recent Studies of the "National Character" of Great Russians. In: *Human Development Bulletin: Papers Presented at the Sixth Annual Symposium Held Saturday February Sixth, International House, Chicago, Ill.* Chicago.

KLUCKHOHN, CLYDE. 1961. Notes on Some Anthropological Aspects of Communication. *American Anthropologist*, 63:895–910.

KLUCKHOHN, CLYDE, AND WILLIAM MORGAN. 1951. Some Notes on Navaho Dreams. In: George B. Wilbur and Warner Muensterberger, eds., *Psychoanalysis and Culture*. New York.

KLUCKHOHN, CLYDE, AND HENRY A. MURRAY. 1953. Personality Formation: The Determinants. In: Clyde Kluckhohn, Henry A. Murray, and David M. Schneider, eds., *Personality in Nature, Society, and Culture.* 2nd ed. New York.

KLUCKHOHN, CLYDE, HENRY A. MURRAY, AND DAVID M. SCHNEIDER. 1953. *Personality in Nature, Society, and Culture.* 2nd ed. New York.

KLUCKHOHN, CLYDE, AND JANINE C. ROSENZWEIG. 1949. Two Navaho Children Over a Five-Year Period. *American Journal of Orthopsychiatry, 19:266–278.*

KLUCKHOHN, FLORENCE R., AND FRED L. STRODTBECK. 1961. *Variations in Value Orientations.* Evanston, Ill.

KNAPEN, MARIE-THÉRÈSE. 1962. *L'Enfant mukongo; orientations de base du système éducatif et développement de la personnalité.* Louvain.

KNELLER, GEORGE F. 1965. *Educational Anthropology: An Introduction.* New York.

KOESTLER, ARTHUR. 1952. *Arrow in the Blue.* New York.

KOMAROVSKY, MIRRA. 1946. Cultural Contradictions and Sex Roles. *American Journal of Sociology, 52:184–189.*

KORNHAUSER, ARTHUR. 1962. Toward an Assessment of the Mental Health of Factory Workers: A Detroit Study. *Human Organization, 21:43–46.*

KOSTIUK, G. S. 1961. Problems of the Child's Personality Formation. In: *Soviet Psychology.* New York.

KOTCHEN, THEODORE A. 1960. Existential Mental Health: An Empirical Approach. *Journal of Individual Psychology, 16:174–181.*

KROEBER, ALFRED L. 1946. History and Evolution. *Southwestern Journal of Anthropology, 2:1–15.*

KROEBER, ALFRED L. 1948. *Anthropology.* New ed., rev. New York.

KROEBER, ALFRED L. 1952. *The Nature of Culture.* Chicago.

KROEBER, ALFRED L. 1953. Concluding Review. In: Sol Tax, Loren C. Eiseley, Irving Rouse, and Carl F. Voegelin, eds., *An Appraisal of Anthropology Today.* Chicago.

KROEBER, ALFRED L. 1954. The Place of Anthropology in Universities. *American Anthropologist, 56:764–767.*

KROEBER, ALFRED L. 1957a. *Ethnographic Interpretations, 1–6.* University of California Publications in American Archaeology and Ethnology, vol. 47, no. 2.

KROEBER, ALFRED L. 1957b. *Style and Civilizations.* Ithaca, N.Y.

KROEBER, ALFRED L. 1963. *An Anthropologist Looks at History.* Berkeley, Calif.

KROEBER, ALFRED L., AND TALCOTT PARSONS. 1958. The Concepts of Culture and of Social System. *American Sociological Review, 23:582–583.*

KUHN, THOMAS S. 1962. *The Structure of Scientific Revolutions.* Chicago.

KUMASAKA, Y. 1964. A Culturally-Determined Mental Reaction Among the Ainu. *Psychiatric Quarterly, 38:733–739.*

KUNKEL, JOHN A. 1965. Values and Behavior in Economic Development. *Economic Development and Cultural Change, 13:257–277.*

KUUSINEN, OTTO, ed. 1961. *Fundamentals of Marxism-Leninism.* Translation from the Russian edited by Clements Dutt. London.

LA BARRE, WESTON. 1945. Some Observations on Character Structure in the Orient: The Japanese. *Psychiatry, 8:319–342.*

LA BARRE, WESTON. 1954. *The Human Animal.* Chicago.

LA BARRE, WESTON. 1958. The Influence of Freud on Anthropology. *American Imago, 15:275–328.*

LAING, R. D. 1960. *The Divided Self.* London.

LAMBERT, RICHARD D., AND MARVIN BRESSLER. 1956. *Indian Students on an American Campus.* Minneapolis.

LAMBERT, WILLIAM W., LEIGH M. TRIANDIS, AND MARGERY WOLF. 1959. Some Correlates of Beliefs in the Malevolence and Benevolence of Supernatural Beings: A Cross-Societal Study. *Journal of Abnormal and Social Psychology*, 58:162–169.

LAMBO, T. ADEOYE. 1964. Patterns of Psychiatric Care in Developing African Countries. In: Ari Kiev, ed., *Magic, Faith, and Healing*. New York.

LAMING, A., GEORGES GRANAI, HENRI PIÉRON, A. LEROI-GOURHAN, E. BUYSSENS, PAUL CHALUS, AND PAUL WERNERT. 1953. *A la Recherche de la mentalité préhistorique*. Paris.

LAMPHERE, LOUISE. 1964. Loose-Structuring as Exhibited in a Case Study of Navajo Religious Learning. *El Palacio*, 71 (no. 1):37–44.

LANDES, RUTH. 1937. The Ojibwa of Canada. In: M. Mead, ed., *Cooperation and Competition Among Primitive Peoples*. New York.

LANDES, RUTH. 1938a. The Abnormal Among the Ojibwa Indians. *Journal of Abnormal and Social Psychology*, 33:14–33.

LANDES, RUTH. 1938b. *The Ojibwa Woman*. Columbia University Contributions to Anthropology, vol. 31.

LANDES, RUTH. 1965. *Culture in American Education*. New York.

LANDY, DAVID. 1965. *Tropical Childhood*. Torchbook ed. New York.

LANE, ROBERT E. 1953. Political Character and Political Analysis. *Psychiatry*, 16:387–398.

LANGNER, THOMAS S. 1965. Psychophysiological Symptoms and the Status of Women in Two Mexican Communities. In: Jane M. Murphy and Alexander H. Leighton, eds., *Approaches to Cross-cultural Psychiatry*. Ithaca, N.Y.

LANGNER, THOMAS S., AND STANLEY T. MICHAEL. 1963. *Life Stress and Mental Health*. New York.

LANGNESS, L. L. 1964. Biography: A Common Denominator. Paper presented to the American Association for the Advancement of Science, Montreal, December, 1964.

LANGNESS, L. L. 1965. Hysterical Psychosis in the New Guinea Highlands: A Bena Bena Example. *Psychiatry*, 28:258–277.

LANGNESS, L. L., AND LESLIE Y. RABKIN. 1964. Culture Contact Stress: Bena Bena Attitudes and Feelings as Expressed in TAT Responses and "Unguarded Moments." Paper presented to the First International Congress of Social Psychiatry, London, August, 1964.

LANHAM, BETTY B. 1956. Aspects of Child Care in Japan: Preliminary Report. In: Douglas G. Haring, ed., *Personal Character and Cultural Milieu*. 3rd rev. ed. Syracuse, N.Y.

LANTIS, MARGARET. 1953–1954. Nunivak Eskimo Personality as Revealed in the Mythology. *Anthropological Papers of the University of Alaska*, 2:109–174.

LANTIS, MARGARET. 1959. Alaskan Eskimo Cultural Values. *Polar Notes*, no. 1:35–48.

LANTIS, MARGARET. 1960. *Eskimo Childhood and Interpersonal Relationships*. Seattle.

LAPIERE, RICHARD. 1959. *The Freudian Ethic*. New York.

LASSWELL, HAROLD D. 1934. *Psychopathology and Politics*. Chicago.

LASSWELL, HAROLD D. 1951. Propaganda and Mass Insecurity. In: A. H. Stanton and S. E. Perry, eds., *Personality and Political Crisis*. Glencoe, Ill.

LECLERCQ, CHRESTIEN. 1910. *New Relation of Gaspesia*. Translated and edited, with a reprint of the original, by William F. Ganong. Toronto.

LEE, DOROTHY. 1959. *Freedom and Culture*. Englewood Cliffs, N.J.

LEE, S. G. 1958. Social Influences in Zulu Dreaming. *Journal of Social Psychology*, 47:265–283.

LEIGHTON, ALEXANDER H. 1945. *The Governing of Men*. Princeton.

LEIGHTON, ALEXANDER H. 1959. *My Name is Legion*. New York.

LEIGHTON, ALEXANDER H. 1960. *An Introduction to Social Psychiatry.* Springfield, Ill.

LEIGHTON, ALEXANDER H., AND JANE H. HUGHES. 1961. Cultures as Causative of Mental Disorder. In: Milbank Memorial Fund, *Causes of Mental Disorders: A Review of Epidemiological Knowledge,* 1959. New York.

LEIGHTON, ALEXANDER H., ADEOYE T. LAMBO, CHARLES C. HUGHES, DOROTHEA C. LEIGHTON, JANE M. MURPHY, AND DAVID B. MACKLIN. 1963. *Psychiatric Disorder Among the Yoruba.* Ithaca, N.Y.

LEIGHTON, ALEXANDER H., AND DOROTHEA C. LEIGHTON. 1949. *Gregorio, the Hand-Trembler: A Psychobiological Study of a Navaho Indian.* Papers of the Peabody Museum of American Archaeology and Ethnology, Harvard University, vol. 40, no. 1.

LEIGHTON, ALEXANDER H., AND JANE M. MURPHY. 1965. Cross-cultural Psychiatry. In: Jane M. Murphy and Alexander H. Leighton, eds., *Approaches to Cross-cultural Psychiatry.* Ithaca, N.Y.

LEIGHTON, DOROTHEA C., JOHN S. HARDING, DAVID B. MACKLIN, ALLISTER M. MACMILLAN, AND ALEXANDER LEIGHTON. 1963. *The Character of Danger.* New York.

LEIGHTON, DOROTHEA C., AND CLYDE KLUCKHOHN. 1947. *Children of the People.* Cambridge, Mass.

LEIS, PHILIP E. 1964. Ijaw Enculturation: A Reexamination of the Early Learning Hypothesis. *Southwestern Journal of Anthropology,* 20:32–42.

LEITES, NATHAN. 1948. Psycho-Cultural Hypotheses About Political Acts. *World Politics,* 1:102–119.

LEMERT, EDWIN M. 1962. Paranoia and the Dynamics of Exclusion. *Sociometry,* 25:2–20.

LENSKI, GERHARD. 1963. *The Religious Factor.* Rev., Anchor Books ed. Garden City, N.Y.

LERNER, DANIEL. 1961. An American Researcher in Paris: Interviewing Frenchmen. In: Bert Kaplan, ed., *Studying Personality Cross-Culturally.* Evanston, Ill.

LERNER, EUGENE, AND LOIS B. MURPHY, eds. 1941. *Methods for the Study of Personality in Young Children.* Washington, D.C.

LESLIE, GERALD R., AND KATHRYN P. JOHNSEN. 1963. Changed Perceptions of the Maternal Role. *American Sociological Review,* 28:919–928.

LESSA, WILLIAM A., AND MARVIN SPIEGELMAN. 1964. *Ulithian Personality as Seen Through Ethnological Materials and Thematic Test Analysis.* University of California Publications in Culture and Society, vol. 2, no. 5.

LEVI, PRIMO. 1959. *If This Is a Man.* Translated by Stuart Woolf. New York.

LÉVI-STRAUSS, CLAUDE. 1950. Introduction a l'oeuvre de Marcel Mauss. In: M. Mauss, *Sociologie et anthropologie.* Paris.

LÉVI-STRAUSS, CLAUDE. 1963. *Totemism.* Translated by Rodney Needham. Boston.

LEVINE, JACOB. 1961. Regression in Primitive Clowning. *Psychoanalytic Quarterly,* 30:72–83.

LEVINE, ROBERT A. 1960. The Role of the Family in Authority Systems: A Cross-Cultural Application of Stimulus-Generalization Theory. *Behavioral Science,* 5:291–296.

LEVINE, ROBERT A. 1963a. Behaviorism in Psychological Anthropology. In: Joseph M. Wepman and Ralph W. Heine, eds., *Concepts of Personality.* Chicago.

LEVINE, ROBERT A. 1963b. Political Socialization and Culture Change. In: Clifford Geertz, ed., *Old Societies and New States.* New York.

LEVINE, ROBERT A., AND BARBARA B. LEVINE. 1963. Nyansongo: A Gusii Community in Kenya. In: Beatrice B. Whiting, ed., *Six Cultures,* New York.

LEVINSON, DANIEL J. 1964. Toward a New Social Psychology: The Convergence of Sociology and Psychology. *Merrill-Palmer Quarterly,* 10:77–88.

LÉVY-BRUHL, LUCIEN. 1926. *How Natives Think*. Translated by Lilian A. Clare. London.

LEWIN, KURT. 1947. Frontiers in Group Dynamics. *Human Relations*, 1:5–41.

LEWIN, KURT. 1948. Some Social-Psychological Differences Between the United States and Germany. In: Kurt Lewin, *Resolving Social Conflict*. New York.

LEWIS, AUBREY. 1953. Health as a Social Concept. *British Journal of Sociology*, 4:109–124.

LEWIS, LIONEL S. 1963–1964. A Note on the Problem of Classes. *Public Opinion Quarterly*, 27:599–603.

LEWIS, OSCAR. 1951. *Life in a Mexican Village: Tepoztlán Restudied*. Urbana, Ill.

LEWIS, OSCAR. 1959. *Five Families*. New York.

LEWIS, OSCAR. 1960–1961. Some of My Best Friends Are Peasants. *Human Organization*, 19:179–180.

LEWIS, OSCAR. 1961. *The Children of Sánchez*. New York.

LEWIS, OSCAR. 1964. Seventh Day Adventism in a Mexican Village: A Study in Motivation and Culture Change. In: Robert A. Manners, ed., *Process and Pattern in Culture*. Chicago.

LEWY, ERNEST. 1961. Responsibility, Free Will, and Ego Psychology. *International Journal of Psycho-Analysis*, 42:260–270.

LI AN-CHE. 1937. Zuni: Some Observations and Queries. *American Anthropologist*, 39:62–76.

LIDDELL HART, BASIL H. 1964. Generalship in the Second World War. *The Listener* 72:333–338.

LINCOLN, JACKSON S. 1935. *The Dream in Primitive Cultures*. Baltimore.

LINDESMITH, ALFRED R., AND ANSELM L. STRAUSS. 1950. A Critique of Culture-Personality Writings. *American Sociological Review*, 15:587–600.

LINDZEY, GARDNER, ed. 1954. *Handbook of Social Psychology*. 2 vols. Cambridge, Mass.

LINDZEY, GARDNER, ed. 1958. *Assessment of Human Motives*. New York.

LINDZEY, GARDNER. 1961. *Projective Techniques in Cross-Cultural Research*. New York.

LINTON, RALPH. 1936. *The Study of Man*. New York.

LINTON, RALPH. 1938. Culture, Society, and the Individual. *Journal of Abnormal and Social Psychology*, 33:425–436.

LINTON, RALPH. 1945. *The Cultural Background of Personality*. New York.

LINTON, RALPH. 1951. The Concept of National Character. In: Alfred H. Stanton and Stewart E. Perry, eds., *Personality and Political Crisis*. Glencoe, Ill.

LINTON, RALPH. 1956. *Culture and Mental Disorders*. Springfield, Ill.

LIPPITT, RONALD. 1940. An Experimental Study of Authoritarian and Democratic Group Atmospheres. *University of Iowa Studies in Child Welfare*, 16:45–195.

LIPPITT, RONALD, AND RALPH K. WHITE. 1943. The "Social Climate" of Children's Groups. In: R. G. Barker, J. S. Kounin, and H. F. Wright, eds., *Child Behavior and Development*. New York.

LIPSET, SEYMOUR MARTIN. 1961. A Changing American Character? In: Seymour M. Lipset and Leo Lowenthal, eds., *Culture and Social Character*. New York.

LIPSET, SEYMOUR MARTIN. 1963. The Value Patterns of Democracy: A Case Study in Comparative Analysis. *American Sociological Review*, 28:515–531.

LIPSET, SEYMOUR MARTIN, AND REINHARD BENDIX. 1959. *Social Mobility in Industrial Society*. Berkeley, Calif.

LITTLE, K. L. 1950. Methodology in the Study of Adult Personality and "National Character." *American Anthropologist*, 52:279–282.

LLEWELLYN, KARL N., AND E. ADAMSON HOEBEL. 1941. *The Cheyenne Way*. Norman, Okla.

LOCKE, JOHN. 1880. *Some Thoughts Concerning Education*. Edited by R. H. Quick. Cambridge.

LOCKE, JOHN. 1959. *An Essay Concerning Human Understanding*. Collated and annotated by Alexander Campbell Fraser. 2 vols. New York.

LOKASCZYK, KURT. 1958. Vom Volksgeist zur Modalpersoenlichkeit. In: *Seelenleben und Menschenbild. Festschrift zum 60 Geburtstag vom Philipp Lersch*. Munich.

LOLLI, GIORGIO, E. SERIANNI, G. M. GOLDER, AND P. LUZZATTO-FEGIZ. 1958. *Alcohol in Italian Culture. Food and Wine in Relation to Sobriety Among Italians and Italian Americans*. New Brunswick, N.J.

LOWY, SAMUEL. 1942. *Psychological and Biological Foundations of Dream-Interpretation*. London.

LUCIAN. 1711. Anacharsis. In: *The Works of Lucian*. Translated from the Greek by several hands. Printed for Samuel Briscoe. 4 vols. London.

LYND, HELEN MERRELL. 1958. *On Shame and the Search for Identity*. New York.

LYNN, DAVID B. 1961. Sex Differences in Identification Development. *Sociometry*, 24:372–383.

MCARTHUR, CHARLES. 1955. Personality Differences Between Middle and Upper Classes. *Journal of Abnormal and Social Psychology*, 50:247–254.

MCCANDLESS, BOYD R. 1961. *Children and Adolescents*. New York.

MCCARY, JAMES L. 1956. *Psychology of Personality*. New York.

MCCLELLAND, DAVID C. 1951. *Personality*. New York.

MCCLELLAND, DAVID C. 1961. *The Achieving Society*. Princeton.

MCCLELLAND, DAVID C. 1964. French National Character and the Life and Works of André Gide. In: McClelland, David C. *The Roots of Consciousness*. New York.

MACCOBY, ELEANOR E. 1961. The Choice of Variables in the Study of Socialization. *Sociometry*, 24:357–371.

MACCOBY, ELEANOR E., AND PATRICIA K. GIBBS. 1954. Methods of Child-Rearing in Two Social Classes. In: William E. Martin and Celia B. Stendler, eds., *Readings in Child Development*. New York.

MCGEER, PATRICK L. 1962. Mind, Drugs, and Behavior. *American Scientist*, 50: 322–338.

MACGREGOR, GORDON. 1946. *Warriors Without Weapons*. Chicago.

MCKINLEY, DONALD GILBERT. 1964. *Social Class and Family Life*. New York.

MACKINNON, DONALD W. 1944. The Structure of Personality. In: J. McV. Hunt, ed., *Personality and the Behavior Disorders*. 2 vols. New York.

MCPARTLAND, THOMAS S. 1960. Frontiers of Sociological Research on Mental Health and Illness. In: Wayne Wheeler, ed., *Social Change and Mental Health*. Parkville, Mo.

MAIER, HENRY W. 1965. *Three Theories of Child Development*. New York.

MALINOWSKI, BRONISLAW. 1922. *Argonauts of the Western Pacific*. London.

MALINOWSKI, BRONISLAW. 1927. *Sex and Repression in Savage Society*. New York.

MALINOWSKI, BRONISLAW. 1938–1939. The Group and the Individual in Functional Analysis. *American Journal of Sociology*, 44:938–964.

MANDELBAUM, DAVID G. 1953. On the Study of National Character. *American Anthropologist*, 55:174–187.

MANDELBAUM, DAVID G. 1954. Psychiatry in Military Society. *Human Organization*, 13 (no. 3):5–15; (no. 4):19–25.

MANGIN, WILLIAM. 1957. Drinking Among Andean Indians. *Quarterly Journal of Studies on Alcohol*, 18:55–66.

MANGIN, WILLIAM. 1960. Mental Health and Migration to Cities: A Peruvian Case. *Annals of the New York Academy of Sciences,* 84:911–917.

MANIS, JEROME G., MILTON J. BRAWER, CHESTER L. HUNT, AND LEONARD C. KERCHER. 1964. Estimating the Prevalence of Mental Illness. *American Sociological Review,* 29:84–89.

MARETZKI, THOMAS W., AND HATSUMI MARETZKI. 1963. Taira: An Okinawan Village. In: Beatrice B. Whiting, ed., *Six Cultures.* New York.

MARGETTS, E. L. 1965. Transcultural Psychiatry. *Canadian Psychiatric Association Journal,* 10:79.

MARWICK, M. G. 1950. Another Modern Anti-Witchcraft Movement in East Central Africa. *Africa,* 20:100–112.

MARX, KARL, AND FREDERICK ENGELS. 1958. *Selected Works.* 2 vols. Moscow.

MASLOW, ABRAHAM H. 1943. A Theory of Human Motivation. *Psychological Review,* 50:370–396.

MASLOW, ABRAHAM H. 1948. Some Theoretical Consequences of Basic Need-Gratification. *Journal of Personality,* 16:402–416.

MASLOW, ABRAHAM H. 1951a. Higher Needs and Personality. *Dialectica,* 5:257–265.

MASLOW, ABRAHAM H. 1951b. Resistance to Acculturation. *Journal of Social Issues,* 1:26–29.

MASLOW, ABRAHAM H. 1954. *Motivation and Personality.* New York.

MASLOW, ABRAHAM H. 1960. Health as Transcendence of Environment. Paper read before the Symposium on Research Implications of Positive Mental Health, Eastern Psychological Association, April, 1960.

MASLOW, ABRAHAM H. 1962. *Toward a Psychology of Being.* New York.

MASLOW, ABRAHAM H., AND BELA MITTELMANN. 1951. *Principles of Abnormal Psychology.* Rev. ed. New York.

MATTHEW, EUNICE S. 1959. What is Expected of the Soviet Kindergarten? *Harvard Educational Review,* 29:43–53.

MATZA, DAVID. 1964. *Delinquency and Drift.* New York.

MAY, ROLLO. 1958. Contributions of Existential Psychotherapy. In: Rollo May *et al., Existence.* New York.

MAYO, ELTON C. 1945. *The Social Problem of an Industrial Civilization.* Boston.

MEAD, GEORGE H. 1934. *Mind, Self and Society.* Chicago.

MEAD, MARGARET. 1928a. *Coming of Age in Samoa.* New York.

MEAD, MARGARET. 1928b. The Role of the Individual in Samoan Culture. *Journal of the Royal Anthropological Institute of Great Britain and Ireland,* 58:481–495.

MEAD, MARGARET. 1930a. Adolescence in Primitive and Modern Society. In: Victor F. Calverton and Samuel D. Schmalhausen, eds., *The New Generation.* New York.

MEAD, MARGARET. 1930b. *Growing Up in New Guinea.* New York.

MEAD, MARGARET. 1930c. *Social Organization of Manua.* Bernice P. Bishop Museum, Bull. 76.

MEAD, MARGARET. 1931. Education, Primitive. In: Edwin A. Seligman and Alvin Johnson, eds., *Encyclopaedia of the Social Sciences,* vol. 5. New York.

MEAD, MARGARET. 1932a. *The Changing Culture of an Indian Tribe.* Columbia University Contributions to Anthropology, no. 15.

MEAD, MARGARET. 1932b. An Investigation of the Thought of Primitive Children, With Special Reference to Animism. *Journal of the Royal Anthropological Institute of Great Britain and Ireland,* 62:173–190.

MEAD, MARGARET. 1933. More Comprehensive Field Methods. *American Anthropologist,* 35:1–15.

MEAD, MARGARET. 1934. *Kinship in the Admiralty Islands.* Anthropological Papers of the American Museum of Natural History, vol. 34, pt. 2.

MEAD, MARGARET. 1935. *Sex and Temperament in Three Primitive Societies.* New York.

MEAD, MARGARET. 1935–1936. Review of Géza Róheim, *The Riddle of the Sphinx.* *Character and Personality,* 4:85–90.

MEAD, MARGARET, ed. 1937. *Cooperation and Competition Among Primitive Peoples.* New York.

MEAD, MARGARET. 1939–1940. The Concept of Plot in Culture. *Transactions of the New York Academy of Sciences,* 2:24–31.

MEAD, MARGARET. 1940. Character Formation in Two South Seas Societies. In: *Proceedings of the American Neurological Association, 66th Annual Meeting.* New York.

MEAD, MARGARET. 1940–1941. Social Change and Cultural Surrogates. *Journal of Educational Sociology,* 14:92–109.

MEAD, MARGARET. 1942a. *And Keep Your Powder Dry.* New York.

MEAD, MARGARET. 1942b. Educative Effects of Social Environment as Disclosed by Studies of Primitive Societies. In: Ernest W. Burgess *et al., Environment and Education.* Chicago.

MEAD, MARGARET. 1943. Anthropological Techniques in War Psychology. *Bulletin of the Menninger Clinic,* 7:137–140.

MEAD, MARGARET. 1946. Research on Primitive Children. In: Leonard Carmichael, ed., *Manual of Child Psychology.* New York.

MEAD, MARGARET. 1947a. Age Patterning in Personality Development. *American Journal of Orthopsychiatry,* 17:231–240.

MEAD, MARGARET. 1947b. The Application of Anthropological Techniques to Cross-National Communication. *Transactions of the New York Academy of Sciences,* 9:133–152.

MEAD, MARGARET. 1947c. The Concept of Culture and the Psychosomatic Approach. *Psychiatry,* 10:57–76.

MEAD, MARGARET. 1947d. The Implications of Culture Change for Personality Development. *American Journal of Orthopsychiatry,* 17:633–646.

MEAD, MARGARET. 1947e. On the Implications for Anthropology of the Gesell-Ilg Approach to Maturation. *American Anthropologist,* 49:69–77.

MEAD, MARGARET. 1948a. A Case History in Cross-National Communications. In: Lyman Bryson, ed., *The Communication of Ideas.* New York.

MEAD, MARGARET. 1948b. The Contemporary American Family as an Anthropologist Sees It. *American Journal of Sociology,* 53:453–459.

MEAD, MARGARET. 1949a. Character Formation and Diachronic Theory. In: Meyer Fortes, ed., *Social Structure.* Oxford.

MEAD, MARGARET. 1949b. *Male and Female.* New York.

MEAD, MARGARET. 1949c. Psychologic Weaning: Childhood and Adolescence. In: Paul H. Hoch and Joseph Zubin, eds., *Psychosexual Development in Health and Disease.* New York.

MEAD, MARGARET. 1951a. Anthropologist and Historian: Their Common Problems. *American Quarterly,* 3:3–13.

MEAD, MARGARET. 1951b. The Impact of Personality Development in the United States Today. *Understanding the Child,* 20:17–18.

MEAD, MARGARET. 1951c. Research in Contemporary Cultures. In: Harold Guetzkow, ed., *Groups, Leadership and Men.* Pittsburgh.

MEAD, MARGARET. 1951d. *The School in American Culture.* Cambridge, Mass.

MEAD, MARGARET. 1951e. *Soviet Attitudes Toward Authority.* New York.

MEAD, MARGARET. 1951f. The Study of National Character. In: Daniel Lerner and Harold D. Lasswell, eds., *The Policy Sciences*. Stanford, Calif.

MEAD, MARGARET. 1952a. Introduction. In: Margaret Mead, ed., *Studies in Soviet Communication*. 2 vols. Center for International Studies, Massachusetts Institute of Technology. Cambridge, Mass.

MEAD, MARGARET. 1952b. Some Relationships Between Social Anthropology and Psychiatry. In: Franz Alexander and Helen Ross, eds., *Dynamic Psychiatry*. Chicago.

MEAD, MARGARET, ed. 1953a. *Cultural Patterns and Technical Change*. Paris.

MEAD, MARGARET. 1953b. National Character. In: A. L. Kroeber, ed., *Anthropology Today*. Chicago.

MEAD, MARGARET. 1954a. Some Theoretical Considerations on the Problem of Mother-Child Separation. *American Journal of Orthopsychiatry*, 24:471–483.

MEAD, MARGARET. 1954b. Research on Primitive Children. In: L. Carmichael, ed., *Manual of Child Psychology*. 2nd ed. New York.

MEAD, MARGARET. 1954c. The Swaddling Hypothesis: Its Reception. *American Anthropologist*, 56:395–409.

MEAD, MARGARET. 1955a. Effects of Anthropological Field Work Models on Interdisciplinary Communication. *Journal of Social Issues*, 11 (no. 2):3–11.

MEAD, MARGARET. 1955b. Theoretical Setting—1954. In: Margaret Mead and Martha Wolfenstein, eds., *Childhood in Contemporary Cultures*. Chicago.

MEAD, MARGARET. 1956a. The Cross-Cultural Approach to the Study of Personality. In: J. L. McCary, ed., *Psychology of Personality*. New York.

MEAD, MARGARET. 1956b. Cultural Differences in the Bathing of Babies. In: Kenneth Soddy, ed., *Mental Health and Infant Development*. 2 vols. New York.

MEAD, MARGARET. 1956c. *New Lives for Old*. New York.

MEAD, MARGARET. 1959a. *An Anthropologist at Work*. Boston.

MEAD, MARGARET. 1959b. Independent Religious Movements. *Comparative Studies in Society and History*, 1:324–329.

MEAD, MARGARET. 1961a. *Cooperation and Competition Among Primitive Peoples*. Rev. paperback ed. Boston.

MEAD, MARGARET. 1961b. National Character and the Science of Anthropology. In: Seymour M. Lipset and Leo Lowenthal, eds., *Culture and Social Character*. Glencoe, Ill.

MEAD, MARGARET. 1961c. Psychiatry and Ethnology. In: H. W. Gruhle and W. Mayer-Gross, eds., *Psychiatrie der Gegenwart*, vol. 3, *Soziale und Angewandte Psychiatrie*. Berlin.

MEAD, MARGARET. 1963a. Culture and Personality. In: Albert Deutsch and Helen Fishman, eds., *The Encyclopedia of Mental Health*, vol. 2. New York.

MEAD, MARGARET. 1963b. Socialization and Enculturation. *Current Anthropology*, 4:184–188.

MEAD, MARGARET. 1964a. *Continuities in Cultural Evolution*. New Haven.

MEAD, MARGARET. 1964b. The Idea of National Character. In: Roger L. Shinn, ed., *The Search for Identity: Essays on the American Character*. New York.

MEAD, MARGARET. 1965a. The Future as the Basis for Establishing a Shared Culture. *Daedalus*, Winter:135–155.

MEAD, MARGARET. 1965b. The Years Between: 1943–1965. In: Margaret Mead, *And Keep Your Powder Dry*. New expanded ed. New York.

MEAD, MARGARET, AND FRANCES COOKE MACGREGOR. 1951. *Growth and Culture*. New York.

MEAD, MARGARET, AND RHODA MÉTRAUX, eds. 1953. *The Study of Culture at a Distance*. Chicago.

MEAD, MARGARET, AND MARTHA WOLFENSTEIN, eds. 1955. *Childhood in Contemporary Cultures*. New York.

MEANS, RICHARD L. 1965. Weber's Thesis of the Protestant Ethic: The Ambiguities of Received Doctrine. *Journal of Religion*, 45:1–11.

MECHANIC, DAVID. 1962. *Students Under Stress*. New York.

MEDALIA, NAHUM Z., AND OTTO N. LARSEN. 1958. Diffusion and Belief in a Collective Delusion: The Seattle Windshield Pitting Epidemic. *American Sociological Review*, 23:180–186.

MEDLEY, ROBERT. 1964. Matisse's "L'Escargot." *The Listener*, 71:438–439.

MEGGERS, BETTY J. 1946. Recent Trends in American Ethnology. *American Anthropologist*, 48:176–214.

MEIER, DOROTHY L., AND WENDELL BELL. 1959. Anomia and Differential Access to the Achievement of Life Goals. *American Sociological Review*, 24:189–202.

MENNINGER, KARL. 1963. *The Vital Balance*. New York.

MERTON, ROBERT K. 1957. *Social Theory and Social Structure*. Rev., enlarged ed. Glencoe, Ill.

MÉTRAUX, RHODA. 1943. Qualitative Attitude Analysis. In: National Research Council, Committee on Food Habits, *The Problem of Changing Food Habits; Report of the Committee on Food Habits, 1941–1943*. Washington, D.C.

MÉTRAUX, RHODA. 1961. Children's Drawings: Satellites and Space. *Journal of Social Issues*, 17 (no. 2):36–42.

MÉTRAUX, RHODA, AND MARGARET MEAD. 1954. *Themes in French Culture*. Stanford, Calif.

MEYER, HENRY J., EDGAR F. BORGATTA, AND WYATT C. JONES. 1965. *Girls at Vocational High*. New York.

MIDDLETON, JOHN, AND EDWARD H. WINTER. 1963. Introduction. In: John Middleton and Edward H. Winter, eds., *Witchcraft and Sorcery in East Africa*. London.

MILGRAM, STANLEY. 1963. Behavioral Study of Obedience. *Journal of Abnormal and Social Psychology*, 67:371–378.

MILLER, ARTHUR. 1965. Our Guilt for the World's Evil. *New York Times Magazine*, January 3, 1965:10–12, 48.

MILLER, DANIEL R., AND GUY E. SWANSON. 1958. *The Changing American Parent*. New York.

MILLER, DANIEL R., AND GUY E. SWANSON. 1960. *Inner Conflict and Defense*. New York.

MILLER, NATHAN. 1928. *The Child in Primitive Society*. New York.

MILLER, NEAL E., AND JOHN DOLLARD. 1941. *Social Learning and Imitation*. New Haven.

MILLER, S. M., AND ELLIOT G. MISHLER. 1964. Social Class, Mental Illness, and American Psychiatry: An Expository Review. In: Frank Riessman, Jerome Cohen, and Arthur Pearl, eds., *Mental Health of the Poor*. New York.

MILNER, ESTHER. 1953. Some Hypotheses Concerning the Influence of Segregation on Negro Personality Development. *Psychiatry*, 16:291–297.

MINER, HORACE M., AND GEORGE DE VOS. 1960. *Oasis and Casbah: Algerian Culture and Personality in Change*. University of Michigan, Museum of Anthropology, Anthropological Papers, no. 15.

MINTURN, LEIGH, AND JOHN T. HITCHCOCK. 1963. The Rajputs of Khalapur, India. In: Beatrice B. Whiting, ed., *Six Cultures*. New York.

MINTURN, LEIGH, AND WILLIAM W. LAMBERT. 1964. *Mothers of Six Cultures*. New York.

MINTZ, NORBETT L., AND DAVID T. SCHWARTZ. 1964. Urban Ecology and Psychosis: Community Factors in the Incidence of Schizophrenia and Manic-Depression Among Italians in Greater Boston. *International Journal of Social Psychiatry*, 10:101–118.

MIROGLIO, ABEL. 1958. *La Psychologie des Peuples*. Paris.

MIROGLIO, ABEL. 1963. Einige Aspekte des franzoesischen Nationalcharakters. *Koelner Zeitschrift fuer Soziologie und Sozialpsychologie, 15:693–710.*

MIZRUCHI, EPHRAIM HAROLD. 1964. *Success and Opportunity*. New York.

MONTAGU, ASHLEY. 1961. Culture and Mental Illness. *American Journal of Psychiatry, 118:15–23.*

MOORE, LILIAN. 1960. *Everything Happens to Stuey*. New York.

MORGAN, WILLIAM. 1931. Navaho Treatment of Sickness: Diagnosticians. *American Anthropologist, 33:390–402.*

MORLEY, SYLVANUS GRISWOLD. 1946. *The Ancient Maya*. Stanford, Calif.

MORRIS, CHARLES W. 1956. *Varieties of Human Values*. Chicago.

MORRIS, RICHARD T. 1960. *The Two-Way Mirror*. Minneapolis.

MOSHER, DONALD L., AND ALVIN SCODEL. 1960. Relationships Between Ethnocentrism in Children and the Ethnocentrism and Authoritarian Rearing Practices of Their Mothers. *Child Development, 31:369–376.*

MOWRER, O. HOBART. 1959. Changing Conceptions of the Unconscious. *Journal of Nervous and Mental Disease, 129:222–234.*

MOWRER, O. HOBART. 1960. "Sin," the Lesser of Two Evils. *American Psychologist, 15:301–304.*

MOWRER, O. HOBART. 1961. *The Crisis in Psychiatry and Religion*. Princeton.

MUI, LORNA HOLBROOK. 1961. Social Structure and Anomia. *American Sociological Review, 21:275–277.*

MULLANE, HARVEY. 1965. Moral Responsibility for Dreams. *Dialogue, 4:224–229.*

MULLIGAN, D. G. 1957. *Maori Adolescence in Rakau*. Victoria University of Wellington Publications in Psychology, no. 9.

MUNROE, RUTH L. 1955. *Schools of Psychoanalytic Thought*. New York.

MURDOCK, GEORGE P. 1945. The Common Denominator of Cultures. In: Ralph Linton, ed., *The Science of Man in the World Crisis*. New York.

MURDOCK, GEORGE P., et al. 1961. *Outline of Cultural Materials*. 4th rev. ed. Behavior Science Outlines, vol. 1.

MURDOCK, GEORGE P., AND JOHN W. M. WHITING. 1951. Cultural Determination of Parental Attitudes: The Relationship Between the Social Structure, Particularly Family Structure and Parental Behavior. In: Milton J. E. Senn, ed., *Problems of Infancy and Childhood. Transactions of the Fourth Conference on Problems of Infancy and Childhood, March 6–7, 1950*. New York.

MURPHY, HENRY BRIAN MEGGETT. 1955. *Flight and Resettlement*. Paris.

MURPHY, HENRY BRIAN MEGGETT, E. D. WITTKOWER, AND N. A. CHANCE. 1964. Cross-cultural Inquiry Into the Symptomatology of Depression. *Transcultural Psychiatric Research, 1:5–18.*

MURPHY, JANE M. 1962. Cross-cultural Studies of the Prevalence of Psychiatric Disorder. *World Mental Health, 14:53–65.*

MURPHY, JANE M. 1965. Social Science Concepts and Cross-cultural Methods for Psychiatric Research. In: Jane M. Murphy and Alexander H. Leighton, eds., *Approaches to Cross-cultural Psychiatry*. Ithaca, N. Y.

MURPHY, JANE M., AND CHARLES C. HUGHES. 1965. The Use of Psychophysiological Symptoms as Indicators of Disorder Among Eskimos. In: Jane M. Murphy and Alexander H. Leighton, eds., *Approaches to Cross-cultural Psychiatry*. Ithaca, N.Y.

MURPHY, LOIS B. 1962. *The Widening World of Childhood*. New York.

MURPHY, LOIS B. 1964. Adaptational Tasks in Childhood in Our Culture. *Bulletin of the Menninger Clinic, 28:309–322.*

MURPHY, ROBERT F. 1957. Intergroup Hostility and Social Cohesion. *American Anthropologist,* 59:1018–1035.

MURPHY, ROBERT F. 1959. Social Structure and Sex Antagonism. *Southwestern Journal of Anthropology,* 15:89–98.

MURRAY, HENRY A., et al. 1938. *Explorations in Personality.* New York.

MURRAY, HENRY A., AND CLYDE KLUCKHOHN. 1953. Outline of a Conception of Personality. In: Clyde Kluckhohn, Henry A. Murray, and David M. Schneider, eds. *Personality in Nature, Society and Culture.* 2nd ed. New York.

MURSTEIN, BERNARD I., AND RONALD S. PRYER. 1959. The Concept of Projection: A Review. *Psychological Bulletin,* 56:353–374.

MUSSEN, PAUL H., ed. 1960. *Handbook of Research Methods in Child Development.* New York.

MUSSEN, PAUL H., JOHN JANEWAY CONGER, AND JEROME KAGAN. 1963. *Child Development and Personality.* 2nd ed. New York.

MYERHOFF, HOWARD L., AND BARBARA G. MYERHOFF. 1964. Field Observations of Middle Class "Gangs." *Social Forces,* 42:328–336.

MYERS, JEROME K., AND BERTRAM H. ROBERTS. 1959. *Family and Class Dynamics in Mental Illness.* New York.

MYRDAL, GUNNAR. 1965. With What Little Wisdom the World Is Ruled. *New York Times Magazine,* July 18, 1965: 20–26.

NADEL, SIEGFRIED F. 1951. *The Foundations of Social Anthropology.* London.

NARAIN, DHIRENDRA. 1957. *Hindu Character.* Bombay.

NARAIN, DHIRENDRA. 1964. Growing Up in India. *Family Process,* 3:127–154.

NAROLL, RAOUL. 1959. A Tentative Index of Culture-Stress. *International Journal of Social Psychiatry,* 5:107–116.

NEAL, ARTHUR G., AND SALOMON RETTIG. 1963. Dimensions of Alienation Among Manual and Non-Manual Workers. *American Sociological Review,* 28:599–608.

NEEDHAM, RODNEY. 1962. *Structure and Sentiment.* Chicago.

NEHER, ANDREW. 1961. Auditory Driving Observed With Scalp Electrodes in Normal Subjects. *Electroencephalography and Clinical Neurophysiology,* 13:449–451.

NEHER, ANDREW. 1962. A Physiological Explanation of Unusual Behavior in Ceremonies Involving Drums. *Human Biology,* 34:151–160.

NETT, EMILY M. 1957–1958. An Evaluation of the National Character Concept in Sociological Theory. *Social Forces,* 36:297–303.

NEUGARTEN, BERNICE L., et al. 1964. *Personality in Middle and Late Life.* New York.

NEWMAN, PHILIP L. 1964. "Wild Man" Behavior in a New Guinea Highlands Community. *American Anthropologist,* 66:1–19.

NEWSON, JOHN, AND ELIZABETH NEWSON. 1963. *Infant Care in an Urban Community.* London.

NIAU, [——]. 1887–1888. *The History of the Devils of Loudun.* Translated and edited by Edmund Goldsmid. 3 vols. in one. Edinburgh.

NOKES, PETER. 1961. Feedback as an Explanatory Device in the Study of Certain Interpersonal and Institutional Processes. *Human Relations,* 14:381–387.

NORBECK, EDWARD. 1961. *Religion in Primitive Society.* New York.

NORBECK, EDWARD, AND MARGARET NORBECK. 1956. Child Training in a Japanese Fishing Community. In: Douglas G. Haring, ed., *Personal Character and Cultural Milieu.* 3rd rev. ed. Syracuse, N.Y.

NORBECK, EDWARD, DONALD E. WALKER, AND MIMI COHEN. 1962. The Interpretation of Data: Puberty Rites. *American Anthropologist,* 64:463–485.

NORTHROP, FILMER S. C. 1946. *The Meeting of East and West.* New York.

NURGE, ETHEL. 1966. *Life in a Leyte Village*. Seattle.

NYDEGGER, WILLIAM F., AND CORINNE NYDEGGER. 1963. Tarong: An Ilocos Barrio in the Philippines. In: Beatrice B. Whiting, ed., *Six Cultures*. New York.

OESER, O. A., AND S. B. HAMMOND, eds. 1954. *Social Structure and Personality in a City*. London.

OESTREICH, NANCY. 1948. Trends of Change in Patterns of Child Care and Training Among the Wisconsin Winnebago. *Wisconsin Archeologist*. 29:39–140.

OLSON, ROBERT. 1957. What's Happened to the Suburb They Called Crestwood Heights? *Maclean's Magazine*, 70 (no. 21):24–38.

OLSON, ROBERT G. 1962. *An Introduction to Existentialism*. New York.

OPLER, MARVIN K. 1956. *Culture, Psychiatry, and Human Values*. Springfield, Ill.

OPLER, MARVIN K. 1959a. Anthropological Aspects of Psychiatry. In: J. H. Masserman and J. L. Moreno, eds., *Progress in Psychotherapy*, vol. 4. New York.

OPLER, MARVIN K. 1959b. The Cultural Backgrounds of Mental Health. In: Marvin K. Opler, ed., *Culture and Mental Health*. New York.

OPLER, MARVIN K. 1963. Scientific Social Psychiatry Encounters Existentialism. *Philosophy and Phenomenological Research*, 24:240–243.

OPLER, MARVIN K., AND JEROME L. SINGER. 1956. Ethnic Differences in Behavior and Psychopathology: Italian and Irish. *International Journal of Social Psychiatry*, 2:11–22.

OPLER, MORRIS E. 1946. A Recent Trend in the Misrepresentation of the Work of American Ethnologists. *American Anthropologist*, 48:669–671.

OPLER, MORRIS E. 1948. Some Recently Developed Concepts Relating to Culture. *Southwestern Journal of Anthropology*, 4:107–122.

OPLER, MORRIS E. 1952. A Current Phase of Separation in Social Science. In: J. E. Hulett, Jr. and R. Stagner, eds., *Problems in Social Psychology*. Urbana, Ill.

OPLER, MORRIS E. 1959–1960. Considerations in the Cross-Cultural Study of Mental Disorders. *International Journal of Social Psychiatry*, 5:191–196.

ORLANSKY, HAROLD. 1946. Jewish Personality Traits. *Commentary*, 2:377–383.

ORLANSKY, HAROLD. 1948. Destiny in the Nursery. *Commentary*, 5:563–569.

ORLANSKY, HAROLD. 1949. Infant Care and Personality. *Psychological Bulletin*, 46:1–48.

OSGOOD, CHARLES E., GEORGE J. SUCI, AND PERCY H. TANNENBAUM. 1957. *The Measurement of Meaning*. Urbana, Ill.

OSGOOD, CORNELIUS. 1951. Culture: Its Empirical and Non-Empirical Character. *Southwestern Journal of Anthropology*, 7:202–214.

OWEN, ROBERT. 1927. *A New View of Society and Other Writings*. Everyman's Library ed. London.

PARK, GEORGE K. 1962. Sons and Lovers: Characterological Requisites of the Roles in a Peasant Society. *Ethnology*, 1:412–424.

PARKER, ARTHUR C. 1913. *The Code of Handsome Lake, the Seneca Prophet*. New York State Museum Bulletin, no. 163.

PARKER, SEYMOUR. 1960. The Wiitiko Psychosis in the Context of Ojibwa Personality and Culture. *American Anthropologist*, 62:603–623.

PARKER, SEYMOUR. 1962a. Eskimo Psychopathology in the Context of Eskimo Personality and Culture. *American Anthropologist*, 64:76–96.

PARKER, SEYMOUR. 1962b. Motives in Eskimo and Ojibwa Mythology. *Ethnology*, 1:516–523.

PARKER, SEYMOUR. 1964. The Kwakiutl Indians: "Amiable" and "Atrocious." *Anthropologica*, 6:131–158.

PARKER, SEYMOUR, AND TOM T. SASAKI. 1965. Society and Sentiments in Two Contrasting Socially Disturbed Areas. In: Jane M. Murphy and Alexander H. Leighton, eds., *Approaches to Cross-cultural Psychiatry*. Ithaca, N.Y.

PARSONS, ELSIE CLEWS. 1945. *Peguche*. Chicago.

PARSONS, TALCOTT. 1951a. Personality and Social Structure. In: Alfred H. Stanton and Stewart E. Perry, eds., *Personality and Political Crisis*. Glencoe, Ill.

PARSONS, TALCOTT. 1951b. *The Social System*. Glencoe, Ill.

PARSONS, TALCOTT. 1952. The Superego and the Theory of Social Systems. *Psychiatry*, 15:15–25.

PARSONS, TALCOTT. 1960. Pattern Variables Revisted: A Response to Robert Dubin. *American Sociological Review*, 25:467–483.

PARSONS, TALCOTT. 1961. Social Structure and the Development of Personality. In Bert Kaplan, ed., *Studying Personality Cross-Culturally*. Evanston, Ill.

PARSONS, TALCOTT, AND ROBERT F. BALES. 1955. *Family, Socialization and Interaction Process*. Glencoe, Ill.

PASAMANICK, BENJAMIN, ed. 1959. *Epidemiology of Mental Disorder*. American Association for the Advancement of Science, Publn. no. 60.

PAUL, BENJAMIN D. 1953. Interview Techniques and Field Relationships. In: A. L. Kroeber, ed., *Anthropology Today*. Chicago.

PEARL, ARTHUR. 1965. Youth in Lower Class Settings. In: Muzafer Sherif and Carolyn W. Sherif, eds., *Problems of Youth*. Chicago.

PEARSON, GERALD H. J. 1959. The Psychoanalytic Contributions to the Theory and Practice of Education. In: Morton Levitt, ed., *Readings in Psychoanalytic Psychology*. New York.

PETERS, R. S. 1958. *The Concept of Motivation*. London.

PETERSON, LEN. 1954. Desert Soliloquy. In: Walter Goldschmidt, ed., *Ways of Mankind*. Boston.

PETTIGREW, THOMAS F. 1964. *A Profile of the Negro American*. Princeton.

PETTITT, GEORGE A. 1946. *Primitive Education in North America*. Berkeley, Calif.

PHILLIPS, HERBERT. 1963. Relationships Between Personality and Social Structure in a Siamese Peasant Community. *Human Organization*, 22:105–108.

PIAGET, JEAN. 1929. *The Child's Conception of the World*. Translated by Joan and Andrew Tomlinson. London.

PIAGET, JEAN. 1932. *The Moral Judgment of the Child*. Translated by Majorie Gabain. Glencoe, Ill.

PIÉRON, H. 1909. L'Anthropologie psychologique, son object et sa méthode. *Revue de l'École d'Anthropologie de Paris*, 19:113–127.

PIERS, GERHART, AND MILTON B. SINGER. 1953. *Shame and Guilt*. Springfield, Ill.

PIOTROWSKI, ZYGMUNT A. 1959. Basic Human Motives According to Kurt Goldstein. *American Journal of Psychotherapy*, 13:553–560.

PLAYNE, CAROLINE E. 1925. *The Neuroses of the Nations*. London.

PLOSS, HERMANN HEINRICH. 1911–1912. *Das Kind in Brauch und Sitte der Voelker*. Rev. ed. 2 vols. Leipzig.

PLUNKETT, RICHARD J., AND JOHN E. GORDON. 1960. *Epidemiology and Mental Illness*. New York.

POLYANI, MICHAEL. 1962. *Personal Knowledge*. Rev. ed. Chicago.

POLGAR, STEVEN. 1960. Biculturation of Mesquakie Teenage Boys. *American Anthropologist*, 62:217–235.

POLGAR, STEVEN. 1962. Health and Human Behavior: Areas of Interest Common to the Social and Medical Sciences. *Current Anthropology*, 3:159–205.

POPE, ALEXANDER. 1963. *Epistles to Several Persons (Moral Essays)*. James E. Wellington. Coral Gables, Fla.

POPPER, KARL R. 1957. *The Poverty of Historicism*. London.

POSTAL, SUSAN K. 1965. Body-Image and Identity: A Comparison of Kwakiutl and Hopi. *American Anthropologist*, 67:455–462.

POTTER, DAVID M. 1954. *People of Plenty*. Chicago.

PRESCOTT, DANIEL A. 1957. *The Child in the Educative Process*. New York.

PRESTON, RICHARD J., III. 1963. Inherent and Imposed Structures and Writings of Edward Sapir M.A. thesis, Wilson Library, University of North Carolina at Chapel Hill.

PROSHANSKY, HAROLD, ed. n.d. *Linking Social Class and Socialization: Toward a Framework for Analysis and Research*. Institute for Social Research, University of Michigan, Ann Arbor.

PROTHRO, E. TERRY. 1960. Patterns of Permissiveness Among Preliterate Peoples. *Journal of Abnormal and Social Psychology*, 61:151–154.

PROTHO, E. TERRY. 1961. *Child Rearing in Lebanon*. Cambridge, Mass.

PRUGH, DANE G. 1960. The Preschool Child. In: Harold C. Stuart and Dane G. Prugh, eds., *The Healthy Child*. Cambridge, Mass.

PYE, LUCIEN W. 1962. *Politics, Personality, and Nation Building*. New Haven.

RABIN, ALBERT I. 1958. Kibbutz Children—Research Findings to Date. *Children*, 5:179–184.

RABIN, ALBERT I. 1961. Culture Components as a Significant Factor in Child Development. Symposium, 1960. 2. Kibbutz Adolescents. *American Journal of Orthopsychiatry*, 31:493–504.

RADCLIFFE-BROWN, A. R. 1952. *Structure and Function in Primitive Society*. London.

RADIN, PAUL. 1936. Ojibwa and Ottawa Puberty Dreams. In: *Essays in Anthropology Presented to A. L. Kroeber*. Berkeley, Calif.

RAINE, KATHLEEN. 1956. *The Collected Poems of Kathleen Raine*. London.

RANK, OTTO. 1952. *The Trauma of Birth*. New York.

RAPOPORT, ROBERT N. 1963. Social Anthropology and Mental Health. In: Albert Deutsch and Helen Fishman, eds., *The Encyclopedia of Mental Halth*, vol. 6. New York.

RASMUSSEN, KNUD. 1929. *Intellectual Culture of the Iglulik Eskimos*. Report of the Fifth Thule Expedition, 1921–1924, vol. 7, no. 1.

RATANAKORN, PRASOP. 1959–1960. Schizophrenia in Thailand. *International Journal of Social Psychiatry*, 5:47–49.

RAUM, OTTO F. 1940. *Chaga Childhood*. London.

READ, MARGARET. 1959. *Children of Their Fathers*. London.

REDFIELD, ROBERT. 1955. *The Little Community*. Chicago.

REICHEL-DOLMATOFF, GERARDO, AND ALICIA REICHEL-DOLMATOFF. 1961. *The People of Aritama*. London.

REID, D. D. 1960. *Epidemiological Methods in the Study of Mental Disorders*. World Health Organization, Public Health Papers, no. 2.

REISS, ALBERT J., JR., AND A. LEWIS RHODES. 1963. Status Deprivation and Delinquent Behavior. *Sociological Quarterly*, 4:135–149.

RENAUD, HAROLD, AND FLOYD ESTESS. 1961. Life History Interviews with One Hundred Normal American Males: "Pathogenicity" of Childhood. *American Journal of Orthopsychiatry*, 31:786–802.

RENNIE, THOMAS A. C. 1955–1956. Social Psychiatry—A Definition. *International Journal of Social Psychiatry*, 1:5–13.

RIBBLE, MARGARET A. 1943. *The Rights of Infants.* New York.

RICE, ROBERT. 1965. Junk. *The New Yorker,* 41 (no. 6):50–142.

RICHARDS, AUDREY I. 1956. *Chisungu: A Girl's Initiation Ceremony Among the Bemba of Northern Rhodesia.* London.

RIESMAN, DAVID. 1950. *The Lonely Crowd.* New Haven.

RILKE, RAINER MARIA. 1949. *The Notebooks of Malte Laurids Brigge.* Translated by M. D. Herter Norton. New York.

RITCHIE, JAMES E. 1956. *Basic Personality in Rakau.* Victoria University of Wellington, Publications in Psychology, no. 8.

RITCHIE, JAMES E. 1963. *The Making of a Maori.* Wellington, New Zealand.

RITCHIE, JANE. 1957. *Childhood in Rakau. The First Five Years of Life.* Victoria University of Wellington, Publications in Psychology, no. 10.

RITCHIE, OSCAR W., AND MARVIN R. KOLLER. 1964. *Sociology of Childhood.* New York.

ROBERTS, JOHN M., MALCOLM J. ARTH, AND ROBERT R. BUSH. 1959. Games in Culture. *American Anthropologist,* 61:597–605.

ROBERTS, JOHN M., AND BRIAN SUTTON-SMITH. 1962. Child Training and Game Involvement. *Ethnology,* 1:166–185.

ROBINSON, HELEN M., MARION MONROE, A. STERL ARTLEY, AND CHARLOTTE S. HUCK. 1964. *Roads to Follow.* Chicago.

ROE, ANNE. 1953. *A Psychological Study of Eminent Psychologists and Anthropologists.* Psychological Monographs, vol. 67, no. 2.

ROE, ANNE. 1961. The Psychology of the Scientist. *Science,* 134:456–459.

ROGERS, G. A. J. 1965. The Hypothesis of Harmony. *The Listener,* 73:261, 264.

ROGINSKIY, Y. Y. 1961. Racial Differentiation and the Psyche. In: V. V. Bunak *et al., Contemporary Raciology and Racism.* Translated by Earl W. Count. Indiana University Research Center in Anthropology, Folklore, and Linguistics, Publn. 17.

ROGLER, LLOYD H., AND AUGUST B. HOLLINGSHEAD. 1965. *Trapped: Families and Schizophrenia.* New York.

ROGOW, ARNOLD A., AND HAROLD D. LASSWELL. 1963. *Power, Corruption, and Rectitude.* Englewood Cliffs, N.J.

RÓHEIM, GÉZA. 1934a. *The Riddle of the Sphinx.* Translated by R. Money-Kyrle. London.

RÓHEIM, GÉZA. 1934b. The Study of Character Development and the Ontogenetic Theory of Culture. In: E. E. Evans-Prichard *et al.,* eds., *Essays Presented to C. G. Seligman.* London.

RÓHEIM, GÉZA. 1943a. Children's Games and Rhymes in Duau (Normanby Island). *American Anthropologist,* 45:99–119.

RÓHEIM, GÉZA. 1943b. *The Origin and Function of Culture.* New York.

RÓHEIM, GÉZA. 1947. Dream Analysis and Field Work in Anthropology. In: *Psychoanalysis and the Social Sciences,* vol. 1. New York.

RÓHEIM, GÉZA. 1949. Technique of Dream Analysis and Field Work in Anthropology. *Psychoanalytic Quarterly,* 18:471–479.

RÓHEIM, GÉZA. 1950. *Psychoanalysis and Anthropology.* New York.

RÓHEIM, GÉZA. 1952. The Anthropological Evidence and the Oedipus Complex. *Psychoanalytic Quarterly,* 21:537–542.

RÓHEIM, GÉZA. 1962. The Western Tribes of Central Australia: Childhood. *Psychoanalytic Study of Society,* 2:195–232.

ROHRER, JOHN H., AND MUNRO S. EDMONSON, eds. 1960. *The Eighth Generation Grows Up.* New York.

ROMNEY, A. KIMBALL, AND ROY GOODWIN D'ANDRADE. 1964. *Transcultural Studies in Cognition. American Anthropologist,* special publication, vol. 66, no. 3, pt. 2.

ROMNEY, A. KIMBALL, AND ROMAINE ROMNEY. 1963. The Mixtecans of Juxtlahuaca, Mexico. In: Beatrice B. Whiting, ed., *Six Cultures*. New York.

ROSENTHAL, THEODORE, AND BERNARD J. SIEGEL. 1959. Magic and Witchcraft: An Interpretation From Dissonance Theory. *Southwestern Journal of Anthropology*, 15:143–167.

ROSS, JAMES BRUCE, AND MARY MARTIN MCLAUGHLIN, eds., *The Portable Medieval Reader*. New York.

ROTTER, JULIAN B. 1954. *Social Learning and Clinical Psychology*. New York.

ROUART, J. 1957. Développement de la personnalité. In: *Encyclopédie médico-chirurgicale*, vol. 1, fasc.37020 A^{10}. Paris.

ROVERE, RICHARD H. 1965. Letter From Washington. *The New Yorker*, 41 (no. 30):116–130.

RUBEL, ARTHUR J. 1960. Concepts of Disease in Mexican-American Culture. *American Anthropologist*, 62:795–814.

RUBEL, ARTHUR J. 1964. The Epidemiology of a Folk Illness: *Susto* in Hispanic America. *Ethnology*, 3:268–283.

RUBINS, JACK L. 1962. A Phenomenological View of Early Development of the Child. *Journal of Existential Psychiatry*, 3:97–110.

RUDOLPH, WOLFGANG. 1959. Die amerikanische *"Cultural Anthropology"* und das Wertproblem. In: *Forschungen zur Ethnologie und Sozialpsychologie*, vol. 3. Berlin.

RUITENBEEK, HENDRIK M. 1964. *The Individual and the Crowd*. New York.

SAHLINS, MARSHALL D., AND ELMAN R. SERVICE, eds. 1960. *Evolution and Culture*. Ann Arbor, Mich.

SAINDON, J. ÉMILE. 1933. Mental Disorders Among the James Bay Cree. *Primitive Man*, 6:1–12.

SAMUELS, ERNEST. 1964. *Henry Adams: The Major Phase*. Cambridge, Mass.

SANFORD, NEVITT. 1964. The College Student in the World Today. *Bulletin of the Bureau of School Service, College of Education, University of Kentucky*, 36:6–19.

SAPIR, EDWARD. 1924. Culture, Genuine and Spurious. *American Journal of Sociology*, 29:401–429.

SAPIR, EDWARD. 1929. The Unconscious Patterning of Behavior in Society. In: Ethel S. Dummer, ed., *The Unconscious*. New York.

SAPIR, EDWARD. 1932. Cultural Anthropology and Psychiatry. *Journal of Abnormal and Social Psychology*, 27:229–242.

SAPIR, EDWARD. 1934a. The Emergence of the Concept of Personality in a Study of Cultures. *Journal of Social Psychology*, 5:408–415.

SAPIR, EDWARD. 1934b. Personality. In: Edwin A. Seligman and Alvin Johnson, eds., *Encyclopaedia of the Social Sciences*, vol. 12. New York.

SARASON, SEYMOUR B., AND THOMAS GLADWIN. 1958. Psychological and Cultural Problems in Mental Subnormality: A Review of Research. *Genetic Psychology Monographs*, 57:3–290.

SARBIN, THEODORE R. 1954. Role Theory. In: Gardner Lindzey, ed., *Handbook of Social Psychology*. 2 vols. Cambridge, Mass.

SARGEANT, WINTHROP. 1961. Profiles: It's All Anthropology. *The New Yorker*, 37 (no. 46):31–44.

SARTRE, JEAN-PAUL. 1956. *Being and Nothingness*. Translated by Hazel E. Barnes. New York.

SARTRE, JEAN-PAUL. 1963. *Saint Génet*. Translated by Bernard Frechtman. New York.

SAVAGE, CHARLES, ALEXANDER H. LEIGHTON, AND DOROTHEA C. LEIGHTON. 1965. The Problem of Cross-cultural Identification of Psychiatric Disorders. In: Jane M. Murphy and Alexander H. Leighton, eds., *Approaches to Cross-cultural Psychiatry*. Ithaca, N.Y.

SCHARR, JOHN H. 1961. *Escape From Authority*. New York.

SCHEINFELD, AMRAM. 1965. *Your Heredity and Environment*. Philadelphia.

SCHNEIDER, DAVID M. 1950. Review of *The People of Great Russia*. *Man*, 50:128–129.

SCHOOLER, CARMI, AND WILLIAM CAUDILL. 1964. Symptomatology in Japanese and American Schizophrenics. *Ethnology*, 3:172–178.

SCHURTZ, HEINRICH. 1903. *Voelkerkunde*. Leipzig.

SCHWITZGEBEL, RALPH. 1964. *Streetcorner Research*. Cambridge, Mass.

SCLARE, A. B. 1953. Cultural Determinants in the Neurotic Negro. *British Journal of Medical Psychology*, 26:278–288.

SCOTT, FRANKLIN D. 1956. *The American Experience of Swedish Students*. Minneapolis.

SCOTT, J. P. 1962. Critical Periods in Behavioral Development. *Science*, 138:949–958.

SCOTT, JOSEPH W., AND EDMUND W. VAZ. 1963. A Perspective on Middle-Class Delinquency. *Canadian Journal of Economics and Political Science*, 29:324–335.

SEARCY, ANN MCELROY. 1965. *Contemporary and Traditional Prairie Potawatomi Child Life*. University of Kansas Potawatomi Study Research Report, no. 7.

SEARS, ROBERT R. 1963. Dependency Motivation. In: Marshall R. Jones, ed., *Nebraska Symposium on Motivation 1963*. Lincoln, Neb.

SEARS, ROBERT R., ELEANOR E. MACCOBY, AND HARRY LEVIN. 1957. *Patterns of Child Rearing*. New York.

SEELEY, JOHN R., ALEXANDER R. SIM, AND ELIZABETH W. LOOSLEY. 1956. *Crestwood Heights*. New York.

SELIGMAN, C. G. 1929. Temperament, Conflict and Psychosis in a Stone-Age Population. *British Journal of Medical Psychology*, 9:187–202.

SELYE, HANS. 1953. The General-Adaptation-Syndrome in Its Relationships to Neurology, Psychology, and Psychopathology. In: A. Weider, ed., *Contributions Toward Medical Psychology*. New York.

SELYE, HANS. 1956. *The Stress of Life*. New York.

SELZNICK, PHILIP. 1957. *Leadership in Administration*. Evanston, Ill.

SEMIN, R. 1961. Les Résistances que l'adolescent turc rencontre pour devenir adulte. *Vita humana*, 4:15–21.

SEWARD, GEORGENE. 1956. *Psychotherapy and Culture Conflict*. New York.

SEWELL, WILLIAM H. 1952. Infant Training and the Personality of the Child. *The American Journal of Sociology*, 58:150–159.

SEWELL, WILLIAM H. 1961. Social Class and Childhood Personality. *Sociometry*, 24:340–356.

SEWELL, WILLIAM H. 1963. Some Recent Developments in Socialization Theory and Research. *Annals of the American Academy of Political and Social Science*, 349:163–181.

SEWELL, WILLIAM H., AND A. O. HALLER. 1959. Factors in the Relationship Between Social Status and the Personality Adjustment of the Child. *American Sociological Review*, 24:511–520.

SEWELL, WILLIAM H., PAUL H. MUSSEN, AND CHESTER W. HARRIS. 1955. Relationships Among Child Training Practices. *American Sociological Review*, 20:137–148.

SHERIF, MUZAFER, AND CAROLYN W. SHERIF. 1964. *Reference Groups*. New York.

SHKLAR, JUDITH N. 1957. *After Utopia*. Princeton.

SHOBEN, EDWARD JOSEPH, JR. 1957. Toward a Concept of the Normal Personality. *American Psychologist*, 12:183–189.

SHOBEN, EDWARD JOSEPH, JR. 1962. Behavioral Aspects of the Self. *Annals of the New York Academy of Sciences*, 96:765–773.

SHOBEN, EDWARD JOSEPH, JR. 1963. Moral Behavior and Moral Learning. *Religious Education*, 58:137–145.

SHORT, JAMES F., JR. 1965. Social Structure and Group Processes in Gang Delinquency. In: Muzafer Sherif and Carolyn W. Sherif, eds., *Problems of Youth*. Chicago.

SIEGEL, BERNARD J. 1955. High Anxiety Levels and Cultural Integration: Notes on a Psycho-Cultural Hypothesis. *Social Forces*, 34:42–48.

SIEGEL, BERNARD J., ed. 1959. *Biennial Review of Anthropology, 1959*. Stanford, Calif.

SIEGEL, BERNARD J. 1962. *Biennial Review of Anthropology, 1961*. Stanford, Calif.

SIEGEL, BERNARD J. 1963. *Biennial Review of Anthropology, 1963*. Stanford, Calif.

SIEGFRIED, ANDRÉ. 1952. *Nations Have Souls*. Translated by Edward Fitzgerald. New York.

SIKKEMA, MILDRED. 1947. Observations on Japanese Early Child Training. *Psychiatry*, 10:423–432.

SILVERT, KALMAN H. 1965. American Academic Ethics and Social Research Abroad. *American Universities Field Staff Reports Service, West Coast South America Series*, 12, no. 3.

SIMMONS, LEO W., ed. 1942. *Sun Chief*. New Haven.

SIMMONS, LEO W., AND HAROLD G. WOLFF. 1954. *Social Science in Medicine*. New York.

SIMPSON, RICHARD L., AND H. MAX MILLER. 1963. Social Status and Anomia. *Social Problems*, 10:256–264.

SINGER, MILTON. 1961. A Survey of Culture and Personality Theory and Research. In: Bert Kaplan, ed., *Studying Personality Cross-Culturally*. Evanston, Ill.

SLOTKIN, J. S. 1953. Social Psychiatry of a Menomini Community. *Journal of Abnormal and Social Psychology*, 48:10–16.

SLUCKIN, W. 1954. *Minds and Machines*. Harmondsworth, England.

SMITH, ALFRED G. 1964. The Dionysian Innovation. *American Anthropologist*, 66:251–265.

SMITH, ERNEST A. 1962. *American Youth Culture*. New York.

SMITH, JOHN MAYNARD. 1958. *The Theory of Evolution*. Harmondsworth, England.

SMITH, M. BREWSTER. 1965. Socialization for Competence. *Items*, 19:17–23.

SMITH, THOMAS V. 1934. *Philosophers Speak for Themselves*. Chicago.

SNYDER, CHARLES R. 1958. *Alcohol and the Jews*. Glencoe, Ill.

SOLOMON, PHILIP, PHILIP E. KUBZANSKY, P. HERBERT LEIDERMAN, JACK H. MENDELSON, RICHARD TRUMBULL, AND DONALD WEXLER, eds. 1961. *Sensory Deprivation*. Cambridge, Mass.

SOLOMON, PHILIP, P. HERBERT LEIDERMAN, JACK H. MENDELSON, AND DONALD WEXLER. 1957. Sensory Deprivation: A Review. *American Journal of Psychiatry*, 114:357–363.

SOMMER, ROBERT, AND HUMPHREY OSMOND. 1960. Autobiographies of Former Mental Patients, *Journal of Mental Science*, 106:648–662.

SOMMER, ROBERT, AND HUMPHREY OSMOND. 1961. Autobiographies of Former Mental Patients. Addendum. *Journal of Mental Science*, 107:1030–1032.

SPENCER, HERBERT. 1963. *Education: Intellectual, Moral, and Physical*. Paterson, N.J.

SPENGLER, OSWALD. 1926–1928. *The Decline of the West*. Translated by Charles Francis Atkinson. New, rev. ed. 2 vols. New York.

SPERGEL, IRVING. 1964. *Racketville, Slumtown, Haulburg*. Chicago.

SPINDLER, GEORGE D. 1952. Personality and Peyotism in Menomini Indian Acculturation. *Psychiatry*, 15:151–159.

SPINDLER, GEORGE D. 1955. *Sociocultural and Psychological Processes in Menomini Acculturation*. University of California Publications in Culture and Society, vol. 5.

SPINDLER, GEORGE D. [1957]. Personal Documents in Menomini Peyotism. *Microcard Publications of Primary Records in Culture and Personality*, 2, no. 13. Madison, Wis.

SPINDLER, GEORGE D. 1963. Personality, Sociocultural System, and Education Among the Menomini. In: George Spindler, ed., *Education and Culture*. New York.

SPINDLER, GEORGE D., AND LOUISE S. SPINDLER. 1957. American Indian Personality Types and Their Sociocultural Roots. *Annals of the American Academy of Political and Social Science*, 311:147–157.

SPINDLER, GEORGE D., AND LOUISE S. SPINDLER. 1963. Psychology in Anthropology: Applications to Culture Exchange. In: Sigmund Koch, ed., *Psychology: A Study of a Science*. Vol. 6. *Investigations of Man as Socius: Their Place in Psychology and the Social Sciences*. New York.

SPINDLER, LOUISE S. [1957]. 61 Rorschachs and 15 Expressive Autobiographic Interviews of Menomini Indian Women. *Microcard Publications of Primary Records in Culture and Personality*, 2, no. 10. Madison, Wis.

SPINDLER, LOUISE S. 1962. *Menomini Women and Culture Change*. Memoirs of the American Anthropological Association, no. 91.

SPINDLER, LOUISE S., AND GEORGE SPINDLER. 1958. Male and Female Adaptations in Culture Change. *American Anthropologist*, 60:217–233.

SPINDLER, LOUISE S., AND GEORGE SPINDLER. 1961. A Modal Personality Technique in the Study of Menomini Acculturation. In: Bert Kaplan, ed., *Studying Personality Cross-Culturally*. Evanston, Ill.

SPIRO, MELFORD E. 1951. Culture and Personality; the Natural History of a False Dichotomy. *Psychiatry*, 14:19–46.

SPIRO, MELFORD E. 1953. Ghosts: An Anthropological Inquiry Into Learning and Perception. *Journal of Abnormal and Social Psychology*, 48:376–382.

SPIRO, MELFORD E. 1954. Human Nature in Its Psychological Dimensions. *American Anthropologist*, 56:19–30.

SPIRO, MELFORD E. 1955. The Acculturation of American Ethnic Groups. *American Anthropologist*, 57:1240–1252.

SPIRO, MELFORD E. 1959. Cultural Heritage, Personal Tensions, and Mental Illness in a South Sea Culture. In: Marvin K. Opler, ed., *Culture and Mental Health*. New York.

SPIRO, MELFORD E. 1961a. An Overview and a Suggested Reorientation. In: Francis L. K. Hsu, ed., *Psychological Anthropology*. Homewood, Ill.

SPIRO, MELFORD E. 1961b. Social Systems, Personality, and Functional Analysis. In: Bert Kaplan, ed., *Studying Personality Cross-Culturally*. Evanston, Ill.

SPIRO, MELFORD E. 1963. *Kibbutz: Venture in Utopia*. Schocken paperback ed. New York.

SPIRO, MELFORD E. 1965. *Children of the Kibbutz*. Schocken paperback ed. New York.

SPIRO, MELFORD E., AND ROY G. D'ANDRADE. 1958. A Cross-Cultural Study of Some Supernatural Beliefs. *American Anthropologist*, 60:456–466.

SPITZ, RENÉ A. 1945. Hospitalism: An Inquiry Into the Genesis of Psychiatric Conditions in Early Childhood. *Psychoanalytic Study of the Child*, 1:53–74.

SRINIVAS, M. N. n.d. *A Study of Disputes*. Mimeographed. Department of Sociology, Delhi School of Economics, University of Delhi.

SROLE, LEO. 1956. Social Integration and Certain Corollaries: An Exploratory Study. *American Sociological Review*, 21:709–716.

SROLE, LEO. [1965]. Selected Sociological Perceptives. In: Stephen E. Goldston, ed., *Concepts of Community Psychiatry*. Public Health Service Publication, no. 1319.

SROLE, LEO, THOMAS S. LANGNER, STANLEY T. MICHAEL, MARVIN K. OPLER, AND THOMAS A. C. RENNIE. 1962. *Mental Health in the Metropolis*. New York.

STAGNER, ROSS. 1951. Homeostasis as a Unifying Concept in Personality Theory. *Psychological Review*, 58:5–17.

STAGNER, ROSS. 1961. *Psychology of Personality*. 3rd ed. New York.

STAINBROOK, EDWARD. 1955. Research on the Epidemiology of Psychosomatic Disease. In: C. H. Hardin Branch *et al.*, eds., *The Epidemiology of Mental Health*. Mimeographed. Brighton, Utah.

STAVRIANOS, BERTHA K. 1950. Research Methods in Cultural Anthropology in Relation to Scientific Criteria. *Psychological Review*, 57:334–344.

STEKEL, WILHELM. 1943. *The Interpretation of Dreams*. Translated by Eden and Cedar Paul. 2 vols. New York.

STENDLER, CELIA B. 1950. Sixty Years of Child Training Practices. *Journal of Pediatrics*, 36:122–134.

STENGEL, E. 1959. Classification of Mental Disorders. *Bulletin of the World Health Organization*, 21:601–663.

STEPHENS, WILLIAM N. 1962. *The Oedipus Complex*. Glencoe, Ill.

STERN, WILLIAM. 1938. *General Psychology from the Personalistic Standpoint*. Translated by Howard Davis Spoerl. New York.

STOETZEL, JEAN. 1955. *Without the Chrysanthemum and the Sword*. New York.

STOKES, CHARLES J. 1963. A Theory of Slums. *Ekistics*, 15:121–124.

STONE, ALAN A., AND GLORIA COCHRANE ONQUÉ. 1959. *Longitudinal Studies of Child Personality*. Cambridge, Mass.

STONE, GREGORY P. 1962. Drinking Styles and Status Arrangements. In: David J. Pittman and Charles R. Snyder, eds., *Society, Culture, and Drinking Patterns*. New York.

STONEQUIST, EVERETT V. 1937. *The Marginal Man*. New York.

STRAUS, MURRAY A. 1954. Childhood Experience and Emotional Security in the Context of Sinhalese Social Organization. *Social Forces*, 33:152–160.

STRAUSS, ANSELM L. 1959. *Mirrors and Masks*. Glencoe, Ill.

STRAUSS, ANSELM L., AND LEE RAINWATER. 1962. *The Professional Scientist*. Chicago.

SUE, HIROKO. 1965. *Pre-School Children of the Hare Indians*. Ottawa. Department of Northern Affairs and National Resources, Northern Co-ordination and Research Centre, publn. NCRC–65–1.

SULLIVAN, HARRY STACK. 1953. *The Interpersonal Theory of Psychiatry*. New York.

SUTCLIFFE, J. P. 1952. Problems for a Theory of Social Learning. *Australian Journal of Psychology*, 4:107–125.

SUTHERLAND, ROBERT L. 1942. *Color, Class, and Personality*. Washington, D.C.

SUTTON-SMITH, BRIAN, JOHN M. ROBERTS, AND ROBERT M. KOZELKA. 1963. Game Involvement in Adults. *Journal of Social Psychology*, 60:15–30.

SYOMUSHKIN, TIKHON. 1952. *Alitet Goes to the Hills*. Translated by B. Isaacs. Moscow.

SZASZ, THOMAS S. 1960. The Myth of Mental Illness. *American Psychologist*, 15:113–118.

SZASZ, THOMAS S. 1961. *The Myth of Mental Illness*. New York.

SZASZ, THOMAS S. 1963. *Law, Liberty, and Psychiatry: An Inquiry Into the Social Uses of Mental Health Practices*. New York.

TANNER, JAMES M., ed. 1960. *Stress and Psychiatric Disorder*. Oxford.

TANNER, JAMES M., AND BÄRBEL INHELDER, eds. 1956–1960. *Discussions on Child Development*. 4 vols. The Proceedings of the World Health Organization Study Group on the Psychobiological Development of the Child, 1953–1955. New York.

TAYLOR, STEPHEN J. L. T., AND SIDNEY CHAVE. 1964. *Mental Health and Environment*. London.

TAYLOR, WILLIAM STEPHENS. 1948. Basic Personality in Orthodox Hindu Culture Patterns. *Journal of Abnormal and Social Psychology*, 43:3–12.

TEICHER, MORTON I. 1954. Three Cases of Psychosis Among the Eskimos. *Journal of Mental Science*, 100:527–535.

TEICHER, MORTON I. 1960. *Windigo Psychosis*. In: Proceedings of the 1960 Annual Spring Meeting of the American Ethnological Society.

TEILHARD DE CHARDIN, PIERRE. 1959. *The Phenomenon of Man*. Translated by Bernard Wall. New York.

THOMAS, WILLIAM I., AND DOROTHY SWAINE THOMAS. 1928. *The Child in America*. New York.

THOMPSON, CLARA. 1950. *Psychoanalysis: Evolution and Development*. New York.

THOMPSON, LAURA. 1950. *Culture in Crisis*. New York.

THOMPSON, LAURA. 1951. *Personality and Government*. Mexico City.

THOMSON, LAURA. 1961. *Toward a Science of Mankind*. New York.

THOMPSON, LAURA. 1965. Freedom and Culture. *Human Organization*, 24:105–110.

THOMPSON, LAURA, AND ALICE JOSEPH. 1944. *The Hopi Way*. Chicago.

THOMPSON, WILLIAM IRWIN. 1962–1963. Anthropology and the Study of Values. *Main Currents in Modern Thought*, 19:37–44.

THWAITES, RUEBEN GOLD, ed. 1896–1901. *The Jesuit Relations and Allied Documents. Travels and Explorations of the Jesuit Missionaries in New France, 1610–1791*. 73 vols. Cleveland.

TOLMAN, EDWARD C. 1948. Cognitive Maps in Rats and Men. *Psychological Review*, 55:189–208.

TOLMAN, EDWARD C. 1949. *The Psychology of Social Learning. Journal of Social Issues*, vol. 5, supp. no. 3.

TOMASIC, DINKO. 1948. *Personality and Culture in Eastern European Politics*. New York.

TRILLIN, CALVIN. 1965. A Reporter at Large. A Third State of Existence. *The New Yorker*, 41 (no. 31):58–125.

TUMIN, MELVIN. 1950. The Hero and the Scapegoat in a Peasant Community. *Journal of Personality*, 10:197–211.

TUMIN, MELVIN. 1952. *Caste in a Peasant Society*. Princeton.

TURNELL, MARTIN. 1950. *The Novel in France*. London.

TURNER, VICTOR W. 1964. Betwixt and Between: The Liminal Period in *Rites de Passage*. In: *Proceedings of the 1964 Annual Spring Meeting of the American Ethnological Society*.

UNDERWOOD, FRANCES W., AND IRMA HONIGMANN. 1947. A Comparison of Socialization and Personality in Two Simple Societies. *American Anthropologist*, 49:557–577.

UNWIN, JOSEPH D. 1934. *Sex and Culture*. London.

USEEM, JOHN, AND RUTH HILL USEEM. 1955. *The Western-Educated Man in India*. New York.

VAHIA, N. S. 1963. Cultural Differences in the Clinical Picture of Schizophrenia and Hysteria in India and the United States. *Transcultural Psychiatric Research*, no. 14:16–18.

VAN DER KROEF, JUSTUS M. 1961. The Acquisitive Urge: A Problem in Cultural Change. *Social Research*, 28:37–59.

VINCENT, CLARK E. 1961. *Unmarried Mothers*. New York.

VOGT, EVON Z. 1951. *Navaho Veterans*. Papers of the Peabody Museum of American Archaeology and Ethnology, Harvard University, vol. 41, no. 1.

VOTH, H. R. 1901. *The Oraibi Powamu Ceremony*. Field Columbian Museum Publication 61, Anthropological Series, vol. 3, no. 2.

WALLACE, ALFRED RUSSEL. 1894. *Malay Archipelago*. London.

WALLACE, ANTHONY F. C. 1950. A Possible Technique for Recognizing Psychological Characteristics of the Ancient Maya from an Analysis of Their Art. *American Imago*, 7:239–258.

WALLACE, ANTHONY F. C. 1952a. Halliday Jackson's Journal to the Seneca Indians, 1798–1800. *Pennsylvania History*, 19:117–147, 325–349.

WALLACE, ANTHONY F. C. 1952b. *The Modal Personality Structure of the Tuscarora Indians*. Bureau of American Ethnology, Bull. 150.

WALLACE, ANTHONY F. C. 1955. Stress, Personality Change, and Cultural Creativity. Paper read at the meeting of the American Anthropological Association, November 17, 1955, Boston.

WALLACE, ANTHONY F. C. 1956a. Mazeway Resynthesis: A Bio-Cultural Theory of Religious Inspiration. *Transactions of the New York Academy of Sciences*, 18:626–638.

WALLACE, ANTHONY F. C. 1956b. Revitalization Movements. *American Anthropologist*, 58:264–281.

WALLACE, ANTHONY F. C. 1957. Mazeway Disintegration: The Individual's Perception of Socio-Cultural Disorganization. *Human Organization*, 16 (no. 2):23–27.

WALLACE, ANTHONY F. C. 1959a. Cultural Determinants of Response to Hallucinatory Experience. A. M. A. *Archives of General Psychiatry*, 1:58–69.

WALLACE, ANTHONY F. C. 1959b. The Institutionalization of Cathartic and Control Strategies in Iroquis Religious Psychotherapy. In: Marvin K. Opler, ed., *Culture and Mental Health*. New York.

WALLACE, ANTHONY F. C. 1960. The Biocultural Theory of Schizophrenia. *International Record of Medicine*, 173:700–714.

WALLACE, ANTHONY F. C. 1961a. *Cultural Composition of the Handsome Lake Religion*. Bureau of American Ethnology, Bull. 180.

WALLACE, ANTHONY F. C. 1961b. *Culture and Personality*. New York.

WALLACE, ANTHONY F. C. 1961c. Mental Illness, Biology, and Culture. In: Francis L. K. Hsu, ed., *Psychological Anthropology*. Homewood, Ill.

WALLACE, ANTHONY F. C. 1962. Culture and Cognition. *Science*, 135:351–357.

WALLACE, ANTHONY F. C., FRED W. VOGET, AND MARIAN W. SMITH. 1959. Towards a Classification of Cult Movements: Some Further Considerations. *Man*, 59:25–28.

WALTERS, RICHARD H., AND ROSS D. PARKE. 1965. The Role of the Distance Receptors in the Development of Social Responsiveness. In: Lewis P. Lipsitt and Charles C. Spiker, *Advances in Child Development and Behavior*, vol. 2. New York.

WARNER, W. LLOYD. 1937–1938. The Society, the Individual, and his Mental Disorders. *American Journal of Psychiatry*, 94:275–284.

WARNER, W. LLOYD, AND JAMES C. ABEGGLEN. 1955. *Big Business Leaders in America*. New York.

WARNER W. LLOYD, MARCHIA MEEKER, AND KENNETH EELLS. 1949. *Social Class in America*. Chicago.

WARNER, W. LLOYD, PAUL P. VAN RIPER, NORMAN H. MARTIN, AND ORVIS F. COLLINS. 1963. *The American Federal Executive*. New Haven.

WATSON, ROBERT I. 1965. *Psychology of the Child*. 2nd ed. New York.

WATTS, ALAN W. 1957. *The Way of Zen*. New York.

WATZLAWICK, PAUL. 1963. A Review of the Double Bind Theory. *Family Process*, 2:132–153.

WAX, MURRAY L., ROSALIE H. WAX, AND ROBERT V. DUMONT, JR. 1964. *Formal Education in an American Indian Community*. Supplement to *Social Problems*, 11, no. 4.

WEAKLAND, JOHN H. 1956. Orality in Chinese Conceptions of Male Genital Sexuality. *Psychiatry*, 19:237–247.

WEBER, MAX. 1930. *The Protestant Ethic and the Spirit of Capitalism*. Translated by Talcott Parsons. New York.

WEGROCKI, HENRY J. 1939. A Critique of Cultural and Statistical Concepts of Abnormality. Journal of Abnormal and Social Psychology, 34:166–178.

WEINBERG, S. KIRSON. 1958. *Culture and Personality*. Washington, D.C.

WEINSTEIN, EDWIN A. 1962. *Cultural Aspects of Delusion*. New York.

WESOLOWSKI, WŁODZIMIERZ. 1962. Some Notes on the Functional Theory of Stratification. *Polish Sociological Bulletin*, nos. 3–4 (5–6):28–38.

WHITE, LESLIE A. 1949. *The Science of Culture*. New York.

WHITE, LESLIE A. 1960. Four Stages in the Evolution of Minding. In: Sol Tax, ed., *The Evolution of Man*. Chicago.

WHITE, ROBERT W. 1959. Motivation Reconsidered: The Concept of Competence. *Psychological Review*, 66:297–333.

WHITING, BEATRICE BLYTH. 1950. *Paiute Sorcery*. Viking Fund Publications In Anthropology, no. 15.

WHITING, BEATRICE BLYTH, ed. 1963. *Six Cultures*. New York.

WHITING, JOHN W. M. 1941. *Becoming a Kwoma*. New Haven.

WHITING, JOHN W. M. 1954. The Cross-Cultural Method. In: Gardner Lindzey, ed., *Handbook of Social Psychology*. 2 vols. Cambridge, Mass.

WHITING, JOHN W. M. 1961. Socialization Process and Personality. In: Francis L. K. Hsu, *Psychological Anthropology*, Homewood, Ill.

WHITING, JOHN W. M. 1964. Effects of Climate on Certain Cultural Practices. In: Ward H. Goodenough, ed., *Explorations in Cultural Anthropology*. New York.

WHITING, JOHN W. M., AND IRVIN L. CHILD. 1953. *Child Training and Personality: A Cross-cultural Study*. New Haven.

WHITING, JOHN W. M. et al. 1954. *Field Guide for a Study of Socialization in Five Societies*. Cambridge, Mass.

WHITING, JOHN W. M. et al. 1966. *Field Guide for a Study of Socialization*. New York.

WHITING, JOHN W. M., RICHARD KLUCKHOHN, AND ALBERT ANTHONY. 1958. The Function of Male Initiation Ceremonies at Puberty. In: Eleanor E. Maccoby, Theodore M. Newcomb, and Eugene L. Hartley, eds., *Readings in Social Psychology*. 3rd ed. New York.

WHITING, JOHN W. M., AND BEATRICE B. WHITING. 1960. Contributions of Anthropology to the Methods of Studying Child Rearing. In: Paul H. Mussen, ed., *Handbook of Research Methods in Child Development*. New York.

WHORF, BENJAMIN LEE. 1956. *Language, Thought, and Reality: Selected Writings of Benjamin Lee Whorf*. Edited by John B. Carroll. Cambridge, Mass.

WHYTE, WILLIAM F. 1955. *Street Corner Society*. 2nd ed. Chicago.

WHYTE, WILLIAM F. 1964. The Slum: On the Evolution of Street Corner Society. In: Arthur J. Vidich, Joseph Bensman, and Maurice R. Stein, eds., *Reflections on Community Studies*. New York.

WIEBE, GERHART D. 1958. Social Values and Ego Ideal: Recollections of the Army-McCarthy Hearings. In: *Psychoanalysis and the Social Sciences*, vol. 5.

WILKINS, LESLIE T. 1965. *Social Deviance*. Englewood Cliffs, N.J.

WILLIAMS, HERBERT H. 1958. *Some Aspects of Culture and Personality in a Lebanese Maronite Village*. Ph.D. dissertation, University of Pennsylvania.

WILLIAMS, RICHARD H., CLARK TIBBITS, AND WILMA DONAHUE, eds. 1963. *Processes of Aging*. 2 vols. New York.

WILLIAMS, ROBERT M., JR. 1947. *The Reduction of Intergroup Tensions*. Social Science Research Council, Bull. 57.

WILLIAMS, THOMAS RHYS. 1959. The Personal-Cultural Equation in Social Work and Anthropology. *Social Casework*, 40:74–80.

WILSON, BRYAN R. 1962. The Teacher's Role—A Sociological Analysis. *British Journal of Sociology*, 13:15–32.

WILSON, GODFREY, AND MONICA WILSON. 1945. *The Analysis of Social Change*. Cambridge, England.

WILSON, MONICA. 1951. *Good Company*. London.

WITMER, EDWIN P. 1951. *An Experiment in the Prevention of Delinquency*. New York.

WITTKOWER, E. D., AND J. FRIED. 1959–1960. A Cross-cultural Approach to Mental Health Problems. *American Journal of Psychiatry*, 116:423–428.

WITTKOWER, E. D., H. B. MURPHY, J. FRIED, AND H. ELLENBERGER. 1960. A Crosscultural Inquiry into the Symptomatology of Schizophrenia. *Review and Newsletter, Transcultural Research in Mental Health Problems*, no. 9:2–17.

WOLFE, ROBERT PAUL. 1963. Report on Replies to the Invitations to a Conference on Anthropology and World Affairs (Wenner-Gren Foundation for Anthropological Research, February 13, 1963).

WOLFENSTEIN, MARTHA. 1951. The Emergence of Fun Morality. *Journal of Social Issues*, 7 (no. 4):15–25.

WOLFENSTEIN, MARTHA. 1953. Trends in Infant Care. *American Journal of Orthopsychiatry*, 23:120–130.

WOLFENSTEIN, MARTHA. 1955a. French Children's Paintings. In: Margaret Mead and Martha Wolfenstein, eds., *Childhood in Contemporary Cultures*. Chicago.

WOLFENSTEIN, MARTHA. 1955b. French Parents Take Their Children to the Park. In: Margaret Mead and Martha Wolfenstein, eds., *Childhood in Contemporary Cultures*. Chicago.

WOLFENSTEIN, MARTHA. 1955c. Fun Morality: An Analysis of Recent American Child-training Literature. In: Margaret Mead and Martha Wolfenstein, eds., *Childhood in Contemporary Cultures*. Chicago.

WOLFENSTEIN, MARTHA. 1955d. Implications of Insight—I. In: Margaret Mead and Martha Wolfenstein, eds., *Childhood in Contemporary Cultures*. Chicago.

WOLFENSTEIN, MARTHA. 1955e. Some Variants in Moral Training of Children. In: Margaret Mead and Martha Wolfenstein, eds., *Childhood in Contemporary Cultures*. Chicago.

WOLFENSTEIN, MARTHA, AND NATHAN LEITES. 1950. *Movies: A Psychological Study*. Glencoe, Ill.

WOLFENSTEIN, MARTHA, AND NATHAN LEITES. 1954. Plot and Character in Selected French Films: An Analysis of Fantasy. In: Rhoda Métraux and Margaret Mead, *Themes in French Culture*. Stanford, Calif.

WOLFF, HAROLD G. 1960. Stressors as a Cause of Disease in Man. In: J. M. Tanner, ed., *Stress and Psychiatric Disorder*. Oxford.

WOLFF, KURT H. 1944. A Critique of Bateson's *Naven. Journal of the Royal Anthropological Institute of Great Britain and Ireland*, 74:59–74.

WOLFF, PETER H. 1961–1963. The Natural History of a Family. In: Brian M. Foss, ed., *Tavistock Seminar on Mother-Infant Interaction*. 1st–2nd, London, 1959–1960. *Determinants of Infant Behavior; Proceedings*. 2 vols. London.

WOLFF, WERNER. 1952. *The Dream, Mirror of Conscience*. New York.

WOLMAN, BENJAMIN B. 1960. *Contemporary Theories and Systems in Psychology*. New York.

WORCHEL, PHILIP, AND DONN BYRNE, eds. 1964. *Personality Change*. New York.

WORSLEY, PETER M. 1957. *The Trumpet Shall Sound*. London.

WORTIS, JOSEPH. 1950. *Soviet Psychiatry*. Baltimore.

WRONG, DENNIS H. 1962. The Over-Socialized Conception of Man in Modern Sociology. *Psychoanalysis and the Psychoanalytic Review*, 49 (no. 2):53–69.

WYMAN, LELAND. 1936. Navaho Diagnosticians. *American Anthropologist*, 38:236–246.

YAP, P. M. 1952. The Latah Reaction: Its Pathodynamics and Nosological Position. *Journal of Mental Science*. 98:515–564.

YAP, P. M. 1963. Koro or Suk-Yeong—An Atypical Culture Bound Psychogenic Disorder Found in Southern Chinese. *Transcultural Psychiatric Research*, 1:36–38.

YAP, P. M. 1965. Koro: A Culture-bound Depersonalization Syndrome. *British Journal of Psychiatry*, 111:43–50.

YARROW, LEON J. 1963. Research in Dimensions of Early Maternal Care. *Merrill-Palmer Quarterly*, 9:101–114.

YARROW, MARIAN R., JOHN D. CAMPBELL, AND ROGER V. BURTON. 1964. Reliability of Maternal Retrospection: A Preliminary Report. *Family Process*, 3:207–218.

YOUNG, FRANK W. 1962. The Function of Male Initiation Ceremonies: A Cross-Cultural Test of an Alternative Hypothesis. *American Journal of Sociology*, 67:379–396.

YOUNG, FRANK W. 1965. *Initiation Ceremonies*. New York.

ZBOROWSKI, MARK. 1949. The Place of Book-Learning in Traditional Jewish Culture. *Harvard Educational Review*, 19:87–109.

ZBOROWSKI, MARK, AND ELIZABETH HERZOG. 1952. *Life Is With People*. New York.

ZILBOORG, GREGORY, AND GEORGE W. HENRY. 1941. *A History of Medical Psychology*. New York.

ZINGG, ROBERT M. 1942. The Genuine and Spurious Values in Tarahumara Culture. *American Anthropologist*, 44:78–92.

Indexes

Index of Names

477

Index of Subjects

Abeokuta, 379, 380
Abnormal, 326–327
    See also Illness
Acadians, 370, 371, 373–374, 375
Acculturation, 24, 124–127
    See also Culture change
Achievement, 39, 103, 317, 423
Admiralty Islands, *see* Manus
Adolescence, 11–15, 33, 59, 174, 219–220, 228, 232–233, 251–255, 256–257, 259, 260, 304–305, 313, 317, 327–328
Adults, 305–306
  in socialization, 162
Affectional warmth, 208, 210
    See also Maternal warmth
Africa, 190, 259, 292, 317, 319, 397
  North, 404
    See also specific tribes
Aggression, 49, 86, 134, 159, 172, 230, 233, 236, 249, 258–259, 270, 278, 280, 293–294, 309, 318
Aging, 306, 317
Agriculture, 393
Ainu, 404
Aitutaki, 237
Alcoholics Anonymous, 344
Alcoholism, 29–30
    See also Drinking, alcoholic
Algonkian Indians, 24
    See also Chippewa Indians; Cree Indians; Menomini Indians; Montagnais-Naskapi Indians; Ojibwa Indians
Alienation, 56, 147–149, 154, 317
    See also Anomie
Alor, 107–112, 117, 193, 269, 291, 299, 323
Alternatives, cultural, 66, 150–151
Ambiguity, 74
American Indians, 184, 260, 304, 388, 391, 392, 393, 394
    See also Eskimo; specific Indian tribes
American Museum of Natural History, 32
American Psychiatric Association, 349
Amish, 384
Amok, 398, 406–407
Amur river, 397
Anal character, 267, 271–272, 294
Anal system, 172, 229, 270–272, 277, 278, 279, 280
Anfechtung, 339
Animal husbandry, 393
Anomia, 149, 154
    See also Alienation; Anomie
Anomie, 137, 152, 179, 352–353

Anthropology, ix, 1–2, 206, 207, 208
Anxiety, 279–281, 336, 353, 354, 395, 399, 410
Apache Indians, 342
Apollonian, 7, 9, 11, 154
Appetite, 176
Arapaho Indians, 260
Arapesh, 42, 73, 100, 102, 150, 151, 229, 268, 285, 287, 300, 307, 419
Araucanian Indians, 260
Archeology, 36
Archetypes, 112, 113, 115
Arctic hysteria, 403–406
Aritama, 394
Art, 37, 59, 101, 281
Artifacts, 64–66
  in socialization, 163, 179–180, 189, 203–205
Asai, 424
Asia, 260, 407
Athapaskan Indians, 260, 403
    See also Apache Indians; Hare Indians; Kaska Indians; Navaho Indians
Athens, 259
Atimelang, *see* Alor
Atomism, social, 138, 139, 402, 411
Attawapiskat, 394
Australia, 260, 261
Austria, 62–63, 64, 160–161, 202, 259, 389
Autonomy, 75, 131, 165–166, 271, 346
Aviators, 398

Baffin Island, *see* Eskimo; Frobisher Bay
Bali, 129, 147, 181, 182, 260, 282, 422
Baltimore, 363
Bang Chan, 147
Baseball, 315–316
Bassa, 48
Bathing, 282
Behavioral epidemics, 386, 395–397
Berdache, 407
Berkeley, 251
Bhagavad-Gita, 347, 350
Biculturation, 212
Biochemical insult, 345
Biography, *see* Life history
Bladder training, 197
Bodily zones, 266–277
Boston, 255–257, 258, 420–421
Bowel training, 197
    See also Anal system
Boys, 198, 219, 222
Brain, 69
Brain disorder, 329